1991

THERAPEUTIC RECREATION PROTOCOL FOR TREATMENT OF SUBSTANCE ADDICTIONS

THERAPEUTIC RECREATION PROTOCOL FOR TREATMENT OF SUBSTANCE ADDICTIONS

By
Rozanne W. Faulkner C.T.R.S.
Seaside, OR

Venture Publishing, Inc.
State College, PA 16801

Cover Design by Sandra Sikorski
Production by Bonnie Godbey
Library of Congress Catalog Number 90-71928
ISBN 0-910251-37-1

Dedicated to my eternal inspiration:

Oh pumpkin so great
What magic is fate

CONTENTS

Part I
Why We Do What We Do

CHAPTER 1 The Leisure Connection   3

The Problem of Abuse   3

Misconceptions   4

The Leisure Connection   6

Definition of Therapeutic Recreation   8

Codes Used in This Text   9

References/Resources   9

CHAPTER 2 Understanding the Person   11

The Typical Profile   11

A Story of Friendship   11

It's Only Natural   12

A Concept of Greater Paradise   14

Learning The Lessons Too Well   15

A Humorous View: The Baby Factory   15

An Anti-Society Viewpoint   16

Togetherness, Foreverness   17

Which Came First?   18

Control   19

The Geographic Cure   19

Denial   20

The Magic Line   21

There Is a Big Difference Between Living and Existing   21

Alcoholic or Addict: Is There a Difference?   22

Habituated Addiction or Addicted Habituation?   23

References/Resources   25

CHAPTER 3 Of Drugs and Addiction   27

A Look Into The Body   30

  The Endorphins   32

  Acetylcholine   34

  Norepinephrine (NE)   34

  Dopamine (DA) and ACTH   34

  GABA and Glutamate   35

  Serotonin (5-HT)   36

  Still Looking   36

Systems   36

  Endogenous Hit and Run   37

  How To Really Spell Relief   37

  The Immune System   37

  A Jump and Skip System?   38

  Systems Control Center   39

  A Final Consideration: A Brain Split   39

Back to Addiction   41

  A New Definition of Addiction   41

  The Impending Disaster: Positive Addiction   43

Substance Addictions: A New Look at Some Old Drugs   43

   Alcohol: A Brief Summary   43

   Other Depressants   46

   Narcotics and Opiate-Like Substances   47

   Stimulants   48

      Cocaine, Amphetamines   48

      Hallucinogens/Psychotominetic   50

      Caffeine and Nicotine   52

      Non-Drug Substance Addiction: Food   52

Process Addictions   54

   Gambling and High-Risk Addictions   54

   Work Addictions   55

   Sex Addictions   56

   People Addictions   56

   Meditation/Spirituality/Positive Thinking   57

   Material Addictions   57

   Leisure Addictions   58

An Addictive Summary   59

References/Resources   59

CHAPTER 4 Understanding Family   63

Faulkner's Family Addiction Cycle   63

   FAC Stage 1: Functional Living   63

   FAC Stage 2: The Blow-Out   63

   FAC Stage 3: The Fireworks   64

   FAC Stage 4: The Sawtooth   65

   FAC Stage 5: The Flatline   65

   FAC Stage 6: The Healthline   66

Someplace Between Function And Blow-Out   68

   Co-Dependency   68

      Co-Dependency via:

         Trauma   68
         The Search for Acceptance   68
         Self Under/Overestimation   69
         Natural Chemistry   69
         Backstage Mother   69
         Is There Anything Else?   70
         Summary   70

Someplace Between Blow-Out and Fireworks   70

   Significant Other Addiction Syndrome   70

      SOAS:
         Controlling the Uncontrollable   71
         Basing Actions on Reactions   72
         The results   73

From Fireworks to Sawtooth to Flatline   74

   Co-Addiction   74

      Parents   75

      Reflections on Child Rearing Practices   76

   Children of Addiction   76

      Correlating Roles and TA   78

      Adult Children of Alcoholics   79

      To Treatment   80

From Other FAC Stages to Healthline   81

References/Resources   82

Part II
How We Do What We Do

CHAPTER 5   Treatment and Therapy   85

Treatment Modalities   87

Therapeutic Recreation as a Support Service   88

     Detox Support   88

     Support for Physical Restoration   89

     Psycho-social Support Service   89

     Dietary Support   90

     Education Support   90

Support Services for Therapeutic Recreation   90

Interfacing with 12-Step Programs   91

References/Resources   94

CHAPTER 6   TNT-A Model Center   97

Computerized Operations   98

Facility Design   100

Detox Program   101

     Client Scheduling After Detox   101

Adolescent Scheduling   105

Basic Family Visitation and Therapy Schedule   105

Outpatient Scheduling   106

After-Care Scheduling   107

Transition Center Scheduling   107

Scheduling The Activity That Takes A Day Or Two   107

Employee Recreation   107

TNT Management   108

The Therapeutic Recreation Team   108

Staff Training   110

Therapeutic Recreation Staff Scheduling   111

Therapeutic Recreation Budget   111

References/Resources   114

CHAPTER 7   TNT-Assessment Model   115

Therapeutic Recreation Programming   115

Getting Started   116

Leisure Skills and Interests   116

Assessment By TRI   118

     # 1: Physical Condition   120

     # 2: Education Ability   120

     #3: Transportation   120

     #4: Economic Situation   120

     #5: Family Support   121

     #6: Personal Stress   121

     #7: Play History Status   121

     #8: Creative Problem Solving   121

     #9: Leisure Skills   122

     #10: Leisure Awareness   122

From Assessment to Evaluation   123

The Treatment Plan   124

The TRI Coding System   124

Determination of Goal Attainment   127

References/Resources   127

Part III
What We Do

CHAPTER 8 Leisure Education   131

Leisure Education Sessions for TRI Items:

    #10: Leisure Awareness   132

    #1: Physical   150

    #2: Education   150

    #3: Transportation   150

    #4: Economic   151

    #5: Family   153

    #6: Stress   155

    #7: Play Status   156

    #8: Creative Problem Solving   157

    #9: Skills   157

References/Resources   158

CHAPTER 9 Skill Development   161

Required Skill Development Sessions   163

Competitive Sessions   164

Self-Competitive Sessions   165

Productive Sessions   166

Social Sessions   166

Individual Pursuits   167

Intellectual Pursuits   168

Creative Sessions: 169

    Art   169

Dance   170

Drama   171

Music   172

Writing   174

Spiritual Pursuits   175

High Risk Pursuits   175

References/Resources   175

CHAPTER 10 Re-Creation   177

Creating a Likely Environment   177

Break Times   178

Style Shop   178

Community Government   178

Clubs and Rap Sessions   179

Special Events   179

Individual Pursuits   180

References/Resources   182

CHAPTER 11 Recreation Therapy   183

401.0   Physical Restoration   183

402.0   Learning Stimulation   184

403.20   Assertive Transport Improvement   186

405.0   Family Relationships   186

406.0   Stress Reduction   187

407.0   Restoration of Developmental Play Behaviors   187

408.0   Creative Problem Solving   188

410.0   Situation Response Awareness   190

420.0	Process Addiction Treatment	191
430.0	Ventilation of Anger	193
440.0	Managing Grief	193
450.0	Trust of Self and Others	196
460.0	Risk-Taking	196
470.0	Anticipations and Expectations Management	197
480.0	Decision Making	197
490.0	Adventure Course	198
	References/Resources	198

CHAPTER 12 Individual Cases   201

The Case of Narron High   201

The Case of Coca Butter   204

The Case of Wildir. I. Shrose   206

The Case of Val Eyum Yum   211

The Case of Bud M. Wiser   215

The Case of Tina Bopper   218

The Case of Tweety Bopper   222

The Case of George Dikkel   222

The Case of Johnny Walker   224

References/Resources   227

CHAPTER 13 Back To The Real World   229

No Space   229

No Money   229

Inadequate Staff Skills   230

No Staff   230

No Time   232

Short Stay   232

One Man Department, Short Stay, No Space, No Money 232

Overwhelming Client Staff Ratio   234

Final Comments   235

APPENDIX   237

Policy: Video Recording   239

Job Descriptions   241

Schedules:

    Clients During Treatment Phase   251

    Therapeutic Recreation Team Manager   252

    Therapeutic Recreation Specialists 1 and 2   253

    Therapeutic Recreation Specialists 3 and 4   254

    Technicians "A," "B," "C," and "D"   255

    Typical Week for Skill Development and Re-Creation   256

    Typical Rotation of Leisure Education Sessions for 9 a.m. Time Slot   257

Other Sources   259

Part I

Why We Do What We Do

CHAPTER 1

THE LEISURE CONNECTION

THE PROBLEM OF ABUSE

Approximately 67 percent of Americans over age 15 drink, with about 15 percent of those drinking heavily (Estes & Heinemann, 1982, p. 37). Estes estimates the number of "alcoholic or severely problematic drinkers to be in the range of 5 million Americans" (Estes, 1982). Other sources have quoted 3 million, 7 million, 10 million, 1 in every 10 drinkers. It is difficult to identify an accurate number, for the nature of the disease is one of secrecy. Without a doubt there are millions of Americans addicted to just alcohol alone, millions more addicted to other substances and combinations of alcohol and drugs.

The consequences of millions of Americans being addicted to chemical substances are staggering. Alcohol and drug abuse is the source of many hospital admissions. ". . .alcohol-related disorders are involved in a large percentage of public & private medical & psychiatric patients" (Estes, 1982, p. 46). There is arguably no specialty area within the health care system that does not treat (either directly or indirectly) addiction-related disorders. In times of crisis, persons who are addicted turn to emergency rooms, family physicians, addiction treatment services, and psychiatry in attempts to get sober or clean. Television offers the constant reminder that fifty percent of fatal traffic accidents result from drinking and driving. Many more traffic accidents occur that do not result in fatalities, and the non-fatalities pass through the emergency room door and into intensive care, surgery, internal medicine, orthopedics, and physical rehabilitation units. Occasionally, alcohol/drug use results in family violence. Battered family members are seen in pediatrics, obstetrics, and psychiatry. When drinking/using, diabetics may forget to take their insulin, persons with cardiovascular disease forget to take their medication, and persons with wounds or broken bones fail to keep the sites clean or follow other simple procedures, changing minor inconveniences into medical crises. Add to these the admissions that result from internal damage of the body's organs caused by sustained alcohol/drug use (e.g., cirrhosis of the liver, hypertension) and it is apparent that there is no area within health care where addiction is not present. Furthermore, practicing addicts, when faced with the choice of paying a health care bill or using that money to buy another drink, fix, or pill, will more than likely choose the latter. Thus, every American who purchases health care or health care insurance is forced to pick up addiction's bar tab.

Health care is not the only segment of American society staggering from the impact of alcohol/drug abuse. Jails are overcrowded. An estimated 50 to 80 percent of the prison space in our country is occupied by persons who committed drug-related crimes and/or were under the influence of alcohol/drugs when crimes were committed. I have little reason to doubt such high estimates. I live in one of those small towns thought to be void of crime and drugs, but a reading of the local newspaper will often reveal an interesting pattern reported in the "Police Log" section. For example, the October 12, 1989 paper reports that my town's crime wave for the week consisted of two arrests and six break-in reports (Police Log, 1989). One arrest was for driving under the influence, so that's fifty percent of the arrests made. Of the break-ins, four were thefts of items valued under $100. Stolen items in these cases included a crab net valued at $40, a radar detector worth $100, two video tapes worth $70, and $97 from a restaurant safe. While I have no way of knowing if these latter incidents were actually substance abuse related, such actions seem to pose too great a risk for too small a return for any sober individual to consider. The other two crimes had at least some value to compensate for the risks. One was the theft of a wrench and air saw worth over $200, and the other, jewelry worth $1500. Perhaps these last two were by persons who earn a living from thievery. Perhaps they were the work of persons attempting to pay for their daily supply of intoxicating substances and who just got lucky. Just for a moment, visualize a map of the United States. See all the small towns which might be expected to have crimes similar to the ones just mentioned. Then see the larger cities where drug use is known to be a contributing source of crimes and gang violence. Then imagine all the prisons overflowing as a result of substance abuse, a problem which can be prevented and treated.

Untreated addiction also plagues the business community. Estimated losses in the work place are too staggering to accurately report. There are the obvious problems of unemployment and inconsistent employment which rob the individual of hope and financial security, not to mention the burden on America's unemployment and social security systems. There is also overuse of sick leave, and failure to report to work on time, both of which disrupt the flow of productivity. There are the problems of white collar crime and misuse of company funds. There are also less obvious costs. I own an American-made car. Though practically new, a number of the automobile's parts fell off, or malfunctioned, shortly after purchase. While all the problems were minor, they caused disruptions in my schedule, created friction between the car dealer's service department, and strengthened my resolve to purchase a non-American-made car next time. Upon moving into a brand new home, the lights would not work; in this case, a highly qualified and experienced electrician had wired the light switch in backwards. Again, this was not a major problem, but it disrupted the my life and prompted a vow never to use that electrical company again. I can't help but wonder if the car rolled through the assembly line, or if the home's wiring finished on Friday afternoons when the persons responsible for performing the work had their minds on getting a drink after work, instead of on what they were doing. What is the cost of the employee who is physically on the job, but has his mind on getting that next drink, fix, or pill? What is the cost of noneffective time use by co-workers, as they attempt to cover for, or counsel, the employee who suffers from addiction? What is the cost of employing the family member drained of energy by the crisis and turmoil encountered at home? The costs of all of these combined probably range in the millions, perhaps billions of dollars every year. The television news blares measures of the United State's slipping economy, the Gross National Product, the overseas trade deficit. One might wonder just how much of our nations collective economic strength is being drained by substance abuse in the work force? This is a problem that can be solved.

All of the above problems are multiplied, for alcoholics/ addicts are also born into families, and create their own families as they progress through life. In many areas of the United States, half of all marriages end in divorce. How many of those divorces are the direct result of alcohol/drug abuse? It is impossible to determine. The State of Oregon asks that no reasons be given, other than mutual incompatibility. Other states ask for citing of specific behaviors as grounds for divorce (i.e., infidelity, mental cruelty, etc.). While all of these behaviors can be symptoms of alcohol/drug abuse, they are not owned exclusively by alcoholics and addicts. Few states grant divorce on the grounds that a spouse drinks too much. This is unfortunate. While no two alcoholics or addicts are alike, if there were a profile of the average alcoholic or addict, it would not be of a man or woman who is divorced. A common characteristic would be a man or woman with multiple marriages. One might argue that if persons who drink or use drugs were not permitted to marry, the divorce rate in this country would be the lowest in the world. (That, of course, will never happen.) No one can deny that substance abuse is a source of family dysfunction. But, the problem of substance abuse can be resolved.

Many observers feel there is something wrong worldwide. Glasser (1975), identifies a lack of role models for our youth and blames the transitory nature of television advertising as the culprit. He believes that the television ad has become the role model for youth, a model without true substance. Other authorities have placed the blame on the emergence of new technology and computerization. Still others point a finger toward political unrest resulting from Vietnam, Watergate, presidential assassinations, Japan's buying power, and the threat of impending holocaust from nuclear buildup. All are compelling sources. Yet, none leaves as clear a trail as alcohol/ drug abuse. If there is something wrong in the world, it may well include a limited supply of alcohol/drug-free thinking available to deal with the presenting problems.

It has become obvious that alcohol/drug addiction is a major problem in our society. Although there is little argument that addiction is a problem, there is a wide variety of opinions about the problem's exact nature and what should be done about it. In the past, a number of solutions have not worked because comprehension of the problem has been limited, filled with inaccurate stereotypes and misconceptions. Since the identification of solutions depends on accurate comprehension of the problem, it is wise to fully comprehend the problem prior to attempting any application of a proposed solution. First, let us clear away some basic misconceptions.

MISCONCEPTIONS

A most dangerous assumption is that solving the problem of addiction is hopeless. Nothing could be further from the truth. It is true that the majority of persons addicted to chemical substances cannot return to "social" use of chemical substances. That does not mean that a person who is addicted must die intoxicated or that the problems caused by addiction cannot be eradicated. Addiction is responsive to treatment. The symptoms can be arrested. It is a problem with solutions. As it is written in the "Big Book" of Alcoholics Anonymous, "Rarely have we seen a person fail who has thoroughly followed our path" (Alcoholics Anonymous, 1976). There are millions of recovering alcoholics today who live effective lives without the use of a drink, fix, or pill. These people are living proof that addiction can be overcome.

There are other misconceptions plaguing the comprehension of addiction. The general public, as well as many researchers, seem to be operating under four principal misconceptions. The first assumption is that young people are getting drunk or high at an earlier age these days than did the generations before them. Second, that more women are becoming addicted in today's society than in the past. Third, that addiction is on the increase. Finally, that one form of addiction is better or worse than another form of addiction. Each of these requires further examination for they shape the purpose and scope of treatment.

Are people taking their first drink, fix, or pill younger today than in the past? The author began working in an alcohol treatment facility in the mid-1970s. At that time, the age of the facility's average first admission was 38. Soon we admitted a 28-year-old, then a 25-, a 21-, a 19-, a 16-year-old. Today it appears that approximately half of all admissions to treatment facilities are adolescents. But does this mean that the first use of alcohol or drugs occured at an earlier age? In the mid-70s, a man was admitted who was in his first treatment attempt. He was in his mid-40s. He was expelled from school when he was in the first grade, as a result of his drinking. He had been drunk at age six, in the 1930s. Are today's youth drinking any younger than that? The true tragedy was not that he got drunk at age six, but that he had to wait 40 years before someone told him he had a treatable disease. Today, a first grader who arrived at school drunk would receive immediate intervention. Thus, it would seem that children are not getting drunk younger, but are being sent to treatment sooner.

While a young person's first drink, fix, or pill may not be taken at an earlier age, today's youth are more likely to suffer greater consequences from intoxication. Changes in laws to protect youth from hard core criminals in prisons have caused youth to fall prey to hard-core criminals who are not incarcerated. It is far safer on the streets to have a child deal and transport drugs than an adult. The man mentioned previously got drunk on his father's moonshine at no cost. Today's drugs cost money. Between child labor laws and minimum wage jobs, about the only way the user can assure an adequate supply is to deal or engage in illegal acts. Human ingenuity has increased the potency of the drugs available which has shortened the length of time elapsing between first use and addiction. Meanwhile, the volume of information being taught in schools is far greater than it used to be. Missing a day of school today is like missing two days in the past. Today's youth find it more difficult to pick up where they leave off after an absence. The mind operating under the influence of a chemical substance must attempt to absorb more knowledge than in the past. The combination of stronger drugs, criminals recruiting youth to deal, and inability to keep up with peers in school, make the choice to succumb to addiction attractive.

Are more women abusing alcohol and drugs? Again, when the author began working in this field, some 15 years prior to publication of this text, men outnumbered women in our treatment facility 10 to 1. Today there seems to be a more equal number of men and women in most treatment facilities. Does this mean that more men than women were getting drunk? Not at all. At that time, it was more socially acceptable for men to be drunk than women, thus it was more acceptable for men to be in treatment than women. Also, the women's role was more home-oriented, making it easier to conceal a drinking problem. A friend once confided that one of his earliest childhood memories was of his grandmother sitting beside a kitchen table. The kitchen table was covered with empty beer bottles. Today's woman is in the public eye. For many, the kitchen table has been replaced by a work desk. Women in the work force find it no easier to conceal a drinking or drug problem than men. Women who remain in the home also find it more difficult to avoid detection. Urban sprawl has moved kitchen tables closer together. Apartments and condominiums have thinner walls than past homes with yards and privacy fences. It may not be that more women are getting addicted today than in the past, but that more women are getting help to overcome addiction now than before.

Is addiction on the increase? If it is on the increase, how could so many of today's swelling ranks have had addicted ancestors in their family trees? Today, researchers are finding more and more evidence to support the theory of a genetic link. Chances are that a person who becomes addicted has a parent or grandparent who was addicted. This genetic factor may weaken the assertion that addiction is "on the rise" beyond the predictable expansion resulting from population growth rates. The perceived increase may be due, in part, to improved public awareness of the problem and improved acceptance of the concept that addiction is a treatable disease. In 1982, Estes stated that "Only a portion of all active alcoholics will seek hospitalization, perhaps as infrequently as one first admission per 300 alcoholics..." (Estes, 1982, p. 41) He also cited a study indicating that of 165 persons who died of alcoholism, only 21 of the cases were known to treatment facilities. With increased public awareness and acceptance, more and more of the unidentified millions are coming to treatment. More and more family members are willing to talk about the problem to friends, and associates. Also, insurance companies have begun to pay for admission to treatment settings. This has made treatment accessible to many more people than in the past. Such developments suggest that what we are seeing may not be so much an increase of addiction in America, but an increase of persons being treated for addiction, an increase of recovery attempts. As a result, it appears that addiction is spreading when in fact it is recovery that is dispersing.

Another factor which has given the illusion that there is more addiction today than in the past is statistical analysis of the problem. Public awareness and acceptance have created a desire to know just how many problem areas are alcohol- and drug-related. Statisticians are more likely to keep records of alcohol-related incidents, and to report the findings. Their reports are also more likely to make the news. A first report tends to carry with it a certain sensationalism. Many feel that because the statistic is new, the problem which the statistic reports is new. For example, if the headline reads "50 percent of all traffic accidents are alcohol-related," suddenly drinking and driving is a problem. The problem existed long before the statistic was reported. It is possible that people have been drinking and driving since the automobile was invented. Before insurance companies paid for detoxification, hospitals were detoxifying people. All too often their symptoms were treated under some other diagnosis so that the insurance company would be obliged to pay for the treatment. When statisticians attempt to collect numbers of alcoholics treated per year in health care, they are likely to find significant increases during the years when insurance companies began to pay for detox and treatment. Does this mean that the number of persons addicted to alcohol increased during those years? This question has no easy answer. However, it is likely that more cases were accurately diagnosed and more people found they could afford to recover in a hospital.

Consider the following quotation: "[It] is one of the most serious addictions among. . .professionals and business men, teachers and persons having large cares and responsibilities" (Morgan, 1974, p. 14). Though the statement sounds all too familiar, it is not about cocaine, crack, or "ice." The drug of concern was morphine. The warning was issued by a doctor in 1902. "[It] is today a greater curse than alcohol, and. . .the majority of them are to be found among the educated *and most honored. . .members of society*" (Morgan, 1974, p. 15). This concern was voiced in 1885 about the use of opium. "At no time in world history has drug addiction been greater" (Freemantle, 1986, p. 314). This is a statement from the here and now, but it sounds identical to the statements made in the past. It must be remembered that prohibition did not occur because of a foolish whim. Alcoholism was a big problem. Prohibition was lifted because it failed to solve the problem. Prohibition neither marked a beginning or an end to alcohol abuse. Nor did the flower power children of the 1960s invent drug addiction. Both problems have been with us for centuries.

All of these quotations indicate that not only has addiction plagued our society for well over 100 years, but that it has been popular to deliberate the "which is worst" question. Public concern seems to shift over the years from one form of drug abuse to another. Perhaps the increasing strength of street drugs will finally solve the problem. The day when all drugs cause immediate addiction, may be the day when all people become unwilling to pay the price of the first drink, fix, or pill. Until that time, debate over which is worse does little more than cloud the issue. Addiction is addiction is addiction. There is no good form of addiction, so why waste time deciding between bad and worse?

To summarize, a number of misconceptions discussed in this section have fraught the study of addiction with confusion and ambiguity. Addiction appears to be increasing because there is increased public awareness of the problem. There is a growing awareness that addiction is a disease, and that it can be successfully treated. It is more socially acceptable to admit to others that an addiction problem exists in the home, and for the person experiencing the problem to seek help. People who keep accident and crime statistics are now noting when alcohol/drug use is involved. Past statistics were inaccurate, thus the new honesty about use results in the appearance of an increase. Those who use alcohol or drugs are not "starting younger." Addiction is not on the increase any more than can be accounted for by the increase in population. There are not more women alcoholics, or more children alcoholics, but a disease that is less hidden. More people are seeking treatment than used too, and they are coming for help sooner. There has also been a change in the acceptability of non-alcoholic drugs, which has permitted more persons to admit their problems.

To say that addiction is not on the increase, but is a long-standing problem does not minimize the problem. It strengthens the problem. Something new may be a fad which will pass without effort. The source of a new problem would most likely be rooted in a recent change. The problem of addiction will not pass without effort. Its source is not rooted in recent changes in parenting, family role model shifts, the national economy, or the effects of Watergate or Vietnam. The problem existed before all those events occurred. A new problem has no history; the history of addiction is a long one. Numerous attempts have been made to solve the problem. No form of treatment, no law, has eradicated the problem. Some have made a significant impact. But simply doing more of what we have been doing will not work. One area which has not adequately been addressed throughout history is one of the most obvious: the linkage between leisure and addiction. It's time to stop substituting one addiction for another. It's time to enjoy and value sober life in balance.

THE LEISURE CONNECTION

Addiction is a leisure disease, and dysfunctional leisure is a symptom of addiction. Naturally, there are many other factors involved in the creation of an addictive personality. But the linkage between leisure malfunction and addiction is astounding. Most people take their first drink, fix, or pill during leisure hours and as part of leisure functioning. In that respect, addiction becomes a function of leisure and a "dis-ease" of leisure. Once embarked on the addiction trail, people frequently abandon forms of leisure pursuits which do not permit alcohol and/or drug use. At this stage, dysfunctional leisure becomes a symptom of addiction.

The leisure connection is obvious. In the words of users, they are attempting to take a "social drink" or participate in "recreational drug use." A first attempt to explain to a person in treatment for addiction that it is possible to be social without a drink, or to recreate without a drug, is usually met with a dumbfounded expression and total disbelief. Upon initial leisure assessment, many addicted persons have no leisure activities that do not involve alcohol/drugs. For many, it is not a case of getting back to leisure pursuits which were crowded out by chemical use—they never had any. For many, the first experience of "leisure" was the first drink, fix, or pill. For these persons the disease of dysfunctional leisure existed long before the ingestion of any chemical substance.

Dysfunctional leisure behavior is often present in family members as well. Persons with poor leisure skills tend to marry persons with poor leisure skills. It is perhaps a function of selecting the known over the unknown, or selecting a partner with common interests (or common lack of interests.) Fourteen common characteristics are shared by many adults who have grown up in alcoholic homes. It is significant that number 5 on this list of 14 is an inability to have fun (Woititz, 1983, p. 66). Difficulty having fun and being spontaneous has also been cited as a characteristic of co-dependency (Beattie, 1987, p. 44).

Among users and abusers, and family members, chemical-free leisure has no value. A practicing alcoholic may stay sober from Monday morning until the work shift ends Friday, but be drunk from Friday after work until Monday morning. For many, use is confined to leisure hours until the later stage of addiction. In fact, the practicing alcoholic/addict does not usually define the alcohol or drug use as a problem as long as the use is confined to leisure hours. Chemical use is often determined to be a problem by the user when it interferes with work. Others may say the person's problem began many years earlier. But as long as use only creates problems during leisure hours (which often hold little significant value to the user), the user will seldom find reason to discontinue use. Since most family involvement occurs during leisure hours, family members often recognize the impact of substance abuse long before it comes to the attention of the user's employer. Many consider the alcoholic/addict's failure to recognize the use problem during free time as denial. If one drops a penny and doesn't bother to stop to pick it up, is this denial? The person fails to stop because the penny has little value to them. To the substances abuser, loss of leisure may be very much like the loss of a penny.

Removal of the chemical substance does not automatically restore a person to functional leisure. The author has asked many persons who were repeating treatment to identify the problem that resulted in a relapse to alcohol/drug use. A common statement given was, "If this is sobriety, I don't want any!" Upon examination, the statement usually reflected a life-style of too much work, too much responsibility, and too little if any leisure. Indeed, a concern voiced by many in later stages of inpatient treatment is how to stay sober/clean during spare time. There seems to be some degree of confidence in an ability to stay sober during working hours. There seems to be an equal degree of doubt about the ability to stay sober when "there is nothing to do." Many persons, even years into recovery find it difficult to "relax,"or permit themselves to enjoy free time. Too often, the solution is to avoid leisure.

Alcoholics Anonymous and groups patterned after AA have been successfully helping addicted persons to recover for many years. An important part of their success is the fact that their meetings are held at times when their members need them most, during leisure hours. Alcoholic Anonymous also provides leisure skill development and recreation participation opportunities for its members, though it is not referred to in those terms. The teaching of leisure skills is conducted as part of the group's informal structure. Members are encouraged to come early and stay late. Much of the before and after meeting time is spent around the coffee pot in social interaction. Car pooling to meetings provides time for one-on-one assistance. It also provides time for leisure participation. Many groups conduct "birthday parties" for members in recognition of maintaining sobriety for a set length of time. Some groups have clubs, bowling teams, and other recreation opportunities for their members. Conventions, roundups and intergroup meetings include picnics, dinners, and/or dances as well as formal meetings. But most of the leisure development skills are shared between members informally. (Please note that this is only one aspect of the 12-step programs which provide benefit to their members.)

Recent research into brain chemistry shows further connection between leisure and drug use. Neuro-chemical substances secreted while an individual is engaged in certain types of recreation are the same substances that are manipulated by drug use. O'Connor's study of leisure (1988) found that norepinephrine is secreted during activities that produce feelings of euphoria; serotonin is secreted when an individual does things that are soothing and calming; dopamine is secreted in socially outgoing situations. Amphetamines interfere with the production of norepinephrine and dopamine. Many hallucinogens have serotonin within their structure (Dusek, 1980). In many ways, the emotional states produced by various drugs, and therefore engendering repeated use, are not unlike the states that occur naturally in the course of leisure activity.

It is important to recognize that people do recover from addiction without improving leisure behaviors. A quick review of the nearest AA Group will most likely reveal how. Visit an open meeting; ask someone to introduce you to the members with 10 or more years of abstinence. Informally chat with them and ask about their life-style. Ask about medical histories. The informal survey may reveal a profile that includes meeting attendance, workaholism, high blood pressure, and heart attacks. The average life span for an alcoholic (recovering or otherwise) is 12 less than the general public (Estes, 1982). It would seem that many persons recover from addiction by working themselves to death. Even though the aspects of dysfunctional leisure have been recognized by recovering persons and by adult children of alcoholics, specialized skills are required to assist a person to overcome dysfunctional leisure.

Alcohol/drug addiction is a leisure disease and a disease of leisure! People pay for the feeling because they don't know how to get it free. That is, they don't know how to play in a manner that produces the desired feeling. It is a matter of leisure disease. The fact that addiction is a disease explains why people don't stop; physical tolerance/dependence prevents it. The characteristics of addiction as a disease of leisure may aid in understanding why many many substance addicts relapse.

Substance addicts who improve their leisure behavior sometimes relapse. Relapses occur because chemical use is *perceived* to achieve a desired state instantly, with predictable results. It is a known. Often the person reaches for a drink, fix, or pill, before remembering there are other options. Sometimes a relapse results from the ego refusing to hear "I can't." In such cases, an improved leisure cannot block a relapse. Healthy leisure can provide incentive for recovery from relapse. The person who drops a $1000 bill instead of a penny, usually stops to pick it up. The ensemble of programs and methods that can assist substances abusers, including Therapeutic Recreation services, are not yet fully in place. However, as the qualities of these sources improve, clients' motivation to stay sober may also improve.

It is also important to recognize that a person who improves leisure functioning cannot return to "social" use of chemical substances. Once damage has been done to the body's ability to regulate chemical substance intake, the damage cannot be reversed. Lasting sobriety is most effectively achieved when the "want to's" are stronger than the "have to's," and both of these are met through abstinence. Functional leisure helps to extend the want to's beyond the have to's. It is the Therapeutic Recreation Specialist's job to help recovering persons develop functional leisure that is in tune and in balance with other lifestyle needs, and discover the good of life which is missed by an intoxicated viewpoint.

Therapeutic Recreation does not duplicate or replace any other form of treatment available for persons attempting to recover from addiction. The leisure connection is strong.

Often, some form of dysfunctional leisure exists before the first drink, fix, or pill is taken. During alcohol or drug use, even accidental participation in functional leisure is curtailed. Left to his/her own resources, the recovering person may select a lifestyle void of leisure, which can lead to stress management problems, relapse, or physical illness. Support groups for recovering persons and for family members do a great deal to amend the effects of dysfunctional leisure. Therapeutic Recreation Specialists, working in unison with other disciplines and support groups, can provide the intensive programming required to eradicate dysfunctional leisure. It is to this end that this text is written.

DEFINITION OF THERAPEUTIC RECREATION

There are almost as many theories and definitions about what Therapeutic Recreation actually is or does, as there are practitioners in the field. The practitioners of this field operate under a wide variety of titles, including Therapeutic Recreation Specialist, Recreation Therapist, Activity Therapist, and Leisure Specialist, etc. This text does not intend to argue one view of this field over another. The author's definition and philosophy are contained in this section. They serve as the framework for the provision of services described in this text. Use the following as a bilingual dictionary. The intent is to help the reader understand what is meant by the terms user, not to persuade anyone to use these terms.

Therapeutic Recreation is an umbrella term commonly used to refer to four interrelated services: Recreation Therapy, Leisure Counseling/Education, Re-Creation, and Leisure Skill Development. These services provide a continuum of care ranging from total dependence upon others for the meeting of leisure needs, to total independence. Therapeutic Recreation is provided to any person who is unable to meet personal leisure needs without assistance, and services are provided until such time as the individual is able to meet his/her own leisure needs without assistance from another.

Recreation is a basic intrinsic need and a human right for all persons regardless of age, race, creed, sex, national origin, mental or physical limitations. Re-Creation makes the difference between living and existing. It occurs spontaneously at any place or point in time. Due to its spontaneous intrinsic qualities, it cannot be caused to happen by another individual. Therapeutic Recreation Specialists are trained to create situations and provide opportunities within which recreation is more likely to occur. The regular occurrence of recreation is the ultimate goal of a Therapeutic Recreation program or service. Leisure and Recreation are terms with interchangeable meanings. Skill Development sessions teach persons how to perform desired activities. (The process of Re-Creation, is widely referred to as "Recreation Participation," a term the author finds too long to be functional.)

The regular occurrence of recreation stimulates a healthful emotional balance within an individual. Maintenance of a happy, healthy emotional outlook significantly increases the speed of recovery from any physical or emotional state of disease. Recreation relieves boredom and allows hospitalized persons and their loved ones to continue a more normal existence. Recreation also vents stress, and thereby helps prevent the onset of many undesirable physical and emotional conditions. It also maintains the internal neuro-chemical balance within the individual.

Leisure Counseling/Education is the use of various activities and techniques to assist an individual in understanding his/her needs for, and the value of recreation and meaningful leisure activity. Leisure Counseling employs counseling techniques to achieve these objectives while Leisure Education uses academic techniques.

Recreation Therapy is the purposeful intervention into the life of a person to assist in the development of social, emotional, and/or physical skills that are prerequisites for engaging in a meaningful leisure lifestyle. The intervention is achieved through specified and measurable objectives. Leisure activities may be utilized as a tool to achieve the specified objectives. In such instances, the Therapeutic Recreation Specialist is not concerned with the potential for recreation occurring within the activity, or the client understanding the need for, or value of leisure in his/her life. Once the specified objective are achieved, the usefulness of the activity ends and the activity can be discarded by the client. (Whenever possible, recreation therapy activities are selected within which there is a potential for recreation to occur.)

The extent and mixture of services to be provided (recreation, skill development, leisure education/counseling, and recreation therapy) is determined by a qualified Therapeutic Recreation Specialist, with as much input from the individual as possible. Goals and objects for the provision of Therapeutic Recreation services are determined by the Therapeutic Recreation Specialist, after an evaluation of the individual's abilities, limitations, needs, and interests. A great deal of discretionary judgment is required to develop and implement an effective plan of Therapeutic Recreation care; therefore, persons responsible for developing such plans should be certified.

Therapeutic Recreation is not a diagnosis or cure for any specific disease. The goal of Therapeutic Recreation is to assist individuals in increasing their leisure independence and the feelings of self-worth and well-being that result from leisure independence. The work of the Therapeutic Recreation Specialist may ultimately assist other disciplines in meeting their objectives (such as increased endurance, improved stress management), but our primary objective is improved leisure. Therapeutic Recreation is not provided to medically unstable individuals where participation may be life-threatening to the individual (such decisions are made in consultation with a medical physician). Therapeutic Recreation is not provided to persons who are able to meet their leisure needs effectively and independently. To do so would only reduce the individual's capacity for self care.

Not all services are full fledged Therapeutic Recreation Services. To be a full service, Re-Creation, Leisure Skill Development, Leisure Counseling/Education, and Recreation Therapy must be available. A service which only provides Recreation Therapy should be called "Recreation Therapy Service" rather than "Therapeutic Recreation Service." A service which provides only leisure counseling/education should be called a "Leisure Education Service," and so on.

What is the endpoint of service, the definition of "cure?" If it is to stop drinking, then Therapeutic Recreation has little to offer. If the goal is to develop and maintain sobriety, through participation in meaningful life, then Therapeutic Recreation has much to offer to the person who is addicted. Sobriety need not be a painful repentance for sins committed. Sobriety is a healthy, happy, rewarding, productive life which is alcohol/drug free. To this end, Therapeutic Recreation has much to offer to the person who is addicted, to his/her family, and to the prevention of addiction problems for future generations (Larsen, 1985).

Professor Gerald Fain, of Boston University, once said, "If it is strong enough to help, it is strong enough to hurt." In the field of addictions treatment, there is no doubt in my mind that provision of Therapeutic Recreation, is strong enough to help. The provision of these services should be provided with skill and forethought, for inappropriate application is also strong enough to hurt. In the past, the provision of "playful" experiences has been viewed as a placebo; Therapeutic Recreation services involved provision of things as powerless as sugar pills. In light of recent studies demonstrating that even sugar pills have the power to reduce pain, the power of play must be reexamined (Ornstein, 1987, p. 73-98). Any substance or process which changes a person's internal view of the external world is profound and powerful. Fun and playfulness must be organized with serious consideration of purpose and outcomes.

CODES USED IN THIS TEXT

One of my personal leisure idiosyncrasies is a love of codes. This text is riddled with them. A reference that looks like (Smith p. 10) is simply a code to a literary source. The complete title from which the information was drawn is located at the end of each chapter. A code that looks like [Ch5; Ch8:100.0, 109.1] is an invention of the author. This code indicates that there is information in another chapter that has a direct bearing on the provision of Therapeutic Recreation services as discussed in the previous section. In the above example, the code "Ch5;" means there is information in chapter 5 that is relevant to the discussed subject. Numbers that follow a chapter reference indicate specific activity recommendations. For example, "Ch8:100.0, 109.1" refers the reader to two activity descriptions in Chapter 8, activity number "100.0" and activity number "109.1." For an explanation of activity code creation, see Chapter 7.

References/Resources

Alcoholics Anonymous (The Big Book). (1976). Alcoholics Anonymous World Services, Inc., Grand Central Station, New York, NY.

Beattie, M. (1987). *Co-dependent No More; How to Stop Controlling Others & Start Caring for Yourself.* Hazeldon and Harper & Row.

Dusek, D., & Girdamo, D. A. (1980). *Drugs: A Factual Account.* Reading, MA: Addison-Wesley Publishing Co.

Estes N. J., & Heinemann, M. E. (1982). *Alcoholism: Development, Consequences, & Interventions.* St. Louis, MO: C. V. Mosby Co.

Freemantle, B. (1986). *The Fix.* New York, NY: Tom Dohorty Assoc. Books, 1986.

Glasser, R. (1975). Life force or tranquiliser? *Society & Leisure.* The European Centre for Leisure and Education. No. 3.

Larsen, E. (1985). *Stage II Recovery; Life Beyond Addiction.* San Fransisco, CA: Harper & Row.

Morgan, H. W. (1974). *Yesterday's Addicts: American Society & Drug Abuse 1865-1920.* Norma, OK: University of Oklahoma Press.

O'Connor, C. (1988, May). Lifestyling. *Leisure's Grapevine,* 2(2), p. 2. Seaside, OR: Leisure Enrichment Sevice.

Ornstein, R. & Sobel, D. (1987). *The Healing Brain: Breakthrough Discoveries About How the Brain Keeps Us Healthy.* NY: Simon & Schuster.

"Police Log," (October 12, 1989). *Seaside Signal,* 85(31) Seaside, OR.

Woititz, Janet. (1983). *Adult Children of Alcoholics.* Deerfield Beach, FL.

CHAPTER 2

UNDERSTANDING THE PERSON

THE TYPICAL PROFILE

When I began my work in addiction treatment, I felt it was important to understand what an addicted person was. Each week our center received 10 to 20 new admissions. Each week, I would listen to the profiles of the new admissions and draw conclusions. The first week, the majority of admissions were men over 50. I concluded that the typical admission was a man over 50. The next week, a large number of women were admitted, so I concluded that an alcoholic could be male or female. The following week, most of the admissions were quite young. The next week, most of the admissions were farmers, and the subsequent week, most of the admissions were white-collar workers. As time progressed, I realized that the "typical profile" was that of a tall, short, boisterously shy guy, who might be a young lady or old woman, who comes from rural urban areas where he/she works or stays at home or has no home, or several homes; with a socioeconomic background of riches or rags, and a religious background from none to priest, or varied, with an education of Ph.D., illiterate, who is physically dehabilitated and in excellent physical condition. Other demographics were too diffuse to identify.

The common threads of addiction are not woven into observable characteristics such as race, sex, creed, or socioeconomic economic status. People who get the disease look like ordinary people. Reports come out all the time from research on alcohol/drug use in various subgroups (i.e., aging, youth, the Jewish community, American Indians, rich people, poor people, etc.) Researchers often express some surprise that the sub-group studied gets the disease too. I have yet to read a report that found a sub-group which is alcohol- and drug-free.

Shared traits exist in the realm of behaviors and attitudes. Persons who are addicted typically misuse a substance and experience discomfort as a result. However, the commonalties lie in the attributes of addiction, not in the people who get consumed by the disease. The common behaviors and attitudes result from addiction; addiction is not caused by common behaviors or attitudes. It is true that many behaviors and attitudes exist before the first drink, fix, or pill is taken. This may well be part of the legacy of an inherited disease; not only is a predisposition for physical dependence on a substance passed down from generation to generation, but also the behaviors and attitudes which result in psychological dependence.

Not all common behaviors and attitudes are present in all persons addicted to a substance. This chapter provides a sampling of the shared traits. None of the following is based on fact; it is based on feelings. The first step to provision of effective Therapeutic Recreation services is the establishment of rapport with the clientele. To do this, the Therapeutic Recreation Specialist must be able and willing to step into the client's addicted awareness and then help the client see the way out. The sampling of feelings contained in this chapter will hopefully assist the Therapeutic Recreation Specialist to feel the world being experienced by the clientele. A client who displays feelings or attitudes described in a particular section of this chapter, may be assisted by involvement in activity referenced in the code at the end of the section. An explanation of the code is contained at the end of Chapter 1.

A STORY OF FRIENDSHIP

Once upon a time, I was bright, witty, intelligent, sensitive... but, I was a little shy too. Sometimes I didn't put my best foot forward. I worried about what others thought of me. I wondered if they knew just how insufficient I felt. Then, I met someone named Jack. He was different.

Jack and I became close friends, and it's easy to understand why. Jack was the kind of guy that brings the best out in his friends. When Jack was around, my best foot stepped forward automatically. I didn't even have to think about it. With Jack, there was no such thing as a dull party. I could always count on him to get something going. Jack was the life of a party, any party, and he always made it look like I was responsible for all the fun! Jack was the kind of special friend who could pick me up when I was down, settle me down when I was wound up. If I couldn't sleep, I'd call Jack. He knew just the thing to do. If I felt overworked, I'd call Jack. He could make the tension go away. Jack could always understand. Jack was always willing to listen. He was always there when I needed him, always concerned, always caring. Perhaps the best part about Jack was that he never talked back. He'd just listen and then agree, always recognizing the wisdom of my words. Indeed, Jack was a special friend and a close companion. I trusted him with my life. When he was not with me, life seemed drab, boring and empty. Without Jack, I was alone, vulnerable.

Friendship is a rare and highly prized commodity, though often sought, it's seldom found. Once a true friend is found, protect and maintain the relationship at all costs. And Jack was a true friend. I'd give my life for him if I had to.

One day, another friend came to me and said that Jack was causing trouble. The "friend" had the nerve to say that Jack was no good for me! That I should never see Jack again! My reaction was predictable. In shock, I lashed out at the person who was attacking my special friend. I defended Jack. After all, Jack was my friend. I knew him. What are friends for?

Anyone who could say such vicious things about Jack was no real friend of mine. From then on I made sure that Jack and I didn't cross paths with this other so-called "friend."

As time passed, Jack seemed to be the only topic of conversation. Other "friends" whined, "Do you have to spend so much time with Jack?" My family began to complain about my relationship with Jack. My co-workers and boss began to complain. Everyone started threatening me. "Either stay away from Jack, or get out!" I felt confused. What was wrong with everyone? Were they jealous? Were they just vicious? How could they even think such things, let alone say them?

It hurt. An attack against a close friend is always taken personally. In anger and hurt, I took a stand. "I'll see my friend Jack anytime I want. If you don't like it then somebody's got to go, but it won't be Jack without me going too!" With that I walked out on my family, my "friends," even my job.

Just getting rid of everyone didn't seem to solve anything. Anger and resentments grew. Sometimes I would go back and try to patch things up, but, sooner or later, it would end up in a fight about Jack.

One day I looked around and realized I had only one friend, one associate, left. My special friend, Jack, was still there. I hung out with some people. They were really Jack's people. About the only thing I had in common with them was Jack. (I didn't realize this until much later.)

Jack depended on me financially. He couldn't support himself. I understood that from the start. It was okay because nobody's perfect. Besides, what are friends for?

Spending time with Jack was expensive and bills began to mount up. Finances became stretched. The loss of everyone I cared for, except Jack, left an empty feeling. I began feeling lonely even if there were people all around. That would be okay, but Jack was changing too.

Jack used to help me sleep. Now he was keeping me awake. He used to help me be the life of the party. Now Jack thought it was funny to make a fool out of me in public places. On top of that, I had noticed old friends were still inviting Jack to their parties, but would cross the street to avoid me! I felt confused, frustrated, angry, frightened. Frightened, because sometimes Jack and I would walk out the door and the next thing I knew it was the next day or the next week. I couldn't remember where I had been, or what I had done. For all I knew I was a murderer and the next knock on the door would be the cops coming to get me. (In a way that would have been a relief.) Life was becoming impossible.

At last I began to see how Jack had betrayed me. At last I realized that all my problems had resulted from my relationship with Jack. In anger I tried to get rid of Jack. But he kept coming back to see me, promising this time would be different, this time we would be like we were in the beginning. He would offer to relieve my loneliness. Jack was sorry for what he had done and he would promise to behave himself. Sometimes Jack would keep his promise for a while. But, sooner or later, Jack would betray me again. Each betrayal seemed worse than the last.

I had always been in control. Now my life was out of control. I was destitute, lost, and alone. I was frightened with no place to hide from me. I would go back to my family and old friends if I could just swallow my pride. Going back meant admitting to them they were right and I was wrong. And pride was all I had left. Going back was also a big risk. I never was much before Jack came along, and now I was less. They might not want me back. Why should they? I had nothing left of value. I said and did so many hateful things when I was with Jack. What should I do? What would you do?

The special friend, named Jack in this story, is known to many by many names. Some call him "bourbon." Others call him beer, whiskey, or sour mash. Some call him pot, cocaine, downers or uppers. A special friend like Jack may come in the form of a liquid, powder, inhalant, or pill. His true name may be alcohol, tranquilizer, barbiturate, hallucinogen, or narcotic. Regardless of his form or name, he is a mind-altering, mood-altering, perception-altering substance. He may appear friendly or harmless, but he is not a friend. He is a betrayer of trust and an unfeeling killer.

What would you do if you discovered your "friend" and trusted companion was a sociopathic killer? What would you do if you discovered you were an alcoholic or a drug addict?

This story has several endings. There are choices. Some swallow their pride and accept help from former friends, family, employers, treatment centers. Some start fresh building new lives while other rebuild their old lives. Some get rid of "Jack" and replace him with a new "friend." Too often the new friend is Jack's twin brother, another addictive substance called by a different name. Some select death as the way out. Some do their best not to think about it.

For those who choose abstinence, the recovery process is long and often difficult. Physical recovery is swift compared to the emotional recovery process. Not only must a person learn to survive without a special friend, while facing problems created by addiction, but this must be done while the person is in a state of grief over the loss of his/her closet friend, Jack. Alcoholics Anonymous's Big Book states that alcohol is "cunning, powerful, and baffling" (pp. 58-59). Many say that they do not understand alcoholism or drug addiction. It is hard to understand if a drug is considered an inanimate object, rather than a living, breathing, feeling relationship between an individual and himself. [Ch8:100.1, 105.X, 106.X; Ch9:244.1; Ch10:34X.X; Ch11:440.0, 430.0, 450.0, 407.0]

IT'S ONLY NATURAL

Everybody's always telling me what to do. It's been that way all my life. Get up. Brush your teeth. Make your bed. Go to school. Do your homework. Go to college. Get a job. Take out the trash. Scrub the bathroom. Meet me at noon. Take Aunt Sally to the eye doctor. Wait here. Go there. Don't drink so much. Do this. Don't do that. Can't they see I'm sick of it? I wish everybody would just get off my back.

Are we born to search for wisdom and prosperity? Is it natural to us to seek knowledge, understanding, responsibility for the sake of being wise, compassionate, and self-sufficient? Do we fill our brains with facts and figures because we instinctively recognize their value? Do we reach for enlightenment because it is in our genes? Do we take on obligations because we are born with a need to be responsible?

If your answer is yes to the above, then I ask you, what picture comes to mind with the word "paradise"? Think about paradise for a minute. The most perfect place in the universe. Imagine yourself in this most perfect place. What do you see around you?

Does your paradise have an alarm clock? Is there a cranky boss or a deadline with you in paradise? Does your concept of a perfect world have five o'clock rush hours or traffic jams? Did you bring your checkbook and bills with you to paradise? While in paradise, did you spend time pushing a shopping cart through a crowded grocery store, or was there an ample supply of ready-to-eat food? Was paradise filled with responsibility, or was it free from all cares, worries, obligations, and concerns?

For most people, paradise is a lazy, warm, abundant place filled with peace, contentment, love, and self-satisfaction. It is not the search for wisdom and prosperity. Paradise represents the possession of wisdom and prosperity, without the responsibilities required to produce them. It is possession of, not the search for, "the good life."

Mankind's natural state has basic inherent desires. Becoming wise, compassionate, and responsible are not really part of the picture, for "being" and "becoming" are two very different animals. Paradise is "being." It is the desire for all the positive aspects without having to work to get them. Mankind, in his natural state, is lazy. Not bad, just lazy. It's only natural to want the "being" without going through the "becoming."

Why do we begin the undesired and sometimes painful search of "becoming"? Consider the fact that all small children wet the bed. Why? Because it is easier to wet the bed than wake up and walk to the bathroom. Why do most children stop bedwetting? Because it does not feel good to sleep in a wet bed. Considering this example, it would seem that we begin the search, assume responsibility for our own well-being, as a solution to a problem, as a means to relieve pain or an uncomfortable situation. Pain is an important aspect of life. Mankind clings to comfort zones. Without pain, most of mankind would be content to accept less than performance at full potential. When physical and/or emotional pain becomes too great, the personal comfort zone is abandoned. Cast out of comfort, the search for a solution to pain begins. The act of finding a solution brings with it improved understanding of the self, the situation, and the way the world operates.

The search for life's solutions is based on trial-and-error experience. Making sure the correct solutions have been found may require repeated trials—repeated trials resulting in comfort, but also repeated trials resulting in pain. Trial-and-error learning is time-consuming. Tribe elders attempt to reduce the time and pain required to learn the basics by establishing rules and regulations. Too many rules diminish self-development. Too many do's and don'ts can become as painful as the trial-and-error learning process they have replaced.

We assume responsibilities because we desire to overcome obstacles that stand between us and our comfort zone, our paradise. As we search, we learn. As we learn, we develop a sense of accomplishment. And as our sense of accomplishment develops, we develop self-worth. After awhile, the quest for knowledge, understanding, and responsibility becomes more important than the means they provide to solve problems. That which begins our search, does not sustain our search.

What has this to do with alcoholism and drug addiction? The alcoholic and the social drinker have the same concept of paradise. Both leave their comfort zones and begin the search for the same reasons. They exercise the trial-and-error process. During the search, the alcoholic discovers that pain can be wiped out by getting drunk or high. Applying the learning to new situations, the alcoholic discovers that all pains, problems, and obstacles can be wiped out by getting drunk or high. The comfort zone is restored immediately. A prescription is written: "At the first sign of suspected trouble, take one and call me in the morning. If pain persists, take another one." And it works!

The solution has side effects and drawbacks. It requires an ever-increasing amount of the chemical to achieve the desired effect. It short-circuits the natural learning process. Over an extended period of time the person only knows one solution for all of life's problems. Furthermore, the person has not learned to solve anything, only to wipe it out. The use of alcohol and drugs only provides temporary escape to the comfort zone. Eventually, alcohol and drugs create physical and emotional pain. But "old habits are hard to break," especially if the repertoire of habits consists of only one. Use may be continued years after the chemical has lost its ability to return the addicted person to the comfort zone.

When it is obvious that the trial-and-error learning process has gone awry, family and authorities increase rules and regulations to correct the situation. More do's and don'ts are added. The severity of consequences for failing to comply with the rules and regulations is increased. Drinking and driving becomes a don't. Then drinking and driving penalties are changed from a $100 fine to a $500 fine. Chemical use is banned in the home. Then penalties for use are increased from confinement to living quarters, to expulsion from the home. An increased quantity of rules and increased consequences of rules may help to push a person out of the personal comfort zone. But do they initiate self-direction? Too often the increased pain only results in application of the known solution—get drunk or high and wipe out the pain.

Such continued use is difficult for the non-alcoholic/addict to understand. The social drinker's experiences with alcohol are not the same as the alcoholic's experiences. Imagine if one were faced with a choice: experience pain for an extended period of time (a week, a month, a year, or more) which might result in learning how to get to paradise; or choose to get to paradise instantaneously. Which would one choose?

Which would one choose if all life's trial-and-error experience indicated that one had gotten to paradise instantly in the past? In the mind of the addicted individual, this is the choice that is presented. It takes a lot of guts not to choose instantaneous paradise. In fact it takes more guts than any individual has.

So how do the addicted recover? How can anyone manage to rise above the temptation of instantaneous paradise and mankind's natural state? The addicted person has no more (and no less) willpower than any other person. No one has the guts or willpower to rise above addiction alone.

Provision of detoxification and treatment programs cannot provide all the power needed to overcome addiction. Family support alone cannot do the job. Alcoholics Anonymous and Narcotics Anonymous cannot do it alone. Almighty God cannot do it alone. Increased rules and regulations cannot do it. But combining the forces of two or more of the above provides the power to arrest addiction. The whole is greater than the sum of the parts.

The more forces added, the greater the whole. The more parts combined, the less energy is required from each of the parts to get the job done. One part cannot be deleted. The individual with the addiction must be willing to be counted as one of the parts. All the forces of the universe cannot overcome addiction without the willingness of the individual who is addicted. All too often the individual is the last to be counted. The person becomes willing only after the pain is too great to be tolerated. [Ch8:100.2, 100.0LPfT; Ch11:408.0]

A CONCEPT OF GREATER PARADISE

At the beginning of life, all of a baby's needs are met by its parent(s). If mankind is totally lazy and searching for only comfort, then a baby is in total paradise. If the baby wants food, it is provided. If the baby can't sleep, someone rocks and sings to it. All needs are met for it. Is the baby content? Not for long. For no apparent reason, a baby will begin to struggle with itself. The baby's mind will engage its body in a battle. The baby will fight to lift its head. Once that battle has been won, the baby will fight with itself to roll from its stomach to its back, from its back to its stomach. After winning that battle, the baby will then fight to sit up, to crawl, to stand, to walk, to run, to jump, to talk, to understand. None of these come easy. The battles are engaged in response to an internal, not external, motivation. If all of mankind's natural desires were simply to live in comfort and avoid pain, we would all be lying on our backsides sucking our thumbs on our seventieth birthdays.

There is a concept of paradise born into us which is greater than that which we are experiencing at any given time. Just like Adam and Eve, we begin life's journey in paradise, without cares and surrounded by abundance. Out of the blue of peace and contentment, we grasp and bite into a new experience. Instantaneously, paradise, as we knew it, vanishes. We are cast out of our previous state of existence into a new world, into added responsibilities, into a journey, a search for greater knowledge, greater understanding, greater good, than previously experienced. As soon as we attain our new state of paradise, we take a bite from another apple and off we go again. Though the learning process may be stressful, and many attempts unsuccessful, we always move forward—not always in a straight line, but never backward. A child that has learned to run, never wants to sit still again.

This is referred to as the concept of a greater paradise. No matter where one is, no matter how much one has, there is an inner voice that whispers, "There is more to life than this. Find it." Hard work, added responsibilities are accepted as a means to attaining a perceived greater paradise.

What has this to do with addiction? When the individual's brain is saturated with chemicals, awareness is sedated. Contact with the concept of greater paradise is lost. While the concept sleeps, there is no need to have more, to be more, than what the individual is. Many will point to the addicted in scorn. "He's a hopeless drunk." "He's just a bum." He's not "just a bum," and he's not "unmotivated." He's doing exactly what anyone would do without an active concept of a greater paradise.

When chemicals are withdrawn from the brain, the concept of a greater paradise is awakened. But there is a quirk of nature that causes problems. The concept of a greater paradise has not been dead, only asleep. Just as a child grows while it sleeps, so too the concept grows as it sleeps.

Without sedation, the concept and person grow at the same rate. The concept of greater good stays just one developmental stage ahead of the person, beyond grasp but within reach. But the addicted person has not been growing at the prescribed rate. When the chemicals are withdrawn, the concept awakens and the addicted individual sees paradise several developmental stages ahead. The first reaction to the revived concept is panic. The person feels a need to catch up with it before it grows any greater. While in the initial stage of recovery, this individual may try to run before learning to walk. Or, it may appear that this greater paradise is beyond grasp and reach. Where the concept of a greater good inspires most of mankind, it can bring despair, depression, panic, and frustration to the person recovering from addiction.

The distance between the individual and the concept of a greater paradise can be diminished. The balance between what is and what is desired can be restored. But this is a process that requires time and patience. Phrases such as "one day at a time," "first things first," and "easy does it" are important to the recovery process. These phrases help the individual focus on making the most of the present while forgetting about the gap between where one is and where one wishes to be. Placing emphasis on making the most of the present speeds the rate of personal growth. The concept of a greater paradise grows at a constant rate. In time, the individual's speeded rate of growth places the concept not in grasp, but within reach.

There is a second aspect of the concept of a greater good. It hates to be sedated. Once awakened, it resists being suppressed. Once a person has been "dried out," has had an opportunity to think clearly for a while, a return to using is never the same. Once awakened, the concept of a greater paradise seizes every possible opportunity to remind the individual of where one is in relation to where one ought to be. [Ch8:100.0, 100.2, 100.3SoLG, 106.2; Ch9:200.0, 23X.X; Ch11:405.2, 430.0, 402.0, 420.0]

LEARNING THE LESSONS TOO WELL

I'm smart. I only had to stick my hand on a hot coal once to know that all things with flames burn. I only had to trip over a curb once, falling and skinning my knee, to learn to look ahead and avoid walking over dangerous terrain. Nobody was there to pick me up when I fell, so I learned real fast to avoid all falls.

I see some people who never learn. I can't understand it. Like Winston over there. He put all his money into starting his own business. I could never do that. What would happen to him if he fails? Then there's Suzanne over there. She's divorced and she's dating again. Can't she see that this new relationship could end in pain just like the last one? And Bill over there, he just got a new dog because his old dog died. What's to prevent this new dog from dying too? Jori just bought a new house. That's a dangerous move with the economy in the shape that it's in. They just go out and stick their hands in the fire over and over. Seems like everyone wants to get burnt. Not me.

I'm smart. I never repeat the same mistake twice. I know how I will end up before I start something. I went to a party one time. I felt like a jerk. Didn't know what to say so I quit going to parties. I had a relationship once. It went bad and I hurt. I can't avoid all relationships, but I'm prepared for it to fail. No one will ever hurt me like that again. I had a dog once. It died. I never got another one. Besides, what good is getting a dog to feed when the world's going to blow itself up? I'm smart. I'm careful. I'm prepared. So how come I feel so empty when I don't have a drink in my hand?

The operative words in this story are unwritten. There is a need for control, a lack of trust. There is a lack of tolerance for imperfection, especially within the self. There is an attempt to eliminate all risks from life. Logic is substituted for emotion. Logic is neat, orderly, and dependable. Emotion and intuition are unpredictable. It is assumed that any outcomes left to chance will automatically result in personal disaster.

Eliminating the risk of pain and failure also eliminates the chance for pleasure and success. Negativity is a habit that is difficult to change. It is the nature of addiction for bad things to get worse and for good things not to last.

Negative thinking is counterproductive to recovery. Doom is a self-fulfilling prophecy. Those who look for trouble find it. Those who prepare for a relationship to end, find the relationship ends. But is it logical to suggest that people not plan ahead? Is it wise to suggest that people leave themselves open to pain and heartache? Not exactly. The key is to refocus the energy. Get people to believe that good things are as likely to occur as bad things (when addiction is arrested). Help them realize that they are strong enough to withstand a negative event should it happen. Errors in judgement occur; failure is not always fatal.

Leisure participation can rekindle positive feelings. It's hard to think of gloom and despair in a room filled with happy, laughing souls. Games that provide an element of chance and risk are a safe place to begin risking oneself. Logic and measures of self-protection should not be abandoned entirely. But there should always be room for a pleasant surprise. [Ch8:100.1, 107.0; Ch9:2X6.X, 247.1, 277.1; Ch10:33X.0, 347.0, Ch11:450.0, 460.0, 470.0]

A HUMOROUS VIEW: THE BABY FACTORY

Where do babies come from? The Baby Factory of course. It is located in the far southeast corner of Heaven and is a *holy* owned subsidiary of Heaven. It follows all of Heaven's corporate policies. The factory is filled with assembly lines which produce, assemble and stockpile everything a person needs for a lifetime on Earth. One entire stockpile system is devoted to alcohol. It is common knowledge that consumption of unapproved alcohol causes alcoholism. Prior to birth, each baby is given an allotment of approved alcohol. The Baby Factory Policy is to give each baby the same amount. It is a full lifetime supply.

Now Heaven is a nondiscriminating, equal opportunity employer. (No one has to work in Heaven, but many do anyway.) Job placement is based on desire, expertise, and experience. Naturally, most of the qualified people who request work in the alcohol unit of the Baby Factory are (or were) practicing alcoholics.

Most Baby Factory employees drink on the job. (There are no rules against it. After all, it is Heaven.) Each morning, everything starts off routine, but as employees help themselves to the alcohol coming down the assembly line, they begin to lose count of the number of bottles they are placing in each baby's allotment. By the end of the day things are pretty confusing. As a result, most babies receiving alcohol allotments in the morning have a lifetime supply of approved alcohol and live out their lives as social drinkers. But by quitting time, some babies have enough to last two life spans and others may only have one approved drink in their stockpile. The paperwork gets fouled up too, so attempts to correct the situation are time-consuming and usually ineffective. Quality control specialists are sometimes able to identify a problem and correct it. Occasionally a baby with an inadequate supply of approved alcohol is recalled. But recalls are time-consuming and parents get irritated when their babies are not delivered when due.

A task force was appointed years ago to find a solution to the problem. The people on the task force spent their lives in committee work and love it. They have little knowledge of alcoholism and have nothing better to do with their time than to sit around and nit-pick issues. To date, they have come up with a few ideas but nothing has solved the problem. When asked for a report, the task force suggests that the easiest thing may be to just let it continue and let the people on Earth correct the problem. After all, if they have found a cure for a number of diseases, Earth people will eventually find a cure for alcoholism. Besides, the practicing alcoholics working in the Baby Factory seem happy, so maybe it's not such a bad problem after all.

Accurate records maintained in Heaven provide certain consistencies here on Earth, clues that researchers use to identify and correct problems. But the sloppy condition of the baby alcohol allotment records have complicated matters. Researchers are now beginning to unravel the mystery of alcoholism. After many dead ends, and thousands of years, researchers now know it is a disease. At this time there is no solution for prevention at the Baby Factory, and there is no cure on Earth.

Meanwhile, down here on Earth, another baby is being born with an inadequate allotment of approved alcohol. Another social drinker is stepping over the magic line. At this moment another human being is dying from addiction. Somewhere, someone is praying, "Dear God, why me?"

When there is a problem without adequate reason, the mind creates an explanation. Fiction takes on a disguise of fact. As long as the fiction explains the situation, then it is believed. The Baby Factory is fictitious, but it seems plausible, for it explains what is known about alcoholism. If an alcoholic is asked, "Why do you drink?" an explanation will be rendered. An explanation no more and no less plausible than the Baby Factory explanation. The truth is that the problem is not drinking. The problem is getting drunk. People get drunk because they drink. Problems resulting from drunken behaviors end when people stop getting drunk. Getting drunk ends when people stop drinking. Job stress, family disputes, financial problems may be sighted as the "cause." But the true "cause" was the choice to take a drink. To cite job, family, or other problems as the cause is as productive as placing the blame on the Baby Factory.

Information about addicted ancestors is often omitted from family histories, making it difficult to accurately trace the disease genealogically. Even so, researchers continue to find mounting evidence that a predisposition for addiction is inherited. This does not mean that every person with an addicted parent automatically becomes addicted. As in the case of diabetes, it means that the disease is more likely to occur. Preventive education should be provided. Substances known to cause problems should be eliminated from the diet before symptoms are experienced. [Ch3; Ch4; Ch8:107.0, 106.0, 105.0; Ch9:207.0, Ch10:307.0, Ch11:407.0]

AN ANTI-SOCIETY VIEWPOINT

Why are there alcohol and drug rehabilitation centers? Why have there been no smokaholic rehabilitation centers until recently? Chain-smoking is also an addiction which is dangerous to a person's health. The key to understanding the need lies in some key phrases which are popular, such as "excessive use," "inappropriate behavior," "irresponsible acts," and a "means to cope which does not work."

"Excessive" by whose standards? The alcoholic's? Is the consumption of 20 bottles of beer a day excessive when an individual usually drinks 24? "Inappropriate" to whom? Do people behave in a manner that he/she feels is inappropriate at the time? "Irresponsible" according to whom? If alcohol is a "means to cope" then it must work quite well for the alcoholic. Why else would one continue to use it as a coping mechanism?

Amounts of drugs or alcohol consumed are excessive as defined by social and cultural norms. Behavior is inappropriate and irresponsible according to society's dictates. The addicted individual may be able to cope (through drug use) with society, but it is difficult for society to cope with the addicted. Treatment centers are often spawned, not out of concern for the addicted, but out of concern for the well-being of society. Until recently, tobacco addicts have been viewed as causing little harm to society, therefore treatment centers were not created to save them from their addiction. Now that it has been discovered that their smoke can harm non-smoking members of society, treatment centers will most likely be created for them.

The addicted person wages a single-handed war against society and social norms. He or she is outnumbered. Even so, this person would win the war if it were not for one thing. There is a part of society and its norms within the addicted. The addicted person stands divided within. As war is waged against society, it is inadvertently waged against the self.

The addicted person suffers repercussions from this personal war which increase as the war continues. The person may suffer a loss of social prestige, loss of family, loss of employment, and loss of personal freedom (as a result of incarceration from arrests and involuntary commitments to treatment facilities). As the addicted continues, the individual's ability to meet personal needs decreases. It becomes an all-or-nothing, win-or-lose battle.

The treatment process is often caught up in the society's-will-over-yours battle. A judge may give someone a "choice," six months on the road or a voluntary admission to treatment. An employer or spouse may offer similar "choices." It is hoped that the treatment center can do something that they have not been able to do: to win the battle; and get the addicted to submit. The addicted person who chooses not to be persuaded into submission at the treatment center is labeled "unmotivated" and/or "unresponsive to treatment." Further social disgrace is piled upon him. He may be "dishonorably discharged" from the treatment facility or refused re-admission, and the win-lose battle goes on. Is it any wonder that there are burned out alcoholics; persons too tired to live and sometimes too tired to drink?

The addicted eventually realizes that society cannot be changed, and is left with only three choices: 1) withdraw from society as much as possible by making lifestyle changes to accommodate alcohol/drug use; 2) die; or 3) live without alcohol/drug use. To the nonaddicted, the least painful alternative may appear to be the last of these; however, for the addicted, living without alcohol/drugs is often the most painful alternative. The number of addicted individuals living as homeless souls on our city streets makes clear the alternative of choice.

Therapeutic Recreation treatment must steer clear of this battle if it is to be effective. A win-win way of life must be modeled before living without alcohol/drugs can be viewed as an acceptable alternative. Freedom and enjoyment of leisure can make a large contribution to the win-win model. Acceptance and appreciation by others of the individual's uniqueness, not as an addict but as a person, helps to create a win-win situation. Facility rules and regulations governing client behavior should be kept to a minimum. But where rules are set, they should be upheld without exception. Making exceptions only rekindles the win-lose philosophy. Alcoholics Anonymous and Narcotics Anonymous are win-win programs. Many people enter the programs because they feel they have lost the battle, and that they have to go. But those who stay sober/clean in the programs go to meetings because they want to. AA and NA regulars develop a win-win way of life. [Ch5; Ch11:430.0, 440.0, 450.0]

TOGETHERNESS, FOREVERNESS

Bufo and I do everything together. We're not clones. In fact we are a couple of opposites. Bufo is outgoing, wild and zany. I'm a deep thinker, shy and reserved. We're a team like George Burns and Gracie Allen. I deliver the straight line and the set-up, and Bufo delivers the punch. Together we keep the world in stitches.

Our skills are balanced too. Bufo makes the money and I pay the bills, keep the books. Bufo makes the decisions and I handle the details. I read the literature, and Bufo explains to me what it means. Sometimes life is a roller coaster, but one of us always has the skills to bail the other out.

Bufo and I never disagree for long. I know what's best for the both of us. Bufo would never last long without me. Sometimes I have to play games and pull a few strings to keep Bufo headed in the right direction. But that's just part of any relationship.

I know everything Bufo is doing and when. I call and check on Bufo to make sure everything is going according to plan. If Bufo is late, I panic. I've been known to call all the hospitals if Bufo's late, to see if Bufo's been involved in an accident. Bufo does the same when I'm late. I find it a little

irritating when Bufo does it to me. It's like Bufo doesn't trust me. I feel pressured. If I bump into an old friend, I can never stop to talk, because I know I'm due home.

Other people don't understand our relationship. They don't see the good side of Bufo like I do. All they see is when Bufo gets loaded and tries to knock my block off. Some say I should leave. They don't understand. Where would Bufo be without me? Where would I be without Bufo? Each of us has only half of what it takes to survive.

Life is not created in a vacuum. Where one dwelleth, so dwelleth another. The problem is called "co-dependency." Co-dependency has existed for centuries. It is only recently that it has been labeled as a problem. In the past of farm life and one-income home life, co-dependency was the rule rather than the exception. There was cause for alarm when the logger or hunter did not return from the woods on time. The skills of the breadwinner were specialized as were the skills of the person who remained in the home. But in today's two income families and single-parent households, the need for independence is greater than the need for dependence. This is not to say that all dependence on a mate can or should be avoided. The type of dependence which results in dysfunctional living, is the type that prevents one or both members of the relationship to grow to full maturity. Today's complex society requires self-sufficient behavior. Independent people depend on each other because they choose to, not because they have to.

My parents were highly dependent upon each other. They were from the old school and lived a traditional lifestyle. Life was structured. Routines were well-established. There was men's work, and women's work. Free time was spent together. If the car needed gas, they both made the trip to the station together. I remember the time my dad was in the hospital for a critical condition. It was the first time my mother considered the possibility of going on without him. She shared her feelings with me. The thought of solitary life was obviously painful, yet there was no doubt in her mind that she would survive without him. "Who's going to take care of me?" This question was not a concern for she already knew, she could and would take care of herself. Dad recovered so I never had the occasion to find out how Mom might have actually functioned without him. There is little doubt in my mind that she would have done whatever was required to survive. If that included returning to the work force (doing typical female things) she would have done so without protest. Three years later Mom died. Dad had a difficult adjustment. Survival required him to learn to do the traditional female things. Though he learned to use pliers for a potholder and a screwdriver for an eggbeater, he became a good cook. While he welcomed opportunities to trade his manly skills for female skills (a widow got her grass cut in exchange for an invitation to her dinner table), there was never any question of who took care of him. Dad took care of Dad as he had all his life. The only need he reached outside of himself to fill, was the need for companionship.

In dysfunctional co-dependency, "Who's going to take care of me if..." is a primary concern. Decisions to stay in or return to unhealthy relationships are often made as a result of a perceived need to be cared for by another. The need for pleasurable companionship takes a back seat to the need to be clothed, sheltered, and fed. There is an attempt to achieve self-actualization through the accomplishments of another. There is an effort to remain blameless by pointing the finger of dysfunction at the other.

There may be some validity to the feeling that each person only possesses half of the skills required to survive. The old adage that "opposites attract" may be true. If, for example, one person is extremely outgoing, and the other is extremely introverted, by joining together, an averaging effect occurs which brings the two extremes back to middle ground. Desolving the relationship then subjects each to lopsided life. Though the averaging effect works, it has seeds of destruction built within it. The outgoing person is given the job of being outgoing, and the introvert the job of being introverted. As the outgoing person practices being outgoing, this person becomes more outgoing. As the introvert practices the introvert's job this person becomes more introverted. Personal strengths get stronger and weaknesses weaker. The distances between the extremes gets wider. If the introvert begins to value introversion, or the extrovert extroversion, then the differences may become a source of friction. If the extrovert begins to practice introversion, or the introvert extroversion, then the fear or replacement creeps in. One partner begins to fear that the other doesn't need him or her anymore. Strategies are developed to stop the partner from developing.

The extrovert—introvert dichotomy is just an example. The division of skills or abilities could be almost anything. It could be a proven track record for making money as opposed to a complete lack of marketable skills in the job market. It could be creative thinking as opposed to logic and sound judgment. Making use of the partner's skills is not automatically unhealthy. For example, I may not be the greatest carpenter. That doesn't mean I have to live with a person who is good with hammer and nails. If my companion likes to hit nails, that's great. But if he hasn't got time to put my book shelf up that's OK too. I know I can do it myself, or hire someone to do it, or live without it. My companion may not type very well. But if I am unavailable, he'll type or find someone else to type for him. If I start thinking that I can't live without his hammering, or he can't survive without my typing, then the relationship is headed for trouble.

Co-dependency can only be solved by both partners being willing to change, or by dissolution of the relationship. Simply breaking the bond of a dysfunctional relationship does not solve the problem. The co-dependent, left to his/her own devices is likely to form a new relationship which is also co-dependent. To break this pattern, the co-dependent must become self-dependent first. Only then can a healthy relationship develop.

In the process of breaking the bonds of co-dependency, persons go through an intermediate stage of pseudo-independence. Self-sufficiency becomes so important that the person attempts to do everything single-handedly. Doing everything alone seems to be the opposite of doing everything together.

Living with the fear of letting others help is no better than living with the fear of doing everything alone. Pseudo-independence is an important middle step back to health. It is not the ultimate solution. The final destination is a relationship in which two people give each other room to grow and are not threatened by the growth which results. In a healthy relationship, dependency is not required but may be chosen for the sake of expediency. An unwritten contract exists in which each depends on the other equally to meet needs which each is capable of meeting independently.
[Ch4; Ch8:100.0BTToAG, 100.2, 105.1; Ch9:2X5.1, Ch10:349.3; Ch11:405.01, 410.0, 420.0, 450.0]

WHICH CAME FIRST?

Which came first, the chicken or the egg? Does it really make a difference so long as there are scrambled eggs for breakfast? Knowing which came first changes very little. So, too, there are many aspects of addiction, such as what causes it, that are interesting to think about but do not really change the outcomes. Knowing what caused the addiction will not erase the addiction.

Sensitivity is one of those "which came first" aspects of addiction. Recovering alcoholics often seem more sensitive to others than many non-alcoholics. They are frequently able to notice subtle posture shifts, subtle changes in voice tone and inflection. They often respond more to how something is said than to the actual content of the statement. A sharp remark may seem to register at 10 times the volume intended by the person issuing the remark. This sensitivity, or "people-reading" ability, is a gift which cuts both ways. The people-reading gift is usually matched with a people-pleasing desire. Some people seem to get caught up in people reading/pleasing during recovery. They become frustrated and have difficulty separating what they want from what others want for them. They also assume that others can read them as well as they can read others. "Why tell him? He could see how I felt." But most of us do not have this gift. We can't see. We must be told.

The curious point is, which came first? Were alcoholics more sensitive to others before they started drinking? Is one of the advantages of alcohol use the fact that it shuts out this sensitivity to others? Or is the sensitivity caused by the drinking experience and by feelings of guilt? Or is it a phenomenon of being adrift in the treatment process? Perhaps some application of the school system to the treatment setting, where to give the answers desired by the teacher meant getting a passing grade? Regardless of when it started or why, the recovering alcoholic who merely attempts to say and do the correct things is missing the point of treatment. The Therapeutic Recreation Specialist who defines a model client as one who also agrees and participates, may also be missing the point. The client who recovers tends to be the client who questions, disagrees, makes mistakes and learns from the experiences. This is less likely to occur as long as the client is focused on pleasing others.

Many persons who are addicted are manipulators. Were they able to manipulate others before they started drinking/using, or was this behavior learned in the process of substance abuse? Is the sensitivity described earlier the reason they are able to manipulate others so well? Again, the answers to these questions do not matter. What matters is that manipulation tactics must end if the person is to experience a full and meaningful recovery.

Honesty is most difficult yet most necessary to the recovery process. Which is the learned behavior, honesty or dishonesty? Did dishonesty develop as part of the denial system, or did the denial system develop as a result of the person never being honest with himself about anything?

Regardless of which came first, when the addicted person decides to abstain, the person must learn to cope with his sensitivity. He/she must learn to be honest, stop people-pleasing, stop manipulating, and face life with trust. Each and every therapeutic recreation session provided in a treatment facility should be designed to support self-direction and honesty. The client who plays a game of cards because he thinks it will please the teacher is no better off than the client who takes a drink to fit in with his friends. The client who cheats at cards is no better off than the client who thinks it's OK to use so long as no one finds out. The client who blames the loss of a game on poor lighting or faulty equipment is no better off than the client who believes everything would be okay if people would quit nagging about the use. Most of all, the client who spends a treatment stay trying to figure out how he/she became addicted is no better off than the chicken who sits quietly contemplating "which came first—the chicken or the egg," while the farmer's wife approaches with stewpot in hand. [Ch5; Avoid activities that encourage intellectualizing.]

CONTROL

Though many addicted persons appear to be easily controlled by external factors, the opposite is true. Persons with addictions have a strong internal locus of control. It is for this reason that one cannot advise a person to "stop drinking" and expect the individual to stop drinking. Control is extremely important to the addicted person. Control is equally important to family members and to persons who grew up with an addicted parent.

The need for control may be exhibited in a number of ways. Attempting to control the quantity of drugs or alcohol consumed is obvious and quite common. In the home, control may be a matter of who sets or breaks the rules. It may manifest itself as a need to know where family members are going, when, and why. It may take the form of decision making for some and attempting to dictate behaviors for others. It may also take the form of attempting to control personal destiny. To control personal destiny does not always require a crystal ball or star chart. It may simply require manipulation of all variables to stack the deck in the person's favor before venturing into a situation. A great deal of time may be spent in rehearsing what will be said and not said prior to an opportunity to say anything. It may be a matter of asking questions about the unfamiliar, or studying the situations from many angles before getting one's feet wet.

Aspects of control have a direct impact on leisure behavior and the selection of leisure options. A person who is consumed by controlling others may find it very difficult to forget about others long enough to become regenerated by a leisure pursuit. The person who fears a loss of control may fear unstructured leisure time or participation in an unfamiliar leisure pursuit. It is difficult to control the unknown. How can the variables be controlled when there are no variables? Being caught with nothing to do is being caught with nothing to control. These are some of the dilemmas presented by unstructured leisure and participation in the new.

It is prudent to exercise some degree of control, to look before one leaps. The type of control referred to in this section goes beyond the wise and prudent level. This type of control saturates every aspect of life. It may prevent people from doing many things that contribute to productive, healthy lives.

The need for control is not a cause; it is a symptom. Need for control may result from a fear of risk taking. Fear of taking risks is a symptom of feeling inadequate and lacking trust. Feelings of inadequacy are a symptom of not taking risks. Uncontrolled situations present the possibility of something happening which cannot be managed, or may require more capabilities than an individual possesses. The inability to control consumption may mean going through life drunk or high, doing things which ultimately result in feeling inadequate. The inability to control consumption may also imply going through life without a drink, fix or pill, facing situations which result in feelings of inadequacy.

The Therapeutic Recreation Specialist cannot wave a wand and make the control problems go away. But helping a person see the possibility of functioning in the unknown without a stacked deck can make a significant difference. [Ch8:100.0, 109.0; Ch11:460.0]

THE GEOGRAPHIC CURE

A new home; a new life. All I do is cut grass and fix things. If the rent were lower, we would not argue about who spends what for what. I think I'll move.

A new apartment; a new life. The traffic is loud and the neighbors can be heard through the wall. We are always arguing because we're too crowded and always tripping over each other. I think I'll move.

A place in the country; a new life. The rent is low and I can't hear the neighbors. We are always arguing because I'm never home and I have the only car. I think I'll move.

A new apartment; a new life. We are always arguing because work keeps me so stressed out. I think I'll get a new job. A new job in a new town. A fresh start. That's what I need.

A new job. A new home. A new town. The same old life. They say I have a drug problem. Perhaps they are right. If the pusher didn't live on the same street, I wouldn't use so much. I think I'll move.

A new home. The same old life. If we didn't argue so much, I wouldn't need to drive clear across town to visit the pusher all the time. I think I'll move and leave the family behind.

Single life. Same old life. If the boss would get off my back I wouldn't have to use so much. I think I'll move to a new town, a new job. . .

The geographic cure is an attempt to solve personal problems by changing environmental factors. Geographic cures take the form of changing marital status, and occupations, as well as changing residences. Geographic cures may be small or large, from moving across the street to moving across the country. The reasons for the move always make sense and are very logical solutions to the stated problem. Geographic cures seldom work because the stated problem is not the real problem. Moving from one locality to another will not end substance abuse, for there is no place on earth where an intoxicating substance cannot be found or created. There are no relationships that are void of stressful moments or an occasional conflict. Even the most perfect living space has some built-in disadvantages. Granted, it is not conducive to recovery to be living with or next door to a pusher or practicing addict. Certainly, a fresh start and a new life might have therapeutic benefits. But the change alone will not solve problems that have their roots within the individual. A change in the outer world is only helpful after there has been a change in the inner world. [Ch8:108.0; Ch11:420.0]

DENIAL

Has the reader ever wondered how to solve the problem of addiction? Most people have. Over the years, the author has heard many ways. The following solutions come to mind as some of the more creative ones. They were suggested by clients during initial stages of treatment.

1. Allow liquor by the drink; when a person can buy just one, then there will be no need to worry about what to do with the rest of the bottle.

2. Paint the walls of bars and taverns in light colors, because blacks, dark reds, and blues cause a person to drink more.

3. Reduce the number of brands and varieties on the market; with so many choices it gets confusing.

4. Allow a man to drink in peace.

All of these are logical solutions, derived by logical methods. But, they are classified here as examples of the symptoms of the disease rather than solutions for the problem.

Control and geographic cures are symptoms of denial. Prior to recovery, denial pervades every aspect of an addicted person's life. It is present during periods of use as well as during periods of abstinence. It is often a key difference between someone being "dry" and "sober." Denial also manifests itself in family members.

Denial can take obvious forms such as refusal to admit there is a problem. Denial is present when a person is willing to admit to "drinking too much," but not to being an alcoholic. Denial is often present when someone seeks help for emotional disturbance, or nervous disorders, but refuses to discuss drinking and/or drug use patterns. A person in denial might say, "I can quit any time I want to. I just don't want to." "When I get that bad I'll quit." "When it becomes a problem I'll quit." "If . . .would just get off my back, everything would be alright." "I can handle it." "I don't need anyone's help." "I'm different." "You can't understand my problem." "If I lived somewhere else, I could control it." "It's not my fault!" "I know a guy who is 90 and drinks every day! It hasn't hurt him." (And I know ten guys who died before they were forty as a result of use, but what difference does that make?)

Less obvious forms of denial are likely to emerge after an encounter with a treatment program. In treatment, support is given for verbalizing, admitting to being an alcoholic/addict. Persons issuing common expressions of denial are confronted. Through this feedback some realize the truth and are assisted along the path of recovery. Others learn to guard their words carefully, discovering that it is easier to say the "right words" than to explain their honest opinions. For some the feedback causes a crack in the armor of denial. When the person can no longer believe his own blanket denial, he moves from statements such as, "I don't have a problem," to "I know I have a problem but. . ." "Yes. . .but. . ." sentences usually express unexpressed denial. The best one I ever heard was, "I know I'm an alcoholic but I'm a different kind of alcoholic. I don't get out of the way when I drink." Within one week of making this statement, the person had been in a blackout, lost his job, and was in jail for public drunkenness. How "out of the way" must one get to be an alcoholic of the regular kind?

Some expressions of denial occur without words. Many addicted individuals discontinue contact with recovering alcoholics/addicts. They drop out of AA/NA, after-care programs, and other structures of support. The expressed reasons are usually time conflicts, personality conflicts, transportation problems, fatigue, and so on. The true reason may well be the fact that attendance makes it difficult to keep the denial system intact. Some may give the reason that "they are not like me." If the "they" in the statement means recovering persons, then the statement is probably true, though not in the way the person had in mind.

Family members are often caught up in denial. "If I just get good grades, then daddy won't get drunk." "If I don't tell anyone, no one will know." "If we move from the pusher's street then everything will be alright." "If I take a second job so there will be more money, then everything will be OK." "If she could just see herself then everything will be alright." "It's not my fault." "It is all my fault." Perhaps the two most common ones are, "If he/she would just quit drinking then everything will be OK," and "If he/she will just go through treatment then everything will be alright." In fact, it is never that easy. Recovery is a change in behavior which results in adjustments for all family members. To this notion, the spouse may snap the reply, "He/she is the one who drinks, not *me*!"

What causes denial? It may be argued that the stigma attached to being an alcoholic or an addict is so repugnant that it is easier to accept almost any other identity. Some would prefer to believe they are mentally ill, rather than addicted. Trembling hands are not a result of alcohol withdrawal, it's just "bad nerves" and a case of the denials. Some find psychiatric treatment preferable to treatment for addiction. Is it socially more acceptable to be crazy than a drunk? Or is it that so many emotional disorders are treated by administering mood-altering chemicals? Perhaps both.

As the public becomes educated that addiction is a disease rather than a curse, the strength of denial should diminish. The stereotype of a drunk in the gutter may always be with us. People under the influence sometimes forget that others can see them. Since the recovering person looks no different than anyone else, they walk the streets unnoticed. Celebrities and public figures who have openly admitted to being in recovery have done a great deal to educate the public to the difference between practicing and recovering from addiction. The day will come when denial is minimal, when a person will admit to being addicted as easily as people today are able to admit to being diabetic.

Some non-addicted shy away from using the terms "alcoholic" and "addict." These are clear-cut terms with powerful absolute connotations. But, addiction is a powerful and absolute disease; only powerful terms have an edge sharp enough to cut through denial. The most powerful weapon that Alcoholics Anonymous has in its arsenal is in their greeting: "Hi, my name is. . .and I'm an alcoholic." There is little room for denial in such a greeting. [Ch11:410.0]

THE MAGIC LINE

In frustration a person in treatment once snarled, "What do people think? They act like I sat down one day and said 'let's see, what do I want to do with the rest of my life? I know, I'll be an alcoholic!' There is a great deal of truth to this statement. Users and abusers start in the same ways and for the same reasons. Many report years of drinking "like other people" before drinking alcoholically. This is often referred to as crossing an invisible magic line that divides social drinkers from alcoholics. Once crossed, a person is never able to return to social use of alcohol.

The social drinker and alcoholic do share the same desire, to drink and get high without suffering painful consequences. A social drinker with a hangover will swear off booze for life only to drink again. The alcoholic will do the same. A social drinker will blame the hangover on "bad booze" or the mix, or the brand. The alcoholic will do the same. A social drinker

may point a finger at others who consume more and whisper that the other guy has a problem. The alcoholic will do the same. No drinker can be positive that alcoholism will not develop as a result of use until he or she is "six feet under."

There are ways to know that one has not yet stepped over the line into the magic world of alcoholism. Many social drinkers set limits and consistently stay within those limits. Alcoholics find staying within the limits increasingly difficult as time progresses. Limits set by social drinkers are usually measured by the drink rather than by the bottle. A limit set by a social drinker is not usually all that can be consumed within a specified period of time. A social drinker reaching his or her limit will not feel compelled to finish an opened bottle. Social drinkers will attend a function where drinking is not permitted and will not feel compelled to pack along a supply or leave the function early. Most importantly, a social drinker does not have others suggesting a reduction of consumption. Social drinkers do not find chemical use at the root of their problems.

Some believe there is a difference between an alcoholic and a problem drinker. An alcoholic is one who abuses alcohol and drinks alcoholically. A problem drinker is one who drinks because he/she has problems. Once the situation is resolved, then the person is able to return to "normal" drinking. He/she can have just one drink without activating the craving for more. Of the hundreds I have known who drank alcoholically, I would classify only one as a problem drinker. There are problem drinkers; persons who, 20 years ago abused alcohol and are now content with a single beer on an occasional warm Saturday afternoon, who have not been intoxicated for 20 years. While each alcoholic would like to believe he/she is that one in hundreds who is just a problem drinker, it is dangerous to assume that the problem drinker is immune to alcoholism. It is possible that a problem drinker is just one who has not yet crossed the magic line. For the problem drinker there is only one safe course of action which will prevent the development of alcoholism. It is total abstinence. For every problem drinker who has returned to social drinking, there is at least one problem drinker who has become an alcoholic. If the thought of total abstinence seems to be an intolerable alternative, then the continued use of alcohol will invariably result in alcoholism. [Ch8:100.0 LPfT]

THERE IS A BIG DIFFERENCE BETWEEN LIVING AND EXISTING

I have worked with a number of special populations. The addicted population has been the only group to respond to the title of this section. Any time I felt a need to get my clients' attention, I would just say, "There is a big difference between living and existing." Immediately the room would get quiet. Bodies would come to attention and lean forward. Eyes would focus and study my face. Someone would mumble "Amen," or a similar comment indicating agreement and identification with the statement.

Existence is life sentenced to routinizes without hope of parole. It is the bottom rung of Maslow's hierarchy, having food, shelter, clothing, and a living hell for the addicted personality. Many look at their neighbors and find it incomprehensible that they survive, for they do the same thing day after day, year after year. Many an addict would find death more appealing if it weren't for the fact that being dead is doing the same thing day after day after day.

To the addict, living is exciting. Living is getting ahead of the game, rather than just keeping pace. It's having all the senses stimulated and all the faculties in action. Living defined in these terms is never knowing the meaning of being content. It's Maslow's hierarchy upside down, with feelings of self-actualization the first priority, and so what if I have to sleep under a bridge tonight?

I've known practicing addicts who sleep under bridges. When I watched a homeless friend being pulled out of an abandoned car, almost frozen to death, it occurred to me that the will to survive was very strong indeed. But "surviving" is more akin to living than existing. To survive in the face of adversity pumps the adrenalin. The addicted pursues the roller coaster ride, getting a rush from going up and going down. The view from the top and bottom are of little interest. The level runs are static, boring, merely existing.

There is a big difference between living and existing. Healthy leisure can breath life into mere existence. Therapeutic Recreation can help persons examine their definitions of boredom and excitement. The struggle to survive may be exciting, but it's not much fun. Boredom can be reformed into opportunities for contentment. [Ch8]

ALCOHOLIC OR ADDICT: IS THERE A DIFFERENCE?

An alcoholic is one who uses alcohol to become intoxicated while a drug addict is one who uses drugs to become intoxicated. Aside from this obvious difference, there are more similarities than anything else. Alcohol is an addicting drug. The behaviors, problems, and emotions produced by addiction are much the same regardless of the properties of the particular drug of choice. A case may be made for differences existing between persons who use stimulants and person who use depressants. There are other differences. Drugs are illegal and typically cost more than alcohol. Many drugs produce a quicker high. Drugs may also result in addiction more quickly, have fewer tell-tale signs, or leave a residue in the body for a longer period of time. Different kind of drugs vary in length and severity of withdrawal symptoms and type and amount of physical damage done to the body. For example, alcohol may require a longer period of detoxification than cocaine. Alcohol use may cause more physical dehabilitation to the body than cocaine. On the other hand, fatalities resulting from first use of crack clearly occur more frequently.

The illegality of drug use tends to make it more secretive. Fear of incarceration may delay attempts for treatment. Many persons addicted to drugs may seek treatment for alcoholism, while denying the use of other drugs.

The high cost of drug use creates a major difference. Alcohol abuse may result in severe financial stress over a period of time. The alcoholic who can spend $100,000 on booze may not exist, while there are those who have managed to spend that much on cocaine in a matter of months. With alcoholism, financial problems keep pace with disintegrating health, deteriorating social status, and so on. When the alcoholic hits bottom, all areas of life are in equal collapse. Expensive drugs can wreak financial havoc long before physical or social discomfort is experienced. Too often the financial trauma creates discomfort for the user's family, and stretches law enforcement resources, while hardly reaching the drug abuser physically. This may make it difficult for the drug abuser to stop since this individual has not experienced the full impact of the problem. Family and authorities cannot afford to wait until the drug abuse "hits bottom" before taking action. If an alcoholic has been arrested for a serious offense (such as check forgery), the person may have also been offensive to family members for a long time. The first reaction of the alcoholic's family is often tantamount to "good, throw the key away." For the addict's family, memories of the nice guy may still be fresh, the penalty of a lengthy prison term (or long term treatment stay) may seem too harsh, and their initial reaction may be to want to bail their relative out. In these ways differences do exist between the addict experience and the alcoholic experience.

In the treatment setting, alcoholics may insist that they have little in common with drug addicts. Prescription pill addicts may insist that they have little in common with drunks and people who buy drugs on street corners. Narcotic addicts may feel their problem is different from all the others. Young clients may insist that their problems can't be helped by listening to older clients, while the older ones may feel they can't be helped by listening to kids "still wet behind the ears." Men can't be understood by women and women can't be understood by men. The rich can't be understood by the poor, and the poor can't be understood by the rich. Doctors' problems are different from lawyers', and lawyers' are different from nurses'. Vietnam vets are different from World War II vets. Homosexuals have problems different from heterosexuals and marrieds are different from singles.

It has been said that a cocaine addict is different, because the cocaine addict becomes addicted to a lifestyle as well as a drug. This may be true, but is it different? The teenage addict may be addicted to a lifestyle of rebellion. The alcoholic may be addicted to a lifestyle of cocktail hours and champagne breakfasts, or happy hours and just "hanging out" with a drinking crowd. Regardless of the drug of choice, recovery requires withdrawal and abstinence from a lifestyle as well as from chemicals.

Years ago, pronounced differences existed between addicts and alcoholics. From the end of Prohibition until the cultural revolution of the 1960s, alcoholics and addicts lived on opposite sides of the railroad tracks. A person had to travel to "dens" of iniquity to find drugs. They were not served at the boss's Christmas party. In those days, the typical alcoholic did not use drugs. In fact, part of the initial attractiveness of Alcoholics Anonymous may have been the implication that a person addicted to alcohol was different. He was not mentally ill. He or she was not some drug-crazed low life; this person was an alcoholic. Narcotics Anonymous got its start in the same way. A person who used drugs was not mentally ill, not just an alcoholic; this person was an addict.

The 1960s brought drugs into popular "recreational" usage. Today, most persons who have had the opportunity to become addicted to alcohol have also had the opportunity to become addicted to drugs. A person invited to a friend's home might be offered marijuana, cocaine, and other drugs as well as alcoholic beverages. Using alcohol as a chaser for pills is also common practice. It would seem the difference between alcoholic and addict has almost vanished. The membership of Alcoholics Anonymous may now be comprised of persons who used only alcohol and got sober prior to the 1960s revolution, as well as persons who have joined since then who feel their drug of choice is alcohol, but have used other drugs as well. Narcotics Anonymous also has a mixture. Members who identify their primary drug of choice as a narcotic are probably outnumbered by stimulant, depressant, and hallucinogen users—most of whom have also used alcohol.

Though most alcohol and drug use is a purely leisure phenomenon, some persons arrive at addiction through medical avenues. The housewife who refuses a social drink, may find herself addicted to physician-prescribed tranquilizers. The assumption that "It's safe because the doctor ordered it," has backfired countless times. Others have become addicted to narcotics after severe injuries requiring extended use of painkillers. It is not known whether addiction by recreation has different treatment requirements than addiction by physician. One thing is certain, the person who makes the rounds to several physicians to gather an adequate supply of physician-prescribed drugs, or the person who hides the number of pills being taken from family members, is acting no differently than the person who buys his or her supplies on the street corner.

Are there differences? There is a grain of truth to each group's complaint that they are different. But the fact that each group makes the same type of complaint indicates how similar they all are. By focusing on differences they are all able to avoid dealing with their common problem of addiction. Being different is a great way to maintain the denial system. There are two solutions. Separate groups can be established for each subgroup. The other way is to take time to clear away the differences before focusing on the real problem. Regardless of differences, that which assists the recovery of an alcoholic also assists the recovery of an addict. Though properties of drugs vary, specifics vary, addiction is addiction. [Ch3; Ch5:Detox]

HABITUATED ADDICTION OR ADDICTED HABITUATION?

The use of appropriate terms is important, right? It is easy to see the vast differences between a Recreation Therapist, an Activity Therapist, and a Therapeutic Recreation Specialist, right? Therapeutic Recreation is not the only field with a number of multi-syllable terms floating about. Another example is provided by the terms alcoholism, drug abuse, substance abuse, and chemical dependency. Alcoholism is supposed to be addiction to alcohol, drug abuse is addiction to drugs, and chemical dependency means addiction to a combination of the above.

The fact is that most terms used in reference to alcohol/drug abuse are inappropriate and/or inadequate. The term "drug abuse" implies that drug use is okay but abuse is not. Both drug addict and alcoholic fall into this trap, when it is decided to use just one. The answer to "how much" is always "just one" or "a couple" for admitting to more than this is unacceptable while admitting to just a little is OK. It has been suggested that more accurate terms are "drug use" and "self abuse" (Newton). This implies that drug use is a progressive illness which results in self destructive behavior. With this interpretation, "just one" is one too many.

The term "rehabilitation" is often used interchangeably with "treatment." Treatment connotes the Medical Model, which is a system of "curing" a disease. The Medical Model is a system in which a physician identifies the problem and prescribes a course of correction for the patient. The patient, and all others involved, passively take orders and do what the physician has prescribed. This is a totally inaccurate approach to alcohol/drug addiction and has been the cause of considerable debate, because the key player is the "patient", not the physician. A disease contracted by personal choice cannot be resolved without personal choice. "Rehabilitation" is not much of an improvement. It comes from the Team Approach Model, which allows discretionary action among allied health personnel. The physician serves as a coordinator and a medical specialist, drawing strength from other specialists to make appropriate decisions. However, this model still does not focus the attention on the patient as the central player. An Alcoholism Counselor, Joe Bennett, once pointed out that "re-habilitation" implies a return to former capacity. Persons in alcohol/drug treatment are seldom returned to anything. He suggested it should be "habilitation." A good point. The alcoholic cannot be restored to social drinking, nor is it wise to return him or her to a social drinking lifestyle. So in most instances the goal is habilitation or assisting the client to a new way of life.

Recovery is another problematic term. No one ever "recovers" the ability to drink and/or use drugs at will. The term "recovery" is used to imply a positive and progressive development toward self-fulfillment without chemical use. What is "recovered" is the ability to function in society and being happy about it.

The term "addiction" is equally misused. Technically, addiction refers to the physical aspects of the disease. A person who develops a tolerance for the use of a substance and experiences withdrawal symptoms when the substance is not administered, is considered to be "addicted." A person who is able to drink his or her friends under the table is considered to have developed a tolerance for alcohol. When this person quits drinking, and the hands shake or hallucinations occur, then the person is addicted to alcohol. Technically, those who do not experience such symptoms but have developed a lifestyle which revolves around alcohol (or some other drug), are said to have a psychological habituation for the substance rather than an addiction. A person who is physically addicted also has psychological habituation. Those who are psychologically habituated usually wind up physically addicted. Some drugs are said to be nonaddictive. Cocaine for example was considered a nonaddictive drug. This statement was made because there was an absence of observable withdrawal symptoms.

The term "habituation" will not be used in this text. The problem is that use of the two terms implies a difference, and addiction seems to connote a more serious problem than habituation. In fact, both are aspects of the same disease; both are equally serious. Habituation, or psychological dependency, is what causes a person to reach for the first drink, fix or pill, after a period of abstinence. Addiction is what causes the person to continue use after the first drink is taken. A great deal of the treatment for addiction is geared toward helping the person break free from the habituative aspects of the disease. Detoxification is geared toward helping the person break free from the addictive portion of the disease. Therapeutic Recreation does little to change the addictive outcomes of the disease; it can do a great deal to change the "habituation" aspects.

Perhaps the only accurate term used in the field is the street term for LSD which is "acid." LSD, like cocaine, may not have the withdrawal problems associated with barbiturates, narcotics, and alcohol. I'm sure that is a relief to the ex-user who is spending the rest of his life thinking that his psychiatric ward is an enemy space station.

There is a critical semantic difference between "drunk" and "alcoholic" and between "junkie" and "addict." Drunks and junkies are hopeless individuals; alcoholics and addicts are persons with hope, for they have a disease from which life can be salvaged. A primary step in the recovery process is the admission by the individual that he or she is an alcoholic or drug addict. These are not negative terms. This text often uses "a person who is addicted" or "the addicted person" as a reminder to the reader that the person is more than a disease; he or she is a unique creation, an individual. No matter how down and out, there still remains a spark of life waiting to be fanned into full flame. The Therapeutic Recreation Specialist must never doubt that the spark exists or quit looking for the right fan.

The confusion, inaccuracy, and misuse of terms is a revealing reflection of our culture's comprehension of the problem. It is also a telling indicator of the state-of-the-art in problem correction. No terms are offered here which are any better than those in use at this time, nor is the purpose of this text to correct terminology. "Habituation" is not used in this text. Characteristics of habituation are referred to as the psychological factors of the addictive process. "Addiction" is used to imply both the physical and psychological aspects of the disease. An "alcoholic" is an addict whose drug of choice is alcohol. An "addict" is one who has a disease called addiction. A detailed definition of addiction is located in Chapter 3, Of Drugs and Addiction.

References/Resources

Alcoholics Anonymous (The Big Book). (1976). Alcoholics Anonymous World Services, Inc., Grand Central Station, New York, NY.

Alcoholics Anonymous (Living Sober). Alcoholics Anonymous World Services, Inc., Grand Central Station, New York, NY.

Beattie, M. (1987). *Co-dependent No More; How to Stop Controlling Others & Start Caring for Yourself.* Hazeldon & Harper & Row.

Curlee-Salisbury, J. (1981). *When The Woman You Love Is An Alcoholic.* St. Meinrad, Indiana: Abby Press.

Langone, J. (1976). *Bombed, Buzzed, Smashed, or... Sober: A Book About Alcohol.* Boston: Little Brown.

Maxwell, M. A. (1984). *The Alcoholics Anonymous Experience: A Close Up View For Professionals.* NY: McGraw-Hill.

Middelton-Mos, J., & Dwinell, L. (1986). *After the Tears; Reclaiming the Personal Losses of Childhood.* Enterprise Center, Deerfield Beach, FL: Health Communications, Inc.

Narcotics Anonymous. (1982). Narcotics Anonymous World Service Office, Inc., Sun Valley, CA: C.A.R.E.N.A. Publishing Co.

Newton, M. *Gone Way Down: Teenage Drug-Use Is A Disease.* Tampa, FL: American Studies Press.

What do you mean I have a problem: The editors interview Father Joseph Martin. (1983, October). *US Catholic*, pp. 27-33.

CHAPTER 3

OF DRUGS AND ADDICTION

In the first version of this text, this chapter was titled, "The Factual Side." The fact is that facts are changing. The challenge of knowing the facts in this area is compounded as we learn more and more. The basic fragments of what is known about addiction and drug action have not changed, but new fragments of truth are continually coming to light. New and old truths are combining in ways that change "factual statements" significantly. All facts based on the theory that the world was flat made sense until Columbus brought back information that just didn't fit the big picture. Then the "facts" changed to fit the new round-world theory. Today, the same factual revisions are occurring, not only in the study and treatment of addiction, but in all health sciences. The research of today, even seems to sometimes contradict itself. Stagner astutely identified the problem when he wrote, "Attitudes not only determine the conclusions we shall derive from facts, but influence the very facts we are willing to accept" (Monroe, 1950, p. 77). This chapter shares the facts which the author's attitudes have allowed her to accept.

A couple of decades ago, a standard definition of addiction was based on the presence of withdrawal symptoms. If there were no withdrawal symptoms, then there was no addiction. This definition fit well with later stages of alcoholism. However, it did little to address the total problem, for it excluded all drugs of known abuse that did not end in withdrawal systems. Also, people were entering treatment earlier in their drinking careers, so fewer severe withdrawal symptoms were being observed. The old definition fed many an alibi: "I'm not an alcoholic! I don't get the DTs!" The old definition was helping people to stay sick rather than to get better. Furthermore, treatment procedures that helped in the recovery of persons who had experienced withdrawal symptoms, also aided the recovery of persons who had not experienced withdrawal symptoms. This was solid evidence that the definition was incomplete. About 15 years ago, I was told that there were five addictions. There was alcohol, drugs, gambling, work, and I can't remember if the fifth was food, sex, smoking, or what. Again the old definition of addiction came into conflict with this five-addiction theory. These factors proved that it was possible to be "addicted" to something without experiencing withdrawal symptoms.

The known facts were reorganized into a new definition(s). The definition I used back then (and continued to use until 1989) was problem-oriented. If a substance caused problems in a person's life, then the person was addicted to the substance.

This definition fit and permitted the inclusion of more than just alcohol and drugs in the list of addictions that resulted in withdrawal.

At the time I was told about the five addictions, I was also told that they were all branches of the same tree. I was cautioned that a person addicted to a substance on one branch of the tree could easily substitute a substance from another branch and become addicted to new substance as well. This precaution carried with it the implication that it was best to abstain from use of all substances on the tree of addictions. My definition of addiction as a problem source and the addiction tree concept was a neat little package and served me well for many years. It looked like this: (See Figure 3.0, page 28).

But the march of new information continued. New drugs of abuse were discovered. As ignorance gave way to understanding of addictive characteristics, people began to identify other substances which were being abused and causing problems in people's lives. The list of addictions grew. It doubled and then tripled. Each one fit my definition so I added a new branch to my tree. One day, not too long ago, a terrible thing happened. . . (See Figure 3.1, page 29).

My tree was all filled. Still, a steady stream of addictions demanded to be given branches on the tree. The list now included such things as food, video games, chronic back pain, smoking, coffee drinking, moving, and several leisure activities. This sent me back to the drawing board in search of a new tree structure and perhaps even a new definition.

As I looked at the branches, I noticed some interesting things. Overeating and undereating were on the same branch. Are they really the same? Alcohol remained a branch to itself, yet was it really that different from some of the other drugs? The drug branch now had five shoots depressants, stimulants, hallucinogens, narcotics, and "designer drugs." Yet hallucinogens are quite diverse in their characteristics. Designer drugs mimic the actions of other drugs. Did they all belong on the same branch?

The search for answers led the author into a newly emerging field of science, called psychoneuroimmunology. This new science is quite overwhelming. Not only does it give us long multisyllabic and unfamiliar words to fathom, but it changes the "facts" that have been the basis of medical practice for centuries. Before sharing a new definition of addiction and basic information about groups of addictive substances, the author will share the information that has brought her to this new viewpoint.

FIGURE 3.0

THE ADDICTION TREE WITH FIVE BRANCHES

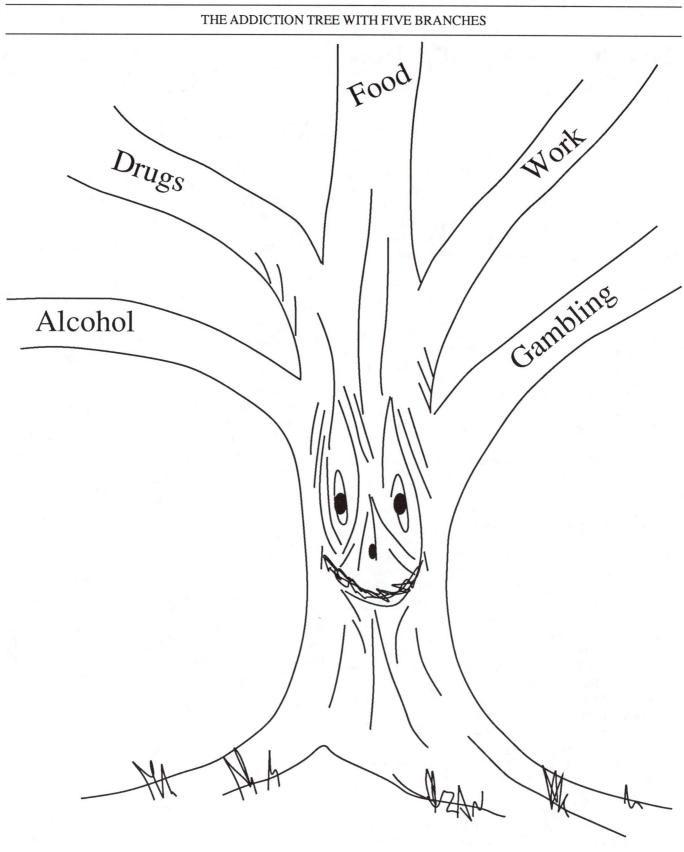

FIGURE 3.1

THE ADDICTION TREE FULL

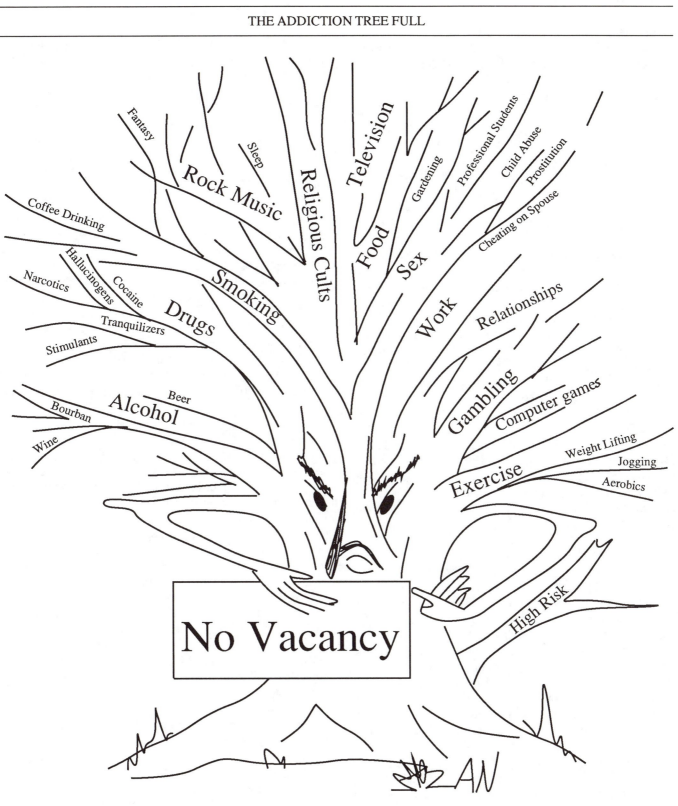

A LOOK INTO THE BODY

Earlier in this century, the atom was known to be the smallest unit of existence. When the atom was shattered, a new world emerged. When man walked on the moon, the stars and planets became part of a changed horizon. Over the last three decades, a new universe has been discovered to exist within each human body. The world of DNA was unveiled in the early 1960s. The mysteries of nerve impulse conduction and hormone action began to be unraveled. Today the exploration of new worlds which exist within and between nerves continues.

It is easy to gaze upon the stars and recognize the infinite radiating from one's personal viewpoint. Looking at a mirror, one forgets that the infinite also exists within. One can see skin and feel the muscle and bone structure under the skin. But the boundless possibilities created by 100+ billion neurons, either firing or not firing in the brain, at any given moment in time, creates a universe so awesome that it defies comprehension.

Research into nerve impulse conduction has been slow to develop because the components involved are so incredibly small. While a nerve may have an extension quite long, the nerve cell body itself is only 0.00788th to 0.0197th of an inch (Davis, 1984, p. 15). *That's* small. But the big area of new research lies at the ends of the nerve's protrusions and what happens between the end of one nerve and the beginning of the next. The space between the end of one nerve and the beginning of the next is called a synapse and is approximately 1/100,000mm, or 0.0000004th of an inch (Clark, 1985, p. 28). But the rascals that tote information across this tiny space are even smaller. A lot smaller. One compound, beta-lipotropin is considered "big." It contains a handful of the amino acid chains that actually do the work. Beta-lipotropin is 10,000 daltons. Since a dalton is about six ten-trillionths of a trillionth of a trillionth of an ounce, I might have made it sound too large when I called it small (Davis, 1984, p. 33).

In addition to smallness, methods of extraction remain primitive. To extract a substance, researchers have had to pulverize, mash, grind, squeeze, and filter brain matter. Since it is difficult to find human subjects willing to sign consent forms for such procedures, animal brains have been the primary source for research materials. (30,000 pig hypothalami hit the blender to produce 18 millionths of an ounce of one rascal known as alpha-neo-endorphin.) (Davis, 1984, p. 52). Without Purée of Brain Humana on the menu, researchers have found the testing of theories a slow go. It is obvious that animal brains do not operate exactly the same way as human brains. This must be remembered anytime an attempt is made to apply animal brain research to human function. Still, factual knowledge gained from the study of animal brain action has led to the creation of important theories about human brain action. Where creative researchers have been able to find ways of testing their assumptions on humans, it appears that what is true for animals is true for humans in many cases. Fortunately, new methods of identifying and testing are being discovered, as well as new substances. So future research may move faster.

A review of basic terms may facilitate discussion of the nerve. The nerve or neuron has a center called a cell body. The cell body has an outer skin or membrane which contains protein and fat molecules. The membrane conducts electrical activity. Within the skin there is cytoplasm containing proteins, sodium, and potassium chloride. Sodium has positively charged electrical particles called ions. Chlorine has negatively charged ions. This permits electrical voltage to pass through the nerve. When this happens it is called a nerve impulse. Closer to the center of the nerve cell is a substance which probably manufactures proteins used by the cell (Clark, 1985). Within that substance is the cell nucleus, and within the nucleus is the cell's DNA.

The nerve is not round. It has one long extension that looks like a tail, called the axon. There are many other branches extending out called dendrites, which are about one twenty-fifth of an inch long. The tips of the dendrites branch out hundreds of times into dendrite spines. This results in approximately 100,000 dendrite spines on each nerve. The end of the axon may also have small branches. At the ends of these are small points called the presynaptic region. Information is sent from the axon's presynaptic region across the synapse to the beginning points of the next nerve's dendrites (the receiving ends of the dendrites are called the postsynaptic region) (Clark, 1985). The synapse is small, yet too wide to permit the electrical activity, nerve impulses, to bridge. Researchers were puzzled. (See Figure 3.2)

Something good comes from everything, even opiate addiction. Based on concepts of chemical actions that have been discussed since 1877 (Julien, 1981), researchers theorized that the opiate molecules were plugging into the brain somehow. They went in search of the receptors and found them. Then they went in search of a reason why the brain would have such receptors and discovered opiate-like chemicals that are manufactured inside the body. These became known as endogenous opiates. It is interesting that the prime focus of attention throughout the research is how endogeneous opiates are like exogenous opiates and how they are different. Had we never stumbled onto opiate addiction, we would have never learned so much about how our brains function. So three cheers for opiate drugs, especially morphine, which has become the standard for comparison and identification of the body's own natural painkiller system. What goes around comes around, it seems. Today, enough is known about the body's internal opiate system to begin speculating about why opiate users become addicted.

It is now believed that information is transported by chemicals that flow from the presynaptic sites on the axon of one nerve, across the synapse, to the postsynaptic region on the dendrites of the next cell. The chemicals that transport this information are called neurotransmitters, neurohormones, and neurotransporters. Neurotransmitters tend to be generated close by. Neurohormones are produced in the adrenal glands and travel throughout the body. A neurotransporter is any substance that transports nerve information; this includes both

FIGURE 3.2

PICTURE OF A NERVE CELL

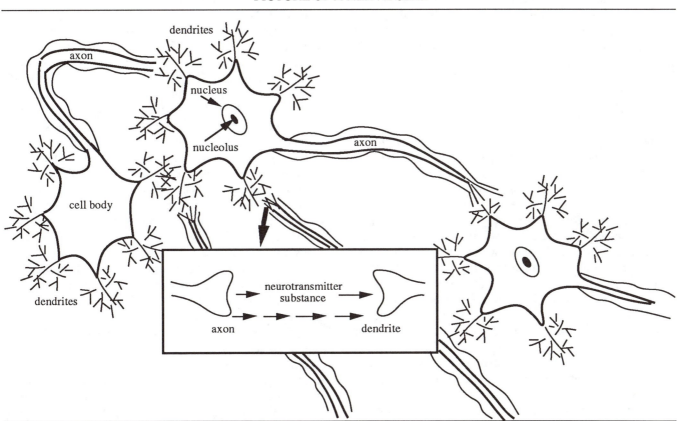

the neurohormone and the neurotransmitter. So whatever they are called, they ferry bits of information across the synaptic bay and dock in the postsynaptic region. The dock is called a receptor.

Science seems to practice convergent thinking. That is to say, researchers tend to look for the one correct answer or solution. In the course of looking, they found an endogenous opiate and ecstatically hoped it was the one and only one, the answer to all questions. But the discovery of a second type of endogenous opiate came quickly after the discovery of the first. Then came another and another. Other chemicals have been discovered floating through the body which are not opiate-like in characteristic. It now appears that there are hundreds of chemicals that serve as neurotransporters, hundreds of "correct answers." Furthermore, the body often uses the same chemical for different purposes in different areas of the body. Endogenous opiates have been found in the bloodstream, indicating they have a possible role as hormones; in the heart, where they may be involved in cardiac reflex activity, as well as various areas of the brain and spinal cord where they function as neurotransmitters (Davis, 1984). With all this floating around inside us there would be mass confusion except for one thing. The receptors are specialized so that only specific chemicals can fit into specific receptors. There are more receptors which accept a specific neurotransmitter in one part of the nervous system and fewer (or none at all) in other parts. In this way the body is able to send information to one part of the brain without disturbing other functions.

The information transmitted is very simple, something of a yes-or-no, do-or-don't type communication. But with more than 100 billion neurons, even simple becomes complex. If each neuron has just two choices (e.g., fire or don't fire), then the total possibilities generated by 100 billion neurons is "two multiplied by itself a hundred trillion times" (Davis, 1984, p. 20). In addition, this is not a one-shot deal. We can't take a single snap-shot of the activity for analysis and assume that we have the total picture of brain activity. We have reviewed only one of the "two multiplied by itself a hundred trillion times" possibilities. Brain activity is continuous. Then there are human brain and animal brain differences to consider. Then there is your brain, my brain, and my first ex's brain. Learning how my brain operates may tell us something about how your brain operates, but I can assure you, it will offer no clues about my ex's. Until we have 100 billion researchers working 'round the clock, our comprehension will be slow to evolve and will remain limited for quite some time.

Neurotransmitters appear to be involved in the body's "fight-or-flight" system, the system that turns off the fight-or-flight" system, the body's pain and repair system, the system that turns off the pain and repair system and the body's immune system. I believe that all of the above are interconnected with an individual's thoughts and emotions. When a person participates in addictive behavior, the person is interacting with specific neurotransporter receptors. But that's not the goal of the behavior. The goal is to produce a desired feeling or effect. So to understand addiction, it is important to understand the internal systems that are being manipulated.

The Endorphins

As previously mentioned, researchers went in search of a molecule produced within the body that might fit the receptor in which morphine fits. The first one was discovered in 1975. It was named enkephalin, meaning "in the head" (Davis, 1984, p. 40). Since then, others have been discovered. Some are similar to enkephalin and others are distinctly different. Those similar contain "enkephalin" in their name. Those which are different are called "endorphins" which is a contraction of the words "endogenous," meaning "inside the body," and "morphine" (Davis, 1984, p. 44). None of these are exact copies of morphine molecules but appear to effect the body in the same general way. In 1986, an exact copy of morphine was found to be produced in the brain, in extremely small quantities (Ornstein & Sobel, 1987).

The names of these rascals are often followed by the word "peptide." A peptide is a small molecular chain of amino acids (Davis, 1984, p. 42). These small chains of amino acids are sliced out of larger structures. The parent structures are called precursors. At least three different types of receptors have been found for the endogenous opiate group. Some nerves may have multiple opiate receptors, permitting different types of endogenous opiates to act on the nerve at the same time (Davis, 1984).

The endorphins are somewhat larger than enkephalins (Clark, 1985). Enkelphins are larger molecules than morphine, heroin, or methadone. All have an amino acid called Tyrosine (Tyr) at one end. Both morphine and enkelphines have chemical structures that result in a negative electrical charge, which attracts it to a positive charge and permits an anionic bond to form. Theory has it that there are sites or pockets on the membrane of the neuron. These "tetrapeptide pockets" are positively charged. The opiate molecule is attracted and fits into, or "bonds" to the receptor sites. The portion of the molecule containing the Tyr amino acid is the part that plugs into the socket. Once the molecule is in place, the information contained in the rest of the molecule is probably transferred to the neuron (Davis, 1984). When an endorphin or exogenous opiate molecule bonds to a receptor site, it inhibits the neuron; that is, it stops the neuron from firing. Thus, these agents are called inhibitory neurotransmitters.

The fact that the enkephalins and endorphins are larger than exogenous opiates suggests that heroin, and the other external opiates, can sneak into places where they don't belong. The brain and body may be a chicken coop protecting its yummy chicks with a 3-inch-mesh wire fence from a wolf (external opiates) who is 2 inches tall. The author has found no research that examines the consequences of this size difference. Still, the point warrants theoretical contemplation.

Endogenous opiates are only found in extremely small quantities. When external opiates are administered, they arrive in massive quantities. (Has the reader ever been in the middle of a drought and prayed for rain? And then got Noah's Flood?)

The fact that the structure of endogenous and exogenous opiates are similar but not exactly the same also says something. The information being transferred may not be exactly the same. While it is true that a volleyball will fit through a basketball hoop and a volleyball can be used to play basketball, a professional basketball team would never substitute a volleyball for a basketball. Why? Because a volleyball is not a basketball. Their inherent properties are different. The professionals prefer the real thing. Not suprisingly, our bodies prefer the real thing too.

Some will say that if the body produces a trace of actual morphine, then injecting externally-produced morphine is exactly the same. Some may even say that the endogenous opiates, which do not have exactly the same structure, act on the body in exactly the same way as external opiates. But even if the chemicals were precisely alike, there is still a big difference in the way endogenous and exogenous opiates are produced.

Endogenous opiates originate in larger precursor molecules. The precursor floats along, minding its own business. Then something happens to break the precursor down. That something is contact with an enzyme. When the meltdown occurs, several fragments are released. For example, pro-opiomelancortin (POMC) appears to be the endorphin precursor (Davis, 1984). Pre-POMC first breaks in two. One fragment contains, among other things, adrenocorticotropic (ATCH). The other fragment is beta-lipotropin. Then, ACTH is broken off from the first fragment, while beta-lipotropin is broken into smaller fragments known as gamma-lipytopin and beta-endorphin. At some point, gamma-lipotropin may be broken into fragments. So the process of creating beta-endorphin results in the release of beta-endorphin, ACTH, and other fragments such as alpha-MSH, beta-MSH, and CLIP. The pituitary gland releases beta-endorphin and ACTH at the same time. Once released from the pituitary, ACTH travels to the adrenal glands where it regulates the release of hormones such as norepinephrine. Norepinephrine becomes a regulator of blood flow by causing blood vessels to constrict. Norepinephrine is part of the "fight-or-flight" system. Meanwhile, the beta-endorphin is busy plugging into painkiller sites in the neurons. (It would appear that whoever set this up did not have much confidence in our ability to win a fight or make a timely escape. Before we even engage in battle, our body is preparing to triage our wounds.)

Now what happens when external opiate painkillers are injected into the system? They rush into the body and immediately plug into the opiate receptors on the neurons. And that's that. That's fast. But nothing else has happened. The pre-POMC molecule is not injected, nor are the other fragments of the precursor molecule. So, it can only be concluded that many of the ingredients the body needs to maintain internal balance are not being provided.

In other words, the pre-POMC is everything the body needs to play ball. When the whistle blows, the POMC-supply-room door opens. Out come the score cards, which are sent to the scorekeepers. Out comes the rule book, which is sent to the umpire and the team is given the basketball. When morphine or heroin is sent into the body, the POMC-supply-room door stays locked. Scorekeepers have no score pads. Umpires have no rule books. The basketball team stands in mid-court, not prepared to play, and is inundated with soccer balls.

What would one do in the shoes of the basketball players? Quit? That appears to be what the neurons decide to do, too. Remember that neurons are not isolated entities. The 100+ billion neurons are interconnected. Many have long axons to form a network of action throughout the body. Stopping the firing of a single neuron in the brain creates a chain reaction that shuts down the operation of many neurons and neurotransmitters throughout the body. When external opiates are introduced, the sensors measure an overproduction of endogenous opiates and shut down the production process that creates endogenous opiates. The use of externally-created chemicals creates internal imbalance. First, there is a flood of too much of one thing, then not enough of anything. When the exogenous drug wears off, there is a lack of endogenous opiates floating around. So the neurons are permitted to fire off faster than usual. Thus, the slightest exposure to norepinephrine or other stimulating neurotransporters causes the neurons to fire, and since one neuron is connected to many others, too many neurons soon reach an excited state. The solution found by the heroin or opiate addict is to deluge his/her system with more soccer balls. The longer this continues, the more out of whack the system gets. After a long run, the basketball players not only refuse to play, they have forgotten how (Davis, 1984).

Enough conjecture. The facts (as known at the time of writing of this text) indicate that the endogenous opiate system is a painkilling system. Studies indicate that it is linked to many other functions. At this point it is difficult to say whether endorphin release causes other phenomena, or if other phenomena cause the release of endorphins, or if other phenomena and endorphin release simply happen at the same time with one having nothing to do with the other. Still, the following is what research has figured out to date.

Poppy juice, the source of opium, has been used for thousands of years as a painkiller. A derivative of opium, morphine, came into use as a painkiller over a century ago. Heroin was created for the same reason, to kill pain. It was hoped to replace morphine and originally billed as a non-addictive drug (Ornstein & Sobel, 1987). Opiates fit into endorphin and enkephalin receptors. It is not surprising that the internal opiates are painkillers. It would appear that they play a primary role in the pain reduction system and a supportive role in many other systems.

Some studies reveal that the endogenous opiates may be involved in other functions. Heroin depresses breathing. Some types of internal opiates may do the same. They may all create euphoria. This euphoria may be a result of stimulation of pleasure zones in the brain, but it seems more logical that the great feeling is primarily a result of "feeling no pain."

Researchers have also discovered a possible connection between endorphins and pain-motivated learning. Increased levels of endorphins may reduce a person's ability to learn from a painful event. At least that's true for some rats (Davis, 1984). Perhaps this explains why an addicted person can hurt so bad during withdrawal and then a few days later say that "just one won't hurt."

Endorphins have been linked to non-opiate drugs too. In a German study in 1987, there appeared to be a connection between alcohol preference and enkephalin levels in animals. They also found a significant reduction of beta-endorphin in the CFS of alcoholics. The exact connection, the how or why, was unclear (Topel, 1987).

"Runner's high" may be a result of endorphin action. Jogging creates stress on the body. The body may respond by increasing the action of its natural painkillers. At least four studies have shown that physical exercise results in increased levels of beta-endorphin and ATCH in the blood. Some believe that the beta-endorphin molecule is too large to pass from the blood stream into the brain (Davis, 1984). Perhaps it is manufactured in the brain as well and scientists just haven't found the correct way of measuring it. Or perhaps when the heart gets pumping from physical exercise, something happens to push the endorphin through the barrier between blood and brain. As a dancer, the author knows from personal experience that perceptions of pain often decrease as strenuous physical exercise increases and a state of euphoria results.

Shock seems to increase levels of endogenous opiates. Electroconvulsive shocks, used to treat some forms of psychiatric problems, increases Met-enkephalin levels in the brains of rats. Trauma that results in a person going into shock may also involve endorphin action. It has been found that naloxone can reverse some of the effects of shock. Naloxone counteracts opiate action. Basic anxiety and stress which are associated with the "fight-or-flight" system preparation have been associated with increased levels of endorphins as well. Increased endorphin levels exist in some people who suffer from anorexia nervosa (Davis, 1984). This may be a result of the stress the body endures as a result of the disease.

Some research has looked at the emotionally evoked state of thrills. Thrills are characterized by that spine-tingling feeling that may come from experiencing something emotionally touching. It could be something very good or sad, or mysterious, or. . .hearing that special song can do it. It has been found that naloxone reduces the intensity of the thrill experience. This may mean that endogenous opiates are involved in producing the thrill experience (Davis, 1984).

The placebo, it turns out, is an inactive substance which does something. For years researchers have tested the action of one substance against a supposedly useless substance to determine results. One group of subjects might get pills containing a new painkiller, while a second group get pills that look identical but only contain sugar or some other inert substance. Well surprise, surprise. While the placebo pill contains nothing of benefit, the act of taking it can result in a reduction of symptoms. Apparently, the subject's belief that the pill is a real painkiller triggers the internal production of opiates, and the perception of pain is reduced. The placebo effect has been observed for a long time. It has been assumed that the reduction of symptoms was a result of imagination, or that maybe the subject was just faking the symptoms to begin with. But the fact is the perception of pain is reduced when a placebo is given. The perception of pain returns when naloxone is administered (Davis, 1984). This indicates that the reduction of pain was not the result of imagination, but of increased levels of internal opiate activity. The placebo effect has been observed in a variety of experiences, not all of these revolving around pain perception. It is likely that other neurotransporters may be involved in addition to endorphins (Ornstein & Sobel, 1987).

Acetylcholine

Acetylcholine has been found from the peripheral nervous system to the brain (Julien, 1981). It may excite muscle action, but it inhibits the autonomic system (Clark, 1985). The autonomic system is divided into the sympathetic system and parasympathetic system. When the sympathetic system is turned on, the parasympathetic system is turned off. The parasympathetic system is a withdrawal system. For example, the parasympathetic portion tends to reverse the fight-or-flight process, permitting the body to relax. The more active one system, the less active the other. The messages of the parasympathetic system are carried by acetylcholine. Parasympathetic neurons are located near the organs they serve (Ornstein & Sobel, 1987). When parasympathetic nerves release acetylcholine, the heart rate slows, breathing is relaxed, and so on. Basically, it does the opposite of norepinephrine and epinephrine.

Atropine binds to acetylcholine receptors without stimulating the cell (Clark, 1985). Thus, problems of high blood pressure are reversed. Eating eggs can increase levels of cholesterol. But before eliminating eggs from the diet, one should know that the consumption of eggs increases the acetylcholine in the brain (Ornstein & Sobel, 1987). It would also appear that Acetylcholine is involved with memory learning (Davis, 1984).

Norepinephrine (NE)

The sympathetic portion of the autonomic system generally prepares the body for action. One part of the sympathetic system is the adrenal glands. Within the adrenal glands are neurons without axons. Here, epinephrine and norepinephrine are released into the bloodstream in order to infuse a general

area of receptors rather than just the guy next door. Both epinephrine and norepinephrine are involved in preparing the body for fight-or-flight (Clark, 1985). Epinephrine acts in the peripheral nervous system but seems to have little action if any in the brain (Julien, 1981). Norepinephrine acts both in body and brain. Norepinephrine is produced in the adrenal glands, but it also is produced in catecholamine neurons in the brain (Julien, 1981). In the body it constricts blood vessels and dilates pupils. It can also speed the heart rate and dilate the bronchi in the lungs. In the brain norepinephrine may be involved in memory learning (Davis, 1984). Many cells which use norepinephrine as a transmitter are located in the brain stem. Therefore, it would appear that norepinephrine has an important regulating function in basic drives such as hunger, thirst and sex (Julien, 1981).

Amphetamines and cocaine are similar in structure to norepinephrine. Amphetamines and cocaine cause increased action of norepinephrine. Exactly how they cause this increase is uncertain (Davis, 1984). Nicotine, muscarine, and atropine also interact with the autonomic nervous system (Clark, 1985). These, too, may cause some differences in levels of norepinephrine and/or epinephrine.

Some hallucinogens are also similar in structure to norepinephrine. These are mescaline, DOM (STP) MDA, MMDA, TMA, myristicin, elemicin. Cocaine and amphetamines appear to be more active in stimulating behaviors and less active in stimulating psychedelic action. The hallucinogens with similarities to norepinephrine seem to result in more psychedelic action and less in the behavior realm (Julien, 1981).

Dopamine (DA) and ACTH

Dopamine is one of those chemicals that the body uses but in different ways. It is a hormone. It is also a neurotransmitter and a precursor. ACTH stands for adrenocorticotropic hormone (fortunately, most simply use the acronym version of the name.) It is produced in the pituitary gland of the brain. As previously mentioned, it is released from a precursor at the same time that the endorphins are cleaved from the same precursor. From the pituitary gland, ACTH travels to the adrenal glands lying on top of the kidneys.

Upon reaching the adrenal glands, ACTH regulates the release of norepinephrine and other adrenal hormones. More specifically, the adrenal glands are stimulated by ACTH to produce dopamine. Dopamine is then broken down to produce norepinephrine (Davis, 1984). During this process, dopamine is being used by the body as a precursor for norepinephrine. But dopamine is also released and allowed to roam throughout the body. When it is roaming around it is being used as a hormone or neurohormone. Both dopamine and norepinephrine are used as neurotransmitters in the central nervous system. A neurotransmitter by definition is something that acts on specific receptors of the nerves, usually produced close to the receptor site. Is it possible that it is produced in specific areas of the brain, as well as in the adrenal glands?

Dopamine has been widely studied and linked to a wide variety of functions. It would appear that social isolation reduces dopamine release (Andreas, 1985). Dopamine may play a specific role in the acquisition of motor learning skills. Performance of two different motor tasks, rotary pursuit and mirror tracing, were studied. Concentrations of dopamine metabolites in the cerebrospinal fluid changed with improvement in performance. (Norepinephrine and serotonin levels were also checked and researchers found no difference in these) (McEntee, 1987). Decreased dopamine levels have also been associated with Parkinson's disease, which has disrupted motor activity as a symptom (Restak, 1984).

Increased dopamine activity is sometimes associated with the experience of symptoms of acute paranoid schizophrenia; prolonged use of cocaine or amphetamines can result in the experience of symptoms similar to acute paranoid schizophrenia. Therefore it is logical that cocaine and amphetamines increase levels of dopamine in the brain. Some studies show that cocaine and amphetamines increase dopamine activity in the brain (Davis, 1984).

Dopamine has been linked to alcoholism by many research studies. The body's inability to produce an enzyme known as dopamine-betahydroxylase, that breaks down dopamine, has been associated with chronic alcoholism. When alcohol consumption stops the lack of the enzyme results in increased dopamine levels (Anokhina, 1985). Findings of other research teams seem to support this finding. In 1985, a study at La Trobe University, Dundoora, Australia, found that disturbance of dopamine status was a consequence of chronic ethanol exposure (Myers, 1985). In the same year, researchers in Hisings-Backa, Sweden, found a higher sensitivity to dopamine during initial abstinence from alcohol after a period of heavy consumption. It was suggested that this higher dopamine sensitivity might result in "a lower threshold for psychotic symptoms and neuroleptic-induced extrapyramidal side effects." Or in other words, an influx of dopamine during initial abstinence from alcohol may cause the audio and visual hallucinations which sometimes occur during withdrawal. Findings also indicated support for the theory that it takes a long period of time to recover from heavy alcohol use (Balidin, 1985). In the same year, a team in Madrid, Spain, found low levels of dopamine and norepinephrine in animals from 12 to 24 hours after the last use of alcohol. They also found the use of naloxone stopped the effects, which indicates endorphin activity is involved too (Guaza, 1985).

Again in 1985, but in Cagliari, Italy, a research team concluded that at least in rats, ethanol causes massive dopamine release in different brain areas. But the real kicker of this study was a second finding. While ethanol caused a massive dopamine release, the alcohol-using rats lost their ability to stimulate dopamine synthesis. I remember the gas shortage of the mid-1970s. Americans had adapted to a lifestyle dependent on oil products and suddenly there was no oil (well, not enough to go around at least). America was dependent on outside sources of oil; when "they" quit sending it and we couldn't produce enough of it ourselves, this country was turned upside down. Everything came to a grinding halt while we sat in long lines at the gas pumps waiting for our ration. So perhaps alcohol is a big oil tanker bringing us a lush supply of dopamine. Suddenly no tankers of dopamine. . .

In short, the Italian rat study showed massive release of dopamine when drinking, and less active dopaminergic transmission during alcohol withdrawal. It was also found that rats given a choice to drink or not drink, chose not to drink so much when treatments that inhibit dopaminergic activity were given (Fadda, 1986).

A 1986 study of the University of Cagliari, Italy, looked at the effect of foot shock stress and ethanol and the combination of the two. When electric shock was applied to the foot of a rat, it produced stress. It also decreased the dopamine concentration by 30 percent. Ethanol decreased dopamine concentration by 20 percent. When foot shock and ethanol were combined, dopamine decreased by 50 percent. So it would appear that the effects of stress are added to the effects of alcohol. But researchers found an interesting difference between the action of foot shock and the action of alcohol. Electric foot shock increased dihydroxyphenylacetic acid (DOPAC) concentration 65 percent, but DOPAC levels were not modified by ethanol. The combination of ethanol and foot shock produced a 30 percent increase in homovanillic acid (HVA), but no change in DOPAC levels. It was concluded that while both ethanol and foot shock activate dopamine release, ethanol decreases dopamine retrieval by nerve terminals (Fadda, 1986).

GABA and Glutamate

The hippocampus is a distinctive part of the brain directly linked to the processing of touch, vision, sound, smell, and also linked to the limbic system. Within the hippocampus are neurons with excitatory receptors stimulated by the neurotransmitter glutamate, and the inhibitory receptors for the neurotransmitter, Gamma aminobutyric acid (GABA). When excitement and inhibition of this area are in balance, all is well. But when something disrupts the balance, epileptic seizures or memory disorders may occur (Restak, 1984). GABA is inhibitory in nature, and if it is prevented from stopping neuronal activity, convulsions may result (Julien, 1981).

PCP use has resulted in massive outbursts of aggressive behavior. The hippocampus and cerebral cortex are thought to be primary sites of involvement which produce these outbursts (Restak, 1984).

Alcohol inhibits the activity of GABA. When alcohol stops GABA from stopping transmissions, a stimulating effect occurs. Initially the areas of the brain governing self-control and judgment are influenced, then the effects extend through the limbic system and the brainstem (Davis, 1984).

Serotonin (5-HT)

Serotonin is also called 5-HT or 5-hydroxytryptamine. Serotonin has been found primarily in the brain (Julien, 1981). Even so, organs that are associated with the production of cells for the body's immune system have nerves with receptors for a number of chemicals including serotonin and endorphins (Ornstein & Sobel, 1987). Serotonin may stimulate the release of ACTH and beta-endorphin (Davis, 1984). And what might release serotonin? Eating carbohydrates appears to increase the brain's supply of serotonin (Ornstein & Sobel, 1987).

Serotonin is associated with relaxed moods. Negative ions (which exist in clean mountain air, at beaches, and around waterfalls) increase serotonin levels (Ornstein & Sobel, 1987). But the picture of peace and tranquility presented by pure air and fresh water might mask a shark or two. Decreased serotonin levels have been associated with increased aggressive behaviors. Increased levels have been associated with suicide and depression (Restak, 1984). Resperin, a drug known to cause profound mental depression, may do so by depleting both norepinephrine and serotonin (Julien, 1981).

There is a collection of cells in the midline of the medulla which produce serotonin. These same cells may be involved in sleep regulation (Restak, 1984). Thus, over- or under-stimulation of these cells might result in insomnia, hallucinations brought on by insomnia, or their reverse, narcolepsy. Acting in other areas of the brain, serotonin may also be involved in sensory perception (Julien, 1981).

Some hallucinogens are known to act on the serotonergic system. LSD structurally resembles serotonin (Julien, 1981). It most likely interferes with the neurons in the brain that use serotonin as a neurotransmitter. LSD reduces the midline area of the brain stem's ability to produce serotonin. LSD may imitate the action of serotonin. Changes in the serotoninergic system may result in hallucinations and changes in reality perception (Davis, 1984).

PCP may cause a rise in serotonin levels in the brain and may elevate levels of tyrosine, which in turn may change levels of dopamine and norepinephrine. It may also decrease GABA levels (Davis, 1984). Other hallucinogens that may act on serotonin levels are dimethyltyptamide (DMT), psilocybin, psilocin, bufotenine, morning glory seeds, and harmine.

Studies to be discussed in detail in the "Alcoholism" section of this chapter indicate that alcoholics have a lowered concentration of serotonin in the central nervous system, and this can be used as a predictor of alcoholism. "Serotonergic dysfunction may exist in alcoholics" (Kent, 1985). In 1987, a study discovered a possible link between the body's serotonin uptake ability and alcoholism. The number of alcoholics studied was small. The study included alcoholics at time of admission to treatment, and after 20 days, as well as recovering alcoholics with 1 to 11 years of sobriety. Lowered kinetics of 3H serotonin uptake well-found in platelets, regardless of length of sobriety as compared to a non-drinking control group. The researchers concluded that this "phenomenon

could be congenital or induced by the previous excessive intake of alcohol" (Boismare, 1987). Researchers in another study by the East Carolina University School of Medicine, also in 1987, arrived at a more definitive conclusion. They developed a test to detect the presence of an impaired serotonin metabolic pathway, and concluded that predisposition toward chronic alcoholism can be detected by measuring "a defect in the metabolism of tryptophan that causes a lowered concentration of serotonin in the central nervous system" (Thomson, 1987).

Still Looking

Marijuana poses a problem similar to the one created by opiate action. Researchers think that the THC in marijuana is somehow plugging into brain receptors. Now the search is on to find the where and how. Once these questions have been answered, researchers will undoubtedly ask why and in so doing, they may discover a whole new world, the endogenous marijuana system (Davis, 1984).

SYSTEMS

What are these 100+ billion neurons trying to do? Naturally, they are involved in doing everything that we do. They regulate and control all physical functions of the body. They allow us to have senses (sight, hearing, smell, taste, touch, hot, cold, hurrah, ouch, etc.), and they allow us to learn, remember, imagine, speak, create, organize, and so on.

The previous brief review of some of the neurotransporters shows how a lot of very simple little things can combine to form an overwhelming complexity. The body would, no doubt, be overwhelmed were it not for its own internal organization. Nerves tend to bunch together, so that there are a lot of nerves in one area of the body and only a few in another. As a result, we tend to think of the nerves being located in the head and in the spinal cord. But the fact is, nerves are everywhere. Not all nerves respond to all neurotransmitters. Specialized receptors permit grouping according to substances used, which are distinguished by common chemical composition. These systems are separate but a part of the total system. The endogenous opiate system transmits information via enkelphins, endorphins, and so on. The cholinergic system uses acetylcholine as its transmitter. The adrenergic system using epinephrine and norepinephrine. The dominergic system uses dopamine, the serotonergic system uses serotonin, and the GABA-egic system uses GABA (Davis, 1984). Exactly what all of these systems do and don't do is still quite debateable. Furthermore, the elements of these systems do not operate independently from one another. They have been grouped into these systems by researchers. The grouping is based on chemical similarities rather than similarities in what they do or don't do.

Not all function comes from neurotransporter actions. Once a chemical has docked in a receptor and its information has disembarked, then what? Well, then an enzyme comes along and chews up the transporter, making the receptor available for use again. A drug may work because it is like a neurotransporter and fits into the receptor. Once in the receptor, it may pass on the same information as the endogenous molecule intended for that receptor. Some drugs, such as naloxone, fit into the receptor but carry no information. It simply prevents the intended neurotransmitter from occupying the receptor. Often some drugs work like enzymes, or by attacking the enzymes instead of connecting with the receptor.

Other non-chemical systems are also involved. Electrical voltage, positive and negative ions, have an important role to play. Timing is also important. Everything in the body has a natural rhythm. The heart rhythm is the most obvious example. But the brain has a rhythm, too (Restak, 1984). Brain waves are just as important as chemical activity. Since this text is not about brain activity, but about addiction, the specifics of how and why the brain functions will be curtailed. However, further independent investigation on these topics is strongly advised.

What are all these systems trying to do? They are trying to keep us safe, healthy and happy. Some might argue that more of the systems are designed to keep us safe and healthy than happy. Perhaps whoever assembled us figured that we were smart enough to figure out our own fun, and didn't have to have an automatic, built-in system for that. A closer look at what the systems seem to be doing follows.

Endogenous Hit and Run

The system is the body's "fight-or-flight" system. It prepares the body for action by increasing muscle tone and sympathetic nervous system activity. The heart rate increases so that oxygen can be pumped to the muscle cells. The liver releases sugar to feed the muscles. The blood supply shifts from skin to muscles. Respiration increases. The individual is ready for hit and/or run. There is sweating and other signs of arousal. Norepinephrine carries the sympathetic system message. Sympathetic neurons are centered in the brain (Ornstein & Sobel, 1987). At the same time, the fight-or-flight system is turned on, the sympathetic nervous system stimulates the adrenal medulla to secret epinephrine and norepinephrine. When the emergency situation lasts a long time, then the hypothalamus stimulates the pituitary gland to release ACTH, which results in the adrenal cortex releasing other hormones, the mineralocorticoid and glucocorticoid. If mainly mineralocorticoid are released the body had made a decision to fight. If mainly glucocorticoid are released, then this reflects a decision to peacefully coexist with the stressor. ACTH and endorphins are released from the pituitary gland at same time in response to stress or a crisis. ACTH prepares for fight or flight while endorphins prepare for Plan B. Self-confidence plays an important role in triggering this system. When a person believes the self is capable of dealing with a difficult situation, then the stress level and the secretion of catecholamine are both reduced. Assurance and a supportive vote of confidence from others also reduces the secretion of catecholamine (Ornstein & Sobel, 1987).

How To Really Spell Relief

Pain is experienced by all people. It is an intrinsic experience that is highly subjective in nature. Any two persons, exposed to the same stimuli, will not experience pain to the same degree or intensity. Pain results from both physical and emotional stimuli. Interestingly, physical pain cannot be remembered. I can remember the last time I dropped a table on my foot. I can remember if it hurt a little bit or a lot. I can even remember the previous time I did the same thing and compare the resulting pain in terms of which time hurt more. But I cannot recall the feeling of the pain. By thinking about the situation, I do not re-experience pain. On the other hand, I can remember emotional pain. I not only remember the degree of intensity, but if I allow myself to focus on remembering the situation long enough, I re-experience the feeling of pain. In fact, if I choose to re-frame the original situation negatively, recollection of the pain can be more intense than the pain originally experienced.

Substance P is considered to be the neurotransmitter of pain impulses. It is a peptide which is found in many parts of the central nervous system (Davis, 1984). The pain system is turned on by any stimulus deemed harmful to the body. This could be physical damage to body tissue such as a cut or bullet hole. This could be an interpersonal conflict or any situation which the mind perceives as threatening to the organism's well-being.

The relief-from-pain system begins powering up at the same time as the fight-or-flight system. It is therefore not surprising that pain (or the presence of substance P) can activate the relief system. The perception of pain is extinguished by activation of endogenous opiates. Morphine seems to stop or reduce the release of Substance P (Ornstein & Sobel, 1987). It is likely that the endorphins act in the same way as morphine. In ability to relieve pain, dynorphin and beta-endorphin are more powerful than morphine (Davis, 1984). The anti-pain system can also be activated by electrical stimulation, acupuncture, even stress and pain itself can turn on the fire extinguishers (Ornstein & Sobel, 1987).

The Immune System

The ability to seal wounds increases when the fight-or-flight system is turned on. Other functions of the immune system which deal with fighting infection seemed to be turned off by crisis. Organs associated with the internal immune system (i.e., thymus gland, spleen, lymph nodes, and bone marrow) have nerve endings. The cells of the immune system contain receptors for neurohormones, neurotransmitters, and neuropeptides. The left cortical hemisphere may be involved. The immune system is linked to the hypothalamus. The hypothalamus regulates shivering, temperature control, blood sugar, lungs and heart control. The hypothalamus is also involved in emotional reactions. The same part of the brain that decides if a person is happy or sad, also decides if this person should fight being physically ill. So, it appears that if one participates in an activity that makes the person feel better emotionally, then the person also becomes stronger physically. Furthermore, the immune system seems to have a brain of its own, for it learns from past experiences. Anticipation of events which caused the system to shut down immunity in the past, may cause it to shut down again as a result of prior experience (Ornstein & Sobel, 1987).

A Jump and Skip System?

As I have read the information available about neuro-chemical activity, I've found an interesting point and an interesting omission. The interesting point is that all these systems and chemicals have been functioning in living matter for millions of years. No one found them until someone bothered to look for them. By the same token, let's not fall into the trap of assuming that what is known is all that exists. There are most likely other chemicals and systems operating that have not yet been detected or identified.

In my mind, the puzzling omission goes something like this: Drug A acts on receptor A which produces painkilling and euphoria. Drug B acts on receptor B which produces excitement of the fight-or-flight system and produces euphoria. Drug C interacts with GABA, serotonin, dopamine, and endorphins, resulting in depressed central nervous system activity, and produces euphoria. Receptors are specialized. Receptors A, B, and C do not do the same things. So how do they all produce euphoria? Almost all drugs of abuse have euphoria as a central component. The interesting omission is a chemical which activates euphoria. It is not likely that euphoria results from an absence of other chemical action, for euphoria is present and paired with endorphin activity, norepinephrine activity, serotonin activity, and so on. Besides, the body does not seem to operate on the absence of sickness. The absence of sickness is not health. The body has an immune system that is activated during times of health and gets turned down or off before we get sick.

While the fight-or-flight, pain generating/reducing, and immune systems have been closely scrutinized, another system most likely exists which has received little attention. We have all observed human beings involved in totally illogical actions. People really do climb Mt. Everest. People do stand in line for hours to ride in a cramped compartment at Disneyland. People do flock to beach towns to spend countless dollars trying to bounce a rubber chicken into a frying pan. The logical minded stops, gawks and asks, "Why do you do this?" No one has an answer. No one stops doing, or climbing, or standing in line either.

I will call this the Jump and Skip system. Though no one has found it exists yet, it is most likely in us to expand our world of knowledge. No one has discovered this system, because no one has bothered to look for it. The system causes us to test the limits of the unknown, just because it's there.

There seems to be an unwritten philosophy that pleasurable states result from the absence of unhealthy activity. Turn off the pain system; turn off the stress and anxiety systems, and joyful life ensues. I would suggest that all that results from the absence of negatives is base zero existence. Some believe the same systems which transport negative emotions also transport positive ones. Ornstein and Sobel (1987) point out that negative emotions don't feel the same as positive ones. Researchers have found areas in the brain which are devoted to the perceptions of pleasurable sensations. There are brain pathways devoted to pleasure. The hypothalamus and limbic systems are involved in the pleasure sensing process (Restak, 1984). Would such areas exist if the pleasure was simply the absence of other system activity? I doubt it. Where there are identifiable pathways, and neuronal centers, there is most likely a system designed to stimulate and use these areas and perhaps a chemical specifically designed to transport its messages.

Ornstein and Sobel warn that "The bored brain may be as damaging as a blitzed one" (Ornstein & Sobel, 1987, p. 213). Several recovering alcoholics have said to me, "I'm sober. I go to meetings. I've faced my problems. So how come I'm still miserable?" Simple. The absence of negatives is not the activation of positives.

Rest and relaxation are important. They strengthen the immune system and the system which turns off the fight-or-flight system. But boredom is not cured by rest and relaxation. The Jump and Skip system is probably a close relative to the fight-or-flight system; it may even use some of the same chemicals for neurotransporters. But purposes of the systems are not the same. The world-expanding Jump and Skip system is most likely activated by curiosity and/or coming in contact with illogical stimuli. When activated, the body is neither signaled to fight nor to run away. If the subject causing curiosity is perceived to have a potential for danger, then the fight-or-flight mechanisms may be activated at the same time as the Jump and Skip system.

To develop the Jump and Skip system, a person must learn to set aside the fight-or-flight system. A person must experiment with challenges such as those found in educational work and leisure pursuits. Sensation seeking (e.g., roller coasters, horror movies, etc.) creates arousal. It has been postulated that participation in sensation seeking does not result in pleasure. "The pleasure may come later when the arousal state subsides" (Ornstein & Sobel, 1987, p. 218). Perhaps. I find it difficult to believe that an adolescent could develop enough self-discipline to sit through an hour and a half of Freddy Krueger, in order to enjoy a few moments afterwards. Perhaps it is the pleasure of the fight-or-flight system. I believe it is the exploration of the fight-or-flight system that is attractive. That need to explore is the activity of the Jump and Skip.

Systems Control Center

It has been suggested that emotions and thoughts are products of nervous system activity. We feel anxious when the fight-or-flight system turns on. We feel depressed when the withdrawal system chemicals are too strong. Yet the control, regulation, and production of neurotransporter chemicals are complex. (See Figure 3.4) Two or more neurotransporters are sent into action for any given function. Fear, for example, may signal the fight-or-flight response shooting dopamine, norepinephrine, epinephrine through our bodies. But it also triggers a build-up of endorphins to kill pain and drops the function of other systems in order to conserve energy. So it seems that the control centers for activation and regulation of all internal systems may be emotions, thought, mediated by logic.

Many years ago, a college professor asked, "If a tree falls in the forest, and there is no one there to hear, does it make a sound?" I had no answer at the time and thought the question frivolous. It now seems that the answer to that question is critical to comprehending the internal state of being and understanding the treatment of addictions as well. The answer is a resounding no. A tree falling only makes a sound if there is someone there to hear it. It makes waves, not sounds. It is the body's internal control center which chooses to interpret the bombardment of waves upon the ear drum as the sound of a tree falling. Until the interpretation has been made there is no sound. The control center, being governed by emotion, may interpret the ear drum's bombardment differently, in which case neither the sound nor the tree have substance for the individual.

For example, my son and I camped in rugged terrain. My son was feeling insecure and fearful as the forest's blackness swallowed the dim light of our campfire. I too was feeling uneasy knowing we had pitched our tent on a game trail, knowing the forest creatures would soon be finding us blocking their way to their water hole. Then we heard an unfamiliar sound. My son's fear caused his internal control center to interpret the noise as the approach of Big Foot. My emotions were being mediated by past experience and logic. My control center interpreted the noise as that of a wild cow (for me, a cow in the wild is far more threatening than an encounter with Big Foot.) After hearing the noise a second time, we concluded that it might be a motorcycle. The first noise brought our bodies to alertness as our control centers dispatched the neurochemical of the fight-or-flight system. The decision to believe the noise was a motor cycle caused our control centers to dispatch the withdraw messengers and we both relaxed back into our chairs to enjoy the stars and dancing flames.

Reality is but a perception created by mixing thoughts and emotions, mediated by logic. Reality is the individualized interpretation of the external bombardment upon our sensors. The interpretation regulates the production and dispatch of the internal chemical systems. A tree falls in the forest. One stands thinking of another place in time and fails to hear it fall. A second stands next to the first and hears a tree fall. A third stands next to the second and hears Big Foot preparing to attack. The first turns to the second and says, this is "boring." The second turns to find the third has run away. Reality is but a perception.

Those who have become addicted have substituted a substance or a process for the internal systems control center. Without use, a falling tree crashes with resounding echo. A couple of drinks and there is no tree. The state of denial, observed in most practicing alcoholics and addicts, is the ultimate proof that reality is but a perception. Family and friends cry, "Can't you see what your drinking is doing to all of us?" The alcoholic truthfully responds, "No." Reality is subject to interpretation for it is only a perception.

A Final Consideration: A Brain Split

Those of us who believe that left and right brain hemisphere functions cause differences, find plenty of evidence to support our claims. Those who don't believe insist that the evidence is grossly overrated. The left hemisphere may govern logic and language. The right hemisphere may govern intuition and creativity (Restak, 1984). The left-brain-dominant person may value paint-by-number approaches to life. The right-brain-dominant person may be very frustrated with a paint-by-number system, always feeling the need to create new lines and spaces. The nation's education system seems dominated by left brains. This is perhaps as it should be. The left-brain-dominant teacher will stick to the facts exactly as written in the book. The right-brain-dominated teacher may be more inclined to disregard the text and create new "facts" which seem to be in harmony with the day's mood, or color of the sky.

I have heard many an alcoholic say he or she felt "different" long before the first drink was ever taken. I would suggest that difference may be the result of a right-brain-dominant person attempting to live in a left-brain-dominant world. Woititz suggests that adult children of alcoholics guess "what normal is" (Woititz, 1983, p. 24). I would suggest that right-brain-dominant persons, regardless of what type of home they were raised in, guess what left brainers want from them.

A study of 50 alcoholic personalities found that EEG output sharply increased at the sight of an alcoholic beverage. Most of the increase was observed in the brain's left hemisphere. The control subjects showed no alteration in EEG output (Bobrov, 1986). Is it possible that right brainers are becoming left brainers with the use of alcohol? The Veterans Administration Medical Center in Pittsburgh, Pennsylvania, studied the split-brain theory in chronic alcoholics. They found brain deterioration, but the damage was not localized to posterior or anterior portions of the brain. It was more like "premature aging of the brain" (Goldstein, 1982). While this study tends to rule out differences between front and back brain involvement, it does not rule out right verses left involvement. In my opinion, it is possible that recovery may be assisted through activities which encourage right brain function, especially at times when the left brain is busy saying, "It's party time!" (Edwards, 1979).

FIGURE 3.4

THE BIO-CHEMICAL TREE/ INTERNAL SYSTEMS

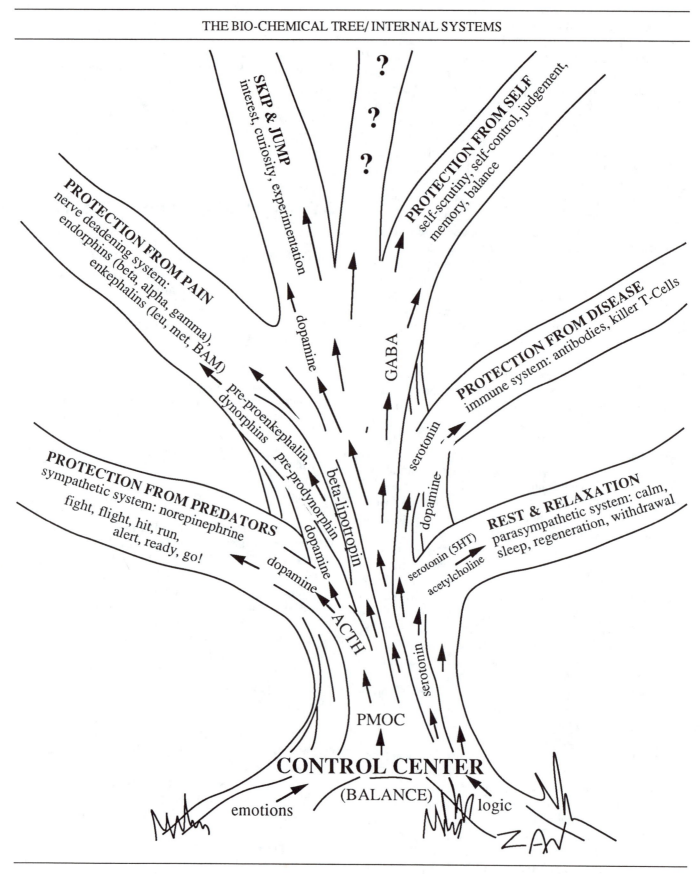

Blackouts are also an interesting phenomenon in alcoholism. During blackouts, the person goes about his/her daily routine, yet remembers nothing about it. When the blackout lifts, the person usually finds him or her self in an unknown. The person usually generates a reason to explain the unknown. Sperry (1968), during studies of split-brain functions, discovered a similar pattern. When a subject's left and right hemispheres were disconnected, and one side of the brain was given information that the other side could not see, the second side created an excuse for the existence of perceptions taken in by the first side. The creation of excuses by an alcoholic have been attributed to the actions of the person's denial system. I would suggest that in many cases, the excuses are not a function of hiding the truth from the self. The excuse results from imbalanced left-right brain functioning. The brain is simply fabricating explanations for things it does not understand.

BACK TO ADDICTION

Many drugs of abuse tend to inhibit various neurotransmitter systems in the brain. The exact mechanisms of the inhibition are not fully understood at this time (Peris, 1986). Even so, enough is known to say there is a connection. Alcohol and drugs act directly on the same systems, such as the limbic system. With chronic use, they will throw internal neurosystems systems out of balance. Some drugs have more action on the endorphin system while other drugs have more action on other systems.

A wide variety of nondrug substances and activities have been nominated for the addiction tree hall of fame. (Davis 1984) mentions "criminal behavior, fascination with electronic media, video games, meditation, playing Rubik's Cube, risk-taking, running, smoking and suicide" (pp. 122-123). Another author nominates sex, gambling, and work (Hatterer, 1980). Even hard rock music may be addicting (Tame, 1984). Other therapeutic recreation professionals have suggested to the author such things as overeating, undereating, moving, shopping/spending money, fantasy, gardening and more, and the list goes on and on. Can all of these be addictions? Before answering yes or no, let us consider the following.

". . .the endorphins have proven to be just as addictive as morphine and heroin"(Ornstein & Sobel, 1987). Rats subjected to large quantities of met-enkephalin or beta-endorphin went through the same withdrawal symptoms as rats receiving morphine when the initial drug action was blocked by naloxone. Alpha-neo-endorphin is over six times as powerful as met-enkephalin. Met-enkephalin is five times more powerful than beta-endorphin. Beta-endorphin is over five times as powerful as morphine. That's not much compared to dynorphin which is 190 times as powerful as morphine (Davis, 1984).

At this time no one is buying endorphins on the street corner. They are too difficult to extract. But researchers are learning how to synthesize them. Remember, it is our tradition to synthesize more addictive than less addictive. Heroin was synthesized to replace morphine, and it is more addictive. Also, watch the TV tonight; the thing that sells pain relievers is the "all new extra strength." Just imagine the television advertisement for "Synthetic Dynorphin! All new. The old kind was 190 times more powerful than morphine, and now it's available to you in extra strength form in a designer, daisy-covered container." This may seem far-fetched, and it appears that the endogenous molecules are actually too large to pass through the blood brain barrier (Davis, 1984). Self-administered endorphin injections, therefore, seem unlikely. But, as has been said many times, "Where there's a will, there's a way."

One might well wonder, has endorphin abuse already begun? Have the wills already found the ways? Pure thought or emotions turn on the endorphin production. This has been proven in studies of the placebo effect (Ornstein & Sobel, 1987). This suggests that even pure thought or emotion capable of evoking beta-endorphin production can be highly addictive. At this time the processes for stimulating the body's endogenous opiates (creating natural highs) are not clearly understood. Some have, no doubt, stumbled onto methods such as physical exertion through running, jogging, weight-lifting, or biking. At this time, the high seems to be transitory. As we learn more and more about the systems within, we will learn more and more about how to increase production of one thing or decrease production of another. When that day comes, we may very well see a client suffering from dynorphin withdrawal symptoms who has never taken the first drink, fix, or pill. If a cost-effective method of producing synthetic endorphins is developed, we may well look back to the good old days when the strongest thing on the market was mere heroin.

So the answer to the question four paragraphs back–"Can all of these be addictions?"– is a resounding "yes." Activities such as gardening, work, physical exercise, meditation can be addictive. It is likely that not all of them stir up the endorphins. But it is not likely that cocaine stirs up the endorphins either. Some may stir up dopamine or norepinephrine activity rather than endorphins. It is becoming apparent that a process can be as addictive as a substance. The problems facing the "workaholic" or the "stress junkie" are not just jokes. They are real diseases. [Ch8:100.0]

A New Definition of Addiction

Old definitions of addiction fall short of their target. Basing addiction on observance of withdrawal symptoms omits the use of some of the most damaging drugs (i.e., cocaine, several hallucinogens). Basing addiction on the compulsion to use or abuse a substance provides a more inclusive definition. Yet it, too, seems to be incomplete. There is more to addiction than just a compulsion to use. Furthermore, what is the definition of "compulsion?" Defining a vague notion by another vague term only sends one chasing through the dictionary. The author's old definition of addiction as something that causes problems, may be too broad and general. It also implies that if there are no problems, there is no addiction. That's a little bit like saying that a cancer cell is not cancer until it multiplies and chews up a vital organ. Determining what is and is not a "problem" is subject to a great deal of interpretation. In 1982, a new definition of addiction was created by Milkman and Sunderwirth (1982). Their theory dealt with the psychological ramifications of avoidance-seeking behavior through satiation or arousal. In their scenario, addiction is a result of dysfunctional relationships between parents and child that develop from birth and during the first few years of life. If they are right, then all behaviors that society has defined as "abnormal," and that someone has identified as dysfunctions between parent and child during early childhood, are addictions. This would include schizophrenia, autism, suicide, and murder among other things. Addiction is not psychosis. The addictive personality has unique characteristics which set it apart from persons who are psychotic, autistic, or criminal. While Milkman and Sunderwirth make a number of points that make a lot of sense, their summation omits the unique aspects of addiction.

Having reviewed a number of definitions, the author has developed a new one:

> *Addiction* is a serious, progressive disease involving the repetitive self-administration of a substance or a process to avoid reality perceptions, through manipulation of internal nervous system processes resulting in damage to the equilibrium of internal biochemical functioning and an inability to relate to the outer world without the use of the selected substance or process.

This is a very long definition, but each word has a purpose and cannot be omitted. Addiction is a *disease* because it has identifiable characteristics. There is a recognizable *progression*. There is progressive physical and psychological deterioration over time. Outcomes are predictable, and the disease can be treated.

As a disease, addiction is like diabetes. The body fails to function normally when a substance is ingested. In diabetes, the body reacts to sugar. In addiction, the body reacts to alcohol, or a drug, or a process. As a *serious* disease, addiction requires medical attention. If it goes untreated, the individual may perish. As a progressive disease, early intervention and treatment are indicated. The survival rate from cancer is better if treatment occurs when only a few cancerous cells are present. Survival rate from addiction is better if treatment occurs before major symptoms are manifested.

The disease of addiction is characterized by *repeated administration*. In initial stages of the disease, repeated use is elective, but as the disease progresses it becomes a compulsion. Since addiction is *self-administered*, the addicted individual is also an essential member of the treatment team. In diseases such as cancer, the individual my assume a passive role and allow the medical team to make treatment decisions and perform corrective procedures. In addiction, the individual must assume an active role in all treatment decisions and procedures.

Addiction is a disease of repeated administration of a substance or a process. *Substance* abuse may include the use of alcohol, drugs, and food, among other things. Such substances, when infused into the system, act by turning on or off nervous system function(s). *Processes*, such as work or physical exercise, turn on or off the same nervous systems just like known substances of abuse. As a repeated, self-administered process, addiction rules out successful suicide. It also rules out the person who blows his or her cork and murders someone. Persons who repeatedly survive suicide attempts may be addicted to suicide. Serial killers may be addicted to murder.

The purpose of repetitive self-administered use of a substance or process is to *avoid reality*. Reality includes problems, boredom, relationships with others, self-limitations, here-and-now lack of money, power, knowledge, spiritual fulfillment. *Reality is a perception.* It is the relationship between the perceived world which exists outside of us and our perception of our ability to interact with the things we perceive. Addiction changes perceptions of reality. Addictive substances and processes give wings to the body, courage to the shy, riches to the poor, and freedom to the slave. Avoiding a negative aspect of reality can be done by making substantive changes in self or environment, or by changing perceptions of self or environment. The easiest change is to simply ignore, or not perceive the negative aspect. Addictive substances or processes permit the person to alter or ignore the undesired perception. In addiction, change is accomplished by *manipulation of internal nervous system* processes that control the organism's ability to perceive reality. Persons wishing to avoid boredom manipulate neurotransporter functions which feed the fight-or-flight system (and perhaps the Jump and Skip system). Persons wishing to avoid stress and anxiety select substances or processes which end awareness of the fight-or-flight system's activity. Persons who find the world too painful, turn on the body's painkilling system. Persons who find reality too demanding, sedate the judgment and control centers of the brain.

Obviously, using a painkiller does not heal the wound. It simply allows the person to forget the wound is there. Manipulation of the body's reality-perceiving systems has two results. As a result of a lack of attention, small reality wounds get infected and get worse. The body's internal systems are designed to operate in harmony with one another. Over-stimulation of one system results in under-stimulation of another. Over time, *internal balance is disrupted* and the body's ability to maintain proper chemical balance can be permanently impaired. *The terminal result of addiction is an inability to produce biochemical equilibrium and inability to relate to the outer world without the use of an addictive substance or process.*

Not mentioned in the above definition, but often associated with addiction, is the concept of tolerance. Substance abuse is often associated with the development of tolerance. Tolerance is a condition in which increasingly larger doses of the same substance are required to produce the same effect. For example, tranquilizers build up tolerance. Initially, one dose provides relaxation. After a while, it takes two doses to provide relaxation, then three doses, then four, and so on. Alcohol builds up tolerance. At first a couple of drinks, and the person is slap-happy. After a while, it may take a couple of cases before the slap-happy effect sets in. The one who is left standing while his or her drinking buddies are under the table, is the one who has developed a tolerance for alcohol and is on his or her way to addiction. Cross-tolerance also evolves. The development of tolerance for one type of depressant often results in tolerance for many other types of depressants (Dusek, 1980).

Can addiction to a process develop tolerance? It would appear that addiction to running develops tolerance and possibly cross-tolerance for other types of physical activity. Addiction to video games may develop tolerance; at least people who get hooked on them seem to play them for longer and longer periods. Old video games are discarded after awhile because they don't seem to "do it" anymore. Addiction to high-risk activities seems to develop tolerance. Bike riding with one hand gives way to bike riding with no hands which gives way to bike riding while standing up, which gives way to racing cars, which gives way to ... Many addictive substances, such as LSD, are known to have no development of tolerance. Likewise there are probably addictive processes that do not build up tolerance. For this reason, tolerance is not part of the definition of addiction, but is a characteristic of the progressive nature of the disease.

The goal of intervention is to arrest the disease. The goal of treatment is to develop a perception of reality that is compatible and a lifestyle that promotes biochemical equilibrium. The goal of recovery is to develop skills and abilities needed to maintain biochemical equilibrium and positive perceptions of reality. Therapeutic Recreation assists in the arrest of the disease by a) helping the individual to understand the disease process, b) helping the individual "detox" from biochemical imbalance, c) helping the individual develop an accurate perception of reality. Therapeutic Recreation assists the treatment process by a) engaging the client in activities which promote biochemical equilibrium, b) assisting the client to develop a balanced lifestyle (which includes balancing of right and left hemisphere brain functioning, c) promoting accurate and positive perceptions of reality, d) supporting objectives of other therapies, and e) helping the client avoid addiction to a leisure process. (See Figure 3.5)

The Impending Disaster: Positive Addiction

As awareness of the existence of process addictions develops, so, too, is support for "positive addiction" growing. The concept suggests that a natural high is better than a substance-induced high. The theory supports substitution of addictive processes for addictive substances. This theory is supported by William Glasser in his book *Positive Addiction* (1976). It is also supported by several others (Fixx, 1977; Egger, 1980) but not by this author. The cry of the early 1960s was to use marijuana because it was a better method of getting high than alcohol. No doubt the attitude that created the problems of morphine and opium addiction, mentioned in Chapter 1, was the assumption that their use were better methods of getting high than previously used compounds. The "positive addiction" theory only supports the same substitution theory which has been attempted over and over and has failed every time. Addiction is addiction is addiction. There is no positive way to be addicted. A "positive" addiction disrupts an individual's internal balance just as much as a "negative" addiction.

SUBSTANCE ADDICTIONS: A NEW LOOK AT SOME OLD DRUGS

Alcohol: A Brief Summary

There is little doubt that alcohol is an addictive substance. Its use is often a serious progressive phenomenon. The desire for a drink escalates to a compulsion. Alcohol develops tolerance. As the disease progresses, blackouts are experienced. During a blackout, a person walks, talks, works, plays, fights, loves, and yet is totally unconscious. When the person awakens from a blackout, he/she remembers nothing of his/her activities that occurred during the blackout. Blackouts are also progressive. The first ones tend to be short—perhaps up to a few hours. At first, the alcoholic learns of blackouts from others who inform him/her of something he/she did. These are usually met with total disbelief and are denied by the alcoholic. As use continues, the frequency and length of blackouts increase. Hours may be spent without success trying to remember what happened during the blackout. It is a frightening experience to remember arriving home from work on Friday, and wake up in a different location on Monday without the slightest idea what happened in between. Withdrawal symptoms also escalate with time. Initially there may be no withdrawal symptoms. As the disease progresses, abstinence results in nervousness and a shaking in the hands. Sleep may be disrupted. With continued use, auditory and visual hallucinations may accompany the shaking and muscle spasms may be experienced. In the final stage of progression delirium tremens (DTs) result, in which the blood pressure may drop to zero and then skyrocket in a matter of minutes. Convulsions may occur.

FIGURE 3.5

A NEW ADDICTION TREE

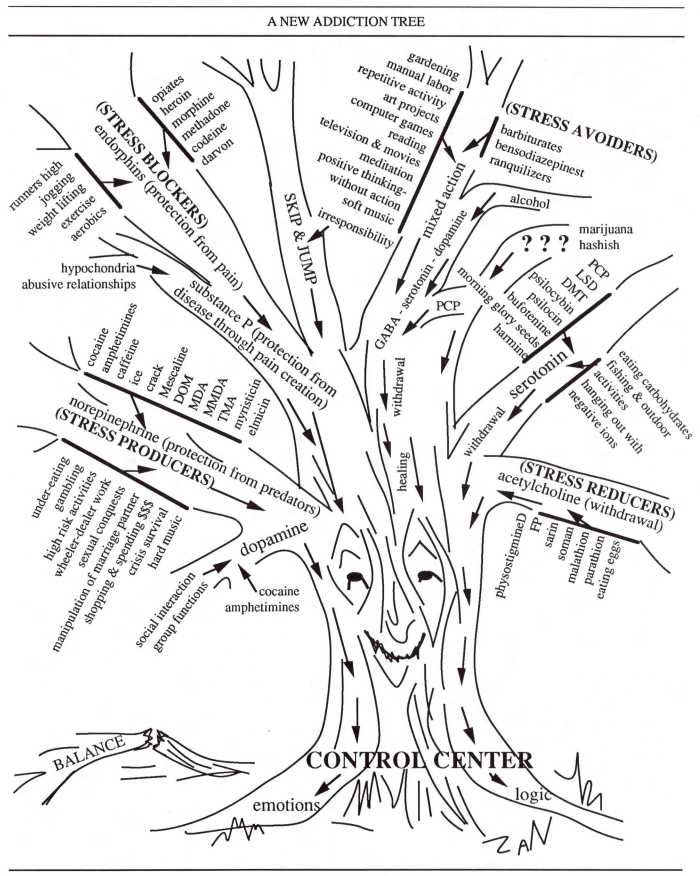

Alcohol abuse results in damage to internal nervous system processes. Alcohol causes changes in the brain as well as in many of the body's other organs. Alcohol has been found to influence and to be influenced by the activity of several neurotransmitter systems. Some systems are more strongly affected than others. But the more alcohol is studied, the more systems are being found that interact with the intoxicating beverage.

Alcohol has been associated with a reduction of serotonin levels. Serotonin uptake is lower in alcoholics regardless of length of drinking or sobriety status. It has been found that lowered concentrations of serotonin may exist in the central nervous system even before the first drink is taken. In fact, a test for lowered serotonin levels can be used to indicate a predisposition towards chronic alcoholism (Thomson, 1987). Studies imply a genetic link (Fadda, 1985). It has been known for some time that an alcoholic most likely has an alcoholic parent(s) or grandparent. However, the findings of serotonic changes do not rule out the possibility that family learning and conditions during early child development could be a contributing factor. One might ask, could lowered serotonin occur when a child or adult child fails to learn how to play and have fun? A leader in the field of linking neurotransmitters to leisure behavior, has concluded that serotonin is secreted when an individual does things which are soothing and calming (O'Connor 1988). People born into homes where alcoholism is being practiced seldom learn to develop adequate play behaviors. Soothing and calming moments usually occur in the eye of Hurricane Drunkeness. The calm is overshadowed by the expectation that the next crisis is coming. The expectation of something bad on the approach would most likely trigger the fight-or-flight mechanisms rather than the production of chemicals which soothe and calm. It would seem that if a person were subjected to the eye-of-a-hurricane experience, year after year, the body would adapt. It would cease to produce chemicals that it has no use for and concentrate on producing chemicals that it has a use for. Thus, the body may very well alter its own ability to produce serotonin as a result of family learning, rather than just the biological inheritance of genes. Once altered, could it be passed to the next generation? Perhaps. One might wonder, whether the test developed for detection of lowered serotonin in this study could be used to detect an absence of play behavior? Has the world-expanding Jump and Skip system been extinguished before it ever got a start?

Why do people drink? It's hard to say. But it has been found that rats who like to take an alcoholic drink have high concentrations of dopamine. Rats who prefer not to drink have low concentrations of dopamine. It seems the higher the concentration, the more they want a drink. Dopamine levels are only one of many factors. It was also suggested that "properties of the opiate receptors of the functions of dopamine and opiate systems determine to a large extent the character of these systems' responses to alcohol and individual alcohol behavior" in rats with a craving for alcohol and in rats with alcoholic rat-parents" (Anokhina, 1985).

Alcohol's ability to reduce the action of GABA results in reduced self-control and judgment. Free at last from an over-developed code of right and wrong and relentless self-scrutiny, the person allows him/herself to enjoy life without care or concern. At the same time, alcohol may be interacting with the opiate receptors of the brain so that the person is truly feeling no pain. Of course these feelings are experienced with limited use. Interaction with other neurotransporter systems result in overuse, and the good times roll at a very high cost to the body's internal mechanisms.

It is possible that intoxication is caused by a specific interaction of calcium and neurotension (Morrow, 1987). Alcohol affects the brain stem and cerebellum, changing calcium uptake and norepinephrine releases (Daniell, 1986). And then there's the action on GABA, changing its ability to regulate critical brain functions.

Dopamine levels are also changed by alcohol use. There appear to be increases in dopamine levels during alcohol use, followed by decreased dopamine and norepinephrine levels when drinking subsides. Decreases are greater during an initial period of abstinence. Decreases in dopamine levels may be greater when withdrawal is combined with stress. Furthermore, alcohol use reduces the body's ability to manufacture an enzyme that breaks down dopamine (Gauza, 1985).

Disturbances in levels of dopamine, serotonin, and GABA in the body are not the total picture. It is possible that alcohol also interacts with the opiate receptors of the brain. Furthermore, alcohol has been found to change the state of the cell's membrane, while the opiates do not (Davis, 1984). Since the membrane is an essential part of the nerve's electrical system, it is not surprising that alcohol has been found to change electrical action. Chronic use results in changes in the coupling between voltage-dependent calcium's ability to enter into nerve endings as well as the ability to release neurotransmitters (Leslie, 1986).

When an attempt is made to stop alcohol consumption, neurotransmitter chemicals cannot function properly. There is too much of this and not enough of that. The cells have been altered so that they can no longer produce the enzymes and electrical charges needed to function properly. Alcoholics Anonymous has maintained that at the end of a drinking career, the person finds him/herself bankrupt "spiritually, mentally, physically." Now science suggests that the person is also bankrupt neurochemically.

To paraphrase a common expression heard in Alcoholics Anonymous circles, "You didn't get sick overnight. You won't get well overnight." Some studies seem to indicate that the longer the span of chronic use, the longer the span required for the neurotransporter systems to recover. In many cases, the end of a 30-day treatment stay marks only a fraction of the time the body needs to heal.

Science continues to look for a quick fix. Serotonergic agents (i.e., L-tryptophan, quipazine, and fluocetine) are being investigated as possible methods of reducing ethanol consumption. They appear to help rats abstain (Zabik, 1984). One study found that simelidine (another serotonin active substance) increased the number of days of abstinence in heavy drinkers without producing an aversive alcohol-sensitizing reaction, or significant depression or anxiety (Hyttell, 1985). Since production of serotonin is known to be stimulated by doing things that are soothing and calming, and these studies suggest that some serotonergic agents may reduce the compulsion to use alcohol, it seems logical that involving alcoholics in soothing calming leisure pursuits should assist in reducing the compulsion to drink.

In 1985, a Polish journal reported a study about the effects of isolation on mice dopamine levels and their desire for ethanol. The researchers found that dopamine release was lower in mice that were isolated for two weeks, and that after two weeks time, the mice began to look for a drink. Providing the mice with ethanol returned dopamine levels to normal. The lowered release of dopamine was not found in group-housed mice, nor did they develop a preference for ethanol (Andreas, 1985).

In the same year, a group of researches in France looked at isolation, serotonin, and alcohol preference in rats. They found that alcohol-preferring rats had lower serotonin levels than non-alcohol-preferring rats. The alcohol-preferring rats were then grouped five to a cage. The grouping reduced both voluntary intake of ethanol and uptake of serotonin at striatal receptors (Daoust, 1985). Alcoholics Anonymous has known from its inception that group action is a more powerful remedy for alcoholism than isolated action. Now, researcher's findings seem to support importance of group involvement in the recovery process. Therapeutic Recreation should be provided in group format as much as possible during treatment. It would appear that discharge to living alone is counterproductive, and that persons who are discharged to isolated settings should be involved in as many hours of group activities as possible. [Ch9: Skill Development in Creative Activities; Ch11:401.0, 460.0]

Other Depressants

Alcohol is a member of a group of drugs known as central nervous system depressants. Many other members of this group are drugs of abuse. There are many drugs in this classification, so they are subgrouped in Figure 3.6.

All depressants have the ability to move an individual from the normal state, through relief from anxiety, through disinhibition, through a sleep stage, through a general anaesthesia stage, through coma, to death. Depressants often act on a variety of nervous system processes rather than on a specific part of the brain. Most depressant users develop tolerance and withdrawal symptoms. The effects of depressants are additive. This means that the use of a second depressant will accentuate the effects of the first depressant. Sedatives are often supraadditive (in other words, one plus one does not equal two but equals five or six). This results in many fatal accidental overdoses.

FIGURE 3.6

CENTRAL NERVOUS SYSTEM DEPRESSANTS

ALCOHOL:	Beer, Wine, Scotch, etc.
BARBITURATES:	Phenobarbital (Luminal), Amobarbital (Amytal), Phetobarbital (Membutal), Secobarbital (Seconal), Pentothal (Thiopental).
NONBARBITURATE HYPNOTICS:	Glutethmide (Doriden), Methyprylon (Noludar), Methaqualone, (Parest, Quaalude, Somnafac, Sopor).
ANTIANXIETY AGENTS: (BENSODIAZEPINES)	Diazepam (Valium), Chlordizaepoxide (Clonopin, Librium), Oxaazepam (Serax), Flurazepam (Dalmane)/ Metprobamate (Miltown, Equanil).
OTHER DEPRESSANTS:	Bromide, Paraldehyde, Chloral hydrate, Ether, Halothane, Chloroform, Alcohol.

Stimulants are often taken to counteract the effects of depressants. But the stimulant action does not return the individual to a normal state of neuronal functioning. Suppose a person has taken too much of a depressant which is acting on receptors for sedation. A stimulant may act on fight-or-flight receptors, causing production of norepinephrine. The person does not go to sleep, because there is too much norepinephrine running around. But the depressant is still active in the sedation receptors. So, rather than using the action of one drug to turn the other drug action off, the person has two systems of opposing natures turned on at once. This is far from normal functioning for the central nervous system (Julien, 1981).

In the past, barbiturates have been used to combat sleeplessness, anxiety, and minor pain. Modern-day uses include low doses to reduce tension and anxiety without inducing lethargy that could lower alertness to potentially dangerous levels, and in moderate doses to counteract insomnia. They have the ability to reduce anxiety, tension, and irritability. They also lower inhibitions, produce euphoria, and induce a perception of well-being.

"Barbs" often find their way into use by persons in search of an addiction. With the exception of pentothal, barbiturates are usually taken orally. Intravenous administration is extremely dangerous. Some, such as phenobarbital, remain active in the person's system for days. Others, such as pentothal, have little action after a few minutes. Barbiturates develop tolerance because the liver develops the ability to metabolize the drug and also, use causes adaptation of neurons in the brain. Withdrawal symptoms, similar to those described for alcohol, can occur after high-dose use is discontinued. Barbiturate detoxification must be very gradual to avoid convulsions (Julien, 1981).

Methaqualone, a nonbarbiturate, has been promoted on the street as the love drug. It is possible that the drug's supposed power in this area is more a result of the placebo effect than actual properties of the drug itself. In view of methaqualone's chemical structure, it would appear that it is actually an anaphrodisiac (or the opposite of something which excites sexual desire). Methaqualone is similar to the barbiturates in its effects, side effects, and withdrawal (Julien, 1981).

The bensoidiazepines have been used and overused to calm the storms of anxiety. This subgroup contains diazepam, also known as valium, which has been one of the most abused prescription drugs on the market. They were developed and distributed in the 1960s in an attempt to provide a drug that would do all the things that addictive drugs would do without being addictive. The diazapams failed to live up to these expectations. They are a seductive group. Physician-prescribed to calm the nerves, they seem safe and harmless. As tolerance develops, the person experiences increased anxiety. Obviously the nerves are getting worse; so two tablets are taken instead of one. That works for a while. Then four tablets are needed to do what two used to do. It is most difficult to convince the user that the thing being taken to calm the nerves is the thing causing the nerves to be agitated.

The person lulled into addictive use usually blames the physician. In fairness to the physician, it should be pointed out that the patient could have called and said, "Hey doc, these aren't working anymore, let's try something different like Transcendental Meditation or acupuncture!" Furthermore, the person who sees a number of physicians in order to gather a large enough supply of prescriptions is a patient, not a doctor, who is out of control.

Treatment for addiction to tranquilizers will not be effective until the person finds a solution for the original malady: too much stress and anxiety in the individual's perception of reality. In the author's opinion, the tranquilizer group has only one saving grace and use. They are highly beneficial during the alcohol detoxification process. [Ch8:106.1]

Narcotics and Opiate-Like Substances

The primary medical use for the group of drugs classified as narcotics is for the relief of pain. These drugs are subgrouped as shown in Figure 3.7. They also relieve diarrhea and coughing. In large doses, narcotics induce sleep. They may also cause respiratory depression, constipation, pupillary constriction, and a loss of psychic energy derived from basic biological urges. Itching often accompanies narcotic use. Nausea and vomiting often accompany heroin use, especially in initial stages of use.

FIGURE 3.7

NARCOTICS & OPIATE-LIKE SUBSTANCES	
OPIATES:	Heroin, Morphine, Codeine, Opium, Dilaudid, Percodan, Demoral, Methadone.
OPIATE-LIKE:	Propoxyphene (Darvon), Pentazocine (Talwin), Fentanyl (Sublimaze).
OPIATE ANTAGONISTS:	Naloxone, Butorphanol (Stadol), Malbuphine (Nubain).

Evidence supporting linkage between opiates and the body's internal opiate system is strong. Narcotics occupy receptors in the body designed for endorphins, enkephalins, and other endogenous opiates. The primary purpose of the system is to block the pain sensation created by activation of substance P. For a detailed look at their action see the previous section in this chapter titled "Endorphins."

As pain relievers, narcotics surpass all other drugs. For this reason, they are still used in hospitals to treat severe pain. Physicians are well aware of their addictive properties, and are usually careful about prescribing them. Recovering addicts find themselves in a bind when health problems result in hospitalization and a medical need for the administration of a narcotic. Under these circumstances the recovering addict should advise the attending physician of the problem and see if some other course of action is an option. If no other option is available and narcotics must be used, then the person should remain hospitalized for an extended period of time to assure complete detoxification prior to discharge.

Heroin is still used in Great Britain as a medicine. In the United States heroin is classified as a Schedule I drug. Schedule I contains drugs with no recognized medical use and a high potential for abuse. Prescription provisions do not apply to Schedule I drugs because their only legal use is for research (Julien, 1981). A heroin addict described the results of heroin use as "a flush of euphoria, elevation of mood, and a feeling of peace, contentment, and safety as the drug relieves from the environment, both internal and external." This is one of the most significant reasons why heroin has the highest addiction potential of all the illicit drugs.

Contrary to common belief, high-dose users of heroin can function adequately (that is if one defines constant constipation, a lack of psychic energy, and a life centered around procurement of a substance, as adequate). The point is that the heroin user may not suffer the same global deterioration of physical and mental abilities that the alcoholic experiences. Financially supporting an opiate high is far more detrimental than the physical deterioration that is experienced. There is also the problem of unsterile needles, overdose, impurities in the street drugs. Keeping the pain system turned off reduces a person's ability to care for wounds that may occur. It also reduces the person's ability to learn from painful situations.

For example, if a person touches a hot coal, the pain teaches the person not to touch the coal again. But if the person has his/her pain receptors shut off, then coming in contact with a hot coal causes a burn but no pain. The person learns little and may get burned over and over again.

Codeine has been used for years as a cough suppressant. Prescriptions are not required to purchase the cough medicine, but the buyer must sign a register as a means of substance control. (Family and friends of narcotics addicts, attention! You are doing him/her no favors by picking up a bottle of codeine containing cough medicine "on your way home." You are not saving a sick person from a trip to the drug store. You are signing your name to the register instead of the addict's, which invalidates the codeine control system. You are supplying a narcotic addict with a narcotic. If the person has a cough, then purchase one of the cough suppressants that does not contain codeine and does not require a signature. If the cough is "too severe" to be treated by a non-codeine product, then suggest he/she see a doctor.)

Propoxphene (Darvon) is structurally similar to methadone. Usually taken orally, it is not as potent as codeine, about equal to aspirin. But in large doses, administered intravenously, it produces an opiate "high." Pentazocine (Talwin) is also a synthetic opiate. Talwin taken orally has the potency of codeine, but when injected, its strength is about one quarter the strength of morphine. The heroin addict or morphine addict will find it a poor substitute due to its lack of strength and may experience mild withdrawal symptoms.

Methadone is a synthetic opiate, and a narcotic which can be taken orally. It can be used to control withdrawal symptoms from other drugs in this group. Its effects last longer and it is less expensive than other narcotics. For these reasons it is sometimes used as a maintenance program for opiate-dependent persons. Methadone is more addictive than morphine, though withdrawal symptoms are less severe. Methadone maintenance does not return the user to a "normal" drug-free lifestyle. It simply reduces the need to commit illegal acts in order to procure the drug of choice. More recently developed synthetic opiates are butorphanol (Stadol), and malbuphine (Nubain) which can cause withdrawals in morphine and heroin addicts.

Opiates may be taken by subcutaneous (skin-popping) or intravenous (main-lining) injections. "Skin-popping" leaves a bluish mosquito-bite mark on the skin for about a day. "Main-lining" can cause permanent damage to the veins. Opiates can also be taken orally, or inhaled, but these methods do not produce as "good" of a "high." Onset varies but usually occurs in about half an hour and lasts for four to five hours. Mainliners report a "rush" experience which occurs immediately. Only a small amount of the narcotic crosses the blood-brain barrier to the endogenous opiate receptors. The remainder stays in the bloodstream in a fat-insoluble form. About 10 times more heroin will reach the brain than morphine. Opiates are rapidly metabolized by the liver before they are excreted by the kidneys (Julien, 1981). Tolerance to any opiate develops rapidly if used on a daily basis. Intermittent use, or "sprees," reduce the speed of tolerance buildup. But "sprees" or "chipping" cannot be maintained for more than a year. By then they have usually given way to daily use. The reason for this is unknown. But this is why a person can be given a narcotic in a hospital, for a few days, and not automatically become an addict. If a person is hospitalized on several occasions, and is given narcotics on each occasion, then the risk of addiction greatly increases.

Cross-tolerance develops within the opiate group. Cross-tolerance does not appear to develop between the opiate group and the depressant group. Effects between the two groups may be additive, for death resulting from the combination of depressants and opiates is common (Julien, 1981).

Withdrawal from opiates is most painful but perhaps least deadly. Bonding of external opiates to receptor sites which turn off pain sensation most likely turns off the body's production of natural painkillers. When the external opiate is removed, there is nothing available in the system to block substance P action. Other neurotransporter systems may be overly sensitive. Heroin withdrawal is characterized by a runny nose, dilation of pupils, stomach cramps, chills, and overall malaise comparable to symptoms of the flu. Symptoms compound themselves in proportion to the amount and frequency of use. Symptoms tend to peak within 24 to 36 hours after the last fix. After a few days, the physical manifestations of withdrawal subside. The psychological effects may last much longer. Medical complications or convulsions do not usually occur. It must be noted that the heroin addict is not usually dangerous to himself or others while using. It is when he needs a fix and does not have one that he/she will do anything, *anything*, to get one. That is when he/she is dangerous.

Opiate antagonists have been and are being developed. The antagonists produce neither euphoria nor analgesic effects. Naloxone is the best known. It is not a narcotic. A shot of naloxone causes immediate withdrawal from narcotic use. It is helpful in overdoses when respiration has been critically depressed. Naltrexone is taken orally and blocks the "high" produced by narcotics. [Ch8:100.2; Ch11:470.0]

Stimulants

Cocaine, Amphetamines

The stimulant group comprises agents which have the ability to "speed" up the central nervous system, most likely through increased production of norepinephrine. Stimulants prevent sleep, and cause reduced appetite. Initially, they produce a sense of improved functioning. The physiological actions are identical to those associated with the arousal of the fight-or-flight system. They include constriction of blood vessels, increased heart rate, increased strength of myocardial contraction, rise of blood pressure, dilation of the bronchi, increased blood sugar, shorter blood coagulation time, increased muscle tension and stimulation of adrenal glands. This is a picture of one who is ready to go, go, go!

Many feel that while under the influence of stimulants they are able to perform Herculean feats. Studies have shown that nothing could be farther from the truth. Researchers have found that with the use of stimulants the individual feels more alert, feels less fatigue. The person has a feeling of being more "up" and more ready to play. Amphetamines produce an elevation in mood, a euphoria, and hyper-optimism. But the ability to accurately evaluate personal performance on a task or to make the necessary corrections to improve performance is reduced. Persons under the influence of amphetamines continue to evaluate their performance on tasks better than they actually did even when presented with evidence to the contrary (Dusek, 1980).

The longer the period of use of stimulants the greater the physical and mental problems which occur. A number of studies have been performed over the years to determine the effects of sleep deprivation. One hardly needs a scientific study to understand the feelings if one has ever made the mistake of staying up all night and trying to work the next day. It is said that after 72 hours of sleep deprivation, hallucinations and irrational thinking begin to set in. The loss of one night's sleep was too awesome for the author to ever consider trying to go the distance to experience the 72-hour results. The negative feelings from lack of sleep are not experienced until drug use has ended. A desire to maintain the stimulated pace, combined with a desire to avoid the inevitable "crash" (depression) after drug use concludes, motivates the extension of use for as long as possible. Psychosis may be an inevitable consequence of high-dose chronic amphetamine use. The amphetamine user may experience lack of sleep, anxiety, and paranoid delusions. He/she may exhibit aggressiveness and irritability. These symptoms do not usually carry over into the non-drug state (Dusek, 1980).

Alternating the use of stimulants and depressants is common practice. It is an attempt to avoid the unwanted nervousness and agitation that accompany use. Both do their job too well and the user becomes a yo-yo—too up, too down. Furthermore, as mentioned in the depressant section, "uppers" and "downers" are not acting on the same neurochemical system, so it is not a matter of having the system too "off" or too "on." It's a matter of having two systems on at the same time. After extended use, stimulant users can become highly excited, highly agitated, and violent when they run out of their drug of choice and feel the need for more.

Administration of stimulants usually begins orally. Cocaine may be inhaled. Some move to intravenous, high-dose injection of stimulants. This produces a quicker and more intense "high." Overdoses from amphetamines are not common and do not usually produce death. Tolerance develops in the aspects of the drug's ability to produce mood elevation and appetite suppression, but not in its ability to prevent sleep (Julien, 1981).

Cocaine is a stimulant, but is legally classified as a narcotic. Cocaine and amphetamines seem to mimic the action of norepinephrine and are structurally similar. It is therefore assumed that they activate the fight-or-flight system. Low doses evoke an alerting response similar to the normal reaction to an emergency or any stressful situation (Julien, 1981).

The cocaine "high" is surrounded by myth. It is billed as the ideal euphoria enhancing leisure pursuits and sexual engagements. The attractiveness has been stimulated by the assumption that cocaine is not addictive. The nonaddictive attribute came from application of the old definition of addiction, which was based on physical withdrawal symptoms. Cocaine does not have physical withdrawal symptoms like alcohol does. The chances of having a convulsion as a result of withdrawal are practically zero. Psychological withdrawal symptoms are severe, a factor which the old definition did not take into account. In terms of the new definition, presented earlier in this chapter, cocaine is highly addictive. Extended use results in damage to neurotransmitter systems which may take years to repair. Extended use of cocaine makes it impossible for the person to relate to reality without the use of the drug.

Cocaine produces a "high" for a very short period of time. The first dose produces an incredible high which lasts for only a few minutes. The high trails off to a slightly lower than average mood in about 20 minutes. A second dose returns the "high" which again trails off to a low. The second high is not as high as the first but the second low is lower than the first. This process continues, with third use producing a high lower than the second and a low lower than the second. After repeated uses the "high" which is produced may be similar to the high that comes from waking up in the morning (not much) trailing off to a black-hole low. Users find themselves in constant need of another dose just to experience some semblance of normalcy. The cocaine crash is inevitable with extended use. Though it is a powerful negative reinforcer, it does not teach people not to use. Instead, it teaches people not to stop (Stone, 1984).

As I think about the "high," I wonder what it is like. To me "high" is something warm and beautiful. How can warm and beautiful come from norepinephrine activity? When I think of norepinephrine activity, I think of the time I was in a plane preparing to land. I heard the wheels unfold and lock into position—all was well. I looked out the window. Instead of seeing the familiar and expected Raleigh-Durham Airport runway, I saw Chapel Hill, North Carolina, and tree tops so close I thought I could touch them. We were coming down at least 15 miles short of the runway! That was a "rush." Though I was 200 feet high, it was not a warm and beautiful experience. Once, as a youngster, I walked through the woods. As I turned and began retracing my steps back to camp, I saw cougar tracks on top of my tracks. The beast had been following me the entire time. That, too, was a "rush," but not a "high." The feeling I experienced on these two occasions was indescribable. It was not a "bad" feeling. Granted I was ecstatic when the plane jolted back to ascending position and when I safely reached camp. The experience did not stop me from flying on planes. Now when I walk through the all too civilized woods and find no cougar tracks atop mine, I am terribly disappointed! Based on this, I would suggest that the norepinephrine experience is an incredible rush, but not an actual "high." A "high" is that unexplainable great, warm, beautiful feeling that might come from completing six rotations of a pirouette with a perfect landing! Perhaps people who mistake a rush for a high have never experienced a true high. Some research suggests that chronic cocaine use may promote beta-endorphine release (Forman, 1988). While this may explain why a cocaine habit is as hard to kick as a heroin habit, it still does not classify cocaine as a substance which induces a true "high." In my mind, there is still a difference between "feeling no pain" and feeling truly high. .

During every natural mass crisis (hurricane, flood, tornado, etc.) people die from heart attacks. Norepinephrine acts on the heart (not figuratively, but literally). The rush of norepinephrine is obviously powerful, and if it hits the heart too hard or too fast, death can follow. It is therefore not surprising that we are hearing on the television news that somebody tried crack (an extra-strength cocaine derivative) and died of a heart attack. It is frightening to think that first use of a substance can result in addiction or death. Crack appears to have the ability to do just that. I predict that it will be a drug of brief impact on the addiction scene. The American population is not in search of death and addiction. It searches for the good feelings without the negative side effects. Still, some lives will be sacrificed to crack. Others will see that crack use is not healthy, and general use will be avoided. The drugs that present the biggest problems are those without absolute and immediate negative results, such as heroin and alcohol. When people can use once without getting into trouble, then they are seduced into repeated use, discounting the horror stories as antidrug propaganda. If all drugs had the immediacy of crack, most potential addicts would be looking for nonsubstance methods of getting high.

Rush or high, cocaine and crack addicts are swelling treatment center populations. Many therapists feel unequipped to handle the onslaught. Alcoholism has been treated for many years. That which works for alcoholism works for treatment of persons addicted to other depressants. But, the cocaine addict does not fit the alcoholic profile. Treatment for stimulant abuse is a relatively recent phenomenon and few guidelines have been published. The creation of Cocaine Anonymous tells me that the basic 12-step program works for stimulant users just as it works for depressant users. Yet the creation of a separate program also implies distinct differences. Persons addicted to processes that result in stress have been widely studied. "Stress junkies" are for real. Though much is known about the result of untreated stress addiction, there seems to be no definitive solution for treatment at this time. Later in this text, I will take some guesses about what might work. [Ch11:420.0]

Hallucinogens/Psychotomimetic

There are a number of drugs in this category, too many to discuss individually. Each drug usually has several street names. The basic rule of thumb is that if it is called a three-letter name, it is a hallucinogen. There are also several names for this group of drugs. Hallucinogens are also known as "psychoactive" drugs and "psychotomimetic" drugs. Psychotomimetic probably says the most, for it implies that the drugs mimic psychosis (Davis, 1984). These drugs are subgrouped by the neurotransporter which they influence, as shown in Figure 3.8. For the most part these drugs were developed in research laboratories by accident, and folks have been trying to find a use for them ever since. Nature does produce a few of these naturally, like marijuana, peyote and mescaline. Most are capable of producing hallucinations, but they are an extremely diverse group in the way they act on the central nervous system.

FIGURE 3.8

HALLUCINOGENS/PSYCHOTOMIMETIC	
Neurotransporter:	*Hallucinogens:*
Acetylcholine:	Physostigmine, DFP, Sarin, Soman, Malathion, Parathion.
Norepinephrine:	Mescaline, DOM, MDA, MMDA, TMA, Myristiciin, Elmicin.
Serotonin:	LSD, DMT, Psilocybin, Psilocin, Bufotenine, Ololiuqui, Harmine.
Arylcyclohexylamine:	PCP, Ketamine.
?	Marijuana, Hashish.

Drugs such as physostigmine, DFP, sarin, soman, malathion, and parathion act by increasing the amounts of acetylcholine available in the synapses. They are known to produce nightmares, confusion, delirium, and agitation. They also slow intellectual and motor functions (Julien, 1981). Norepinephrine-active hallucinogens are mescaline, DOM (STP), MDA, MMDA, TMA, myristicin, and elemicin (an extract of nutmeg). They produce basically the same effects as amphetamines and cocaine.

Drugs that appear to interact with the serotonin system are lysergic acid diethylamide (LSD), dimethyltryptamide (DMT), psilocybin, psilocin, bufotenine, ololiuqui (morning glory seeds), and harmine. LSD requires extremely minute quantities (about a billionth of a gram) to produce an effect. It induces psychological changes without major alterations of physical functioning. It seems to distort reality perceptions. While there may be no withdrawal symptoms, the altered view of reality can cause a user to climb inside and refuse to come back out (Davis, 1984). Tolerance develops rapidly. Cross-tolerance develops between LSD, mescaline, and psilocybin. Initially, LSD was investigated as a potential cure for some forms of mental illness. It came into popular use after one of the experimenters, Timothy Leary, began experimenting on himself and publicizing his results. I remember the uproar when, in the late 1960s, Leary visited my college campus. He spoke to the students. The auditorium filled and overflowed. I listened with hundreds of others to a speaker hastily hung in a hallway. Since then, part of me has always wished I had gotten there early enough to get a seat where I could have seen him as well as heard him. (The other part of me has always been thankful that I did not experience his full impact, only his voice). He was an eloquent speaker and a master of persuasion. After 20 years, I can still hear his voice booming, "Turn on, tune in, drop out." Many of my colleagues did. And what happened to Leary? Fortunately, he took his own advice. I also remember trying to process his message for days after his talk. In all his force and furor, he never said exactly what LSD did. LSD can negatively impact the psychological state of the user and permanent damage to the brain may occur. Persistent flashbacks can occur months after use. Though death by overdose is rare, "bad trips" may precipitate psychotic episodes. Stringent laws governing the use, sale, and manufacture of LSD appear to have reduced its availability. Today, the fascination with LSD use seems to be waning. Perhaps it is no longer popular because it is no longer available; perhaps it is no longer available because those who championed its use have all dropped out.

Mescaline (Peyote) is found in a cactus and psilocybin is found in mushrooms. Though mescaline is structurally similar to norepinephrine and psilocybin is similar to serotonin, they both develop cross-tolerances with LSD. Both distort time and space perceptions the same way as LSD. Users may experience flight-fright-fight reactions. Lower doses seem to induce mental relaxation, while higher doses may result in perceptual alterations and hallucinations.

Phencyclidine, also known as PCP, peace pill, crystal, hog, horse tranquilizer, and angel dust, was synthesized in 1956. Early research focused on its pain-relieving aspect. It was never marketed as such for humans due to its side effects. It has been used as an anaesthetic for some animals. Ketamine is similar to PCP, but lacks some of the side effects. It has been used as an anaesthetic on humans (Julien, 1981). At this point, PCP does not appear to interact with the endogenous opiate receptors. PCP's exact action on the nervous system is still debatable. It has been linked to serotonin levels, increased tyrosine (a precursor for dopamine and norepinephrine), and decreased GABA levels (Davis, 1984).

PCP can be taken orally, smoked, snorted, or taken intravenously. PCP use can result in mental states similar to those found in schizophrenia. At low doses it can cause agitation, excitement, and poor coordination. Catatonic rigidity and blank staring may also occur. Users may also experience altered perceptions of body image, feelings of estrangement, and disorganized thinking. They may exhibit drunkenness,

drowsiness, or apathy. Extremely violent and hostile behavior has also been known to occur (Davis, 1984). Oral overdoses can result in coma which can last days, followed by confusion which can last weeks, followed by psychosis which can last months. Overdose can also result in critically depressed respiration. Overdose can be fatal. Chronic users risk long-term paranoid psychosis, severe depression and anxiety.

THC is the psychoactive agent found in marijuana and hashish. Improved cultivation techniques continue to increase the amount of THC contained in a marijuana plant. Marijuana contains approximately one percent THC, while hashish contains 5 to 12 percent. The effects begin within minutes of smoking it and can last about five hours. The THC residue remains stored in the person's system for up to 30 days after the last use. It is not very water-soluble, but is very fat-soluble; it tends to be deposited in fatty tissues. THC easily penetrates the brain and concentrates in the liver, kidneys, spleen, lungs, and testes. Tolerance does develop with marijuana use. Classic withdrawal symptoms have been observed in research settings using extremely high doses. Most people who use marijuana do not use a high enough dose to experience withdrawal symptoms (Julien, 1981).

Marijuana has been around since before 2700 B.C. Public opinion has always tended to be against its use. Researches have had a difficult time determining what is wrong or right with it from the start. They have had an equally difficult time figuring out how it operates in the body. It obviously does something, but it does not appear to act on the same neurotransporters as the other drugs (Davis, 1984). While I have suggested that another neurotransporter system may exist, which I call the "Jump and Skip" system, I sincerely doubt that marijuana activates it. It may turn off the "Jump and Skip," but it certainly does not turn it on.

Researches have found that THC can be used as a mild pain reliever. It may decrease epileptic seizures. Glaucoma patients may be helped by THC because it may decrease pressure of fluid behind the eyes. It may also decrease resistance in the airways of the lungs and serve as an anti-vomiting agent for cancer patients receiving chemotherapy (Julien, 1981). However, I doubt that these are the reasons why marijuana is purchased on the street.

Back in the sixties, those who embraced Leary's "turn on, tune in, drop out" life style did so with LSD in one hand and a joint in the other. I would suggest that the "tune in" aspect of pot is the brain being tricked into thinking that something significant is going on when in fact nothing is happening. The body "drops out." Those who use are often quite content to sit and do very little for long periods of time. Marijuana does not appear to have serious withdrawal symptoms. Under my new definition it is an addictive substance because it alters perceptions of reality. Extended use results in disengagement from aspects of the non-using world. Motivation to do becomes extinguished.

My personal experience has led me to believe that marijuana use should not be condoned for persons seeking recovery from addiction. I have heard two persons promise, "I promise

I will never use alcohol, or drugs, or marijuana again." (Naturally, the "nevers" resulted in broken promises and relapses.) The interesting thing is that there had been pressure from family on both persons to give up alcohol and drugs. There had been no outside pressure to give up marijuana. In fact, marijuana could have been used as a bargaining point, "I'll give up alcohol and drugs if you won't say anything about marijuana use." But it was not. It was voluntarily thrown into the deal by both addicted persons. To me, this implies that the addicted person views marijuana effects as being the same as use of other addictive substances. I had the opportunity to discuss marijuana use with one of the individuals who had issued the promise. The conversation occurred after the person had been sober for about three years. I asked the person why marijuana use had been lumped in with the other abuse substances and why use had been curtailed. The answer was, first of all, "It never did that much for me." Secondly, "If I smoke a joint I wind up getting a beer and I'm off and running again." Perhaps marijuana use activates the addiction disease cycles. Perhaps marijuana simply decreases the individual's inhibitions to the point where he/she forgets that he/she can't drink just one. Perhaps it's a problem of activating old habits. Just as a cup of coffee needs a cigarette, a joint may need a beer. Whatever the reason, marijuana use is contraindicated for the addicted population.

The psychological effects of the hallucinogens differ greatly from individual to individual. There are many factors that will determine whether or not the user will have a "good trip" or a "bad trip." The persons surrounding the individual, the person's own frame of mind, other people, all play an important part in determining the quality of the "trip." The fact that the thing that is experienced is called a "trip" when the person actually travels nowhere provides further evidence of the distorted perception of reality which occurs.

In general, hallucinogens impair intellectual processes; the subject cannot or will not perform given tasks, may have difficulty concentrating on a subject of choice. Attempts to react logically to intrusions from the outside world may show disorganized thinking. All types of psychological tests (perceptual, cognitive, and motor) taken during a hallucinogenic experience reveal impaired function. Tolerance to the hallucinogens develops rapidly. Those who use hallucinogens for "kicks" must either space their "trips" or take ever-increasing doses to receive the desired effects. [Ch8:100.2; Ch11:402.0, 408.0]

Caffeine and Nicotine

Both coffee and cigarettes are addictive substances. There are social users and then there are addicted users. They have been acceptable because they do not change the individual's perception of the outer world. Aside from clogging others' nostrils and lungs, there is little damage done to non-smokers and non-coffee drinkers. The primary site of damage is within the person who smokes and/or drinks coffee. Caffeine and nicotine damage vital organs. They also alter the internal nervous system, which can eventually result in chemical imbalances.

I've heard many a recovering addict say that his/her drug of choice was far easier to give up than cigarettes. Until recently, much of the difficulty has been in the social acceptability of smoking. The ban on smoking in public places and offices is difficult for the smoke addict, but it may also help the person to see that life is possible without a puff. The well-meaning nonsmoker who pressures the smoker to quit, does no good. It's like pouring the liquor out of the alcoholic's bottle. Detoxification programs are needed for smokers, followed by treatment and attendance in 12-step programs.

Non-Drug Substance Addiction: Food

Overeating and undereating have been around at least as long as alcohol. Those who have struggled with the curse of too much fat have received the same type of "helpful" advice as alcoholics. "Just don't eat so much." "It's a matter of willpower." Actually, it's a matter of addiction. Not all who eat are addicted. Not all who drink are alcoholics. The addiction of overeating is the repetitive self-administration of food to avoid reality perceptions through manipulation of internal nervous system processes, resulting in damage to the equilibrium of internal biochemical functioning and inability to relate to the outer world without the use of food.

I am a foodaholic. Nowadays people look at me and say, "I wish I were thin like you and could eat anything I wanted." They don't like to hear that I'm a recovering foodaholic, that I stay thin by not eating everything I want. It is easier to believe that losing weight is a hopeless battle, so why bother to try? Many who practice overeating and know that I am a recovering foodaholic are uncomfortable being around me. While I say nothing about their weight, looking at me is a reminder that fat can be overcome. But it isn't easy and it doesn't happen overnight.

It would appear that the "drugs" of food are contained in chocolate, sugar, and flour. Something in butter may also be addictive. I remember a popcorn binge. My weight kept rising and every morning I would get off the scales swearing that I would never eat popcorn again, only to find myself popping it that night. In sheer desperation, I glued a picture of an ugly fat woman and the name of a fat person who I knew was miserable on my popcorn storage container. I remember night after night of pacing the floors. Opening the cupboard door, reaching for the popcorn container, seeing the message and closing the cupboard door. Within minutes, the process would start all over again. Some nights I ate popcorn. Some nights I didn't. Finally I broke free. Now I eat popcorn five or six times a year. A one night binge always leads to the desire for a repeat performance on the next night. I refuse to do it twice in a row. I still remember that battle and I don't want to go through it all over again.

Later in my food career, I got hooked on creme horns. These are a pastry with pie crust rolled around a wad of icing. The local grocery stores began stocking them in six-pack format. I would buy a package of six with my groceries. The first one would be gone before I left the parking lot. By the time I got home half of them were missing. Embarrassed by my over consumption, I felt it only wise to hide the evidence. So I would quickly eat the other three and hide the wrapper at the very bottom of the garbage in the trash can outside. Somehow it seemed that as long as my husband didn't know I had eaten them it would be OK. (Sound familiar?) One day I realized the severity of my problem. It had been an insane day at work so I decided to get away from it all and do my grocery shopping during my lunch break. I found myself staring at an empty shelf where the creme horns were suppose to be. I couldn't remember the other items on my shopping list so I left. Within minutes, I found myself in a second grocery store staring at a second empty shelf! That day I turned the town upside down in search of a creme horn, and there were none to be found. With each disappointing stop, I became angrier and angrier! I regained my senses the next day. I also discovered that a good sugar binge resulted in experiencing mild withdrawal symptoms. I would become nervous, jittery after the stuff wore off. Since then, creme horns have been on my danger list along with popcorn, cheesecake and birthday cake icing. Yes, I still use, but with great caution. I have to be willing to fight the battle before I eat the first one. Six-packs are strictly off-limits.

I used food to change my perception of myself and my relationship to the outer world. When things didn't go my way, I ran for food rather than dealing with the problem. When the outer world filled with uncertainty, I climbed into that secure and lazy feeling which accompanies a too-full belly. An accomplishment was always celebrated with a feast.

I have been told that overeating is genetic. Fat people have fat children. The brain has a control system in it which governs how much is eaten. Some brains are set too high allowing us to eat too much. If we don't give the body as much food as the brain thinks it wants, then we stay hungry (Ornstein & Sobel, 1987). Our bodies don't metabolize fat as well as normal people's. It could be genetic. Research has found genetic links in mice. Furthermore, it is possible that increased levels of enkelphins caused those mice to gain the extra weight. It is also possible that the additional weight gain put stress on the little mice bodies causing increased production of endorphins (Davis, 1984). I have chosen to reframe the fat-metabolizing factor. Rather than using it as an excuse to remain fat, I say my body is so efficient at processing and storing that I need to eat less than the average guy.

No doubt my family's tradition of feasting for leisure, for family gatherings, for organizing work parties had something to do with my problem. My mother often shared her memories of childhood family adventures. They ate great cheese in Tillamook. They sat on huge boulders to eat lunch while hiking a beach trail. Her brother's antics at her aunt's resulted in a dinner of baked robin. Every memory worth the sharing contained a food of some sort. The first stop on our outings to the beach was the bakery for sheep herder's bread (it was there that I learned to solve my problems by eating creme horns, at age seven.)

A close friend, also a recovering foodaholic, confided to me that she used fat to hide in. While growing up, fat made her feel less attractive to a sexually molesting father. Upon reaching adulthood, she found fat was a great way to keep people at a distance. She let go of her fat when she let go of her need to keep people away.

Treatments for obesity have been varied. Persons have wired their teeth together and stapled their stomachs. Fat has been surgically removed. Crash diets of all types have been tried. Muscle-torturing exercise regimes have been attempted. Few have gained lasting benefits from any of these. There are no easier, softer ways. Many are turning to Overeaters Anonymous, a 12-step program similar to Alcoholics Anonymous and finding recovery, one day at a time.

I hope that in sharing my creme horn antics has allowed the reader a chance to laugh. I hope the reader can also see just how similar food addiction is to alcoholism. In fact, overeating may be a method of manipulating endorphin levels in the body, so perhaps it is more akin to heroin addiction than alcoholism.

What of the undereater? I also have been too thin. In times of severe trauma, such as the death of a loved one, I guess I forget to eat because it is one of those rare times in my life that I am not hungry. It takes me some time to remember that people are supposed to eat to live, instead of always living to eat. My lack of eating during trauma is somewhat different from addictive under-eating, known as anorexia. Persons with anorexia seem to have an over-weight complex. They choose to lose (weight). No matter how many pounds they take off, it is not enough. They may starve themselves to near-death and still feel fat. There seems to be an altered body perception, a feeling that society will not accept them because they are fat, no matter how thin they are. Anorexia may mask inhibited anger and depression. Persons with anorexia may lack tolerance for physical discomfort. There is deep-seated denial. The person cannot or will not believe that a lack of food could be deadly. There may be an indirect connection between anorexia and endorphins. The addicted runner may exhibit many of the same personality characteristics as the anorexic (Davis, 1984). During my Therapeutic Recreation internship, I worked with a young girl who had anorexia. She always liked coming to the gym. She'd get a basketball and, unless I stopped her, which I did, would run up and down the court bouncing the basketball for the entire session. I always felt that her goal was not to play the game, but to see how many calories she could burn off. She had a vacant stare, one that I now associate with the look of a practicing addict.

The control of weight is complex. The hypothalamus controls appetite and absorption of food into the body (Ornstein & Sobel, 1987). It is my opinion that food addicts use food to stimulate the hypothalamus to alter moods and perceptions of self and to avoid uncomfortable situations which exist in the outside world. The self-administered manipulation of the internal systems produces health problems. Eating instead of acting allows difficult situations to get worse. If overeating or undereating goes unchecked, the body loses its ability to function and death ensues.

Are overeating and under-eating two extremes of the same continuum? Are endorphins manufactured by the stress of overeating? Do anorexics experience an endorphin-produced "runner's high" from the stress of undereating? Are they two different animals? Does overeating fall on the depressant branch of the addiction tree, while undereating falls in the fight-or-flight group next to the amphetamines which suppress appetite? (Flip a coin. I did, and it came out listing over-eating with the depressants and under-eating with the stimulants.) [Ch8:100.0; Ch11:408.0, 420.0, 410.0]

PROCESS ADDICTIONS

It must be asked, can a person really get "hooked" on something which is not injected or ingested into the body? What actually causes the heroin addict to get high? It is not the heroin molecule. What actually causes the drinker to get drunk? It is not the alcohol molecule which causes the change in behavior. The heroin user feels high as a result of a molecule fitting into specific receptors in the brain. The effects of drinking result from molecules fitting into receptors in the brain. These receptors were not designed for heroin or alcohol molecules. They were designed for molecules produced within the body. Production of these natural molecules result from natural processes. Since the molecules produced within the body are more addictive than heroin and other external substances, it is logical to assume that any process which can cause the body to generate molecules intended to fit into those same receptors has to be a potentially addictive process.

If the purpose of addiction is to alter perceptions of reality, can a process alter reality precepts in the same way? Again it must be asked, what causes a substance to alter perceptions of reality? The actual substance does not produce a change in the perception of reality anymore than a tree falling in a forest produces sound. It is action of stimuli on the brains receptors which the body's control system (emotions, thought, mediated by logic) interprets as reality. Thus any process which can create production on internal chemicals has the potential to alter perceptions of reality. If a heroine molecule can fit into receptors and produce a perception of "feeling no pain," then a process which causes the body to produce endorphines which fit into the same receptors will produce the same perception.

Aside from gambling, few process addictions have specialzed treatment programs available to treat the problem. This text primarily addresses substance addictions. It is unlikely at this time that a therapeutic recreator working in an alcohol/drug treatment facility will have a client whose "drug of choice" is a food or a process. For this reason, only limited review of the process addictions is provided. But it is important to know something about the process addictions to provide adequate treatment for the alcoholic or drug addict. When a person realizes that a drug is causing a problem, he/she may become involved in a first-order scenario which leads to substituting a different type of addiction into the vacuum created by the absence of a drug. Process addictions are often viewed as "healthier" than drug and alcohol use, thus the substitution may be encouraged and welcomed by therapists and family members alike. Glasser's *Positive Addiction* (1976) supports this type of substitution as does...Fixx's *Complete Book of Running* (1977). *I cannot agree. Addiction is addiction is addiction! Therapeutic Recreation Specialists must be very careful in program design and leisure education sessions and discharge planning to avoid open or unconscious support of process addictions.*

In attempting to place process addictions on the appropriate branches of the addiction tree, I found a problem of double negatives. "He does not have no fun," actually means he has fun. Yet the person issuing the remark actually means no fun. "Is it not true?" is another highly perplexing sentence for me. If I respond "yes" does that mean yes it is not true and therefore false, or does it mean yes it is true? Many potentially addictive processes are engaged in only when the person is under the influence of drugs or alcohol. When a person uses a depressant prior to engaging in a stimulant-type process, is the person addicted to a depressant or a stimulant, or both? Pragmatically, I have chosen to discount the process if it is performed under the influence of a substance. If the substance addiction is treated first participation in the process addiction may subside, at least temporarily.

Consider the alcoholic who must take a drink to get up enough nerve to engage in a process. When the alcoholic stops drinking, the participation in the process is also stopped. But as the alcoholic progresses through treatment and recovery, he/she may find strength within to participate in desired processes without a drink, fix or pill. That's great; that's what treatment is all about. But that also opens the door to participating in desired and potentially addictive processes and getting hooked on those processes. Treatment must be designed to encourage persons to develop the ability to participate in desired activities. However, it must also prepare addictive personalities to avoid process addictions. [Ch8:100.0; Ch11:420.0]

Gambling and High-Risk Addictions

Gambling is a serious disease. I failed to recognize the severity of gambling until I visited Las Vegas. Looking into the blank faces of those in the casino at three in the morning told me that gambling drains life. Though purely psychological, it is no less addictive than heroin.

Regulation has been attempted by legal methods. Laws preventing gambling are only partially successful. Gambling continues in black market enterprises and in neighbors' game rooms. When dice are unavailable, the compulsive gambler bets on life. Many an entrepreneur has gone bankrupt betting his or her bottom dollar on insane business ventures. This is not to say that all high-risk business ventures are addictive. The person who engages in a high-risk venture backs that venture with him/herself as well as money, and then follows the venture through to conclusion, is probably not an addict. The person who gets involved in several such ventures, and regardless of success or failure, jumps into more of the same, is most likely addicted to the gambling process involved, rather than searching for wealth and health. [Ch8:100.0; Ch11:420.0]

Work Addictions

Work addiction may be encouraged by the short sighted. Working 60 hours a week instead of 40 brings home a larger paycheck if one is being paid by the hour. That's more money for the family to spend and the stores to collect. Employers who pay by the task rather than by the hour are delighted to discover a workaholic on the payroll. It's delightful to see employees burning the midnight oil on their own time! But overwork brings imbalanced living. Imbalanced living brings physical health problems, distracted thinking, and turmoil from those who feel neglected. As hours of overwork increase, efficiency and effectiveness decrease. The workaholic is a shining star in the organization until overwork results in a careless mistake which throws a monkey wrench into the entire operation. Organizational contributions diminish as the shining star gets hospitalized for stress-related disorders, and the workaholic finds difficulty being productive when the lonely family escapes from solitary confinement.

To appreciate the full ramifications of work addiction, it must be noted that "work" can occur without monetary compensation as well as for financial reimbursement (Hoyt, 1989). The person who cleans out the ashtrays 17 times an hour in a home where no one smokes does not get paid for his/her labors, yet work is occurring just the same. It has been suggested that work addiction occurs due to feelings of low self-esteem and as a means to avoid reality (Robinson, 1989).

In his book *Work Addiction,* Robinson suggests that many adult children of alcoholics are predisposed to work addiction (1989). He lists the same characteristics which identify adult children as characteristics of work addicts. To this list he adds (a) attention- and crisis-seeking behavior and complaint about the results, (b) avoidance or aggravation of conflicts with only rare initiation of solutions to the conflict, (c) fear of rejection and frequent rejection of others, (d) fear of failure coupled with steps taken to defeat success, (e) criticism of others and inability to accept criticism, and (f) poor time management (Robinson, 1989). To Robinson's list, I would add one critical characteristic: the fear of getting trapped with nothing to do. Too many projects are taken on. This minimizes the risk that comes with a single project. A single project eventually gets completed, leaving the person with nothing to do. Workaholics manage to carry their work with them wherever they go. This alleviates the fear of sitting in a doctor's reception room with nothing to do. Work-sacks are carried on vacations. The work projects are seldom utilized, for the fear of nothing to do has caused the workaholic to overstructure and overcommit

the days alloted for rest and recreation. The vacation is spent at a blinding pace: Up at dawn, packed and out of the motel by 8:00 in the morning, driving 600 miles and touring eight museums before check-in at the next motel. Ferries and other long boat rides are usually avoided because they limit access to something to do. If the rider runs out of things to do, he/she must wait for the boat to dock before getting more!

The results are an array of physical and behavioral symptoms. The lifestyle produces fatigue and stress. Headaches, indigestion, stomach aches, ulcers, chest pain, hyperventilation, nervous tics, high blood pressure, and dizziness may result (Robinson, 1989). The body's immune system may be depressed, permitting minor allergies to flare into major health problems. A minor cold develops into bronchitis or pneumonia. Behaviorally, the person may have temper outbursts, experience insomnia, find it difficult to concentrate or to sit still, become forgetful, and experience mood swings from euphoria to depression (Robinson, 1989). Professional help is often sought to cure the symptoms rather than the cause. A doctor's advise to "slow down" is staunchly rejected, for that means a fate worse than death (sitting around with nothing to do). But a doctor who prescribes a tranquilizer, now there's a doc who knows the score! Alcohol and depressant use are often discovered as methods to control the symptoms without giving up the cause. Some find substance addiction as a result of workaholism. Some substitute work addiction for substance addiction. Addiction is addiction, and a healthy, balanced life is not found in either.

Yes, in addition to being a food addict, I am also a work addict. Relapses are quite common and I must always guard against them. There are times when I have abused work to avoid pain and discomfort. There have also been times when I have barreled into a project just to get a rush. At such times it is impossible to distinguish me from my work. I would divide work addiction into two types. Stress avoidance and stress seeking. Hard-core work junkies use work for both.

Stress avoidance workaholics can't sit down and chat because we are too busy. We can't play because we are too busy. We'll deal with the problem at home tomorrow because right now we are late for work, or have a deadline. The pain of conflict and grief are eradicated by focusing on the task at hand. Repetitive work fits the avoidance bill best—cleaning, playing host at the party, "working" in the garden, around the house, in the woodwork shop, or chopping wood. Getting paid to avoid life is even better. Assembly-line work, and other jobs where few decisions are required, fit the bill. Doing a job so many times we can do it in our sleep is a perfect hiding place. Perfection is demanded. The more perfect a thing is, the more time is consumed. The more time consumed, the less time is left to face real world problems. When cut off from our work hiding place, we feel vulnerable. Off the job we hide in the garden, in an art project, or in cleaning the all-too-clean. The process is as important as the outcome. Stress avoiders take no short cuts, leave no stone unturned. Stress avoiders cry, "Look to someone else, I'm busy!"

Stress seekers are looking for thrills, for validation that our lives mean something to someone. We seek new horizons to conquer. Sales are ideal for some (not me). Talking a person into buying a product that the person doesn't actually need is a true sign of personal superiority. Management jobs are also attractive. Pitch that new proposal. Get the company to buy my idea. (That's more me.) Other stress seekers find heaven waits in real estate sales, used car lots and political arenas. Many find small-business entrepreneurial endeavors ideal. Stress-seeking work addicts are natural born wheeler-dealers. The stress-seeking workaholic will not be found puttering around in his/her garden when forced to take some time off. He/she is out there riding motorcycles, shooting whitewater rapids, racing cars, jumping out of planes. Process is less important than outcome. How something gets done is of little consequence; getting it done quickly is important. Most important is who is responsible and who gets the credit. The stress-seeking workaholic cries, "Look at me, look at me!" He/she lives in the job and the total human identity becomes the job. Tolerance develops rapidly. To get the desired charge, bigger and bigger projects must be taken on. If the path to bigger and bigger is blocked, the stress-seeker may turn to sabotage, causing the existing to crumble so that it can be rebuilt. Making the big deal, jumping 50 buses on a motorcycle never quite makes the small child within feel nurtured, loved, secure. (But perhaps jumping 51 will).

It might be argued that the stress avoiders are accessing the same or similar internal systems as the depressant drug users and overeaters; likewise, the stress seekers access systems similar to stimulant users. Work cuts off the stress avoiders' and the stress seekers' perception of non-work-related problems. Of course, the inability to perceive does not make the problems go away. The lack of attention causes problems to grow. Work addiction is deadly, both physically and emotionally. Even so, it may be a long time before we see, "For treatment call 1-800-WORK-ADDICT" flash across our television screens. Addicts seldom stop use voluntarily. With the exception of cases involving fraud, legal authorities seldom get involved in the apprehension of work addicts. Employers seldom ask employees to reduce their dedication to their jobs. Families complain but seldom demand a halt to the behavior, for it may mean potential reduction of social status and financial support. [Ch8:100.0, 100.1, 100.2, 100.3; Ch11:420.0]

Sex Addictions

It was a winter day with blistering winds chilling my bones even though I was in the car with my heat turned full blast. Pulling up to a stop sign, I glanced to the right to see a prostitute. In short mini-skirt attire she paced her corner, cold and very much alone. She patiently waited for an invitation, willingly risking AIDS, syphilis, or a knife in the back. Whatever need brought her to that corner that day, it was far greater than mine.

Healthy sex is healthy. But not all sex is healthy. Some adults find themselves compelled to become sexually involved with children. Some feel compelled to "cheat" on marital partners. Some singles feel compelled to pick up strangers at singles clubs, finding no real satisfaction from an encounter, only a compulsion to repeat the function the next night. These examples indicate an inability to establish meaningful interpersonal ties with another.

Some seek escape in sex. Others see in it a chance to control the destiny of another. Still others seek an ego boost, a chance to prove personal desirability. None of these motives have anything to do with the type of sex that evolves from a caring interpersonal relationship.

Though perhaps too simplified a classification, I would place those who abuse sex to avoid formation of interpersonal relations into the stress avoiders group, and those who abuse it to validate self-worth into the stress seeker group. [Ch8:100.0, Ch11:420.0]

People Addictions

Co-dependency is addiction to a specific person. Some people avoid intimate involvement with one person by getting hooked on groups of people. The group may be a gang. It may be a cult. It could be a church. People addiction may also manifest itself in meeting attendance. In my years of employment in health care management, I often wondered if my organization had caught a plague of meeting addiction. I remember giving one day a week over to various meetings. We were so busy meeting and identifying problems, there never seemed to be enough time to solve our problems. Twelve-step programs also fall victim to meeting addicts. In Alcoholics Anonymous jargon, a person who attends the program to avoid problems rather than solve them, is referred to as being "on" the program rather than "in" the program. Wherever group addiction occurs, there is a marked decrease in personal problem solving activity. Participation in the group functions is viewed as a cure-all which requires no individualized action outside the group. While engaged in the group, there is euphoria. Difficulties are left behind. When the group is abandoned, even temporarily, cold harsh reality sets in. The person has two choices: find the controls on the reality air conditioner, or avoid the scene by returning to the group. Persons who are not addicted to meetings or groups make small individual adjustments between group functions. Persons who are addicted often make no individual change attempt.

Characteristics of people addiction include lack of individual decision making and lack of personal identity. Treatment requires time. First, addicted individuals must go through a "detoxification period." This may take years. During detox, persons addicted to a person, or to a group of questionable health (e.g., gangs or cults) should be encouraged to transfer their dependency onto a healthy group. The fact that

Alcoholics Anonymous has identified a difference between being "in" or "on" the program indicates that some help is available through 12-step programs. Over time, the person should then be encouraged to initiate individualized action. Wherever possible, the person should be encouraged to attend larger meetings rather than small ones. The person who is addicted to meetings is a potential disruption to group process. In a group of 10 or less, the person can be a source of frustration to the other group members. In large groups the person has less opportunity to be disruptive to the healthy process.

People addiction often involves manipulation and control of others rather than focusing on self-control and self-change. The compulsion to manipulate others may result in an array of serious disorders. Hypochondria may be an addiction to illness. There are those who develop a lifestyle which revolves around being ill. Perhaps some people are addicted to production of substance P, the neurotransmitter which produces the pain sensation. It is equally possible that experiencing the symptoms of illness is undesirable. The goal of hypochondria may be to manipulate the behaviors of others. If the goal is to manipulate others, then hypochondria is a symptom of people addiction. The desire to manipulate and control others may also manifest itself in multiple suicide attempts. As the song says, "If you don't love me, I will kill myself." As previously mentioned, successful suicide is not an addiction because it only happens once. Some people reach the point of blackness where it seems foolish to sustain life. People who seek death as a logical solution are probably not addicted to suicide even if the attempt fails. But then there are those who cut their wrists just enough to make a big mess, but not enough to assure success. They always make sure that someone will find them before it is too late. This group is attempting to manipulate others rather than end life. This type may be addicted to manipulating others through suicidal attempts. Sometimes the manipulation fails and the person dies, although that was not their intention. In the same vein, some forms of violent and criminal behaviors may be viewed as addiction to manipulation of others. Serial killers, spouse beaters, and child molesters may all experience a compulsion to commit their acts out of a desire to manipulate others. [Ch8:100.0; Ch11:420.0, 410.0, 480.0]

Meditation/Spirituality/Positive Thinking

Spiritual development is an important aspect of personal growth. Meditation and positive thinking unlock many doors for the recovering person. However, hungry sharks lurk deep within the wells of all three. Consider the man who seeks God's guidance prior to making a decision. Is that a spiritual addict? No. While it may be a repetitive action, the purpose of the action is not to avoid reality. Instead, it is an attempt to tune into reality and to make the best possible interface with reality. On the other hand, there is the man who prays, and

prays, and never takes action or gets results. This is a man addicted. Where spiritual principles are applied, improvement always follows. The addicted person seldom finds improvement, but continues his/her acts.

Meditation is a powerful tool. It alters body chemistry in ways that we have yet to understand. Use of meditation is recommended in the twelve steps of Alcoholics Anonymous. But the twelve steps also indicate that actions are required after meditation. The twelfth step states that the results of meditation and activity conducted in the other steps, members should "carry this message to alcoholics and practice these principles . . ." (AA, 1976, p. 60). To carry is action. To practice is action.

Mild doses of meditation bring the mind, soul and body into balance; its use for this purpose is strongly recommended. The more meditation is practiced, the deeper into altered states of perception one is able to slip. The use of meditation to experience "head trips" is not recommended on a regular basis. People can "turn on, tune in, and drop out" with meditation. The person who is addicted to meditation develops a preoccupation with the trip itself. Problems are avoided, actions of a worldly nature are abandoned. The primary purpose for meditation must be to restore the balance and energy needed to resolve real-world situations.

Positive thinking is critical to the recovery process. My life seems to be a self-fulfilling prophecy. When I think bad things will happen to me they do (usually because I unconsciously cause them to happen). When I think good is coming, it does. So it is very important for addicted people to believe that good things can happen, that recovery is possible, that happiness is attainable, and so on. Ah, but what of the person who is so convinced that good abounds that he/she can't see the problems at hand? Positive thinking can anesthetize the system. It can induce hypnosis to the point that a person really cannot feel pain, either physically or emotionally. When used to avoid rather than to overcome pain, positive thinking functions exactly like denial and is an addiction. Healthy positive thinking permits a person to feel and see negative aspects of life and then correct them. Positive thinking addiction is "I have no problems." Healthy positive thinking is "I can overcome my problems." There is a big difference in the actions which result from the two statements. One who has no problems has no action. One who can overcome problems is very busy improving life. [Ch8:100.3; Ch11:420.0, 460.0, 470.0, 480.0]

Material Addictions

Shopping and spending money appear to be addictive. When in pain, the addicts of this group cry out, "Charge it!" The new appears more important than the need. A closet full of clothes cannot drive the blues away. Only a brand new outfit can do that. A television in every room is not enough when the ad comes out for one with a new feature. As high tech fills showroom shelves with new innovations, the shopping addict finds an unlimited supply from which to select. When television was invented, radio producers feared extinction. When videos became available, movie theaters forecasted gloom for their industry. When cassette tapes came in, records were thought to be on the way out. Today, record-breaking spending is occurring at movie theatres, while in homes people shuffle stereos, radios, video players, televisions and the cassette deck to one side in order to make room for the new compact disc player. Nothing has replaced anything. Undoubtedly, the purpose of many a remodeling project is to add storage space for our "stuff" rather than to add living space. *When Society Becomes An Addict* is a book title that explains many of the strange rituals being conducted in this country every day.

Electronics technology has produced many potentially addictive "substances." Television has replaced many a babysitter. It has the capacity to hold a person's attention and block out all awareness of reality. Computer and video games are also addictive substances. There are those who are able to play just one or two and go about their business. And there are others who can't quit once they start. [Ch8:100.0; Ch11:420.0]

Leisure Addictions

Leisure, as all Therapeutic Recreation Specialists know, contains a full gamut of activities. Some are passive, some are active, some relaxing, some exciting. Many have already been reviewed or alluded to in previous descriptions of process addictions. If the reader has been "skipping and jumping" through this section, then stop. The reader may even want to read every word of this section twice over.

Physical exercise has been identified as potentially addictive. During my workshop tours, Therapeutic Recreation Specialists who work in addiction treatment have informed me that they have observed persons hooked on running, jogging, biking, weight-lifting, and aerobic exercise. A friend related to me that he was hooked on running. Even during a severe case of the flu, he got up and ran for miles in the winter wind and rain. "I just had to get that feeling." Just for fun, I substituted some drug names for the word "running" into some of the passages in *The Complete Book of Running* which describe the "benefits" of running. Suddenly the passages sounded very familiar. They sounded exactly like the excuses that practicing addicts use to continue use of their drug of choice. "To [use] is to live. . .Everything else is just waiting," could be not only the statement of a drug junkie describing the feeling of a fix, but of a runner talking about running (Fixx, 1977).

Gambling addiction is known to be serious. How many of the table games we use in Therapeutic Recreation are modified versions of gambling games? Card games are. "Wheel of Fortune" is a modified version of roulette. Entire kingdoms used to be won or lost in the final roll of the backgammon dice. Has the danger of such games been removed by the modification of the gambling aspect? Are there persons who find playing a table game a method of avoiding reality? I fear the answer is yes.

Puzzles seem more inherently addictive than cards. There is tolerance build-up. The person who begins with a 50-piece jigsaw puzzle soon wants a 500-piece puzzle, and then one with 5000 pieces. Today, computer and video games seem to be giving puzzles a good run in the addictions race. If one doubts this, then one should go to the nearest arcade and look into the blank-blitzed gaze of the video users. The look is identical to the look I've seen on the faces of alcoholics and gamblers.

High-risk activities abound in leisure—from snow skiing to waterskiing; from racing cars to mountain climbing, whitewater rafting, and scuba diving; wind surfing, sailing, surfing, snow mobiling. Putting one's life on the line is a rush which can be highly addictive. Tolerance develops as rapidly as performance skills. The nonaddicted snow-skier winds down the hill enjoying the beauty of the descent and ascent alike. The addicted skier is angered by those who stop to admire the beauty. He/she barrels down the slope in break-neck speeds, does a double back-flip off a mogul and despises the slow climb to the top. When the trip down fails to produce a hair-raising experience, the slope is abandoned for more difficult terrain. When the extreme danger slope is navigated without a rush, the addicted skier tries it with one ski instead of two.

Work-substitute activities and projects that are productive in nature have already been mentioned in the section dealing with work addiction. Hobbies can also be addictive. Once some hobbyists begin a hobby, they cannot put it down. It could be a quilt, or the construction of a model. It could be weaving a basket or making wooden trinkets. They all block out awareness of the world outside the activity and result in a product that makes the creator feel proud.

I am an artist and a dancer. I would therefore like to omit the arts and performing arts from the list of addictions. But I can't. If people can get hooked on running and aerobic exercise, then they can get hooked on ballet, jazz, and all forms of dance. Painting, sculpture and other forms of art can be great places to hide from reality. Involvement seals out reality just as much as video games and watching a juicy television movie. Drama is the ultimate reality escape where a person can actually take on the life of another. Music has been demonstrated to have the ability to produce "thrills." It activates internal neurochemical systems (Davis, 1984). Specific types of loud rock music have the ability to turn a raw egg to a boiled one and may have a similar effect on the brain (Tame, 1984). It therefore must be included on the list of potentially addictive processes along with the other arts.

So what is left? Reading a good book? Sorry, reading can provide a powerful reality escape. Avid readers know that a good book is most difficult to put down.

I can go no further. Other potentially addictive processes exist in leisure, but I am getting too depressed to continue. I would like to be able to offer a substance or process which is free of addictive potential. It would appear that none exist. It is some consolation that nonleisure processes also lack freedom from potentially addictive contents. There is no easier, softer way. There is no risk-free drink, fix, pill, substance, or process that, once taken, makes addiction disappear. A Therapeutic Recreator working in addictions treatment hands out potentially addictive processes in every therapeutic recreation session. If the abuse potential is not considered, if program structure permits process abuse, more harm than good may come from the experience. Skilled supervision is necessary if clients are to use leisure to recover instead of becoming abused by leisure. [Ch8:100.0; Ch11:420.0]

AN ADDICTIVE SUMMARY

A dear friend for many years, an alcoholic and codeine addict used to say in his AA talk, "If you give me a drink of water at the same time three days in a row, and I don't get it on the fourth day, I will go into the DTs." His statement would always bring the house down in laughter. The more I learn about the body's ability to self-produce potentially addictive neurotransmitters, the more I recognize the wisdom of my friend's words. The list of potentially addictive substances and processes is beginning to appear endless.

Some substances can be avoided. Total abstinence from alcohol and drug use is the best course of action. But food use cannot be avoided. Life without work offers a sterile existence at best. Life is equally meaningless without leisure pursuit. People shrivel without human companionship. Group support is critical to the recovery process. If all potentially addictive processes were avoided, life would not be worth living. Boredom, far more damaging to the body than any addiction, would set in. So the solution for process addiction is to aim for balance.

Balance is not a word in the addicted person's vocabulary. Therapeutic Recreators must help this population create a definition of the word balance as well as to help them develop the structure and skills that can provide the needed balance. We cannot say, "Here's an addictive process, be careful that you don't use it too much." This is a population with demonstrated inability to determine what "too much" is.

The provision of structure and balance is critical to the recovery process. Yet what is structure? What is it that is being structured? For the most part, it is time devoted to any given function. The treatment day and the choice of activities must be structured to provide balance. What is to be balanced? Is leisure the balancer of work? Not when the activities performed on the job have the same inherent qualities as activities performed during leisure. Balance comes from allowing all internal nervous systems to function in harmony with one another. Nonaddicted persons seem to be able to provide structure and balance to life without thought. It is just automatic. Addiction burns out the automatic circuits. So balance and structure must be provided manually until such time as the internal automatics resume the ability to self-regulate these functions.

A final guiding principle is one of purpose. *When a process or substance is used to avoid dealing with the world outside of the self, then trouble will soon be knocking on the door. The purpose of healthy activity is to restore balance and generate energy which is then used to deal with the world outside of the self.* The body is a tea kettle to which one adds water (substance) and heat (process). Keep adding water, and the fire will be put out. Keep adding heat, and the water will evaporate. No good comes from an excess of either. But keep the two in balance and make use of the results, and something warm ensues that sheds a winter's chill.

References/Resources

Alcoholics Anonymous (The Big Book). (1976). Alcoholics Anonymous World Services, Inc., Grand Central Station, New York, NY.

Andreas, K., Dienel, A., Fischer, H. D., Oehler, J., & Schmidt, J. (1985). Influence of social isolation on ethanol preference behavior and dopamine release in telencephalon slices in mice. *Polish Journal of Pharmacology and Pharmacy,* 37(6):851-854 (23747/86877)

Anokhina, I. P. (1985, August 4-10). Dopamine and opiate systems peculiarities as a basis of development of alcohol dependence: Role of genetic factors. Alcohol, Drugs & Tobacco: An International Perspective. Past, Present & Future. Proceedings of the 34th International Congress on Alcoholism & Drug Dependence: Vol. II. Calgary, Alberta, Canada, pp. 165. (Reprints available from ICASA, P.O. Box 140, CH-1001, Lausanne, Switzerland. 29837/88418)

Baldwin, B. A. (1987, October). Eliminating neurotic overtime. *Pace Magazine,* Piedmont Airlines, NC.

Balidin, J., Alling, C. Gottfries, C. G., Lindsted, G., & Langstrom G. (1985). Changes in dopamine receptor sensitivity in humans after heavy alcohol intake." *Psychopharmacology 86,* 1-2:142-146. (Hisings-Backa, Sweden, 20688/85248)

Bejeret, M. D. (1972). *Addiction, An Artificially Induced Drive.* Springfield, IL: Charles C. Thomas Publishing.

Bobrov, A. (1986). Psychophysiological and medical aspects of the problem of personality changes in alcoholism. *Psiklologicheskii Zhurnal,* 7(2):89-95 (29764/87581)

Boismare, F., Lhuintre, J. P., Daoust, M. N., Moore, N., Saligaut, C., & Hillemand, B. (1987). Platelet affinity for serotonin is increased in alcoholic and former alcoholics: A biological marker for dependence. *Alcohol & Alcoholism,* 22(2):155-159 (33454/93595).

Clark, J. (1985). (The) nervous system: Circuits of communication. NY: Torstar Books.

Daniell, L. C. (1986). Correlation of rates of calcium uptake and endogenous norepinephrine release in rat brain region synaptosomes: Alteration by ethanol. *Dissertation Abstracts International*, 47(2):585-B (29980/88561)

Daoust, M., Chretien, P., Moore, N., Saligaut, C., Lhuintre, J. P., & Boismare, F. (1985). Isolation and striatal (#H) serotonin uptake: Role in the voluntary intake of ethanol by rats. *Pharmacology Biochemistry & Behavior Journal*, 22(2):205-208 (Faculty of Medicine of Rouen, Dept. of Pharmacology, Saint-Etienne du Rouvray, France, 21490/84319.)

Davis, J. (1984). *Endorphins: New Waves in Brain Chemistry*. Garden City, NY: The Dial Press: Doubleday & Co., Inc.

Dusek, D., & Girdamo, D. A. (1980). *Drugs: A Factual Account*. Reading, MA: Addison-Wesley Publishing Co.

Edwards, B. (1979). *Drawing on the Right Side of the Brain*: A Course in Enhancing Creativity and Artistic Confidence. Los Angeles, CA: J. P. Tarcher, Inc.

Egger, G. (1980). Alternative view. 1980 Seminar of the South Australian Foundation on Alcoholism & Drug Dependence. *(Conference Paper) Adelaide, Australia (12148/73420)*

Estes, N. J., & Heinemann, M. E. (1982). *Alcoholism: Development, Consequences, & Interventions*. St. Louis, MO: C. V. Mosby Co.

Fadda, F., & Gessa, G. L. (1985). Role of dopamine in the CNS effect of ethanol. In: S. Parvez, Y. Burov, et al., *Progress in Alcohol Research*: Vol. 1, Alcohol, Nutrition & the Nervous System, Utrect, The Netherlands: VNU Science Press, pp 147-161. (Study from University of Cagliari, Institute of Physiology & Pharmacology, Cagliari, Italy. 32593/88034)

Fadda, F., Mosca E., Meloni R., & Gessa, G. L. (1986). Ethanol-stress interaction on dopamine metabolism in the medial prefrontal cortex. Alcohol & Drug Research 6(6):449-454 (University of Cagliari, Italy: 28992/87863)

Fixx, J. (1977). *The Complete Book of Running*. (Psychology of Chapter 2, Running to assist sobriety, pp. 29-30) Random House.

Forman, L., & Estilow, S. (1988). Cocaine influences beta-endorphin levels and release. *Life Sciences*, 43(4):309-315 (2665/ADO2516)

Frontiers of Medicine: Foundations for the Future. (1986). NY: Torstar Books.

Frykman, J. H. (1972). *A New Connection: An Approach to Persons Involved in Compulsive Drug Use*. San Francisco, CA: The Scrimshaw Press.

Glasser, W. (1976). *Positive addiction*. NY: Harper & Row.

Goldstein, G., & Shelly, C. (1982). *Multivariate Neuropsychological Approach to Brain Lesion Localization in Alcoholism*. Addictive Behaviors 7(2):165-175 (14695/72673)

Guaza, C., & Borrell, S. (1985). Brain catecholamines during ethanol administration, effect of naloxone on brain dopamine and norepinephrine responses to withdrawal from ethanol. *Pharmacological Research Communications* 17(12):1159-1167 (Institute of Neurobiology, CSIC, Madrid, Spain, 26621/86600)

Hatterer, L. J. (1980). *The Pleasure Addicts: The Addictive Process - Food, Sex, Drugs, Alcohol, Work, and More*. NY: A. S. Barnes & Co.

Hawley, R. J, Major, L. F., Schulman, E. A., & Linnoila, M. (1985). Cerebrospinal fluid 3-methoxy-4-hydroxyphenylglycol and norepinephrine levels in alcohol withdrawal: Correlations with clinical signs. Archives of General Psychiatry 42(11):1056-1062 (VAMC Neurology Service, Washington DC: 24563/86013)

Hoyt, K. (1989). The concept of work: Updating a point of view. *Career Planning and Adult Development Journal*, 5(2), 24-26.

Hyde, M. (1978). *Addictions: Gambling, Smoking, Cocaine Use*. NY: McGraw-Hill.

Hyttell, J., & Larsen, J. J. (1985). Neuropharmacological mechanisms of serotonin reuptake inhibitors. In: Research Advances in New Psychopharmacologic Treatments for Alcoholism: Proceedings of the Symposium, Toronto, 4-5, Oct 1984, New York, NY: Elsevier Science Publishers BV (30982/87896)

Julien, R. M. (1981). *A Primer of Drug Action*. San Francisco, CA: W. H. Freeman & Co.

Kent, T. A., Campbell, J. L., Pazdernik, T. L., Hunter, R., Gunn, W. H., & Goodwin, D.W. (1985). Blood platelet uptake of serotonin in men alcoholics. *Journal of Studies on Alcohol*, 46(4):357-359 (University of Kansas, 23246/85436)

Leslie, S. W., Woodward, J. J., Wilcon, R. E., & Farrar, R. P. (1986). Chronic ethanol treatment uncouples striatal calcium entry and endogenous dopamine release. *Brain Research* 368(1):174-177 (30011/87248)

Linnoila, Jacobson, Marshall, Miller, & Kirk. Liquid chromatographic assay for cerebrospinal fluid. Life Sciences 38(8):687-694 (25664/86863)

Littleton, J. M., & Padonis, C. (1985). Biochemical effects of ethanol on central neurotransmitter function. Alcohol & Alcoholism 20(1):77-78 (22716/85070)

Machlowitz, M. (1980). *Workaholics: Living With Them, Working With Them*. Reading, MA: Addison-Wesley Publishing Co.

McEntee, W. J., Mair, R. G., & Langlais, P. J. (1987). Neurochemical specificity of learning: Dopamine and motor learning. Yale Journal of Biology & Medicine 60(2):187-193 (reprints avail. from pub. journal.(32619/91913)

Meyer, D. G., Peterson, D. M., & Frank, J. W. (1983). *Drugs & The Elderly Adult*. Rockville, MD: National Institute on Drug Abuse.

Milkman, H., & Sunderwirth, S. (1982). Addictive processes. *Journal of Psychoactive Drugs, 14(3):* 177-191.

Monroe, W. S. (Ed.). (1950). *Encyclopedia of Educational Research*. New York: The MacMillan Co.

Morrow, E. E., & Erwin, V. G. (1987). Calcium influences on neurtensin and beta-endorphin enhancement of ethanol sensitivity in selectively bred mouse lines. *Alcohol and Drug Research*, 7(4):225-232 (32251/91546)

Myers, W. D., Mackenzie, L., Ng, K. T., Singer, G., Smythe, G. A., & Duncan, M. W. (1985). Salsolinol and dopamine in rat medial basal hypothalamus after chronic ethanol exposure. *Live Sciences,* 36(4):309-314 (La Trobe University, Dundoora Australia, 20685/83921)

National Clearinghouse for Alcohol & Drug Information, Rockville, MD (References followed by numbers such as (32251/91546) are available in abstract form from National Clearinghouse. The first number indicates Record Number, with second being the Accession Number.)

O'Connor, C. (1988, May). Lifestyling. *Leisure's Grapevine, 2(2)* p. 2. Seaside, OR: Leisure Enrichment Service.

Ornstein, R., & Sobel, D. (1987). *The Healing Brain: Breakthrough Discoveries About How the Brain Keeps Us Healthy.* NY: Simon & Schuster.

Peris, J., & Dunwiddie, T. V. (1986). Inhibitory neuromodulation of release of amino acid neurotransmitters. *Alcohol & Drug Research,* 6(4):253-264 (2558186691)

Restak, R. M. (1984). The Brain. NY: Bantam Books.

Robinson, B. E. (1989). Work addiction: Hidden legacies of adult children. Deerfield Beach FL: Health Communications, Inc.

Role of neurplasticity in the response to drugs. (1987). *National Institute on Drug Abuse Research Monograph 78.* U. S. Dept. of Health & Human Services, Public Health Service, Alcohol, Drug, & Mental Health Administration. (For Sale by the Superintendent of Documents, U. S. Government Printing Office, Washington DC)

Schaef, A. W. (1987). *When Society Becomes An Addict.* San Francisco, CA: Harper & Row (Catbird)

Schaef, A. W., & Fassel, D. (1988). *The Addictive Organization.* San Francisco, CA: Harper & Row (Catbird)

Segal, B., Ph.D. (Ed.). (1987). *Perspectives on Person-Environment Interaction & Drug Taking Behavior.* NY: The Haworth Press.

Snyder, C. R. (1978). *Alcohol & The Jews.* Glencoe, IL: Free Press.

Sperry, R. W. (1968). Hemisphere disconnection and unity in conscious awareness. American Psychologist. 23: 723-33.

Stone, M. (1984). *Cocaine: Seduction & Solution.* NY: Crown Publishers.

Stuart, M. S, and Orr, L. (1987). *Otherwise Perfect: People & Their Problems with Weight.* Pompano Beach, FL: Health Communications, Inc.

Tame, D. (1984). *The Secret Power of Music: The Transformation of Self & Society Through Musical Energy.* Rochester, VT: Destiny Books.

Thomson, S. M., & McMillen, B. A. (1987). Test for decreased serotonin/tryptophan metabolite ratios in abstinent alcoholics. *Alcohol: An International Biomedical Journal,* 4(1):1-5 (32129/91423)

Topel, H. (1987). Alcohol, endorphins and opiate-precursors: Critical questions in alcohol research. *Auchtgefahren, 3* (1):1-15 (32710/92004)

Tuchfeld, B. S. (1983, Summer). Social involvement and the resolution of alcoholism. *Journal of Drug Issues.*

Weil, A. and Rosen, W. (1983). *Chocolate to Morphine: Understanding Mind Active Drugs.* NY: Houghton Mifflin Co.

Woititz, J. G. (1983). *Adult Children of Alcoholics.* Enterprise Center, Deerfield Beach, FL: Health Communications, Inc. (Catbird)

Wood, G. W., & Elias, M. F. (Eds.). (1982). *Alcoholism & Aging: Advances In Research.* Boca Raton, Florida: CRC Press.

Zabik, J. E., Binkerd, K., & Roache, J. D. (1985). Serotonin and ethanol aversion in the rat. In: Naranjo, C. A., & Sellers, E. M. (Eds.). Research Advances in New Psychopharmacological Treatments for Alcoholism: Proceedings of the Symposium, Toronto, 4-5, Oct 1984, New York, NY: Elsevier Science Publishers BV (32609/87895)

CHAPTER 4

UNDERSTANDING FAMILY

FAULKNER'S FAMILY ADDICTION CYCLE

Addiction does not exist in a vacuum. All alcoholics and addicts have (or had) parents. Many are or have been married (often more than once). If they are not children, then it is common for them to have children. The designing of treatment procedures for the addict without considering the dynamics of family involvement will fall short of the target. Treating the addict without treating the family sabotages recovery efforts. I have developed the FAC (family addiction cycle) to provide a general overview of the dynamics involved (See page 65). Recommended interventions in this model are not intended to be all-inclusive. Lists of primary needs are related to leisure and the provision of Therapeutic Recreation services. At this time, the majority of Therapeutic Recreation professionals who work with addictive personalities, do so in substance abuse treatment settings. As such, the following scenario focuses on substance addictions. However, it also applies to process addictions.

FAC Stage 1: Functional Living

In the beginning, there was family. For purposes of the model it is assumed that the family has interactive patterns which are life-supportive. Healthy function of the family unit may have been abandoned generations before the alcoholic or addict was born. But every model needs a starting point. This seemed to be a positive place to begin. The stage is represented by an out-of-round circle. (See Figure 4.0)

FIGURE 4.0

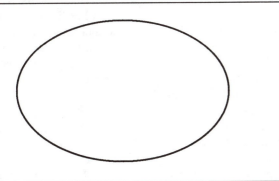

This means it appears about the same as other circles and will function about the same, except that it does not roll quite as far or quite as fast as round circles. (Functional living is not exactly the same as healthy living.) The out-of-round circle is accepted by round circles as being the same, yet there is something not quite right about the out-of-round circle. It feels different from the other circles and the other circles feel different from it.

In FAC Stage 1, family members function. No one is happy all the time. No one is unhappy all the time. Life comes and goes without the assistance of an abused substance. This is the time for preventive action. The seeds of addiction may be sown and waiting to blossom. Although addictive substances may not be used, family members may have dysfunctional leisure habits. Communication may not be as open and honest as it could be. The negative costs of substance abuse may not be clearly understood.

Therapeutic Recreation professionals working in substance abuse treatment rarely come in contact with families during Stage 1 of FAC. Community Recreators see these families regularly. School systems do too. Until recently, the community has been under the misguided assumption that once a family is Stage 1 they will always be Stage 1. This assumption is far from accurate. Again, Stage 1 is the time for prevention. Therapeutic Recreation professionals working in substance abuse should serve as catalysts and resources for prevention. Leisure Education should begin in the elementary grades of the school system. The development of healthy leisure attitudes is as important as the development of alcohol/drug awareness.

FAC Stage 2: The Blow-Out

One day the functional family is rumbling along, and one of the members experiments with a drink, fix, or pill. Or perhaps the member(s) have been drinking "socially" for quite some time and now the use has turned to abuse. (See Figure 4.1)

FIGURE 4.1

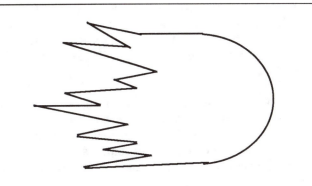

The "blow-out" may happen overnight, but most often it is a gradual slip into dysfunction. Intervention is required at the earliest stage possible to prevent the spread of the infection. Many treatment facilities have intervention specialists or teams.

These professionals are specifically trained to help the alcoholic or addict and the family become motivated to make changes. But the intervention team cannot take action until someone asks for help. Therapeutic Recreation Specialists are seldom part of the intervention team, but may play a role in intervention just the same. (As a point of clarification, I do not think Therapeutic Recreation Specialists should be on the intervention team. We have too many other equally important things to do.) Therapeutic Recreation Specialists who serve as a resource for community recreation and school systems may indirectly stimulate calls for intervention. They should assist the community in developing "Latch Key Kids" programs. They should help community recreation personnel recognize the signs of substance abuse displayed by family members. Community recreation should not be in the business of "intervention." But recreation personnel can identify problems and be ready to refer to appropriate sources when the time is right.

The signs of a family moving from function into blow-out are numerous. There is increased withdrawal and isolation. Words which once flowed freely become guarded. Joy and laughter are washed from the eyes. Minor inconveniences trigger emotional reactions which most of us reserve for major catastrophes. There is either too much energy or not enough. Children arrive at the school or community center far too early and stay far too late. Children may also hover. They may select a kindly coach or authority figure and follow them. It may be obvious by the drooping expression that the child wants something. But if asked, the child withdraws, saying nothing or denying there is a problem.

If successful intervention occurs, the substance abuser becomes involved in detox and then a treatment program. At this point the Therapeutic Recreation Specialist should become active in the treatment process for the abuser. Details of therapeutic recreation involvement are contained in later chapters of this text. Meanwhile, the role of community recreation and schools should make a transition. Family members now need support and hope. They need people who will listen without casting judgement or retaliating with hasty advice. Therapeutic Recreation Specialists working with the alcoholic/addict, should provide Leisure Education to family members. If the treatment structure does not provide family contact at this stage, then self-study guides addressing family leisure needs may be provided. [Ch8:100.0, 100.1, 100.2, 100.3, 100.4; Ch9; Ch10]

If early intervention leads to treatment, the third stage of this model is skipped. Successful treatment may occur with limited family participation. After detoxification, successful treatment may be provided on an outpatient basis. If active substance abuse is pursued, then the family progresses to the "fireworks" stage.

FAC Stage 3: The Fireworks

The "fireworks" for which this stage has been named are the kind that happen when someone pours water on an electronic circuit board rather than the pretty kind viewed on the Fourth of July. (See Figure 4.2)

FIGURE 4.2

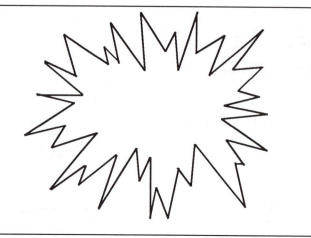

Has the reader ever ridden in a car with a flat tire? Most who have find it a most uncomfortable ride. Everything gets bumped and jousted from its proper position, even one's internal organs. Imagine riding in a car with a flat tire for 10 or 20 years! This is what happens when addiction goes unchecked. This is the Fireworks Stage. Surprisingly, it only takes a relatively short period of time to create total family dysfunction. Obviously, the longer active use continues the more destructive it is to family function.

If treatment does not occur at this stage, then children grow up but not out of dysfunction. As adults, they start families of their own and pass the dysfunction on to a new generation. Over and over, children become adults without ever knowing what normal, healthy family function is like. Basic developmental steps of play and social interaction may be missed entirely.

If the addicted person enters treatment after all members of the family have adopted dysfunctional lifestyles, then the entire family requires treatment. Without such treatment, actions of family members will undermine the recovery process even when that is not the intention. There is simply too much fear, too much pain, anger, and resentment to be overcome without assistance. Attempts to stifle the fear, pain, and resentment consume the day, ending opportunities to play. Internal imbalance results. All interaction becomes unhealthy and stimulates increased family discord.

When the fireworks begin, community recreation programs can lessen the body count by providing a safe harbor for family members. The Therapeutic Recreation Specialist can assist family members to release the anger and resentment. Most of all, Therapeutic Recreation Specialists can help the family understand the value of play and support leisure functioning. [Ch8:100.0, 100.1, 100.2, 100.3, 105.1, 105.2, 105.3; Ch9; Ch11:430.0, 410.0, 460.0, 470.0;]

FAC Stage 4: The Sawtooth

Without treatment, the family becomes too dysfunctional to survive as a unit. It breaks apart producing the "Sawtooth." (See Figure 4.3)

FIGURE 4.3

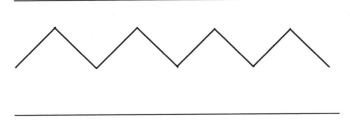

Together, all the scrapes and scars from years of abuse form an abrasive edge that cuts the self as well as any other individual who makes the mistake of wandering too close. Rigidity sets in; the best defense becomes a good offense.

If the family is in treatment at the Sawtooth Stage, then it is wise to separate family members. They only know how to sabotage each other. The types of treatment for family members are similar to the types of treatment provided to the addicted person. A full range of Therapeutic Recreation services are required to restore leisure functioning. With treatment, individual family members learn to smooth and soothe their abrasive edges during parallel activities. (By parallel, I mean the same type of service provided to the client is also provided to the family, but in separate sessions.) Once the anger and resentment are vented, once leisure functioning has returned, then client and family members may be brought together in joint activities. [Ch11:430.0, 410.0, 460.0, 470.0; then Ch8:100.0, 100.1, 100.2, 100.3, 105.1, 105.2, 105.3; Ch9; then Ch10]

FAC Stage 5: The Flatline

The Flatline may be a highly positive or negative stage. (See Figure 4.4)

FIGURE 4.4

It depends on whether treatment has been received. With treatment, the Flatline represents a clean, smooth surface upon which a new life can be built. The Therapeutic Recreation Specialist assists in the rebuilding of the family, through provision of joint activities.

Negative Flatline is the sound of life coming to a halt. It is the sound the heart makes when it is no longer pumping. Too often the body continues to function, while the "person" is no longer present. The treatment team is frustrated by the family member who has flatline. He/she comes to sessions when requested; responses are given upon demand. But the treatment team always feels they have failed to reach him/her.

A syndrome has been observed and studied in the helping professions for many years. It is called burnout. Burnout occurs in firemen, police, emergency room personnel, and in Therapeutic Recreation Specialists, too. Wherever there is a job performed by a person with high expectations for success, where accomplishments fail to be apparent, where a mistake in a decision can have adverse consequences, where compensation does not equal exertion, there can be burnout. The greatest cause of burnout is being on-call, or waiting for a crisis to happen. The fireman cannot predict the time of the next fire. While he appears to be "relaxing" at the firehouse, he is not relaxed. He is waiting for an accident to happen. Anticipation of crisis removes relax-ability.

Many people not in the helping professions also suffer from burnout. The family member does not have to work in a firehouse or an emergency room (though some do) to experience burnout. During the Fireworks Stage, the spouse is "on the job" twenty-four hours a day. The "job" is taken on with high expectation—that of living a "normal" lifestyle. During the Fireworks Stage, results from actions fail to be apparent. No matter what is attempted, substance abuse continues. No matter how tightly pennies are pinched, or how much money is made, there is not enough money to meet financial obligations. Exertion seldom provides rewards. With assumption of the caretaker role comes the assumption that an error in personal judgment will have disastrous consequences. Most of all, life becomes a process of waiting and anticipating the outbreak of the next crisis.

Family members often experience severe burnout. It results from anticipation of recurring stressful events, which can erupt at unpredictable times. The resolution of a stressful event does not mean the end of the stress, for the person knows that another similar event is just waiting to happen. It is not surprising that family members experience burnout. They live with addiction. One day everything is great. The next day, crisis strikes without provocation. The next day everything may be great, but the person soon learns to anticipate another crisis which may or may not strike at any time, any place, any way.

When someone enters burnout, he/she feels tired even after a good night's sleep. People often comment about personal appearance, suggesting that appearance denotes physical illness. The person feels like they are working harder and harder to accomplish less and less. Cynicism increases. Feelings of sadness occur for no specific reason. Thinking and the daily routine become disorganized, resulting in forgetfulness. Irritability increases and others, more often than not, fail to live up to personal expectations. The person withdraws from social circles and social interactions. The schedule gets too busy to accomplish small items like writing a letter to a friend. Physical aches and pains seem to linger. A feeling of disorientation occurs when time is spent "off the job." Joy becomes elusive. Jokes stop being funny. Sex becomes a duty rather than a pleasure. A chance meeting with a friend brings an awkward moment with little to say (Freudenberber, 1980, pp. 17-18).

Burnout moves through stages. Enthusiasm and hope for creating a solution wane, and self-doubt takes their place. Self-questioning begins. "Am I right for this?" "Do I know enough?" "Is this where I really want to be?" Frustration and disillusionment set in. The final stage is one of apathy. Initially the person feels the pain of others and the self. In the final stage of burnout, the person is incapable of feeling anything. There is no pain. There is no pleasure. There is no hope for tomorrow or that a solution is possible. Life is reduced to robotics.

Burnout is the body's way of self-protection from this type of continued stress. As burnout continues, the ability to experience both positive and negative emotions reduces. By the final stage, the person does not care about anything anymore. There is total disengagement from life. Disengagement is different from detachment. Detachment is the removal of the self from a specific situation. Disengagement is the retraction of the self from all situations.

Texts on burnout recommend early intervention. The final stage of dulling apathy is most difficult to counteract. The person who experiences job burnout may find some relief by changing jobs. The person who burns out on life has little left to change.

It is difficult to treat a family member, or anyone who is in the final stage of burnout. There is no motivation, thus no desire to change. Climbing out of apathy means feeling again, and life feels better without pain. As with a painkilling drug, it is only the perception of pain that has been abandoned. The body is still being subjected to the actions of stress. The thing that hurts is still there. Physical and mental integrity will be damaged if the person remains in this stage.

Early intervention in the syndrome can reverse the problem. Little is known about how to reverse the final stage of burnout. I fear I have little to add. Creating an awareness of the problem is the best source of revival. When a person is able to see the physical damage which can no longer be felt, a desire to change might be kindled. When a person is able to realize that blocking out the bad feelings also blocks out the good feelings, then motivation toward growth might resume. The treatment team is obligated to present an option; only the individual can decide to make a change. Once the final stage has been reached, it can take a long, long time and a lot of patience to reverse the process. Expecting the burnout victim to immediately show signs of caring, or enthusiasm, or to

actively participate in an event, is unrealistic. The Therapeutic Recreation Specialist attempting to deal with a family member in the final stage of burnout should develop a long-term plan of treatment. [Ch8:106.1; Ch9]

FAC Stage 6: The Healthline

With treatment, the family can rise from the ashes. It can become healthier and stronger than it ever was. While this is cause for celebration (without a drink, fix, or pill), it is not a time to forget the lessons of the past. The Family Addiction Cycle takes years to get from functional living to healthful living. In the course of those years, a new generation will have been spawned. The Healthline Stage signals that it is time to begin education and prevention for the next generation. (See Figure 4.5)

FIGURE 4.5

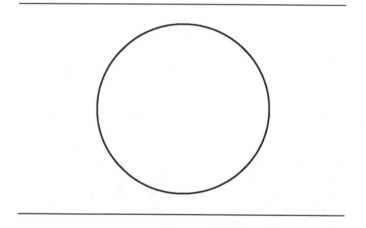

Reaching the Healthline Stage is reaching a time to reevaluate life goals. Careers selected during previous stages may no longer meet personal or familial needs. More time together may become more valuable than more time apart. Time for play and time for doing nothing may develop value where in the past they were seen as terror-provoking experiences. Types of leisure needs also change. The need to grow and branch out may motivate pursuit of new leisure skills. "I'm sober. So what?" signals the beginning of this reevaluation process. Therapeutic Recreation Specialists are not usually involved in making the adjustments needed during this stage. It is a matter of timing. The re-examination stage may occur for some during the final after-care sessions. For most, it occurs years after contact with the treatment facility has ended. Occasionally, a former client will return to visit the treatment facility during this stage. Brief assistance in clarifying the former client's restlessness with the known can be helpful. Clients and family members who attained leisure independence during previous stages will have the skills required to negotiate this stage.

FAMILY ADDICTION CYCLE FLOW CHART:

STAGE 1: FUNCTIONAL LIFESTYLE
GOALS: **PREVENTION** of addiction through development of healthy leisure attitudes and alcohol/drug education.

STAGE 6: THE HEALTHLINE
GOAL: **PREVENTION & FINE TUNING,** by family members. Provide support for healthy lifestyles. Education and prevention for the next generation. Re-Creation by family members.

STAGE 2: THE BLOW-OUT
GOALS: **INTERVENTION** to prevent spread of infection. Problem identification, detox and treatment. Provision of Safe Harbor Activities for non-addicted family members. Provision of self-evaluation opportunities and support for all.

STAGE 5: THE FLATLINE
GOAL: **RESTORATION,** to assemble the separate units back into a family. Provide joint Recreation Therapy, Leisure Education and Re-Creation. Initiate potential for healthy family interaction.

STAGE 4: THE SAWTOOTH
GOALS: **TREATMENT** for all family members separately. Parallel Recreation Therapy, Leisure Education and Recreation.

STAGE 3: THE FIREWORKS
GOALS: **INTERVENTION & SEPARATION**
Problem identification and resolution for each family member. Separate family to stop unhealthy interaction patterns. Focus each individual on self-evaluation, self-improvement and self-recovery. Inpatient treatment as needed.

SOMEPLACE BETWEEN FUNCTION AND BLOW-OUT

Co-Dependency

Co-dependency is a term that was coined in the late 1970s. A variety of definitions exist. Some definitions are as broad as the number of persons who live or have lived with a substance abuser. Beattie defines it as allowing another's behavior to affect personal behavior and becoming "obsessed with controlling that person's behavior" (Beattie, 1987, p. 31). It has been suggested that traits for co-dependency exist before involvement with a person who is addicted. Co-dependents do not always marry alcoholics or addicts. Sometimes co-dependency evolves between professionals and their clientele. A co-dependent often has multiple (at the same time) or repetitive (one after another) relationships with persons who are seriously ill (Beattie, 1987, p. 31). The grouping of all persons who have personal or professional relationships with seriously ill people under a single label may be over-simplification and highly dangerous. A single label implies a single method to remedy the situation. With an expanding list of substance and process addictions, it must be asked, is there anyone who is not an addict or a spouse of an addict, or a child of one or both, or has an occupation working with ill people? Are all of these persons in need of treatment for co-dependency?

Which came first, the chicken or the egg? Were there personality traits in the spouse which caused the person to be attracted to an addicted partner? Or did the emotional and behavioral patterns develop as a result of living with addiction? It seems to be a raging debate with no end in sight (Beattie, 1987, p. 32). Does it matter? Perhaps. Let us take a page or two to examine some scenarios about how co-dependency traits may exist prior to exposure to addiction.

Co-Dependency via Trauma

The small child within nestles securely within a perfectly round circle-type family. Suddenly the family is struck by crisis: a fatal car accident, terminal illness; security is crushed. The small child within is tossed into a cold, harsh world while the self attempts to deal with excruciating pain of grief. The ordeal sucks every ounce of strength from the body. Nothing really matters. Judgment becomes clouded and confused. The small child within is floundering and turns to others for help. Other family members are consumed with their own grief; no help is available. Well-intentioned friends who have not experienced a trauma of similar proportions say such stupid things in times of crisis that it is impossible to turn to them for support. Friends who have experienced similar situations remember the sting of their own crisis each time they look into the new victim's eyes. Placing self-survival first, they quickly whisper, "It just takes time," and scurry away. The trauma of

grief is compounded by the trauma of isolation. Then along comes M. Right. M. Right says, "Follow me. You don't have to think or hurt anymore." M. Right is selected, not by attraction but by the process of elmination. Co-dependency evolves. The rules of co-dependent relationships are welcomed. There is no discussion of problems. That's great. It prevents reopening of the grief wound and prevents M. Right from saying something that might show a lack of understanding. Expressions of feelings are off-limits. That's great too, for the only feeling the trauma victim has is severe pain. Honest communication, selfishness, and rocking the boat, require energy. The trauma victim has no energy, so avoidance of these is also welcomed. The trauma victim feels all too human, vulnerable, and imperfect, so escape into addiction fantasy is embraced. Playfulness and having fun have always occurred spontaneously. Now trauma has extinguished fun's pilot light, so the absence of playfulness is accepted.

Time does heal grief. Self-function returns with healing. Healing restores energy and desire. The co-dependency rules become abrasive. The former trauma victim is trapped. The desire to press new shoots of life toward the sun are thwarted by M. Right's code of dysfunctional living. Leaving M. Right means abandoning the only person who was there when needed. Separation from M. Right also means being alone in a traumatic situation again. "Perhaps I could do for M. Right, what M. Right did for me?" Enter full-blown symptoms of Co-dependency and FAC Stage 3 fireworks.

The most effective tool for this scenario is prevention. Development of support groups for trauma victims has been a relatively recent development. There are now support groups attached to hospice programs. There are also support groups for family members and victims of rape and violent crimes. With proper support, grief is still painful, but not so destructive. Undoubtedly such groups reduce the number of potential co-dependents wandering the streets. [Ch11:440.0]

Co-Dependency via The Search for Acceptance

To feel appreciated and accepted by others is a basic human need. The highlight of my 20-year high school reunion was having a number of former classmates tell me that I was always "different." It was great to hear them say it. When we were in school together, they always made me feel different, but they never would come out and say it. The lack of words seemed to imply that being different was bad. When I heard them say it, being different seemed to carry a compliment. Perhaps it was my viewpoint that changed. Today I don't see being different as being good or bad, just different.

Some are born with right hemisphere-dominant brains, while most of the world operates under left hemisphere domination. While most of my classmates found pleasure in the soda shop after school, I found it in ballet class. One of the greatest afternoons of my teen years occurred when gazing up at a very old tree. The fact that it had not moved from that spot for hundreds of years was an earth-shattering revelation to me. My peers found my ability to watch a tree (stone-cold sober) quite peculiar, just as the reader might, if a left brain-dominated person. A discovery so great demands to be shared. Obviously, I received little appreciation for my discovery that trees don't move, nor did I feel a sharing of something in common which leads to feelings of acceptance. The fact that I come from a right-brain family probably prevented my demise. I could share my "tree's don't" discoveries with my parents and not only get appreciation for my discovery but a challenging response such as, "Next time ask the tree how he feels about it." There were a good many right-brain operators in my dance classes, too. I only felt "different" walking the hallowed halls of the three "R's." Even there I gravitated toward the art and drama classes, where others were unable to detect my differences because they were "different" too.

Feeling different in this way can have a number of sources. There are socioeconomic differences. (I remember feeling different when I realized that my parents had been married for over 20 years while many of my classmates' parents were divorced. Or the time when a discussion arose about credit cards and my folks didn't have any—they always paid cash.) There are internal chemical and brain functions which are different. They cause some of us to like some things and dislike other things. What is interesting to me may bore you and what is viewed as an accomplishment by you may seem to be no big deal to me. Some are different by being too smart while others are just smart enough to know they aren't smart enough. Some may feel too talented, or not talented enough. Some may feel too physically fit to fit, while others feel too unfit to fit. Some may have disabilities or repetitive childhood illness which causes them to feel different.

Feeling different means feeling a lack of acceptance or appreciation. Suddenly, there is M. Right, feeling different too, but perhaps for different reasons. Or perhaps M. Right appears to be the same as other peers but seems able to appreciate the unusual or peculiar, able to accept a person who could watch a tree. Wow! M. Right really knows a good thing when he/she sees it! M. Right seems to be accepted by everyone. If I hang out with M. Right, and keep my mouth shut, then others will think I'm normal too! Enter co-dependency. [Ch11:450.0]

Co-Dependency via Self Under/Overestimation

Co-dependency literature seems to indicate that the typical co-dependent has low self-esteem. No doubt once this individual is involved in addiction, the person's self-esteem gets squashed. It's easy to see how self-doubt could spawn a co-dependent relationship. Feeling incapable of surviving without M. Right is an automatic setup. But some co-dependents do not fit the low self-esteem profile prior to involvement with addiction. Persons with careers that require self-confidence and personal risk taking are sometimes co-dependents too. In the process of being co-dependent, some take drastic actions and attempt to exert control over others. Are those really the actions of a person with low self-esteem?

Overestimation of personal strength and ability may result in co-dependency as easily as underestimation of self capabilities. The person who overestimates the self may develop a relationship with M. Right. M. Right's problems may be recognized and discounted with, "I'm strong enough to survive his insanity," or "I can cure him." After the Blow-out Stage, it is discovered that "I can't cure or handle M. Right." That shocking revelation leads to panic, to feelings of helplessness, and to low self-esteem. The truly strong ego may accept defeat and move forward more quickly than the untested ego that has never previously encountered defeat.

Some hide feelings of low self-esteem in actions that mimic high self-esteem. In such cases there is a need for recognition. The goal of involvement is to say, "Look at me! Look what I did! I cured M. Right!" A truly self-confident person does not care who gets the credit for the "cure" as long as conditions improve. [Ch11:410.0, 450.0]

Co-Dependency via Natural Chemistry

There is much ado about "natural chemistry" between a man and a woman. For all the discussion, it is probably the least understood mechanism of our human system. Perhaps when the "Jump and Skip" system is discovered, the "natural chemistry" element will be discovered as well. Perhaps it is just a matter of sharing common likes and dislikes, or feeling appreciated and accepted. I don't think so. Many alcoholics can swear they can spot another alcoholic a mile away. I believe them. There just seems to be a special energy emitted which seems to allure some and repel others. Sensitivity toward chemical attraction would predispose one for contracting co-dependency. The only solution would be to learn to keep walking. [Ch11:420.0]

Co-Dependency via Backstage Mother

The backstage mom is a phenomenon that exists in schools of the performing arts. Regardless of the daughter's desire, Mom insists that she take whatever steps necessary to become a great dancer, musician, or artist. When the daughter is talented and wants to do, it is a rewarding relationship for all concerned. But the "backstage mother" title has been designated for moms with daughters who have no desire to perform. Most likely, there are "back-goal dads" too. Convinced that the son is destined to be a great athletic star, the dad coaches, practices, pushes, and manipulates to turn junior into a goal-line hero.

Backstage mom and back-goal dad attempt to fulfill their dreams through their children's efforts. Results are often disastrous. I always shudder when a new student arrives at my dance studio and mom says, "I always wanted to dance, but no one ever gave me lessons." I always point out that it's not too late. Adults can learn to dance. True backstage moms do not pursue my offer. Backstage moms and back-goal dads are co-dependents though addiction is not part of their lifestyles. Eventually the child grows up. If he/she is good, then the child moves away from the parents and takes the vicarious experiences with him/her. If he/she is not very good, then parents' dreams of success are shattered.

Living life through another's efforts is a wonderful way to gain accomplishment without taking personal risks. The addict's life is filled with excitement, as he/she survives falling from a plane only to be arrested for littering. Just listening to the recounting of a drunken antic is exciting. The spouse who would not dare risk such adventures may savor the excitement vicariously. The spouse experiences life through the adventures of the addict just as the parent lives through the child. It is a great way to pass the time until the addict's behavior creates personal trauma or risk for the spouse. Then there is a real dilemma. If the user recovers, the excitement for the spouse ends. If the user continues, the excitement is too close and threatening. Perhaps it is logical to end this relationship and start fresh with a new exciting addict. [Ch8:100.0, 107.1; Ch9; Ch10; Ch11:410.0, 420.0]

Co-Dependency via Is There Anything Else?

The adult raised in a dysfunctional family may unconsciously seek out and form relationships with addicts and alcoholics. The adult child may not desire the same type of relationship that his/her parents had. Selection of a mate is based on the known. If all that is known is dysfunctional patterns of behavior, then what else exists? Development in an intoxicated family usually results in low feeling of self-esteem. So when M. Right walks in, he/she may represent a known which is "all I deserve." M. Right's behaviors reinforce the feeling that "this is all I deserve." Low self-esteem becomes lower. The known patterns of behavior become strengthened. It is a difficult cycle to break. Physical abuse does not break the cycle; it reinforces it. [Ch8:100.0, 107.1; Ch11:410.0, 420.0, 450.0, 460.0, 480.0, 430.0, 440.0]

A Co-Dependency Summary

These scenarios indicate that there are a number of ways in which traits for co-dependency may develop before the first fix, drink, or pill is taken. Within all the scenarios, the person is able to function within normal parameters until involvement with the addicted personality. Would the person have developed co-dependency had a willing partner not come along? It

is difficult to say. Not all trauma victims become co-dependents. Feeling different is one of the most common feelings shared by humanity. Is there anyone alive who has not felt unaccepted or unappreciated at least once in a lifetime? Some do feel the natural attraction and do not stop to investigate the potential outcomes. Since there are many addicts out there, the chances of bumping into one at the right time to set off the chain reaction are extremely good. It is clear that once the personality has been exposed to addiction, co-dependency symptoms will develop and the partner's ability to abstain will not automatically end the co-dependency symptoms.

Is it fair to assume that all persons in a relationship with an addicted person are co-dependent? Therapeutic Recreation Specialists, are you a co-dependent? If you answer "no," are you automatically in denial? If you are working in a substance abuse treatment setting, then you have relationships with addictive personalities. The prime motive for becoming a health professional is the desire to help other people. There can be a very fine line between helping and rescuing. Be sure you know which side you are on. Unless one is ready to say that all people who work in substance abuse are co-dependents, one cannot assume that all who are in relationship with addictive persons are co-dependents.

Regardless of why or when, co-dependency is self neglect. Co-dependency is the development of diffuse boundaries between the self and another. Co-dependency is permitting the replacement of personal values and needs by values and needs of another. Co-dependency is a compulsion to manipulate and control the life of another. [Ch8:100.0, 100.1, 100.2, 100.3, 105.1; Ch9; Ch11:420.0, 405.0]

SOMEPLACE BETWEEN BLOW-OUT AND FIREWORKS

Significant Other Addiction Syndrome

No matter how well adjusted one is before involvement with a practicing alcoholic/addict, one will get sick. The term I have coined, Significant Other Addiction Syndrome (SOAS), represents this phenomenon. SOAS results from application of logical automatic impulses to solve problems created by illogical, irrational emotional situations. Living with a person addicted to and using alcohol/drugs is illogical. Those of us who do it, do so because of emotions rather than logic. SOAS does not occur in crazy people. It occurs when normal healthy people are plunged into irrational circumstances. Sane people adopt crazy behaviors in order to survive in an irrational environment.

As a child I was indoctrinated to a Cinderella mind set. I was supposed to fall in love and , against all odds, live with my prince happily ever after. No one ever lives "happily ever after," especially when Prince Charming gets drunk/high on a regular basis. When reality does not seem to live up to how I think life is "supposed to" be, positive values give way to doubt and confusion.

Emotions get the other person in the situation. When both positive and negative emotions are experienced simultaneously, life becomes consumed by pain. When charged emotions fail to solve problems, there is a rebellion against feelings and a turn to logic. When logic fails, there is panic and the other person enters into the Significant Other Addiction Syndrome. The other person gets deeper and deeper into SOAS by:

1. Attempting to communicate with a mind that's MIA (missing in action).

2. Attempting to control the uncontrollable.

3. Basing actions on reactions. [Ch11:410.0]

Outcomes are pain, resentment, anger, regret. Life fills with negativity. Anticipation of tomorrow is anticipation of intolerable fear, helplessness and inadequacy. Feelings of self-worth extinguish. Love becomes a four-letter word. Addiction strains trust, respect and communication to the limit and SOAS destroys them. Some afflicted with SOAS continue to hurt years after life with the addicted person has ended.

Living with addiction causes SOAS. But that which starts it does not sustain it. SOAS is a self-feeding syndrome only made worse by continued association with practicing alcoholics/addicts. SOAS does not cause addiction. The actions of the significant other do not cause consumption of, nor abstinence from alcohol/drugs. SOAS can slow the progress of recovery from addiction. On top of that, SOAS causes additional crisis and trauma to the family unit.

The other person cries out in words and actions, "See what you are doing to me?" This is spawned by the incredible lack of communication that occurs when one person sees the world from the inside of a chemical and the other from the outside. Hang around open AA meetings long enough and you will hear an AA tell his story over the grumbling of the significant other: "That's not the way I remember it." Of course recollections differ. What one sees with unaltered perceptions is totally different from what someone else sees with altered perceptions. The fact that the two viewpoints differ does not mean that one is right and the other is wrong. Both can be right. That is why addiction is so destructive to the relationship. Sharing of common experiences is a key to keeping any relationship healthy. The practicing alcoholic/addict may be in the same room with the other person, but the two are not sharing the same experience. When one person says "apples" and the other thinks "oranges" communication cannot occur no matter how hard the two try. Sometimes the addict's other decides, "If you can't beat 'em, join 'em." (Then one says "apples" while thinking "oranges" and the other thinks "banana," but neither really cares. Obviously, this solution increases the fruit basket selection but has limited long-range potential.)

All attempts to communicate are well-intentioned. But as the effects of addiction increase, attempts to communicate become increasingly frustrating to both the addicted individual and the significant other. At first the other person addresses the problem timidly. He/she questions out loud. "What is wrong with us?" "Why do I feel so lonely?" "Where is our money going?" "Why are the children acting like this?" When the questions fall on deaf ears, then the significant other begins to supply the answers. "You are drinking too much." "You are spending too much time drinking." "You are spending too much money on booze." "The children are suffering because of your drinking." To hear the statements means a change of behavior and acceptance of the guilt trip. So most find it easier to just take another drink, fix or pill and slip back into oblivion. If the person is prevented from slipping back into oblivion then he/she turns the tables on the other person: "Why is it always all my fault?" "If you would quit your nagging. . ." "Who the hell are you to tell me what to do?"

As the fireworks progress, actions are tossed into the verbal battle. The other person's nonproductive actions are usually a product of the thought, "If I can't tell him/her how much I suffer, then I will show him/her." To graphically display the suffering, the significant other may demand separation. The ways this person may attempt to prove inability to cope are varied. It may take the form of solemn silence, passive submission, tearful outbursts, or allowing the house to fall into disarray. The significant other may seek medical attention for real or imaginary health problems (usually unrelated to alcohol/drug use in the home). Admissions to psychiatric wards and suicide attempts are also possible.

Leaving home or kicking the user out, can be productive. These methods are more often unproductive when the other person yells ". . . and never come back!" while thinking "He/she'll be back. This will show him/her." Family members are subjected to a great deal of stress, which takes its toll physically and emotionally. It can result in true physical and emotional illnesses which require treatment. SOAS is conning oneself into thinking one is sick in order to get one's point across to others. All actions are unproductive when the motive is "I'll teach him/her a lesson. I'll show him/her. Then he/she'll have to quit drinking." Only the significant other can look within to find the true motive for the action. If it is found that the internal motive is "showing him/her," then the person should stop; the action will be counterproductive. It will only block honest, open communication, build resentments, and hurt the self and intoxication will continue. It is a disease.

SOAS: Controlling the Uncontrollable

A common characteristic identified in co-dependency is the assumption of the caretaker role (Beattie, 1987, pp. 34-45). When it is obvious that a situation is out of control, then it is logical to assume that control is needed. When substance abuse is out of control, then it is obvious that the person who is abusing should control his/her consumption. If the person cannot control him/herself, then someone else has to do it. "If you won't, I will. If I can't, then maybe God will." The wand of prayer is tapped three times and nothing happens *immediately*. "So if God won't, I will."

The significant other's attempts at controlling the situation are doomed from the beginning. The flaw in logic was back at the first conclusion. The real problem was not a lack of control. The real problem was and is addiction, and addiction is in control. The person is not in control of the addiction. Addiction feeds and grows on everything it contacts. The person and situation are not out-of-control. They are being controlled by the disease. When the other person chooses to take control, then he/she, too, becomes controlled by the addiction. At this point both Prince Charming and Cinderella think they are in control, when in fact both are being controlled by a substance.

Assume a significant other has one unobligated hour. There are a number of ways to use an hour. If this person is attempting to control the uncontrollable, he/she will only be able to think of things which relate to past, present or future aspects of the addiction. He/she will rationalize that by doing so, he/she will find a way to stop the influence of addiction.

If looking at the past, he/she will remember past hurts and resentments which cannot be changed. Often the time will be spent trying to figure out what caused the substance abuse, and whose fault it is. Would one sit down and watch one's own home burn to the ground while trying to decide what caused the fire? Knowing how it started will not put out the fire, nor will it stop the substance abuse. Since the true source of the problem is almost impossible to determine, the hour will most likely end with more questions than answers. Attempts to place the blame result in fault-finding rather than fact-finding. Fault-finding results in digging up petty resentments against other family members as well as against oneself, and then these are blown out of proportion. The hour will end with a sense of fatigue, frustration, guilt, and alienation from friends and family.

If looking to the present, the hour will be spent in plotting the next move. Favorite pastimes are trying to prevent the use of the substance and looking for evidence of its use. Prevention takes the form of watching the addicted's every move, trying to catch him/her in the act. If this effort is successful, life is miserable. The addicted individual will be angry, say it's the other person's fault for spying, lie and swear he/she did not do it, even when the chemical is in hand. If the addict is not caught, it means one of two things. Either there was no use, or there was use that was not detected. Since it is humanly impossible to keep another person in view twenty-four hours a day, there is always a fear of failure to detect use. Time must be split between trying to catch him/her in the act, searching for evidence of use, and looking for signs that of impending use. If the time was spent in this manner and there was no use, then the time has been wasted. If use did occur, then the other person is too exhausted to think straight or take positive action. The addicted's protests sound believable. The disease has had a "fun run," but little has been accomplished.

Exercises of control are varied. Trying to keep money and valuables hidden and out of the addicted's possession is a challenging pastime. Addicted individuals have an uncanny knack for hiding substances and finding money. The other person can spend an hour hiding valuables. As soon as everything is hidden, the big question pops to mind, "Have they been found?" Constant rechecking is required to allay the fear; rechecking leads to moving things to new hiding places. Then when the items are needed, the significant other can't remember the last hiding place. If something can't be found, it is uncertain if the items have been misplaced or found.

Another pastime is worry about what will happen if . . ? Time spent worrying about how to survive the next bout often breeds uncontrollable fear. The mind seems most fertile when creating future disasters. "What if the sky should fall?" cried Henny Penny. Henny Penny must have been the hen of an addicted rooster. The significant other will feel exhausted from considering (and attempting to prepare for) all negative possibilities. "What if there is no more use?" is never a consideration. Energies become channeled into, "I can't go through it again." The significant other becomes obsessed with the thought, "I should be able to do something."

Fortunately there are only twenty-four hours in a day. Twenty-four chances to spend an hour. Twenty-four chances to control or be controlled. The addicted's other can do something, lots of things. Instead of dwelling on the addiction, attempting to control the addiction, the hour can be spent on a hobby, or productive work, on cleaning, sleeping, pleasurable conversation with a friend, self-improvement, a surprise for the kids, and so on. When is the spouse truly in control? When he/she is able to spend time pursuing other matters, without thought of addiction. As long as time is spent in the activities previously described, he/she is as out of control as the practicing addict. Both are ruled by the substance. [Ch 8:100.0, Ch 9]

SOAS: Basing Actions on Reactions

In dealing with the practicing substance abuser, the first most natural reactions are fight or flight, to run away or defend the self by hitting first (not necessarily hitting physically, but emotionally). The spouse who does not get a divorce, has chosen not to run. If the significant other misses the chance for the first hit, then he/she will hit in retribution. If this automatic impulse is followed, then a battle ensues that eventually destroys the entire relationship.

There is an alternative: by-pass the automatic reactions, take manual control. Do not act on first impulses. When dealing with addiction, action based on first impulse is not action, but reaction, and will invariably inflame the situation. The significant other needs to act, not react. When substance abuse begins, the addict begins the approach toward family destruction. Like a locomotive that starts off slowly, he/she quickly gains speed and momentum. The other person looks up to find the addicted barreling down the tracks with awesome, unstoppable force. The significant other looks down to see his/her feet planted on the tracks, and then looks behind to see that the tracks are missing. If automatic impulses for flight had been followed, this person would be miles from this spot. To follow the impulse to fight means to remain standing on the tracks and try to stop the train with bare hands. Results of "fight" are obvious. The other person gets flattened and the train derails anyway. To survive, the other must learn to override the automatic impulses—get off the track, let it pass. It wasn't the other's own choice to start the train in motion. The train may stop on its own before running out of track. If it derails, then at least the other is in one piece and can administer first aid, sift the wreckage for salvageable parts, help pick up the pieces, call for help, or just walk away.

The addicted personality is also very good at manipulating automatic responses to his/her advantage. The spouse who acts on first impulse will most likely regret it later. Any decision, small or large, should be given twenty-four hours to simmer. A delayed response is less likely to be an automatic response. [Ch 8:100.2, Ch 9]

SOAS: The Results

The results of communicating with a mind that is missing in action, attempting to control the uncontrollable, and basing actions on reactions are disastrous. The ego is crushed. He/she becomes jealous of time and attention devoted to an inanimate object. The self becomes devoured by fear. Healthy perspective is lost. He/she feels alone, lonely, isolated, and worthless. As the family member assumes responsibility for everyone's problems and solutions, the caretaker role is adopted. A job so great demands being right all the time. Of course everyone makes mistakes, and when the caretaker is incorrect he/she feels incompetent, guilty, and embarrassed. At the same time all this is occurring, there are also attempts to hide the problem; these are naturally accompanied by a feeling that he/she is the only person in the world to ever experience the problem.

Hiding the problem has serious consequences for all concerned. The other's denial system is two-fold. "He/she drinks too much, but he/she's not an alcoholic," is the first denial. "I'm not sick, he/she's the one with the problem," is the second denial. Naturally, addict and significant other support each other's denial system. The other person will make excuses for the addicted person's actions (or lack of action). Even after the addicted person recovers from denial, the significant other may continue denial. It may be difficult to apply a term such as "alcoholic" in a description of the partner. There may also be unwillingness to tell the children about the partner's involvement in a 12-step program. The other person may cling to blaming all of the problems of the world on the addicted partner, assuming no self-responsibility. The other person thus borrows the thinking of the 7-year-old caught in the act: "He made me do it!" [410.0]

These are all ego defense mechanisms. Convincing others (and ourselves) that something is someone else's fault, is a method of avoiding blame and punishment that is learned very early in childhood. Refusing to accept that the partner is an alcoholic or an addict may have a number of sources. If the significant other has a stereotype of an alcoholic or addict being someone who sleeps under bridges, then being the partner of such a person has little social prestige. Loving the partner and not wanting to say "bad things" about him/her may also be a factor. Part of it may come from the old "hear no evil, see no evil, speak no evil" ethic. "Behind every successful man there is a good woman." Does this imply that behind every unsuccessful person there is a bad partner? The pill that may be hardest to swallow is, "I got myself into this mess." The fact that the partner is a substance addict is not as ego-deflating as the fact that the other person got tangled up with an addict. It is especially devastating when a spouse divorces an alcoholic/addict and remarries, only to discover that the second mate is also addicted. [Ch11:460.0, 450.0]

Being jealous of a spouse's lover seems easy to understand, but feeling jealous over an inanimate object? In fact, this is quite common. When a person spends more time, money, affection, with another than with his/her regular partner, the partner usually gets jealous. In the case of the substance addict, the "lover" is a drink, fix or pill. The partner becomes jealous, feeling that someone else (or in this case, something else) has taken his/her place in life. One significant other confided, "I wish it was another woman. At least then I could understand it. I could compete for his attention. I could do something!" [Ch11:450.0]

Fear is an intricate part of the syndrome. Anxiety attacks are common. Anxiety is unrealistic fear. That is to say that the amount of fear experienced is greater than the source should logically produce. Here's an example:

> "Swallowed by fear, I found myself in the darkest corner of the house. All the lights out. All the doors locked. All the shades pulled. I was afraid to let the dog and cat out. And still I could find no safety. I felt as if he could float through the walls and get me. He was not the kind who was violent. He had never laid a hand on me. Yet I was terrified, as if there were a rapist with a gun pounding down the front door. I can still remember how frightened I could become, without reason."

Fear is an intricate part of SOAS; an unrealistic, unreasoning fear of the unknown. It is generated and fed by a power source that is difficult to comprehend and impossible to control. The other person feels powerless. Life seems unmanageable and unpredictable. Past experience has taught that calm always precedes a storm. "What are you afraid of?" The other person may express a fear that the partner will drink again, or simply respond, "Everything!" The second answer may be closer to the truth. The use of alcohol/drugs is not the true fear. "What will happen if…" is the true fear-provoker. There is fear of personal ability to cope. Internal warning signals have advised the other person that he/she is on the edge. It may only take one more negative experience to push him/her over the edge. The internal warnings do not supply information about what results if the person is pushed over the edge. They just keep flashing, "Warning, danger, warning, danger. . ." There is fear of loss. Loss of food, shelter, clothing, money, physical, emotional, spiritual well-being, and self-esteem. There is fear of death and physical injury, of self and other family members. There is fear of further social degradation resulting from still another embarrassing situation. There is fear of the unpredictability of human nature. The actions of the addicted are unpredictable, but the automatic responses evoked are also unpredictable. [Ch11:450.0, 460.0]

SOAS changes perspective. The significant other's suffering can consume all sense of perspective. Substance abuse becomes the only topic worthy of consideration. All of life is negative and fearful. Every word is scrutinized for hidden manipulations. It's just "little ol' me" against the world. Good things that might happen do not require further consideration. The altered viewpoint becomes a filter. Negatives are permitted into awareness while positives are screened out. This altered perspective is active not only in the home, but in all aspects of life. The promotion at work is discounted, but the irritated glance of a coworker registers. The children's good deeds are dismissed, but their breaking of the cookie jar is remembered. The television shows forecasting gloom and despair carry real-world power, while the show that ends with everyone living happily ever after is quickly forgotten if watched at all. Each person's senses are being bombarded with stimulation everyday. The mind is only able to attune to a small portion of the incoming messages (Maltz). When in denial, all evidence of a problem is screened out. When fearful, all signs of safety and security are overlooked. When feeling angry, or depressed, all access to sunlight is blocked from view. This is one reason why the significant other continues to suffer even after the partner has entered recovery. A change in perspective can end the suffering before active abuse ends. In most cases, the significant other is unable to change his/her perspective independently. Something positive has to slip through the filtering system before anything changes. Ongoing group support is necessary to maintain a healthy perspective once adjustments have been made. [Ch11:470.0]

FROM FIREWORKS TO SAWTOOTH TO FLATLINE

My perspective would like to believe that the cavalry arrived. Help came at the Blow-Out Stage for most, a few suffered the Fireworks. No one got to the Sawtooth Stage. Unfortunately, my filtering system has some holes in it. I know that in today's real world, the opposite of this scenario is still true.

Obviously, difficulties described in the previous section have consequences. The person subjected to adversity for extended periods of time, becomes trapped in coping behaviors. Rigid methods of operation result. Positive anticipation

of something good results in disappointment so many times that the person learns not to expect anything good. When nothing good is expected, nothing good is received. Attempts at communication are abandoned. Distrust rules supreme. Living becomes mechanical. The family circle breaks apart. Family members go their own separate ways. Little is solved because the breakup of the circle exposes abrasive behaviors which saw through any new relationship that might otherwise be formed.

Many substance addicts enter treatment at this point. The family that has physically broken apart is of no concern to the treatment facility. The addict is treated as an independent entity. The family receives no treatment. Sometimes a remarriage will restart the cycle, and the family will receive help on the next go round.

When a person is in the Sawtooth Stage, changes do not occur quickly. Behavior patterns are chronic and require more time to adjust than a short-term treatment program has to offer. Emphasis should be placed on motivating the person toward long-term involvement with a source of help. Twelve step support groups offer hope for those who are not in a hurry to be healed. After-care programs also provide the extended time required.

Without help the family members will Flatline negatively. Sometimes, the family has broken apart but are still physically dwelling under the same roof. Treatment teams who are subjected to constant intervention by a spouse, are dealing with a family member who is in the Fireworks Stage. When the treatment team finds it extremely difficult to contact the significant other, they are dealing with a family member who is in the Negative Flatline Stage. While it is important to always reach out to others in need of help, it is also important for the Therapeutic Recreation Specialist to concentrate on helping those who are ready to be helped. Keep in mind that response to treatment varies and is highly dependent on the stage of involvement. The Therapeutic Recreation Specialist should keep a close check on personal levels of involvement and burn-out. Addiction has enough victims. We need models of health, and wholeness.

Co-Addiction

This chapter looks at the family of a person who is addicted to a substance, and is based on the premise that the family members are clean and sober. This is not always the case. Sometimes the significant other's greatest concern is "Who is going to go drinking with me when he/she gets out of treatment?" Many social drinkers marry alcoholics. As the disease progresses, the significant other either gets so disgusted with the situation that he/she never wants to drink again, or the person also becomes addicted. Many family members feel a need for something extra to get through the crisis of the day. That something extra may be discovered in a tranquilizer, which can lead to prescription pill addiction. Sometimes the relationship was formed on the mutual preference for substance abuse. Sometimes the person who goes into treatment has a significant other with chronic symptoms of addiction and no desire to change. Both may enter treatment at the same time. When this occurs, the chances of co-dependency existing are very strong.

Where two or more family members are involved with substance abuse, then it may be assumed that the family missed the Blow-Out Stage of the cycle, and is experiencing the full fury of the fireworks stage. Inpatient treatment is critical if the recovery process is to have a chance to get started. Intervention attempts with family members not in treatment should also be explored. Attempts to rebuild the family must be delayed until substances abuse ends for all members of the household. [Ch2; Ch3]

Parents

For purposes of this discussion it is assumed that the parents are clean and sober.

The parents of an addicted individual experience the same basic feelings and problems as the significant other. They go through the same stages of the family addiction cycle. There are differences in emphasis. Our society and our laws hold parents responsible for the actions of their children. Parents typically experience feelings of guilt, responsibility and a sense of failure far greater than the significant other. Parents are often viewed as the source of the problem by schools, neighbors, and other family members. Most damaging is the fact that most parents hold themselves responsible for the problem. Fingers pointed by others only support the personal assumption. Because of the feelings of guilt and responsibility, persons who are addicted find parents easy marks. I have listened to hundreds of recovering alcoholics tell how they got sober. I have yet to hear one that began drinking because mom or dad forced him/her to take a drink. Some parents unwittingly provide motive and opportunity. But unless a parent is planning to supervise the youngster twenty-four hours a day throughout the child's entire life span, opportunity cannot be avoided. Furthermore, the parent who tries to do just that will be branded as overprotective and the cause of emotional trauma to the child. Obviously, I view parenting as a difficult situation made more complex by addiction. It takes so many years to raise a child, that by the time we get enough feedback to know how to do it, we are too old to be doing it.

Parents become trapped trying to figure out who is to blame while the fire continues to rage. Addiction is a product of inherited traits, family learning and social environment. No one is totally to blame. No one is totally off the hook. Parenting is not a matter of teaching behaviors. It is a matter of helping a child to modify inherent behaviors. The child who is predisposed to introversion will never enjoy being an extravert. But he/she does not have to grow up to be a hermit or feel bad about enjoying his/her own company. Through mediating

applications of inherent qualities to outside interactions, the parent is able to assist the child in developing a functional lifestyle. The parent can help, but cannot cause the child to develop.

If the addicted individual is underage, the parents are legally responsible for the person. The significant other can provide a choice: "Stop or get out." The parents of an addicted child legally cannot throw the child out of the home until the child becomes of age. Quality halfway houses are an option where they exist. For the most part, parents must find positive and negative enforcements within the home environment.

Teenage years have always been problem years for parents. They become especially difficult when substance abuse is involved. Transactional Analysis (TA) provides insight into the problems and solutions for teen years. According to TA, there is a Parent, Adult, and Child in each of us from birth. Most often, the Child within is represented as a bad little rascal. Nothing can be further from the truth. The Child is our natural Skip and Jump system which keeps life alive and creative. It is only when the Child does not get a chance to play that maladaptive behavior sets in. At any rate, TA tells us that communication patterns develop between the internal Parent, Adult, and Child in each of us. Parents by definition communicate with children. Adults only talk to adults (Berne, 1961). During teen years, the Parent is busy operating out of his/her parent and the child shifts into adult expression. Communication ends. Initially the Parent tries to get the kid back into being a child. Eventually the Parent shifts to his/her Adult, and Adult-to-Adult communications begin. It is critical to the addiction recovery process that the Adult-to-Adult communication pattern be established as quickly as possible. (The teen and parent both need to learn to let their Child out for healthful play, but not when honest communications are being attempted.)

It is critical that parents assist addicted teens to identify alternatives and consequences but not to make decisions for teens nor assume responsibility for their decisions once made. The teenager must know what the parent will or will not do prior to selection of an alternative. The parent must make a commitment to do or not do and then live with that commitment. If, for example, an alternative is to drink, the teen should know prior to selection of that alternative, whether the parents will bail him/her out of jail if necessary, pay attorney fees, and so on. If the parents tell the child they will not bail him/her out, then they must not, no matter how painful it is to see him/her behind bars. The greater the communication before the choice is made, the easier it will be to live with the consequences afterward.

Rapid replacement of articles can reduce negative consequences of behavior. The teen who is given a new car on Monday, wrecks it on Tuesday, and finds its replacement in the driveway on Wednesday, has not experienced any consequences as a result of his/her actions. Some parents may play a guessing game. If the wrecked car was a result of the teen's irresponsible actions, then the car will not be replaced. If it resulted from a friend's poor judgment, or the accident was caused by the other guy, then the car will be replaced. The attempt to link negative consequences to negative behaviors can result in the child learning that "it's not my fault" is the solution to avoiding consequences. Addicted individuals seem to be born with the ability to be caught red-handed and find a logical explanation that relinquishes their responsibility for the situation. Perhaps the lesson addicted children need to learn is that negative situations have negative consequences regardless of who caused the situation. Regardless of what caused a car to crash, a wreck has negative consequences. [Ch8:100.3]

Reflections on Child Rearing Practices

My father had a high school education. He never read a book on psychology or child development but he had a knack for staying calm, saying the right thing, making the right decisions at the right times. (I never thought so at the time. I recognized his wisdom years later.) Growing up, I always knew if he approved or disapproved of my actions before I acted. I always knew he would not bail me out if I failed. I always knew he would not stop me from trying something simply because he did not agree. It takes something special to say to one's child, "If you jump off that bridge, you will get hurt, and I won't pick up the pieces." Then give the child a hug and let him/her go jump off the bridge. Dad was that kind of a person. Once, in a reflective mood, I asked him how he managed to survive me. Specifically, how he managed to stay calm while allowing me to make my own mistakes. He shrugged his shoulders and said, "After a child is 10, you've done all you can do. Either you've taught them what they need to know or you haven't. It's too late to go back and try to change anything." I don't know why he chose 10 as the magic age. I don't know if I fully agree with his logic. I do know his view kept him strong and sane during adverse conditions. It worked for him. I think it worked for him because down deep, he believed in himself. His value system was tested and unshakable. He practiced what he preached because he knew it worked. In trusting himself, he was able to trust me. In trusting that things would eventually work out, he remained calm. Knowing that he trusted me, and that I was free to make my own choices, I found it unnecessary to jump off many a bridge.

In today's complex world, it is easy to lose faith in ourselves. There are so many opinions on how to raise children. There are so many experts providing opposing views on what is good and what is bad for children. When even aspirin is suspect, it is difficult to believe we have made the right selections in child rearing practices. When the child becomes involved in addiction at age 12, it is easy to believe that the wrong child rearing practices were selected.

The past cannot be changed. If a person could go back and relive the choices, they would probably make exactly the same choices and decisions as were made originally. Why? Because for each decision, given the options available at the time and given everything known at the time, the choice made was the best decision to make at the time.

"What would have happened if. . .?" "If only I had. . ." Chances are very good that the selection of a different approach would not have prevented the child's addiction. Parents would still be looking for a way to live with an addicted child and wishing a different option had been selected. "If only I had. . ." is a symptom of grief. The heart wants to believe that something could have altered the outcomes. It wants something tangible to affix the blame. There is no recorded crisis in history in which someone did not stop to think, "If only I had. . ." Part of the acceptance that must occur is to recognize that even given the "If only I had. . .", nothing would have changed.

The real problem is in the here and now. The past cannot and need not be changed. The real problem now is losing faith in the value of the choices that were made in the past. If parents lose faith in themselves, they convey a lack of trust and hope to their addicted offspring. Without trust in self, how can anyone survive? The battle is lost before it is begun.

Children of Addiction

Much of what is known about growing up under the guidance and supervision of an addicted parent comes from the adults who experienced the disease as children. Being subjected to the substance abuse behaviors of parents often results in common characteristics when adulthood is attained. Home function is governed by don'ts, with the real biggies being don't tell, trust or feel. Promises are made to be broken. The home's energies are focused on the whims of the user. Normal play development is disrupted. [Ch8:107.1]

Healthy play development is spontaneous. It is noisy and disorganized. Highly experimental in nature, playfulness clangs tins cans together. Short attention spans cause roaming from one activity to another. Children interact with one another with rambunctious zeal. All of this tries the nerves of even the calmest parent. When stress is always present, spontaneous outbreaks of natural play behavior are quickly extinguished. Family members learn to tip toe for fear of awakening a sleeping giant. It's difficult to have fun in silence. [Ch11:407.14]

As the child grows, he/she begins to recognize and become embarrassed by the problems of addiction. Healthy friendships are abandoned when others start asking too many personal questions, or when visits to other children's homes mean an obligation to invite friends into the substance abusing home. Patterns of maladaptation form. Children develop roles rather than personalities. Emotional neglect becomes a way of life. [Ch8:109.0; Ch11:450.0]

Eventually children get involved in the Fireworks Stage. If help does not arrive they too can fall victim to the Sawtooth and negative Flatline Stages. Those who survive become adult children. Many find relief through practicing addiction. Many find comfort in the known and marry substance abuse. Unless help arrives, no one teaches them to relax or play. [Ch8:106.1, 107.1; Ch11:407.0, 420.03]

The child of addiction may come to the treatment center to visit dad/mom. This is healthy. It breaks the rules of "don't tell." But children need more than a brief visit. They need an opportunity to play and interact playfully with the parent. They need to learn about the disease of addiction; what has happened to them and why.

Many people who are in treatment for addiction have children who do not visit. Some facilities may have a minimum age requirement for visitors. What is a child? A non-entity, or a thinking, breathing, feeling part of the family unit? Is there a magic age when children suddenly become "old enough to understand?" Is a child ever too young to be affected by an unstable family environment? Some believe that the seeds of addiction are planted during the first months of life (Milkman & Sundewrith, 1982, p. 178). Until this theory is totally ruled out, a child will never be too young to receive treatment.

Both addict and partner want the best for the child. "The best" too often takes the form of protecting the child from the truth. Arguments are reserved for after the child falls asleep. Children are sent away when alternatives are discussed and decisions are made. Children are excluded from the treatment process. The partner may jump to conclusions, overreact, try to control the environment because of a desire to protect and shelter the children. The partner's decision to break up the family unit or to stay with the substance abuser may be based on what is considered to be best for the children, without input from the children. As long as parents shelter and think for the children, their children will learn to think for others and the cycle of caretaking will continue.

What does the child see and hear? Twice as much as parents think. Children are curious. Children pretend to sleep through arguments, pretend to be watching television, when in fact, they are eavesdropping. If parents should succeed in hiding the problem, then the child wakes up one day to find the parents happy and the next day to find stress and irritation are rampant. One day it's OK to make noise while playing and the next day parents are yelling and screaming at the slightest sound. One day the home is filled with apologies and promises that "it" will never happen again, and the next day "it" happens. Daddy looks happy, goes away and comes back sick. Or Daddy is sick, goes away and comes back happy. Mommy says Daddy's never coming back. Just when the shock wears off from Daddy being gone, he comes back. What does the child experience? Some children have an intuitive nature and a greater ability to detect mood changes than most parents. Children are experts in detecting subtle differences in voice tone. To a child, "no" in one tone means do it again; in a second tone it means wait a minute before doing it again; and in a third tone it means wait till no one is looking. The child may be the first to recognize that alcohol/drug abuse is a problem again. The parent's attempt to break the bad news to the child may be cut short by the child saying "I know that." Children can feel like their intelligence is being insulted too.

For the most part, children experience the same feelings as adults, though they may express the feelings differently. Primarily, the child experiences feelings of confusion, fear, and betrayal. The child is instinctively aware of his dependence on his parents. His total emotional and physical survival depends on them. When parents falter, children become afraid. If asked what they fear, they might respond, "I don't know." The fear of the unknown, the fear for their own survival is greater than their vocabulary. The child may direct anger toward the nonaddicted parent. The significant other may be perceived as a total authority figure to the child. If the parent is able to control every aspect of the child's life, and make the child behave, then why is the nonaddicted parent not controlling the addicted parent? In frustration the child may turn to the same behavior as the partner. The child may attempt to control the parents. The child may attempt to punish the parents. Sometimes feelings of isolation and exclusion are expressed through attention-getting behaviors, acting out, temper tantrums, regression, pouting, whining and crying. The child may assume he/she is the problem and demonstrate behaviors that demand punishment. Broken promises fill the child with distrust. [Ch11:450.0, 430.0, 440.0, 460.0, 470.0]

The stress resulting from parents dealing with addiction robs energy. The addicted parent is preoccupied with alcohol/drug consumption and recovery and has little time to play with the child. The nonaddicted parent is often too tired, too stressed out to pay attention to the child. The child feels unimportant and insignificant. [Ch9; Ch10; Ch11:402.0]

There are times when children reach their limits. They just can't take any more. Provision of an escape hatch, a place to go where they can forget about everything for a while is important. A safe harbor for such times can be a relative or friend's home, or a hobby or class of special interest at the community recreation center. It could be sitting in a big old tree where the negative ions are plentiful. [Ch8:106.3; Ch11:406.0]

All children need hope. Promises to never do "it" again feed distrust and extinguish hope. Hope comes from learning to live with situations, not from avoiding them. Hope comes from finding the positive in a day rather than the negative. Hope comes from being able to identify progress and growth within the self.

Sometimes crisis creates holidays. On national holidays, work stops, school stops, people unwind and get lazy. Living with a problem is not an excuse for sloppiness in thought or actions. Having a crisis is not an excuse for a holiday. The reason for the child's inappropriate behavior should be recognized but the act should not be excused. The old, "he pooped in the lobby because his Daddy's an alcoholic" is not acceptable. The message given to the child's logic is "I have to behave myself except when Daddy's drinking." It's a short step in logic from there to "I have to behave myself except when I'm drinking." In times of crisis, the child may not feel like going to school or picking up his/her toys. The child may not be able to concentrate on the task at hand. But he/she should be expected to try. Parents must also be expected to try. Parents must find the energy to devote to a child even during times of crisis. "I'm too tired" cannot be the only comment the child hears. Fifteen minutes a day is not much time. But 15 minutes packed with attention and energy devoted solely to the child can make all the difference in the world. [Ch8; Ch9]

Attempts to recognize the child's feelings may result in allowing the child to make decisions concerning family directions. Children should be included when alternatives are discussed. Their feelings should be heard. But the adults in the family should make the final decisions. Allowing the child to make decisions about actions of the parents encourages the child to think he/she is able to control the parents. It also sets the child up for failure. The child should not be obliged or encouraged to assume responsibilities that have been abdicated by the parent. This only leads to further family dysfunction.

Correlating Roles and TA

Claudia Black, in her book *It Will Never Happen To Me*, describes roles that children develop as a result of living in alcoholic homes (1982). She found that most children adjust in ways that do not attract attention to themselves. They develop roles that allow the family to "appear" normal to the outside world. Black labeled these roles as "the Responsible One," "the Adjuster," and "the Placater." A few children develop behaviors which negatively attract the public's attention through acting out. These are the ones most often seen in the principal's office and by juvenile courts. It would seem that the roles Black identified have a correlation to the Parent, Adult, and Child portions of the personality which are identified in Transactional Analysis.

Consider the Responsible One. Black found this role often performed by an only or oldest child. The Responsible One assumes responsibility for himself and other family members as well. One might suspect that teachers and neighbors, not aware of the family drinking problem, say that the Responsible One "is quite mature for his age." But maturity really has nothing to do with it. This is a kid who is developing a strong Adult at the expense of his/her Parent and Child. I have known persons, "quite mature for their age," who have logically found suicide as a solution for a meaningless life. All too often the "mature for his/her age" Responsible One is rewarded with additional responsibilities. The need is less responsibility, and more playfulness. During activities, the Responsible One should not be given the duties such as passing out supplies or being captain of the team. This only strengthens the role. It's often tempting to utilize the Responsible One's skills, for he/she may volunteer for the task and may be one of the few in the group that the leader can depend upon to get the job done. [Ch11:410.0]

Consider the Adjuster, defined as one who finds it easiest to simply follow directions. Consequences of acting on directions are not considered. It would seem that this is a Child without benefit of a functioning Adult. Without the Adult, what choice is available but to grow up functioning as dictated by a warehouse full of Parent tapes. Black states, "This coping pattern allows the child to appear more flexible, more spontaneous and, possibly, more selfish than others in the home."

This sounds very much like the TA description of a person whose Child has been too tightly restricted. The Adjuster needs to participate in activities which develop logic. Educational game software for computers may be of assistance. The computer game that only does what the user dictates, forces the user to take charge of the situation. Since the computer is a one-player interactive device, there is no one around to ask advice. Development of self-trust and risk-taking are also important factors. [Ch8:109.0; Ch11:450.0, 480.0;]

The Placater is described as the family comforter. According to Black, the child is always willing to listen and comfort others who are upset. In other words, this kid runs around mothering people. It is likely that such a kid has a strong Parent, and virtually nonexistent Adult and Child. If the Adult were functioning, the kid would occasionally ask, "Is my mothering helping the situation?" If the Child were functioning, the kid would be demanding to be mothered rather than mothering. The Placater is most likely an intuitive and insightful person. Perhaps getting the Child to literally look in a mirror and comfort what he/she sees would be highly beneficial. [Ch8:107.0, 108.0; Ch10; Ch11:407.0, 408.0]

One point seems clear. In homes where alcohol/drug use is a problem, or has been a problem, the young person seldom has the opportunity to develop all three parts of the personality equally. None of the above "roles" has a strong, healthy Child active within. This should be no surprise. The Child has a very difficult time. Playfulness is seldom encouraged around a sick person. Most often the Parent tapes compile information telling the Child to be quiet. True play is loud and unpredictable. How can a person develop good feelings about playing while growing up around someone who has the flu for several years?

Sobriety seldom brings an end to the ban on play. Few parents ever say, "Okay he/she has quit drinking. You can play now. Be loud. Be wild. See what you can get into." The most typical tape is, "He/she has quit drinking, but don't do anything that might cause him/her to start up again." As a result, noise and play levels continue to be restricted on into recovery.

When a kid grows up and has a kid, then what? Our culture has been unkind to play for centuries. Combine the basic cultural bias of pro-work/anti-play, with the Parent tapes of "Shhhhhh don't wake up Daddy." Add to that the eruption of a genetically inherited disease known as addiction, and one might wonder why Kid II, son of Kid I, doesn't seem to play like other kids?

What can be done? Intervention is important. Visiting hours at a treatment center can be an opportunity to observe family interactions. It is also an opportunity to structure and model healthful interactions. Parents need time together to discuss nonchildish things. If children are brought to the treatment center, the parents' attempts to establish adult-to-adult interactions results in making the child feel excluded. If the parents attempt to meet the child's needs for inclusion, the parents fail to reestablish their bonds with each other. If staff provide a "children's hour," then children are kept busy while parents are free to renew their bonds. Meanwhile, children are receiving what they need to grow strong and healthy. After the separation hour children and parents should participate in a joint activity. When needed, staff may provide parenting sessions which assist client and partner to meet the children's needs in the home.

Adult Children of Alcoholics

The adult child is a person who grew up in a home where addiction was practiced. Threads of the adult child syndrome are woven throughout previous chapters of this text. It is discussed here to aid in understanding the family, and to avoid mixing characteristics of substance abuse with characteristics of the adult child. Many children from addictive homes grow up to become substance addicts. Many others avoid alcohol and drug use, but manage to marry substance abusers. The Therapeutic Recreation Specialist is well-advised to know the characteristics of the adult child and be prepared to deal with them in the client, in the family, or even in other staff.

Adult children have basic characteristics. They know their childhood was "different." This feeling of being different is carried into adult life (Woititz, 1983, p. 46). Being able to recognize a lack of normalcy does not mean understanding what is "normal." In addition to the lack of understanding of what normal is, there also seems to be a desire to be "normal" (Woititz, pp. 24-28). As previously mentioned, I was never "normal." As a youngster I watched "Leave It To Beaver," and assumed that show represented normal family interaction for Americans. I have a friend, who is an adult child, who also watched the show while growing up and assumed it was "normal family" functioning. The interesting difference is that I always felt sorry for Beaver, because his life was so dull. My friend envied Beaver and wished to change places. So in addition to guessing what is appropriate family function, I would suggest there is also the desire to be what is being guessed about. Adult children who spend time guessing about what is considered appropriate and inappropriate by "normal" people subject themselves to constant stress. Since there is no such animal as a "normal person," it must be frustrating attempting to duplicate something that does not exist. The attempt results in another characteristic, that of seeking the approval of others (Woititz, pp. 44-46). The process of behaving in ways perceived appropriate by other people and wondering if appropriateness is being attained, would also result in limited leisure pursuit, limited pleasure derived from leisure pursuit, and limited understanding of what leisure is all about. It must be difficult to enjoy leisure pursuits which meet personal needs, when the goal is to be like other people and do what other people do. The purpose of leisure is to meet intrinsic needs, not needs that are appropriate for others. Attempting to do what others do may be considered a lack of risk-taking. The greatest risk that the adult child needs to take is the risk of being him/herself. [Ch8:100.1, 106.1, 109.0]

Adult children are characterized as persons who can start a project easily but will finish it only with great difficulty (Woititz, pp. 28-30). (This may be a trait common to many non-adult children too.) Where this characteristic exists, it is important to select projects carefully. A project that is too large and complex dooms the person to failure every time. Adult children are also impulsive, selecting a project before fully considering all factors involved (Woititz, pp. 50-54). The fast plunge into selecting a course of action may be one of the main reasons why things that have been started don't get finished. A person with this problem may have a history of learning a wide variety of leisure skills, never staying with anything long enough to acquire the benefits. Therapeutic Recreation services should monitor selection of Leisure Skill Development sessions, making sure that too many are not attempted at any given time. It may also help to ask the person why a specific choice was made, what factors were considered in the selection process, and so on. The exact reasons given are not as important as getting the person to look at how decisions are made. [Ch11:480.0]

According to Woititz, adult children have difficulty making honest statements, and tend to judge themselves severely (Woititz, pp. 30-37). They also take themselves too seriously, and may overreact to changes caused by factors beyond their control (Woititz, pp. 37-39, 44). These traits will show themselves during participation in any aspect of the Therapeutic Recreation services and should be dealt with rather than ignored. Of course, some ways to deal with a problem may be more appropriate than others. Telling a person who tends to judge him/herself too harshly that he/she is a liar, may not be the best approach. Confrontation should be gentle, providing ego support along with feedback about undesirable behavior. Taking the self (or taking life) too seriously is deadly. Seriousness constricts the flow of creativity that is needed to solve serious problems. [Ch8:107.3; Ch11:407.12, 407.15, 407.16]

The characteristic of loyalty may be observed during team activities. The adult child is often loyal and protective of another person, even when there is no reason to be loyal (Woititz, p. 49). This may be a result of avoiding the risk of disloyal behavior. Disloyalty risks conflict. It also risks being stuck with no one to be loyal to. [Ch8:109.0]

The fifth characteristic noted by Woititz is that adult children "have difficulty having fun" (Woititz, p. 66). It is most interesting to note that it is the only one of the 13 characteristics discussed which is not followed by further explanation (Woititz, p. 37). Later in the text she suggests borrowing a kid to teach the adult child how to play. This introduces the chance that the adult child will only select a dysfunctional child who does not know how to play, and each will sit gaping at the other, wondering the proverbial, "Are we having fun yet?" [Ch8:100.0, 100.1, 100.2, 100.3, 105.2, 107.1, 107.2, 104.3, 109.0; Ch9; Ch10; Ch11:407.0, 408.0, 410.0, 450.0, 460.0, 470.0]

Eleven of the 13 characteristics of the adult child have been discussed. (The first 11 were: guessing normal, follow-through problems, lying, severe self judgment, fun problems, taking self too seriously, overreaction to changes, approval seeking, feeling different, loyalty, and impulsiveness.) (Woititz, p. 4). I would suggest that the final two characteristics (being super responsible or irresponsible, and difficulty with intimate relationships) are the results of the other 11 characteristics (Woititz, pp. 39-43, 47-49).

Formation of an intimate relationship demands honesty. If also demands the ability to finish what has been started, and accept changes that occur in the relationship and in the partner. An intimate relationship becomes too intense if taken too seriously; it smothers without fun and playfulness. Constant second-guessing and approval-seeking chokes the life out of a relationship. Spontaneous interaction is a must for a healthy intimate relationship. Impulsive behavior is different from spontaneity. Impulsiveness is an extreme which constantly keeps the partner adjusting to the unexpected. Spontaneity is a free-flowing, trusting condition that breathes life and openness into a relationship. [Ch8:105.2, 107.3, 109.0; Ch11:405.0, 407.0, 430.0, 460.0]

To Treatment

When a person arrives at the admission booth of a substance abuse treatment facility, the extent of family involvement must be determined. If early intervention has brought the client in prior to the Fireworks Stage, then the family may still have many positive bonds. The treatment center may focus on basic family education. If at one of the other stages, the center must focus on healing needs of the family before client-family interactions can be expected to be supportive. This is more easily said than done, since the family does not enter treatment.

Often times, family members appear very strong and healthy at the time of admission. However, as time progresses, the family members seem to fall apart. This often results from what might be called "the Family's Recovery Myth," or "If he'll just stop, everything will be OK."

When one's house stops burning and the home is ashes, is everything OK? No. When the fire stops, the only thing left intact is a wide range of emotions. There are feelings of relief, thankfulness, joy because the fire has stopped. There are feelings of anger, violation, resentment, unfairness, because something important has been taken away without permission. There are feelings of physical and emotional exhaustion. Firefighting uses up energy reserves, and looking forward toward rebuilding seems an insurmountable task. There is fear. "Can I learn to live and be happy in a new house? What will happen to me if I rebuild and another fire wipes me out?"

When the addicted person goes to a treatment center, most families initially experience a tremendous sense of relief. Removal of the individual from the home is perceived as an opportunity for physical and emotional rest. The relief also comes from the assumption that the magic wand has been waved and now everyone will live happily ever after. The relief does not last long. Maintaining family and business routines while short-handed is difficult. It is especially difficult when the routine that has been established is warped and nonfunctional - add to that the normal emotional letdown that is experienced after any crisis. The time is also consumed by visiting hours, phone calls, and so on.

Admission to treatment may bring some feelings of embarrassment for family members. "What will I tell the neighbors?" Tell them the truth or don't tell them anything. Where is it written that because someone lives next door, they must know everything? Most likely they are as relieved as the family that the person has gone for help.

After the initial feelings wear off, the family begins to experience anger, resentment and guilt. Feelings that have been suppressed, or not satisfactorily expressed, rise to the surface. The family has been waiting for a substance-free moment to tell the person how much they have been hurt. They may seize the first visiting hour to do just that. There are two reasons why this never meets with satisfactory results. First, the person in treatment is not in a position to hear it. For him/her, the battle has just begun. Just making it through the new routine of the day without substance use is a major accomplishment. The second reason deals with the family's desired outcome. Why bring up past hurts? What can be accomplished? By bringing it up, can the past be erased? No. If he/she says "sorry," the family will respond, "Sorry isn't enough." What is enough? An assurance that he/she will never do it again? He/she can't give that.

The myth begins to break down. The person is alcohol/drug free, but the family still hurts and nothing can be done to change that. The person is alcohol/drug free and still can't meet the family's needs; alcohol/drug free, but still can't promise to stay that way. The treatment team confides that there is no cure. The family feels confused and frustrated.

In the past, the myth that everything would be OK as soon as the addicted individual stopped, had played an important role in the family's survival. It provided the one shred of hope available to the family. The myth not only conveyed hope for a better tomorrow, but it contained a solution to all problems and a definite endpoint. The myth implied immediate results. It was a rallying point for physically and emotionally exhausted individuals. "If I can just manage to survive to this point, then everything will be good and I can rest." As the myth breaks down, fear is added to anger, resentment, and confusion. The family, still exhausted, loses sight of a definite endpoint. Treatment causes growth. Growth causes change. The family sees the change. The question pops up, "Will he/she be someone that I can live with after this change occurs?" The fear is compounded for the significant other who has only known his/her partner while under the influence of alcohol/drugs. The fear of the future and fear of a return to substance abuse, compounded by the fear of change, produces fear of the unknown. Attempts to make the unknown a known generate more confusion, doubt, and panic.

The brain is a computer operated by the mind. If a computer is fed a program such as, "Start with 1, then go to 2, then go to 3, then go to 1," it will create a loop, spinning 1,2,3,1,2,3,1,2,3,1... into infinity. While the person with the addiction is nestled into a treatment program with a logical progression, the family members sit at home alone attempting to solve all the unknowns. The attempts result in programming loops. The mind spins to exhaustion and solves nothing.

An attempt may be made to break the loop by adding new information into the program. The source for new information is the visiting hour. Visitors greet their loved one and promptly place every action under a microscope. Every aspect of the individual is observed and interpreted and added to the spinning program. The result is unsatisfactory. The new information is interpreted in such a way as to add new fears, and the program still loops back on itself. For example, if a patient is five minutes late, it may be interpreted that "He/she doesn't want to see me." When this conclusion is added to the spinning program, it comes out saying, "He/she will never want me. He/she's going to leave me after all I've been through." If the person in treatment is observed smiling and happy, the family might conclude that, "He/she's happy. He/she was never happy with me." Again, the out-of-control program jumps to a fatalistic conclusion.

At this point the addict's partner wants most a display of affection, some reassurance that there will be a caring relationship after treatment. There is a need for closeness. Each time the partner attempts to sit closer, the person in treatment pulls his/her chair away. Conversation seems strained until another person who is in treatment enters the room. Suddenly the partner is sitting alone while the person he/she has come to see is laughing and joking with another. The information is fed into the warped program and feelings of jealously boil out. The partner forgets that he/she used the first visiting opportunity to vent anger. He/she does not realize how awkward the loved one feels being reviewed under a microscope.

While the person with the addiction is in treatment, he/she may see loved ones moving from a positive position of support and control to a negative position of anger, resentment, anxiety, jealousy, and hopelessness. He/she typically does not see that the initial positiveness was based on unrealistic anticipation of relief, and a myth. What is seen is that as he/she gets a clear head, everyone around him/her is going bonkers. Unless the family gets assistance in working through their feelings, discharge day threatens to be doomsday. A person with an addiction, unsure of his/her ability to cope with and be accepted by a drug-free world, goes off to live with strangers (who are supposed to be his/her family) who are filled with fear, doubt, anger, panic, anxiety, insecurity, and are reacting unpredictably.

The provision of "homework" for family members can help resolve the problems of the Family Recovery Myth. Homework should consist of self-evaluation tools, educational information, and tips for leisure functioning. At this point, unoccupied time is dangerous, so anything that reduces unobligated time or structures free time toward productive uses is helpful. The homework keeps the person occupied while at home, leaving less time to worry about the progress of the client. It also supports concepts that the client is learning while in treatment, providing new and productive information to discuss during visiting hours.

FROM OTHER FAC STAGES TO HEALTHLINE

Successful family treatment depends on recognizing the family members' unique needs and meeting those needs. The information provided in this chapter is only a general guideline. There are few absolutes in anything. It is certain that all family members are not alike. The provision of services should be based on individualized assessment of needs and interests. This may sound like an overwhelming task, but it's really not that bad. Family members respond to opportunities for self-analysis and independent study. Visiting hours and Re-Creative experiences may be structured to contain therapeutic value. Naturally, to do the job recommended in this text requires time and staffing for Leisure Education, Skill Development, and Recreation Therapy. Many facilities are not capable of staffing these for the families at this time. The practitioner is encouraged to do whatever is possible, for even a little is better than nothing.

There is one thing that all Therapeutic Recreation services can do. All too often the treatment process ends at a FAC Stage where the family unit has been dissected and left in shambles. Therapeutic Recreation can help to reunite the family unit. Family participation in a card game, a picnic, or some other special event prior to discharge is important. A few moments of pleasure in each other's company can kindle the desire to resolve differences.

References/Resources

Al-Anon Family Groups. Al-Anon Family Group Headquarters, Inc., Madison Square Station, New York, NY.

Al-Anon. *The Dilemma Of The Alcoholic Marriage.*

Alateen - Hope For Children of Alcoholics. Al-Anon.

Beattie, M. (1987). *Co-dependent No More; How to Stop Controlling Others & Start Caring for Yourself.* Hazeldon and Harper & Row.

Berne, E. (1961). *Transactional Analysis in Psychotherapy.* NY: Ballantine Books.

Black, C. (1982). *It Will Never Happen To Me: Children of Alcoholics as Youngsters, Adolescents, Adults.* M.A.C., Denver, CO.

Black, C. *Repeat After Me.* M.A.C., Denver, CO.

Bradshaw, J. *Bradshaw on: The Family, A Revolutionary Way of Self-Discovery.* Enterprise Center, Deerfield Beach, FL: Health Communications, Inc.

Deutsch, C. (1982). *Broken Bottles, Broken Dreams: Understanding & Helping Children of Alcoholics.* Columbia University, NY: Teachers College Press.

Edelwich, J., & Brodsky, A. (1980). *Burn-out: Stages of Disillusionment in the Helping Professions.* New York, NY: Human Sciences Press.

Faulkner, R. W. (1988). *Addictionaide Series.* Seaside, OR: Leisure Enrichment Service.

Forum, The Al-Anon's Grapevine.

Freudenberger, H. J., & Richelson, G. (1980). *Burn-out: The High Cost of High Achievement.* Garden City, NY: Anchor Press, Doubleday & Co., Inc.

Kerr, B. (1974). *Strong at the Broken Places: Women Who Have Survived Drugs.* Chicago, IL: Follett Publishing Co.

Maltz, Maxwell. *Psychocybernetics.*

Middelton-Mos, J., & Dwinell, L. (1986). *After the Tears; Reclaiming the Personal Losses of Childhood.* Enterprise Center, Deerfield Beach, FL: Health Communications, Inc.

Milkman, H., & Sunderwirth, S. (1982). Addictive processes. *Journal of Psychoactive Drugs,* 14(3):177-191.

Miller, A. (1975). *The Drama of The Gifted Child; The Search for the True Self* (Original Title "Prisoners of Childhood") NY: Basic Books, Inc.

Nar-Anon. Nar-Anon Family Group Headquarters Inc., Palos Verdes Peninsula, CA.

Robinson, B. E. (1989). *Work Addiction: Hidden Legacies of Adult Children.* Deerfield Beach, FL: Health Communications, Inc.

Seixas, J. S. (1979). *Living With A Parent Who Drinks Too Much.* NY: Grenvillow Books.

Wegscheider, S. (1981). *Another Chance: Hope & Health For the Alcoholic Family.* Science & Behavior Books, Inc.

Whitfield, C. L., M.D. (1987). *Healing The Child Within; Discovery & Recovery for Adult Children of Dysfunctional Families.* Enterprise Center, Deerfield Beach, FL: Health Communications, Inc.

Woititz, J. G. (1983). *Adult Children of Alcoholics.* Enterprise Center, Deerfield Beach, FL: Health Communications, Inc.

Part II

How We Do What We Do

CHAPTER 5

TREATMENT AND THERAPY

Phases of assistance for addiction can be divided into Prevention, Intervention, Detoxification, Treatment, and Support for Recovery. The process of change which leads to recovery, usually begins with some sort of crisis. In crisis, the family and substance addict are most vulnerable to intervention. The crisis becomes stabilized by a detoxification attempt. Stabilization of crisis is often confused with crisis resolution, causing many substance addicts to leave detoxification programs without entering treatment programs. Where crisis has been stabilized but not resolved, a second intervention and detoxification are often required. A delicate balance must be maintained to get the client from detox to treatment. Treatment represents a change, an unknown, which is frightening. The crisis is past. A promise that this time will be different seems to be the least painful solution. In my opinion detoxification programs that are housed separately from treatment programs increase the fear of the unknown and discourage treatment attempts, unless treatment facility staff are able to bridge that gap. During detox, the client must be encouraged to maintain an optimistic and realistic viewpoint: There is a problem; it has a solution. The solution is treatment. Treatment is not punishment; treatment is worth the effort.

One might argue that the best system is one in which the detox program is separate but a part of a freestanding addiction treatment center. This reduces red tape for transferring clients from detox to treatment. It permits the client to see what is in store for him/her, reducing the fear of the unknown. It improves continuity for staff, permitting a view of both pre- and post-detox behaviors. It also permits earlier establishment of rapport with the client and the family. And it provides medical competency during the treatment phase, should a client go into "delayed withdrawals."

Many addicted persons do not go through detox programs. They go through withdrawal at home. The person able to withdraw at home is no more or less addicted than the person who goes through a detoxification program. However, self-detoxification can be more dangerous. The majority of persons who experience life-threatening symptoms as a result of withdrawal are relatively few. It depends a great deal on the type of substance abused, length of use, and quantity consumed. But should medical complications occur, it is best to have medical attention in immediate proximity, rather than a phone call (and perhaps a "please hold") away. Severe withdrawal symptoms are usually the result of an abrupt end of substance abuse. In detoxification programs, other drugs are substituted for the drug of choice and then the substituted drug is withdrawn gradually, thus reducing the likelihood of severe withdrawal symptoms. Some home detox programs provide prescription drugs to be administered at home. A family member is usually placed in charge of dispensing the drug. In my opinion this is an extremely dangerous practice and should be done as an exception rather than the rule. First of all, it reinforces the family member's role as caretaker, a role that needs to be abolished. Secondly, it assumes that the user has no supply of the substance of choice hidden in or near the home. Should the user use while the family member is dispensing the detox medication, the client is getting an increased rather than a decreased supply. Persons who have a history of becoming physically abusive, or who use a substance known for inducing violence, should never be detoxed at home. To do so is to risk physical harm to client or to family members, and a potential lawsuit to the facility. So at the very least, allowing a family member to dispense detoxification drugs is counterproductive to therapy; at most, it is provoking a dangerous situation for all parties concerned.

Therapeutic Recreation personnel are primarily employed to assist in the treatment phase. Treatment programs can be found in a wide variety of settings, places, and formats. Some are attached to general and psychiatric hospitals, while others are freestanding. Some are government supported, while others are private (both for-profit and nonprofit). Formats vary from purging and puking to intensive education and psychotherapy. The length of stay ranges from a few days to a year or more. For the purposes of this text, treatment programs that exceed a month are considered "long term."

There are positives and negatives to any length. The longer the person is in treatment, the more help can be provided; the longer the stay, the greater the monetary cost, the greater the risk of institutionalization, and the more difficult the task of community reentry. An employer may be willing to grant a leave of absence for a few days, even weeks, but cannot be expected to hold a job open for several months, or a year. The family is placed on hold, too. The longer the absence the greater the problems of mending family ties. Family members have a great need to get on with their lives. During long-term treatment, the family turns to others to fill the roles once reserved for the client. When the client returns, he/she finds no niche to fill in family functioning, no job, no unbroken ties with his/her former community. In some cases, the client has developed ties to a community so hostile to recovery that the breaking of those ties is advisable. Examples include the client who sells drugs for a living or has a spouse who sells drugs; clients who are addicted to substances known to require extended periods for detoxification and have already broken all ties with the family, may also benefit from long-term treatment. Clients who have gone through short-term treatment programs repeatedly without producing extended periods of sobriety may also benefit from long-term treatment. Heroin addicts, chronic alcoholics, and adolescents are often candidates for long-term treatment.

In the past, most treatment has occurred on an inpatient or residential basis. There are a growing number of outpatient treatment programs. In cases where the family addiction cycle is at the Blow-Out Stage, outpatient treatment can be effective. It avoids the problems caused by taking the client out of the family, job, and community. It also provides here-and-now information to therapists. The client does not have to focus on the problems that occurred before entering treatment, nor guess what problems may await after treatment. Treatment may focus on the problems of the day.

When the family is in the Fireworks Stage, the family needs time apart to help break the unhealthy patterns of inter- action. When all social circles revolve around substance use, time out in a treatment facility can stimulate a break from those circles. It can also signal to the circles that use, that the client is making a change. While many are welcomed home from treatment by a "friend" with the drug of choice in hand, this is more of a test than a failure to understand. The "friend" is saying, "Tell me. Are you still one of us or not?" The client who takes a stand for sobriety by rejecting an opportunity to use, is usually left alone after that. Attending some type of therapy on an outpatient basis does not send as strong a message to friends who are still using.

In conclusion, it seems clear that all forms of treatment, short-term, long-term, inpatient, outpatient, can be beneficial. Naturally, all forms also have inherent limitations. The key is proper placement. The form of treatment must be selected to match the client's needs. Yet in the real world, people who need inpatient treatment get involved in outpatient programs. People who need long-term treatment occupy beds in short- term programs. Some Therapeutic Recreation programs should be designed to compensate for inherent problems of the form selected. Where the client has healthy family and community ties and is in a long-term inpatient program, Therapeutic Recreation services should be provided which will help main- tain those ties. All forms of treatment risk creation of depend- ency on the treatment facility that can lead to institutionaliza- tion. Therapeutic Recreation services must always be de- signed to minimize the formation of dependency.

Attempts to use psychoactive drugs to treat addiction are often unsuccessful. The replacement of alcohol with a medi- cally prescribed depressant may appear to produce short-term benefits, but provides no long-range solutions. A psychiatrist may identify mood swings and prescribe a drug such as lithium. Lithium is known to eliminate the extreme highs and lows in manic-depressive disorders. But lithium may have serious side effects if used in conjunction with alcohol or other drugs. (Just one drink may not cause problems, but who ever heard of an alcoholic drinking just one?) The source of the mood swings must be carefully examined. The person who is too up and then too down for no apparent reason is quite different from the addict who is too up or too down for a reason. The person who is too up when heroin is freely flowing and too down when the supply is exhausted, has good reason to experience mood swings; the heroin must be withdrawn before

any other form of treatment is initiated. Persons with true psychiatric disorders do abuse substances. But the presences of a natural chemical imbalance causing psychiatric symptoms can only be determined after the person is well into the substance abuse recovery process.

There are a growing number of drugs now on the market that are designed to treat specific types of addiction. The oldest, methadone, is a less expensive drug which may be legally substituted for illegal and more expensive opiates such as heroin. Methadone, more addictive than heroin, provides a "maintenance" system. It does not attempt to solve the individual's problem. It allows the addict to be managed in society. A person on methadone has not yet become a function- ing, responsible, contributing part of society; however, the person no longer has a need to commit crimes in order to procure drugs. Methadone users avoid use of contaminated needles. This offers a partial solution for reducing the spread of diseases such as AIDS. Methadone has its place in treat- ment, as a last resort (Nelkin, 1973).

Anabuse is quite different from methadone. Anabuse does not have psychoactive properties. It has physical proper- ties. Anabuse reacts violently when mixed with alcohol. An alcoholic, having taken an anabuse tablet in the morning, has a choice during the day. He/she can abstain, or can risk dying before getting drunk. Mixing alcohol and anabuse can result in death. Anabuse moves the physical pain from the with- drawal phase to the first drink. Knowing this, an individual is less likely to take the first drink. The purpose of anabuse is to buy time, time that is desperately needed to replace unhealthy automatic reactions with healthy reactions. It provides motiva- tion and time to learn how to say "no" to a drink.

However, anabuse has its flaws. The individual's system must be alcohol-free before anabuse can be introduced. It only works if it is taken, and if the person taking it believes it works. Most alcoholics do not learn from vicarious experience. They are not very good at "taking your word for it." Some die trying to find out if anabuse really does work. It can also be used as a solution to the age-old problem, "How can I get these guys off my back so that I can drink in peace?" A false sense of security can be produced in family members. If the family believes the alcoholic is taking anabuse when he is not, they will relax and leave him alone to drink in peace. Anabuse pills can be replaced with other pills, or slipped under the tongue until no one is looking. Nevertheless, for the alcoholic who sincerely desires sobriety, its use is highly beneficial. There are many alcoholics sober today who would not be sober without the use of anabuse.

Naloxone derivatives, such as Trexan, may be used to assist the recovery of heroin addicts. It occupies neuron receptors so that heroin cannot occupy the receptors. Where heroin overdose has occurred, a treatment of naloxone sends the addict into immediate withdrawal, which restores respira- tion. Trexan, provided in daily doses, prevents the addict from feeling the effects of opiate use. It is assumed that the addict will not waste his/her money on drug use if use does not result in getting high. In blocking the internal receptors, naloxone is still manipulating internal chemistry. The receptors are designed to be occupied by endorphins. What happens to the endogenous opiate production systems when receptors remain blocked by foreign chemicals for extended periods? The long-term effects of extended Trexan use have not yet been fully studied. Like anabuse, Trexan is a helpful tool in the recovery process. And like anabuse, it has its flaws. It, too, comes in the form of a tablet, which does not work if it is not taken.

Researchers are now experimenting with dopamine-like and serotonin-like chemical structures that may reduce the person's desire for alcohol consumption. Such substances will be helpful additions to the recovery arsenal. Will they solve all the problems? No. A tablet will never teach an individual how to live or develop healthy interactions with others. This is a poly-drug world. What is to prevent the anabuse user from getting "high" on opiates, or the trexan user from getting drunk? Will the pill that removes the craving for alcohol also take away the need to hide from reality? A common characteristic of adults who were raised in alcoholic homes is that they try to imitate "normal" behavior by guessing what normal is (Woititz, 1983, p. 4). A number of chemicals may be developed to end the craving for substances of abuse, and to block the effects of substances once used. But if only the chemical side of addiction is treated, then we will have millions wandering our streets not using, but guessing about what they should be doing. I once knew a recovering alcoholic who read every research report published on alcoholism, hoping for the day when a pill would allow him to drink "like other people." I asked him how he would feel if drinking a can of beer had the same effect as drinking a soda pop. He found the thought disgusting. He wanted a pill that would allow him to get the buzz without the negative consequences. After that discussion, he quit reading the research. I quit believing a pill could solve the problem. Health is more than the absence of symptoms. Something more must happen so that those afflicted can stop guessing about what is normal, stop needing a chemical high, and start celebrating their own uniqueness.

Regardless of the type of treatment provided, continuous support and reinforcement are required after the treatment phase. Alcoholics Anonymous, (AA), and other twelve-step programs provide the needed support. Narcotics Anonymous (NA) was founded on the same principles, catering to those that consider their primary substance of choice to be a drug other than alcohol. Cocaine Anonymous is, as the title implies, a twelve-step program for cocaine addicts. For family members, support is provided through such organizations as Al-Anon (family and friends of alcoholics) and Nar-Anon (family and friends of drug addicts.) Other substance addicts find support in OA (Over-eaters Anonymous) and Nicoholics Anonymous (for recovering cigarette smokers). Process Addicts have GA (Gamblers Anonymous), and persons with emotional disorders may find support in EA (Emotions Anonymous). All are programs of support, honesty, and encouragement to continue the long process of recovery.

After-care is being provided by an increasing number of treatment facilities. It is recognized that recovery is a very long process. After-care helps the client to make the transition back into the community and family after an inpatient stay. It also reinforces the application of functions learned in treatment to events that occur during the day-to-day routine. An individual's readiness is a key to learning. Many aspects of treatment may be discounted because the client is not ready to understand the value of some aspect. After-care permits the client to review concepts discussed during treatment after discharge, when something happens to create the readiness. Many aspects of leisure education are influenced by readiness. The need for leisure revisions seems a low priority during treatment. Upon discharge, a lack of meaningful leisure activity can take on crisis proportions; suddenly, readiness is created. After-care is the avenue by which to resupply the needed information.

TREATMENT MODALITIES

Many therapies and disciplines have been involved in the treatment of addiction. It is beyond the scope of this text to discuss all of them. Group Therapy and psycho-social counseling are important avenues for recovery. Clients must develop insight into their behaviors. The development of insight does not return a person to social drinker/user status. It provides the individual with choices and options for the development of a meaningful life. A wide variety of counseling approaches exist. The ones I find most in tune with the provision of Therapeutic Recreation services are here-and-now approaches such as Reality Therapy and Gestalt Therapy. The Alcoholics Anonymous approach is also a here-and-now approach. Transactional Analysis also provides insight into the behaviors exhibited in addictive personalities. Assertive Training is a must for anyone working in a therapeutic setting. A working knowledge in Client-Centered Therapy is also a must. Detailed descriptions of these are beyond the scope of this text. Should additional information be desired, the reader may consult the references at the end of this chapter. The texts listed are ones the author has found extremely helpful.

Nursing and medicine always play an important role. Clients have sometimes spent years manipulating their internal mechanisms. By the time the client arrives in treatment, his/her body functions are a network of confusion. A client may look fit, yet be in such bad physical condition that even walking is dangerous to his/her health. Only the medical community has the skill to unravel the internal functions and get the body on a path toward health. Physical appearance does not always tell the whole story.

Education specialists are especially important in the care and treatment of adolescents. Many students have fallen behind their grade level and require special attention to get them back on track. Many have undiagnosed learning disabilities that can be identified by education specialists.

Vocational evaluation and rehabilitation specialists are also important. Feelings of self-sufficiency and self-responsibility are closely tied to occupational pursuits. Some clients have jobs which literally drive them to drinking. Some clients have never found their niche in the workplace and don't know where to begin to look.

Therapeutic Recreation may function as a supportive service to assist other disciplines to accomplish their objectives. Conversely, other disciplines may function as supportive services for accomplishing Therapeutic Recreation's objectives. Full-service Therapeutic Recreation is most likely to be found in facilities where recovery is defined holistically and the facility employs an interdisciplinary approach to treatment. Where recovery is defined as the absence of substance use, Therapeutic Recreation is limited in its effectiveness. The absence of substance use results in existence; the goal of Therapeutic Recreation is to change existence into living.

THERAPEUTIC RECREATION AS A SUPPORT SERVICE

The primary purpose of Therapeutic Recreation is to assist clients in developing substance-free leisure that is meaningful and healthy. To do this, clients must learn skills needed to participate in new activities. They must learn the value of leisure and the role that leisure plays in their life-styles. Clients must also be equipped with leisure retrieval skills (skills, attitudes, and behaviors which permit a client to initiate leisure involvement). Therapeutic Recreation must also provide the client with skills needed to prevent the client from substituting a process addiction for a substance addiction. Finally, Therapeutic Recreation must do all of the above for the client's family members to prevent the extinction of new leisure behaviors after discharge. This is a lot for any one service to do. Yet there is much more that Therapeutic Recreation can and should do. Therapeutic Recreation should also function as a support service for other disciplines.

As a support service, Therapeutic Recreation should support the goals and objectives of other treatment team members and of the center as a whole. Support services for other disciplines' objectives should be designed to function within all Therapeutic Recreation programs and activities. When separate programs are created to meet other disciplines' needs, then time for attainment of leisure objectives becomes diminished. The Therapeutic Recreation Specialist is forced to choose between assisting other disciplines or meeting the client's leisure needs, or attempting to do both, which may result in doing neither very well. When support for nontherapeutic recreation goals is infused into all Therapeutic Recreation programs and activities, the Therapeutic Recreation Specialist may assist other disciplines in achieving their objectives while selecting programs and activities that meet the clients' needs. In this way, the Therapeutic Recreation Specialist is

able to do both at the same time. With this in mind, it should also be pointed out that some support objectives may require separate sessions, such as those found in Chapter 11. But these have a direct impact on the client's ability to be leisurely.

What type of goals and objectives am I talking about? Some of the critical ones include improving a client's understanding of addiction, which goes beyond helping the client understand the linkages between addiction and leisure; assisting in the development of this understanding, which becomes a support service for substance abuse counseling; assisting a client to get in touch with his/her feelings, improve self-esteem, self-identity, ego, which is a support service for psychology. Increasing physical endurance, coordination, agility, and so on, is a support service for physical medicine. Improving family interactions, which go beyond meeting family leisure needs, is a support service for family counseling and/or social work. Activities for ventilation of anger and resentment are support services for counseling. Helping a client become motivated to learn is a support service for educational specialists. Confronting denial is a support service for substance abuse counseling. Helping a client to detach, let go, or live one day at a time is support service for AA/NA and other twelve-step programs. Helping a client stay sober/clean by making changes in leisure is not a support service; this is what Therapeutic Recreation is all about. If Therapeutic Recreation is not aggressively helping clients understand and change leisure behavior, then the Therapeutic Recreation service is not providing Therapeutic Recreation.

Team composition and center-wide goals vary from facility to facility. This makes it impossible to provide an accurate and detailed description of all the functions Therapeutic Recreation might perform as a supportive service. The following provides a general overview of support service function for goals that are typically found in a substance abuse treatment setting.

Detox Support

Most clients are not in the mood to play games (at least recreational games) during detoxification. The detoxification process can be supported through the creation of a compatible environment. As previously mentioned, persons withdrawing from depressants may be assisted by the provision of a calming, soothing environment—plants, aquariums, and artificial waterfalls. (By artificial I mean the type of waterfall where water spills from one small pond or container to another and is then recirculated by a pump. This discharges negative ions from the water, which produces a soothing, calming effect on the brain.) Depressed clients may feel more depressed by a calming environment, so determination of who sits by the waterfall and who doesn't cannot be based strictly on the client's drug of choice.

Therapeutic Recreation can also assist by matching clients with common interests and initiate interaction between the matched clients. This reduces feelings of isolation. Feelings of isolation (at least in rats that have been studied) seems to increase the desire for a drink. Stimulant users may benefit from movement and laughter. However, care must also be taken to prevent clients from overexertion. Precise amounts of exercise should be prescribed by the physician in charge of the client's detoxification program.

Because depressant users and stimulant users may have opposing needs during detoxification, they may aggravate each other if on the same detoxification unit. The client in search of peace and quiet is no match for the client who can't sit still for a second. Removal of stimulant or depressant users from the detox unit for a portion of the day may be the solution. But taking the client off the unit must be handled carefully. Assurances must be made that the client does not have access to any intoxicating substances, a list which may include housekeeping and maintenance supplies. Even more dangerous are potentially poisonous substances, that are not intoxicating, but which the client thinks might be intoxicating.

If processes are used to assist detoxification, then what has been accomplished? Medical detoxification consists of substituting another drug for the client's drug of choice. Gradual withdrawal of the substituted medication then provides a gradual end to intoxication. If a process is used to assist the process, then it too must be gradually withdrawn. If the process is not withdrawn then the client has been given a substitute addiction and may never achieve internal balance. The withdrawal from a process, such as sitting by a waterfall, or exercising, may continue into the treatment phase. But by the time a client is discharged, he/she must be functioning on a balanced schedule.

Support for Physical Restoration

Provision of assistance to the detoxification process, as described above, should be considered part of the support services to the physical restoration process. This category also includes helping a client relax so that he/she can get a good night's sleep without the use of a drink, fix, or pill. Many clients are physically unfit when they enter a treatment facility. Alcohol users tend to lose muscle tone. Stimulant users tend to have good muscle tone but have not been eating regularly. Improving physical fitness, agility, endurance, and coordination can be assisted by Therapeutic Recreation services.

As anyone can attest, trying to "get back in shape" in a short period of time has painful results. Age also plays a big factor. When I was 18, I could skip my exercise for an entire summer and return to my previous level of functioning in a week. I couldn't understand why "warming up" was such a big deal. I couldn't feel any benefit from a bowling game. At 40, it is a different story. If I exercise once a week I lose ground. I have to exercise at least three times a week to make progress. If I miss a week, I lose two months' worth of function, and I can't move without a lengthy warm-up. My annual trip to the bowling alley produces sore muscles. When I was 18, my

muscles got so sore that I could hardly walk, but that didn't stop me. Today if I feel half that sore on my first morning stretch, I don't get out of bed. Trying to get back in shape has become emotionally painful for me. I try not to miss a session because the struggle of getting "it" back is so difficult. The good news is that my precision is better than ever, my endurance is better, and the pleasure derived is far greater than ever before. Based on my personal experience, I would suggest that dealing with the 18-year-old after detox is dealing with the physical condition that existed prior to admission. Dealing with the 40-year-old is dealing with the physical condition that existed at admission plus the dehabilitation that resulted from restricted activity levels during detoxification. If the 40-year-old does not receive regular exercise during treatment, then the prospect of getting back in shape after discharge will be an ordeal both physically and mentally.

Some clients have more severe physical problems. Wounds and nerve damage may have occurred as a result of an accident during intoxication. Often, minor injuries become major because the person has not taken proper care of the problem. Clients who appear fit may have internal problems such as high blood pressure or liver disease. For this reason all aspects of improving physical fitness must be accomplished with care and under the direction of the physician. (I must add that when I was younger, I found the physician's guidelines too conservative. Now, having experienced the stiffening effect of a bowling game, I think he might have been too liberal. It pays not to second guess the physician, unless it is to err on the side of safety.)

Excessive dehabilitation compounded by medical problems may require the expertise of a physical therapist. Exercise programs for mild dehabilitation can be safely provided by Therapeutic Recreation personnel provided that the personnel have been trained in safe body mechanics. Maintenance programs to prevent dehabilitation during treatment can also be provided by Therapeutic Recreation. The restoration of physical fitness is a lengthy process. A short treatment stay may not provide enough time to restore a client to optimal physical functioning. Therapeutic Recreation can provide a starting point and Leisure Education sessions can be used to encourage continuation of physical exercise after discharge.

Psycho-social Support Service

Many clients are admitted deep in denial of their disease. In order to break the denial, all staff, regardless of their discipline, must help the client see through the denial. The Therapeutic Recreator may be attempting to provide a Leisure Education session, a skill development session, or a needs assessment. If the client is in denial, nothing good will come of the session. There are two ways to handle denial. One is through confrontation. The other is through playing along with the client until he/she has enough rope for a self-hanging. Direct confrontation usually results in disruptive behavior. Denial is an ego defense. In my opinion when direct confrontation is used both therapist and client enter into an "I'm OK, you're the one that stinks" dialogue. When the therapist wins, the client's already fragile ego is bruised even more. The client wins by leaving treatment early, or by deciding to play along, agreeing with everything and hearing nothing. Obviously, there may be a softer, easier way. A firm, assertive stance may be appropriate. Follow rules and regulations to the hilt; get the client to agree to disagree. Then give the client ample opportunity to look in the mirror. The self-administered leisure assessment can help the client look in the mirror. As the client speaks, repeat back to the client key phrases that he/she has said which show the denial system in action. Confront by calmly, verbally identifying discrepancies between what the client says and does, what the client says and others see. Allow the client to see him/herself through others' eyes.

Therapeutic Recreation can also assist clients to improve self-esteem and identity. All activities provided should have the power to do this. When a counselor identifies a client who needs to improve self-esteem, then that need can be met through whatever activity the client is scheduled to attend. By using the firm, assertive approach to denial, the therapist has demonstrated respect for the client. It is then much easier to help the client strengthen his/her self-esteem. Participation in leisure will also assist restoration of internal balance. This will also help the client feel better about him/herself.

Ventilation of anger and resentment can be assisted in a variety of ways. Facets of negative emotions tend to lodge in different areas of the brain and body. "Talking it out" is an important step. But talking only relieves the part of the emotion housed in the language portion of the brain. Physical exertion dislodges other portions of the negative emotion. Art and creative processes can dislodge still other portions. When a person needs to vent, the person should be permitted to vent in as many ways as possible. Specific "venting" sessions, such as those mentioned in Chapter 11, should only be scheduled when adequate staff and resources exist within the Therapeutic Recreation service.

Family involvement is another important aspect. Where Therapeutic Recreation services are provide to help the family develop leisure skills, it is not a supportive service. Where Therapeutic Recreation is used to alleviate marital discord, or enhance family communication, it is a supportive therapy and should be guided by Family Counseling Specialists. Recreation events such as a Friday night dance, or a weekend picnic, can do a lot to alleviate marital discord, but one-on-one processing of family problems should be left to family therapists.

Dietary Support

Dietary goals should also be supported in Therapeutic Recreation. While eating is part of leisure, knowledge of what's good to eat and what's not good should be left to the experts. Where Leisure Education sessions teach "wellness" concepts, which include eating habits, the session content about eating should be reviewed by the facility's dietary team. Where clients are on special diets, Therapeutic Recreation should assist the client in sticking with the diet during outings, picnics, and other activities.

Education Support

Many clients in treatment for addiction cannot read. Some cannot read because they were too busy getting drunk or high to pay attention in the classroom. Some cannot read because of undiagnosed learning disabilities. As with physical restoration, learning to read is a lengthy process, one that takes more time than a short treatment stay permits. It is not the job of a Therapeutic Recreation Specialist to teach the three R's. Therapeutic Recreators can help to identify clients who need assistance. They can also help to make learning fun. Becoming motivated to overcome a learning disability or reading problem is half the battle. Leisure Education sessions can be designed to encourage the use of free time to learn how to read after discharge. Where the treatment program is long-term and Educational Specialists are employed, Therapeutic Recreation can provide support for the learning process. The adolescent's classroom assignment can be turned into a game to provide needed repetition of the material in a fun way. Specific content of educational games should be supervised by the Educational Specialist. With coordinated effort, great progress can be made. Therapeutic Recreation services can also support educational programs by encouraging adolescents to complete homework assignments before involvement in Re-Creation sessions. (Recreation Therapy, Leisure Education, and other activities specified as part of the client's "treatment" should not take second place to education. The faster the client receives "treatment," the faster he/she will be able to focus attention on educational tasks. But Re-Creation is something that happens during "free time." For the adolescent, "free time" is the time remaining after the homework is completed.)

SUPPORT SERVICES FOR THERAPEUTIC RECREATION

Other disciplines can be valuable in reinforcing appropriate leisure behaviors. Instilling a change in any type of behavior is a twenty-four hour-a-day job. Other staff may turn to Therapeutic Recreation during a conference with, "He needs something to do." That statement indicates an awareness of the problem. It also indicates a lack of understanding about what to do or how to go about doing it. Educational sessions for staff can provide the needed information about how to help a client find "something to do" without creating client dependence on staff for meeting leisure needs. Many times, "He needs something to do," can be handled immediately by the staff member who identifies the problem. That person can provide the client with a list of available Re-Creation options. If that does not solve the problem, then the staff can encourage the client to participate in Leisure Education sessions.

Staff of other disciplines who have healthy leisure habits should be encouraged to share their health with clients. It is important for the client to see that all people need leisure pursuits. To know that a psychologist is going out to eat with his family after work is helpful. To know that the nurse is going sailing, is also helpful.

There are many jobs in an organization that are difficult to fill. They tend to be aid and assistant positions where the pay is relatively low and the work far from glamorous. Persons who fill such positions are usually not qualified to lead an intensive Recreation Therapy session, or provide an effective Leisure Education session. They are not usually qualified to assess a client's leisure needs. But many do have valuable leisure skills that they can teach to others. Helping with a Re-Creation session can put some life into their jobs and some excitement into Re-Creation sessions. Some personnel who work second and third shift can extend Therapeutic Recreation coverage into the hours when clients need it most. For example, a nursing aide may be a difficult position to fill. If an applicant has a hobby such as aerobic exercise, then he/she may find leading an hour of aerobic exercise as part of the evening work routine very attractive. Therapeutic Recreation personnel can train the nursing aides to provide such activities safely and therapeutically. Such leadership should occur within highly structured guidelines, closely monitored by Therapeutic Recreation specialists. The result is a satisfied employee doing a job notorious for discontent, and provision of a needed Recreation session at a needed time without overstressing the Therapeutic Recreator's work schedule. The more communication that occurs among staff in a facility, the better the quality and quantity of services that can be provided.

INTERFACING WITH 12-STEP PROGRAMS

In writing this segment, I have found a number of excuses to get up from my word processing equipment. I have been told that many perils exist from dissecting and analyzing "the program." While I agree, I also find that any text about Therapeutic Recreation for substance abuse treatment is totally inaccurate if twelve-step program operation is omitted. The following is my opinion and not meant to be a thorough review or an authoritative statement.

Typically, 12-step programs such as Alcoholics Anonymous, Al-Anon, Al-Ateen/Atot, Narcotics Anonymous, Nar-Anon, Cocaine Anonymous, Gamblers Anonymous, Adult Children of Alcoholics, have some common characteristics. The Therapeutic Recreation Specialist should attend open meetings (session open to public attendance) to fully understand the function of twelve-step programs. Most twelve-step programs are based on hope, sharing between members, honesty, 12 ongoing steps to recovery, and 12 traditions that guide

provision of services. Most 12-step programs are based in spiritual principles, with the individual member being charged with the responsibility to define the source of the spiritual power. Twelve-step programs further define day-to-day function for members through slogans and repeated phases such as "Easy does it," "First things first," "One day at a time," "Detach," "Let go and let God," and "Accept what cannot be changed."

Sometimes friction occurs between providers of Therapeutic Recreation services and followers of twelve-step programs. This is unfortunate, for all of the aspects of twelve-step programs are compatible with Therapeutic Recreation. Therapeutic Recreation can be designed to support twelve-step program functions. Where Therapeutic Recreation services are designed to interface with twelve-step programs, the quality of Therapeutic Recreation programming is greatly improved.

The substance abuse population does not learn through ordinary channels. Being told what to do to get well does not cut it. Being shamed into submission does not work either. The population learns through experience, emulation of others, and hope. In twelve-step programs, no one tells anyone what to do. Members recover by being treated in a respectful manner. They learn by comparing their experiences with the experiences of others. They are given hope that recovery is possible. There is a basic "If he can do it, I can do it," atmosphere. The Therapeutic Recreation service "delivery system" is improved when these practices are duplicated.

Therapeutic Recreation personnel must model leisure behaviors both on and off the job. Nothing breaks rapport with a client faster than to see a staff member preach the value of leisure while in a state of over-work fatigue. Nothing does more harm than a staff member's insistence that a natural high is best, while the staff member attempts to survive a morning hangover or watches the clock in anxious anticipation of happy hour time. Each member of the Therapeutic Recreation staff is a model of meaningful leisure. (If you have not got it, you can't give it away.)

Treating the client as an equal member of the treatment team is very important. Permitting self-assessment is advised. Recognizing the client's integrity and intelligence is critical. Whenever a client is found to have leisure skills, he/she should be employed to teach or share his/her skills with other clients. Demonstration and simulation should be utilized instead of lecture, pen, and paper activities wherever possible. When lecture must occur, having the materials presented by a discharged client or member of a twelve-step program is preferable. If this is not possible, then lecture should be kept to a minimum followed by participant discussion. The answer given is seldom as effective as the answer discovered.

Care must be taken in the provision of Leisure Education and Leisure Discharge Planning sessions. Methods that ask the client to project what he/she plans to do after discharge, are in conflict with the "one day at a time" philosophy. Twelve-step programs support a here-and-now approach to life. Leisure Educators who ask clients to delve into past leisure experiences or project future leisure needs invariably are confronted by a client who refuses to participate on the basis that such activity is in conflict with his/her "program." Nine times out of 10, the client who takes this stand is using the twelve-step program as an excuse to avoid participation. This is most frustrating for the Therapeutic Recreation specialist because he/she knows the client needs the session content and also knows the client is right. To avoid the setup, most Leisure Education sessions can be formatted into here-and-now approaches to the content. In this way, twelve-step programs are supported and reinforced, the client loses a potential excuse to participate, and the quality of the Leisure Education session is greatly improved. For example, "What did you do for leisure before admission?" can be rephrased to "What did you do for leisure today?" Before admission, the client may have used alcohol or drugs for leisure. If the point is to help the client see the leisure addiction connection, then it's OK to ask the question of leisure prior to admission. But if the goal is to improve leisure functioning, then it is better to ask the question in the here and now. What did you do today? This is a question that can be dealt with. The client who did not have time for leisure pursuit because of an overcrowded therapy schedule, will not have time for leisure after discharge when work is substituted for therapy. Learning to find leisure within twenty-four hours is the most significant leisure skill that can be taught. "How do you balance your life?" Wow! If a client is twenty, that question asks for a brief report of balance encompassing 7,300 days of living. (If the client is forty years old, that's 14,600 days of life.) Is it any wonder why responses seem vague or too general to be useful? On the other hand, "How did you balance your life today?" That is a question that is highly specific. A client can respond, learn and improve. Improvement can be measured by how the client balances the next twenty-four hours.

Not all past and future projections can be omitted from the leisure education process. For adult children, dealing with childhood learning about leisure is important because it impacts how the adult interacts with free time in the here and now. Such sessions should be prefaced with statement about why the here and now is being temporarily discarded. Sessions dealing with leisure planning for post-discharge use are also important. It is also important to realize that no one really knows what the needs of tomorrow will be until tomorrow comes. It is wiser to plan future "options." Creating an option for the future does not mean a person has to do that thing. It means that the person is prepared to do when the time is right. "What are you going to do when you leave here?" Answer: "I don't know." "What are your options for when you leave here?" The answer to this question can be fully developed. Also, the process of planning for future options should include a doing in the here and now. If a desired option is to learn to paint, then the client should determine if a step can be taken today toward learning to paint. If something can be done today, then it should be done. If nothing can be done, then the option is set aside for another day. In these ways, Leisure Education and Discharge Planning become highly effective and supportive of twelve-step program function.

In general, Leisure Education seeks to analyze rather than accept leisure behavior. The process of intellectualization of twelve-step program functions have led to relapses. Twelve-

step programs suggest that it is not as important to understand why something works. It is only important that it works and that doing makes it work. Leisure Education tends to dissect and analyze leisure. If a client is to make leisure work for him/her, then it seems necessary to understand why it works. But overanalysis is dangerous; understanding must accompany doing. If I spend the entire day learning that exercise will improve my life, then I have not improved my life, only my understanding. For my life to improve, I must put my improved understanding into action. For this reason, I believe that Leisure Education alone should not be considered the solution for leisure dysfunction. Leisure Education is only a step toward leisure improvement. Participation in leisure is the solution to leisure dysfunction. Furthermore, the person who participates in a healthy leisure, does not need Leisure Education. It is not necessary to understand why leisure works, if the person is busy making leisure work.

Twelve-step programs and Therapeutic Recreation can interface with the use of slogans and symbols. In my opinion the posting of "Easy Does It" on a Therapeutic Recreation wall helps to reinforce the concept. Development of Therapeutic Recreation slogans and posting them throughout the facility is also helpful. "Living or Existing? Make a Difference," would be a good one to support Therapeutic Recreation function. Posting symbols of balance would also be helpful. Creative art sessions in which slogans are made into art project would be an excellent interface of Therapeutic Recreation and twelve-step programs. Creating art projects with the numbers 1 through 12, helps to remind clients of the 12 steps and 12 traditions. Any activity or display should be broken into 12 segments whenever possible. A pizza or cake should be sliced into 12 pieces. An exercise course should have 12 stations. A board game with 12 squares is better than a board game with any other number of squares. A bulletin board divided into 12 segments is also better.

When members of Alcoholics Anonymous achieve a designated length of sobriety, the accomplishment is often recognized by giving the person a "chip." The chip, resembling a poker chip, is often color-coded. The color coding system symbolizes stages of recovery with white representing beginning, yellow suggesting proceed with caution, red representing danger, green indicating growth, and blue representing spiritual achievement. If color coding were used in Therapeutic Recreation services to indicate levels of achievement or degrees of difficulty, the colors used could be selected to match the colors of progression used in the chip system. A year of sobriety is often recognized by a "birthday party." The concept that life begins with the first day of sobriety can also be therapeutically reinforced through Therapeutic Recreation. Clients who grumble that they have never done a leisure activity before can be met with the idea that they have never lived before their sobriety date. New ways for new days is a logical selection.

Application of slogan content may be improved through participation in Therapeutic Recreation services. The client who cheats during a game may be confronted with, "This is an honest program." The client who turns play into serious business may be reminded that, "Easy does it." The client who demands instant activity too grandiose to be provided, or demands perfection beyond the scope of possibility, may be cautions to "Accept the things you cannot change." The client who is ready to play but has not gathered the needed equipment may be reminded, "First things first." The client who desires to be a great musician but avoids taking music lessons should be reminded, "First things first." "First things first" deals with the establishment of realistic priorities. Leisure Education, Leisure Discharge Planning options, should always be reviewed for priorities. Small steps come before big ones. Therapeutic Recreation Specialists must always remind themselves of the "first things first" priorities. Though leisure may be the highest priority in my life, it should not be the client's highest priority. Staying clean and sober is priority number one for the client. Healthy leisure supports sobriety, but leisure pursuit cannot take first place in the client's life or process addiction is soon to follow. Participation in twelve-step programs is a priority of the first kind. Therapeutic Recreation schedules should not compete with twelve-step meeting schedules.

The Twelve Traditions govern the way twelve-step programs operate. The traditions insist on a voluntary, nonprofessional approach to provision of services. In this way Therapeutic Recreation will always differ, for we strive to be a profession well-paid for services provided. The Twelve Traditions demand separation, declining support from outside sources. This is another area in which Therapeutic Recreation differs from twelve-step programs. While one may see the value of autonomy and agree that Therapeutic Recreation would be far better off if we followed AA's Fourth, Fifth, Six, Seventh, Tenth, and Eleventh Traditions, we simply have come too far to turn back now. The Twelfth Tradition demands that members remain anonymous when dealing with the public. Again, Therapeutic Recreation differs. We are free and are often encouraged to splash our names across the headlines in order to create awareness of Therapeutic Recreation's plight. But the purpose of anonymity as indicated in the original printing of the Twelfth Tradition was a principle of "immense spiritual significance" (AA, p. 568). It is believed that anonymity reminds members "to place principles before personalities" (AA, p. 564). Though Therapeutic Recreation Specialists do not maintain anonymity, we can support the Twelfth Tradition by placing principles before personalities in all our affairs. Therapeutic Recreation personnel must also closely review the traditions and be very careful not to breach them. Twelve-step program members' anonymity should not be broken by a careless slip of a TR's tongue. Twelve-step groups' autonomy should be recognized and supported. Donations of Therapeutic Recreation facilities and supplies should not be made in a way that breaches the groups' autonomy or traditions. (Facilities and equipment can be rented for the exorbitant fee of $1 per year, but not given free of charge. The $1 rental charge is a way of saying that there are no strings attached.) There should be no attempts by Therapeutic Recreation personnel to "infiltrate" a 12-step group, for the purpose of promoting Therapeutic Recreation, gathering volunteers, and so on. Where a member of a 12-step program wishes to volunteer, his/her services should be welcomed. But there is a big difference between accepting assistance from individual members and recruiting group involvement.

The Eleventh Tradition requires members to increase membership through attraction rather than promotion. This is a principle which Therapeutic Recreation would be wise to adopt. Promotion is an attempt to sell leisure to others. Creating an atmosphere so leisurely that it attracts those in need of our service is far more contagious.

Twelve-step programs have developed a format for provision of services that would be wise for Therapeutic Recreation Services to adopt. Many facilities operate with ongoing groups. This means that clients are admitted on different days, enter programs at different times, and are discharged at different times. This creates a steady flow of new clients into therapy sessions. Development of trust, continuity, and open interactions within an ongoing group can be difficult. Twelve-step programs have been operating ongoing groups for years. The newcomer sits down next to the person with 30 years of sobriety/clean time and both come away with their cups filled. The meeting format permits both new initiates and "old timers" to benefit. Meetings open with an introduction that provides a brief statement of purpose, and a review of the Twelve Steps and Twelve Traditions. This orients the newcomer and provides a reminder for those who have heard it before. The introduction is followed by a discussion or sharing of a members' experiences. This provides the new information for those who have attended enough to be familiar with the information contained in the introduction. Those who are new to the group are expected to assume a follower role. Those who have progressed into the program are expected to participate. Those who have an extended period of participation are expected to lead the meetings. In Therapeutic Recreation services, ongoing groups can be handled in the same way. A brief introduction to leisure philosophy can be provided at the beginning of each session to help orient new admissions. Clients reaching the midpoint of treatment should be expected to participate in discussions and activities. Clients preparing for discharge should be expected to lead and teach others what they have learned from the involvement.

The most difficult aspect to analyze is the 12 steps that form the backbone of the recovery process. Again, the intent is not to explain how or why they work, but to show how Therapeutic Recreation services can support them. It is strongly recommended that all Therapeutic Recreation personnel review Chapter 5, "How it Works," of the Alcoholics Anonymous *Big Book* as well as information about the 12 steps as used in other 12-step programs. The First Step has three words in it that Therapeutic Recreation can help the client investigate. The words, "admitted," "powerless," and "unmanageable," require individual definition. To admit to anything requires honest communication with self and others. It also requires development of trust and courage. Thus any activity or process provided by Therapeutic Recreation that helps the client to develop a realistic view of his/her behavior, helps the client share personal feelings with others, supports the first step. Any activity that assists the client in breaking from denial also supports the first step. Clients with difficulty following rules and procedures often display aspects of "powerlessness" and unmanageable living. Helping the client to identify these and discuss the feelings associated with the words is most helpful. The Second Step involves turning personal will over to an intangible force. The Third Step deals with aspects of control and trust. The Client's awareness of control needs can be heightened by looking at who sets the rules during a game. The Fourth Step requires self-evaluation. Leisure Education sessions that help the client identify personal leisure needs, also equip the client with skills needed to perform a fourth step inventory. The Fifth Step requires the client to share results of self-evaluation with others. To do this the client must develop trust in self and others. He/she must also develop skills in communication of feelings. Sharing the results of leisure self-assessment is a way of practicing for the Fifth Step. The Sixth Step requires that the person become willing to be healed. Lingering illness may have some benefits. Health must be deemed more valuable before a person is willing to give up unhealthy ways. Participation in meaningful leisure can make health more rewarding, more valuable, making it easier to become willing to give up dis-ease. The Seventh Step involves asking the higher power to remove shortcomings. A Therapeutic Recreator is not a god. But practice at asking for what a person really wants can be achieved through Therapeutic Recreation involvement. The Eighth Step requires a person to make a list of persons harmed and become willing to set things straight. Therapeutic Recreation can provide here-and-now practice for this step. When a mistake occurs, it should be accepted and corrected. Excuses for inappropriate behavior or for failure should never be accepted. Therapeutic Recreation staff can model this type of behavior as well as expecting it from the clientele. The Ninth and Tenth Steps deal with actually doing the Eighth Step. The Eleventh Step requires the person to pray and meditate. How can a person become quiet enough to do either if his/her fear of free time keeps the person constantly on the move. An effective Leisure Education program that teaches the client that it is OK to relax and do nothing once in a while also equips the client with the skills needed to do this important Eleventh Step. The Twelfth Step asks the person to share his/her recovery with others and continue to recover. Again by assisting clients to interact with each other, and by helping the client to develop healthy leisure habits, the stage is being set for the Twelfth Step.

Where there is adequate staffing and financial resources for Therapeutic Recreation, specific programs can be designed to support twelve-step program objectives. But again, these should not be instituted if it means curtailment of programming that assists clients in the development of meaningful leisure. Creative art projects can be designed to help the client deal with meanings of words such as "powerless" and a power greater than the self which is part of the second step. Games can be created as well. Adventure/challenge courses can also be used to help clients define the terms used in the Twelve Steps in meaningful ways. Aspects of power, control, honesty, and trust come into play when a client reaches the point of a challenge exercise where he/she cannot succeed alone. In these and many other ways, Therapeutic Recreation can interface and become supportive of 12-step programs.

References/Resources

Alberti, R. E., & Emmons, M. (1978). *Your Perfect Right.* CA: Impact Publications.

Alcoholics Anonymous (The Big Book). (1976). Alcoholics Anonymous World Services, Inc., Grand Central Station, New York, NY.

Atwater, E. (1981). *I Hear You: How to Use Listening Skills For Profit.* Englewood Cliffs, NJ: Prentice-Hall.

Axline, V. (1964). *M. Dibs: In Search of Self.* Reading, MA: Houghton Mifflin.

Berne, E. (1982). *Games People Play.* NY: Ballantine Books.

Berne, E. (1961). *Transactional Analysis in Psychotherapy.* NY: Ballantine Books.

Berne, E. *A Layman's Guide to Psychotherapy & Psychoanalysis.* NY: Ballantine Books.

Dyer, W. (1977). *Team Building: Issues & Alternatives.* Reading, MA: Addison Wesley Publishing Co.

Fast, J. (1970). *Body Language.* NY: Pocket Books Co.

Faulkner, R. W. (1988). *Therapeutic Recreation In Health Care Settings: A Practitioner's Viewpoint.* Seaside, OR: Leisure Enrichment Service.

Feder, B., & Ronali, R. (Ed.). (1980). *Beyond The Hotseat: Gestalt Approaches to Group.* NY: Brunner Mazel.

Friedman, A. S., & Beschner, G. M. (Ed.). (1987). *Treatment Services for Adolescent Substance Abusers.* National Institute on Drug Abuse, Rockville, MD, U. S. Dept. of Health & Human Services, Alcohol, Drug Abuse & Mental Health Administration. (DHHS Publication No. (ADM)87-1342.)

Frykman, J. H. (1972). *A New Connection: An Approach to Persons Involved in Compulsive Drug Use.* San Francisco, CA: The Scrimshaw Press.

Galassi, M. D. & Gallasi, J. P. (1977). *Assert Yourself: How To Be Your Own Person.* NY: Human Science Press.

Gendlin, E. T. (1978). *Focusing.* NY: Bantam Books.

Glasser, W. (1975). *Reality Therapy: A New Approach To Psychiatry.* NY: Harper & Row.

Grant, P. H. (1978). *Holistic Therapy: The Risk & Payoffs of Being Alive.* NJ: Citadel Press.

Gunn, S. L. (1975). Leisure counseling: Analysis of play behavior & attitudes using TA & gestalt awareness. *Expanding Horizons III,* University of Illinois.

Gunn, S. L. (1976). Leisure counseling: Using techniques of assertive training and values clarification. *Expanding Horizons IV,* University of Illinois.

Kelly, C. (1979). *Assertion Training: A Facilitator's Guide.* CA: University Association.

Kid, J. R. (1977). *How Adults Learn.* NY: Association Press.

Knowles, M., & Knowles, H. (1973). *Introduction to Group Dynamics.* Association Press.

Larsen, E. (1985). *Stage II Recovery; Life Beyond Addiction.* San Francisco, CA: Harper & Row.

Maxwell, M. A. (1984). *The Alcoholics Anonymous Experience: A Close Up View For Professionals.* NY: McGraw-Hill.

Narcotics Anonymous. (1982). Narcotics Anonymous World Service Office, Inc., Sun Valley, CA: C.A.R.E.N.A. Publishing Co.

Newton, M. *Gone Way Down: Teenage Drug-Use Is A Disease.* Tampa, FL: American Studies Press. (Makes the point that there is no such thing as "drug abuse." There is only drug use and self abuse.)

Nelkin, D. (1973). *Methadone Maintenance: A Technological Fix, George Braziller.* NY.

Nierenberg, G., & Calero, H. (1981). *How to Read a Person Like a Book.* NY: Cornerstone Library.

O'Morrow, G. (1974). Team practice and the therapeutic recreation specialist. *Expanding Horizons II.* University of Illinois.

Perls, F. S. (1969). *Gestalt Therapy Verbatim.* Moab, UT: Real People Press.

Rosenblatt, D. (1975). *Opening Doors: What Happens in Gestalt Therapy.* NY: Harper & Row.

Schaef, A. W., & Fassel, D. (1988). *The Addictive Organization.* San Francisco, CA: Harper & Row.

Seabury, D. (1974). *The Art Of Selfishness.* NY: Pocket Books. (Non CD Specific.)

Tuchfeld, B. S. (1983, Summer). Social involvement and the resolution of alcoholism. *Journal of Drug Issues.*

Woititz, J. G. (1983). *Adult Children of Alcoholics.* Deerfield Beach, FL: Health Communications, Inc.

Wooden, H. (1976). The use of relaxation training & biofeedback as an adjunct to TR. *Expanding Horizons IV.* University of Illinois.

Wubbolding, R. E. (1988). *Using Reality Therapy.* NY: Harper & Row.

CHAPTER 6

TNT-A MODEL CENTER

Therapeutic Recreation exists within health care systems. Therefore, it may be necessary to create a framework before appropriate Therapeutic Recreation experiences can be discussed. This chapter provides a framework for discussion by briefly describing the TNT Addiction Center, its structure, and its Therapeutic Recreation System (See p. 103). The Center is fictitious. It can be assumed that standard operating procedures are employed for any function not mentioned. Since the TNT Addiction Center lives only in the heart of a recreator, all aspects of the center are developed in favor of providing maximum benefit to the recovery process, and maximum benefit to provision of Therapeutic Recreation services. In the real world, many policies and procedures are developed to assure survival of the organization, such as third-party reimbursement practices. Such differences must be remembered when attempting to incorporate aspects discussed in this book into a program that exists in the real world. In addition to the following narrative, job descriptions, schedules, and other specifics are located in the appendix.

The TNT Addiction Center is a 100-bed, private for-profit, specialty hospital. It exclusively serves alcohol and drug-addicted individuals. TNT has a 12-bed Detoxification Unit, a 44-four bed Inpatient Adolescent Treatment Unit, and a 44-bed Inpatient Adult Treatment Unit. There is also a Transition Center. The transition center is similar to a motel, providing a place for family members to stay when needed. Some clients stay at the transition center after discharge from inpatient treatment. The TNT Center also provides outpatient treatment services and after-care programs. Both voluntary admissions and involuntary commitments are accepted.

The length of stay is flexible. Duration of treatment is highly dependent on the type of drugs used and the availability of healthy family/community support. Most clients complete the detox program in 3 to 10 days. The inpatient program usually takes an adult six weeks to complete, and an adolescent twelve weeks to complete. (Adolescents spend half of their time in a school program.)

AA/NA principles are merged with the treatment program. Persons are required to complete AA/NA Steps One through Five before discharge from the inpatient program. Many privileges are restricted until the client completes Step One, which involves breaking down the denial. Family member contact outside of sessions, is not permitted until after this initial stage of treatment has been completed. Persons will not be discharged for failing to admit they are addicted. Instead

they can be held on restricted status indefinitely or until they do admit they have a "problem." After completion of the first step, treatment is terminated for persons who do not show significant progress on a weekly basis. Persons having completed the inpatient program attend after-care for one year. Relapses are handled on an individualized basis. Detox services are usually provided. Readmission to inpatient treatment is a team decision. Alternatives to inpatient readmission are usually found and often employ the use of out-patient treatment or the transition center. Involuntary commitments are only accepted for first admissions.

The treatment team consists of personnel who have been specially trained in addictions treatment. Being a qualified nurse, doctor, psychologist, Therapeutic Recreation Specialist, is not enough. Each must also be a certified alcoholism counselor or the equivalent. This provides common ground for communication as well as a united direction for treatment.

Several teams operate to provide needed services. As a Therapeutic Recreation Specialist, I am not qualified to address the specifics of other professionals which comprise a team. Therefore, I will use terms such as "counseling," to imply a general field of expertise. The "counseling" function may be provided by an alcoholism counselor, a group therapist, a family therapist, a psychologist, a social worker, a gestalt therapist, a psycho-social nurse, a reality therapist, and so on. This is not to suggest that one is automatically better or worse than the other. The point is to indicate that other valuable services are being provided along with Therapeutic Recreation. The same is true with any reference I might make to "medical" or "nursing." These functions may be provided by a nurse, a doctor, a nurse practitioner, a physician's assistant, and so on. I am not qualified to say which is most appropriate, only that Therapeutic Recreators are not trained to handle these functions.

At the TNT Center all functions are handled through interdisciplinary team action. The Intervention Team includes education and counseling specialists who are skilled in communication with family members, employers, and intoxicated individuals. The Detox Team consists of medical personnel. The Treatment Team consists of medical, counseling, and Therapeutic Recreation staff. The Recovery Team consists of education specialists, work rehabilitation specialists, leisure specialists, occupational therapists, physical therapists, and many others. The recovery team staffing is primarily provided through contracted services. Most of the recovery team staff are not directly employed by the TNT Center. They are employed in other facilities and in the private sector. They are called in on a case when needed. This permits a highly individualized approach to each client's specific needs. The client with a good job never sees a work rehabilitation specialist; the client without a job may spend hours with work rehabilitation specialists. The client with a physical disability may spend hours receiving therapy at the nearest physical rehabilitation center. The client who cannot read will spend hours in a school classroom. The amount of "recovery" services provided on the grounds of TNT depends on the average number of admissions which require the specific service. Wherever possible, recovery team services are provided off-campus. This permits continuation of the recovery service after the client is discharged from TNT. In many cases, those services listed as recovery service require far more time to achieve maximum benefits than the inpatient treatment stay allows.

All teams function in all aspects of TNT Center services. The treatment team and the recovery team may be operational even during detox or intervention. The intervention team may be called in during after-care. Prior to admission, the prospective client is managed by the intervention team. Other teams function prior to the client's admission when requested by the intervention team. Upon admission, the client's program is directed by the detox team. Other teams function by the request of the detox team. The treatment team begins functioning with the client as soon as the detox team determines the client to be medically stable. The therapy team may call in some recovery team services as soon as initial evaluations are completed. Most of the time, clients require time in therapy before participation in non-physical recovery services can be productive. The treatment team functions during inpatient treatment, outpatient treatment, and after-care.

At TNT, there is no family treatment team. Family members receive services from the same teams that provide services to the clients. Provision of family services is important, and listed in each staff's job description. Upon entry to treatment, there is usually total blockage of communication between family members and client. To break the provision of services into separate staff and teams only creates more distance and miscommunication.

I remember one client I had in group therapy. For weeks he railed about his mean wife. From the client's sharing, my mind created this picture of a 300-pound cave woman who slept with a club in hand. From his sharing of events, the object of treatment seemed to be to equip the client with survival skills. All attempts to assist seemed to be at an impass. Family services were handled by a separate division in the facility. It was three weeks before I accidentally met this cave woman who turned out to weigh about 93 pounds, and wouldn't know what to do with a club if you gave her one. I had been sucked into the client's denial system and his need to blame the problem on something outside of himself. Effective therapy did not begin until the session after the group and I had met the big-little Mrs.

The TNT Center organization places equal emphasis on quality care and cost-effective operations. Efficient operation is always a prime concern. An item with a $10 price tag is only purchased when it is proven to do a better job than a similar item with a $5 price tag. To conserve on costs, the Center employs highly qualified staff. Quality/ongoing staff education is emphasized. There is nothing more expensive than employing a person who does not know what he or she is supposed to be doing. Administrative costs are reduced through the reduction of administrative and secretarial positions. Management and secretarial tasks are combined with front line tasks. Organizational decisions are made at the lowest possible level. A matrix system of organization is used. Computers are utilized by everyone. The facility design cuts wasted steps wherever possible. Employees are trusted. People are only hired because they are needed. Once hired they are valued for what they contribute.

COMPUTERIZED OPERATIONS

TNT's fully-automated and computerized system is the key to efficiency. All routine communications and operations are handled by computer. This includes recording, reporting, scheduling, admitting, treatment planning, monitoring, coordinating, discharging, as well as supply replacement, budgeting, payroll, and so on. Computers are programmed to recognize and identify individuals by their fingerprints. Employees check in and out of the workplace by touching a fingerprint sensor. The computer records the time of arrival and exit, determines the number of hours worked for each employee and deposits pay into the employee's bank account accordingly.

The Therapeutic Recreation service depends on the computer to document all aspects of client involvement. This begins with referral of the client to the service. The Therapeutic Recreation Assessment may be entered into the computer by the client, or the client may use a pencil and paper format, if desired. Either way, the results are entered into the computer as a file is created for the client. The treatment plan is typed into the client's computer file. Then the Therapeutic Recreation Specialist uses the computer to match Therapeutic Recreation programs which are available to the objectives listed on the client's treatment plan. When activities are selected to meet the needs, the client agrees with the plan, and all is in order, the Therapeutic Recreation Specialist has the computer print out a copy of the client's schedule. The schedule is given to the client. The computer automatically enters the client's name onto the attendance list of each assigned activity. The individualized program of care is developed, documented, and put into action within minutes.

Client attendance in activities is also tabulated by the computer. The person in charge of the activity enters the code for the activity, then each person in attendance touches the fingerprint sensor. After the activity, the activity leader enters comments about the client's response, progress, identified needs, and so on. When it is time for a progress review, or a discharge summary, the Therapeutic Recreation Specialist sits down at the computer and reviews the client's activity. Since treatment plans are also filed by computer, the Therapeutic Recreation Specialist uses the computer to compare a client's attendance record with the treatment plan and to determine whether the client's plan is being implemented, and whether appropriate results are being obtained.

Computerized data reflects quality as well as quantity. Educational sessions are followed by computer programs that test the individual's knowledge. Such scores are automatically filed and waiting for review. Unusually low or high scores are automatically brought to the attention of the appropriate person(s).

Coding of descriptive information provides data about anything that can be heard, seen, or touched. Coding permits quicker filing of information than can be done by using pen and paper. It also permits rapid summarization of data after they are filed. Collection of data for monthly reports, employee evaluation, program evaluation, quality assurance, is no longer a chase through reams of paper found in countless offices. It's simply a matter of pushing the right buttons.

Quality assurance is carefully monitored by the computerized system. The TRI system is used, which is discussed in the next chapter. The TRI addresses 10 areas at the time of assessment. Scores obtained from each area are automatically weighted and tabulated by the computer. The sum of the 10 areas provides a number used in quality assurance evaluations. The computer automatically averages the scores for clients at time of admission and again at time of discharge. The difference between the admission and discharge scores is used to establish an overall rating of quality for Therapeutic Recreation services. Once per month, the Therapeutic Recreation Team Manager, reviews a random sample of cases who made greater gains (according to the numbers) and reviews a random sample of cases making smaller gains than the average. Occasionally this review results in identification of patterns. Clients receiving one particular activity may appear to make greater gains than clients not receiving that activity. When this is noticed, studies using control groups are developed to see if the activity in question is actually doing something significant. Differences may also be noted when clients receive the same activity but from different leaders. In this case, co-leading is provided between the leaders to standardize the presentation of the session. The TRI scores at discharge are also compared to statistics about lengths of sobriety, which are gathered after discharge. This also gives important information about which programs are more helpful than others. (See Figure 6.1 following page)

In addition to the monitoring of the TRI numbers for general quality assurance, the computer helps in ongoing program evaluation. Leisure Education sessions are meant to develop client awareness of leisure needs. Routinely, clients are tested to see what is known about leisure prior to involvement in Leisure Education, and retested after involvement. This helps identify the Leisure Education sessions that are most helpful. Skill Development evaluation is handled the same way. Clients are tested to see how many leisure skills they know before involvement in Skill Development sessions and how many after. Then clients are contacted after discharge to see how many of the skills learned are being put to use. Re-Creation sessions are the easiest to evaluate. Since the purpose of a Re-Creation session is to have a good time, and since attendance is voluntary, the number of persons participating at the end of the session (not the beginning) is tabulated. These numbers are translated into percentages by the computer. The Therapeutic Recreation Team Manager monitors the percentage of clients attending the sessions who were available to attend. Occasionally the percentage attending with interests in that area is computed. Clients are also asked to rate the Re-Creation sessions on a "What would you rather do, this or this" type scale. Therapeutic Recreation Specialists usually conduct and monitor these types of program evaluations. They find such evaluations provide needed feedback about what they are doing.

The fingerprint system also provides controlled access to sensitive information and to restricted areas. A fingerprint is required to access computerized information. Each fingerprint is assigned a level of clearance. For example, the fingerprint of a client may permit access to review but not change his/her treatment plan and attendance record, but the client could not access a friend's records. A Therapeutic Recreation Specialist could access specific information about assigned clients but not unassigned clients. Any employee could access and review, but not change, his/her own payroll records. Only payroll employees can change these records. Locked doors are unlocked by an approved fingerprint. The identity of a person entering a restricted area and time of entering are automatically recorded. Such a system would be highly beneficial to Therapeutic Recreation. Consider a room filled with exercise equipment. Entry by a client is permitted at the touch of his finger, but the touch could also trigger a video camera surveillance system. A touch of the finger could permit usage of equipment for clients classified as physically independent. The touch of a client who has medical precautions, on something such as an exercise bike, would cause the bike to shut down after a designated number of minutes of use. Disappearance of equipment is matched to persons entering the area prior to the disappearance. Once clients or employees are discharged from the facility, their fingerprints are removed from the computer files, barring back-door access to the Center.

In the world of paper, it is difficult for a Therapeutic Recreation Specialist to evaluate and develop treatment plans for 20 clients. By permitting capable clients to access themselves, using interactive computer assessments, and by processing the resulting information by computer, a Therapeutic Recreation Specialist can easily handle over 40 clients with greatly improved quality. With 40 clients, and computer assistance, the Therapeutic Recreation Specialist still has time to implement the plans, something which is difficult to do for 20 without the computer's assistance.

The original version of this text was written in 1986. At that time this vision of computerized operation seemed like a fantasy that would take centuries to reach the practical world. Three years later, all the technology exists in the here and now. The hospital without a computer is becoming the exception rather than the rule. The use of computers to control access and to turn equipment on and off is available, although the price tag

FIGURE 6.1

MONITORING Q.A. WITH TRI SCORES FOR SUBSTANCE ABUSE SCALE (TOTAL POSSIBLE POINTS = 100)			
TIME PERIOD	*# RECORDS EXAMINED*	*AVERAGE TRI SCORE ADMISSION/DISCHARGE*	*GAIN/LOSS DURING TX.*
SPRING 1989	50	44.6	68.9	+ 24.3
SUMMER 1989	50	52.1	79.4	+ 27.3
FALL 1989	50	74.2	91.6	+ 17.4
WINTER 1989	50	30.5	48.8	+ 18.3
TIME PERIOD	*# RECORDS EXAMINED*	*AVERAGE TRI SCORE DISCHARGE/6 MO. POST*	*GAIN/LOSS 6 MO. POST DC*
FALL 1989	50	68.9	78.9	+ 10.0
WINTER 1989	50	79.4	94.5	+ 15.1
SPRING 1990	50	91.6	94.2	+ 2.6
SUMMER 1990	50	48.8	45.1	- 3.7

CONCLUSIONS:
1) Leisure Independence Levels, as measured by TRI, at time of admission fluctuate, showing seasonal trends.
2) Largest gains indicating greatest benefit from inpatient TR Services, appear to be those admitted at the dependent level, as measured by TRI.
3) Clients discharged at the semi-independent and independent levels, appear to continue to make gains after discharge, as measured by TRI.
4) Clients discharged at the dependent level do not appear to progress after discharge.

RECOMMENDATIONS:
1) Maintain present TR programming for clients admitted with TRI score greater than 40.
2) Review needs of clients admitted with TRI score 39 or less, to determine if new inpatient programming can be developed for this group.
3) Automatically refer all clients with discharge TRI score of 50 or less to Outpatient Therapeutic Recreation Services.

for full-scale implementation is still too high. (Spending over a $1000 to secure something that has a $100 value is what is meant by "too high.") However, the costs of computerization continues to drop while the cost of other types of equipment increases, so the day may come when computerized security exists in hospitals. Great advances have been made in computerized assessment for Therapeutic Recreation. Still in the experimental stage, some programs permit the clients to assess their own leisure interests. Other programs, such as the TRI, permit the Therapeutic Recreation Specialist to load assessment data, write treatment plans, give clients schedules, monitor quality assurance data and perform other management functions. None of the systems are fully automated at this time. The recent developments in laptop computers means that a computer can go anywhere. The Therapeutic Recreation Specialist can now input and retrieve data at poolside, on the ball field, or on a hike, as well as in the office. New technological designs permitting mainframe-like computers to interact with desktop computers further increase the options and possibilities for efficiency and convenience.

There are still many of us with an aversion to computer dependence. Computers can generate fear of the unknown and feelings that we might be replaced by them completely. The younger work force has grown up with a healthy diet of computer games and has no such fear. They do not remember the panic that once struck with the shrill cry, "The computer is down again!" The younger generation sees the computer as an extension of the self, an avenue for bigger and better creations. Computers are here to stay. Therapeutic Recreation Specialists must grow through computer implementation. The fact is that every facet of providing Therapeutic Recreation services, that normally takes time away from client interactions, can be done by computer. We must begin thinking of how this technology can help now, if it is to become helpful tomorrow.

FACILITY DESIGN

Another key to efficiency is in the facility's design. Supervision and communication are aided by design. Most of the Therapeutic Recreation area is in view from the reception desk. Video cameras permit monitoring of other areas from the reception desk. Areas are grouped by noise levels. Storage is designed for efficiency. Clustering of functions saves time so often wasted by walking halls and walking between buildings, and also reduces the "them against us" employee factions found in more dispersed organizations. Design can aid cooperation between organizational divisions. For example, picnic tables are located in close proximity to both Therapeutic Recreation and Food Services. Picnics are welcomed and held frequently, with the work shared equally between Therapeutic Recreation staff and Food Service staff because it is not a long "out of sight, out of mind" walk to the picnic area. The same is true for provision of refreshment for special events. Leisure Education areas are in close proximity of Group Therapy rooms. Therapeutic Recreation Specialists have offices in close proximity to the Group Counselors offices. (See Figure 6.2, p. 103)

DETOX PROGRAM

The primary emphasis of the detoxification program is medical stabilization of the client's physical condition. Transfer from detoxification to treatment is a medical decision. There are no set schedules for meeting client education, therapy, and leisure needs. Client participation in all activities is dependent on the client's medical status, which may vary from hour to hour.

Therapeutic Recreation Specialists introduce themselves and begin the assessment process as soon as the client is medically ready. Depending on the client's condition, some clients may be permitted to join educational sessions, Leisure Education, and Re-Creation sessions after the first day. Others may not be ready to participate for several days. Recreation supplies are distributed as indicated. All attempts are made to prevent boredom, to help the client feel welcome, and to help the client preview the activities awaiting in the treatment phase.

Prevention of boredom is an important and challenging aspect of Therapeutic Recreation programming during detox. If the client has nothing to do, he/she will sit and focus on the physical discomfort being experienced. This intensifies the perception of the discomfort. He/she will also think about what is happening at home. Things were left undone. The family may find they don't need the client. The client begins to think it is better for all concerned to discontinue treatment and go home. Keeping the mind occupied with a leisure pursuit makes the time pass more quickly. The client focusing on leisure involvement is less likely to focus on reasons for leaving treatment or the physical discomfort being experienced. Yet most clients lack the skills to keep themselves occupied in interesting leisure pursuits. Withdrawal symptoms may disorganize thinking, cause problems focusing the eyes to read, or cause trembling of the hands, which makes it difficult to hold a pencil. During withdrawal, the nervous system is waking up from sedation. A loud, unexpected noise can startle the client, causing the person to jump from his/her chair.

It would seem that those experiencing alcohol withdrawal, and withdrawal from other drugs that have reduced the body's natural ability to produce serotonin, would benefit from soothing, calming environments. Even though the client is receiving drugs to keep the fight-or-flight system from waking too quickly, the person still lacks the internal chemical production that regulates this system. Sitting in an atrium where there are lots of plants and an artificial waterfall should help a great deal.

At the same time, it also seems that persons who have used a drug that has calmed and soothed them to a point of considering suicide, should not benefit from an atrium of plants and trickling waters. Persons who feel clinically depressed may experience increased feelings of depression in an environment that is overly soothing and calming. Cocaine and stimulant users have exhausted their system's norepinephrine productions. During withdrawal they may feel the need for more stimulants. Laughter and mild exercise (assuming medical stability is present) may be the most appropriate source of help for their withdrawal symptoms.

As mentioned in Chapter 3, isolation may increase the desire to drink. Attempting to detox in a private room is probably the ultimate in isolation. The development of a buddy system during detox should reduce feelings of isolation. Two clients who realize they are fighting the same battle of withdrawal together, will not feel isolated even though they are in separate rooms. Sitting in an atrium with another client is preferable even though the clients choose not to speak to one another.

Videotaped introductions to the treatment center are also valuable during detox. They help the person clear away the unknowns about treatment. They structure thought toward positive outcomes. While the person is learning what is in store for him/her during treatment, the mind remains too occupied to consider what is happening at home. Videotapes may be preferable to live introductions provided by a staff member. First of all, the videotape can provide pictures of activities and events that can only be described by a staff member. The Videotape is available for viewing when the client is ready to see it. This could be the first day after admission or at three in the morning of the third day. When the introduction is provided in lecture format, it is presented at a time convenient to the staff which is seldom the time that the client is ready to hear the information. Finally, a videotaped presentation saves time and money. The personal touch can be provided by a staff visit in which the client's questions are answered.

Client Scheduling After Detox

During treatment, clients use alarm clocks to wake up. During the first week of treatment, clients are given an additional wake-up call at 6:00 a.m. on weekdays. After the first week clients are on their own unless they specifically request a wake-up call in addition to the alarm clock. This system immediately sets a tone for self-responsibility. Wake-up calls are issued automatically by computer. At the designated time the computer sends a signal to a doorbell chime located in the designated room(s). Clients may request the wake-up call earlier or later than the standard time. It does not matter to TNT when

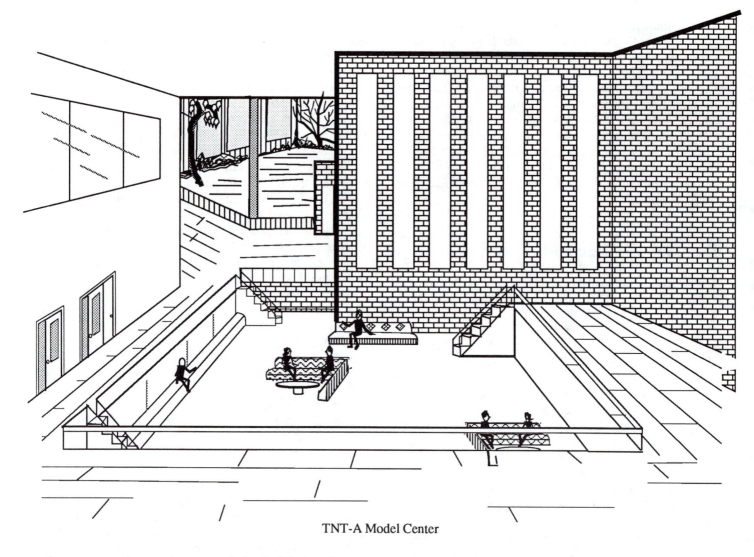

TNT-A Model Center

they get up, so long as they get to their scheduled sessions on time. Clients may also take advantage of the wake-up service after discharge. If this is elected, the computer dials the client's home phone at a designated time. Upon answering the phone, a recorded message is played. The recorded message gives the time, the date, and the thought for the day from Alcoholics Anonymous's *Twenty-Four Hour Book.* At the end of the thought for the day, the discharged client may leave a message such as "I'm doing fine," or "Call me, I have a problem." The discharged clients' messages are forwarded by computer to appropriate therapists.

On weekdays after wake-up, there is time to brush the teeth prior to exercise. The half-hour exercise session is mandatory during the first week of treatment. After that, participation is optional but strongly encouraged. The majority of clients participate throughout treatment. Then it's a mad dash to the showers and then to breakfast.

Medications are distributed between exercise and breakfast. Doctor's appointments are scheduled when clients pick up their medications. Anyone wishing to see a doctor makes arrangements at this time. After the client touches the fingerprint sensor, a nurse helps the client enter the specifics of the

request and estimated length of time required into the computer. The physician's schedule has been divided into blocks of time ranging from 10 minutes to an hour. After requests have been taken, the computer cross matches clients' schedules with physician's time blocks and schedules the appointments. The computer has been instructed to prioritize the client's schedule. First it tries to set appointments during the client's free time. If this is not possible then appointments are scheduled so that the client is pulled from different types of sessions during his/her treatment stay. It will not make an appointment during a therapy time unless it is an emergency. Any client who has not requested an appointment during the previous 10 days, is automatically scheduled to see the physician for a brief review. This system takes the place of traditional rounds. It keeps the physician in touch with the clients, while allowing him/her to spend available time with those who need him/her most. When time permits, the physician makes informal rounds in the recreation area during skill development time slots. The physician is able to use the recreation computers should questions arise. He/she also changes activity level classifications at this time, as needed.

FIGURE 6.2

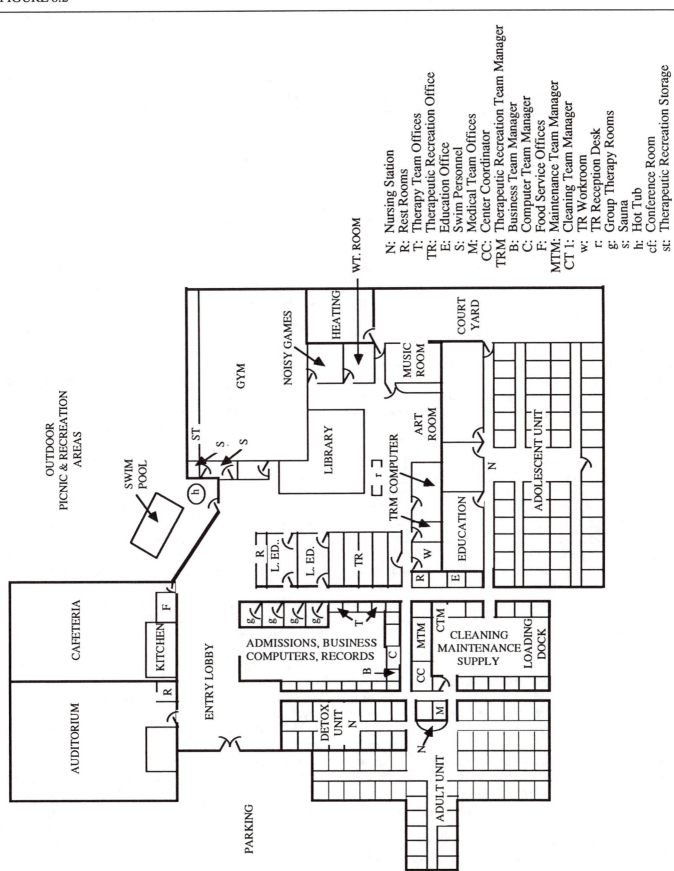

N: Nursing Station
R: Rest Rooms
T: Therapy Team Offices
TR: Therapeutic Recreation Office
E: Education Office
S: Swim Personnel
M: Medical Team Offices
CC: Center Coordinator
TRM Therapeutic Recreation Team Manager
B: Business Team Manager
C: Computer Team Manager
F: Food Service Offices
MTM: Maintenance Team Manager
CT 1: Cleaning Team Manager
w: TR Workroom
r: TR Reception Desk
g: Group Therapy Rooms
s: Sauna
h: Hot Tub
cf: Conference Room
st: Therapeutic Recreation Storage

Community meetings are held in the cafeteria while clients are finishing breakfast. These are chaired by an elected client. At least one staff member from each service area attends. It is an opportunity for clients to give their input to organizational policies, procedures, and changes. Announcements concerning the day's routine are made by the elected client when possible. Last-minute changes are shared by staff. Physician appointments are distributed to clients at the end of the community meeting. A meditation period and a reading from Alcoholic Anonymous's *Twenty-Four Hour Book* concludes the community meeting. This schedule has provided the client with a simulation of how the morning should begin after discharge. There has been time for nurturing the mind, body, and soul as well as communication with the "family." Since this population is habit-forming, the development of a routine such as this will become a habit with a good chance of continuation after discharge.

At TNT, the client population is divided into eight groups, averaging 11 clients per group. After the community meeting, four of the groups go to group therapy, while the other four groups are scheduled for Leisure Education. At 10:30 a.m., the groups reverse. Those who have been in group therapy go to Leisure Education. Those who have been in Leisure Education go to group therapy. Lunch begins at 11:30 a.m. Most are not available for lunch until noon. Adolescent groups attend Leisure Education two days a week. On the other three days, most attend a school program during Leisure Education times.

There are various educational lectures and films, from 1:00 to 3:00 p.m. Educational lectures are given by the Center coordinator, the physician, group counselors, team manager, and nursing personnel. Educational films are shown in the Therapeutic Recreation area by recreation technicians. Clients attend the lecture or film of their choice until they have seen all that are required at least once. Adolescents attend the school program during this time slot, after completing attendance in the required sessions.

On Thursdays all clients are required to attend a discussion of the Twelve Steps and Twelve Traditions. Discussions of different aspects are offered at the same time. Clients are expected to begin with a Step One discussion but then advance at their own rate.

From 3:00 to 4:30 p.m., Skill Development Sessions are held on every weekday except Wednesdays. A variety of Skill Development sessions are offered simultaneously. The number and type of skill development sessions required for a client to attend depends on the results of the Therapeutic Recreation assessment. Group Therapists and other staff often join the sessions. Clients having completed required sessions attend sessions of interest to them or use the time for Re-Creation . Some adolescents receive special assistance meeting school requirements during this time. The amount of time used for school is negotiated between the Therapeutic Recreation Specialist and the teacher, and handled on an individual basis.

On Wednesdays, a special seminar is given by clients who are finishing their inpatient treatment stay. After the seminar, representatives from the client population join the Therapeutic Recreation staff meeting. The representatives help plan future events, and help identify and solve problems related to Therapeutic Recreation programming.

Recreation Therapy and special individualized Therapeutic Recreation sessions are scheduled at various times. Sometimes the sessions are scheduled during Leisure Education times. This permits the group counselor to either open the topic that the Recreation Therapy session is designed to treat, or to process the topic that was presented in the Recreation Therapy session. Sometimes it is deemed too intense to have an intensive Recreation Therapy session back to back with a group therapy session. In these cases, the Recreation Therapy session is scheduled during an afternoon time slot. Sometimes the group counselor co-leads the Recreation Therapy session with the Therapeutic Recreation Specialist.

Dinner and medications call begins at 4:30 p.m. If desired, clients may return to the recreation area after dinner. During this time, specific activities are often conducted by client recreation leaders. Special events are held on Wednesdays. Clients are required to attend AA/NA meetings each night for the first 10 days of treatment. After that attendance is optional but most continue to attend nightly. Those who choose not to attend are confronted during group therapy sessions. Recreation facilities are closed during AA/NA meeting times and then reopened. Recreation technicians provide transportation to and from meetings, which are held off-campus. Clients are encouraged to make the getting to and from the meeting a leisurely event. Exercise sessions for relaxation purposes are held nightly. Participation is optional after the first 10 days, but the majority of the clients find it helpful and attend on a regular basis.

On weekends, one hour of exercise is held after the community meetings. On Saturdays, clients without visiting family are free until 3:00 p.m. During this time, some join a recreation activity organized by a client recreation leader, or pursue an individual interest. Some assist in preparations for the evening activity. Counselors make rounds to help clients connect with the feelings that result from not having visitors. At 3:00 p.m., they may participate in a skill development session. Clients are required to attend an educational session. After dinner, there is an AA/NA meeting held on the grounds and open to the public. There is a special event held after the meeting. The special event is open to all clients, their visitors, outpatients, persons who attended the AA/NA meeting and members of the Employee Recreation Club.

On Sundays, a spiritual meditation/prayer session is held between the community meeting and the exercise session. After exercise, all clients are required to attend a Twelve Step and Twelve Tradition discussion session. Several sessions are held at the same time and led by nurses. Clients without visitors are free from lunch until 3:00 p.m. There is a required educational lecture in the late afternoon. There is a skill development session available at 3:00 p.m., followed by dinner and an AA/NA meeting in the evening.

Clients are eligible for passes after completion of AA/NA Step Three. Members of Groups 1-4 may leave the Center on Saturdays from noon until 6:00 p.m. Members of Groups 5-8 leave the Center on Sundays from noon until 6:00 p.m. Overnight passes are also provided after the midpoint of the treatment stay. Upon return from pass, the client and family are interviewed by a Therapeutic Recreation Specialist. This "Leisure Review" focuses on identification of problems encountered during the free time away from the Center, and finding solutions. All clients go on pass with a plan for leisure. The interview tends to focus on the client's ability to follow through on the leisure plan. Other problems which are identified are referred to the client's counselor.

Adolescents are usually separated from adult clients. Youngsters in treatment have a tendency to idolize and emulate the adult who is most worldly and knows the most four-letter words. Such adults do not always encourage recovery principles in the youngsters. Adolescents are always supervised by unit personnel until the final phase of treatment. Though adolescents eat at the same time as adults, they are seated separately. Though they come to recreation at the same time, they are usually involved in a different activity or in a different area from adults. They are not permitted to attend the special events until they are in the final phase of treatment. They have their own "Special Events" on Tuesday and Friday nights.

ADOLESCENT SCHEDULING

As previously mentioned, the adolescent unit is primarily self-contained. Weekday scheduling simulates a school day at home. Leisure Education, Group Therapy, and Traditional Education are provided during the "school hours." Leisure Education sessions are designed to help the client understand his/her need for leisure pursuit. They also help the client deal with the problems encountered when attempting to develop a healthy social life in a world that often revolves around alcohol and drug use.

Special attention is devoted to how the client uses his/her free time after school and before dinner. Many of the clients have been "latch key" kids. Parents have worked and left the children to their own devices after the school bell rings. For these clients, it is important to restructure this time period. (Not all latch key kids wind up in treatment for addiction. But where children are in treatment for addiction, and no one has been in the home to greet them after school, then it can be assumed that what the child found to do during that time was nonproductive.) Clients are taught a series of exercises that can be done immediately upon arrival home from school. The exercises are designed to be done inside on rainy days and outside on sunny days. They do not require specialized equipment. The purpose of the exercise is to relieve the body of excess energy that builds up from sitting in a school desk all day. New admissions are taught the exercises in a structured, supervised group. After a couple of weeks, clients are expected

to do the exercises in their sleeping quarters. Doors remain open during this period. Staff check to see if the client has done the exercises. After the client finishes his/her exercise session, homework is next on the list. Next the client is expected to clean up his/her room. When the client finishes these items he/she may have some free time. Free time may be spent watching television, playing games, or participating in activities available in the TNT Center's Recreation Area. The gym is usually open for adolescents from 3:00 p.m. to 7:00 p.m. Adolescents are not usually able to complete their "after school" tasks until 4:30 p.m. But knowing there is something more fun to do than homework and cleaning the room is part of the simulation of a typical day at home. If the client is presented with a choice of homework or nothing to do, then homework will be selected without resistance. If the client must choose between fun and homework, then the client may pull every trick in his/her book to bypass the homework and get to the fun. Members of the adolescent treatment team are very active during this period dealing with behaviors which erupt. Eventually the client learns to do the exercise, homework, cleanup routine as quickly as possible. Since this is a habit-forming population, the routine, once established, is likely to carry over into the home after discharge.

Skill Development sessions are provided during evening hours and on weekends. Clients often attend Family Therapy and Family Leisure Sessions on weekends. Interactions between clients and family members are identified and dealt with in this way. Counselor and Therapeutic Recreation Specialist often co-lead weekend sessions to provide maximum benefit to clients and to family members.

BASIC FAMILY VISITATION AND THERAPY SCHEDULE

While on the detox unit, communication between family and client is channeled through the detox staff. Direct contact and communication is not permitted. While the client is working on Step One, communication is permitted only when approved by the treatment team for a specific reason or purpose. Initially, there is little to be gained, and much to be lost, through interaction between clients and family. At the time of admission, emotions are often very high. Destructive patterns of noncommunication and denial have been established. Separation allows the situation to cool down. It allows the client to focus on treatment needs, and to sort out personal needs from family needs. During this time the family begins participation in their own outpatient therapy program.

The separation also reduces the client's opportunity to leave treatment before detoxification is complete. Unwittingly families often help clients leave treatment by providing transportation and excuses such as, "I have to leave because my child's sick," "There are financial problems," "The plumbing broke," "My wife will leave me if I don't." Such problems do occur, but in most cases the problems can be solved without the client leaving detox. In most cases solutions are simplified without the addicted person complicating matters by using alcohol/drugs. Where co-dependency is active, the no-visitation rule will be difficult to live with. During the separation, family therapy can focus on here-and-now problems created by the separation as examples of co-dependent action.

Upon completion of Step One, visiting hours are Tuesdays, 3:00 p.m. to 8:00 p.m.; Thursdays, 6:00 p.m. to 9:30 p.m.; Saturdays, 9:00 a.m. to 11:00 p.m.; and Sundays, noon to 6:00 p.m. Families are not allowed to visit the entire time. In the beginning, visitation is permitted through participation in highly structured activities, with only a few minutes of free time available. Specific visiting hours are scheduled by the client's treatment team. Steps are taken to assure that family members and client have an opportunity to communicate with each other, and to have fun together as well. The time is increased and the degree of structure decreases as the treatment stay progresses. If a client has an appointment, or session, during visitation hours, visitors attend the appointment with the client. This permits observation of family interactions by staff. It also provides a feeling of inclusion and shared experience for family members, which is most helpful in the recovery and relationship rebuilding process.

Families are required to attend sessions each time they visit. Educational sessions are designed to develop new patterns of communication between client and family, create awareness and insight into past behaviors, understand the disease concept of addiction, and the family addiction cycle. Families are also required to attend therapy sessions and Therapeutic Recreation sessions. Leisure Education sessions are provided to create an awareness of personal and family leisure needs. Skill Development sessions allow the family to learn the same leisure skills as the client, providing common ground for rebuilding relationships. Family members are also encouraged to find meaningful leisure activities to engage in while the client is attending AA/NA Initially a spouse may experience an overwhelming sense of isolation while the client devotes the majority of his/her free time to a twelve-step program. The development of separate leisure pursuits can subdue the impact of the isolation. Recreation sessions permit opportunities for positive shared experiences needed to rebuild the strained relationships that have become unbalanced by a predominance of negative experiences.

On Tuesdays, family members with approval of the treatment team may attend the skill development sessions that begin at 3:00 p.m. If they attend the 3:00 p.m. session, then they may eat dinner with the client. All family members are required to attend an educational session from 6:00 to 7:00 p.m. with the client. They are free to visit until the closed AA/NA meeting(s) begin at 8:00 p.m. Families are encouraged to attend the closed Al-Anon/Nar-Anon meetings which are also held at the Center.

On Thursdays, clients are required to attend therapy sessions with spouses, from 6:00 p.m. to 7:00 p.m. Children attend "Kid's Group" while their parents are in the therapy

session. Children and parents then join together for a Therapeutic Recreation Session. Then attendance in open AA, NA, Al-Anon, Nar-Anon, Al-Atot, Al-Ateen meetings held at the center is encouraged for the entire family. They are encouraged to attend a different meeting each week. Children may attend meetings with parents or attend their own meetings. Some children with special needs remain in the Recreation area for therapy.

Kid's Group is a combination of special programs provided for visiting children while parents are in meetings. Kid's group uses recreation experiences specifically designed to educate them about addiction and the purpose of treatment, give them a chance to express and evaluate feelings, and provide support. During Kid's group, the cardinal rules are See, Feel, Tell, and Laugh. Children who are identified as having major adverse emotional/behavioral reactions to the addiction are referred to the psychologist for evaluation. Families with children pay a one-time charge per treatment stay. Most parents pay the fee gladly, since their children are getting the special attention they need at a cost equal to that of a babysitter.

On weekends, all clients and their visiting family members must attend the Family Education and Therapy sessions on Saturdays, from 10:30 a.m. to noon. Members of groups 5-8, must attend Family Leisure Education from 1:30 to 3:00 p.m. on Saturdays while groups 1-4 must attend on Sundays. Groups 1-4 must attend skill development on Saturdays while groups 5-8 must attend on Sundays. At the discretion of the treatment team, family members may arrive at 9:00 a.m. on Saturdays, and join the exercise class. They may be permitted to eat lunch and dinner at the Center and stay for the AA/NA meetings(s) and participate in the Saturday night special event. Kid's group is available on Saturdays. On Sundays, at the discretion of the treatment team, family members may arrive at noon for lunch, and for dinner, but they must leave by 6:00 p.m.

OUTPATIENT SCHEDULING

It is assumed by TNT Center definition that family support is healthy for clients who enter the outpatient treatment program. For this reason, the outpatient family-oriented program is less structured than in the inpatient program. Family members' needs are assessed and treatment is provided based on the results of the assessment. Some need assistance in meeting leisure needs. Many do not. Often family member needs can be met at the same time as the client's needs are being met.

The outpatient program has the same content as the inpatient program. Outpatients who can arrange their work schedule to permit daytime treatment often join in inpatient sessions. The same sessions are repeated during evening hours for outpatients who work during the daytime hours. Outpatients are scheduled for Skill Development sessions as needed. All are encouraged to attend special events.

Specialized sessions are held during evenings and weekends. The sessions are available to outpatients and inpatients alike. Some discharged clients make use of the groups as part of their after-care program. The special sessions address specific problem areas. For example, one group is specifically designed to meet the needs of Vietnam vets. Another group deals with managing problem children in the home. Another group deals with problems faced by women alcoholic/addicts. One group deals with career problems and another with leisure problems. There is another group for victims of abuse. Some groups permit family participation, others do not.

AFTER-CARE SCHEDULING

The goal of after-care is to help the client bridge the gap from a structured, sheltered environment to routine life. Clients and family are encouraged to continue attending the Family Leisure Education programs and the special events. Discharged clients are also urged to attend group therapy sessions on Thursday nights. Clients and their spouses are encouraged to continue attending the couples group, which is held on Tuesday nights. Individual sessions are scheduled as indicated.

Over the course of a year, the client and family is weaned away from dependence on the Center. At first, after-care attendance is strongly encouraged by staff. Clients are expected to participate at least once per week. Then they are expected to participate twice per month, then once per month. Staff monitors community support systems which are developing for the client. As the client develops his/her own support system, the Center's staff withdraw their support. By the end of after-care, transition back to the community is complete.

TRANSITION CENTER SCHEDULING

The transition center is separate but a part of the TNT Center. Discharged clients who have jobs but no healthy family ties, and no place to stay, utilize the transition center. For these clients, the transition center functions as a temporary group home. For the most part, clients are required to initiate activities independently. If the client feels the need for a therapy session or additional Leisure Education or Skill Development, then the client must contact the appropriate staff and arrange an appointment. Sometimes clients without jobs stay at the transition center. Clients may be transferred to the transition center before all objectives on their treatment plan are met. When this happens, the client continues participation in portions of the inpatient program until maximum benefits have been achieved. The recovery team is very active with transition center clients. Work rehabilitation counselors provide support and encouragement for the client as the client undergoes the job interviewing process. Family members who must travel long distances to attend family programs also stay at the transition center.

Transition center clients participate in Therapeutic Recreation schedules established for inpatient, outpatient, or after-care, depending on their needs. Sometimes clients initiate special requests for Therapeutic Recreation services. These requests sometimes result in private consultations with a Therapeutic Recreation Specialist. Sometimes the request is best met by contracting services from a Therapeutic Recreation Specialist who is self-employed. The determination of who, where, and when, is handled by the client's primary Therapeutic Recreation Specialist from the treatment team.

SCHEDULING THE ACTIVITY THAT TAKES A DAY OR TWO

Some Therapeutic Recreation activities require more time than a routine schedule permits. Sometimes it seems "fun" to take the clients to a fair or some exhibit in the community and that, too, requires a whole day. Such trips should be closely scrutinized. At TNT, "fun" is not reason enough to pull a client from therapy. "Fun" of equal quality can usually be provided on the grounds, at a reduced cost, for a shorter period of time. (All too often, a day trip is spent in boredom getting to and from the "fun.") Clients are only pulled from the routine schedule when the experience cannot be duplicated on the grounds and when the "therapy" of the outing is greater than the therapy which occurs during the routine schedule.

Adventure-based programming is a good example. Courses such as Ropes, Inward Bound, Outward Bound, Project Adventure, and others have benefits to therapy that cannot be duplicated in a classroom or a conference room. Outdoor risk taking, camping, rafting, hiking, mountain climbing, and other activities, also offer tremendous benefits. To achieve the benefits usually requires a full day or more. When such an outing occurs, the treatment team goes on the outing along with the Therapeutic Recreation staff. Group Therapy is held under the stars instead of under fluorescent lighting. Where other therapists are unable to go on such outings, Therapeutic Recreation personnel have been co-trained so that therapy objectives can be satisfactorily met while the clients are absent from the Center.

EMPLOYEE RECREATION

Employees are not permitted to use recreation equipment nor facilities unless they join the Employee Recreation Club. Employees are not eligible for the club until they have completed probationary periods. In the eyes of nonrecreation employees, the creation of an Employee Recreation Club changes recreation from an attractive nuisance to a job benefit. Without such a club, employees share equipment and facilities with clients without sharing in the cost of upkeep and replacement. Supervisors often find that work is not being done because employees are in the recreation area. Policies developed to prevent the misuse of recreation by employees result in antagonism between employees and Therapeutic Recreation staff.

At TNT, membership in the Employee Recreation Club is a privilege that must be approved by the employee's supervisor. Membership fees help support Therapeutic Recreation services. The Center's administration pays the membership dues for employees that they wish to recognize for having done a superb job. Employees may select an individual or family membership. Membership allows access to all equipment and facilities that could be found at an athletic club but at a greatly reduced cost. Facilities are also available at times when community facilities are closed, making them attractive to second and third shift personnel. Club members may participate in some activities planned for clients such as exercise sessions and special events. Some time slots are exclusively for club members, such as the time when clients are attending AA/NA meetings. Skill Development sessions are held for employees on Tuesday nights. Leisure Education sessions and other specialized programs are conducted by the Therapeutic Recreation Manager on Thursday nights. The most attractive advantage to membership may be access to the swimming pool. Special events, tours, and excursions away from the Center are also planned and organized by the club membership. For off-campus activities, the Therapeutic Recreation Manager serves as a consultant to the club. The Employee Club has its own elected officials who actually do the legwork of organization.

TNT MANAGEMENT

TNT utilizes a team approach to providing treatment. The treatment team consists of a Group Counselor, a Medical Specialist, and a Therapeutic Recreation Specialist. The Medical Specialist is usually a nurse from the client's unit. The treatment team is assigned while the client is in detox, but does not have authority over the client's plan of care until the client has completed detox. While in detox, the client is under the care and supervision of the physician and his medical team. Non-medical needs are usually met by intervention team members.

The Center's organizational needs are also met through the team approach. Each discipline forms a team responsible to the manager of that discipline. Staff with client interactions are also assigned to interdisciplinary teams, such as the intervention team, the treatment team and the recovery team. The discipline team manager is responsible for assuring that quality care is provided to all clients receiving the services of that discipline. The interdisciplinary team manager is responsible for the coordination of care being provided to each client on the team.

Management is also provided by team effort. Organizational policies and procedures are formulated within the various teams. Any change of procedure must be communicated to all staff. Changes which impact on more than one team must

be approved by all teams that will be affected. There is an attempt to gain consensus whenever a decision is made. If all persons involved cannot agree the majority rules, provided that (a) the Center coordinator is in favor, and (b) the appropriate team manager(s) is (are) in agreement. For example, if the majority of team managers desire a change in a Therapeutic Recreation procedure, the Center coordinator and the Therapeutic Recreation team manager, must agree to the change before it can be implemented. On the other hand, if only the Center coordinator and the TR team manager want the change, it cannot be implemented until the majority of other team managers are in favor. There are always exceptions to the rule. Where a change is required to assure the safety of clientele, or to assure compliance with accrediting standards, the team manager may make the change even though no one favors the change. During management meetings, each team manager is obligated to share the views of their respective team members as well as their own view. Each team manager has two votes on an issue. One vote is based on what their employees feel is best for them and the client. The second vote is based on what the team manager feels is best for the Center and the service he/she represents.

Personnel working in the Center on a contractual basis, are treated as equal members of the appropriate team. They follow the same rules and regulations as other employees. They are also eligible for some employee benefits such as the Employee Recreation Club. At TNT, Therapeutic Recreation contracts services from community recreation centers, community colleges, and private leisure education firms to provide a full range of services to the clientele. Therapeutic Recreation staff employed by TNT serve as liaisons between other team members and providers of contracted services. (See Figure 6.3)

THE THERAPEUTIC RECREATION TEAM

The Therapeutic Recreation Team consists of one team manager, five Therapeutic Recreation Specialists, two full-time technicians, and two part-time technicians. There are also several contracted services which provide staffing for the swimming pool, instruct Skill Development sessions, and lead adventure-based programming.

The Therapeutic Recreation team manager, serves as part of the Center's management team. The manager also maintains the services organization and direction. The quality and efficiency of services provided are closely monitored. Staff education is provided as needed. The manager also conducts Therapeutic Recreation programs for family members, aftercare, and clients in treatment as needed.

Certified Therapeutic Recreation Specialists evaluate client needs, plan and implement individualized treatment plans, and lead Leisure Education sessions. They provide Recreation Therapy, which is often provided within a Re-Creation session. Therapeutic Recreation Specialists also supervise technicians. One Therapeutic Recreation Specialist is assigned to

FIGURE 6.3

TNT ORGANIZATIONAL CHART

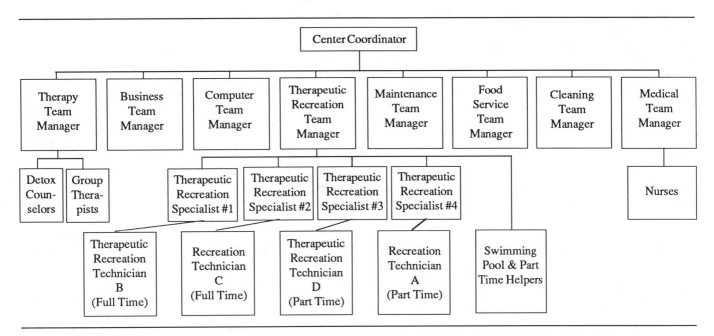

FIGURE 6.4

TNT MATRIX CHART

FUNCTION	TEAM LEADER	THERAPY	BUSN.	COMP.	TRS	MAIN.	FOOD	CLEAN	MED.
Adult Inpatient	Group Therapist #1	GT #1	BS #1	CS #1	TRS #1	M #1	FS #1	CL #1	RN #1
Adolescent Inpatient	Nurse #2	GT #2	BS #2	CS #2	TRS #2	M #2	FS #2	CL #2	RN #2
Sp. Events	TR Tec. B	*	*	*	*	M #3	FS #3	CL #3	TEC #3
Out Patient Therapy	Group Therapist #4	GT #4	BS #4	CS #4	TRS #4	M #3	FS #3	CL #3	RN #4
Recovery Bound Programming	TRS #3 *	*	*	*	M #1	*	CL #3	*	
Detox Programming	Med. Team Manager	Detox Cns. #1	BS #3	CS #3	*	M #2	FS #1	CL #2	RN #3
Transition Center	Nurse Team Manager	*	*	*	RecTecA	M #1	FS #2	CL #1	TEC #2
Family Programming	Detox Counselor #4	GT #3	BS #2	CS #2	TRS #4	*	FS #3	CL #3	*
Program Evaluation	Computer Spec. #2	GT Mgr.	BS Mgr.		TR Mgr.	M Mgr.	FS Mgr.	CL Mgr.	MD Mgr.
Cost Accounting	Business Spec. #2	GT Mgr.	BS Mgr.		TR Mgr.	M Mgr.	FS Mgr.	CL Mgr.	MD Mgr.

clients in groups 1-4. A second Therapeutic Recreation Specialist is assigned to clients in groups 5-8. The third Therapeutic Recreation Specialist substitutes for the others as needed, and conducts special Recreation Therapy programs. The other two Therapeutic Recreation Specialists manage outpatient and after-care treatment plans and programs. Responsibilities are rotated among Therapeutic Recreation Specialists on an annual basis. This prevents burnout, and provides cross training, and a needed break from the routine.

Technicians instruct Skill Development sessions and organize Re-Creation sessions. Secretarial functions are combined with traditional recreation functions in one of the full-time technician positions. Duties, functions, and qualifications, are identified in the job descriptions, which are located in the appendix. (See Figure 6.4)

STAFF TRAINING

All staff receive extensive training before assuming full responsibilities. New employees are paid on a trainee scale. Salaries are increased at the completion of each phase of training. The employee sets his/her own speed. The training can be completed in less than six months. Persons who have not satisfactorily completed the full training program after two years are discharged.

New employees enter the system as a client. They are admitted, spend one night on the detox unit, one night on the adult unit, and one night on the adolescent unit. The Therapeutic Recreation Specialist spends the remainder of the first month becoming acquainted with the Center as a whole. New employees then review organizational, administrative, and safety policies/procedures. They are also indoctrinated into the disease concept of addiction. The reviews are managed by computerized learning programs, which test the knowledge gained by the employee and also educate the employee. An increase in pay is automatically added, by computer, to the employee's training salary when the employee satisfactorily completes the policy/procedure review.

Next the employee spends one day in each service area, from cleaning to management, from maintenance to billing, from group therapies to medicine. One day is spent with each nursing shift, in each unit. An extra day is spent in any department operating two or more shifts. When completed, there is another increase in pay, and the employee begins training in his/her own service area.

Training in Therapeutic Recreation begins with computerized introduction to "departmental" policies and procedures. After key policies and procedures have been satisfactorily assimilated, the employee begins client contact by performing tasks of a Therapeutic Recreation Technician. One week is spent observing the TR team manager, and with each technician. Part-time positions are reviewed first allowing time to complete the policy, procedure and format review, if necessary. An increase in pay accompanies the completion of this phase.

The new Therapeutic Recreation Specialist then begins to assume job responsibilities under direct supervision of the TR team manager. The new employee also begins training with group counselors. The new employee attends Group Therapy Sessions, spending one month with each group counselor. An increase in pay is given when the TR team manager feels that direct supervision is no longer necessary. A final increase in pay is given when the rotation with all group counselors is completed. This completes the training phase. The Therapeutic Recreation Specialist's salary is now at step 1 for the Therapeutic Recreation Specialist grade. Prior to this point the employee has used the title of TRS-t (the small "t" standing for trainee). Now the employee uses TRS-R (the "R" standing for registered by the Center). The rights to employ discretionary judgment, and to participate in corporate share distributions, are withheld until the person becomes a TRS-R.

In addition to the above, a new TR team manager also spends a week performing the tasks of each Therapeutic Recreation Specialist. A new team manager also receives training in computer programming if needed. The team manager also engages in a computerized review of accrediting standards, as well as the results of past program evaluations.

Therapeutic Recreation Technicians complete the same first phase of introduction to TNT. Time in other service areas is spent performing technician functions. They spend one week observing each Therapeutic Recreation Specialist and the team manager. They complete a computerized review of each function of their job, which highlights safety. Upon satisfactory completion of a review for provision of a specific activity, the technician can begin conducting the activity under the direct supervision of the TR team manager and/or a Registered Therapeutic Recreation Specialist. The technician may assume independent activity after the TR team manager has reviewed the new employee's work and determined it safe and satisfactory. Increases in pay occur after the first phase, after the observation phase, after 50 percent of the responsibilities have been assumed independently, and after all responsibilities have been assumed.

All new employees follow the same basic orientation format. After the initial training, each team manager assumes responsibility for monitoring and improving the quality of programming through staff education. Educational sessions are routinely provided. Individual attention is provided as needed. Emphasis is placed on perfecting details of sessions rather than expanding the number of sessions. Emphasis is also placed on improving employees' knowledge of addiction and of new developments in the field. Extensive training is provided to nurses and group counselors, by Therapeutic Recreation, and their involvement in Skill Development sessions, general recreation, and specials events are always helpful and complimentary to the goals of Therapeutic Recreation.

Throughout the employee's career at TNT, standards of performance are used for evaluating the employee's work. Monitoring of an employee's performance is an ongoing process. A formal evaluation is completed annually, with the information used to determine merit awards. Standards of performance are primarily based on personnel policies and job descriptions. Measurement is provided by data stored and tabulated by the computer.

Increases in salary are awarded to employees who exceed established standards of performance. If all Therapeutic Recreation personnel exceed the standards, then all are given raises. In addition, employees who exceed standards are eligible for merit awards. Merit awards are not distributed by "department" but across the Center as a whole. A maximum of one third of TNT's employees who exceed the standards are given merit awards, which consist of TNT stocks. Merit decisions are made by the management team. Employees who meet the standards are not given salary increases, nor merit awards, but they are permitted to keep their jobs. Employees who do not meet the standards are discharged.

TNT provides money and incentive for employees to participate in educational opportunities away from the Center. Fifty percent of the cost of attending a workshop or educational experience that is directly related to the work performed by the employee is paid by the Center. Where that training leads to certification as an Alcohol Counselor or the equivalent, the Center pays a bonus upon receipt of the certification. Therapeutic Recreation Specialists are expected to have their certification as a TRS prior to employment. No bonus is given for receiving certification within their own field, only for cross training which leads to certification in another discipline's field. A nurse could receive a bonus for becoming a certified Therapeutic Recreation Specialist; counselors could receive bonuses for becoming certified nursing assistants, and so on. Fifty percent of educational costs and bonuses are also provided to persons who receive training for the next position up the ladder. The Therapeutic Recreation Technician receives assistance from the organization to become a certified Therapeutic Recreation Specialist. The certified Therapeutic Recreation Specialist receives organizational assistance to train for TR team manager. The team manager receives assistance to become an administrator. In this way, the organization has no dead-end positions and no employees who feel trapped in their jobs.

THERAPEUTIC RECREATION STAFF SCHEDULING

Therapeutic Recreation is not an 8-5 job. Each Therapeutic Recreation team member has a different schedule. This permits provision of services seven days per week from 7:00 a.m. until 11:00 p.m. All Therapeutic Recreation staff work on Wednesday and Thursday afternoons to provide an opportunity for interaction and continuity. Sample schedules are located in the appendix.

The position of TR team manager is a full-time position. Only 75 percent of the manager's time is routinely scheduled. The remaining time is scheduled at the manager's discretion. The flexibility is necessary in order to review each aspect of the Therapeutic Recreation Service on a regular basis. The manager may elect to arrive at 6:30 a.m. one week to review the exercise program and to catch up on paperwork. The manager may choose to come in late and stay until 11:00 p.m. the next week to review the evening program. The manager may work Saturday the next week and Sunday the next.

Therapeutic Recreation Specialists also hold full-time positions. Thirty-seven hours are scheduled. The remaining three hours are selected by the employee. Recreation technicians work the hours that are scheduled for them. Specific functions are assigned for each block of time. General functions that appear on the schedule are detailed one week prior to the undertaking.

Therapeutic Recreation team meetings are multipurpose. A Wednesday meeting follows treatment team conferences, which are about client needs and progress. Highlights of the conferences, such as needed changes in approach to clients, are shared with the Therapeutic Recreation staff. Organizational problems and issues are identified. Most are resolved at the Thursday Therapeutic Recreation meeting. Those that may affect Center operations are scheduled for review in the next Wednesday Manager Meeting. Representatives from the client population join the last part of the meeting. The clients help plan events and schedule activities for the next week. Clients also help identify organizational problems and suggest alternatives for Therapeutic Recreation procedures. Thursday's Therapeutic Recreation meetings are reserved for sharing decisions made about issues presented on Wednesdays, and for inservice training programs. They are sometimes used for organizing and preparing for major events, as well as engaging in group cleanups.

THERAPEUTIC RECREATION BUDGET

The budget is divided into basic line items of salaries, education, supplies, and equipment. Salaries are broken into subcategories of staffing levels plus contracted services. The education budget is subdivided into in-house training and consultation and off-campus education. The supply budget represents routine items that are used and discarded, while the equipment budget represents larger reusable items. Supplies are divided into subcategories of Office, Re-Creation, Leisure Education, and Recreation Therapy. The budget for office supplies is greater than that of a traditional budget due to the extensive use of computers by clients as well as staff.

Swimming staff and supplies are broken out to permit improved monitoring of costs. The most expensive piece of equipment to install, staff, and maintain is a swimming pool. Therapeutic values derived from a pool in an addictions treatment setting do not always justify the cost. However, in a competitive market, the sight of a swimming pool can attract clients away from other facilities. It also makes the Employee Recreation Club an attractive proposition. The combination of therapeutic use for clients, marketing advantages and employee benefits justifies the cost of the swimming program.

Adequate staffing for the pool is mandatory, since it is also the greatest liability. Drownings are hazardous to the financial security of the organization, and not beneficial to clients either.

Salary costs are given in terms of "low," "medium," and "high." (If TNT existed, an accurate figure could be cited. But since TNT does not exist, employees do not exist.) The "low" figure represents the entry-level pay for employees. The "high" represents the salary one might collect after being employed at TNT for several years. "Medium" represents the midpoint between the two. (If all employees began on the same day, paid at the "low" rate, and were give a 10 percent raise each year, they would surpass the "medium" salary in three years.) Salaries are also broken down into levels of staff employed by Therapeutic Recreation. "Contracted" represents money appropriated for employment of persons to provide special Skill Development sessions. Such services may come from a variety of sources at varying costs. The average cost is given. When contracted services exceed the average cost, then fewer hours of services can be provided. When the actual cost is less than average, then more hours of service can be purchased. The total amount spent for contracted services would not exceed the appropriated amount.

"FTE" stands for Full-Time Equivalent. One FTE equals one person working 40 hours per week, or two people each working 20 hours per week, or 40 people each working one hour per week. "Rate" indicates the hourly rate of pay.

The expense budget is somewhat easier to estimate than the revenue budget. Sources of revenue can be listed. But then it must be guessed about how many people will actually pay the estimated amount and when. Sometimes, Therapeutic Recreation personnel are told they can have a certain number of dollars to spend, or can have a new position, but when the time comes, the money isn't there. This is usually because the initial guesses made when the budget was developed were off-target. Census plays a critical factor. If it is guessed that all of the beds will be filled and only half of that number actually become occupied, then there is no money for expansion. Hospitals try to keep routine services going even when the census is down. Sometimes even routine services have to be cut in order to survive. It pays for Therapeutic personnel to be sensitive to the timing of requests. When census is high, ask for that new position. When census is low, offer to provide an event that will bring the hospital into the public's eye and perhaps generate an influx of admissions.

"Cost per client day" indicates the amount of the room rate charge that would have to be allocated to Therapeutic Recreation to provide the services described in this text. The room rate charge is the primary source of income for a Therapeutic Recreation Service. It is based on the assumption that TNT has a total of 100 beds, and are able to average a census of 80. The budget only includes direct expenses. Employee benefits, housekeeping, utilities, and so on, must be added to the stated amount to determine actual costs. (See Figure 6.5)

FIGURE 6.5

DIRECT EXPENSE BUDGET FOR THERAPEUTIC RECREATION

SALARIES:	FTE'S	LOW			HIGH		
		rate	annual*	budgeted**	rate	annual*	budgeted**
Team Manager	1	$12	24,960	24,960	$25	52,000	52,000
TR Specialists	4	$ 7	14,560	58,240	$17	35,360	141,440
Technicians	3.5	$ 5	10,400	36,400	$10	20,800	72,800
Part Time Pool	1.5	$ 5	10,400	15,600	$ 6	12,480	18,720
SALARY TOTAL:	10			$135,200			$284,960
STAFF EDUCATION:	10		$400	$4,000		$400	$4,000
SUPPLIES:							
Office & Computer				$3,000			$4,000
Activity				1,800			5,000
Swim Pool				1,500			3,600
SUPPLY TOTAL:				$6,300			$12,600
EQUIPMENT:							
Repair				$600			$1,800
Replacement				600			2,400
EQUIPMENT TOTAL:				$1,200			$4,200
TR BUDGET TOTAL:				$146,700			$305,760
100 Beds at 80 Percent Occupancy for 365 days:			29,200 (patient days)				29,200
COST PER PATIENT DAY:				**$ 5.02**			**$10.47**

*   hourly rate multiplied by 2,080 hours, equals annual salary.
** annual salary multiplied the number of FTE's (full time equivalents) equals budgeted amount.

FIGURE 6.6

REVENUE & EXPENSE BUDGET FOR THERAPEUTIC RECREATION

REVENUES:

Gift Shop Sales (Profit)		$ 500
Publications, Workshops, Business Consults, Recovery Bound		6,000
Family Recreation Charges		7,200
Employee Recreation Club		14,100
Outpatient Charges (24 billable hours per week)		31,200
TOTAL MISCELLANEOUS REVENUES:		$59,000

TOTAL TR EXPENSE:	(low) $146,700	(high) $305,760
– less Misc. Revenue:	– 59,000	– 59,000
REMAINING EXPENSE:	$87,700	$246,760

FINAL COST PER PATIENT DAY:	**$3.00**	**$8.45**

Additional sources of revenue can be grants and contributions. These are usually limited or nonexistent in a private, for-profit facility. Other sources of revenue can come from individual charges for services rendered in outpatient treatment programs, family programs, children's programs, and after-care. By-products of Skill Development sessions can also be sold. For example, a gift shop may be stocked with note cards carrying designs created during craft classes. Talented staff can sell copies of successful sessions on videotape. Program write-ups can also be sold to other centers. Cassette tapes for exercise and relaxation can be sold to clients for use after discharge. In developing these sources of revenue, staff must be very careful not to spend more in production than the item has a potential in bringing in. Client confidentiality must also be carefully guarded. (See Figure 6.6)

The TNT Addiction Center utilizes a variety of revenue sources to defray the cost of Therapeutic Recreation. Most of the sources bring in revenues for other service areas in addition to Therapeutic Recreation. The amounts listed below in the revenue budget are the portions allocated to Therapeutic Recreation.

Gift shop sales include the sale of exercise cassettes and videotapes, and arts and crafts from Skill Development sessions. Leisure supplies and equipment are also sold. These are purchased from wholesalers and sold at regular retail prices. Where an art project is made by a client and sold by the Center, profits from the sale are split between the client and the Center. T-shirts are also sold. The majority of sales are made to visitors and employees rather than clients.

Local businesses have also donated profits from videogames placed in their shops. Such a game takes up little space and gives the shopowner the image of a concerned citizen. The loss of profits from one machine is well worth the advertising provided by having the machine in his/her shop. Placement of the videogames in the shops and retrieval of the money is handled by a local vending company.

The Center is active in educating the public about alcoholism and drug addiction, its causes and its treatment. Therapeutic Recreation conducts workshops for community groups, businesses, and other professionals on topics such as "Leisure and Alcoholism," "Leisure and the Recovery Process," and "Employee Fitness and Recreation." Therapeutic Recreation also consults with businesses to provide Employee Leisure and Retirement Counseling to their employees. These are provided for a fee which goes to the support of the Therapeutic Recreation Service.

A one-time charge is made for family members who participate in the specialized programs for children, significant others, and so on. Revenues from the family charges are divided between the teams providing the services (Therapeutic Recreation, Food Services, Therapy and Education services). Outpatient, after-care, and transition center clients are charged by the hour for services rendered.

The Employee Recreation Club has a membership fee. Part of the revenue is used to pay for Special Events held for the employees. Part of the revenue is allocated to the Therapeutic Recreation Service to pay for supplies, facilities, and staff time used by the club members.

If TNT were a nonprofit organization, the Therapeutic Recreation program could be supported by profits from bingo games held regularly in the community, or sponsored by a church. An annual event such as a tennis or golf tournament could be developed to support the program.

References/Resources

Alcoholics Anonymous, *Twenty Four Hour Book* (p. 292)

Faulkner, R. W. (1984). *Therapeutic Recreation In Health Care Settings: A Practitioner's Viewpoint.* Seaside OR: Leisure Enrichment Service.

Faulkner, R. W., & Cheth, R. *TRI for IBM PC.* Seaside, OR: Leisure Enrichment Service.

CHAPTER 7

TNT-ASSESSMENT MODEL

THERAPEUTIC RECREATION PROGRAMMING

"Programming" is a word used so often in Therapeutic Recreation that it has almost lost its meaning. For the purposes of this text it will be used to mean the process of selecting, grouping, organizing, scheduling, providing, and evaluating activities to accomplish a desired objective. "Activities" is also a word with too many meanings in this profession. For the purposes of this text, the term "activity" will be used to mean a single unit of leisure experience (i.e., a game, bingo, craft session, an exercise class, a party, a ball game, etc).

In community recreation, programming is usually organized around common interests of participants and around common activities. Programming for persons interested in sports takes the form of organizing activities, such as softball, into leagues, practice times, tournaments, and so on. Programming for persons with artistic interest involves selecting specific types of craft and art classes appropriate for specific age groups and abilities. In Therapeutic Recreation, activities are sometimes organized in the same fashion as in community recreation. This usually results in a strong Recreation Participation service and a piecemeal approach to Recreation Therapy and Leisure Education. Some organize activities around each client's treatment plan. While this provides strong individual programming, group activities often get lost.

Some believe the solution is a "cafeteria" approach. This concept when applied to Therapeutic Recreation programming implies that if a wide variety of activities are served, the client will select what he/she needs. The cafeteria approach has its merits and its flaws. This approach shows a strong belief in the client's abilities and treats the client as a reasoning, responsible human being, which is very important. It does not take into consideration the client's fear of the unknown, which is its major flaw. Clients who have recently experienced emotional trauma tend to cling to the familiar. Engaging in an activity which is unfamiliar can be an ego risk and threatening. Without encouragement, support, direction, and/or intervention, a client during the treatment process will base choices on familiarity rather than on what is best for him/her.

At the TNT Center, programming is designed similar to a college curriculum structure. Colleges do not invent courses after students arrive on campus. They have predetermined curriculums, meeting common needs with core courses. The structure is individualized with electives and independent studies. The system is further tailored to the student's individuality by requiring a certain number of electives. With electives, students may choose from an available list. No one at the college cares which ones are selected as long as the numbers add up properly. Activities which meet the client's identified needs are required "core courses." Activities which meet the client's interests are "electives."

Therapeutic Recreation treatment plan goals emphasize development of leisure skills which clients can utilize after discharge. Key to the provision of services is the client's ability to meet his/her leisure needs without assistance. The development of healthy attitudes about leisure is of primary importance. This is accomplished through Leisure Education Sessions, which are considered part of the core courses.

Clients are seldom motivated to develop leisure skills. Negative attitudes developed in childhood and general misinformation create a barrier to leisure participation. Provision of Leisure Education sessions is important to unlock mental barriers and allow the client to escape from boredom. Leisure Education allows the client to explore the value of leisure within his/her lifestyle. It helps the client understand the way substances have been substituted for meeting leisure needs and it allows the client to give him/herself permission to play without a drink, fix, or pill.

It is important for clients to be discharged at their optimal level of physical and mental fitness. Too much spare time can be dehabilitating. Re-Creation participation such as table games, ball games, swimming, and special events, are never required but always available during spare time. The leisure battle is truly won when the client discovers the therapeutic recreative value of leisure for him/herself. Recreation participation permits the client to discover that he/she can have a good time without a drink, fix, or pill. He/she can get his/her mind off of "it" without becoming intoxicated. Though Re-Creation participation is considered highly beneficial and therapeutic, it is not considered a therapy or treatment. Sessions are considered as electives or part of the "student body's extracurricular" functions. The benefits of Re-Creation are intrinsic. It is impossible to determine if a truly recreative experience has occurred without attaching electrodes to the client's brain, or withdrawing fluids to measure levels of neurotransmitter substances. However, problems encountered in evaluation of results do not reduce the value of the experience. Therapeutic Recreators can create an environment conducive to stimulation of the recreative experience and take the client's word that something changed inside the client as a result of the experience.

The development of new, meaningful leisure interests are also important. Skill Development sessions, treated as "electives," instruct clients on how to participate in leisure activities that are new to them. Clients are required to participate in at least one Skill Development session per week. Participation in familiar "extracurricular" activities is optional. It is important to begin new activities while in treatment. The "getting started" is the most difficult part of acquiring a new leisure pursuit. Clients who get their feet wet while in treatment are more likely to follow up on the activities after discharge. Skill Development sessions are often offered at the same time as Recreation Participation sessions. In that way, clients who know how to perform an activity can assist in teaching the activity to others when appropriate. For example, a trip to the bowling alley may be a Re-Creation session for some clients and a Skill Development session for others. Those who know how to bowl and go because they enjoy bowling are receiving a Re-Creative experience. Those who go but don't know how to bowl are receiving a Skill Development session. Once they learn the basics of bowling, they may decide to continue participation because bowling meets intrinsic needs.

Recreation Therapy is something of a horse of a different color. All other forms of Therapeutic Recreation programming are designed to equip the client with leisure skills and interest for use after discharge. In Recreation Therapy, activities are used to treat specific problem areas of client behavior. The activity is selected for its ability to act as a catalyst for change. The therapist does not select the activity on the basis that the client might enjoy it, or desire to participate in the activity after discharge. Recreation Therapy includes the use of specific activities to meet specific needs such as improving communication skills, getting in touch with feelings, ventilating anger, and developing trust in self and others. The client's need for such activities is not immediately apparent. It usually takes a week or two of group therapy before the client's inner needs can be accurately identified. Recreation Therapy can be thought of as the provision of pre-leisure skills. In the college curriculum format, it is part of the required course content for the major area of study. Clients who are distrustful major in development of trust in self and others. Clients who are filled with anger, major in the ventilation of anger, and so on.

Leisure Education, Re-Creation, Skill Development, and Recreation Therapy combine to create the Therapeutic Recreation Service. All programs are available. Not all clients need all of the programs. The exact mix of programs for the client is determined by the initial evaluation and the creation of an individualized treatment plan. As therapy progresses, the mix of services is adjusted to meet newly identified needs. Just as the colleges require participation in basic core courses before selection of majors, the Therapeutic Recreation Service begins by addressing the basics before attempting to identify specific needs.

GETTING STARTED

Before any of the above can be provided, the client must be brought into the system. This begins with referral from the physician. At TNT, the referral form contains information needed to begin the assessment process as well as verification of permission to begin work. The referral gives factors about the client's physical condition, including carefully noted precautions, and the level of physical activity which the physician considers safe for participation. It also provides information

about length of time since detoxification, and type of drug used prior to admission. This information is important to know. At TNT, Therapeutic Recreation protocols are used to assist detoxification. The protocols tend to substitute a process for a substance. Use of these is noted on the referral so that the Therapeutic Recreation Specialist may pick up where the detox program left off, withdrawing the specific process until balance is achieved.

The referral also contains information about family members and basic demographics. Sometimes the family is referred to service just as the client. Sometimes there is not enough known about the family to make a referral. When there is a lack of information, only the name and relationship of the person who accompanied the client to admission is listed. Demographics include the client's age, marital status, number of children in the home, city of residence, and the client's education level and occupation. Pending court cases are mentioned as well as driver's license status. The referral also contains the client's room number so that the Therapeutic Recreation Specialist knows where to look for him/her. Most of this information has been loaded into the computer by the admissions clerk. The computer is programmed to transfer the information to the Therapeutic Recreation referral automatically when the physician makes the referral. (See Figure 7.0)

Each day, each Therapeutic Recreation Specialist has a scheduled time for meeting new clients and for doing assessments. The time is begun by checking the computer for a listing of the new referrals. Armed with the referral information, the Therapeutic Recreation Specialist goes to the client's room to meet, greet, and assess. The new referrals are in their rooms, for other TNT staff know the Therapeutic Recreation assessment schedule. During the informal interaction that leads to the assessment, the Therapeutic Recreation Specialist compares comments made by the client with information from the referral. By the time the assessment process actually begins, the Therapeutic Recreation Specialist knows if this client is capable of completing the assessment independently, or will need assistance of some type. The Therapeutic Recreation Specialist knows if the client should be given the pencil and paper format of the assessment, or the interactive computer format. Since the Therapeutic Recreation Service at TNT uses laptop computers, clients may complete the interactive computer format in their rooms, while the Therapeutic Recreation Specialist meets and greets other new referrals.

LEISURE SKILLS AND INTERESTS

The Therapeutic Recreation Specialist usually uses the interest inventory as part of the meeting and greeting time spent with the client. Leisure interests tend to be a nonthreatening area of discussion. Once the client has shared information on this topic, and the information has been received with care, interest, and support, he/she is more willing to reveal more sensitive information. The client's interests are an important aspect of programming. Making use of the information also depends on

FIGURE 7.0

SAMPLE REFERRAL FORM

NAME: _____ MEDICAL RECORD #: _____ ADMISSION DATE: _____
ROOM #: _____ CASE COORDINATOR: _____

ADDRESS: _____ PHONE: _____

BACKGROUND INFORMATION:
DRIVERS LICENSE#: _____ revoked _____ suspended _____ restricted _____ non-driver _____

DATE OF BIRTH: _____ EDUCATION: _____ OCCUPATION: _____

LIVES WITH: _____ Relationship _____
_____ Relationship _____
_____ Relationship _____

ACCOMPANIED TO ADMISSION BY: _____

CHEMICAL ABUSE HISTORY AS REPORTED UPON ADMISSION:

CLIENT: _____

FAMILY MEMBERS: _____

TYPES OF SUBSTANCES USED PRIOR TO ADMISSION: _____

DETOX PROTOCOL IN USE/USED: # _____ POST DETOX TIME: _____

MEDICAL PHYSICAL STATUS:

TRI ITEM #1 PHYSICAL: 1 2 3 4 anticipated length of time before rating changes: _____

COMMENTS/SPECIAL RESTRICTIONS:

PRECAUTIONS:

ORDERS:

_____ REFERRED TO THERAPEUTIC RECREATION FOR EVALUATION TO BE FOLLOWED BY TREATMENT IF NEEDED.

_____ THE FOLLOWING FAMILY MEMBERS ALSO REFERRED TO THERAPEUTIC RECREATION SERVICE FOR EVALUATION, FOLLOWED BY TREATMENT IF NEEDED: _____

OTHER COMMENTS/INSTRUCTIONS:

REFERRED BY DR. _____ DATE: _____

the resources available to the Therapeutic Recreation Service. If rapid assessment of interests is needed, the client's interest may be determined in categories of activities, rather than through knowledge of specific activities. Ask, "What do you like to do such as. . ." and give three examples of activities which you consider belong to a particular group of activities. This helps to jolt the client's thinking, avoid generalities such as "nothing much," and helps to understand how the client categorizes activities. Some principal interest categories are Competitive, Noncompetitive, Productive, Social, Individual, Intellectual, Creative, Spiritual, and Other. Information extracted by the leisure interest inventory is used in the selection of "electives." The process of getting the interests down on paper is perhaps more important to the client than to the Therapeutic Recreation Specialist. I say that because in the system I am describing, the client decides which interests to pursue. The Therapeutic Recreation Specialist only determines how many pursuits are adequate. This permits the Therapeutic Recreation Specialist to focus time and energy on meeting the client's needs. (See Figure 7.1)

ASSESSMENT BY TRI

The assessment is usually the first contact between Therapeutic Recreation Specialist and client. Too often it is the last. Some clients do not stay in treatment long enough to process the traditional paperwork. It is important that the initial contact not only collect data, but also set the stage for future treatment, and provide immediate assistance for leisure improvement. The TRI (Therapeutic Recreation Information) System accomplishes these objectives. (See Figure 7.2)

TRI is designed to recognize the client as a partner in the treatment process. It respects the client's individuality, and implies that he/she is a responsible, reasoning, independent individual. At the same time it does not set the client up to fail by giving him/her a project that is beyond the individual's capabilities. TRI provides measurement, feedback, flexibility, and structure while consuming a minimum amount of the Therapeutic Recreation Specialist's time. TRI is the hub of the Therapeutic Recreation structure. It does not determine everything there is to know about the client. It determines how the Therapeutic Recreation Service might best assist the client into recovery. All Therapeutic Recreation activities are coded into the TRI system. Since all programs exist because they impact on the needs identified by the assessment, treatment planning is almost automatic. Unoccupied time is structured immediately.

The TRI System is based on 10 assessment areas referred to as "items." Scoring of each item is primarily based on self-report, but should be verified and modified by other sources of information whenever possible. There are five possible answers for each of the 10 items. The combination of scores from the 10 items provides an overall estimate of the client's level of Leisure Independence. By reassessing the client at the end of treatment, the TRI score provides an estimate of progress

made during the time which has lapsed between assessments. The scores for each of the 10 items identifies specific areas of needs for which Therapeutic Recreation programming may be required.

For the TRI System to work effectively, it is critical that Therapeutic Recreation programs be developed to address the needs identified by the assessment process. Otherwise there is no need to ask the question in the first place. (The difference between a Therapeutic Recreation assessment and a gossip session, is that a Therapeutic Recreation assessment provides needed information to assist the client's recovery. A gossip session provides interesting information the disclosure of which benefits no one. One should verify which of these is being provided.)

If programs do not exist to address the needs of a TRI assessment item, then the item should be deleted. If programs exist that do not relate to the TRI assessment items, then new items should be developed to steer appropriate clients into the existing programs. The TRI System only allows for 10 items. Therefore, substitutions must be made instead of adding more items. The number of items has been limited for a good reason. Ten items with five possible solutions requires that at least 50 activities be offered. Most activities need to be performed more than once to produce desired benefits. In a 30-day (or shorter) treatment program there simply isn't time to ask a client more than 10 questions. If items must be omitted, it is suggested that items unrelated to increasing leisure independence be the first to go.

There are five possible levels (or scores) for each TRI Item. The highest level for an item is the "Independent" level, and is given a score of 4. The next highest level is the "Semi-Independent" level, which gets a score of 3. Then comes the "Dependent" level, with a score of 2, followed by the "At Risk" level with a score of 1. The fifth possible level for each item is "None of the above, or Unknown." This level is given a raw score of "0." If the answer for the TRI Item does not fit in any of the levels of scoring for any reason, it is given a 0. When developing a treatment plan for a "0", the goal becomes to reevaluate the TRI Item area using some other source of information before initiating a program plan. Additional sources of information may be an extended period of observation, a lengthy standardized Therapeutic Recreation assessment, or consultation with members of other disciplines.

In actual use the raw scores of 4, 3, 2, 1, and 0 are weighted and then the scores for each item are added together to give an overall number on a 100-point scale that reflects the client's overall position of Leisure Independence. To simplify matters, the scores from TRI are demonstrated without weighting. When the TRI is used in conjunction with computers, the raw scores are automatically weighted. The weighting assists in the selection of a starting point for programming.

Since TRI forms the backbone of the Therapeutic Recreation Service being described, a brief review of the TRI Items is necessary before activities supporting the assessment results can be described. The reader should note that this is a very brief review. Full explanation is beyond the scope of this text.

FIGURE 7.1

LEISURE SKILLS INVENTORY*

INSTRUCTIONS: *Satisfying is defined as something which is enjoyable, meaningful, worthwhile, or just plain fun.*
In column (A) list three (3) personally satisfying things that you know how to do during your free time. List only activities which do not require a drink, fix or pill, in order to participate. **In column (B)** *estimate the number of hours per week you could do the activity without getting bored.* **In column (C)** *place a "1" in front of the one most satisfying to you. Place a "2" in front of the next most satisfying, a "3" in front of the third most satisfying, etc.* **When finished, circle the activities which you find relaxing. Thanks for your continued cooperation.**

(A)	(B)	(C)
1. OTHER-COMPETITIVE: such as team sports, playing poker, car racing,		
2. SELF-COMPETITIVE: such as jogging, snow skiing, video games,		
3. PRODUCTIVE: such as gardening, fishing, woodworking, knitting, home decorating,		
4. SOCIAL: such as dining with others, table games with family, visiting with friends,		
5. INDIVIDUAL: such as walking, listening to music, singing in the shower,		
6. INTELLECTUAL: such as crossword puzzles, learning new information, debating current events,		
7. CREATIVE: such as playing music, creative writing, painting pictures,		
8. SPIRITUAL: such as meditating, reading inspirational books, attending church,		
9. OTHER: such as high risk activities, and anything that does not fit above.		

* Reprinted from TRI by permission of Leisure Enrichment Service.

TRI Item #1 addresses the client's medical stability and physical condition for leisure participation. The item's purpose is to identify temporary states of physical "dis-ease" (detoxification complications, nutrition deficiencies, illness, injuries, or physical impairments) which temporarily or permanently restrict leisure participation. Though the client is asked to score this item, the final official score should be based on all information available from the medical team. It should then be reviewed by the medical director before any programming action is taken. Any discrepancies between the client's view of his/her physical condition, and the medical view of the client's condition should be dealt with as part of the client's therapy program. All Therapeutic Recreation activities having a physical component should be reviewed by the medical director, or his designed and assigned to a level corresponding to the TRI Item levels for this item. In this way, clients are not permitted to press beyond their limits. Clients who score "Independent" on this item are encouraged to continue exercise through Re-Creation to prevent dehabilitation while in treatment. The clients who scores "Semi-Independent" may be assigned a goal to increase physical fitness to the "Independent" level by discharge. Clients who score "Dependent" on this item have physical or medical problems that can be inflamed by overexertion. The goal for this group becomes the provision of safe, nonstrenuous activity. Rest and relaxation are encouraged. The dangers of overexertion are stressed. When the health problem is resolved, the client should be given increased activity until he/she is able to participate in activities of the "Semi-Independent" level. Clients who score "At Risk" on this item have health problems or physical impairments that clearly interfere with leisure participation. "At-Risk" clients may initially need bed rest, then physical therapy. It is unrealistic to assume that Therapeutic Recreation can restore physical fitness during a short treatment stay. The goal becomes the provision of leisure pursuits that do not require physical exertion until the client becomes ready.

TRI Item #2 addresses education ability. Whenever possible, the client is given something to read out loud and the score is based on his/her ability to perform the task. Clients who score "Independent" and "Semi-Independent" in reading skills are permitted to complete the remainder of the assessment independently. Independent clients are encouraged to use the Therapeutic Recreation library and to learn new leisure skills through reading. Clients who score "Dependent" have reading skills adequate for the day-to-day routine at home. Their primary choices of reading materials are newspapers and magazines. Clients who are "Dependent" or "At Risk" in reading are assisted in the completion of the assessment form. Pen-and-paper type Leisure Education sessions are avoided unless a specific goal has been established by the treatment team to improve the client's reading skills. Adolescents who are "Dependent" or "At Risk" usually have such a goal established for their treatment. In these cases, the Therapeutic Recreation Specialist works closely with the Education Specialist to select the appropriate level of reading materials for the client.

TRI Item #3 looks at the client's access to transportation to and from leisure pursuits. The purpose of the item is to develop realistic alternatives for post-discharge leisure. Clients who have their own car and an unrestricted driver's license are considered to be "Independent." No special programs are required. Clients who score "Semi-Independent" (have a temporarily restricted license or shared transportation) are treated the same as "Independent" clients if living in an area with good public transportation. The more "Dependent" the client becomes on others for transportation, the more the client needs to develop assertive behaviors that will allow him/her to ask for transportation to leisure pursuits. As dependence on family for transportation increases, the family's need to understand the value of leisure pursuit increases. The client who is "At Risk" has no driver's license, no car, no close friends or family with transportation—and no changes are expected in the near future. For the "At Risk" client, the goal becomes to assist the client in developing leisure plans that are not transportation-dependent. Inadequate transportation will severely limit post-discharge leisure activities. Most leisure needs must be met through AA/NA participation and activities available within walking distance. Development of assertive skills remains helpful.

Transportation plays an important part in leisure participation. The best planned recreation program is worthless if the participant has no way to get there. Persons who must depend on others for transportation also must depend on others for many other services. After a while, a person may feel like a burden to others. They may feel guilty asking for so many "favors." The first item they will stop asking for is transportation for leisure. Assertive skills must be developed to help the person ask for transportation to leisure without feeling guilty. Leisure Education for family will help the family understand the need and become more willing to provide the transportation. Persons scoring "Dependent" and "At Risk" may become frustrated by exciting leisure plans if they have no way of getting to the events. AA and NA have many leisure aspects built into their programs, and members are accustomed to providing transportation for others. It is therefore wise to meet as many needs as possible through these functions.

TRI Item #4 addresses the client's economic situation. How much money a client earns is of little concern. The critical question is how much the client has left for leisure purposes. The information from this question is used in many ways. During treatment, clients are steered toward Skill Development sessions for activities that match their economic level. Economics of leisure are addressed in at least one Leisure Education session. Some clients are able to stay sober or clean when broke, but get into trouble when there is money left over. For these persons the answer is spending more on leisure so that less is left. Clients who score "Independent" on this item are free to choose any activity available at the Center. At the opposite end of the scale, clients who are "At Risk" are helped to find meaningful leisure pursuits for very low costs.

TRI Item #5 deals with family support for leisure. Answers to this item provide information for Therapeutic Recreation programming for both the client and the family. The client who is "Independent" on this item probably does not need Therapeutic Recreation intervention. Sessions that help the client value leisure time with family are important to reinforce and maintain healthy habits. The "Semi-Independent" client belongs to a family that is willing to be together in an alcohol/drug-free environment, but the family members may have few common leisure interests and/or lack understanding of the value of leisure. For these families, Therapeutic Recreation involvement can be most productive. Most clients enter treatment at the "Dependent" level where family relations are strained. Time spent together tends to be strained. Parallel programming is required to allow client and family members opportunities to vent their frustrations without inflicting wounds on each other. Once this has been accomplished, then the client and family may join together for Skill Development and Re-Creation sessions. This adds memories of good times together back into the relationships. Clients who are "At Risk" have no family contact, or contact is with family member(s) who abuse alcohol/drugs. Special care is taken to provide activities for the client to engage in during visiting hours.

TRI Item #6 identifies levels of personal stress. This item is designed to assist in the selection of leisure pursuits that are conducive to stress reduction. There are many forms of relaxation methods available. Most of them require practice and repetition to be effective. Persons who have displayed stress symptomology prior to detoxification, or those who have become dependent on alcohol/drugs to relieve stress, may need more practice time in stress reduction techniques than most short-term treatment programs permit. For this reason, such individuals should be referred to a Stress Reduction Specialist after discharge. Leisure itself is a great stress manager. Any activity on which the client is totally able to focus attention can produce relaxation. Total focus of attention is measured by a loss of awareness of the passage of time, or failure to respond to interjected questioning. Persons who develop the ability to use a leisure pursuit as a relaxation method, must also be cautioned not to use the activity to avoid dealing with reality. The difference between using an activity for relaxation and for avoidance is that the relaxed person accumulates regenerated energies that may be used to solve the problems which have been causing the stress. The person who seeks avoidance moves from one relaxing activity to another relaxing activity without stopping to face the problem which is producing the stress. Stress reduction methods (other than utilization of appropriate leisure activity) should be performed by the most qualified person on the treatment team. A Therapeutic Recreation Specialist may provide stress reduction techniques provided that additional specialized training has been received in this area. Clients who score "Independent" know how to manage their stress and therefore no special programming is provided. Clients who score "Semi-Independent" have a variety of alcohol/drug-free ways to relax, but still find times when stress is a problem in life or times when getting adequate

sleep is difficult. For these clients, the provision of practice time may be all that is needed. Clients who have difficulty sleeping at night and/or have difficulty alleviating stress without chemical use should receive the full attention of Therapeutic Recreation programs that are designed to relieve stress. The client who finds a loss of sleep intolerable and finds it impossible to sleep without chemical use, is "At Risk." The expertise of the entire Treatment Team should be brought to the assistance of this type of client.

TRI Item #7 is called "Play History Status." It addresses the needs of clients who have missed developmental leisure levels during childhood as a result of growing up in an alcoholic home. Clients are considered "Independent" if they can recall childhood memories such as inviting friends into the home to play; playing games, going on family outings, and/or roughhousing with parents; exploring the world at home by tapping different objects to see what sounds result, and by taking objects apart; exploring personal abilities at home such as stacking blocks or objects to see how high they will stack before falling down, or climbing from one piece of furniture to another to cross a room without touching the floor; finding pleasure in sunbathing, taking a nap, or just being lazy. These forms of play were typically accepted and encouraged by the parents. "Semi-Independent" clients can remember doing about the same things but do not remember parents encouraging such activities. "Dependent" clients remember avoiding doing such things around the home. "At Risk" clients find it difficult to remember positive play experiences which occurred in the home and/or while parents were present. Early childhood trauma often blocks memories of childhood. When a client cannot remember playful activities, the chances are the memories are associated with painful emotional events.

TRI Item #8 deals with the client's ability for creative problem solving. This item addresses the person's capacity for divergent thinking (finding as many correct answers as possible) as opposed to convergent thinking (finding the one correct answer). The ability to consider alternatives and solve problems is critical to the development of a healthy leisure lifestyle. The Therapeutic Recreation Specialist can only assist the client up to a point; the Therapeutic Recreation Specialist cannot go home in each client's suitcase. The best-designed plan for meeting future leisure needs is imperfect. The future is unpredictable; needs change. What will happen when the leisure plan develops a flaw? A person good in developing alternatives will find a way to adjust the plan. The person who is good at following instructions, but not good at identifying alternatives, will be stopped by the flaw. Providing divergent problem-solving opportunities during the treatment phase can be productive, but to make significant gains will take time. Establishing a contact person to assist in redesigning leisure plans after discharge is indicated for those persons lacking the ability to generate alternatives. The ideal contact person would be an AA/NA member from the client's community who is a good leisure problem-solver. The next best would be linking the "Dependent" or "At Risk" client to a skilled community recreation contact. Another alternative would be a follow-up system coordinated by a Therapeutic Recreation Specialist in the treatment facility.

TRI Item #9 is based on completion of a Leisure Skills Inventory (see 7.1). The client's needs for Leisure Skill Development are addressed in this item. This is perhaps the most difficult area of need to assess because it is so easy for the Therapeutic Recreation Specialist to impose personal value judgments on the evaluation of the client's list of leisure interests. For example, some adults are couch potatoes. They go to work, come home, and sprawl out on the couch for the remainder of the evening, day after day after day. Is that good or bad leisure? Granted, when a person has been admitted to a treatment program for addiction, the chances of him/her being a well-adjusted couch potato (or anything else) are slight. Still, when it comes to determining if the client has adequate leisure skills, one must remember that adequate refers to his/her lifestyle and internal chemical composition, and not mine. The anorexic client is a good example. Persons with anorexia tend to be physically active. The physical activity helps to burn off those calories. For the anorexic, the development of leisure skills that permit the person to become a couch potato is very healthy. The person who is always busy and active because unmanageable stress levels prevent the person from sitting still, would also benefit from developing couch potato abilities.

To determine if the client has adequate skills for healthy leisure pursuit, TRI Item #9 asks the client to evaluate the list of activities on the Leisure Skills Inventory Form. To establish the client's level of independence in leisure skills, a series of questions must be answered. Are the activities the client knows how to do (when sober) satisfying? Are there activities listed which maintain physical fitness and are consistent with the client's physical/medical condition listed in TRI Item #1? Are the costs involved in participation in the activities consistent with the client's economic level as measured by TRI Item #3? (The typical cocaine addict may have lots of activity skills, all requiring significant funds to participate. By admission, the supply of abundant funds has been exhausted, leaving the cocaine addict without drugs and without satisfying leisure pursuits.) Before activities listed can be deemed "adequate," it must also be determined that transportation is adequate (as measured by TRI Item #4) to get the client to and from the activity. Activities of choice must also be consistent with discharge destination and family support (as measured by TRI Item #5). The list of activity skills must also contain activities that reduce personal stress. Those who are "At Risk" or "Dependent" in personal stress (as measured by TRI Item #6), do not have adequate leisure skills, regardless of how many activity skills have been listed. Activities listed on the Leisure Skill Inventory must also be checked for repetition. When the passive interest is watching others while jogging, the competitive interest is jogging with others, and the noncompetitive interest is jogging alone, then the client may be a jogging addict rather than an individual with a wide variety of leisure interests. (The client may also be in denial and simply does not want to admit that his/her leisure is inadequate.) Along this same

vein it must also be determined that different activities listed are actually different. Jogging, aerobics, weightlifting, and biking are different branches of the same tree. They are different activities, yet they have the same purpose and impact on the body. For the purposes of developing a balanced lifestyle, these are all considered variations of the same leisure interest. Finally, it must be determined that the client has been able to list enough skills to fill his/her free time. And how much is enough? Some suffer from a lack of free time in the daily routine, others suffer from too much. Some with overcrowded schedules manage to find free time somehow; others find more tasks to fill the day to avoid having free time. To establish a minimum for this determination, there should be enough activity listed to fill four hours per week if the client is employed fulltime. Those without fulltime employment should have enough activity to fill two hours per day or 14 hours per week. There have been 10 areas addressed to determine adequacy of leisure skills. The client with a Leisure Skills Inventory able to get a positive on all of the above test questions is considered to be "Independent" on TRI Item #9, indicating that the client's leisure skills are adequate to meet his/her needs. For this person, the teaching of new leisure skills is not necessary. The client who has managed to get the "OK" on 7 of the 10 is considered to be at the "Semi-Independent" level. The client who has 4 to 6 of the areas intact is considered to be at the "Dependent" level. Three or less, and the client is considered to be "At Risk."

This may seem too complex for a client to review and make a determination. The Therapeutic Recreation Specialist is far better equipped to evaluate the content of the Leisure Skills Inventory. Some clients are able to process the content. The attempt to process may help the client to see that there is a lot more to leisure than he/she realized and may then become willing and motivated to attend Therapeutic Recreation Sessions. Because of the complexity of scoring, some clients may feel overwhelmed. Becoming overwhelmed and frustrated may create a desire to avoid Therapeutic Recreation sessions. The Therapeutic Recreation Specialist must make an educated guess about how the client will feel in attempting to evaluate the Leisure Skills Inventory. Where there is the slightest concern that the process might result in frustration, the Therapeutic Recreation Specialist and client should go through the evaluation process together. Typically, most clients have a relatively blank Leisure Skills Inventory to evaluate. Complexity is greatly diminished when no leisure skills exist, adequate or otherwise.

TRI Item #10 is the final item and one of the most critical. Fortunately, it is easier to score than Item #9. This item addresses Leisure Awareness. The purpose of this item is to determine the need for Leisure Education sessions and also the type of Leisure Education sessions. To accurately determine the Leisure Awareness level, results of TRI Item #9 (Leisure Skills) and TRI Item #8 (Problem Solving) should be considered as well as the client's response to the Leisure Awareness question. The Leisure Awareness question asks if leisure is an important aspect of life. It also asks the client to give an example of participation in at least one leisure pursuit that regenerated his/her energy. If the client knows that leisure is important, can describe an event in which recreation occurred, and has a healthy Leisure Skills Inventory and good problem solving skills, then the client is "Independent" in Leisure Awareness. There is no need for Leisure Education sessions for this individual, other than a few basic ones that help him/her understand the leisure/addiction connection. Therapeutic Recreation Specialists find their jobs difficult because few clients are independent in leisure awareness. Still, the possibility cannot be ruled out. At the same time, when a client is independent in Leisure Awareness, treating him/her as if he/she were not independent is highly counterproductive. Clients who admit that leisure is an important aspect of life, but feel guilty taking time for leisure are considered to be "Semi-Independent." For this group, just one good Leisure Education session dealing with leisure guilt can catapult them to the "Independent" level of leisure functioning. Many clients do fall into this group. Clients are considered to be "Dependent" when they indicate that leisure is an unimportant aspect of life, due to a lack of personal time to participate in leisure. The client who indicates that leisure is an important aspect of life, but cannot provide a specific example of participating in an alcohol/drug-free leisure pursuit that regenerated his/her energy, is also considered to be "Dependent." The client who says something is unimportant and then gives an excuse for not doing it, is no better off than the client who says something is important but does not do it. The "Dependent" client needs intensive Therapeutic Recreation services and Leisure Education. Benefits can be derived from the provision of these services, and it usually takes the entire treatment stay to produce results. The client who is "At Risk" in leisure awareness is the client who has no idea what leisure is or does. Also "At Risk" is the client that says leisure is unimportant in his/her life and offers no excuses for his/her position. This is the "My mind's made up, don't confuse me with facts" client. Clients who are "At Risk" need intensive Therapeutic Recreation services; however, benefits derived are questionable. Often, the client is not really ready to hear what the Therapeutic Recreation Specialist has to say. The most appropriate avenue is exposure to Therapeutic Recreation services and a plan to repeat the needed Leisure Education sessions for the client after discharge. Usually the "At-Risk" client is the one who comes back after discharge and says, "I wish I would have paid more attention to what you were saying."

To summarize, the TRI addresses 10 areas referred to as items. Each item has five statements listed. The client selects the statement which seems most reflective of his/her position. The statement selected determines the "score" received on the item. Scores range from 4 to zero, with 4 meaning the client is at an independent level of leisure functioning in this area, 3 indicating a semi-independent level, 2 demonstrating a dependent level, 1 suggesting an at-risk level, and zero indicating that the level of function is unknown. When a zero turns up, the Therapeutic Recreation Specialist attempts to develop a treat-ment plan that does not require immediate use of information from the unknown area. Too many zero's, and the goal of the initial treatment plan is to determine the levels in areas marked by zero's. This often means going to the use of a more in-depth assessment tool, or observing the client in a variety of activities. Many times the zero's are a result of denial or of the client's avoidance of the truth.

FROM ASSESSMENT TO EVALUATION

Assessment is different from evaluation. Assessment is the collection of data. Evaluation is the interpretation of the data that have been collected. Whenever possible, the client takes the lead during assessment. The Therapeutic Recreation Specialist takes the lead during evaluation. Data collected during assessment are treated as opinions. There are a number of opinions to be considered. There is the opinion of the client as indicated on the self-administered TRI assessment form. There are the opinions of the physician and admissions staff, represented on the referral form. There is the opinion of the Therapeutic Recreation Specialist. Agreeing "opinions" are rare. The Therapeutic Recreation Therapist attempts to negotiate agreement with the client. When this is not possible, the Therapeutic Recreation Specialist gets the client to agree to disagree. Evaluation scores are the Therapeutic Recreation Specialist's opinion, not the client's. Treatment plan objectives are selected for areas where the client and the Therapeutic Recreation Specialist agree to scores which indicate there is a need. Work on other needs is postponed. Usually progress in the agreed-upon areas, combined with progress in other therapies, resolves the disagreements.

In the process of moving from assessment to evaluation, scores are weighted. Weighting provides more descriptive numbers. (The sum of the 10 TRI Items' raw scores adds to 40 if all items are scored at the "Independent" level; but what is a 40?) After the weighting process the sum of the 10 TRI Items, if all scored at the "Independent" level add to 100. One hundred provides a connotation of completeness; the best one can do. There is a second reason for the weighting process. The weighting permits the scores to reflect the possibility that Therapeutic Recreation can do more to resolve some of the areas than some of the other areas. Conversations with other Therapeutic Recreation professionals suggest that this weighting reflects programming trends in the field at this time.

The larger the weight, the larger the potential contribution of Therapeutic Recreation to resolving the problem. While Therapeutic Recreation can play an important role in improving a person's "Physical" condition, there are many other factors and disciplines involved in any improvement that might occur. In the areas of Leisure Skills, Play Status, and Leisure Awareness, Therapeutic Recreation is the key discipline involved in an improvement. For this reason, "Physical" has been given a maximum weighted score of 10, while Leisure

Awareness, Skills, and Play Status have been given 12's. Family Support, Stress, and Problem Solving fall into the same category as Physical, and are all given 10's. The others, Transportation, Education, and Economic, are given 8's. These items are sometimes beyond the control of an entire Treatment Team. They are important factors, but improvements are often slow. Very often programming for these areas is designed to help the person to accept what cannot be changed, rather than to seek actual improvement.

The evaluation score is calculated by multiplying the raw score from the assessment form (4 if independent, 3 if semi-independent, 2 if dependent, 1 if at risk, 0 if unknown) by a weight number. For example, the evaluation score for TRI Item #1 is the raw score (if independent, then it is 4) times 2.5. Therefore, the evaluation score for Item #1 is 10 if the person is independent. Weights are shown for each level for each TRI Item. (See Figure 7.2 on the following page)

THE TREATMENT PLAN

The Evaluation Scores are shown at the top of the treatment plan. The treatment plan is based on these scores. Too often there is room for improvement in all areas evaluated. The treatment day is too short to address all areas in need at once. Choices must be made. Priorities must be set. Three factors contribute to the selection of objectives. The first factor is the availability of Therapeutic Recreation programs and activities to address identified needs. Since TNT has a full range of services, this factor is not a consideration. The second factor is the client's recognition of the need for improvement in a given area. Without the client's cooperation, nothing beneficial will result. Therefore, areas where Therapeutic Recreation Specialist and client agree to the score should be given a higher priority than those where there is disagreement. The third factor is a determination of the areas that can be changed the most by involvement in Therapeutic Recreation. This is noted by the weighting system. In this way, those areas which have

been given larger weights should be selected over those with lower weights. (See Figure 7.3 below)

In this example, the client's opinion or scores varied significantly from the Therapeutic Recreation Specialist's scores for several items. Economics was scored high by the client. The Therapeutic Recreation Specialist noted that the referral form indicated the client was unemployed, so marked the item as an unknown. The client marked him/herself independent on transportation and family status. The Therapeutic Recreation Specialist also noted that the referral form indicated no family accompanied the client to admission and the client's driver's license had been revoked. The Therapeutic Recreation Specialist was unable to get the client to change his/her scoring where there were differences of opinion. There were only four areas assessed in which there was agreement. Of those areas the one with the highest weighting was Item #10, Leisure Awareness. The client scored "Dependent" on this item, meaning it needed a lot of work. The first treatment plan focused on improvement in Leisure Awareness for these reasons.

Once the goal is selected, the next step is to select activities to meet the objective. At TNT, this process is speeded along with the use of the TRI coding system. After the goal has been selected, which in this case is to increase Leisure Awareness by one level as measured by the TRI, then the Therapeutic Recreation Specialist reviews activities which are coded to meet Leisure Awareness needs and schedules the client to participate in the selected activities.

THE TRI CODING SYSTEM

In the TRI coding system, all activities offered by the Therapeutic Recreation Services are assigned a number. The number is a code which summarizes how well the activity meets a given evaluated need. Some activities meet a variety of needs. The activity is coded for all needs met by the activity, as the activity is provided at the facility. An activity may have the

FIGURE 7.3

TRI Item:	Opinion of Client	Rating TRS	(Level)	Final Wght. Score	Maximum Possible
TRI PORTION OF TX PLAN WITH CLIENT AGREEMENT NOTED					
1. Physical	3	3	(3)	7.5	10
2. Education	3	3	(3)	6	8
3. Transportation	4	0	(0)	0	8
4. Economic	0	1	(1)	2	8
5. Family Support	4	0	(0)	0	10
6. Stress	4	1	(1)	2.5	10
7. Status (Play)	4	2	(2)	6	12
8. Problem Solving	2	2	(2)	5	10
9. Leisure Skills	3	2	(2)	6	12
10. Leisure Awareness	2	2	(2)	6	12
TRI Total Score:				**41 out of**	**100**

FIGURE 7.2

TRI WEIGHTING SYSTEM FOR SUBSTANCE ABUSE SCALE

TRI ITEM # / LABEL	INDEPENDENT	x WEIGHT	=	SCORE
1. Physical	4 points	x 2.5	=	10
2. Education	4 points	x 2	=	8
3. Transportation	4 points	x 2	=	8
4. Economic	4 points	x 2	=	8
5. Family Support	4 points	x 2.5	=	10
6. Stress	4 points	x 2.5	=	10
7. Status (Play)	4 points	x 3	=	12
8. Problem Solving	4 points	x 2.5	=	10
9. Leisure Skills	4 points	x 3	=	12
10. Leisure Awareness	4 points	x 3	=	12
Maximum Score for Independent Level:				**100**

TRI ITEM # / LABEL	SEMI-INDEPENDENT	x WEIGHT	=	SCORE
1. Physical	3 points	x 2.5	=	7.5
2. Education	3 points	x 2	=	6
3. Transportation	3 points	x 2	=	6
4. Economic	3 points	x 2	=	6
5. Family Support	3 points	x 2.5	=	7.5
6. Stress	3 points	x 2.5	=	7.5
7. Status (Play)	3 points	x 3	=	9
8. Problem Solving	3 points	x 2.5	=	7.5
9. Leisure Skills	3 points	x 3	=	9
10. Leisure Awareness	3 points	x 3	=	9
Maximum Score for Semi-Independent Level:				**75**

TRI ITEM # / LABEL	DEPENDENT	x WEIGHT	=	SCORE
1. Physical	2 points	x 2.5	=	5
2. Education	2 points	x 2	=	4
3. Transportation	2 points	x 2	=	4
4. Economic	2 points	x 2	=	4
5. Family Support	2 points	x 2.5	=	5
6. Stress	2 points	x 2.5	=	5
7. Status (Play)	2 points	x 3	=	6
8. Problem Solving	2 points	x 2.5	=	5
9. Leisure Skills	2 points	x 3	=	6
10. Leisure Awareness	2 points	x 3	=	6
Maximum Score for Dependent Level:				**50**

TRI ITEM # / LABEL	AT RISK	x WEIGHT	=	SCORE
1. Physical	1 point	x 2.5	=	2.5
2. Education	1 point	x 2	=	2
3. Transportation	1 point	x 2	=	2
4. Economic	1 point	x 2	=	2
5. Family Support	1 point	x 2.5	=	2.5
6. Stress	1 point	x 2.5	=	2.5
7. Status (Play)	1 point	x 3	=	3
8. Problem Solving	1 point	x 2.5	=	2.5
9. Leisure Skills	1 point	x 3	=	3
10. Leisure Awareness	1 point	x 3	=	3
Maximum Score for At Risk Level:				**25**

potential of meeting 100 needs. Most likely it is only used for two or three purposes at the most. The activity is coded for the two or three uses, not for the 100 potential uses.

The code has three digits followed by a decimal point, followed by one and sometimes two more digits. (See Figure 7.4) The first digit of the series indicates the major heading, or type of program. The next digit indicates interest categories. The next digit shows if the activity meets an area of need identified by the TRI assessment system. The digit following the decimal point shows the level of leisure independence which is the score received on that item during TRI assessment. Additional digits are used to reference specific formats so that two formats meeting the same basic needs do not get confused. This is only used when such confusion can make a big difference.

The "major headings" for the categories noted by the first digit of the code are Leisure Education, Skill Development, Re-Creation, and Recreation Therapy. All activities provided are grouped under one of these headings. A "1" in this position indicates that the activity is used as a Leisure Education session (meaning that the session is primarily designed to develop the

client's awareness and understanding of his/her leisure needs). A "2" means it is used as a Skill Development session (meaning that the session is primarily designed to develop skills needed to perform a given leisure activity). A "3" means the listed activity is used for Re-Creation participation (an opportunity to experience leisure and to derive the benefits provided from a Re-Creative event). A "4" means the activity is used as a Recreation Therapy tool (as an intervention designed to restore the participant to a healthful state).

The next digit indicates interest categories. A zero listed in this space indicates that it appeals to a wide variety of interests. Codes in this digit are primarily used for Skill Development sessions and Re-Creation sessions. A "1" in the second digit position means that the activity is other-competitive in nature. It could be physical or it could be a table game, but it strongly pits one person or team against another, and there is a clear winner or loser at the end. A "2" means the activity is self-competitive. It includes forms of physical exercise and games where there is no clear winner or loser at the end. A "3" indicates productive activities. It includes work substitutes and/or activities that result in an end product. This

FIGURE 7.4

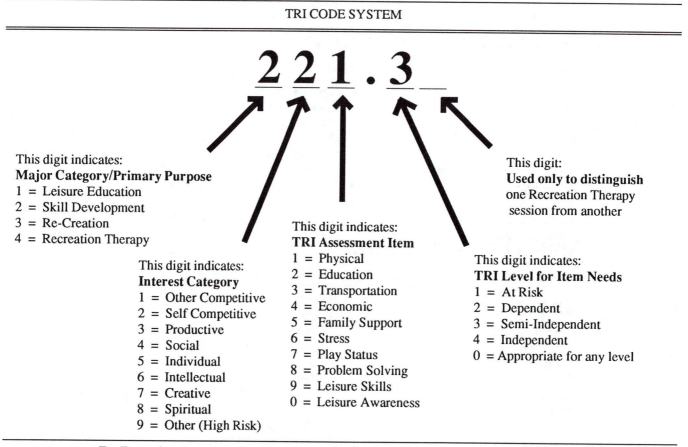

TRI CODE SYSTEM

$$2\ 2\ 1\ .\ 3\ \_$$

This digit indicates:
Major Category/Primary Purpose
1 = Leisure Education
2 = Skill Development
3 = Re-Creation
4 = Recreation Therapy

This digit indicates:
Interest Category
1 = Other Competitive
2 = Self Competitive
3 = Productive
4 = Social
5 = Individual
6 = Intellectual
7 = Creative
8 = Spiritual
9 = Other (High Risk)

This digit indicates:
TRI Assessment Item
1 = Physical
2 = Education
3 = Transportation
4 = Economic
5 = Family Support
6 = Stress
7 = Play Status
8 = Problem Solving
9 = Leisure Skills
0 = Leisure Awareness

This digit:
Used only to distinguish
one Recreation Therapy
session from another

This digit indicates:
TRI Level for Item Needs
1 = At Risk
2 = Dependent
3 = Semi-Independent
4 = Independent
0 = Appropriate for any level

For Example:
221.3 = A skill development activity which is self-competitive to be used for a client
scoring on TRI Item #1 (physical) at the semi-independent level.

category includes but is not limited to gardening, fishing, hunting, woodworking, sewing, and craft projects for which a pattern or a model of the end product is provided. A "4" indicates social activities. It includes activities where the primary focus or purpose is for people to come together and to interact with each other. A "5" indicates individual pursuits. These are activities which are done alone and tend to isolate persons from interaction with others. Watching television could be considered an individual pursuit because a person watching TV does not interact with others who are in the same room (until commercial break at least). A "6" indicates intellectual pursuits. These are activities which stimulate thought processing. A "7" signals creative activities. This includes but is not limited to forms of art, dance, drama, music, writing, where there is experimentation in the medium selected, and the end product is not a primary concern or is initially unknown. An "8" indicates spiritual pursuits. This includes activities which cause a person to feel close to a power greater than the self as well as the traditional pursuits of reading the Bible and attending church services. A "9" indicates "high-risk" activities.

The digit before the decimal indicates the TRI Item number taken from the TRI assessment system. A "1" indicates physical, a "2" education, a "3" transportation, and so on. A zero indicates TRI Item #10, Leisure Awareness. Each possible score that a client could receive on the TRI assessment is also indicated in the code as the digit after the decimal. In this position a "1" indicates an activity of a client "At Risk" on the TRI item noted in the digit preceding the decimal point. A "2" indicates the "Dependent" level, and so on. Where there is a zero in the TRI Item score position, it means the activity is beneficial for all levels, or that all levels can be dealt with in that activity.

For example, a 100.2 code means the activity is used as a Leisure Education session, interest category does not matter, the session address TRI Item #10, Leisure Awareness needs for clients who have scored at the "Dependent" level. In the example in the treatment plan section, this activity would be appropriate for the client in the example, and the session would be scheduled to meet the client's needs. The 100.2 activity might have a title such as "Hop Scotch." The activity name does not matter, for the Therapeutic Recreation Specialist knows that "Hop Scotch" is designed to meet a need which the client in question needs to have.

The coding system also helps the client to function independently. If the client knows he/she must attend at least one Skill Development session per week and knows his/her interest category, then the client can select sessions which may be of interest. The client may be given a list of scheduled activities. Looking down the list the client may find an activity named "Herbolgargantuous." The title is an unknown to him/her (and to me too). But the client also sees that Herbolgargantuous is a 222.2. That tells the client that Herbolgargantuous is a Skill Development session that is noncompetitive, involving reading skills at the "Dependent" level. The client now has information upon which to base his/her choice of attendance.

A treatment plan using the TRI system may look something like the following. Note that only one "work" goal has been set though there are many identified needs. A second goal is set which is a maintenance goal. It is important to help clients maintain their level of independence while in treatment. If a client is independent or semi-independent in a specific area, then it involves little work on the part of the Therapeutic Recreation Specialist to monitor maintenance of independence. The client does most of the work, and that pays off in self-esteem. (See Figure 7.5 on the following page)

DETERMINATION OF GOAL ATTAINMENT

Goal attainment is determined by a re-administration of the TRI assessment. The second time around, the client will be more open. Agreement to work on new areas may be negotiated. Conferences with the interdisciplinary team may identify needs for Recreation Therapy sessions before progress on other TRI Items can be achieved. This information is used to revise and update the client's treatment plan on a regular basis. As one goal is achieved, another is selected. In short treatment stays, the client may be discharged before all identified needs have been met. A discharge summary that lists goals achieved and those yet to be attained, provides important information for after-care workers, community resources, and so on. The client should also be given such a summary. In this way, the client can develop his/her own self treatment plan after discharge as needed.

References/Resources

Faulkner, R. (1988). *TRI Information System For Pen & Paper*. Seaside, OR: Leisure Enrichment Service.

FIGURE 7.5

SAMPLE TRI TREATMENT PLAN

Initial Assessment Results:

TRI Item:		Opinion of Client	Rating of TRS	(Level)	Final Wght. Score	Maximum Possible
1.	Physical	3	3	(3)	7.5	10
2.	Education	3	3	(3)	6	8
3.	Transportation	4	0	(0)	0	8
4.	Economic	0	1	(1)	2	8
5.	Family Support	4	0	(0)	0	10
6.	Stress	4	1	(1)	2.5	10
7.	Play Status	4	2	(2)	6	12
8.	Problem Solving	2	2	(2)	5	10
9.	Leisure Skills	3	2	(2)	6	12
10.	Leisure Awareness	2	2	(2)	6	12

TRI Total Score: 41 out of 100

Client was admitted on Jan. 7, 19__, and self administered the TRI Scale for Substance Abuse on Jan. 8, 19__. Differing opinions which existed between client's self scores and Therapeutic Recreation Specialists scores were discussed with client on Jan. 10, 19__. Client agreed to the following plan of care:

Initial Treatment Plan:

TRI Item:	TRI Score/ (Level) Score		TRI Score Goal	Goal Description, Method & Date to be Accomplished
3 Transportation	(0)	0	2+	Determine accurate level. Have client place phone call to Division of Motor Vehicles, in presence of a staff member by 1/15/__.
5 Family Support	(0)	0	2.5+	Determine accurate level of family support through interview with client's family and/or review of case with assigned family therapist by 1/15/__.
6 Stress	(1)	2.5	2.5+	Increase client's ability to manage stress by at least one level as measured by TRI through participation in at least one #106.1 & three #206.1 Therapeutic Recreation Activities by 1/20/__.
10 Leisure Awareness	(2)	6	3+	Increase client's understanding of Leisure by at least one level as measured by TRI, through attending at least four #100.0 Therapeutic Recreation Activities by 1/20/__.

TRI Total Score: 41 to be increased at least 10 points to 51 by 1/20/__

_____ _____ _____ _____
Client Signature   Date   Therapeutic Recreation Specialist Signature   Date

Plan of Care approved by Dr. _____ Date _____

Part III

What We Do

CHAPTER 8

LEISURE EDUCATION

Leisure Education may be defined as sessions designed to help the client understand the role and value of leisure pursuit. Leisure restores balance to life. It makes the difference between living and existing. It restores energy needed to resolve problems and be effective on the job. Participating in leisure requires granting the self permission to play. When clients understand how important it is to play, then it becomes easier to give the self permission to play. Knowing how, where, and when to participate in a leisure activity does not cause a person to participate. A client must understand the need, the value, and the role of leisure, before voluntary participation will occur. This is especially true when recommended leisure pursuits are a change from the norm for an adult. The awkward feelings generated by participation in a new experience can override intrinsic desires to participate, unless the desire is supported by understanding and awareness of needs. Provision of Leisure Counseling/Education is important to the understanding of leisure needs. It is an important first step. The important last step, that keeps people coming back for more, is the deep intrinsic awareness that "I feel better coming out than I did going in." This insight usually occurs spontaneously after Re-Creation has occurred.

There appears to be a hierarchy in the development of leisure awareness. First the awareness that leisure is for adults as well as kids must be created. Then it must be realized that leisure is more than watching television or playing a game (yet there is nothing wrong with TV or games as long as it does not destroy balance). The ultimate awareness is that Leisure is for oneself, that one has a need for it, and that one can make time for it.

Once a person becomes motivated to participate in leisure, then the big question is, in what area? Since literally thousands of leisure pursuits exist, the client must be assisted in narrowing the available choices. The goal becomes finding the right activity to meet the client's needs. Since individual needs change over time, it is important to provide the client with the skills required to identify needs and select activities that meet those needs. Values Clarification sessions can be effective in this process.

After leisure has been attempted, the realization of guilt feelings may surface. These are effectively dealt with by recognizing that it is a common reaction and by looking at sources of guilt (e.g., old sayings warning persons of the evils of play, unspoken family rules from childhood, associations with concepts of selfishness and laziness). Clients who indicate leisure is important but are unable to give specific examples may be doing so only to please the Therapeutic Recreation Specialist. In TRI Item #10, which identifies levels of Leisure Awareness, the client who gives lip service to the value of leisure pursuit but does not practice it, is assigned to the "Dependent" level.

Certain Leisure Education sessions are important for all clients, regardless of levels of leisure independence or individualized needs. At least one session should be devoted to Therapeutic Recreation activities and services available at the treatment facility and the facility's definition of leisure pursuit. At least one session should be devoted to the use of leisure to achieve a balanced lifestyle. At least one session should be devoted to understanding the inter-relationship of alcohol/drug use and leisure. After the client has gotten his/her feet wet in participation, at least one session should be devoted to the prevention of substituting a leisure pursuit for alcohol/drug use and becoming "addicted" to an activity. (Jogging, running, weight lifting, and biking have been used more than once as substitute addictions.) The tree-of-addictions concept should be discussed as part of this session. The body's chemistry, which is altered by drugs and by leisure participation, should be discussed. Clients should be encouraged toward "balance," "variety," "moderation," in selection of leisure pursuits. Most important, clients should be given guidelines and lists of warning signs to assist them in identifying abuse of a leisure pursuit. Finally, all clients require sessions devoted to leisure planning. Clients should not wait until discharge is pending to decide how to manage their leisure. Clients should be planning their day's leisure throughout the treatment stay. Group planning sessions can provide peer support for plan implementation. Ideally, monitoring of the client's leisure planning and plan implementation should be conducted daily. Where this is impossible, it should be done not less than weekly.

At the TNT Addiction Center, a full range of Leisure Education sessions are available and are listed in this chapter. Core sessions that all clients receive are listed with the TRI code of 100.0. (The "1" indicates Leisure Education. The next digit is a "0," which indicates that it does not matter what type of activities the client enjoys doing. The next digit is a "0," indicating that the sessions relate to the tenth item of the TRI assessment, Leisure Awareness. The "0" after the decimal point indicates that it does not matter what the client's score or level of independence on Leisure Awareness is.) The 100.0 sessions are required sessions for all clients and are offered each week during scheduled center-wide educational time slots. Many clients attend them before being transferred from detox to treatment.

Most adult clients at TNT remain in treatment for 6 weeks, and adolescents for 12 weeks. Adult clients are scheduled to attend Leisure Education sessions five days per week. Adolescents are required to attend three Leisure Education sessions per week. The other two days each week, they attend a school program. Adolescents with an early discharge may join adult groups to complete required sessions at an accelerated rate.

Independent clients, and those who have completed the required Leisure Education rotation, are required to check in at the beginning of the session. Most go to other areas of the Therapeutic Recreation facility, pursuing other aspects of the service. Those clients who have completed all aspects of the Therapeutic Recreation program, simply check in and share their day's leisure plan. Then they leave.

Introductory sessions should be void of physical activity so that they may be provided to all clients regardless of medical condition. Introductory sessions should also be passive in nature, for most clients will not feel like becoming active initially. Even so, lecture should be kept to a minimum. Many of the formats in this text employ lecture because it provides a better graphic display on a typed page. In the real world, lectures which must occur should be augmented with audiovisual materials wherever possible. Points should be listed on a flipchart or chalkboard. The use of overhead projectors is also helpful. Videotapes of activities available within the Therapeutic Recreation Service are highly effective. Where forms are used, volunteers should be available to assist clients with reading and writing difficulties. Leisure Education session formats indicated in this chapter might seem detailed, but they are general outlines, since each group of participants asks different questions. At TNT, copies of the lecture are available to clients upon request. In this way, clients can share the information with their families if desired. The same sessions are offered for outpatient groups. The success of each session depends on the session leader's expertise and knowledge of group dynamics. Most sessions are conducted by Therapeutic Recreation Specialists. The Therapeutic Recreation team manager should conduct the introductory session, which describes Therapeutic Recreation Service policies and procedures, and may lead other sessions as well. The following are the basic content of these sessions. (For explanation of numbering code see Chapter 7)

LEISURE EDUCATION SESSIONS FOR TRI ITEM # 10: LEISURE AWARENESS

100.0 Introduction to Recreation and the Therapeutic Recreation Service

Things which are important to us have many names. For example, list a name for a motorized vehicle. (Allow group to share several names such as automobile, car, jalopy, sedan, wagon, Ford, Chevy, etc.) For another example, let's list names for alcohol on the board. (Continue until a comfortable interaction pattern has been established between group and session leader. Different examples can be used, but it is important to select examples which are familiar to the clients. The mood and tone for the group must be established while dealing with the known before moving into the unknown. The

clients will judge the session leader's expertise on knowledge of the field of alcohol and generalize it to other subject matter. It is therefore important that the session leader add a few unusual terms for alcohol to the client's list.) Recreation also has many names. Name some:

Recreation	Leisure	Spare Time
Therapeutic Recreation	Activity	Free Time
Recreation Therapy	Play	Fun

When I say one of the above what comes to your mind?

Eating	Reading	Travel	Cards	Swimming
Crafts	Jogging	Drinking	Kids	Relaxing
Sports	Hobbies	Parties	Sleep	Exercise

I could continue listing things all day and still not scratch the surface. But just the few we have listed demonstrate three key points:

1. Leisure means different things to different people.
2. Recreation for one is not recreation for another.
3. Everyone has it.
4. Everyone needs recreation.

I know I said there were three, but I just had to add a fourth. For some, sports are fun and for others, sports are a pain. For some reading is recreation and for others reading is work. For some, drinking is a hobby and for others, it's a full-time job.

I cannot get rid of spare time. I can't work twenty-four hours a day for the rest of my life. I'll talk about the fourth point in detail later. For now let me say that if we didn't need it, how come we have so many words for it? How come we have so many kinds of it?

It will be difficult communicating with each other as long as you are thinking of one meaning and I am thinking of another. I'm passing out some definitions. While you are at TNT please think in terms of these meanings.

RECREATION: Something that you remember with a smile, that you do because you want to. It feels good from the inside out. Something that you do that makes hours fly by like minutes. Something that you do that fills you with energy. You may feel tired at the beginning but afterward you battery is recharged. You may feel tired physically but it's a good, relaxed kind of tired. Recreation is the difference between existing and living. It can be anything from sleeping, to eating, to sports, to skydiving, to driving, to art, to listening to music, to. . .

LEISURE: Your non-work time. Time when recreation is possible.

LEISURE EDUCATION:	Sessions like today's, designed to help you understand your leisure and the value of recreation in your life.
RECREATION THERAPY:	Using an activity to improve a specific aspect of yourself and/or your life. For example, if you have problems handling stress, there are activities that can calm you. If you are out of shape, there are physical exercise activities that can help strengthen and tone your muscles. If you have problems relating to yourself or others, there are activities which can help that too.
THERAPEUTIC RECREATION:	An umbrella term indicating that a hospital or treatment facility is attempting to provide Recreation, Recreation Therapy, and Leisure Education for its clients.
SPARE TIME:	Time on your hands. Empty, boring, wasted time. The goal is to turn spare time into free time.
FREE TIME:	Unobligated time. Time you can use to enjoy life. All of leisure should be free time, not spare time.
PLAY:	Recreation. Doing what comes naturally. Feeling good.
FUN:	Recreation.

It will also help communication to be as specific as possible. "I need something to do" can mean any one of a thousand things. If you leave the choice to me, I will probably give you the wrong thing. After all, my chances of making the right selection is one in a thousand. "I need something to do like playing cards" helps. At least we can focus on the type of card games I have on the shelf instead of giving you a basketball or a paint brush. But playing cards is still a broad request. I still don't know if you mean you want to play bridge, poker, old maid, or some other card game. In other words, if you have a leisure need, come to me. Be as specific as possible when asking for what you want. If I don't have it, I might have something similar, or I might be able to get it with a little time. (The recreation equipment check-out system is explained as well as the equipment sales from the gift shop.)

Recreation plays an important part in our lives. But most of us have been taught to view recreation negatively. Through subtle tones, sayings, and behaviors, we have received messages such as:

"Stop that, you are acting childish."
Meaning: Play is for children. There is something wrong with acting like a child. What do children do? They play.

"It's okay to play when your chores are finished." Meaning: It's only okay to play when you are too tired to play and there is nothing "better" to do. Most people look to retirement as their time to play, but then it's been so long they can't remember how to play.

"Idle hands are the devil's workshop." Meaning: Taking time out to relax will cause terrible things to happen.

"What are you doing, KILLING time?"

It's against the rules to commit murder in this facility. So please don't kill time while you are here. There are hundreds of these messages floating around. Can you think of some more of them?. . . Yet what is life worth without play time? Wake up in the morning. Why? So I can go to work. Why? So I can make money. Why? So I can pay my bills, so that I will have a place to sleep, so that I wake up in the morning and go to work. This can become a boring rut, and boredom is a true killer. I must have something to look forward to. Someplace the cycle must be broken, so that I can have time and money for myself, time and money for fun. Not after I retire, for if I don't relax today, I may not live to see retirement. If I don't play today, I will be too set in my ways to learn how to play when I retire. The Leisure Education courses offered here are designed to help find the time, the money, and the fun that is rightfully yours. The classes only offer ideas. It is up to you to make the ideas fit into your life. Play is a basic human need just like thirst, hunger, and air. I can't shut them down completely. But I can do them and feel guilty about doing them. Because we have a need to play but don't feel good about playing, we trick ourselves into playing. We justify our behavior. Here are some popular examples:

It's not for me, it's for the kids.
The old food on the table trick.
It's not my fault I had a good time.

Let's look at each of these. "It's not for me, it's for the kids." How many times have you used this one? Kids need to play and everyone knows that, so it's OK to play with them. Have you ever seen an adult play with a child? Wrestle, play ball, make faces, go to a playground and swing with the child? I like going down the slide with my kid. Make sand castles with them at the beach? Take a child to a movie? Take a child to the beach or on a picnic, or for a hike? Play a table game with them, read a book to them? Take them sightseeing or to a fair? I see some heads nodding. But understand it's not just for the kids. It's for the kid and the adult. It's food, it's healthy, and it's fun for both.

Have you ever done things with kids that you wouldn't be caught dead doing without a kid? If you have, then have you used the kid as an excuse to have some fun yourself. That's okay as long as the kid's concept of fun matches your concept of fun. Beware; a child can be damaged by a parent who must meet his or her leisure through the child. For example, suppose I always wanted to play the piano, but I never did. So I have my child take piano lessons. That's good if the child wants to learn to play the piano. But if the child does not want to play the piano, then there is a problem. In this example, I should take the piano lessons instead of the child.

The old "got to put food on the table" trick, is not a harmful justification, just dishonest. How many people do you know who garden to put food on the table, go fishing to put food on the table, go hunting to put food on the table? Be honest. Have you ever added up the cost of the seeds, the fertilizer, the water, the time, the property taxes on the land used to garden, and the cost of preserving the produce? In most cases, if you added it all up and divided it by the pounds of produce used from the garden, it would be cheaper to go to the store and buy the produce. Note I said "pounds used from the garden." Gardeners often grow 10 times more produce than they can ever use. If a true gardener has two years of produce left from last year, will he or she skip a year of gardening? No.

Consider the cost of serving a fish dinner caught by a fisherman. How much did it cost if you consider the time, license, gas, equipment, etc.? Especially if that fish was caught in Alaska? The same is true for the hunter. In most cases, the meat supplied from the market is much cheaper than the meet supplied by the sportsman.

Don't misunderstand. I am not against gardening, fishing, and hunting. I'm against dishonesty. The truth is that the gardener gardens because he likes to garden. The fisher and hunter, fish and hunt, because they like to fish and hunt. They all have a need to be outdoors, feel a part of nature, feel the peace and serenity of a non-manmade world. The point is that it's good to garden and fish and hunt. Not because it is work that puts food on the table, but because it is recreation and it feels good. It is just as valuable to just sit or walk outdoors, as it is to fish, hunt, or garden. Sitting is probably cheaper, but it is a vicarious experience, not an active experience.

"It's not my fault I had a good time," is the final justification, and a real biggie. How many of you have danced at a party? How many of you have ever danced sober and clean? How many of you have done wild and crazy but fun things while drinking or drugging that you would never do sober? What starts the ball rolling? A decision to get out-of-control drunk or high? Or a decision to have some fun? Once the decision is made to have fun, then a drink, fix, or pill is taken as a method to achieving the goal of having fun. How many fun things have you tried to do sober? How many while drinking? You see. It wasn't your fault you had a good time, it was the alcohol or drug that caused the fun. This is dangerous and dead wrong. You had a good time because you let yourself have a good time. Blaming drugs or alcohol for a good time is just another way to trick yourself into meeting your basic thirst for fun. I promise you, if you have ever had fun drunk or high, you can have even more fun sober and clean. It will just take some time and practice.

There is a catch-22 in having fun. Having fun is not automatic. Just as I had to learn how to eat when I was a baby, I have to learn how to have fun. Learning how to have fun, is not fun. Doing a thing sober is a totally new experience from doing the same thing while intoxicated. I might make a fool of myself. If I am sober, the fear of acting like a fool gets in my way. If I'm drunk, I probably won't know I made a fool out of myself, and if I do know it, I can blame it on the bottle. Doing it sober is risky. Not only do I know I have made a mistake, I can't blame the mistake on the bottle. But I can't learn to do it right unless I am are aware of my mistakes and learn to make the needed corrections.

Fun is much more fun sober than it is drunk. But it takes time to learn how to have fun. I would suggest giving yourself the learning time you need. Fun without excuses, fun without drugs, fun for the sake of fun is worth it. Start now.

It is especially hard for me to break into a new kind of fun when everybody knows how except me. Here at TNT everybody is in the same boat. Helping you to find what kind of fun fits you, is my real job. Putting drug-free fun into your life is your real job. We can both do our jobs better by getting started today, not tomorrow, not when you feel better, not when you get home, but today. Are there any questions or comments about what I have said, or about leisure and recreation in general?

This is an introduction to recreation, to leisure in general, and to the Therapeutic Recreation program here at TNT. It is one of four required Leisure Education sessions. The other sessions are designed to explain how leisure fits into recovery from substance abuse.

Here at TNT, Therapeutic Recreation Services are designed like a college curriculum. Everyone is required to attend a few basic classes. Then depending on your needs and interests some sessions are required and others are optional. All activities are numbered. The numbers mean:

100.0's:	Basics, required
100.1 and up:	Leisure Education sessions, required for some but not all persons. The determination is based on the results of the TRI Assessment which you have or your Therapeutic Recreation Specialist will soon help you complete.
200's:	Skill Development sessions. These teach how to participate in different types of Leisure Pursuits. You are welcome to participate in as many as you can. You are required to attend at least one per week. There is only one Skill Development session required for
200's cont'd	all. It is the 200.0 session which teaches you how to monitor your heart rate. You are expected to attend even if you know how to do this. At this session we will give you guidelines for safe participation in all physical

activities and exercise programs offered here at TNT. (The digit which indicates interest category is also pointed out and discussed.)

300's: Recreation Participation sessions are provided for your pleasure and enjoyment. You are not required to participate in these but may miss a lot of good times if you don't.

400's: Recreation Therapy sessions are special sessions designed to meet your special needs. Not all clients are required to attend them. If you see a 400 session listed on your schedule, then you are required to attend it.

Let me take a moment to define "required" as it relates to recreation. (New unsharpened pencils are handed out.) Recreation is Re-Creation. It is something that happens inside of you. The Therapeutic Recreation Staff can't make you have a good time. We can't require you to recreate. We do require your body to be present at certain sessions. What happens after that is up to you. When it comes to recreation, people are very much like this pencil I have just given you. As it is there isn't much you can do with it. But there's magic inside this pencil. All I have to do is sharpen it and there is no limit to the number of things it can do. The sessions we offer here are the pencil sharpeners. Come to the sessions, sharpen your skills, then use them to do whatever you want.

The TNT Center has a lot to offer. The number of choices existing for leisure pursuit can be overwhelming. Completion of the TRI Assessment makes it easier to choose the sessions that are right for you. If you have not completed the TRI by now, please see me after the session. I have extra TRI forms or can schedule help if needed. The TRI asks about 10 areas. You are to select the answer for each area that best matches your situation. Then your Therapeutic Recreation Specialist will review the areas with you. Together, you will develop a plan for attending Therapeutic Recreation classes which will be the most helpful to you. It is at this point that some sessions will be required for some and not for others. Your cooperation in this process will assure that the sessions selected are right for you. Sometimes you and your Therapeutic Recreation Specialist may not agree about the activities that you need. When you disagree, we will try to start working on areas in which there is agreement. Sometimes our sessions are difficult to describe. Your Therapeutic Recreation Specialist knows what they are like. Please trust your TRS. Our staff is here to help you. If a session is recommended which does not sound like it meets your needs, give it a try anyway. You might be pleasantly surprised. If at the midpoint of treatment, you feel you are not benefiting from Therapeutic Recreation Participation, please contact me. Attempts will be made to adjust your Therapeutic Recreation program.

(Specific rules, regulations, expectations, and costs are then discussed. Family involvement is discussed. The fingerprint attendance system is explained as well as the individualized treatment plan. Then a videotape is shown. The video gives a general overview of equipment, facilities, activities, and so on. The video shows people participating in various activities, laughing, and having a good time. It also shows people making mistakes, laughing, and having a good time in the learning process. The session is concluded with a question-and-answer period and an invitation to attend upcoming General Recreation events.)

The next required Leisure Education session will be [title], and will be held tomorrow, same time, same station. These sessions are held every week. But please, be here tomorrow if you possibly can. The sooner you get these in, the sooner everything we have to offer will make sense. I would like to close with my favorite story.

Once upon a time, many years ago when time began, there was a cave man. His name was Cave Man. He had no need for any other name, since he was the only cave man he had ever met. Cave Man was not alone. He lived with Cave Woman, and their son, Cave Boy. Cave Boy was named Cave Boy because they had not yet invented the word son. I mean we are talking basic.

Each morning Cave Man, Cave Woman, and Cave Boy were awakened by the first morning light. It would stream in from the cave entrance and rest on their faces for a gentle fleeting moment. Cave Man liked it. Once he tried to catch the sun ray in his hand, but as soon as he opened his hand to peep in to see it escaped. Ah but as quickly as the ray disappeared, so too the day disappeared. Cave Man, Cave Woman, and Cave Boy had to be up and quick about it.

Each day began with work and ended with work. There were tree limbs to make into pointed sticks. There were stones to be gathered and made into the basic necessities of life. They always woke up hungry, but there was never any food until after the hunt. Sometimes the hunt took them far from home. Sometimes the hunt would take them so far away that they would not find their way back. Then they would have to find a new place to live, make new pointed sticks and gather new stones. The work was long and hard.

They were lucky to find food and shelter before the night attacked them. Each day was the same as the last. It ended with exhaustion. Each night, Cave Man would say to Cave Woman and Cave Boy, "There has to be a better way. There has to be a faster way. There has to be an easier way. We must find a better, quicker, easier way." This was all Cave Man said before he drifted into sleep drugged by exhaustion. As he slept he would dream of the things he would do if he had time. He would dream of relaxing and having fun. He would dream of watching the sun come up as his family sat close to him. He would dream of sleeping on a soft bed all day long. He would dream of running through the forest for the sheer joy of running. He would have dreamed of many more things, but the sun's first morning ray would always interrupt his dreams.

The years passed. The cave family slowly learned ways to do things quicker, easier than before. Each night Cave Man would say, "We must learn to do things quicker, earlier."

Years passed. Cave Boy grew up to become Cave Man II. Each night Cave Man II ended the long weary day as his father had taught him. Cave Man II would say to his family, "We must find quicker easier ways to do things." Cave Man II's family found ways to do things a little quicker, a little easier.

Years passed. Cave Man II's son became Cave Man III. Cave Man III's son became Cave Man IV, and on and on it went with each generation finding quicker, easier ways to do things, each generation falling asleep at night to the words, "There must be a better way. A quicker, easier way." On and on it went through the years until here we are today.

Here we are. We have microwaves and supersonic jets, and precooked food in prepackaged packages. We can drive to stores to get our food. Our food can be on the table in minutes. Everything needed to support life is at our fingertips. Are we happy about it? Do we see our inventions as the miracles that Cave Man I might have considered them to be? No. We seem to feel as if we are missing something, and we are.

You see, Cave Man I told his son what we needed to do. But he always fell asleep before he told his son why he needed to do things quicker. What to do has been passed down through the generations, but not why. So here we sit. Our goal has been accomplished. We no longer have to struggle to put food on the table. But instead of taking time to watch the sun come up, be with each other, appreciate the beauty around us, and run for the sake of running, what do we do? We continue to invent machines that make life quicker and easier. We continue to make money so that we can spend money on machines that will make things quicker and easier.

We all have a need to play. The need has been there since time began. But this is really the first time in history that we have a choice. If we have a machine that will put dinner on the table in ten minutes, do we really need a machine that will put dinner on the table in one minute?

Is it better to spend our money on a new one minute machine or keep the old machine and use the money on something that is fun? We have done what the Cave Man told us to do. Isn't it about time to do what he really wanted us to do?

(Note to session leaders: This session may be broken into several shorter sessions if needed.)

100.0   Your Leisure and Internal Chemical Needs

The goal of this session is to assist clients to broaden their definition of addiction and help them see how leisure fits into the overall scheme of things. If the session is provided in lecture form it can become overwhelming for "neurotransmitter" and other multisyllable terms must be discussed. Instead, it may be preferable to make a game out of the content.

List short phrases that describe the actions of the body's internal systems, on separate cards. Write the names of the neuro-chemicals on cards. Write the names of leisure activities on cards. Shuffle the cards together and pass all but one card out to participants. (If there is a large number of participants,

form teams with one stack of 3 X 5 cards per team). The card not passed out is placed on a board in front of the group (or in the center of the table, if a small group). Players then take turns attempting to match cards in the player's control with the card on the board. If the first player or team cannot match a card in the hand with the card on the board, then the player takes one card from the hand and places it on the board to the side of the original card. The next player may attempt to match either of the two cards now on the board. If the player is able to match something in his/her hand with the card on the board, then the card is placed directly under the original card and the player gets a point. As the game progresses, it may become apparent that two separate groupings of cards on the board actually belong together. The first player who is able to combine the groups gets to add points to his/her score equal to the number of cards in the combined groups. Play continues until all cards are on the board, and properly grouped. When the group stalls, the leader provides information about the internal systems' function and leisure pursuits until players have enough information to continue the game. The winner of the game is the one who ends with the most points. [Ch3]

This format may also be used to demonstrate the connection between substance abuse and leisure. [Ch1]

100.0 The Balancing Act

(The following session is presented in lecture format. However, it is most effective if it is accomplished through group interaction. It is presented here in lecture format because it's easier to present in written form.)

Excesses do not provide a healthy lifestyle. The substitution of one excess for another is easy and it happens a lot. Is substituting the excessive use of pills for the excessive use of alcohol any better? Is the excessive use of beer any better than the excessive use of vodka? It is easy to substitute excessive work for alcohol or drug use. Some use all the time they used to spend drinking and drugging on sleeping. Is that any better?

In my opinion, spending all my time working, or sleeping, or playing, is better than using drugs or alcohol. But spending all my time doing one thing, no matter what it is, will eventually produce some unwanted side effects. This session is about leisure, so that's about all we ever discuss. But please don't leave thinking that you should spend all your time playing. To play all the time creates an imbalance just as working all the time or drinking all the time. Having said that, let's spend all of this session talking about leisure.

Excessive use of one activity during leisure is not healthy. Ever stumbled into a new hobby, or a new game, and started doing it, and doing it, and doing it, and doing it? What happens? One day the thought of doing it turns my stomach and I never do it again.

Repetition of an activity improves skill in performing the activity. As long as the learning process is going on there seems to be a tolerance for the repetition. I may be doing the same thing but I am learning something new. Once the learning process is complete, the challenge disappears and the activity itself usually becomes boring. You may leave here with a whole new bag of hobbies, activities, and games. Realize they won't last forever. Sooner or later new ones will have to be found.

Some activities maintain interest longer than others. Outdoor activities often become a lifetime pursuit, perhaps because we can never do them all the time, year-round. Take snow skiing for example. Most people who snow ski long enough to overcome their fears, will continue to ski and look forward to skiing for years and years. There are two reasons. First of all, learning to ski is a very long process. The other reason is a person can't ski all the time, year-round. Eskimos, who spend the entire year in snow, probably have a hard time understanding why anyone would want to ski for fun.

Learning several new activities at the same time is not fun. When in a period of life when everything seems new, then there is a need for something very old and familiar during leisure. This is a need you might have right now. Your whole lifestyle might be changing and I'm standing here preaching new things for leisure. It's okay to take some time out and do some leisure activities that you know, that you have done so many times you don't have to think when you are doing them. But the opportunity to learn some new leisure things is available now and it might not be available when you need it later on.

Balance is important. Balance in leisure is important. Have you ever had days when you were around so many people that all you wanted was to be alone? Have you ever had days when you were by yourself and you felt like you needed to be with someone so bad you would be willing to help your garbage man dump the trash? Have you ever had a day so noisy that you would gladly pay a million dollars for five minutes of silence? Have you ever had so much silence that you had to turn the TV and radio on at the same time for relief? Have you ever sat so long that you could not listen to the lecture? All you could think of was getting up out of the chair? Have you ever walked so long that you had to sit?

Not only is balance important in leisure, but leisure is the great balancer of life. I may not be able to control how many people I see at work, or how long I sit. I can control what I do with my leisure. By selecting a leisure activity which is totally opposite from what I have been doing at work, I can restore balance. But I can only select the "right" activity if I have a wide variety of activities from which to choose.

Let's combine forces and see how many things can be listed for each of these categories. Give me some things that can be done alone.

(The form titled "Balance" has been placed on an over head projector. Pages of paper have been placed over the transparency to block all information except the section being dealt with. As participants suggest activities the suggestions are written in under the category being discussed. The Therapeutic Recreation Specialist adds ideas when the group comes up short. But give the group time. A moment of silence may be required to get the ball rolling. After the first category is dealt with go to the next category. When participants have become involved and are responding, have them demonstrate or role-play the activity and allow others to guess what it is before listing the activity on the board. This puts some fun into the session and will help clients remember the session content. After the session place the transparency, backed with a white page of paper, in a copy machine and make copies of it for all participants. Then wipe the transparency clean in preparation for the next session.) (See Figure 8.1 on following page)

What happens when there are two or more persons in the same household? What happens when you have been working all day in a noisy, crowded setting and your family has been home alone all day? Or when you have been home alone all day and your spouse/significant other has been in the crowded setting? What happens between the two of you as one feels a need to rush out the door and the other a need to rush in? Many family squabbles have occurred at the door. Both persons must be aware of their own balance needs as well as each other's. Balance differences must be reconciled. What are some ways to do this?. . . (Allow the group time to respond, and ask less vocal participants if they can give a personal example of the situation, what happened, and what alternatives might have been available.)

Recognition of the problem is half of the solution. Taking some personal quiet time immediately after a rushed day is important. Personal quiet time can be the long way home in the car. It can be a walk around the house before walking into the house. It can be a long shower before talking to anyone. It can be time stretched out on the couch for a few minutes. As long as family members understand the purpose of these moments of separation, they will respect quiet time. Of course at first it will be hard to respect the space at first because it might remind them of the times of substance abuse. (Open discussion of comparison of withdrawal from family to participate in substance abuse if it has not already come under discussion. Encourage participants to select a different form of withdrawal during recovery. For example, the person who hid the bottle in the bathroom should not attempt to find quiet time in the bathroom during initial stage of recovery.)

Many adults avoid doing new things. It is uncomfortable doing the unfamiliar. The fear of the unknown often stops me from doing what I need to restore balance. How many of you avoid doing new things? What can be done about it? (Again allow time for group response. Try to draw out the participants who have not yet shared. Most likely, they are remaining silent because talking in a group is an unknown, unfamiliar activity which is being avoided.)

Like so many problems, recognizing and admitting that something is being avoided because it is new or different, is half the battle. Nothing stays new unless I avoid doing it for the first time. (Place the statement on the overhead projector, "It is unknown until I make it known.") Accept the discomfort in the knowledge that the discomfort will pass with time.

Before you leave, I would like to summarize the points of this session. An important aspect of maintaining a happy healthy life is balance. Drugs and alcohol cause problems by destroying balance in daily routines. Looking forward to a drug and alcohol-free life may feel like looking into a huge

FIGURE 8.1

BALANCE FORM

INSTRUCTIONS: List as many things to do as you can in each of the following areas

Alone: With Spouse: With Friends: With Family:

_____   _____   _____   _____
_____   _____   _____   _____
_____   _____   _____   _____
_____   _____   _____   _____

Calm/Relaxing: Quiet: Exhilarating/Active: Noisy:

_____   _____   _____   _____
_____   _____   _____   _____
_____   _____   _____   _____
_____   _____   _____   _____

Spiritual: Self Improvement: Creative: Just Plain Fun:

_____   _____   _____   _____
_____   _____   _____   _____
_____   _____   _____   _____
_____   _____   _____   _____

That Change The Scenery: That Stay At Home:

_____   _____
_____   _____
_____   _____
_____   _____

void or vacuum because the balance has been destroyed. It is important to have a lifestyle that balances work and leisure. It is important to balance leisure pursuits. Have some new things to do and some old things. As interest is lost in one activity, find another one to take its place. Don't try to do the same activity all the time no matter how much it is liked. Use leisure to balance life. On days when I feel peopled out, I use some of my leisure alone. Try to reconcile differences in leisure needs. At home, find ways to use your leisure to balance your life and allow your family to do the same. While here, practice balancing leisure needs with your roommate taking the place of family. Don't let the fear of the unknown stop you. Before discharge, have something listed in each of the categories we have discussed, that can be done and enjoyed the first week after discharge. You may not have time to do them, but know they are there if needed to restore life's balance.

This is a here-and-now program. Start looking at the balance that exists today. Everyone is required to attend the Leisure Planning session 100.0 each week. The first session provides methods to monitor daily leisure balance. After that the session gives you a chance to share how you are balancing with others and to hear how others are balancing. Remember there is a big difference between living and existing. Balance makes the difference. [Ch3]

100.0 Beware! The Tree of Addictions Grows: Substance Abuse and Leisure Abuse Are Interrelated

The goal of this session is to introduce the concept of process addiction and what can be done to prevent it. If not handled correctly, it can become a session which provide an excuse for not participating in leisure activities. It is therefore wisest to delay presentation of this session until midpoint of the treatment process.

If a large dry-ease board (a chalkboard substitute that permits use of colored felt-tip markers) is available, then use it to draw a tree trunk. If not, place newsprint on the wall and draw the trunk of a tree. Have the names of addictive substances and processes written on cards, large enough to be seen by the group. Have blank cards available, for there is always someone who suggests a new form of addiction.

Open the discussion by talking about the addiction tree and get the group to generate the names of different types of addictive substances or processes. Then shuffle the cards and divide the group into teams. Give an equal number of cards to each team. Draw a branch onto the tree trunk in order to structure thinking. Have each team sort through their pile of cards and find addictive process or substances which they think belong on the same branch. The unused cards may be passed to other teams. Get the teams to go to the tree and tape their cards to the addiction tree which is being created. Let them draw additional branches as needed. Where there is disagreement about which substance or process belongs on which branch, have persons/teams give their reasoning and let the group as a whole make the final decision. Help the group see the relationships and list the contributing sources on the branches, trunk, and roots of the tree. [Ch3]

Discuss the client's vulnerability to addiction by other substances and processes, especially those located closest to the person's drug of choice as listed on the addictions tree.

Take the group through visual imagination. It is now winter. The leaves of addiction are dropping off, as a result of admission to treatment. (Take the substance addictions being treated by the facility from the tree and drop them on the floor.) But spring will soon come. Not all the leaves have fallen. Those that remain are trying to grow at this moment. How can you get rid of the rest of the leaves? How can you keep the other leaves from growing back?

Encourage daily monitoring of personal activities to maintain balance, which will prevent many leaves from growing back. Point out that any substance or process used to avoid uncomfortable situations can be added to the tree of addictions. Explain why Therapeutic Recreation Services is structured to encourage a variety of leisure interests and ask for cooperation. After the group has had a chance to take in the information, take all the leaves from the tree. This represents barren existence. Ask the group to react to the feeling of looking at a leafless tree. The point is that abstinence from all potentially addictive substances is not possible and not healthy. Have a duplicate set of the original cards. Ask the teams to sort through the cards and separate all those that it is wisest to totally abstain from using. (The discard pile should contain alcohol and drugs.) Other addictive processes and substances are returned to the tree with each participant putting up a card and offering the group a verbal warning. For example, food may be returned to the tree with the warning "Eat to live, don't live to eat." Leisure pursuits may be returned with warnings such as, "Play to live, don't play to avoid life."

Persons who show denial of process addictions or who are observed abusing leisure should become involved in more in-depth Recreation Therapy sessions on the topic. [Ch3; Ch11:420.0]

100.0   Leisure Planning for Today

The Leisure Planning session should be repeated by clients on a regular basis. The session monitors the client's ability to plan leisure that meets his/her needs and to implement the plan. Toward the end of the client's stay, the same planning process is used to develop Leisure Discharge Planning options.

The session consists primarily of participant interaction. Discussion is focused with responses to basic questions, such as the following:

> How much time for leisure did you have yesterday?
> What did you do with that time?
> Did you encounter any problems in your leisure?
> Were you able to maintain internal balance?
> How much time do you expect to have today?
> What are your leisure needs today?
> What internal chemical systems were activated yesterday?
> Which internal chemical systems do you expect to activate today?
> What do you plan to do with your time available for leisure to meet your needs?
> How will you balance your life today?

At the end of the discussion session, each client completes a written statement, "Today I will use may leisure to_____." This is followed by a leisure plan for the day which includes breaks between sessions, meal hours, scheduled Therapeutic Recreation times, and evening hours. The plan is signed off by the session leader and brought back to the next Leisure Planning session. [Ch11:420.02] (See Figure 8.2)

100.1   Leisure, What Is It? One Man's Fun is Another Man's. . .

This session is designed to help clients widen their view of what leisure is and can be. Magazine sweepstakes packets, which comprise the majority of junk mail received these days, are saved and then passed out to begin the session. These packets contain stamps with pictures of magazines and a brief review of the contents of the magazines.

The majority of the magazines deal with leisure interests and provide a very thorough review of what type of activities are available to adults. They also provide a good way of getting involved in a new interest. The biggest barrier to leisure involvement is often fear of the unknown, followed by lack of information about how to make the activity a known. By reading a magazine about a potential leisure interest, the person can become involved in the activity as a vicarious spectator, which is an extremely low ego risk position. While in that position the person can learn about the activity through reading, which makes the activity a known. The magazine also has advertisements and resource listings for needed supplies. All this makes it easier for the person to move from an interested bystander position to active participation. The session, however, focuses on discussion of the wide variety of leisure opportunities that are available and encourages participants to expand the list represented by the magazine stamps.

FIGURE 8.2

DAILY PLANNING FORM
(Everything Gets Done One Day At A Time)

Name:_____   Date:_____

THINGS TO DO FOR ME: FOR FAMILY/FRIENDS   FOR WORK/SCHOOL/TREATMENT
  I need to: I need to: I need to:

_____   _____   _____

  I want to: I want to: I want to:
_____   _____   _____

  Most important thing is: Most important thing is: Most important thing is:
_____   _____   _____

_____   _____   _____

SCHEDULE FOR TODAY

6 _____	6 _____	6 _____
7 _____	7 _____	7 _____
8 _____	8 _____	8 _____
9 _____	9 _____	9 _____
10 _____	10 _____	10 _____
11 _____	11 _____	11 _____
12 _____	12 _____	12 _____
1 _____	1 _____	1 _____
2 _____	2 _____	2 _____
3 _____	3 _____	3 _____
4 _____	4 _____	4 _____
5 _____	5 _____	5 _____
6 _____	6 _____	6 _____
7 _____	7 _____	7 _____
8 _____	8 _____	8 _____
9 _____	9 _____	9 _____
10 _____	10 _____	10 _____
11 _____	11 _____	11 _____

ACCOMPLISHMENTS

_____

_____

Next, guests from the community are invited to share unusual hobbies in the "EALP" Competition (Extraordinary and Awesome Leisure Pursuits). Facility staff, former clients, and members of the local 12-step programs should be encouraged to participate in EALP. Each contestant tells what they do and why they do it in less than five minutes. (Due to logistics, many contestants are on videotape.) Participants of the session vote to select the week's most Extraordinary and Awesome Leisure Pursuit. Each winner of a competition is considered a semifinalist and sent an award certificate from the TNT Client Government. Every three or four months, a finalist is selected from the semifinalists. The finalist wins $25 and is invited to demonstrate the leisure pursuit at a special event. The finalists are also added to a display called the "EALP" Hall of Fame. This event appeals to interesting people who have trained fleas, collections of cobwebs, and so on.

The point of the session is that a wide variety of leisure interests are available and that nothing should be ruled out as a potential leisure pursuit. Many clients fear participation in a standard leisure event, such as ballroom dancing, for fear of appearing foolish. When people are seen who are sane, sober, productive in life, yet have bizarre leisure hobbies, the fear of participating in the standards is significantly reduced.

The session is concluded by getting each participant to make his own definition of leisure, what is acceptable and not acceptable leisure behavior. An attempt is made to get a contract signed by each client committing to leisure pursuit. If there are enough magazine market stamps to go around, then each participant should be encouraged to paste one of the stamps on the contract, selecting one that he/she feels might be interesting to pursue. (See Figure 8.3)

Objectives of this session may be further supported during Skill Development sessions where art projects are produced. Art projects may be created to represent the most extraordinary and awesome leisure pastime known to the creator, or a leisure pursuit which interests the client. The magazine stamps may be used to make collages and mini-mobiles. Art projects may be created to be given to winners of the EALP contest as trophies.

100.1   Leisure As Related to Work and Substance Abuse

The problems of work addiction are discussed or developed into a table game. The purpose of the session is to help the client see that overwork has no lasting benefit. Content may be drawn from Robinson's *Work Addiction* (1989).

100.2   Leisure Values Clarification: Living versus Existing

A number of values clarification formats are available. It would be difficult to say that one is more beneficial than another, nor could one easily devise a better format than the others that are available. Any format that helps the client evaluate what he/she truly values in life is appropriate (Stumbo, 1989).

100.2   Drawing From Paradise

The purpose of this session is to help persons achieve their dreams through living one day at a time. Each participant is given two sheets of paper of equal size. On the first sheet, participants are asked to draw a picture of "paradise." The drawing should fill the entire page. On the second sheet, participants are asked to draw a picture of "personal reality." Differences between the two are discussed. Then the question is asked, "When will you begin to make paradise a personal reality?" Help participants see that being permanently in "paradise" is an unrealistic expectation, but that portions of the dream can be pursued in the here and now. Have participants cut a window in the drawing representing "personal reality." Place the personal reality picture over the picture of paradise. Have participants move the window in the reality drawing around until some aspect of "paradise" appears in the window that is realistic to attain in the here and now. For example, if a person drew a sunset in the paradise picture, then the window of the reality page may be placed so that the sunset is visible in the "personal reality" of today. Then attempt to get a commitment from that participant to actually take time out of the day to watch the sun set. Try to find something in each client's "paradise" that can occur in the here and now. If nothing can be found then look for a realistic step that can be taken in the here and now that will bring the client closer to some aspect of his/her paradise. [Ch2: "It's Only Natural," "Concept Greater Paradise"]

Variations of the "Draw a Picture of. . ." format can be employed to investigate a wide variety of abstract terms. Participants can be asked to draw a picture of leisure, sobriety, joy, sorrow, serenity, acceptance, unmanageable, powerless, control, and so on. The results of the drawing should be shared with other participants. This develops the client's ability to share a portion of the self with others. The leader must make sure that there is no laughter of nonacceptance during the process. Laughing with a person is OK, but not at the person. Should a client feel his/her offering has been labeled unacceptable by others, then the session leader must intervene, helping the client to express his/her true feelings to the group and getting the group to respond with support.

Drawing of any abstract term brings new meaning to the term. Drawing comes from a different part of the brain than language. It therefore taps internalized thought/feeling processes that are not tapped by verbal exchanges. For purposes of this format, it is not important what the person draws, but what the person says he/she has drawn. Skill in drawing is of no concern.

Persons who are uncomfortable drawing should be given a pencil with a good eraser. Scrap paper that has a mark, a wrinkle, or a flaw is less intimidating than a clean white page.

FIGURE 8.3

SAMPLE LEISURE CONTRACT

LEISURE CONTRACT

I, _____, do hereby enter into this contract with myself and with the intention of completing all obligations noted below.

Today I will take _____ of my time and spend it on me. I will use this time to:

_____learn something new	_____relax	_____be surprising
_____improve my fitness	_____do nothing	_____be silly
_____talk with someone just for fun	_____exercise	_____be playful
_____appreciate what I have	_____laugh	_____be expressive
_____do something unplanned	_____listen	_____be inspired

_____ _____ _____

_____ _____ _____

_____ _____ _____

_____ _____ _____

I agree to take this time because I deserve it, because it is my time, because I need the time to re-charge my energy, live a balanced life, and because I want to feel better.

Signed:_____ Date:_____

Witnessed by:_____ Date:_____

Some therapists overcome the client's discomfort of drawing by allowing clients to cut and paste pictures from magazines. However, it is suggested that the cut-and-paste process is governed by noncreative centers of the brain, and therefore does not result in the same experience as drawing.

It can be helpful to record the date on the drawings, and keep the drawings on file. Have clients draw a picture of . . . at the beginning of the treatment phase. Have them repeat the process toward discharge and compare the drawings. Allow clients to self-evaluate their work. Help them to see changes that have occurred as a result of the treatment process.

100.2 Time, Priorities, and Leisure: Finding Time for Fun

Today's session looks at how you have been spending your time. The purpose is to find time for leisure. (Pass out blank Time Finder Forms.) (See Figure 8.4, p. 144)

The form contains a blank schedule for a week. It starts with Monday, and continues through Sunday. There are colored pencils on the tables.

Think of a routine week before you were admitted. Think about the way you spent your time when you were drinking or drugging. First, lightly shade in the time you spent working and write "work" on the space. Only shade the regular blocks of time that you are working. Do not shade the regular blocks of time that you are not working. Do not shade in lunch times . . . Use a different color to shade in the regular times you sleep. Write "sleep" on these areas. . . Use a different color to shade in the time spent dressing, bathing, etc. The time left unshaded is your leisure time. Do not shade it, but write in what you usually did with the time. . . Use one of the stamps on the tables to indicate the times you usually took a drink or used a drug. Then draw an arrow from that drink/drug through the hours that you were under its influence. There are stamps that say "beer," "wine," "mixed drink," "narcotic," "barbiturate," "tranquilizer," etc. There are also smiley faces, clown faces, skull-and-cross-bones stamps, etc. Take your pick. They are self-inking stamps. Just push down. (While participants are stamping, the other clients are rounded up and brought back into the group.) Now that everyone has a completed form, let's discuss it.

SAMPLE DISCUSSION QUESTIONS

1. First of all, is there anything on it that surprises you, or that you had not thought about before?

2. Look at your week and tell me how it makes you feel?

3. What will happen with the time that you used to reserve for using alcohol or drugs?

4. If you go back to doing the same things without the alcohol or drugs, how will it feel?

5. How many see a need to make some changes in the way you have been spending your time?

6. How many want some fun in your life?

7. How many know how to make the changes and know how to put some fun in your life? (If anyone does, ask them to share their plans with the group.)

I'm passing out a new form exactly like the one you just finished. On the new form, make the changes that will pack more meaning, satisfaction, and fun into your week.

Everyone has time for leisure. Time for leisure comes from making free time out of spare time. Spare time comes in two sizes, large and small. Large is like a Saturday, or a weekend. Small is like a lunch hour or coffee break. I would like everyone who will have large blocks of time after discharge, to move to the right side of the room. I would like everyone with mostly small blocks of spare time to move to the left side of the room. If you will have both, or don't know, then pick the one you want to work on. Sit down in groups of two, or three, or four or more and discuss the questions that are written on the chalkboard.

SHORT BLOCKS OF TIME

1. Why is your schedule so chopped up? Is it a result of external forces, or a result of your own planning?

2. Is all the rushing from place to place necessary?

3. What can you do with 10 minutes that is pleasurable?

4. Where can you combine small blocks into larger blocks?

5. How can you make room for AA or NA attendance?

6. Is your daily routine stressful? How can you decrease the stress?

7. What are the advantages of large blocks of time?

8. How and where does family fit into your schedule?

LARGE BLOCKS OF TIME

1. What usually happens when you have a whole day with nothing to do?

2. If you enjoy a whole day with nothing to do, tell why and tell what you do with it.

3. If you dislike what usually happens during a whole day with nothing to do, tell why and what you do.

4. Why is it sometimes difficult to find something worthwhile to do with a large block of time?

5. How can large blocks be broken down into small blocks?

6. What are the advantages of smaller blocks of time?

7. How does family time fit into your schedule?

(The Therapeutic Recreation Specialist spends times with each group, helping groups to focus on common issues. Then participants are brought back together for a summary. Ask one person to share the ideas of their group. Go to the next. Ask them not to repeat. If the idea or suggestion has already been made, then pass. Just add new ideas. The Therapeutic Recreation Specialist should help the group realize that many have purposely chopped up their schedules by finding excuses to step out for a drink. Different ways to work, different places to eat lunch, getting to work fifteen minutes earlier may provide pleasurable breaks from routine. Meditation or carrying a picture of a beautiful serene place can be most calming and only takes a minute. The problem with a whole day to spend is that there are very few cheap things to do that will take a whole day. I can find one thing to do for twelve hours or I can find twelve one-hour things to do for twelve hours.)

The longest journey begins with a single step. The same is true of a large activity if I only have small blocks of time. If I want to cruise around the world, I can start now. If I only have five minutes, I don't have enough time to go around the world, but I do have enough time to make a phone call and have travel brochures mailed to my home. Just planning and dreaming about the trip over an extended period of time can actually be more fun than the trip itself.

Turning spare time into worthwhile time usually requires planning. Time gets wasted by trying to think of things to do. At the same time, if I plan just one thing you could be frustrated if my plan does not work out. For example, If I wait until Sunday to build a deck onto my house that day, I probably won't have the supplies I need. I will either spend the day shopping or just sitting wishing I had the supplies. If I have an advance plan to build the deck on Sunday, then I can have all the supplies I need. But come Sunday, I might sit around frustrated because it's raining, or some friends dropped by, or I just don't feel like deck building. To solve this problem I carry index cards around with me. As I think of something I

FIGURE 8.4

THE TIME FINDER FORM: WEEKLY TIME USE STUDY

	MON	TUES	WED	THURS	FRI	SAT	SUN
1 a.m.							
2							
3							
4							
5							
6							
7							
8							
9							
10							
11							
12							
1 p.m.							
2							
3							
4							
5							
6							
7							
8							
9							
10							
11							
12							

would like to do, I write it down when I think of it. When I am in the mood to shop, I buy the supplies I need to do the things listed on my cards. When I have some time to play, but don't know what to do, I pull out the cards. The cards remind me of what I have available. I can pick the one which fits my mood. Index cards work better for me than notebooks because they are easy to carry around, I can sort them, shuffle them into piles, throw them out, and add to them. The trick is to be prepared for some free time but at the same time, maintain flexibility. Create options, not musts.

Let's move from the past to the future. Take a look at the one-day schedule I am passing out. (See Figure 8.5)

At the top of the schedule write the day of the week that you think you will have the hardest time refraining from alcohol or drug use. For example, if you cannot imagine doing anything on a Friday evening except joining the old gang for happy hour, write Friday at the top of the page.

(Ask for a volunteer to share their difficult time slot. Ask if anyone else has the same time slot. Match clients with common time slots into groups. Have them discuss alternative time uses.)

The page has three columns next to each time slot. List one alternative before you leave today. Before you are discharged, I want you to have listed three different ways that you can use your old happy hour time slot. This was time you used to allocate to yourself. Don't throw this time away by working. Make it something you can do that will make you feel good. Keep at least part of it as time for yourself. Make it realistic. Make it something you are willing to do and are able to do the first time your "Friday Happy Hour" time rolls around after discharge. Make it something you would really like to do and can look forward to doing. It can be anything except doing exactly what you used to do without using drugs or alcohol.

If you have more than one time slot that is of special concern, you are welcome to take a form for each of your problem time slots. You can leave this session as soon as the first plan for the first problem time is complete. Have a good day! Remember, there is a big difference between living and existing. Having leisure options makes the difference.

FIGURE 8.5

ONE DAY SCHEDULE

ONE TOUGH DAY FORM

DAY_____   **Problem time of day from**_____ **to**_____

Plan of Action #1 _____   Alternative #2 _____   Alternative #3 _____

_____   _____   _____

_____   _____   _____

_____   _____   _____

100.2   Haven't Got Time Or Won't Take Time? A Matter of Priorities

The purpose of this session is to look at setting priorities for leisure. The principles apply to setting priorities for anything. But the primary concern here is leisure. Too often, there seems a point where there are more things to do in twenty-four hours than can ever be done. I must pick and choose, doing some and leaving others. I must set priorities. Setting priorities seems difficult sometimes. For me, it's hard to accept that I can't do it all perfectly in the given period of time. Often I do not consciously set priorities. But if I don't set them, then . . . Let's see what happens.

(Ask for a show of hands of participants who feel good at setting priorities and sticking to them. Then ask for a show of hands of participants who do not believe they set priorities. Select one participant from each group. Ask them to come up to the front. Ask them to make a list of priorities for the day and schedule in times to accomplish each priority. Follow the request by asking the person who does not feel experienced in setting priorities to just doodle on the priority list. While the two are writing or doodling, get another participant to go up and interrupt one of them and make small talk. Most of the time, the person who is to interrupt will talk to the person who is doodling. If the person who is making the priority list is really good at sticking to priorities, he/she will politely ask the person who is interrupting to go away. If the person allows the interruption, then get the group to give advice about how to get rid of the interruption. Discuss the action with the group. Point out that disruptions are attracted by a lack of personal priorities. Point out that follow-through depends on ability to assertively manage interruptions. Point out that the doodler, without priorities, had his/her priorities set by the person who interrupted.)

Outside influences are unexpected events. If I get a phone call from a friend who says, "Come over and. . .," I will answer yes if I haven't anything more important in mind. One phone call, one visit, one chat, might not cause any problems. But, if I make ten unexpected stops in a day, I will look back and feel frustrated because I didn't get anything done that I wanted to do.

(If the person who was good at setting priorities had time to make a list, see if he/she is willing to share the list with the group. If so, get the group to discuss the list. See if leisure was on the priority list. Regardless of whether it was or was not listed, get the group to discuss whether it should be. Finally, get the group to estimate the amount of time that gets consumed in an average day by interruption or unexpected events. What happens when the list is not accomplished? Does it get carried to the next day, or into consuming personal leisure time? Help the group to see that sometimes a priority must be considered more important than leisure but then additional time for leisure must be scheduled the next day or everything will get out of balance.)

Priorities must also be set for leisure. How many have felt a time when it was important to relax and be lazy? (Get someone who admits a need to relax to come to the front. Ask him/her to pretend to be relaxing and respond as he/she would normally respond. Then role-play a phone call or the entry of a friend and ask, "What are you doing?" The client will most likely say, "Nothing." Help the group to see that equating relaxing with doing nothing removes relaxing from the priority list. The control of the time is given over to the interruption.)

Taking time to relax and to be lazy is important to maintaining balance. How can interruptions during times set aside for relaxing be managed? (Get the group to make suggestions.)

Where are your leisure priorities? Is time for yourself important to you? Are you important to you? Is time with the family important to you? Is it important to find new fun things to do? Are these part of your recovery program or part of your time that's left over after everything else is completed?

(Pass out Leisure Priority Forms. Get each participant to list five aspects of leisure that are of personal importance. Assist participants in assigning priorities and have them share their lists.) (See Figure 8.6)

Can you meet your leisure priorities today? Why or why not? (Help participants set realistic expectations for the day's leisure. Priorities that are unrealistic for today should be reviewed to see if there is some aspect or variation of that priority that can be met at the present time.)

Today's session has looked at who sets priorities and what happens when priorities are not set. As a group we have considered ways to manage interruptions. We have looked at making leisure a priority in the day's routine, and at priorities for personal leisure. We have not looked at setting too many priorities. Briefly, I will just say there is an art to setting the right number of things to do in a day. Too few and I set myself up for boredom or being victim of others' priorities. Too many and I set myself up for frustration and failure. Reviewing priorities set and priorities accomplished and why helps to improve the ability to set the right number and get things done.

In closing, I would like to say that making leisure a priority in the day makes a difference between living and existing.

100.3   Sources of Leisure Guilt

This session expands on the content of session 100.0: Introduction to Recreation and the Therapeutic Recreation Service. It is designed specifically for those clients who admit to feeling guilty when they attempt to participate in leisure. Participants should share with each other about feeling guilty. Encourage specific examples. Hearing that others have experienced the same guilt feeling is very therapeutic. The session leader should help the participants see that feeling guilty about leisure is normal. Where clients are able to identify "why" they feel guilty, that is helpful but not totally necessary. Help them to see that their sources of guilt should not stop them from participating in leisure. It is okay to feel guilty about taking time out to enjoy life, so long as the guilt feeling does not stop the person from leisure pursuit. Have the group memorize a statement such as, "There is a big difference between living and existing."

Leisure is worth the guilt." Then get participants to commit to saying this to themselves each time they start feeling guilty about participating in leisure pursuits.

100.3   Matching Needs, Skills, and Activities with Activity Analysis

This session uses a videotape to give examples, explain and describe the process of activity analysis. Participants are then assisted in developing an individualized list of criteria for performing activity analysis. Criteria are listed in the form of questions which the client can ask before becoming involved in a new activity or experience. This reduces the risk of involvement in the unknown and increases chances of successful experiences. For example, if a client feels a need for more physical activity and new social contacts, then the following criteria may help his selection:

> Is drinking involved?
> Will the time interfere with my 12-step program?
> Will the cost fit in my budget?
> Will it provide physical exercise?
> Will it get me involved with people?
> Will conversation with others be automatic?
> Will there be someone there I can follow in order to learn how to go about doing what needs to be done?

Using the above as a guide, the client may find that swimming or bowling fits his/her needs, while a social event held in a tavern does not.

The session should also suggest ways to find new activities. "Clearing houses" for such information would include specific yellow page listings of the phone book, community recreation centers, community colleges, newspapers, libraries, AA members, and stores that sell specific recreational equipment. At TNT, clients are also shown how to use the computers to access the activity analysis system, resource information, and contacts.

FIGURE 8.6

LEISURE PRIORITIES FORM

INSTRUCTIONS: List the most important leisure things you want to do, or work toward.
(#1 should be the most important, #2 the second most important, etc.)

#1_____

#2_____

#3_____

#4_____

#5_____

100.3 Will Yesterday's Fun Be Fun Tomorrow?

The TNT Center preaches a here-and-now philosophy. Forget the past. Forget the future. Make the most of today. But this session will spend time looking back. It is important to look at old patterns and habits. By looking at my past, I can make a choice to keep what I see or change it. If I don't look at them, then I will use today to do the same things I did yesterday, even though I do not enjoy what I am doing.

Today's session deals more with patterns than specific activities. But to see the patterns we need to start with specifics. (Pass out Leisure Satisfaction forms. A copy of the form is placed on the overhead projector.) (See Figure 8.7)

Start here, with column A. List as many activities, things, experiences as you can. In other words, what you did to fill your spare time and your free time. In the top half of the column, list what you did before you started using alcohol or drugs. In the bottom half list the things that you were doing prior to admission. How did you fill your time? This is not meant to be an all-inclusive list. Remember, there are no right or wrong answers to this, only accurate and inaccurate answers. Accurate answers are more helpful than inaccurate ones. . .

Everyone have something down? Next complete column B. How often did you do this activity? Once a day, once a week, once a month? If you have not done this thing in the last year, mark an X next to it. . .

Now think about how you felt when doing each activity that you have listed. Try to avoid the use of the words "good" and "bad." Did you feel happy, sad, relaxed, energized, bored, frustrated, excited. . .? Write the word that best represents the feeling, as you remember the feeling, in column C. In column D, interpret the feeling that you remembered. If it was a positive feeling, mark it with a plus. If it was a negative feeling, mark it with a minus.

Columns E and F call for explanations. In column E, explain why you stopped doing any activity marked with an X. In column F, explain why you marked the activity with a plus or minus. For example, if I put down that an activity was frustrating and marked a plus next to it, then I would explain why feeling frustrated is a positive experience for me. . . You have about five more minutes to work on these.

(The Therapeutic Recreation Specialist selects four persons from the returning group. The selection is based on the completed forms which were left behind. Each of the four is given a card. One card has a "++" and a "-", one a "+ -", and the other a "- +". Then the session is continued.)

It is time to move and move on. If you have not completed the form, then try to spend some time finishing it tonight. First, look at column A of your form. If you feel that there are enough activities listed, please get up and move to the left side of the room. If you feel there are not enough activities listed, please move to the right side of the room. Take your form with you.

(Physically moving people around the room provides a break, a needed stretch, and forces communication with different people. In this session, it also visually demonstrates a key point. Most of the participants will move to the "not enough activity" side of the room. If a participant does not comment on this point, then the Therapeutic Recreation Specialist should verbalize the observation.)

Now stay on your side of the room and sit down with three or four people who are standing next to you. Take a minute to tell your group the type of activities you were doing.

(This provides a safe, nonthreatening topic to open discussion. It also helps participants to hear what others were doing. If their activities were the same as others, then there is a feeling of having something in common. If the activities were different, then there is new information about a different way to fill time.)

For those of you who feel you have an adequate number of activities, find out if the group sees future participation in the activities as realistic, and why. For those of you who feel you do not have enough activities listed, what will it take to add activities. What can you do? You have about five minutes. Then I want one person from each group to summarize the points.

(Requesting a summary at the end encourages participants to listen to the discussion. It also allows a sharing of ideas from one group to another, expanding the number of points that can be covered.) The summaries have generated some ideas, given some solutions, and identified problems, not solved all of them. Now that we have done, that let's move on. The solutions will come before you are discharged.

Look at your form again. How many participated in the same types of activities before you started drinking or drugging as you did when you were drinking and drugging?

How many can see a difference between activities listed under the "before" and "during" sections in terms of variety? How many can see a difference in terms of amount of energy consumed by doing the activities? Was there more or less energy consumed while using?

(These questions can lead to some interesting discussions, if time permits. The important points are for participants to recognize that most lifestyles change with alcohol/drug use.)

Okay, it's time to look at your form again and to stand up and move again. Look at satisfaction levels represented by the pluses and minuses. I gave someone a card with two pluses on it. Please hold up the card. When I say go, everyone who listed pluses for most activities "before" and pluses for most activities "during" will move over to the person holding up the plus-plus card.

Who has the minus-minus card? Hold it up please. Everyone who listed mostly minuses for "before" and mostly minuses for "during" will go over to that particular group. Who has the plus-minus card? Everyone who listed mostly pluses for "before" and mostly minuses for "during" go over to that group. I repeat, pluses for "before," the top half of the form, and minuses for "during," the bottom half of the form.

Who has the minus-plus card? Everyone who had mostly minuses for "before" and mostly pluses for "during" go to the corresponding group. That should be everyone that's left. Ready to move? Go!

FIGURE 8.7

LEISURE SATISFACTION FORM

INSTRUCTIONS: The purpose of the following is to look at the results of ways you have used free time in the past. By doing so, needs for future activities may become clear. "Activities" means anything you did with your time by personal choice. Begin by listing activities in **Column A** first. Then complete columns B-F. In **Column B**, indicate how often you did each activity. Once a day? Once a month? If you cannot remember doing it in this last year mark an "x". In **Column C**, indicate how you felt when doing the activity. Did you feel relaxed? Uncomfortable? Happy? Frustrated? Excited? Bored? In **Column D**, mark "+" if you consider doing the activity a positive experience. Mark a "-" if it was a negative experience for you. In **Column E**, note why you have not done any activity marked with "x". In **Column F**, note why you have marked the activity with a "+" or "-".

A (Activities I did before I (ab)used alcohol/drugs)	B	C	D	E	F
1					
2					
3					
4					
5					
6					
7					
8					
9					
10					

A (Activities I do when I'm drinking or using drugs)	B	C	D	E	F
1					
2					
3					
4					
5					
6					
7					
8					
9					
10					

(Some fun can be added to moves by playing tape recorded music during the moves. Music with familiar associations, such as theme songs from Perry Mason, Dragnet, Lone Ranger, Jaws and Batman can add levity.)

I am giving each of the four groups some questions to discuss and answer. Please write some of your answers and key points down. If we run out of time, your answers will be posted on our "Leisure Is For Everyone" bulletin board. There will also be an open leisure question-and-answer session tonight for clients and family. You are welcome to bring some of the points up at that time.

PLUS PLUS (++) DISCUSSION QUESTIONS

1. If the same activities are listed in both sections, is there a difference between how often the activities are done as indicated in column B?

2. Are there activities listed under "before" that have been discontinued? Were they discontinued because of alcohol/drug use?

3. Has alcohol/drug use had an impact on your leisure?

4. Which of your previous activities do you plan to continue and why?

MINUS MINUS (- -) DISCUSSION QUESTIONS

1. Could any of your previous activities become positive experiences? Why? How?

2. Why has leisure been a negative experience for you? What can you do to change this?

3. What kind of experiences would you like in your leisure?

PLUS MINUS (+ -) DISCUSSION QUESTIONS

1. Can you resume activities that you were doing before you started using alcohol/drugs?

2. If you resumed these, would you find doing these satisfying now? Why?

3. What are the advantages of resuming previously satisfying activities as opposed to finding new activities?

4. Will you need to supplement your past activities with new activities? How?

MINUS PLUS (- +) DISCUSSION QUESTIONS

1. Will you find the same satisfaction in activities you did when using alcohol/drugs, now that you are not using alcohol/drugs?

2. What are the dangers in attempting to participate in the same activities without drinking or using drugs?

3. Why were activities before you started using alcohol/drugs negative to you?

4. What do you need in order to make leisure positive?

I have a homework assignment for you. One of things discussed today was how often you did the listed activities. It is also helpful to consider what percent of your total time was used doing these activities. Take some time tonight to think about it. If I did activity #1, one hour a day every day, then that accounts for 1/24th of my time, or 4 percent of my day. What did I do with the other 96 percent of my time? If you add up all the time spent that is represented on this form, does it represent 20 percent or 50 percent or 100 percent of your time? What percent of your time has been spent on things so insignificant that you can't remember doing them? If you don't like the way the big cookie of time is crumbling, what can you do to change it? Another tough question to consider: Which was more satisfying--the feeling produced by the drug, or the feeling produced by the activity you were doing? Have you ever given yourself a chance to feel good without using alcohol or drugs? How and when?

(The final questions are listed in a handout which is passed out to exiting participants. The handout also suggests contact with the appropriate Therapeutic Recreation Specialist to review the homework assignment and discuss issues raised during the session. The Therapeutic Recreation Specialist who has led the session enters a time and session code into the computer. After participants leave, the session leader reviews the attendance record which the computer has automatically generated and adds any observations about client responses to the session. After the review, the computer automatically transfers pertinent information to each client's Medical Record. This process is repeated at the end of each session.)

100.4 Maintaining Leisure Independence During Treatment

On rare occasions, a client is admitted with a good understanding of his/her leisure needs and how to meet them. For these clients, the goal is to maintain Leisure Independence. Developing a program of Leisure Maintenance is helpful. The independent client may provide leadership to Skill Development sessions and Re-Creation sessions. He/she may have needs that are met through individual hobbies. These should be continued during treatment. Developing a plan of Leisure Maintenance assures continuation of healthy habits. The client may check in with a Therapeutic Recreation Specialist on a regular basis just to say, "All is well."

LEISURE EDUCATION SESSIONS FOR TRI ITEM #1: PHYSICAL

101.0   Designing Your Fitness Maintenance Program for Use Now and After Discharge

All clients should receive guidance about what activities will provide physical fitness for them during treatment and after discharge.

101.1   It's Possible and It Feels Good to Be Physically Fit

Some clients are so physically unfit that it is depressing. While they may not be physically ready to enter a physical improvement program, they can begin to be motivated toward physical improvement. This session could be handled by a videotape that shows others who once thought they were too old, too fat, too sick, too. . . now enjoying health and fitness. The session should also include cautions about attempting to get too fit too fast, explaining the value of gradual improvement over time.

101.1   Physical Impairments Can Be Overcome

Occasionally, addiction has resulted in a physical disability, or a physical disability has resulted in addiction. Too often the person is unaware that life can continue in spite of a disability. Provision of an overview through films, books, or videotapes of persons who are active in spite of physical disabilities can be a great motivator, especially when the model of fitness is a person with a greater disability than the physical disability experienced by the client.

LEISURE EDUCATION SESSIONS FOR TRI ITEM #2: EDUCATION

102.0   Guest Speaker Adults Expanding Knowledge

The best format for this session might be a videotape prepared by an Adult Education Specialist at a local community college. Within the tape, time should be devoted to the needs of persons at each level. The goal of the session is to motivate persons who cannot read to learn to read, and to motivate persons who can read to expand their boundaries through educational experiences.

102.2   It's Never Too Late to Learn

The biggest obstacle to learning to read is motivation. This session helps participants become willing to try. All persons who are measured dependent in TRI #2 should be brought together. The purpose of the gathering could be anything. Helping the clients see that they have peers who cannot read is important to breaking the barriers to learning. During the session, give clients the opportunity to share how difficulty in reading influences leisure experiences. Clients who respond to the session and indicate a desire to improve reading skills should be referred to an Adult Education Specialist. Part of the daily leisure planning should include small steps to overcoming the reading problem. (Making contact with the Adult Education Specialist is considered a "small step" which can be accomplished during a treatment day. If an Adult Education Specialist is not on staff at the facility, then a phone call can be placed to a specialist at a community college.)

LEISURE EDUCATION SESSIONS FOR TRI ITEM #3: TRANSPORTATION

103.1   Discovering Leisure Close By and By Mail Order

Sources of leisure not requiring transportation are discussed in the session. Catalogs of supplies and equipment can be distributed.

103.2   Assertive Car Pooling for Leisure Pleasure

The purpose of this session is to provide the client with the skills needed to arrange transportation. Participants should be encouraged to look at the costs involved in providing transportation. Then develop a list of services that can be fairly traded for transportation. (For example, a car wash is usually welcomed by a busy driver.) Participants should then participate in role-playing situations where they must assertively ask for transportation. [Ch11:441.0]

The session may also address the question, is leisure worth the trouble? If the client does not believe that leisure has value, then the client will use a lack of transportation as an excuse to avoid leisure participation. To help clients see the value of leisure, the leader may play devil's advocate, taking a stand that leisure is not worth the trouble of arranging transportation. If handled correctly, the clients will find themselves insisting that life will be meaningless without leisure pursuit, and that the hassle of finding transportation is minor compared to the benefits that can be gained.

103.3 Transportation: A Factor of Leisure Discharge Planning

Discussion of the relationships between leisure, transportation, and family interactions can be beneficial. Have clients draw a map of typical daily routines. Use a different colored pen to indicate the path of each member of the family (or persons who are expected to provide transportation). Share the results with the group. Help clients to see from the map where provision of transportation for leisure can be handled without interference of other's routines and where provision of transportation can disrupt other members' activities. See if ways can be found to prevent disruption yet provide transport of leisure.

LEISURE EDUCATION SESSIONS FOR TRI ITEM #4: ECONOMICS

104.0 Fun and Money

This session begins with a game called "Drinkin' and Druggin' For Dollars." It is a guessing game that results in matching costs of alcohol/drug use to the cost of participation in selected leisure activities. The game has two rounds. In the first round, a large game board is placed in front of the group. There is either a drug, an alcoholic beverage, a dollar amount, or leisure activity hidden behind each number. The goal is to match items of equal cost. The first participant selects three numbers. The numbers are removed from the game board to reveal either a certain number of bottles of beer, an amount of drugs, or a leisure activity. The game board would look something like this: (See Figure 8.8) The participant who called out the numbers must then guess if it is a match. A match occurs when the two items revealed cost the same amount of money. If the participant correctly states "no match," then the numbers are placed back over the numbers and the next participant takes his turn. If the participant correctly matches them, then the items are taken from the board. The person who matches is then given a choice. The person can "cash in" (be given play money equaling the dollar amount), or keep either of the match cards from the board. Then the next participant takes a turn. If the participant makes an incorrect call (i.e., says it is a match when it is not), he/she must select and answer a question from the money pot. The money pot contains questions such as:

What can you do for fun that is free?
What would you do if you had a million dollars?
What is the biggest waste of money you can
    think of?
What is a leisure pursuit you can do for $10 or
    less?

The first round continues until the game board is cleared. If time permits, more expensive activities can be put up on the board and distributed to participants in the same manner.

In the second round, participants generate a list of luxurious vacations and assign costs to each. The list may look something like the following:

A night with tickets to a Broadway show in
    New York . . . . $ 400
One week in the Bahamas . . . . . $ 600
A second honeymoon on a yacht . . . $1,500
Snow skiing in the Alps $2,000
Deep sea diving lessons in Australia . . $2,500
One week of peace and quiet at home
    without the kids $5,000

Then, one by one, the vacations are auctioned off to the highest bidder. Participants may bid money or prize values from first round winnings. They may also bid "X" week's supply of their drug of choice. Before bidding begins, each participant must place in front of him/her the amount previously spent in one week on their drug of choice.

After the game, discuss the cost of alcohol/drug use versus the cost of recreation. Because one has spent $1,000 on drug use does not mean that the person actually had $1,000. Discuss how much of the alcohol/drugs were procured through trade, borrowing, stealing. Help the group to realize that non-cash-and-carry methods cost time. Alcohol/drug use also reduces work performance, which can reduce income. Help participants weigh factors and then commit a percent of the money once used for alcohol/drugs to be used for leisure.

Traveling around the world is realistic. It may take 20 years, but the longest journey begins with a single step. Anyone who can find enough money to stay drunk or high, can find enough money to do any leisure activity known to man. Anything is possible if a goal is set and then implemented, one step at a time, one day at a time.

What does it cost to play? How much is play worth? Identify inexpensive ways to play. For example, a picnic, or watching planes land at an airport can be fun and inexpensive. Hobbies are less expensive and more fun if they are not prepackaged. Community recreation programs and community colleges provide opportunities for developing new leisure skills at reasonable costs.

FIGURE 8.8

DRINKIN' AND DRUGIN' FOR $$$$			
2 Glasses Wine	2	3	$1.50
5	1 Bowling Game	7	8
9	10	11	12

Is there a family commitment to spend money on leisure? Why? How can a commitment to spend money on fun be developed? If there is a commitment to spend money, is it only for joint participation activities? There needs to be money for each members leisure aloneness time as well as family togetherness functions.

Differences between start-up costs and maintenance costs should also be discussed. Purchase of lessons and supplies is usually much more expensive than routine costs of continued participation. Identify some activities that require lessons and/or equipment which are expensive at first, but once purchased, cost little to continue. Identify activities that are expensive to maintain. For example, oil painting is costly when purchasing enough paint and brushes to get started. But once these supplies are purchased, they last a long time and usually only one tube of paint requires restocking at a time. Thus, initial costs are much higher than maintenance costs. On the other hand, bowling requires rental of the alley each time. Initially, shoes and ball can be rented for a low start-up cost, but as bowlers get involved, they desire their own shoes and ball, which can increase the cost of participation down the road. Activities that are expensive to maintain should be identified as well as activities that are inexpensive to maintain. This can be accomplished through group discussion.

104.1   Leisure at a Reasonable Price

Participants join together to discover low-cost leisure pursuits through participation in a game of "Cheaper Yet." Participants are divided into two teams. Play begins by the leader naming a leisure hobby or activity. The first team (decided by the flip of a coin) offers the name of an activity that costs less to do but is basically the same as the activity named, or a way to do the named activity at a reduced cost. The second team must offer the name of an activity or cheaper method of participation than was given by the first team. Play continues, each team being challenged to find a "cheaper yet" option until one of the teams becomes stumped. The last team to give an answer is given 100 points, and the leader offers a new leisure hobby or pursuit. Play continues for a specified period of time. The team with the highest number of points wins. A list of the winning responses is maintained throughout the game. At the end of play, copies of the list are made and passed to all participants. The remainder of the session is spent discussing sources of cost-free activities which are available. Leisure opportunities available through public facilities are pointed out. Twelve-step program functions are also available at low cost. The newspapers usually have a listing of public events and club meetings, many of which are free. There is a difference between living and existing. A lack of money is no excuse for merely existing.

104.2   Economic Changes Mean Leisure Adjustments

This session is designed for clients who have used an expensive drug which has depleted financial resources. The best format would be a guest speaker who is well into recovery from an expensive drug habit. A person who made it to the top, to the bottom, and is well on the way back to the top. After the talk, a discussion of how to make leisure adjustments should follow. The discussion should stress acceptance, patience, and making the most of what one has. Focusing on the loss only intensifies the loss.

104.2   Leisure Opportunities at Your Library and Other Public Facilities

This session is most effective using a video that interviews staff in public facilities. The video can show the librarian describing the resources available at the library, show the outside and the inside of the library, and indicate the library's location on a map. In this way, the library becomes a known to clients. Having seen it, they are more likely to take advantage of it. If the librarian comes to the Center to lecture, then participants only have his/her word for what is there and the library still feels like an unknown. It is also more time-efficient in the long run. Once the video is made, then there are no schedule conflicts, off days, or anything else. The session leader just has to turn the video on, and can attend to some other details while the video is running.

104.2   Developing a Leisure Budget

In this session, clients are assisted in developing a realistic budget to meet their leisure needs.

104.3   The Average Cost of Leisure

Clients may be out of touch with the costs of alcohol/drug-free leisure. This session is designed to help clients become aware of the costs so that realistic plans may be developed.

104.4   Are You Getting Rich to Enjoy or Relapse?

Some clients have a knack at making money. Yet each time they have cash to spare, they relapse. The session asks clients to evaluate their substance abuse career by drawing a time line. Years are listed across the bottom and the words "poor," "okay," "rich" are listed on the vertical axis. The client graphs the highs and lows of his/her past financial situation. (See Figure 8.9)

FIGURE 8.9

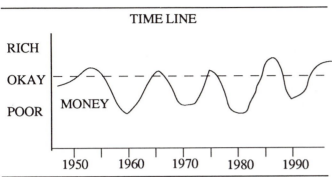

TIME LINE

Next the client tries to correlate heavy substance abuse with the time line. Is substance abuse at its greatest during periods of financial abundance? If so, what are the options? One option is to stay poor. That's not much fun. Another option is to burn off excess cash through pursuit of expensive leisure activities. The graph might also be indicating the results of workaholism. The client makes money rapidly as a result of workaholism, but then is too exhausted to continue the pace and resorts to substance abuse as a means to ending the insane pace. If this is the case, then the participant is encouraged to not work so hard, not try to make so much so fast; learn to enjoy the getting there. The group should discuss all options thoroughly.

This session can avoid use of pencil and paper. The years can be marked on poster paper and placed on the floor, at equal distances, in a straight line. Participants line up along the same line, holding a streamer that stretches from the first year to the last year. Then each participants takes a turn at creating his/her personal time/money line. Times of low financial income are marked by the participant standing on that year (or sitting down) and lowering the streamer. Times of high financial income are marked by the person standing in the appropriate place on the time/money line, standing tall and raising the streamer chest high. (Holding the streamer above the head is not recommended for it is an uncomfortable position to maintain for any length of time. To demonstrate extreme highs a participant can stand on a stepladder, and extreme lows can be demonstrated by dropping the streamer to the floor.) Props such as party hats, balloons, toy handcuffs, broken toy dolls, may be used to mark the times of heavy substance abuse. Props

such as flowers may be used to mark periods void of substance abuse. This provides a far more graphic display of the points and will be remembered longer. It cannot be kept, placed in the pocket, and shared with others after the session.

LEISURE EDUCATION SESSIONS FOR TRI ITEM #5: FAMILY

105.1 Value of Leisure Aloneness

Being alone is different from being lonely. Too often persons who live by themselves omit the amenities of daily life because it's "just for me." Decorating the house for a holiday should be done for self-pleasure as much as for others. Eating by candlelight is pleasurable alone as well as with others. Setting the table for dinner rather than eating out of a container is important. Most people who live alone see these things as extra work and trouble. But when the extra work is not done, the person wonders why they feel so depressed. This session discusses these ideas and the group is guided to the realization that the self is always worth the effort, no matter how many are or are not coming to dinner. The session also investigates the role of friendship, volunteerism, and work relationships to maintain balance in lifestyle. A good friend, even 3,000 miles away can prevent aloneness from being lonely.

Times alone are times for self-gratification. Have the group list times, places, reasons that cause lonely feelings. Then have the group brainstorm about things that can be done (alone) to remove the loneliness, things that provide feelings of self-pride. (See Figure 8.10)

105.2 Fun and the Opposite Sex

The purpose of this session is to break down stereotypes and unrealistic expectations, and to develop honest, open communications between men and women. Participants are separated into a men's group and a women's group. The groups are given the following to complete. (See Figure 8.11)

The women then share and discuss their list with the men and the men share with the women. The consequences of projecting an image are also discussed. Participants are encouraged to present an honest, accurate image of themselves

FIGURE 8.10

THE ALONE BUT NOT LONELY FORM

A LONELY TIME FOR ME IS:	A LONELY PLACE FOR ME IS:	A REASON I FEEL LONELY IS:
I can use this time alone to:	I can change this place of loneliness by:	I can resolve this reason for being lonely by:

FIGURE 8.11

FUN AND THE OPPOSITE SEX

WOMEN'S GROUP		MEN'S GROUP	
Men always like	_____ .	Women always like	_____ .
Women like men that	_____ .	Men like women that	_____ .
Men expect women to	_____ .	Women expect men to	_____ .
On a date a man must	_____ .	On a date a man must	_____ .
On a date a woman must	_____ .	On a date a woman must	_____ .
Pet peeves on a date	_____ .	Pet peeves on a date	_____ .
Pet peeves about men	_____ .	Pet peeves about women	_____ .

and to have faith that the right person will be attracted to the projected image. The discussion also focuses on the stressfulness of a "first date." Ways to decrease the stressfulness are suggested, such as selecting a familiar activity. Inexpensive things to do on a date are discussed as well as the concept of dating one's own spouse or significant other.

The group may also discuss the importance of sharing common leisure interests. Many times a relationship is formed because both like or dislike the same leisure pursuits. Too many common leisure pursuits can support co-dependent functions. Too few common leisure interests strains the relationship. A healthy relationship is one of balance. Some leisure pursuits are participated in jointly. Some are participated in independently. Healthy relationships share independent pursuits by talking with each other about the events which occurred. It is important that both members of the relationship are able to value and appreciate each other's interests, even if one member does not desire to participate in a pursuit of the other's interest.

To illustrate this point, I recall one day my husband walked in laughing to himself. After five years of happy marriage, he said, "Do you realize we have absolutely nothing in common?" As I started to think about it, I began to laugh too. He was right. No computer dating service would have ever matched us up! Yet we were happy. He spent his leisure in social and competitive activities. I spent mine in isolated, creative, noncompetitive activities. But it worked, for the night I enjoyed my dance class was the night he enjoyed his team bowling league. Afterward we both felt great, filled each other in on what great things the other missed. I enjoyed listening to his league antics and he seemed interested in my triple-pirouette success. Our relationship would not have been half as interesting had we both done all the same things. What new information would we have had to share? Of course it would not have worked had we never spent time together sharing, or had a few things that we always enjoyed doing together (Seabury, 1974).

105.2 Family Leisure: What Is It, How Does It Work?

One of the characteristics of an Adult Child is that this person guesses what normal is. It is difficult to develop healthy family relationships if there is no model of health. An outing to a crowded park can help provide examples of functional and dysfunctional family relations. To be effective this must be handled in small groups. Unleashing 50 people on the park will disrupt the natural flow of events. Participants should be given a list of things to look for. At the park, participants should sit at tables or on picnic blankets, positioned in places where other park users can be observed without making the observed feel uncomfortable by being watched. Participants must also be positioned so that the leader may observe all participants. Once the logistics have been dealt with, have participants watch for the basic give-and-take which occurs in healthy families. Watch for examples of the parents who play with their children at the park and for parents who are only there to supervise their children. See the difference in the children. Return to the facility and process the observations.

105.3 Family Leisure

This session discusses the difference between assertive, passive, and aggressive responses. It then uses role-plays to help clients practice assertive responses to meeting their leisure needs. Role-plays help clients learn to manage situations such as the following:

Situation #1: Joe is invited to a friend's house. It turns out to be a surprise birthday party and Joe is the guest of honor. Everything is going along great until the gifts are opened. Joe's friends have given him a case of beer, a fifth of vodka, a bag of pot, and an ounce of cocaine. Joe's friends start helping themselves to the gifts as soon as they are opened. Naturally, his friends want the birthday boy to try out his gifts. As the role-play begins, Joe is unwrapping the presents. How can Joe assertively manage the situation? (After the role-play add that Joe's wife was at the party and embarrassed by the situation. How should Joe handle the situation?)

Situation #2: Fred has worked ten hours today. He has worked ten-hour days for the last six days. Fred has attended four AA meetings this week. He's tired and looking forward to a nice, quiet evening at home. All he can think about is a snooze on the couch and watching his favorite TV re-run. As Fred walks in the door, his wife says, "You're late. Hurry and change your clothes. The Reardons, the Van Burans, and the Duseldorfins are coming for dinner. They will be here any minute." How can Fred assertively manage the situation?

Situation #3: Samantha likes being with her friends. Every Friday her friends eat together and then play scrabble until midnight. It is the only night they can all get together. Samantha wants to be with them but is bored stiff with scrabble. She feels like she will be sick if she sees one more scrabble letter. How can Samantha manage the situation? (After role-play ask how situation would differ if Samantha was with family instead of friends?)

Situation #4: Any time Jill goes out with anyone it's the same old story. They say, "What would you like to do?" She says, "I don't know, what would you like to do?" Then they say, "I don't know what would you like to do?" Then she says, "I would maybe like to go to a movie." They say, "What do you want to go see a stupid thing like that for?" How can Jill assertively manage the situation? (How would the situation differ if Jill is with her husband rather than a date?)

In addition to practicing assertive behaviors, participants are also being given an introduction to drama. At the end of the session, participants who show a flair for role-plays are invited to attend the Drama Skill Development sessions offered at TNT. (For additional resources on Assertive Training, see the references from Chapter 6.)

105.3 Meeting Son and/or Daughter's Needs

Clients who are parents can benefit from sharing with each other the problems of parenthood. They can also benefit from interacting with their children with the Therapeutic Recreation Specialist's guidance. Playfulness should be encouraged during game participation. Clients may need help in learning how to release the parent role in order to play with the child, and they need help learning how to make the transition back into the parent role. Clothing signals may be required. Just as the businessman's loosening of his tie means it is time for informal down-to-earth interaction, the parent may need to develop a gesture which lets the child know it's time to play, or that playtime is over.

LEISURE EDUCATION SESSIONS FOR TRI ITEM #6: STRESS

106.0 Coping with Burnout

Burnout results from extended periods of stress. Even the person who scores independent in stress management as measured in TRI Item #6, has a potential for burnout. Other clients may already be experiencing some of the burnout symptoms. Experience suggests that there are ways to postpone the arrival of the final stage of burnout, but there is no way to avoid its arrival, other than removal of the sources of stress. Recovery from the final stage of burnout is a long and gradual process. The body is never able to tolerate previous levels of stress, just as the alcoholic's body is never again able to tolerate intoxication.

The first step to resolving burnout is to recognize the symptoms, know the dynamics of the stages. After the concept is introduced and defined, participants should be given an opportunity for self evaluation of some sort. Most burnout literature provides checklists and self-evaluation tools. I cannot recommend one over another, nor can I create one which I think is better.

When participants have identified their burnout stage, the next step is to identify primary sources of stress that are producing or may produce burnout. Stress levels can be significantly reduced by ending several small sources of stress, or by eliminating a large source of stress. All of life's stressors can never be totally avoided. Care must be taken in this portion of the session. Some clients may jump to the conclusion that the solution is to avoid all stress. This solution returns the person to the comfort of denial and not dealing with problems that arise. What is needed, is to bail out of functions that produce stress but few benefits to staying sober/clean. For example, entertaining the spouse's business clients at home may be a source of stress. Perhaps the stress can be avoided by entertaining them at a restaurant. Sharing the dislike of entertaining with the spouse may produce stress which should not be avoided.

Finally, methods to combat burnout must be discussed. Reduction of stress is important. Finding new and creative ways to interact with the stressors is helpful. Increasing the amount of time designed for relaxation in the day's routine helps. Finding activities which totally get the mind off of the stressors for an hour also helps. Recreation experiences help, too.

The final stage of burnout is one of disengagement from all living matter. When a client has reached this point, the client must be brought back into the flow gradually. Help the client find a nonstressful way of taking an interest in living again. Avoid placing the client in positions of responsibility to others, such as leader of a Skill Development session, or president of the Client Government. When the client volunteers for such positions, the client is on the road back from burnout. (Ch4: "Flatline"]

106.1 What Causes Stress and What Causes Relaxation

A discussion of stress should include how the fight-or-flight system is turned on and off. The release of the stress chemicals is not automatic. The brain's perception of the degree of potential danger determines the amount of chemicals produced. Practice makes perfect. The more the brain practices seeing danger in situations, the more chemicals are produced each time. Anticipation of trouble produces stress chemicals. The more time a person has to worry about an upcoming event, the more stress is placed on the body. Assuming that the event will automatically result in negative outcomes increases the degree of danger perceived by the brain. It is therefore important to manage stress before and after a stressful event.

Managing stress before an event takes place, means dealing with uncomfortable situations as soon as possible. Postponement only adds intensity. When waiting for trouble, it is important to keep the mind occupied with a nonstressful image. Relaxation training using mental imagery can be put to use at such times. Participation in recreation is also helpful to keep the mind in a positive focus. Believing that the self is competent and can handle the situation, that the outcome can be beneficial to the self, is critical.

Managing stress after the fact requires releasing any negative emotions which resulted from the event. Temper tantrums help to vent the negativity. Physical exercise drains the chemicals from the body. Then the mind requires refocusing onto positive aspects of living. Again, leisure pursuits can help restore the balance. Finally, the body requires rest. Activities which produce sleep, rest, relaxation, are needed to complete the cycle. If unnecessary sources of stress are eliminated, and necessary stressors are managed, then health is maintained.

The previously described cycle of stress management should be compared to stress management methods which employ the taking of a drink, fix, or pill. The use of substances to control stress blocks the person's awareness of stress, but not the action of stress on the body. Personal choice is diminished with awareness. Substance abuse prevents the person from learning how to manage stress. It prevents the person from accurately judging the situation, reducing chances for positive outcomes and increasing chances for negative outcomes. All methods of controlling stress which are substance-free are learning opportunities. The person learns by doing, how to manage stressful situations. Thus as time passes, the stress associated with specific types of events becomes less and less. All substances that reduce the perception of stress interfere with the learning process. For example, a person might be afraid to get up before an audience and talk. If the person makes the speech sober, the stress level may be extremely high the first time. After several speeches have been made, the person may experience no stress at all. If a person makes the speeches with the help of a tranquilizer or a drink, then the stress of the event remains the same. Making one's 50th speech is the same as the first. Furthermore, all substances which have

calming action are also addictive. Eventually, the lack of a drink, fix, or pill is more stress-producing than the event which is being avoided.

This session should end with participants making a commitment to doing a stressful event without the use of a substance. Wherever possible, the event should be performed before the session ends. Persons who are "afraid of talking" in front of a group should be asked to at least stand up before everyone and say, "Hello." Persons who are "afraid" of appearing foolish, should get up before the group and make a foolish face. Discuss the results. Help the group to see that they lived through the event. Then get each one to do it again. Discuss the results and see if the second time was easier than the first time. Ask the group to close their eyes. Imagine breathing in calm and goodness, and exhaling panic and fear. It is important to model participation in stress followed by a relaxer.

106.2 Alternative Methods of Relaxation

Provide samples of activities which have potential to produce relaxation. Selections should be from available skill development sessions in the fields of art, movement, music, outdoor activities, reading, and so on. Use pictures to show how the environment can be controlled to produce a relaxing effect (Danskin & Danskin, 1988).

106.3 Matching Leisure Relaxers to Stress Producers

Discussion should identify specific stress producers known to the group. Then assist the group in identifying different leisure pursuits which can vent the stress. Timing should also be discussed. A relaxing pursuit should always follow a stressful event. Some form of relaxation should always precede attempts to sleep.

LEISURE EDUCATION SESSIONS FOR TRI ITEM #7: PLAY STATUS

107.1 Childhood Play: Lessons Learned about Leisure

Values and purposes of childhood play are discussed. "It's OK to play" is the central message of the session. Since clients score "at risk" on TRI Item #7 by indicating an inability to remember childhood play, the session is formatted in a way which does not require personal recollection. If the client's group therapist/counselor feels the client needs to remember these events, then sessions can be devised to unlock the doors. Such sessions should be co-led. [Ch4: "Children of Addiction"]

107.2 Recall Memories Associated with Balloons and Cotton Candy

Have the group recall childhood play behaviors. Touching of childhood play supplies often triggers memories. Clay being molded by the hands, brings visions of the past to the mind. Songs sung in childhood are also associated with events. Help participants remember the good times and how parents reacted to them. Help participants rewrite the scripts of the past giving group support to the concept that play is good for us. For those who are willing, actually participate in childhood play and discuss the appropriateness of such play in adult life. [Ch4: "Children of Addiction"]

107.3 Appropriate Times and Places for Kids Play

Attitudes and feelings about appropriateness of play in life are discussed. Many are taught that it is okay for children to play, but proper adulthood requires non-playful functioning. Transactional Analysis theory, which insists that there is a *child* in all of us regardless of age, can be presented to justify the need for adults to play as well as children. Participants may divide into subgroups and see how specific examples can be generated of when adult play is appropriate and when it is not appropriate. For example, placing a whoopie cushion on the boss's chair before asking for a raise is probably not appropriate. Placing a whoopie cushion on the boss's chair for his/her fortieth birthday celebration might be appropriate. Timing of adult play demands evaluation of the consequences and concern for other's needs.

Each client should leave with a list of ideas about how his/her Child within needs to play, and ways in which that play need can be met. [Ch4: "Children of Addiction"]

LEISURE EDUCATION SESSIONS FOR TRI ITEM #8: CREATIVE PROBLEM SOLVING

108.1 Leisure Planning Assistance

Clients who are at risk in creative problem-solving will need more structuring of their programs. They will also need assistance in identifying alternatives when the plan does not go as intended. This session should be provided daily. It should focus on providing feedback about what to do when the plan gets off course and suggest methods of making plan corrections. The client who remains dependent on this type of assistance at discharge should be linked up with community support for continued assistance. The source of assistance may be a private Therapeutic Recreation Consultant, or a 12-step program sponsor with good problem-solving skills. Discharge planning should be more structured for this group of clients. By discharge, the client should have a list of qualified Skill

Development teachers who operate in the community, complete with addresses and phone numbers, and have a list of preselected Skill Development sessions for post-discharge involvement.

LEISURE EDUCATION SESSIONS FOR TRI ITEM #9: SKILLS

109.0 What's the Risk?

The purpose of this session is to help clients become aware of the levels and types of risks which are involved in leisure participation. Risks are involved in all aspects of life. Each person unconsciously sets a level of risk which he or she is willing to take. That which is risked is physical safety and ego safety. If the person has set a low level of acceptable risk-taking, then feelings of personal achievement are greatly limited. Stress is often experienced because performing routine functions often require the performance of tasks which have personally been defined as risky. If a person has set a high level of acceptable risk-taking, then the chances of serious trauma (either physically or emotionally) are great. [Ch2; Ch4]

The feeling of risk tends to diminish with repetition. Those seeking low-risk functioning tend to cling to activities which are known. Those seeking high-risk experience tend to increase the level of difficulty or constantly seek new experiences in order to continue feeling the rush. I once met a fellow whose high-level risk-taking caused his friends to constantly ask him if he was suicidal. He told me that the only risk rush that doesn't wear off with repetition is helping other people. (He also shared that he never took a risk that he did not think he could survive.)

Have clients evaluate their risk-taking levels. Have them decide if their levels are acceptable or if they feel a need to narrow or expand their definition of acceptable risk-taking. Provide a list of Skill Development sessions offered at the facility. Have each client evaluate the activities based on if he/she considers involvement to be high or low risk. Share and discuss the findings.

109.2 Learning New Things and Learning Creative Activities

This session helps participants learn how to learn. Some learn by watching others. Some must take classes to learn. Some do best by jumping into the middle and learning by trial-and-error. The question may be asked, "How do you enter a swimming pool?" Some dive straight into the cold water and take the adjustment all at once. Such persons will most likely prefer to plunge into the middle of a new activity and get the adjustment over as soon as possible. Others tip toe into a pool of cold water. They prefer gradual adjustment. These persons will most likely want to observe others doing a new activity, then attempt simple segments of the activity, then enter full participation. The point of the session is that it is OK any way it is done, so long as new activities are learned.

Many people have stereotypes about the requirements for being creative. It is important for participants to understand that everyone is creative. Practice increases creative abilities. Development of internal balance demands getting in touch with creative powers as well as with emotions and logic.

109.3   The Leisure Audio-Visual Library

Since individual interests vary widely, it is impossible to have all activities available for client participation. The sessions that are provided may be augmented by cassette tapes and videotapes. Ideally, a large selection should exist. Cubicals with audio and video equipment and headphones permit several participants to make use of the AV library at the same time. The cubicals also reduce the problem of loaning out expensive equipment that seldom gets returned, or comes back damaged.

This session teaches clients proper use of the equipment, how to find the materials of choice, when the equipment is available for use, and so on. Samples of the audiovisual materials should be demonstrated to whet participants' appetites. After all, an extensive library is of no value unless it is used. Materials could include the following:

114.4   Overview of Affluent Leisure Competitions (e.g., Polo)
119.1   Overview of Other-Competitive Non-Physical and Physical Activities
124.3   Overview of Health Club Memberships: How to Join and What They Offer
129.1   Overview of Self-Competitive Non-Physical and Physical Activities
134.1   Patio Vegetable Gardening
134.3   Overview of Hunting Clubs: How to Join and What They Offer
134.4   Custom Home and Living Space Designs
134.4   Overview of Affluent Leisure (e.g., Travel, Fishing in Alaska)
139.1   Overview of Productive Activities
144.4   Overview of Volunteerism and Philanthropy
145.2   Overview of Social Activities
145.3   Overview of Family Activities
154.3   Overview of Travel Clubs and Guided Tours: How to Join and Advantages
155.1   Overview of Collecting Things
155.1   Overview of Individualized Leisure Pursuits (e.g., Hobbies, Puzzles, Games for One)
156.2   Overview of Relaxing with Music from Center Library
156.2   Relaxing with Nature
157.1   Overview of Joining Creative Writing Clubs, Little Theater, Guilds

162.2   Reading and Math Mazes, and Puzzles
164.1   Overview of Taking Advantage of the Public Education TV Channel
164.4   Overview of Travel Planning: Meeting AA Worldwide
171.3   Introduction to Ballet (or Tap Dancing)
172.2   Overview of Creative Writing and Poetry
174.3   Overview of Community Sources for Dance Classes
174.3   Overview of Community Sources for Music Lessons
174.4   Overview of Affluent Leisure (Opera, Concerts, Theatre)
174.4   Overview of Creative Hobbies that are Expensive
176.2   Relaxing With the Arts
179.1   Overview of Arts and Crafts
179.1   Overview of Creative Writing Activities
179.1   Overview of Dance
179.1   Overview of Drama
179.1   Overview of Music and Song
189.1   Overview of Spiritual Activities
194.3   Overview of Outdoor and Adventure Clubs: Finding, Joining, Advantages
199.1   Overview of Outdoor Activities
199.1   Overview of Risk Taking Opportunities

109.4   Leisure Rap

Leisure Rap is an opportunity for participants to share knowledge and leisure information with each other. As a Leisure Education session, the structure of a Leisure Rap session is modeled. Participants are assisted in discussing leisure topics. Clients who are independent in Leisure Awareness and have skills in a specific area are recruited to lead Leisure Rap sessions which occur during Re-Creation participation times.

References/Resources

Crawford, M. E. Leisure counseling & drug addiction, a prescriptive approach. *Practical Pointers.* AAHPERD, Washington DC, 3(6).

Cudnohofsky, F. W. (1978). Leisure education with the alcoholic. *Expanding Horizons V.* University of Missouri.

Danskin, D. G., & Danskin, D. V. (1988). *Quicki-Mini Stress-Management Strategies For You, A Person With A Disability (or Even if You are Not Disabled - Right Now!).* Manhattan, KS: Guild Hall Publishing.

Eason, J. (1972). Life-style counseling for a reluctant leisure class. *The Personnel & Guidance Journal,* 51(2).

Edelwich, J., & Brodsky, A. (1980). *Burn-Out: Stages of Disillusionment in the Helping Professions.* NY: Human Sciences Press.

Edwards, P. B. (1975). *Leisure Counseling Techniques: Individual & Group Counseling Step By Step.* Los Angeles, CA: University Publishers.

Gunn, S. L. (1976). Leisure counseling: Analysis of play behavior & attitudes using TA & gestalt awareness. *Expanding Horizons III,* University of Illinois.

Gunn, S. L. (1977). Leisure counseling : Using techniques of assertive training & values clarification. *Expanding Horizons IV.* University of Missouri.

Faulkner, R. W. (1988). *Addictionaide Series.* Seaside, OR: Leisure Enrichment Service.

Freudenberger, H., & Richelson, G. (1980). *Burn-Out: The High Cost of High Achievement.* NY: Doubleday & Co., Inc.

Geba, H. B. (1985). *Being at Leisure- Playing at Life: A Guide To Health and Joyful Living.* State College, PA: Venture Publishing, Inc.

Godbey, G. (1989). *Leisure in Your Life: An Exploration, Revised Edition.* State College, PA: Venture Publishing, Inc.

Henderson, K., Bialeschki, M. D., Shaw, S. M., & Freysinger, V. J. (1989). *A Leisure of One's Own: A Feminist Perspective On Women's Leisure.* State College, PA: Venture Publishing, Inc.

Hitzhusen, G. (1972). Recreation & leisure counseling for adult psychiatric & alcoholic patients. *Therapeutic Recreation Journal.* 7, p. 78.

Kelly, C. (1979). Assertion training: A facilitator's guide. CA: University Associates.

O'Connor, C. *Lifestyling* (For C.D. Adolescents), Lifestyle Consultants, Cohasset Stage, Chico, CA.

Robinson, B. E. (1989). *Work Addiction.* Deerfield Beach, FL: Health Communications, Inc.

Seabury, D. (1974). *The Art of Selfishness.* NY: Pocket Books.

Self Disclosure & Team Building Activities For Chemical Dependency and Prevention Groups. (1989). Therapeutic Recreators For Recovery, Algonquin, IL.

Stumbo, N., & Thompson, S. (1989). *Leisure Education: A Manual of Activities & Resources.* State College, PA: Venture Publishing, Inc.

Westland, C. (1982). *Playing, Living, Learning: A Worldwide Perspective on Children's Opportunities to Play.* State College, PA: Venture Publishing, Inc.

CHAPTER 9

SKILL DEVELOPMENT

The purpose of Skill Development sessions is to develop activity skills for use in leisure during treatment and after discharge. Basically, these are "how to" sessions. They are very important, for most clients and family members do not have adequate activity skills. Leisure Education sessions help the participant understand why he/she should play. Understanding why does not make a change in behavior until the participant understands how. For example, I once felt a need to branch out. To grow I needed a new leisure interest, one that would place me in a different environment and require more risk taking than I had been accustomed to. During a shopping trip to a mall which had a rink in the center of it, I was exposed to ice skating. As I watched, I knew that ice skating would meet my needs. This was the Leisure Education portion of the process. But making a decision that ice skating would meet my needs did not change my life. Before I could branch out, I had to learn how to ice skate. The process of branching began with my first lesson. (For what it's worth, my ice skating ended abruptly nine months later. After six months of lessons, numerous falls, and bruises, I was able to skate forward and backward, on two feet and on one foot. I went on my first maiden voyage. In confidence I set out onto the ice without assistance! Two hours later and no falls! Wow was that great? No. For two hours, I had been skating around the rink, around, and around, and around. It occurred to me that I spent most of my life going in circles and to travel in circles during leisure was redundant and irritating. I left the rink and, to this day, some 20 years later, I have yet to experience a desire to strap on the skates. I continue to enjoy watching a good skater spin as a rope tightly twisted, but it never sparks a desire to do it myself. I have no regrets.) For me, ice skating accomplished the objective. It was an adventure, a challenge. It changed my life by giving me the confidence I needed to take on bigger adventures (ones which proceed in a straight line). I have also seen people respond to similar needs without taking lessons. I remember a gal in an expensive outfit atop a small ski slope. She strapped on the best skis that money could buy, pointed them straight down the hill, zoomed past me and other skiers, past the lift, through the bales of hay marking the edge of the run, and tumbled into the trees. She brushed the snow from her face, gathered up her skis, and walked back to the lodge never to be seen on the slopes again. The point is, going from recognition of a need to successful doing, takes action based on instruction. The activity skills taught in Therapeutic Recreation should be for leisure pursuits that can be continued after the treatment stay is over. They should also be taught with the understanding that the activities are meeting transitory needs. Most of the time, activity interests discovered during treatment will not last a lifetime. But the feelings of competence from successful participation will last and open the doors to participation in new leisure interests as needed. For this reason, providing Skill Development sessions in the treatment setting is an important part of the Therapeutic Recreation Service.

Provision of Skill Development sessions should be based on participant interests. Interest identification can be awkward. Interest inventories may often provide little assistance. Inventories which ask if the person likes or dislikes, or has ever done a long list of activities, consume more time while providing very little useable information. The client struggles through a long, boring pencil and paper assignment. Occasionally the client looks up and smiles, seeing the name of an activity which sounds interesting: "Oh! I've always wanted to try that, do you have it here?" The Therapeutic Recreation Specialist smiles and responds, "No." Most of the time, the activities identified by an interest inventory, are activities which are unavailable in the treatment setting. The interaction provides a tone of mild frustration. Often the long inventory list results in no functional interests. This tends to make the client feel inadequate, a feeling that is contraindicated in the treatment process. Sometimes the client states interest in an activity which is offered at the facility. All too often the first time the client participates is also the last time. The client mumbles something about the activity being different from the previously encountered version, and wanders off. Certainly, the clients' interests are important. But what causes a person to be interested in a specific activity? (See Figure 9.1 on the following page)

The client's desire to develop skills in a specific activity is sparked by a combination of things. Why is anyone motivated to learn a specific activity? First of all, the prospective participant develops an awareness of the existence of an activity. With that awareness comes preconceived notions about what the activity is like. If the concept of the activity is such that it seems personally appealing (i.e., fits with the client's self-image) and/or the client perceives that the activity will meet his/her needs, then the client becomes willing to participate. This is the portion of the formula that is influenced by Leisure Education sessions. Once involved in the activity, the client makes a decision to like or dislike participation. This decision is influenced by both activity content and process. The content of an activity consists of the inherent physical properties of the activity itself, properties which can be extracted through activity analysis. But the activity process is leader-dependent. The process is dependent on the leader's confidence, the leader's enjoyment of the activity, and the leader's group dynamic/teaching skills.

A good example of this point is the time I helped an elementary school coach provide an all-school fitness program. I relieved another volunteer. The content of the activity at my station was to follow a predetermined course and run or walk

FIGURE 9.1

CAUSES OF ACTIVITY "LIKE" OR "DISLIKE"

PARTICIPANT Self Dependent	ACTIVITY CONTENT Activity Dependent	ACTIVITY PROCESS Leader Dependent*
Perceived PERSONAL APPEAL	**1** "This activity looks like the kind of thing I would like." or "It looks like something that does not match my image of me."	**2** "I like the way the activity is conducted; therefore, I like the activity." or "I dislike the way it's done, so I dislike the activity."
Perceived PERSONAL NEED	**3** "It might not look appealing but I know it will be good for me." or "Participation does not appear personally beneficial to me."	**4** "This is structured and I need to learn structure." "This will help learn patience." "This will help me learn organization."
RESULTS	1 + 2 + 3 + 4 = Degree of Activity Like or Dislike	

* Process dependent on leader's confidence, enjoyment of activity, and group dynamic/teaching skills.

the course three times, with the fastest time winning. The volunteer I relieved was a strict disciplinarian and highly competitive. Naturally, I'm the fun-for-all and all-for-fun type. Though the content did not vary, the process did. Under the leadership of the previous volunteer, the students did not talk and their faces were marked with fatigue, stress, and seriousness. The ones that came in first strutted about. The one that came in last fell to his knees sobbing. I got the groups laughing before they ever started. I structured a one-for-all, all-for-one attitude. Getting to the winner's circle was good, but just finishing was fantastic. Well, there was talking between students while they ran. Leaders yelled encouragement as they lapped the slower ones. When the last runner crossed the finish line, everyone applauded. The times were a little slower for my groups than for the first volunteer's group. I would say, so what? The first volunteer would say a lot. All too often, the participant's like or dislike of an activity is dependent on process rather than content. Unfortunately, the participant who dislikes the process assumes it is the content that is distasteful. The student who fell to his knees sobbing, probably thinks he dislikes "fitness" programs, especially racing, and will do whatever possible to avoid that type of activity in the future.

Staffing is also a challenge. I have yet to meet a person employed in the field of Therapeutic Recreation who is able to teach all types of activity skills. The person who knows how to teach athletic skills may be completely at a loss attempting to teach music skills. The person who knows how to teach art skills is often at a loss attempting to teach swimming skills, and so on. At the same time, the staff member with true expertise

in a particular type of activity may make a terrible instructor for that activity. My love of painting makes it difficult for me to teach beginners to paint. I must constantly fight my desire to snatch the paint brush out of their hands and do it myself. Having advanced-level skills in dance can also make teaching beginning levels boring. (In the private sector, I can tolerate beginning levels because there is the hope that the students will continue and I will get a chance to teach advance levels. But in the treatment facility, all there is, and ever will be is a moving sea of beginners.) Regardless of skill level of the instructor, teaching the same activity over and over leads to burnout. The leader begins to feel in a rut. As repetition continues, the leader begins to dread conducting the session. When the enthusiasm evaporates from the leader, it also drains from the process. The participants react to the process by feeling bored and they begin to dread attending the session.

Providing variety is a most difficult aspect of programming. Each client is different. Activity skill development needed by one client is seldom the same as the skills needed by the next. It is impossible to have a thousand activities on hand at any given time. The client's stated interest is usually process-dependent rather than content-dependent. This means that even though the same activity may be provided within the treatment facility, it may be different as a result of the way it is conducted. A person may have enjoyed participating in an activity in the past because it met internal needs which are no longer there. On top of these, are added the basic mechanics of staffing. Finding qualified instructors with not too much or too little skills to teach the sessions is often beyond the capability of the organization's structure. If this is accomplished, then there is the problem of repetition resulting in burnout, which depletes the process portion of the activity provided.

Solutions are at hand, though none is exactly perfect. Ideally, a wide variety of activities should be available to clients to meet individual interests. Attempts should be made to provide Skill Development sessions in areas that are of interest to clients. First of all, it is helpful to identify categories of interests rather than specific activity interests. Less time is consumed by assessing interest categories. Categories of interest are more constant over time. In my ice skating example, ice skating was a new activity for me. The category was not. I am drawn to self-competitive activities which contain aesthetically pleasing movement. I branched out without changing branches. Knowing the client's category of interest means that substitution of specifics is possible. The service does not have to stock one thousand activities so that specific interests can be met. The service can offer a representative sample of each category and most clients will find something of interest. Problems of staffing may still be present, but somewhat reduced. The problem of leader burnout is trimmed, for substitutions within the category can be made to keep things interesting for the leader.

The categories of interest I have found most revealing are used in this text. Activities are categorized as Other-Competitive, Self-Competitive, Productive, Social, Individual, Intellectual, Creative, Spiritual, and High Risk. "Physical," "Active" and "Passive" are not used in this breakdown. Too many activities have components which are physical, active, or passive to make them meaningful categories. For example, ballet, football, swimming, yardwork and rock climbing are all physical activities. It is unwise to assume that any one of these can be substituted for another with satisfactory results. What is active or passive really? Is the person who jumps out of his chair and shouts at the football players on television, participating in an active or passive pursuit? To substitute an activity for this person, would you give him an hour of television watching cartoons, or a table game which simulates football? All activities have levels of participation that are passive and active. To make these separate categories provides little information to assist in the selection of appropriate activity. (Knowing if a person's level of participation is passive or active can be beneficial; however that information is usually revealed on the first participation attempt. Besides, the trauma of treatment can cause active participants to regress to passive status.)

It is especially important to detect tendencies toward high-risk pursuit, since risk-taking can be highly addictive and deadly. When a person has been involved in high-risk activities, determine if he/she requires a depressant prior to participation. In my opinion, the person who takes a depressant prior to participation is not at great risk of addiction to high-risk pursuits. Most likely he/she will need encouragement to take any risk at all when sober. [Ch8:109.0; Ch11:460.0] On the other hand, the person who uses stimulants in conjunction with high-risk ventures is a hard-core stress junkie and may be at risk. [Ch11:420.0]

To assess client interests, clients are given examples of activities that are contained in each category. This leading approach results in answers. Too often the old standard, "What do you like to do?" gets the response, "Nothing." Indeed, many clients do nothing, having no leisure interests. Many times clients really don't understand how broad the topic of leisure is. They actually do many things but don't realize that the things they do are considered part of leisure pursuit. By giving a few examples, the client is able to respond to the examples and add activities that he/she associates with the examples. This system also helps the Therapeutic Recreation Specialist understand how the client categorizes leisure interests. This information is very important. Unusual associations of activities within a given category are often the result of process appeal rather than content appeal. [Ch7: "Leisure Skills & Interests"]

At TNT, Skill Development leaders are selected on their expertise in activity categories. To extend the variety which can be offered, recreation assistants, part time staff, staff from other departments, volunteers and clients are utilized. Staff from the second and third shifts are especially helpful for extending opportunities for skill development beyond the routine 9-5 day. Videotapes and instructional books can also expand opportunities for skill development opportunities. All Skill Development sessions offered, regardless of leadership source, remain the responsibility of the Therapeutic Recreation Service. As such, guidelines must be set to assure safe and therapeutic provision of the sessions. The session content and process must be monitored to assure maintenance of quality and safety. [Ch5: "Support Services for TR;" Ch6]

REQUIRED SKILL DEVELOPMENT SESSIONS

The only required session for all clientele is session 200.0, Finding and Taking Target Heart Rate. This session provides guidelines for monitoring exertion during physical activities while in treatment. It is the responsibility of each client to monitor his/her own progress and stay within safe limits of exertion. Naturally, all staff are aware of the guidelines set for the client and help the client to stay within the limits as needed. Again, exact levels and guidelines for participation should be set by the medical team. Physical activities and classifications listed in this text are only examples and should not be used without medical approval.

Additional Skill Development requirements vary from client to client. All clients are expected to learn at least one new activity per week. Which activity that is, is entirely up to them. Clients who are at risk or dependent in leisure skills are placed on a structured program which may require additional involvement in Skill Development sessions within specific categories of interest. Clients who are dependent in other areas of assessment may be required to attend specific Skill Development sessions which address identified needs. The number and variety of Skill Development sessions must be large enough to support the TRI assessment findings. There is a concentration on activities to support the dependent and semi-independent levels, since this is the area where the greatest gains can be made within a relatively short period of time. Clients who are independent, by definition have skills. It is therefore unnecessary to provide more skills (it might be a nice touch, but not necessary). Clients who are at risk may not be ready, or may require highly individualized attention. [Ch7]

Some activities may meet a variety of needs. For example, a client who has inadequate leisure skills, and has a need to improve ability to live alone, may benefit from developing skills in hobbies which can be done alone. The client who needs to reduce stress and improve physical fitness may benefit by learning leisure skills which are physically demanding yet provide relaxation. For this reason, most Skill Development sessions have two purposes, to meet a need identified in TRI assessment item 1 through 8, and to expand the client's repertoire of leisure skills. Rather than listing every activity twice, the Skill Development session is listed to meet the needs identified in TRI items 1 through 8, with the understanding it can also be used to simply expand the number of skills the client has. Whenever possible, the client should be allowed to choose participation in activities of interest as well as meet his/her needs. [Ch7] For example, the client who is out of shape and needs to improve his/her physical condition, as measured by TRI Item #1, may meet this need while expanding his/her list of leisure skills by selecting participation in one of the following:

211.2   How to Play Miniature Golf
211.2   Beach Ball Volleyball from Sitting Position
211.2   How To Play Shuffleboard
221.2   New Games For Fitness
221.2   Aerobics Designed for Persons Over 60
221.2   How to Swim for Fitness
221.2   Introduction to Tai Chi
231.2   Indoor Gardening
241.2   Low Cost Party and Family Games for Exercise
241.2   Social Dance Class (Slow Dancing)
241.2   Picnic Games for Mild Exercise (Water Balloon Toss)
251.2   Walking for Health and Fitness

Persons who are in good physical condition, could maintain their fitness through participation in:

211.4   How to Play Tennis
221.4   High-Impact Aerobics
241.4   Social Dance (Fast Dancing)
271.4   Introduction to Folk Dancing

The person who needs to improve relaxation skills could choose from the following skill development sessions:

226.2   Relaxation through Physical Exercise
226.2   Relaxing with Water Exercises
236.2   Relaxing while Growing Things
256.2   Relaxing with the Help of a Pet or Aquarium
256.2   How to Relax with Music
256.2   How to Relax with Nature

The remainder of this chapter supplies ideas for possible skill development sessions. Lists are not intended to be all-inclusive.

COMPETITIVE SESSIONS

Competitive sessions are actually "other-competitive," but the "other" is omitted to prevent clients from asking too many questions. The truth is, it is difficult to find a non-competitive activity. The question is, who does the participant compete against? Another person, or him/herself? Sometimes the answer is both. When an activity is other-competitive or both self- and other-competitive, it is listed as "Competitive." Even though these sessions are competitive, the competitiveness is not stressed. Participants tend to overexert themselves when competition is emphasized. The following provides a sample of other-competitive activities which might be taught at TNT.

211.2   How To Play Shuffleboard
211.2   How To Play Croquet
211.2   Beach Ball Volleyball
211.2   How to Play Miniature Golf
211.3   How to Bowl
211.3   How to Golf
211.3   How to Play Volleyball
211.3   How to Play Competitive Water Games

This last category includes games such as water polo, water volleyball, and water basketball. Swimming races are also included in this category. There are non-swim races as well as swim races. There are bubble contests, floating contests, and splashing contests. These are games performed in the water that require teams or result in naming a person as a winner.

211.3   How to Participate in Team Swims
211.4   How to Play Tennis
211.4   How to Play Frisbee™ Games
212.2   How to Speed Read
214.1   How to Play Low-Cost Team Sports
214.1   Let's Play Cards and Table Games

The basic rules for participation in popular board games and card games are taught in this series. Clients who are skilled in a particular game are used as instructors for the session. In addition to using client instructors, other clients, knowledgeable of a particular game, are paired with beginners, sharing the same hand or game piece. In this way, several games can be taught at the same time. Special attention is given to teaching backgammon, chess, and bridge. These three games have a complexity which maintains participants' interests for years. They often provide a purpose for social gatherings after discharge (e.g., bridge parties and clubs.)

214.4 How to Play Polo
215.3 Competitive Games for Family Fun
216.2 Using Sports and Other Competitions to Reduce Stress

Stress reduction comes from refocusing energies on a nonstressful event. It also comes from physical movement which drains the energy that feeds the stress.

217.1 How to Laugh and Make It Funny

Laughter is not fully utilized by many. Most of us participate in inhibited laughter which does little for our internal systems. Gut-wrenching, bellowing laughter brings oxygen into the lungs and activates internal chemical transmissions. This is the type of laughter which is taught in this session.

218.2 How To Play Backgammon
218.3 How to Play Chess

SELF-COMPETITIVE SESSIONS

Self-competitive sessions are those often referred to as noncompetitive. The self-competitive process requires the participant to recognize his/her present level of ability and then press the self beyond the existing level.

221.2 Aerobics Designed for Persons over 60
221.2 Introduction to Tai Chi
221.2 New Games For Fitness
221.2 How to Swim for Fitness

Skill Development sessions held in the swimming pool are designed to teach people everything except how to swim. Swimming lessons are avoided because most know how to swim. If an adult does not know how to swim, then the first step is to overcome the fear of water. (After that, swimming lessons are easily attained anywhere there is a pool.) At TNT, poolside Skill Development sessions teach people ways to have fun in water and get some healthy wet exercise. Stretching and aerobic-like exercises performed in the water are especially valuable for persons with limited range of motion.

221.3 How to Rumba Dance
221.3 Low-Impact Aerobics
221.3 Introduction to Martial Arts

Clients are introduced to the principles and philosophies of various forms of self-defense, such as Karate and Tae-Kwon Do. There are aspects of competitive activity in the Martial Arts but the primary thrust is self-competition. The basics are offered for mild exercise. Participants are given information about where to find lessons in the community. In the community, many Martial Arts Centers are alcohol/drug-free centers. Many sponsor tournaments which are also alcohol/drug-free events, pleasurable to watch as well as to participate in.

221.4 High-Impact Aerobics
222.2 Progressive Repetition Reading Game
224.1 Home Exercise Programs

Videotapes may be made at the facility or purchased from a vendor. The contents should be scrutinized for safe body mechanics. This session provides participants a chance to work out to videos which may be used after discharge. The goal is to help clients select the right video to meet their needs and to get in the habit of using it.

225.3 Non-Competitive Games For Family Fun
226.2 Relaxation through Physical Exercise

Relaxation is produced from focusing the energies on the event at hand rather than on thinking about a stressful situation. It is also reduced by the physical movement itself. The exercise program can vary in content. It should be done to music. The pace may be fast at the beginning but should be very slow at the end. [Ch9: Creative Sessions: Music]

226.2 Relaxing with Water Exercises

Water is a natural relaxer. A dip and a stretch, and a float, followed by time in a hot tub is a great way to relax.

227.1 Kid Games for Adults

Some "Adult Children" need to learn missed play developmental levels. When the client has blocked out the antics of childhood, his/her ego is saying things are too painful to be remembered. I believe the developmental play can be reestablished without delving into the painful past. This can be accomplished by getting persons to look at and participate in some of the kid games that adults play. The whoopie cushion is one of those adult kid games. Practical jokes and gags are the content of this session.

227.2 Hide and Seek and Climbing Games

This session teaches games of childhood. It includes climbing trees, playing red rover, and hide and seek. The leader must play as an equal. Process the activities afterward.

227.2   Hop Scotch, Leap Frog, and School yard
        Games

Some "Adult Children" may have forgotten how to play kid games. This session permits reexperiencing those activities and may recall lessons learned about leisure during early childhood. To be effective, the leader must participate with the clients, not act as an overseer. [Ch11:407.22, 407.23]

228.2   How to Play Computer Games
228.3   New Games for Problem Solving

PRODUCTIVE SESSIONS

231.3   Gardeneering

At the time of admission, gardeners know how to grow gardens. Farmers know how to farm. Flower lovers know how to grow flowers, and house plant lovers know how to grow house plants. It is a waste of precious treatment time to teach the gardener about gardening. In the Gardeneering series, outdoor gardeners and farmers learn to adapt their skills to indoor vegetable gardening and to patio gardening. Small greenhouse construction and use are also taught. The additional knowledge can come in handy for the farm lover who has moved to a city life. It is also helpful for the person who can keep occupied during the warm weather but can find nothing to do when the outdoor growing season is over.

The Gardeneering series includes a session about herbs. Myth and folklore surrounding herbs are shared as well as the basic propagation of herbs. Songs which make reference to herbs are also shared during the session. Home-grown herbs stimulate the quality of some other leisure pursuits. Cooking becomes more rewarding. Food tastes better when the "right" fresh herbs are used. Persons becoming interested in herbs can find hours of activity in the collection of information about herbs. (Care is taken to select herbs which do not have psychoactive properties.) Other sessions in the series include Japanese Gardening, the Non-Gardener's Paradise, and Chop Stunts. In the Non-Gardener's Paradise, participants learn basics of rock gardens and zero-maintenance yards. Chop Stunts provides the basics for shrub and tree trimming and pruning to achieve unusual effects. Persons who develop an interest in any of the above are encouraged to join garden clubs after discharge.

231.3   Working with Wood, Saws and Hammers
232.2   Writing Letters for Freebies
234.1   Cooking Class
234.2   Calligraphy

Calligraphy is learning to print artistically. At TNT, the lettering is used to make personal greeting cards. Birthday cards, holiday greetings, and "Thinking of You" cards are tops on the lists. Basic italic calligraphy is taught. Those who become interested may select different fonts from books that are usually available in craft stores and libraries.

234.2   Cake Decorating

Cake decorating can cost, but usually is cheaper than purchasing decorated cakes from a bakery. At TNT, clients decorate their own refreshments for special events and make all party favors for special events.

234.2   How to Sew Clothes
234.2   Tie Your Own Flies for Fishing
234.3   Customizing Your Home

Clients learn basic drafting skills. They draw a floor plan of their existing home, then they find ways to remodel it to make it more pleasurable. Developing leisure spaces is the focus of the new design. Participants are permitted to dream and scheme in the process. Before the session ends they are encouraged to find one thing they can do to improve the leisureability of their home that is within their resources. It may be to change the curtains to permit more sun into the home. It may be to clean out a corner to make room for a new hobby. It may be to create a calm, relaxing place.

235.1   Crocheting/Knitting/Needlepoint
236.1   Fishing

Clients are taught to cane pole fish, and tie their own flies for fishing. Casting contests are held. In this way, the clients develop the skills they need to participate in inexpensive fishing for both fun and relaxation.

236.2   Relaxing While Growing Things

This session helps persons who have never gardened before get started. Plants and seeds which sprout during the treatment stay go home with the client.

SOCIAL SESSIONS

Social sessions teach social interaction skills as well as how to plan and organize social engagements that are not centered around alcohol/drug use. Persons who have all their interests in the social category should be encouraged to take additional Skill Development sessions in individual activities.

241.2   Low Cost Party and Family Games for Exercise
241.2   Picnic Games for Mild Exercise (Water
        Balloon Toss)
241.2   Social Dance Class (Slow Dancing)

A party at home can be more fun if there is something to do. Dancing is something to do. Social dance without a drink, fix, or pill, presents a real problem to many. NA and AA Conventions provide alcohol/drug-free opportunities to dance. Many a newcomer has nearly shaken him/herself to death, or developed serious foot disorders, in anticipation of the social dance hour. Practice in treatment can take the edge off of the experience. At TNT, clients are taught the basic social dances that are currently popular. (In other words, the waltz and polka are out.) Persons who become interested in social dance are encouraged to continue lessons after discharge. Arthur Murray and similar dance studios, though expensive, provide excellent programs for learning social dance starting in a sheltered environment, at the person's own pace; from there the participant can move up, and out. Some studios provide alcohol/drug-free dance parties that meet many social needs. Going to a lounge to dance is not recommended. But, should a person become "trapped" into a trip to a lounge, dancing can remove the individual from the table where the drinks are ordered, served, and consumed.

241.3   New Games for Fitness
241.3   Picnic Games for Moderate Exercise
241.3   Square Dance

Square dancing is introduced at TNT. Participants learn a few basics and have some fun. Many communities have square dance clubs. Participation in the club often leads to clean and sober social fun. Some clubs take their dancing very seriously. The seriousness sometimes drains the fun.

241.4   Social Dance (Fast Dancing)
245.1   How to Start Pen Pal Letter Writing

This session helps clients get started in reaching out to others. It is especially good for those who have primary interests in individual pursuits but know they need to develop social skills.

245.2   Cooking for Large Groups
245.2   New Games to Meet Your Family Leisure Needs
245.2   The Dating Game

Participants pretend to visit a dating service. The first thing they must do is to complete a profile. The profile shares a brief introduction about the self which potential dates may read and decide if they want to pursue a relationship. The profile must describe the client, the type of person the client wants to date, and what type of relationship is desired. The group may discuss the profiles. Discussion is focused on helping clients to put their best foot forward.

Next, the group suggests first date expectations and concerns--places to go, things to do; when and how to explain a history of addiction and treatment. The group also discusses places to go (other than bars) to meet new people.

245.3   Family Activities
247.1   Playing Pictionary™ and Charades
247.1   Shouting Contests

Many adult children equate raising the voice with danger, yet Spivey Corners, North Carolina, has become nationally known for its Hog Hollerin' Contest. Anyone who has visited the Stone Mountain Georgia Laser Light Show has felt the wonderful power of the rebel yell when the new South rises to the tune of Dixie. Anyone who has attended a Tae-Kwon Do

tournament has seen the force of the shout productively harnessed. This session permits clients to see that shouting can be fun. Shouting requires inhaling oxygen and resonating vocal chords, which can produce healthy side effects. [Ch9: Creative Sessions: Music] It has been suggested that "The individuals who are most likely to survive are those who are 'aggressive, irritating, narcissistic and demanding'. . ." (Ornstein, 1987, p. 68). It is most difficult to be aggressive and irritating when a shout comes out a whisper.

This session helps clients see that there is value in raising the voice. A shout does not always mean danger. Sometimes it's fun to shout. Patterned after a hog calling contest, each participant attempts to give his or her best shout. Then the group is divided into teams. An attempt is made to offer up the best group shout. After the shouting has reached its best, a discussion follows. Feelings experienced by shouting are investigated. Appropriate times for shouting are discussed. Participants are also taught to communicate the purpose of a shout to friends and family.

247.1   Yarn Spinning and Telling Fisherman's Tales.

Storytelling is an adult variation of kid's play. In this session, participants experience the freedom of lying through their teeth--the bigger the tale, the better; the less truth, the better. Yarn spinning, when everyone knows it is a lie, is an acceptable way of stimulating the flow of creative juice.

249.2   Planning Alcohol/Drug-Free Social Gatherings

This session is linked with Community Government activities. Participants practice organizing special events in the facility. They are given guidelines and bases to cover in the planning of an event. These include inviting others, making sure everyone knows it is a substance-free event, and so on.

INDIVIDUAL PURSUITS

Sometimes Individual Pursuits have to be taught. These are usually taught in a group setting. The purpose is to provide the skills for safe, independent functioning during Re-Creation times. Persons who have all their interests in the Individual Pursuit category should be encouraged to take additional Skill Development sessions in the Social category.

251.2   Walking for Health and Fitness

While almost everyone knows how to walk, few know how to walk to gain maximum benefits for health and fitness. Usually, one quick class will make the difference. The class should teach warm-up stretches. It should address proper attire and footwear. The speed at which a person walks determines the aerobic benefits. Adjusting posture and gait provides muscle tone. By lifting the pelvic section, the back becomes properly aligned and the stomach develops muscle tone. By pressing back on the front of the thighs with each stride, the legs get exercise. Keeping the hips from swinging, and keeping the heels on the ground as long as possible develops muscle tone in the back of the legs. Keeping the shoulders immobile while swinging the arms tones the arms.

251.3   Outdoor Gardening
254.1   How to Go Fly A Kite

Kite flying is a calming pursuit which gets a person outdoors. In this session, clients are taught to make their own kites and then to fly them.

255.1   How to Play One-Player Games
256.2   How to Relax with Music (see "Creative")
256.2   How to Relax with Nature
256.2   Relaxing with the Help of a Pet or
        Aquarium
257.1   Joining Creative Writing Clubs, Little
        Theatre, Guilds
257.2   Making Mud Pies
259.1   Collector's Corner

Many things or any thing can be collected. The Collector's Corner introduces participants to the hobby of collecting. Sessions focus on how to get started, what to watch out for, in the practice of collecting stamps, antiques, coins, and other things. It also teaches how to organize collections.

Participants are also encouraged to select an item which is special, or meaningful to them, and start collecting it. One person might find a collection of keys and padlocks interesting. Another person might enjoy collecting rocks. Someone else might enjoy collecting ceramic frogs. Another may enjoy collecting outrageous comments. Enjoyment of a collection hobby is dependent on the meaningfulness of the item collected to the collection's owner.

259.2   Learning to Play Individual Activities
259.2   Outdoor Photography

Taking pictures has a number of benefits. Most important of all, it causes the person to stop and really look at what is going on around him/her. When the photographer frames a picture in the viewfinder of the camera, that picture is also being framed in the mind. It can then be recalled at will. Without stopping to frame a picture, the mind does not capture the beauty that is all around. The camera also provides a purpose for the introvert to get involved in otherwise uncomfortable situations. I know there have been times when I was uncomfortable about going to some social engagements alone. Not knowing anyone at a formal dinner, or wedding, provides a feeling of potential entrapment. That's when I take my camera. It gives me an excuse to reach out to people I don't know. I also take risks when I am playing photographer that I would never take when my camera is out of film. Without my camera, I cling to the backside of a viewpoint which is 500 feet

straight down to the view. When I have my camera, I'm hanging off the ledge, braced by my left toe hooked around a root, just to get that perfect shot.

The outdoor photography class teaches participants to see their surroundings rather than taking it all for granted. Participants are taught to select an object for the subject and then find the most pleasing angle and view. Macro-photography is also taught. A blade of grass with a drop of dew can be something to step on—or admire.

INTELLECTUAL PURSUITS

Classes in Intellectual Pursuits are encouraged for those who feel inadequate about intellectual abilities. Persons who operate on an intellectual level all the time may also participate in the classes. For them it is a Re-Creation experience; time spent in a comfort zone. Should a person who is totally out of touch with his/her feelings, who always sees the logical side, select the intellectual category as his/her required Skill Development session, the selection should be permitted. The person should also be encouraged to select Skill Development sessions in other categories. His/her overdependence on intellectual pursuits should be pointed out. A quest for balance should be supported.

262.2   Games That Practice the 3 R's
264.4   How to Make a Travel Plan
265.1   How to Operate a Computer for Fun

Participation in the computer fun sessions results in development of a basic working knowledge of home computers. Participants learn to like and use pre-packaged programs. They also learn to develop their own simple programs and save them on disks. A wide variety of educational programs as well as games are available. Participants are also taught to access and review portions of their own medical files which contain their treatment plan, attendance, and treatment goals. (The TNT computer system is designed in such a way that the client cannot tamper with his/her file or access sensitive information.) Persons who become interested in computer fun are encouraged to attend computer classes offered at community colleges after discharge. Persons are also cautioned to structure their time carefully, for some do get hooked on computer game use. [Ch11:420.0]

266.1   How to Design Stress-Free Environment at Home
266.1   How to Select Reading Materials for
        Stress Reduction
268.2   Math Games (How Many Ways to Add # to
        Get Given #)
268.3   How to Use Computers/Fun and Divergent
        Thinking

CREATIVE SESSIONS

The Creative classification includes a wide variety of art, music, drama, writing, and dance activities. Because of the diversity within this category, each will be discussed separately. Just as in Intellectual pursuits, there are those who cling to Creative pursuits. Persons who find their comfort zone in the Creative section should be permitted to take Skill Development sessions. They should also be encouraged to balance their lives by taking some Social and Intellectual Skill Development sessions.

CREATIVE SESSIONS: ART

Art contains a wide variety of mediums. Since art is highly individualistic, the fact that one is living alone or with others is of little importance. Art can be created at home, at a hospital, a halfway house, or in a prison cell. It can be an expensive hobby or one of minimal cost. In addition to creating art, opportunities for involvement include taking classes, participating in art shows, and appreciating the work of others. Classes may be offered by craft shops, recreation departments, art museums, community colleges, and by private artists as well.

Many people are afraid to try their hands in an artistic activity for fear of failure. There is an expectation that the first attempt must turn out perfect. Experienced artists have learned that the value of art is in the doing, with most end products being less than anticipated. The willingness to accept failure is an important key. Beginning artists need encouragement to try. They need to focus on the process rather than the outcome. Did the hour pass quickly, or was the hour boring and frustrating? That is the most important consideration.

Beginners have three favorite excuses for not getting involved in art. "I'm not talented." "I'm not creative." "I'm not artistic." However, the only valid reason for not participating in an art session is "I've tried it and I don't like it."

In my opinion, "natural talent" has little to do with a quality end product. Most people with natural talent are lazy and never fully develop their full potential. Practice and repetition are keys to success. Being creative is a form of problem solving. Creativity is a matter of generating alternatives and trying them until one works. It's a matter of giving the self permission to experiment. Being artistic means that the person has practiced and investigated a particular art form long enough to develop technical skill. Art is not just for women unless Van Gogh, Raphael, and Angelo were male impersonators.

It is the job of the Therapeutic Recreation staff to modify client stereotypes associated with art participation. Some people do not like art and that's acceptable. But it's not acceptable for persons to put themselves down or hold negative viewpoints about themselves. Therapeutic Recreation staff should not accept, "I'm not creative" or "I'm not artistic." They should only accept, "I don't like it" or "I choose not to try."

There seems to be two types of artists. Those with patience and those without. Such activities as needlepoint and crochet take hours of repetitive work before progress is identifiable. Many find only frustration in spending hours to produce one square inch of work. For those without patience, painting, calligraphy, and pottery have more appeal.

Provide quality supplies. How can a beginning artist be expected to turn out a decent painting with a paint brush that would turn a great master's work into a piece of trash? An expensive paint brush can last for years, if cleaned after each use. A cheap one will last long enough to paint one sorry picture. The same is true for other art supplies.

Assembly line crafts are not creative. Pre-cut-pre-packaged-attach-A-to-B's meet the need to be productive. But, they lack opportunities for self-expression. They eliminate opportunities to risk making mistakes. Though they appeal to the person who lacks confidence in creative abilities, completion of the package never seems to develop confidence. Unless some risk is taken, confidence cannot be developed.

The following formula has been developed to help get beginners involved in art. Low, medium, and high-risk projects should be available. Beginners should begin with low-risk projects and advance to high-risk ones. Risk results from the investment of time and money. The cost of time and materials multiplied by the perceived risk of failure can be calculated. Dividing that amount by the value of the end product results in the risk factor number.

FAULKNER'S RISK FORMULA

$$Risk = \frac{(\text{Amount of Time} + \text{Material Cost}) \times (\text{End Product Expectation})}{(\text{Perceived Risk of Failure})}$$

1 = LOW   2 = MEDIUM   3 = HIGH

To use this formula, a one, two or three is substituted for each factor contained in the formula. The number that is produced is the degree of risk. Using this formula for selected art projects, I can determine if I am providing a variety of risk-taking opportunities for clients. For example, I consider ceramics to be a low-risk project. (Figure 9.2, see p. 166) Time and material costs are high, but there is a model to follow and assurances that if the client does as told, the end project will turn out exactly like the model. The value of the end project is high. As a result, persons who are low risk takers in art, will attempt ceramics. Any project which has an end sample project on display with clear steps to the accomplishment of that end project, is a low-risk activity. Any project with the end product on display, but with no clear guidelines on how to achieve the end project, is a very high-risk venture. Trash art is a medium risk activity. There is no end project on display. There are no clear steps set for achievement. Thus the risk due to these factors is high. But trash art does not demand expenditure of time or money for supplies. The concept that if you start with trash and end with trash, then nothing has been lost, causes people to risk creative participation. Since only trash went into the project, any project that results in something can be directly attributed to the person's creativity. So trash art is a great creative confidence builder. The highest risk activity is one like painting. In painting, the supplies cost money. Time and energy are also spent. The results almost never match the intention. To get people painting, no end product should be demonstrated. Persons should be told to try to paint without thinking of any picture—just let it happen. The highest risk of all is a model which is in reality or in the mind's eye, for a copy is never as good as the original.

274.1 Drawing
274.1 Paper-Mâché Projects
274.1 Trash Art
274.1 Rubbings
274.1 Flower Arranging
274.2 Clay Modeling/Sculpture/Carving
274.3 Ceramics
274.3 Crocheting/Knitting/Needlepoint
274.3 Painting Pictures/Pastels
274.3 Photography
274.3 Pottery
274.3 Stained Glass
274.3 Weaving
277.2 Finger Painting and Basic Graffiti
278.2 Trash Art
278.2 Using Modeling Clay (How Many Shapes Can You Make?)
279.2 How to Design Living Spaces
279.2 How to Make Costumes and Your Own Patterns
279.2 How to Tie-Dye

CREATIVE SESSIONS: DANCE

Dance is an action of the soul. Movement can create new states of consciousness, new views of reality. Every person has a dance inside just waiting to be expressed. Take special care selecting music for a dance session. The movement of the body seems to heighten receptiveness to content of lyrics and melodies. Sometimes when I teach dance, the last tune I use plays in my mind for an hour after class. I take great care to make that last selection a piece of music I enjoy listening to.

Teaching dance requires skill in dance and skill in teaching. Although some basics may be provided through the use of videotaped instruction, videotapes cannot replace hands-on teaching. They can, however, provide the client with an understanding of what the style of dance is all about and give guidance to teaching for those with dance skills. A full line of videos are available. (See other references) I recommend beginning level videos, those endorsed by associations, over those led by movie celebrities.

271.3 Introduction to Ballet, Tap Dancing

TNT provides basic introduction to the performing arts, ballet, jazz, tap, modern, etc. The session is designed to help participants learn what to expect. Many dance studios offer adult beginner classes. All dance studios are cigarette/alcohol/drug-free centers. They support healthy treatment of the body. If one becomes interested, hours of free time can be consumed in a meaningful way. (It also consumes money in tuition fees.) (Featherstone, 1970).

FIGURE 9.2

FAULKNER'S RISK FORMULA APPLIED TO ARTS AND CRAFTS		
STARTING RISK	**TYPE OF PROJECT**	**THEORETICAL FUNCTION**
LOW	Ceramics,	LEFT BRAIN
	String Art,	LEFT BRAIN
	"Project" Crafts,*	LEFT BRAIN
MEDIUM	Trash Art,	RIGHT BRAIN
	Free Form,**	RIGHT BRAIN
HIGH	Drawing,	RIGHT BRAIN
	Painting,	RIGHT BRAIN
	Woodworking	RIGHT BRAIN
	Sculpture	RIGHT BRAIN
	Model in Mind's Eye,***	RIGHT BRAIN
HIGHEST	Model is Reality,***	LEFT TO RIGHT

*   Attach A to B and the results will look exactly like this type of craft.
**   Experimentation with a media, emphasis on process rather than results; no finished project example available.
*** A copy is never as good as the original; results never match the intention.

271.4 Introduction to Folk Dancing (275.0)

Participation in folk dancing does not require expertise in dance. It is fun. It is social. It also provides a sense of cultural identity, a feeling of knowing your roots. The Irish in me responds to the Irish jig, and with that response, I learn something about myself. The German in me responds to the "Chicken Dance" (which I was recently informed is actually the "duck dance"). I have no Spanish in my bloodline, yet I find the Mexican hat dance refreshing. Most folk dancing in this country is of European influence. All countries dance, and a person can travel the world in an hour by learning portions of various folk dances (Harris, 1970).

278.2 Creative and Social Movement (Explore Movements and Directions)

Exploration of movement is particularly helpful in freeing expression of the creative spirit. Modern dance exercises may be used. The best technique to get people to express themselves through movement is to just help them get started. It could be as simple as swinging one's arms forward and back. Once everyone is doing this tell them to swing them a different way. Teach a couple of steps. For example, step forward and hop. Once everyone is doing this, put on some music and ask participants to add an extra step. Be vague and unclear. They will all come up with a different understanding of the instructions and then support the differences. Another way is to imagine floating in water and swaying with the currents, then imagine something closing in and pressing against the imagined motion. Lastly, imagine getting hit and contract the body. Put on music and tell participants to do all the previous motions as they think of them. Creative movement can also begin with experimentation. Take a shoulder and see how many different ways it can be moved. Repeat the process with the head, a knee, a foot, a hip, and so on.

CREATIVE SESSIONS: DRAMA

Drama has value in, during, and after treatment. Many clients enjoy being the life of the party. In drama, they find out they can be the life of the party without a drink, fix or pill. Drama provides opportunities to practice new skills and behaviors, to try on different personalities, to experience the feelings of others. Pretending to be someone else can unlock doors barred by denial and help a person get in touch with the inner self. In addition to the therapeutic value, drama can be a lifelong leisure pursuit. Many communities have active amateur theater groups. Drama should not be used with psychotic clients. There is a chance that they will take on the imaginary role and not be able to return to the real world.

278.2 Drama: How Many Different People Can You Be?

This session selects a popular television or movie character. Participants are asked to portray the character "differently." For example, how would Rambo act if he were a woman? How would Rambo act if he were 9 or 90?

278.2 Mime and Mimicry

This session asks participants to act out situations or events, and to portray characters without words. Participants might be asked to share what they have done during the day without using words. This could involve guessing games. Guess what I'm pretending to do. Guess what emotion this is.

279.2 Script Writing

Standard script formats are used which help participants learn the ground rules needed for participation in drama groups after discharge. If participants are comfortable with the idea, a video camera can be used to record skits. If participants are not comfortable being videotaped, a few members of the audience should write down the action and some of the good lines. Individuals who show a flair in creative writing sessions are often invited to the drama sessions to take notes. When a skit accidentally turns out to be a quality product, a script is developed from the video, or the notes. (Drama leaders review scripts and prevent any one actor from having more lines than any other. Some characters are written in with just one line for those clients who are really uptight about the thing. There is also room built-in for those who wish to be seen, but not heard.) The skit is then rehearsed from the script and presented to the center as a special event. The "just for fun" concept should always be emphasized.

279.2 How to Act and Participate in Drama

There is a difference between plays offered by community groups and skits in treatment facilities. A play, in a community theatre, may be rehearsed for months. Emphasis is placed on perfection, memorizing lines, and so on. The name of the game in treatment is ad-lib impromptu. Drama classes do not use prepared scripts. Participants may develop scripts and present skits at special events. When skits are performed for the treatment center, the scripts are kept simple and used as guidelines only. Participants carry their scripts with them and are prepared to improvise when someone forgets a line.

Drama sessions focus on short role plays and improvisations. Situations for dramatic activities can be selected by the activity leader or developed through group interaction. Scenes can be set up by asking some participants to write a sentence or two describing a place. These are collected and placed in a jar. Some participants are asked to describe an event or situation. These are collected and placed in a second jar. The remainder of the participants are asked to describe two characters and these are placed in a third jar. The group then selects a time of day. A place and a situation are drawn from the jars. Approximately one-third of the participants select a character to portray from the third jar. The "stage" is set according to the time, place, and situation, and the action begins. The remaining two-thirds of the participants serve as the audience. After a few minutes, the activity leader calls for a conclusion and the actors must find an ending for the skit. At the end of the skit, audience and actors interact, discussing alternative plots and actions that could have developed. A new situation, place, and time are selected, and a second third of the participants draw characters to play. A second skit develops, and the process is repeated.

Drama may be used in a variety of ways. A descriptive passage from a book or story may be passed out and several participants read or act out the same passage. Each participant can select a different method of conveying the passage to the group. One participant may act it out. Another may read it as if it were a sarcastic joke. Another may read it as if it were an angry scene. Another may read it as if it were a love scene. Drama may also be used as Recreation Therapy. [Ch.11]

CREATIVE SESSIONS: MUSIC

People can be divided into two kinds, those who play and those who wish they could. Those who wish they could, listen to those who play. Regardless of active or passive participation, music is an important avenue of communication. Musical tones and the speed of the tones interact with internal system processes. Lyrics lodge in our memory banks, reinforcing viewpoints of perceived reality (Tame, 1984).

In the past, music was often under-utilized by many Therapeutic Recreation Services. Playing a musical instrument takes skills which many of us do not have. There are a wide variety of musical instruments. Most cost more than the budget allows. Clients who don't know how to play, can't learn in the period of a short treatment stay. The advent of the keyboard synthesizer has changed much of this. The keyboard is a relatively inexpensive instrument which can produce a variety of sounds. It is portable and storable. It is capable of making a beginner's plunks sound good, thus providing incentive for the client to continue after discharge. Obviously it is no substitute for a qualified Music Therapist, but it sure beats sitting around listening to a record player.

275.1 How to Sing-A-Long

Sing-a-longs are participatory. TNT has developed song books which contain a variety of popular songs. Participants may select country and western favorites, rock, or just about any type of music. Lyrics are screened to make sure the themes of the songs are positive. Persons who become interested in singing are encouraged to join church choirs or barber shop quartets after discharge.

275.3 How to Develop Family Sing-A-Longs

Listening to music together is a way of family sharing. Many families have adjusted their schedules to displace the trauma of alcohol/drug use on weekends. Bringing the family together to sing, during a time previously reserved for fight-or-flight preparations, can be highly beneficial. Each family member can bring his or her selection of favorite songs to the family sing. Family members may take turns selecting their favorite song for the entire family to sing. This assists in the development of family unity and cooperation. It also provides a non-threatening avenue for self-expression. Clients are cautioned not to attack other family members for their selections. The child who selects a sad or resentful song should not be told to find another song. The entire family should accept and show support for the child's feelings by singing the song with him/her. The type of song selected will change when the underlying feelings change. The sad song child will receive immediate assistance when other family members select happy songs to sing.

276.1 How to Lip Synch to Vent Stress

Singing out loud causes oxygen to be pumped by the lungs. The larynx is highly sensitive to emotions and singing changes the tension on the larynx. Almost every internal system of the body is affected when a person sings (Tame, 1984, pp. 136-137). Unfortunately, many of us have become convinced that our voice sounds like a dying cat. This session helps participants understand that the sound that goes out is not important. It is the making of the sound that matters.

The session begins with playing a familiar record or cassette tape. Participants are given the lyrics and pretend to be the singer, mouthing the words to themselves. The leader gets participants to act like the singer, using appropriate facial and body expression. Participants then note their own pulse and respiration rate. Next the leader discusses the impact of singing on the body. Then the songs are sung to the record again. This time the volume is turned up. Participants are encouraged to belt it out, loud and clear. Participants recheck their pulse and respiration rates. The session ends with participants comparing the difference in feelings experienced between whispering along with a song and belting it out.

The best songs I have found to vent anger and frustration are those which really scream. Janis Joplin was a master. Elvis often hit those releasing chords. Barbra Streisand, Billy Joel, and Leon Russell have been known to hit them too. Singing the Blues can have the desired effect. It is not so much the volume or loudness, but the selection of chords and the length at which chords are held. (When singing along with Janis's, "Oh Baby," I have to take a very deep breath, furl my eye brows and let it all out. That prolonged grinding exhale seems to scour the frustration and stress right out of my system.)

276.1 How to Select Music for Stress Reduction

Music which is fast tends to increase respiration and heart rate. Music which is slow tends to reduce them. Prior to the session, music is organized according to the number of beats per minute. "Average" is considered from 60 to 75 beats per minute. This is about the same as the average rate at which the heart beats. "High" is over 75 beats per minute. "Low" is under 60 beats per minute. Slow-beat music is often accompanied by sad song lyrics. These are screened out. The goal is to relax participants, not depress them.

A room which has soft lighting and is likely to have few interruptions is selected. At the beginning of the session, participants monitor their heart rates. Music is selected which has beats lower than the lowest heart rate in the room. Participants listen to the music for 15 minutes. During this time, participants are free to stretch out on the floor and close their eyes. They may doodle on a piece of paper if desired, but they may not talk to one another. (It can be uncomfortable to be in a group setting and do nothing. This is why the options are provided.) At the end of the 15 minutes, participants recheck their heart rates. Most of them will have lowered their heart rates. Discussion focuses on the difference in heart rate as well as the difference in feelings that may have occurred. (Participants should feel more relaxed.) The use of soft lighting and assurance of limited interruptions is also pointed out.

Relaxation is also produced by the actual pitches that vibrate the ear drums. Many hearing nerves have long axons that reach throughout the body. In addition to speed and volume, there are the actual harmonic vibrations that produce relaxation. Much of the "New Age" music masterfully utilizes the sounds that produce relaxation. Its effects are amazing. (I have used it successfully to counteract the preschool-Halloween-sugar-fix syndrome in many dance classes. I have to be careful about using it in other dance classes, for too much of it makes students too lazy to dance.) (Tame 1984).

The session concludes with a discussion and review of the points. Lists of music titles which produce relaxation and which fall in the "low" rate category are passed out. In this way, participants my purchase their own music after discharge. Cassettes of relaxing music are available through the TNT library check-out system for use during the treatment stay.

277.1 Home-Made Rhythm and Kazoo Band

Participants learn to make and play hand-made instruments. Jars with varying amounts of water are plunked. Pot lids clank together. If an old-fashioned wash board can be found, it is added to the rhythm section. Rubber bands stretched tightly over a box provide the string section. (Though I have never had luck with them, paper over a comb is suppose to make a musical sound.) Bells of varying types and sizes are fun. Party favors which produce noise can be included. Kazoos and other cheap instruments can also be added. The group learns to play and produce some musical rhythms. Songs such as "Jingle Bells" and "Row, Row, Row Your Boat" are the artillery for the great orchestral production.

277.2 Making Sounds: Acceptable, Unusual, Loud, and Strange

The group experiments with making different sounds. The body is treated as a primary source of musical sounds. Knee slapping, hand clapping, and foot tapping are basics. Other sounds can be produced by slapping the forearms and chest. The mouth is a wonderful instrument. It oinks, it squeaks, it pocks, bops, and plinks. Get participants to see how many unusual noises they can make. Then participants are organized into rhythm and melody sections and songs are produced. The session seeks to encourage creativity, experimentation, and lowering of personal inhibitions.

279.0 How to Make Music a Therapeutic Force

This session provides a summary of the impact of music on a person's life. It helps people select music that is therapeutic. Group discussions about music can be interesting for those who do not play or sing. The impact of music on a person's life is discussed.

The type of music participants enjoy is discussed. The leader encourages a balanced selection of listening materials. Some music should be fast paced; some should be slow. Music with negative lyrics should be avoided. The body's response to various types of music should be discussed (Tame, 1984).

Many songs have interesting lyrics which often go unnoticed. Discussion can bring out the meaning of the lyrics. Some people have a specific song or type of music that "puts 'em in the drinking mood." Through discussion, participants become aware of any music triggers in their lives and are encouraged to avoid them.

To stimulate group discussion, songs of opposing messages or philosophies are played and discussed. Usually only a portion of each song should be used, or the session tends to drag. A true song of love may be played followed by a song of co-dependency. The difference is discussed.

Participants are asked to recall a song from the past. Usually the entire song cannot be remembered. Only the lyrics which were most significant at the time are remembered. Participants should attempt to recall songs about both work and leisure. They should attempt to recall favorite songs from childhood and adolescent years. They should attempt to recall songs which support substance abuse. If the remembered portion is negative, or supports abuse, the group helps the person to rewrite the song, making it positive. Then the group sings the rewritten song at least three times to load the new version into the person's memory bank. Whenever possible, the new versions should be written down. The new versions should be practiced before bedtime every night. Persons who respond to this process may benefit from Recreation Therapy sessions which use the same format to deal with specific topics in-depth. [Ch11:405.01, 407.2]

279.2 How to Play Keyboard, Guitar and Drums

TNT also provides basic lessons in guitar, drum, and keyboard playing. Learning to play a musical instrument is a very long process and beyond the confines of a treatment stay. The purpose of the lessons are to help interested persons get started. The lessons are beneficial in terms of developing interest and the confidence to try. Persons who become interested are encouraged to continue lessons through private and public sources after discharge.

CREATIVE SESSIONS: WRITING

272.2 Creative Writing and Poetry

In my opinion, writing is an excellent leisure pursuit for persons who are limited by physical health, transportation, economic, family support, community, and discharge destination. Persons who are "Independent" in creative problem solving are more likely to respond to creative writing activities than persons who score "At Risk." It is also an excellent avenue of communication for persons who have difficulty expressing themselves verbally in a face-to-face situation. Creative writing is not recommended for a person scoring "At Risk" on Education. As a form of communication, I have noticed that many clients refer to the practicing addict's self as "i" and to the recovering self as "I." At TNT, emphasis is placed on self-expression rather than on technical skills. Various formats are used to stimulate participation. In some sessions participants select a topic. Sometimes the topic is assigned by the activity leader. Sometimes a story is begun and participants must finish it. Sometimes participants write a topic and give it to the person next to them to write about. Topics often ask the participant to see the world from a different viewpoint. For example, participants might be asked to write a short story or poem about how the world would look if they were a pencil. Sometimes each participant is given a starting point. Each starting point is different but when linked together they create a strange group story.

277.1 How to Write About Events in a Child's Life

Though the child written about is fictitious, the writer will put his/her childhood learning into the story. Use of the first person can be an emotionally provoking experience for the writer as well as the reader. Each member of the group should write a short story about a child (a few paragraphs at most). Then the stories should be shared with the group. Depending on the writer and the story, the original story should be rewritten. Some writers may be encouraged to make their stories more forceful. Others writing stories of hopelessness or with non-therapeutic endings should be encouraged to rewrite the ending of the story. (Nothing can be done to change the past, but each of us has the power to change our understanding of the past and to change the here and now.) The new endings should tell a story of overcoming.

279.2 How to Write a Song

Participants begin by selecting a song known to them and rewriting the lyrics. Next participants select 12-step program slogans and set them to music, using the slogan as the chorus and creating verses that fit with the slogan.

279.2 How to Write Sounds of Leisure

This session creates an opening of awareness. Many people tune out the sound of life which surrounds them. This eliminates the ability to experience the pleasure that is present in the daily routine. It also limits the writer's creativity. This session also helps persons with spelling difficulties. It demands that the individual develop the ability to distinguish between different consonant and vowel sounds.

Participants think of a sound made during a leisure activity. The sound is then written down. Usually the sound requires creation of a new word. The word is shown to the group. First participants attempt to make the sound that the word represents. Then the participants attempt to guess the leisure event which produced the sound. Here are some examples:

Click-ah-Kreek: Sound of a door opening on a hot tub experience designed for two.

Chajunk: Sound heart makes under hot water after a Click-ah-Kreek.

Kafump-quuawah: Sound of shoe being sucked from foot by Oregon hiking trail mud.

(Kafump-quuawah) X 4: Sound of an elk on an Oregon hiking trail.

Kafump-quuawah! Splat. Kafump-quuawah! Splat: Sound of Oregon hiker's victorious return into the home.

v-v-v-V-V-V-v-v-v: Sound of a hummingbird passing.

v-v-v-V-V-PFMK!: Sound of a kamikaze hummingbird flying into the window glass.

ahh, ha-ha-ha-he-he-e-e-e: Sound induced by trial-and-error matching of letter sounds to kamikaze hummingbird sounds.

Participants benefit from repeating this session. The first time, they have paid little attention to the sounds made during leisure experiences. After the first session, participants tune into the sounds. On the second session they have more sounds to share.

SPIRITUAL PURSUITS

Spiritual pursuits comprise an important interest category. Clients in a treatment facility usually come from a wide variety of church affiliations. Non-church sponsored facilities have no basis to provide spiritual programs due to separation of church and state. Still this is an important aspect of life which should not be overlooked.

HIGH RISK PURSUITS

Provision of outdoor and high-risk activities is strongly recommended. However, due to logistics and conservative agency policies, it is not stressed in this text. Challenge and adventure courses such as Project Adventure, Inward Bound, and others, are a method of bringing the lessons of the outdoors onto treatment center grounds. I am not in a position to recommend one product over another. I do believe that many of these courses are safer than off-campus outings. I believe it is wiser to purchase a manufactured system rather than building one from scratch without assistance. I recommend the purchase of products from companies that maintain safety records and provide training. In this way, the risks are greatly reduced. Where such activities are not possible, risks may be taken through Creative session participation.

299.2 Diving

Teaching people to dive head first into a swimming pool is used to develop risk-taking abilities. Diving is also a self-competitive activity.

299.2 How to Go White Water Rafting Safely
299.2 How to Camp Out and Cook Over an Open Fire
299.2 How to Rock Climb and Rappel

With skill and equipment, rock climbing and rappelling can be taught where no rocks exist. A side of a building can make a good substitute.

References/Resources

Brenner, A. (1980). *The TV Scriptwriter's Handbook.* Cincinnati, OH: Writer's Digest Books.

"Dance Video Review." (1988, March). *Dance Magazine.*

Edwards, B. (1979). *Drawing on the Right Side of the Brain.* Los Angeles, CA: J. P. Tarcher, Inc.

Featherstone, D. F. (1970). *Dancing Without Danger: The Prevention &* Treatment of Ballet Dancing Injuries. NY: A. S. Barnes & Co.

Fitness, exercise, and dance instructional videos, from Taffy's-By-Mail, Cleveland, OH.

Harris, J. A, Pittman, A., & Waller, M. S. (1969). *Dance A While: Handbook of Folk, Square & Social Dance.* Minnesota, MN: Burgess Publishing Co.

Hull, R. (1983). *How to Write a Play.* Cincinnati, OH: Writer's Digest Books.

Leviton, D., & Santoro, L. C. (Eds.). (1980). *Health, Physical Education, Recreation & Dance For The Older Adult: A Modular Approach.* Reston, VA: American Alliance for Health, Physical Education, Recreation & Dance.

Liebler, W. (1988, March). Mechanics of the spine. *Dance Magazine.*

Mayer, R. (1985). *The Artist's Handbook of Materials & Supplies.* NY: Viking Press.

Ornstein, R., & Sobel, D. (1987). *The Healing Brain.* NY: Simon and Schuster.

Performing arts buyers guide, from Stage Step, Philadelphia, PA.

Programming Trends in Therapeutic Recreation. Published bimonthly by Creative Leisure Services, Denton, TX.

Shepherd, M. (1981). *Calligraphy Made Easy: A Beginner's Workbook.* NY: Perigee Books.

Tame, D. (1984). *The Secret Power of Music.* Rochester, VT: Destiny Books.

CHAPTER 10

RE-CREATION

Re-Creation is the fun part of the Therapeutic Recreation Service. Some professionals refer to it as diversion. I object to labeling Recreation as "diversion." True, Recreation diverts one's attention from the negative to the positive. But it does much more than that. Too often the diversion label spawns the quick-something-anything-to-keep-'em-occupied-until-I-have-time-to-figure-out-something-worthwhile-to-do style of programming.

Provision of Re-Creation can be justified in terms of diversion, providing a respite from mentally fatiguing activity. It can be justified in terms of providing time to practice new behaviors and integrate new learning. It can be justified as an opportunity to develop social interaction skills. But these are merely justifications. The primary purpose of Recreation is to provide opportunities for the individual to experience the critical differences between surviving life and living life. Recreation is the ultimate, the final outcome of all Therapeutic Recreation Services. Recreation is the process of intrinsic regeneration. Talking about leisure does not restore internal balance. Doing it does. Re-Creation is just like sex. One can talk about it, and hear about it, and read about it until blue in the face, but it remains meaningless until it is experienced.

Re-Creation is therapeutic but it is not a therapy. A therapy is a process which is designed, controlled, contrived, and manipulated by a therapist to provide predetermined benefits. Re-Creation is a spontaneous outburst of the inner self. The desired experience cannot be produced upon command and the outcomes are unpredictable.

A therapy results in changes which can be observed and therefore measured. It is difficult to observe an intrinsic experience. Re-Creation can only be measured by highly sophisticated tests which measure changes in neurotransmission. Short of that, a positive response to the question, "Did you have a good time?" is a simplistic, yet efficient measure. It is difficult to measure the power and intensity of any aspect of the inner self. If dealing with the inner self is avoided while treating addiction, the treatment is negated.

At TNT, the Re-Creation service delivery system is designed for "Independent" clients. "Independent" clients play a key role in selecting and providing activities as well as participation in activities. Theoretically, there are an infinite number of activities which might result in the occurrence of a recreative experience. In the Therapeutic Recreation setting choices are limited by the staff's and clientele's imagination, by equipment, facilities, space, expertise, time, and money. Therapeutic Recreation personnel have the responsibility of selecting activities which are most likely to succeed in igniting the recreative spark. To prevent the frustration of thinking up neat things to do which cannot be done, program limitations must be identified prior to planning. A pre-selection list can provide guidance. It is a list of all the activities which can be done (or cannot be done). Program planning becomes a simple and non-creative matter of picking something from the list. Maintaining a list of previous activity evaluations can guide and stimulate thought. It must also always be remembered that the recreative experience is an elusive bird. If an activity successfully produced recreation once, it might do so again, but it might also bomb. A list of the limitations does not limit creativity and may serve as an adequate starting point (i.e., cost not to exceed a set amount, length not to exceed a specified amount of time, etc.). The more client involvement in the planning and selection stage, the greater the chance that the selected activity will produce recreation.

Regardless of the types of activities offered or programming approach selected, there is a momentum that develops within Re-Creation programming. One good activity builds up clientele expectations. Those who expect to have a good time are more likely to have a good time. With positive momentum, participants will anxiously attend and have a recreative experience even if there is no activity offered. Just as one good experience sets the stage for another good experience, so too does a bad experience create negative momentum. "If you thought last night was bad, wait until you see this one!" Beware of ruts! An activity which is new to the clientele but routine to the staff is the most efficient form of activity which can be provided. But if the staff become bored with the routine, they will infect the clients with a negative, boring momentum. Though it is difficult to predict when recreation will occur, it seldom if ever occurs when one is bored.

At TNT, participation in Re-Creation is voluntary. Activities are coded as the 300 series, which are similar to extracurricular activities at a college. Most are scheduled or available for free time use. Schedules of events are posted on bulletin boards. They are also announced each morning at the Community Meeting. (For an explanation of the code numbers used in this chapter, see Chapter 7.)

CREATING A LIKELY ENVIRONMENT

The environment is the atmosphere within which activities are conducted. It is difficult to re-create in an environment akin to a prison cell. Creating an environment conducive to leisure should address all factors perceived by the senses. Therapeutic Recreation Staff need to work with other facility employees to create and maintain a therapeutic environment.

Visually, the facility should be decorated to feel warm and comfortable. A lounge should have lounge-able furniture. Plants and greenery help significantly. Areas should feel inviting. Shelving and cabinets are expensive and the Therapeutic Recreation Service often has a shortage of places to put supplies. Disarray is not therapeutic. Clutter should be reduced through order and organization. Equipment shelved behind plexiglass doors is better than in cabinets with wooden doors. Equipment out of sight goes un-used. Frantic searches for the right piece of equipment turns storage areas into disaster areas. Cabinets which are dark and deep swallow everything. Equipment which is moved frequently should be permanently stored on carts. The carts can then be stored in the deep dark closet spaces.

The auditory environment also needs attention. Rooms that echo are distracting. Interruptions, phone rings, door slams, and intercoms are also disruptive. Noise of leisure can also be disruptive. Without management, persons pursuing noisy games and social interactions disrupt moments of quiet contemplation and relaxation. Separate rooms should be used for quiet and noisy pursuits. Times of quiet and noisy leisure participation may be alternated.

Music should also be controlled. All background music and music brought in by clients should be reviewed. Songs which condone substance abuse should be prohibited. Songs which paint a picture of a world about to blow up should also be discouraged. Only music which corresponds to the average heart beat or lower should be permitted for any length of time. [Ch9: Creative Sessions: Music]

Odors are also an important consideration. It is difficult to enjoy leisure surrounded by smelly things. The smell of cleaning fluids, craft supplies, new carpet, musty costumes, dusty paper, etc. should be avoided as much as possible. Strong perfumes and colognes can also be distractive to some people.

BREAK TIMES

Many centers try to pack too much into the daily routine. The cost of a day in treatment is high; the number of days per treatment too short. There is not much choice about it. The client gets up with day break and runs from session to session until bed time. The client eventually reaches a point in the day when he/she cannot take any more information in. From that point on, all therapeutic value is lost.

The length of attention may be expanded. Breaks are important. Most facilities allow ten to fifteen minutes between sessions. But what do clients do with this time? Usually nothing which revives the senses. Teach clients to stretch, to move, to laugh, or to sing on breaks. One minute of such activity is worth an hour of "rest."

STYLE SHOP

The Therapeutic Recreation Service contracts with local beauticians and barbers to operate a beauty/barber shop. Tips about make-up, clothing, and cologne selection are also given on an informal basis. (Repeat: Tips about cologne are given; the cologne itself is a controlled substance.) A new feeling on the inside often needs a new look on the outside. The style shop is the place to find the new look.

COMMUNITY GOVERNMENT

The Community Government is an essential part of the TNT Center operations, and the Re-Creation program. It is similar to a student body government in a college. The Community Government conducts Community Meetings every morning following breakfast and a Senior Seminar on Wednesday afternoons. Meeting attendance is mandatory. The morning meetings are the primary vehicle for communication of changes. The Senior Seminars are part of the treatment program. At the seminar, clients preparing for discharge deliver speeches, which evaluate their own growth and the center's program. Participation in all other government functions and the holding of governing offices are voluntary. Governing officers consist of a president, vice-president, secretary, treasurer, detox liaison, and a group leader from each therapy group. Group leaders are clients elected by the members of the therapy group they represent. All other officers are elected by the clientele at large. To be eligible to hold an office, a client must have completed AA Step Three, or have the permission of this treatment team.

The duties of the president include presiding over Community Meetings and Senior Seminars. The president serves as a spokesman for the client population when needed. For example, if TNT has a rule that is disliked by the clients, it is the president's duty to point out the problem to the center's management team. The president is consulted by the center's management team before making changes in policies and procedures. The president is responsible for communicating and sharing any such privileged information with the other clients. Though the president is designated as chief communicator, all officers are invited to attend designated management and Therapeutic Recreation meetings. All officers are encouraged to give and receive feedback on operational issues. The vice-president assists the president in the conduct of his duties. The president usually asks the vice-president to conduct half the meetings.

The secretary is in charge of the Awards and Honors program. Acting on behalf of the client population, the officers develop certificates which recognize clients (and sometimes staff) for remarkable deeds performed during the week. The awards are given out as part of the Senior Seminar ceremony. Some of the awards are humorous, others serious. Certificates are given to winners of talent competitions, tournaments, etc. Some certificates are given out to recognize clients for their good deeds, such as being most helpful to new clients. Some certificates are given out as a form of humorous confrontation, such as awarding the title of "Ms. Bizzy Bee" to the person who is avoiding her own problems by telling others what to do. It is the secretary's responsibility to meet with the other officers, have them select the winners of the awards, and to prepare and present the certificates.

The secretary is also responsible for checking the computer listing of clients for dates of birth, and having someone surprise appropriate clients with a Happy Birthday song on the appropriate day. The secretary also sends appropriate clients invitations to the monthly birthday party.

The treasurer manages a Community Government budget. The budget can be used to pay for Community Government recreation functions (i.e., refreshments, special events, theatre tickets, cash prizes for contest winners, video rental). The treasurer is responsible for organizing cleanup committees for each special event. A specified amount of money is allocated to the Community Government budget after each special event, provided that the facilities used are left neat and clean. An additional amount is contributed to the fund on a weekly basis for keeping the center and grounds neat. (The specific amount is determined by the housekeeping team. Clients are not expected to scrub floors and wash windows. They are expected to put equipment away, place trash in trash cans, and clean up spills.) The treasurer does not handle any money. He does keep the books, approve purchase orders, and get deposit information from the housekeeping team.

Group leaders are responsible for the Re-Creation needs of their respective groups. Though recreation supplies and equipment are sold through the TNT's gift shop, equipment is also available for check-out. Group leaders check-out equipment from portable locked storage units which are secured in their rooms. Group leaders are responsible for equipment under their control. Any equipment which is lost or stolen is replaced with money from the Community Government budget. (At TNT, recreation equipment such as table games, deck of cards, basketballs, are not left in the day room. Equipment left out tends to be abused rather than used. It only serves to collect dust and get shredded by visiting children.) Group leaders also control an assortment of music cassettes, cassette players, rented video movies, and video games. Group leaders often organize tournaments, ball games, and social events.

CLUBS AND RAP SESSIONS

Skill Development sessions should be supported with Recreation Participation opportunities utilizing the same skills taught in Skill Development sessions. Many clients are independent enough to lead such events. Clubs and rap sessions are opportunities for clients with common leisure interests to get together and do or talk about their interests. Clubs and rap sessions may be scheduled at the same time as corresponding Skill Development sessions. The following is a list of possible clubs and rap sessions which could be offered:

311.4 Sports Club
314.1 Let's Play Cards
317.1 Laugher's Club and Laughing Contests
321.4 Joggers Club
322.2 Readers Club
324.1 Home Exercise Programs Club
334.3 Interior Decorating

334.3 Woodworking Shop Hours
342.2 Pen Pal Letter Writers Club
347.1 Gamer's Club, Table Game and Card Tournaments
347.1 Shouter's Club and Shouting Contests
347.1 Yarn Spinners Club
362.2 Current Events Debate Club
374.3 Photography Club
376.1 Lip Synch to Vent Stress Club
377.1 Rhythm and Kazoo Band
378.2 Mime and Mimicry Club
389.4 Spiritual Club
349.4 Leisure Rap: What's New in Family Activities
349.4 Leisure Rap: What's New in Water Fun Games
359.4 Leisure Rap: What's New in Collecting Things
359.4 Leisure Rap: What's New in Individual Activities
369.4 Leisure Rap: What's New in Computer Fun
369.4 Leisure Rap: What's New in High Tech
379.4 Leisure Rap: What's New in Creative Activities
389.4 Leisure Rap: What's New in Spiritual Activities
399.4 Leisure Rap: What's New in High Risk Activities
399.4 Leisure Rap: What's New in Outdoor Activities

SPECIAL EVENTS

Care is taken not to schedule any major event in competition with AA or NA Meetings. Many special events are open to members of the Employee Recreation Club, outpatients, and family members as well as clients. Community Government officers are involved in the selection and planning process of special events. Group leaders are usually asked to find at least three other clients to help in the preparations of major events. In this way one third of the center's population becomes actively involved in an event. A wide variety of special events are offered, such as:

315.3 Card Tournaments (Spades, Bridge) for Client-Family
315.3 Volleyball Tournaments for Client-Family Participation
341.4 Social Dance Night (341.3)
325.2 Square Dance
325.2 Family Swim Night
325.2 Family Bowling Night
345.0 Birthday Parties

Birthdays are usually celebrated once a month. All clients and staff having birthdays during the month are honored. The theme for the celebration is inspired by the lives of famous persons or celebrities who also have birthdays in the same month. Cake and ice cream are served. The birthday cake is quite large and a by-product of a cake decorating skill development session held earlier in the day. The birthday celebration usually includes a dance, a skit, a tournament, or a picnic. For example, February might be a Presidents' Party & Wood Choppin' Contest. Another month might be the Fred Astaire Birthday Party and Dance (complete with a Fred Astaire Movie.)

345.0   Holiday Celebrations

To prevent ruts, unusual holidays are identified for a theme and either a party, game, skit, or dance is built around the theme. Sometimes the holiday is celebrated all day with special foods and decorations for breakfast, lunch, and dinner. The following are some unusual holidays which can be creatively celebrated:

HOLIDAY SCHEDULE:

January 19:	Robert E. Lee Day
February 7:	Daniel Boone captured by Indians in 1778
March 2:	Texas Independence Day
April 3:	Pony Express Inaugural Run, 1860
May 10:	Fred Astaire Birthday, 1899
June 11:	King Kamehameha Day
July 23:	Ice Cream Cone introduced, 1904
August 27:	Confusius born 551 B. C.
September 26:	American Indian Day
October 24:	United Nations Day
November 6:	John Phillip Sousa born, 1854
December 17:	Wright Brothers Day

345.0   Theme Parties

Social interaction parties are usually accompanied with a theme. A come-as-you-are-not party can be fun. It is also therapeutic for it helps clients to define their personalities. By identifying what they are not, they are saying what they are. Persons come to the party dressed as someone they do not ever want to be.

Bring your own whatever parties are can also be fun and therapeutic. Persons bring something to the party that they brought to the treatment center on the day of admission. Something that seemed necessary at the time and now seems pretty ridiculous. The "something" can be an item or a representation of an attitude. It is shared with other participants.

Masquerade and costume parties are equally interesting. TNT maintains a costume closet. Clients assume fantasy identities while wearing costumes. Many a shy person becomes an extrovert when wearing a mask. Such behavior

changes are dealt with in group therapy sessions on the following day. (Attempting to process this during the event reduces opportunities for Re-Creation to occur.)

345.2   Picnic and Special Event Planning
345.3   Family Picnics

Held in season are the joint productions of Food Services, Therapeutic Recreation and Community Government. Clients assist in menu selection, food preparation, and game or entertainment selection.

345.3   Live Entertainment and Dance Night

Community groups may provide entertainment from time to time. During the year, musicians, magicians, singers, and the like donate their talents to the Therapeutic Recreation Service. Once a year, the Therapeutic Recreation Services hires one group to perform at the Center's annual reunion and birthday bash. The group which is employed to entertain is the group who has been most helpful during the previous year. The group also receives an award for their support which is publicized in local papers. Many of the groups who provide entertainment for the center are groups who are trying to establish professional careers in the performing arts. Both the money and the publicity are greatly appreciated by the groups.

375.3   Talent and Non-Talent Competitions Open to Client and Family

Client Centered Shows are both popular and therapeutic. They are open to employees, clients, family members, and Twelve Step program members. The Center's drama club provides shows on occasion. Talent shows which are held, are usually divided into three categories. Participants may enter the talent show and attempt to win an award for the competitive Best Talent category, or the competitive Worst Talent category. Participants may also perform in the noncompetitive sharing category where no judging occurs. Fashion Shows, TV Spoofs, and Gong Shows are also held. These tend to be humorous renditions of serious events.

391.3	High Risk (Diving, Horseback Riding, Adventure Courses)
391.3	Participation in Outdoor Activities
391.4	Rock Climbing
399.3	Marshmallow Cook-Out
399.3	Whitewater Rafting
399.3	Overnight Hike and Camp-Out

INDIVIDUAL PURSUITS

There is a combination library/lounge area in the heart of the Therapeutic Recreation area. During free time, clients may browse, lounge, read, listen to music, use computers, watch videos, or play card/table games in the area. Cubicals along the sides of the library permit use of equipment which produce noise without disturbing others. Some cubicals have a video player and monitor with headphones. Some have compact disc and cassette players with headphones. Some have computers with headphones. Some are stocked with writing paper and a small desk. All cubical lack doors, but have signs. The user may post a sign which says "Do Not Disturb." Other signs are humorous, inviting interaction with others. The signs help clients to express their needs to others and provide a method which can be duplicated in the home and office. Books and magazines may also be checked-out to be used in their rooms. Reading materials range from fiction to bibliotherapy. The alcohol/drug section of the library is extensive. So is the recreation and leisure pursuit section. There is also a wide variety of short stories, magazines, and newspapers available.

The arts and crafts area is open when skill development sessions are not being offered. During skill development sessions, persons may use the room, but only if interested in doing the type of creative art which is being taught during the session. At other times, clients may pursue their own interests or complete a project which was started during a skill development session. The art area has individual lockers. A client can store a project and needed supplies in the locker and return to it whenever desired.

There is a Noisy Game room which contains ping-pong tables and card tables. The room has large windows opening to the library, but the room is soundproofed. Persons not wishing to pursue leisure quietly are encouraged to spend time in the Noisy Game room.

The Peace Room is open. Only one person at a time is permitted to use the room. The Peace Room contains an aquarium, soft lighting, and comfortable furniture. Relaxation tapes and inspirational readings are always on hand in the Peace Room.

The Therapeutic Recreation computer room is open for individual pursuit when skill development sessions are not in progress. The stage and auditorium are also available for client use. These areas are scheduled to be open only when a staff member is available to supervise the areas. The same is true for physical exercise areas.

Physical exercise equipment and facilities are available for free time use. There is a weight room for individual exercise and a gym for ball games. The swimming area is open when sessions are not in progress and when a lifeguard is on duty. There is a hot tub adjacent to the swimming pool and weight room. Other outdoor facilities include a fishing pond, the Peace Path, joggers exercise path with exercise stations, golf practice, and tennis area. There is also a challenge course, but it is off limits to clients during free time. There are also picnic tables and benches, places to sit and think about exercising, or just think about not thinking.

The Therapeutic Recreation area and the TNT Center are adequately stocked for participation in any recreation pursuit except two. There are no addictive substances available and there is an inadequate supply of televisions. There is a television in each client's room in the detox unit. There is one television in the adolescent unit and one in the adult unit. They are programmed to show education films for all but two hours per day. Community Government is in charge of selecting the programs for the two hours.

LIBRARY:

362.2 Games That Practice the 3-R's
362.2 Reading and Math Volunteers Schedule
362.3 Library/Audiovisuals Unsupervised
362.3 Library Unsupervised
362.1 Jigsaw Puzzles and Non-Word Mazes
362.1 Picture Library and Comic Books
362.2 Crossword Puzzles
362.2 Magazine Library and Comic Books
362.3 Book Library with Topics for Each
      Interest Category
362.4 Instructional Library of Leisure Pursuits
382.1 Assisted Reading of AA and Spiritual Materials

RELAXATION SCHEDULE:

356.2 Relaxing with Music
356.2 Relaxing with the Help of a Pet or Aquarium
356.2 Relaxing with Nature
326.2 Relaxing with Water Exercises
326.4 Relaxing Physical Exercise
326.4 Relaxing Water Exercises
376.2 Relaxing with the Arts
386.4 Relaxing with Inspirational Readings

INDIVIDUAL PURSUITS REQUIRING LEADERSHIP:

321.2 Mild Morning Exercise
311.2 Lazy Sports
311.4 Swimming Races
311.4 Tennis
311.4 Team Sports (Soccer, Unsupervised
      Volleyball, etc.)
312.2 Team Speed Reading Contest
316.4 Sports and Other Competitions to Reduce Stress
321.3 Bowling
321.3 Water Fun
321.4 High Impact Aerobics
351.2 Walking for Health and Fitness
351.3 Nature Hike
371.4 Modern Dance/Ballet/Jazz Advanced Class

INDIVIDUAL PURSUITS NOT REQUIRING LEADERSHIP:

311.3 Gym Schedule
321.2 Gym Schedule
325.2 Video Game Hours

336.1   Indoor/Outdoor Gardening
345.4   Visiting Hour
349.4   Game Room and Lounge Hours
351.2   Open Swim Hours
351.2   A.M. Walk
351.3   Weight Room Schedule
358.4   Computer Programming and Computer
        Play Time
364.1   Public Education Channel Schedule
368.2   Backgammon and Other Game Check-Out
368.3   Chess and Other Game Check-Out
368.4   Divergent Thinking Challenges and
         Games Check-Out
374.1   Crafts Room Schedule (Paper-Mâché,
        Trash Art Projects)
374.3   Art Room Schedule (Painting, Sculpture, etc.)
389.1   Spiritual Activities Schedule
389.4   Chapel/Church Hours

References/Resources

Edginton, C. R., Compton, D. M., & Hanson, C. J. (1980). *Recreation & Leisure Programming: A Guide For The Professional.* Philadelphia, PA: W. B. Saunders.

Faulkner, R. W. (1981, August). Therapeutic holiday experience. *Programming Trends In Therapeutic Recreation.*

Monroe, M. E. (1971). *Reading Guidance and Bibliotherapy in Public Hospitals, and Institutions Libraries.* Madison, WI: Library School of University of Wisconsin.

Sessoms, H. D., & Stevenson, J. L. (1981). *Leadership & Group Dynamics in Recreation Services.* Boston, MA: Allyn & Bacon, Inc.

Thomas, R. B. (1986). *The Old Farmers Almanac.*

CHAPTER 11

RECREATION THERAPY

Recreation Therapy is the purposeful intervention into the client's life to achieve specific objectives. The recreation activity is used as a tool to make the intervention. Activities are selected because they meet the needs, not because they are fun for the participants. Whenever possible, an activity is selected which is appealing, but that is not the primary concern. Recreation Therapy is part of the required program for those clients in need. Some clients may need a large number of Recreation Therapy sessions. Other clients may not need any. Once the intervention has achieved the desired outcome, the activity may be discarded. It is not something the client is expected to pursue as a leisure hobby after discharge.

Many needs met through Recreation Therapy are not determined by the initial TRI assessment. They are identified by interdisciplinary team functioning and by the Therapeutic Recreation staff after observation of the client during involvement in Therapeutic Recreation Services. For example, the need to develop trust in self and other is very important, but there is no reliable way of determining this need at the time of admission. All clients seem distrustful to some extent as a result of embarrassing the treatment process. Ordinarily trust of self and others improves over the first week. Provision of Recreation Therapy for this problem should be reserved for those who remain distrustful after the adjustment period. Observations indicating need for Recreation Therapy should be substantiated by other interdisciplinary team members.

Coding for Recreation Therapy varies slightly from coding used in other services. The first digit "4" indicates it is a recreation therapy program or activity. The next digit does not stand for interest category. If the "4" is followed by a "0" then the listing relates to items assessed on the TRI. The TRI Item number follows as in the other categories. When the "4" is followed by a number other than "0" it indicates treatment for a problem not listed on the TRI assessment. Two digits are listed after the decimal point in the code. The first is reserved for the TRI Item score, which may or may not be used. The last digit simply distinguishes one activity from the next to prevent confusion. This may also be done with the codes used in Leisure Education, Skill Development, etc., but is not really necessary. The substitution of one leisure education session for another with the same code should not make a significant difference. The substitution of one Recreation Therapy format for another can make a big difference.

Recreation Therapy should be led by a certified Therapeutic Recreation Specialist who is competent in group process and substance abuse counseling. If the Therapeutic Recreation

Specialist lacks experience in leading a specific session, there should be co-leading until confidence and skills develop. Depending on the type of session, the appropriate co-leader could be a more experienced Therapeutic Recreation Specialist, a Group Therapist, a Nurse, a Challenge Course Instructor, and so on.

There are many types of Recreation Therapy sessions that could be appropriate. Those listed in this chapter should be considered a brief sample. Some clients may have special needs that must be met through development of individual programs. Provision of customized programs and one on one is time consuming. It also risks setting the client apart from the others. With this population, that can be interpreted as "See I'm different. I'm special." Feeling unique and requiring special attention often feeds an alibi system rather than a recovery system. To summarize, the following is a only a sample. Where additional types of sessions are needed, create them as part of the standard program. Create unique experiences for clients only when the client's specific needs cannot be met through ongoing programs, such as those suggested in this text. (For an explanation of the code numbers see Chapter 7)

401.0 PHYSICAL RESTORATION

Physical conditioning is a thread of programming woven through the entire Therapeutic Recreation structure. A program of physical exercise and conditioning is designed for each client. It is accomplished through selection of appropriate Skill Development and Re-Creation sessions. The physical conditioning program design is accomplished through defining limits of participation at the time of admission and increasing the level of activity as the individual's physical condition improves. The majority of clients are able to follow the guidelines without assistance. For them, a Recreation Therapy Physical Restoration program is not required.

401.01 Supervised Physical Restoration

On occasion a client may have other deficits that prevent self-administration of a physical conditioning program. I recall a chronic alcoholic whose drinking had damaged this person's ability to remember and follow instructions. He was unable to follow directions to enter a room, even though he was standing in front of the room when the instructions were given. Someone had to physically lead him into the room. Such a client cannot be expected to administer his own program. I have also seen cocaine users, who cannot comprehend the need for limited activity. Adolescents may understand the need for limits but ignore them simply as part of their pathology. For these clients, no special activities are required. A selected method of supervision is required to see that the client follows his/her program. For the chronic alcoholic who cannot find his way, all that may be required is a staff to lead him to the exercise session and position him behind another client who will be doing the same type of activity. For the person who cannot believe the limits have a purpose, the Therapeutic Recreation Specialist may need to confront. There may need to be a creation of awareness of consequences of actions. There definitely needs to be interdisciplinary support. For the adolescent, here and now choices may need to be created. The adolescent either follows the rules or spends the time reading the history of the French Revolution.

401.02 Disability Rehabilitation

On occasion a client enters treatment with a physical disability. He/she may have passed out lying on their arm, deadening the nerves. He/she may have been involved in a car accident, causing a permanent physical impairment. Using a mixer of alcohol and machinery sometimes results in the loss of a limb. For these clients, Therapeutic Recreation must work closely with Occupational and Physical Therapists to develop a program of physical rehabilitation. In many cases, the client has not received adequate physical rehabilitation because he/she has believed the effort was hopeless. The Therapeutic Recreation Specialist must devise a plan of activity that proves to the client that he/she can lead a full and meaningful life with a disability. Then specific physical activities must be selected to support the objectives of the Occupational and Physical Therapy treatments.

402.0 LEARNING STIMULATION

The client in addictions treatment may be a school drop-out. He/she may have been a classroom clown or a behavior problem to the school. He/she may have learned to survive by manipulating authority figures. All of these behaviors may have resulted from coping with a mild undiagnosed learning disability, rather than functions of addiction. When a client has a history of problems with the educational system, or when a client shows an aversion to learning, then the presence of a learning disability must be ruled out first before any other actions are taken. If the aversion to learning is not a result of a learning disability, then the next thing to look at is a lack of "fitting" into the educational system. This may have resulted from a right hemisphere dominated individual failing to feel appreciated by a left hemisphere dominated structure. When this is ruled out, then the cause may be emotional trauma caused by the practice of addiction in the home environment. It may also be caused by growing up in a culture that does not value educational learning.

The purpose of Recreation Therapy is not to teach reading, writing, and arithmetic. The purpose is to assist the team in identifying the source of the problem, to assist the client in identifying the source of the problem, and to find methods to stimulate the client's desire to learn. Therapeutic Recreation may also act as a supportive service to Educational Specialists. Where there is "homework" or practice of specific materials

needed, the Therapeutic Recreation Specialist may design specific activities that provide the needed practice in a fun and enjoyable way.

402.01 Learning Disability Identification

(The following materials have been reprinted by permission from *The Zanity Adventure Series*.)   There are a wide variety of specific types of learning disabilities. Mirror vision, one of the better known types, is where a word or letters in a word are seen backwards and/or upside down. Most children exhibit mirror vision when initially learning the letters of the alphabet. But most children learn the difference between a "p" and a "b" quickly and move on. Person's with mirror vision disability learn the difference only with great difficulty. Once learned, knowing the difference cannot be taken for granted. Relapses may occur from time to time even into adult life. A person with a disability may write "p" for "p" one time and "b" for "p" the next. Numbers may also reversed. A "6" may be written as a "9," "387" may be remembered as "783." Writing words or syllables backwards is also a variation of the problem. "bl" may be written as "lb." Sentences may come out middle first, and the first last. A person meaning to write "What I think she said," may write or say "Think she what I said." A person may think pink and say orange. Left may be indistinguishable from right. Others may have no difficulty with language skills but have great difficulty with math computations. Again, all of the above are simple errors that all children experience during initial learning phases. The difference between normal error and a learning disability is the length of time and practice required to correct the problem.

Learning Disabilities are characterized as dysfunction in a specific area of learning educational skills. Manzo defines dyslexia as "a severe and specific learning disability, highly resistant to instructional intervention and characterized by 'nongenerative' learning" (Manzo, 1987, p. 408). The concept of generative verses nongenerative learning is an interesting one. Under normal circumstances learning increases or "generates" between instructional periods. When there is a learning disability, there is little if any increase in learning that occurs between instructional periods.

Though widely studied over the last twenty years, researchers fail to agree about causation, diagnostic methods, or treatment. Some believe that it is an inherited disorder (Manzo, 1987). The entire concept of learning disabilities is relatively new. Prior to the late 1950s, failure to thrive in school was attributed to other factors. Thus it is difficult to identify generational patterns. Other theories about the cause of dyslexia include incomplete neurological development, very specific neurological dysfunction, being born with too many brain cells in the wrong places, damage to nerves tying the left and right hemispheres together, scar tissue on the surface of the brain, chemical imbalances, and unequal sizes of the left and right hemispheres (Manzo, 1987). It has been attributed to inner ear problems. It has been attributed to malformed eye problems. Persons with learning disabilities may possess the ability to see to the side without turning the head or looking to the side (Geiger, 1987). I have heard of improvements created through the use of glasses with colored lenses. Manzo, in his article *"Psychologically induced dyslexia and learning disabilities,"* attributes the problem to emotional disturbances in 15 to 20 percent of the cases. I have found that letters are more likely to be properly sequenced after the client receives adequate sleep than during times of inadequate sleep. Since emotional trauma often results in sleeplessness, relapse of spelling abilities may coincide with times of crisis. If Manzo is correct, and there is an emotional source to some dyslexia, then feelings of inadequacy resulting from repeating stupid errors only heighten the initial emotional distress, which only escalates the number of stupid errors, which increases the emotional distress, etc.

Border's Classification divides dyslexia into two types. Dysphonetic Dyslexia is the inability to hear a word in the standard way. Dyseidetic Dyslexia is the inability to remember the visual shape of a given word (Manzo, 1987). Just as speech problems can be classified as expressive aphasia (able to understand language but not speak it) and receptive aphasia (unable to decode incoming language), I believe there may be expressive and receptive dyslexia. Some persons with expressive dyslexia may see, hear, and store the word image in the brain correctly, but then be unable to retrieve it from memory, unable to write or say it correctly. Some persons may have receptive dyslexia where the visual or auditory word image comes into the brain garbled. As with aphasia, effects of receptive dyslexia might be far more severe than the effects of expressive dyslexia.

Researchers and educators agree that dyslexia differs from retardation; learning disabilities are different from developmental disabilities. Unlike a child with developmental disabilities, the child with a learning disability accomplishes early child development tasks on schedule. The child learns to roll over, sit up, crawl, stand, run, and talk within "normal" time frames. All indicators point to a normal healthy child until the child reaches school and is confronted by the "three R's."

In short, I believe there is no single source or cause of learning disabilities. Some may experience the problem for one reason, while others experience it for other reasons. Exact etiology is less important than problem identification and treatment. Suspect a disability when an aversion to learning is observed. Suspect a learning disability when the client reports doing extremely well in some educational areas, such as math, and extremely poor in another area, such as reading. Suspect a disability when nongenerative learning patterns are observed.

402.02 Attitude Adjusters

Regardless of etiology or specifics of the disability, the pathology tends to be the same. The child is treated as a normal and bright until confronted with the "three R's" While the child sits at his desk, trying to figure out why it is called the "three R's" instead of "R.W.M." (Reading, Writing, Math), authority

figures surround the child and begin to search for a standard "L.D." diagnosis. Unfortunately the "L" usually stands for "lazy" and "D" for "dumb."

Many learning disabled individuals manage to survive school, but leave with the assumption that they are lazy and dumb. These assumptions are counterproductive to addiction treatment goals. In this case, the Therapeutic Recreation Specialist must set up situations in which the client can discover that he/she is not really dumb and/or lazy after all. If the presence of an undiagnosed learning disability can be determined, that information, combined with examples that indicate that the client is not lazy and/or dumb, can really change attitudes for the better. The desire to learn will be stimulated. [Ch11:410.0, 450.0]

402.03 Games for Success

Some clients have learned to avoid areas of learning that are difficult and practice areas that are easy. To address the needs the process must be reversed. Overcoming disability means a lot of time and concentrated effort in the affected area. But the client will resist practice in the needed area. To overcome this problem the Therapeutic Recreation Specialist should use games that contain both the material which the client desires to avoid and the material that the client finds enjoyable. Board games that have an element of chance are excellent, for the client thinks luck may allow avoidance of the difficult area. Fortunately, luck results in the client practicing the needed materials. Success is assured for the client also lands on subject matter that is easy for him/her. The majority of time will be spent on the needed material because the client is very quick at solving the problems in the area that is not affected. The feeling of success resulting from actually working on the area of need stimulates the client to continue work on the area. The success experienced by work in the gifted area generalizes over to the affected area and again learning is stimulated.

402.04 Behavior Modification

The client who has learned to cope by being a back seat clown or by acting out must be put on a program of behavior modification. Attention seeking behavior must be ignored. Offers to help, which remove the client from the activity, must be refused. Interdisciplinary team function must be united in its approach to the client's behavior.

402.05 Creative Applications

Clients who have been turned off by the system rather than by a disability should be taught using the principle of Adult Education regardless of the client's age. Where a client appears to be creative, formatting learning into activities that appeal to right hemisphere dominated individuals may be of assistance. Art classes such as calligraphy may stimulate reading skills. Allowing students to learn while moving or sitting in unusual positions may make a difference. Giving a teen the permission to sit on his head while reading may get the book read.

402.06 Learning of Value

Clients who have failed to thrive in school because of addiction being practiced in the home may benefit from the Therapeutic Recreation program for restoration of developmental play. Concentration on learning stimulation should be postponed until completion of these activities. [Ch8:107.0; Ch9:207.0; Ch11:407.0]

Clients who have been raised in an environment where education was not valued must learn to value learning. The primary reason to learn must be because it feels good to learn. The internal Jump & Skip system must be activated. Recreation Therapy must be designed to create curiosity about the world in which space is being occupied. Once this has been activated, the best source of information is a book, and learning stimulation has been activated. (Preaching and lecturing should be avoided. The session must be hands on, experiential.) [Ch8; Ch10]

402.07 Computerized Learning

Many computer programs are available to support learning stimulation in all areas of knowledge. Educational computer games are an excellent method of providing needed support for educational objectives.

403.20 ASSERTIVE TRANSPORT IMPROVEMENT

Clients who depend on others for transportation to leisure events may require additional practice in arranging transportation. Drama role plays of assertively asking others to provide transportation are helpful. Here are a couple of examples:

Zeb has asked his friend to drive him to work every day for a month. Zeb is looking somewhat irritated about the situation. Zeb now needs transportation to the bowling alley. How would you handle the situation?

Gertrude wants to go to a social tonight. Her regular sources of transportation are unavailable. The only people she knows with cars that might be available are practically strangers. None of them have been invited to the social. How would you handle the situation?

Clients with special needs in developing assertive transportation should be assigned duties which require making arrangements for special events. If AA members sometimes provide client transportation to off-campus meetings, then the client should be assigned to contact an unknown AA member (known to the staff but unknown to the client) and arrange his/her own transportation. If a special event requires use of the facility van, then the client should be assigned to communicate times of departure, etc., to the van driver.

405.0 FAMILY RELATIONSHIPS

Development of open communication and healthy relations with family members is helpful to recovery. By the time the client enters treatment, family relationships are usually void of positive shared experiences. The Therapeutic Recreation Specialist seeks to reunite families through involving them in positive recreation experiences. Many family goals may be accomplished through family participation in Leisure Education, Skill Development, and Re-Creation sessions. On occasion additional assistance is needed, especially when the client is a co-dependent or adult child.

405.01 Songs-of-Relationships

Many popular love songs are songs of co-dependency rather than love. Have participants listen to songs and determine if they are really love songs or dependency songs. (Here's a hint: "I will die if you ever leave me" is not a song of love.) Have participants discuss what is wrong with the songs. Then have participants write new words to the songs, changing them from songs of dependency to songs of love.

405.02 Haveta-Supposedta-Can't

The purpose of this session is to assist clients exercise their freedom of choices. While session content is applicable to all aspects of life, only those relating to family friction, which effects leisure interaction, are dealt with in this session.

To start the game, clients write things they think family members expect them to do. Cards are in "finish-the-sentence" design with some cards saying, "I have to_____," other cards saying, "I'm supposed to_____," and still others saying, "I can't_____." Participants are asked to keep their responses within the realm of family relationships and leisure participation. After sentences are completed, cards are collected and shuffled. Cards are passed to the first player. The player draws a card and reads it. Then if the player can rephrase the sentence to indicate personal choice in doing the task, then the player may discard the card. If the player cannot rephrase the statement, the player must keep the card. Then the next player takes a turn. The play continues until all cards have been drawn. At the end of playing, the person with the least number of cards in front of him is the winner.

An example of the rephrasing process: the statement "I have to make my bed." This can be rephrased to, "I choose to make my bed." Discussion may follow to determine if the person really has a choice or really has to do the task. In most cases, the person has a choice. Not doing the task has consequences, but freedom of personal choice is still there. "I'm supposed to be friendly," can be rephrased to "Others are friendly when I am friendly" or "I choose to be friendly when others expect me to be friendly." Fact is, there are no real "supposed to's" in life, other than those I impose on myself. "I can't talk to people" can be rephrased to, "I choose not to talk to people." In reality, there are very few absolute "can'ts." "I can't jump off of tall buildings" is actually not true. "I choose not to jump off of tall buildings because I don't like the feeling associated with the landing" is true. "I can't drink" is actually false. "I choose not to drink" is true. "I can't drink without getting into trouble" is one of the few "can'ts" that are true. "I can't relax" is a nowhere statement and is false. "I choose not to relax" gives the person a direction to go. For if I can choose not to, then I can choose to. In the same way, "I can't get along with my family" is false. "I choose not to get along" is true, and the person may choose to continue not getting along or choose to get along.

Too many internalized have to's, supposed to's, or can'ts, take the fun out of life and cause family friction. Helping the person see that there are always personal choices creates a feeling of freedom and the doing of tasks becomes less painful.

405.23 Drama for Family Roles and Fun

Clients may have specific problems in developing relationships. These may be identified in group therapy sessions. Based on information and direction provided by the client's Group Therapist, specific role plays may be developed to help the client understand and deal with his/her problem. The role plays should be videotaped and then reviewed by the client and his/her Group Counselor.

406.0 STRESS REDUCTION

Where Therapeutic Recreation Specialists are trained in providing guided imagery and other forms of relaxation techniques, these may be provided in addition to the provision of relaxing activities. [Ch8:106.0; Ch9:206.0; Ch10]

407.0 RESTORATION OF DEVELOPMENTAL PLAY BEHAVIORS

Some clients may require sessions beyond those provided within other Therapeutic Recreation programs. Recreation Therapy sessions are designed to dig deep into the client. They should only be offered when the Group Counselor feels the Client is in need, and most of all, is ready for the given experience. [Ch8:107.0; Ch9:207.0]

407.11 Creative Writing About Events in a Child's Life

This session is formatted the same as the Creative Writing Skill Development session. The difference is that the event is real and the client is the child. Stories written by a client during the Creative Writing Skill development session may be brought to this session for further investigation. [Ch9:277.1]

407.12 Ridiculous Situations

The goal of this session is to reduce inhibitions, to free up playfulness. Participants begin by role playing and performing impromptu skits of the most ridiculous situations they can think of. These are short. They are videotaped and reviewed by the participants. A discussion follows about why the situations were ridiculous—ridiculous by whose standards? Participants are then challenged to perform harmless yet embarrassing or ridiculous things in public. The challenge might be to drop food on the table while eating. The challenge might be to stand up in the lunch room, get everyone's attention, and make a silly face. The group reforms after the challenges have had time to occur. Group members discuss how it felt to do the things. They tend to find out that it was embarrassing but not deadly. They also find out that it was fun. The discoveries are applied to leisure behavior in general. Clients who failed to perform a ridiculous stunt are given group support and encouraged to try again.

407.13 Drama: Role Playing Kids Play

Adults pretend to be kids during the session and play. The play is videotaped. Clients review the tape and discuss how it felt to play like a kid. They discuss how they thought it would look to others if they were caught playing like a kid. They discuss how their play actually looked on the videotape. Participants are encouraged to value the feel of play more than the look of play.

407.14 Pot and Pan and Noise Making Things

A development play level involves making noise. Participants are given the opportunity to clang and bang things that most children clang and bang. Adults tend to resist disorganized banging, so efforts to turn the clangs and bangs into musical rhythms are acceptable. The Therapeutic Recreation Specialist should not initiate the organization. The session should be totally unstructured banging until the participants choose to organize it.

407.15 Costume Party

Dressing up like big people is a developmental play stage. Clients are given a box of strange clothing and costumes, strange hats, shoes and accessories and are told to dress up. Role playing of the person they have dressed up like is encouraged.

407.16 Tele-Joke

Much of adult play is joke telling. Some seem to have a knack for it, others don't. Most of the ability comes from practice and abandonment of self-conscious behavior. In this session, joke books are passed out. Each participant reads a joke. The group gives tips about how to say it to make it funny. When skill and confidence are built, the participants are required to tell a joke a day. They are required to call someone on the telephone, tell them a joke, and hang up.

407.21 Songs of Youth

The purpose of this session is to help participants develop self-awareness. This session is introduced in the Creative Music Skill Development session. [Ch9:279.0] Persons who responded to that session and have a need for the session are required to attend this session. It investigates songs and lyrics that have become part of the self-identity system. The format may also be used to address other needs. [Ch11:410.09, 420.0]

Participants are asked to recall the first song they can remember and sing it. The portions of the lyrics that can be remembered are written down next to the client's age at the time of hearing the song. Then the next song that can be remembered is shared and written down along with the person's age. Then the next, and the next, etc.

When the list is complete, the list is reviewed. Places and events that are recalled when the song is sung are noted. Periods of life when few songs are remembered are compared to periods when many songs are remembered. A lack of memories during a period is sometimes caused by blockage. Something traumatic happened and the mind has blocked out memory of the trauma and memory of the good as well.

Sometimes the lyrics of remembered songs become self-fulfilling prophecies. They say "This is the way life really is." Sometimes the words of a song are accepted into the self-identity system accidentally. The tune was appealing and so the words were remembered even though the words were not representative of personal beliefs. Participants review all aspects of the self-fulfilling prophecy concept. Where clients find changes are needed in remembered lyrics, the words of the favorite old songs are rewritten and sung repetitively.

407.22 Playing with Building Blocks

Playing with building blocks and piling things on top of other things are two activities in a developmental play stage. Participants engage in unstructured play with building blocks. When play triggers a recollection of childhood experiences, the memories are shared. Structure is kept to a minimum. No rules or instructions are provided with the building blocks other than to play with them.

407.23 Silly Games, Kid Games, and Doing Silly Things

This is a session of just "horsing around." The goal is spontaneity. Rule setting by Staff and clients should be kept to a minimum. The session seeks to re-establish another basic developmental play stage, one that leads to feeling accepted by others.

408.0 CREATIVE PROBLEM SOLVING

The addicted personality has found only one solution to all problems. To get drunk/high. No one can be with the addicted person to help guide him/her through every situation that will present itself and require a different solution. No treatment center provides an answer for every question that arises during the life-long recovery process. A treatment center can teach methods of finding alternatives and answers.

In the Creative Problem Solving Series, activities are selected that encourage participants to generate alternatives or to find an alternative that deviates from the norm. (The norm in the world of alcoholism is a drink.) A number of sessions exist in previous chapters that address this need. The following sessions should be reserved for those clients where skill in problem solving is critical. This may be a result of family influence, geographies, or a number of other factors.

408.21 Color Me Not

Participants are given coloring books. They must do something with them, anything accept color them in the usual manner.

408.22 Read Me Not

Participants are given old books and magazines. They must do something, anything with them except read them.

408.23 Create-a-Game

The purpose of this session is to broaden the client's view of acceptable leisure pursuits. This session begins by identifying the greatest source of creative fun potential, the self. Participants are divided into groups of six to eight. Each group is given a duplicate handful of objects. Participants are given about fifteen minutes to make a new game. Then the new games are presented.

408.24 Half Deck

Participants develop a game that is playable using only half of a deck of cards.

408.25 Sentence Malpractice and Old Story New Ending

A sentence is begun and participants generate as many endings as possible. A short story is begun and participants provide as many different endings as possible.

408.26 Ana-Ma-Grammy

Participants attempt to rewrite words or phrases by substituting symbols for syllables. For example:

(Lightening Wells, the name of the TRS
who taught this session to the Author.)

408.27 Adventure Courses (How Many Ways Over the Obstacle?)

408.28 Traditional Games

Many over-the-counter games develop creative problem solving. Strategy games such as Backgammon, Risk™, Chess, and Stratego™ are helpful.

408.31 New Pathways

This is something of a treasure hunt in reverse. Participants know where the end point is. The goal is to see how many different ways can be found to get to a designated point. All methods and paths are acceptable so long as they do not disturb other concurrent sessions, violate center rules, or contain unsafe modes of operation. If competition is desired, participants may be divided into groups. The group returning with the most number of pathways found in fifteen minutes wins.

408.32 Creative Movement

After a brief warm-up, participants explore movements. Each person demonstrates his usual walk. Then participants are challenged to see how many different ways they can walk: long strides, short strides, knees bent, on tippee toes, forwards, backward, sideways, etc. Then arms are swung back and forth. Then participants are challenged to find how many different ways they can swing the arms. Then the participants see how

many different ways they can combine arm movements and walks. Any body part can be used. Adults can find a lot of suggestive ways to move the hips.

408.33 Impromptu Adventures

Drama can provide excellent avenues for creativity. This session is similar to a skill development session in format. [Ch9: 279.2] Persons who are in need of Creative Problem Solving and who showed an interest in the Skill Development session should be scheduled for this session. There are differences between the sessions. The Skill Development session seeks to inspire dramatic usage of leisure time. The Recreation Therapy format seeks to use drama as a tool to the development of alternatives and choices.

Have each participant write down a place and time on a 3 X 5 card and put the cards in a pile. Shuffle the pile. Have each participant write down a character on another card and place them in a pile. Shuffle the pile. Have each person write down a situation on a card. Place these in a pile and shuffle. A place may be a country, a building, a mode of transportation, a type of land formation, etc. A character may be a television personality, an animal, a member of a particular occupation, or a family position such as sister, brother, mother, father, etc. A character may not be the name of an actual participant. A situation may be a problem, special event, or an action. It is the reason why these characters are coming together. The leader selects the top card from the pile of places and the top card from the pile of situations. These are read out loud. Then character cards are passed out to all who are willing to participate, but not more than half of the group. Participants role play the characters they have drawn and attempt to develop the action that might be occurring in the given place, time, and situation. If no "problem" exists, the leader interjects one. Before participants can arrive at a solution, action is halted. Players hand their character cards to observers and exchange places. The new players must resolve the situation. Discussion follows, asking original players if the situation was resolved the way they were planning to resolve it. Then alternative ways of doing things are solicited from all participants. The procedure may be repeated as time permits with selection of new places and/or situations for the card piles.

408.34 Trash Art

Trash art is the use of items that others have discarded as supplies for art projects. In Skill Development sessions, it is used to teach people to enjoy art inexpensively. [Ch8:278.2] As Recreation Therapy, the purpose is discover how many uses can be found for a piece of trash. A plastic milk jug may become an animal body, or cut into pieces for a mobile, or used as a canvas to paint on, or turned into a penny bank, or the top may be cut to create a scoop.

This session should be the last session provided to increase problem solving skills. It should be held in the art room where adequate supplies are available. To start, each participant should be given one disposable item. Each participant's item should be different from the next. Begin by asking each, how many different uses can be thought of for the item. Record the number of responses given. The number of responses given becomes a measure of how well the Recreation Therapy sessions have met the Creative Problem Solving Need. Clients who are able to give seven or more ways to use the object, are re-rated on TRI Item #8, at the Independent level. The client has received maximum benefits and is discontinued from creative problem solving therapy. Listing four to six solutions places the client at the Semi-Independent level. Discontinuing these clients from service is something of a judgment call. It depends on individual needs for creative problem solving abilities. Clients who provide fewer than four answers should repeat creative problem solving formats.

After the re-evaluation of need, clients are permitted to make an art project out of their item, adding other pieces of trash. Clients are encouraged to use as many pieces of trash as they can in their project. This second phase attempts to see how many different items can be used.

410.0 SITUATION RESPONSE AWARENESS

Good communication depends on listening skills and self-expression skills. Many people fall victim to habits of talking and saying nothing, listening without hearing. To change communication patterns one must first become aware of the existing patterns. Communication skills can be dealt with during almost any leisure activity that requires the presence of more than one person. A variety of awareness games and new games have been developed for the specific purpose of helping participants develop communication skills and self-awareness in fun ways. In addition to these, the activities in this series can be most helpful. To achieve maximum benefits, all self-awareness sessions should be videotaped and replayed for participants.

410.01 I Yi Yi

This game is played while some other activity is going on. Each participant is given twenty-five small tokens that are carried with them. The object is to get as many tokens as possible within a specified amount of time. One token can be collected from another participant by catching the person in the act of saying "you," "should," "have to," "supposed to," or "can't."

The game creates an awareness of how much an individual uses these terms. It also creates an awareness of personal reaction to frustration. For example, some players, after being caught too many times, once too often, give all their tokens away. "If things don't go as intended, is this what you do? Give up? If people don't understand, do you choose to just agree to get them off your back?" Some get angry. "Is there another way of handling the situation, besides getting angry?" Some refuse to talk. "Is winning so important that you deprive yourself of pleasurable participation?"

410.02 Grab It

Grab It is an adaptation of Spoons. It can be played with any number of participants, but ten is a nice size. Participants sit in a circle. If there are ten players, then ten matching sets of playing cards are used. A matched set is four aces, or four kings, or four nines, etc. If there are ten players, then nine spoons (or other objects) are placed in the center of the circle. Cards are shuffled and dealt, four cards to each participant. At the same time, all players pass one card to the right, and accept one card from the left. The process continues as fast as possible until someone gets four cards that match. The person with the match grabs a spoon. As soon as one person grabs a spoon, then everyone grabs a spoon. The person who does not get a spoon is "eliminated." One matching set of cards and one spoon are withdrawn. The remaining cards are shuffled and a second round is played. The process is continued until only one person is left.

Persons who are "eliminated" are out of the round but not out of the game. Persons still playing the game cannot talk to persons who have been "eliminated." A person who has been "eliminated" can trade places with a person who is still "in" the game if he/she can get the player to verbally respond. The heckling begins as soon as someone is eliminated. As the heckling begins, the therapy begins. Some players are easy marks for a heckler. Some hecklers resort to all kinds of cunning tricks to get what they want.

Review of the videotape and a discussion follow the game. Individual responses to heckling are discussed. How easy it is to answer without thinking. Some clients get angry when caught in a response. Some clients deny they responded. Items such as these are all discussed. After behaviors and interactions during the game are discussed, then the focus is changed to everyday behaviors. "Is this the way you handle. . .in your daily routine?" A client may say that their reaction to the game was unusual, then in the following day, catch him/herself in the same response pattern over and over again.

Warning: This game is no tea party. Persons who are "At Risk" in physical health should not participate. The game can get wild with chairs and people flying through the air to grab that last spoon. The game should be played in an uncluttered area, away from windows, sharp corners, etc.

410.04 Finding What's Missing

Clients are taken for a ride. (Sorry, couldn't resist using the phrase.) The ride is just far enough away to provide a ten-to-fifteen minute return walk back to the facility. At the end of the ride, each participant is given a note pad and pen. Before getting off the van, they are asked to list everything they saw, felt, heard, and smelled during the trip. Next, participants are asked to pretend to be scientists visiting this area from another world and to record everything they can about the area as they return to the facility on foot. The group then walks back to the facility, exploring every inch of it. Participants are asked not to talk with each other, except to share discoveries. Upon return to the facility, the experience is processed. Notes about the ride out are compared with notes about the walk back. Riding in an automobile produces feelings of separation, preoccupation, and boredom. Walking permits a person to experience the life that abounds all around, inducing feelings of inclusion, interest, and awareness.

410.06 Creating Good Space

A circle must be on the floor. The circle should be about the size of a circle on a basketball court. Signs are placed on participants (Miss America banner-style), indicating positive and negative experiences. One person wears a special banner and is called the "Conductor." Participants take turns. Persons representing the initial problems or negative experiences are placed inside the circle. The good that a participant desires is represented by the persons wearing positive banners and these persons are placed outside the circle. The goal of the game is to get the good in the circle and the undesired out. Rules: All participants are free to move around. Negatives may move within the circle, blocking the entry of good from the circle, and helping other negatives to enter. The same is true for positives. The Vacuum Rule is that the same number of persons must be inside the circle at all times. Thus when one is put out of the circle, another may enter. Undesired problems may enter whenever there is space and are standing in back of the Conductor. Problems may be disabled by the Conductor by using some type of assertive behavior. When the problem is disabled, the banner may be removed from the person and the person can re-enter the circle but has a negative or positive force representation. The group is not given the following information. To "win," the Conductor may disable all negatives. Or, organize participants outside the circle so that all problems remain in view. Then assertively remove a problem from the inner circle and make it join the group of negatives outside the circle. This allows good to fill the vacuum (symbolizes trust that good will enter life if given a chance). The Conductor may hold hands with good that is in circle to keep it from being pushed out (symbolizes creation of good habits, regular practice of a habit during daily routine). Or the Conductor may step out of inner circle and select good and push it in, forcing someone to step out of the circle (symbolizes detachment). Note length of time for problem resolution. After the game is played, leader helps group to process the methods of dealing with problems as related to the game experience. The leader helps participants relate it to real life experiences.

In the next round, the game is repeated with another participant being Conductor. Note length of time for resolution, which should be less than first round. Process the difference in length of time so that group can see the value of learning from others.

In the third round, the game is played with a new Conductor. The Conductor is given an assistant named "Friend." Note length of time required for resolution. Process the difference between trying to achieve an objective alone and achieving the objective with help. The group is asked to apply the learning to their way of dealing with life.

Note that game may be used to enhance creative problem solving. It also helps clients understand the value of group support derived from group therapy or attending 12-step programs. It helps to understand how to inject leisure into a daily routine or how to remove a process addiction from the daily schedule. Game may be designed to help a specific Conductor work through alternatives and discover "first things" really need to go first. Variation can be designed to help a client who thinks the best thing is to leave treatment early to see the value of staying.

410.09 Music's Self-Fulfilling Prophecy

This session can be used in a variety of ways. It can be used to identify work addiction or co-dependency tendencies, or adult child functions or to develop general self-awareness. The basic format is to select popular records or albums and listen to the words in a group. Sometimes the lyrics are difficult to hear so it is helpful to have the key phrases written down and passed out to participants. Then discuss the attitude behind the song. When discussion is complete, rewrite the words to the songs making them in line with recovery objectives.

420.0 PROCESS ADDICTION TREATMENT

Special sessions may be designed to resolve specific process addiction. Many times participation in many of the other formats in this text will help. There needs to be specific information conveyed about the specific process addiction in this session.

420.01 Nothingness

The exercise of "nothingness" is actually a Leisure Education session. However, in my opinion, the content is so powerful that it should not be led by everyone or provided to everyone. The session leader should, in addition to being a Therapeutic Recreation Specialist, be well-trained in group dynamics and counseling techniques. Therapeutic Recreation Specialists, who do not have these skills, should co-lead the session with a group therapist or counselor until skills are fully developed. Only hard core leisure avoiders and clients who have failed to respond to other forms of Therapeutic Recreation programming should be involved. Clients who are severe process addicts, especially workaholics, may benefit from provision of "nothingness." The session may be used to treat family rigidity, co-dependency, work addiction, and food addictions. Actually, any client who feels a need to substitute process or substance out of a fear of unoccupied time may benefit from this session. Any client who is concerned about what he/she will do when there is nothing to do, is a candidate for this session.

Before conducting the activity with clients, provide the activity for the Therapeutic Recreation Staff. It is a good way to train leaders. It is also a good way to help staff understand the function of leisure. Besides, if a staff hasn't got it, the staff can't give it away. This exercise will separate those who have it from those who say they have it.

The activity of "nothingness" is just that. But it forces the client to face content that produces extreme anxiety. Participants are placed in a room with minimal adornment. No books to read, no slogans on the wall, no window views to gaze at. Participants are asked not to talk to each other. No length of time is specified. No music or activities are provided. Leaders sit in silence with participants. For hard core process addicts who fear being trapped with nothing to do, the minutes will grind like hours. Leaders must be sensitive to a client's body language. Breaking the silence too soon defeats the purpose. Allowing the "nothingness" to continue too long is cruel and unusual punishment. The goal of the activity is to help clients face their fear. When the silence is broken, the big question is what happens when nothing happens. Why must nothingness be avoided?

For some, the fear has been unrealistic. Nothing has happened when there is nothing to do. Recognizing this will permit the person to relax. The work bag need not be packed for a trip to an appointment that means time in a waiting room. Vacation schedules need not be so tightly scheduled that life gets squeezed out of the daily routine.

For others, the fear results from the mind wandering into a minefield. As long as the person is busy, the problems and pain of the past, present and future are avoided. The minute that "nothingness" occurs, all the unhappiness attempts to rise to consciousness. Those who are really fighting to hold emotional difficulty at bay will become angry at the leader for subjecting the participants to the pain of "nothingness."

The Therapeutic Recreation Specialist can handle the clients who discover that doing nothing is not so bad. The counselor is needed for those who get angry with the leader, and those who have too much pain arising to awareness.

Many clients say they do "nothing" in their spare time. This exercise helps them realize that they seldom do nothing. Discussion after an experience of "nothingness" can focus on the difference between doing nothing and doing something unworthy of remembering. And because the client is usually doing something rather than nothing, it makes sense to do things that are worthy of remembering.

Where it is the counselor's opinion that "nothingness" is dangerous to the clients health--stirring up memories too painful to be dealt with--then the client and Therapeutic Recreation Specialist together can identify ways to avoid "nothingness" through meaningful leisure pursuit, while counselor and client can agree to deal with the problem areas in appropriate sessions.

Some clients have simply formed a habit of always doing something. For them, the session can help them see just how difficult it is to sit still. The inability to relax and do nothing is often an earmark of workaholism. The client may wish to change the habit. Without a few moments of relaxation, the body is never totally able to regenerate itself. Therapeutic Rec-

reation Specialist and client may negotiate a contract, with the client agreeing to do "nothingness" for one minute a day or for whatever length of time he/she can tolerate. Then the length of time should be gradually increased until the client feels capable of doing nothing for just as long as he/she desires.

This is a good exercise for family members too. Most family members in the Fireworks stage cannot do nothing for a second. They are far too busy worrying about their loved one. Those who admit to the inability to keep their mind off their loved one's problems can begin making progress by recognizing the need to think about the self rather than the loved one. Those who deny being controlled by addiction might benefit from a dose of "nothingness."

420.02 Process Addiction Withdrawal [Detox]

A sudden end to an addictive process may be as hard on the body as a sudden end of substance abuse. After all, both process and substance are stimulating the same neuro-chemical systems within the body. Because the body does better with gradual withdrawal from a substance, it can be assumed that the body will also need gradual withdrawal from a process. An individual unable to stop substance abuse independently will probably not be able to stop use of a process independently either. Little if any research exists on process addictions. I would theorize that a person could be withdrawn from a process in two ways. The first way would be to gradually reduce the number of hours in which the client is allowed to perform the process. The second way would be to substitute a similar process and then gradually withdraw the use of that. While the first seems the simplest, I have had Therapeutic Recreation Professionals report that clients get quite aggravated when cut off from a desired process. They are always pushing for more rather than less. Perhaps explaining process addiction to the client so that he/she can understand the problem would help. Where process substitutes are known, provision of a substitute is recommended. In this way the frame of reference is broken, and hopefully the process can be withdrawn before a new "overdoing it" habit is formed. Productive activities may be substituted for work. One form of calming, soothing activity may be substituted for another. Perhaps laughter can be substituted for physical exercise. Perhaps weight lifting can be substituted for jogging and then the amount of time spent weight lifting can be decreased. Then again, perhaps not.

If processes are used to assist the substance detox phase of treatment, then the process that was utilized should also be gradually withdrawn. For example, the client who found it beneficial to sit by an artificial waterfall eight hours a day should have his/her waterfall sitting time gradually decreased over ten days to a maximum of one hour a day.

The goal of recovery is balance. Too much of anything means not enough time for something else. Perhaps a third method of process "detoxification" would be to allow the client to participate in the activity of choice as much as desired, but he/she must get an equal amount of the opposite activity into the day's schedule. This rule may force self-responsibility in activity selection and self-monitoring. Both are very valuable to the recovery process.

420.03 Process Addiction Monitoring

The addictive personality does not know what "too much" is. "You are jogging too much" is the same as saying "You are working too much," which is the same as "You are drinking too much." Clients must be made aware of the risk of overdoing an activity. They must also be given methods to identify and define what is too much.

Clients must learn to monitor their activities to ensure balanced living. The key difference between activity use and abuse is purpose. When a client uses an activity to avoid problems or interactions, then the activity will be abused. When a client engages in an activity to regenerate energy and gain fresh perspective on the problem, then the activity participation is healthy and helpful. At first, balance will be mechanical. As habits are established, balance will become automatic. The frequent use of the following checklist or similar tool will assist the establishment of balance and prevent a single process or substance from consuming life again. (See Figure 11.1 on the following page)

430.0 VENTILATION OF ANGER

Punching bags, athletics, and physical exercise are good forms of anger ventilation. Activities that vent the anger of one person directly onto another person should be avoided. Nerf™ ball free-for-alls can vent anger without seriously hurting others. Some people need to strike out but are so afraid of hurting someone or something that they cannot even throw a soft ball at someone. The best they can do is give it a gentle toss. Large wet sponges thrown against a wall are ideal for such individuals. They are told in advance that they cannot hurt anything or anyone and are continuously encouraged to throw with greater and greater force. They are encouraged to imagine that the wall is a person, place, or thing that makes them angry and to nail him, her, or it right between the eyes. This not only helps the person to release the anger, but it helps the person become aware of the things that cause the anger. A Nerf™ ball or a wet sponge is not aerodynamic. They require exertion to go any distance. This permits the release of pent-up energies quickly. The Therapeutic Recreation Specialist helps guide the person's anger by providing feedback such as "You are really throwing hard now, what are you imagining?" Where a person is the source of the anger ask for reasons. Too often it is not actually a person but a result of intoxication that has created the anger. Help the person see that addiction is the culprit, not the victims of addiction.

Shouting contests also vent anger. Many people feel uncomfortable raising their voices. Shouting and screaming are natural releases of tension. A suppressed scream is internalized and only adds pressure. [Ch9: 247.1]

440.0 MANAGING GRIEF

My higher power must want more detail in this text than I had originally planned. Yesterday, pictures of my dead aunt and uncle unexpectedly arrived in the mail. As I sat down to write this section, the phone rang. A former work comrade's husband has died. She will be trying to walk down that same long empty hall I tried to walk after my husband died.

Grief is difficult to understand if not personally experienced. If you have experienced it, then I don't have to tell you what it's like to be on the surviving end. If you haven't experienced it, then there is no way I can really explain it to you. It is the instant shattering of the past, present, and future.

It can be experienced in small doses when a sentimental possession is lost or stolen, when the family moves to a new home, even when a frustrating job is given up for a new one. The end of a behavior pattern or habit, even though it was undesirable, can result in grief. The ending of anything can trigger grief.

Death of a family member is far more traumatic. Strength of the relationship intensifies the results. Prior experience with grief teaches how to handle the trauma. When in proper order, a person is provided practice with managing grief, which prepares a person to survive the difficult ones. Usually grandparents and distant relatives die first. Grief is experienced in mild forms. Then parents die after a person has established a supportive relationship with a mate. The grief for the average parent is more intense than the grief felt for the average grandparent. By the time the spouse dies, the person knows what to do and what not to do to survive grief. But when deaths occur out of natural order, or when the person has remained intimate/dependent on the parent or grandparent, then the natural immunity to grief has not had a chance to develop. The person becomes helplessly trapped in grief.

Death of a family member is traumatic regardless of the quality of the relationship. From my observations it seems to be more difficult to move through grief when the relationship has been filled with friction rather than love. When someone I love dies, I lose the presence of the person, but remain surrounded by the love. When someone I have argued with dies, I lose the chance of clearing the air with the person and fail to feel the supporting love.

Many attempt to avoid grief through a drink, fix, or pill. The pain can be postponed but never avoided. When I was five, my grandmother died. My mother told me to cry. I didn't. Thirty-five years later a picture of Granny arrived in the mail. I cried. I had a good friend in grade school. On the way to college, my radio blared his name and that he had been killed in Vietnam. I turned the radio off and went on as though nothing had happened. Last summer, I found his name on the War Memorial in Washington, DC and I cried. The picture of my aunt and uncle also brought tears. The tears were for my uncle. He died twenty years ago, and I didn't cry. My aunt died last year and crying for her then left no tears for today. I cried for my dad on the way to his intensive care bed. I sobbed through his funeral and began to smile shortly thereafter. I also

FIGURE 11.1

PROCESS MONITORING FORM

NAME:_____ PROCESS:_____ DATE:_____

STRUCTURE:

1. Number of hours spent in process:

    MON   TUES   WED   THURS   FRI   SAT   SUN

    ____   ____   ____   ____   ____   ____   ____

2. Did I realize how much time I was spending in this process?

3. No matter how long I do the process, do I always walk away wanting more?

4. Have others commented about how much I participate in this process?

VARIETY & BALANCE:

5. Have I spent an equal amount of time doing things which are the opposite of this process?

6. Am I able to participate in this process and meet my obligations and responsibilities too?

PURPOSE:

7. Am I participating in this activity to recharge my energy or to avoid dealing with the undesirable?

8. After participation, do I deal with my problems, or do I just dream about the next opportunity to participate in the process?

9. Is my life improving or disintegrating as a result of participation in this process?

CONCLUSION:

10. Based on the above I should:

    _____   Continue Process without concern
    _____   Continue Process within limits #_____
    _____   Discontinue participation

(LIMITS: 1 = Reduce time spent in process by 50 percent. 2 = Measure time spent in process. 3 = Cancel a time period for each extended time period. 4 = Ask others why they have commented about participation. 5 = Add an equal amount of time in an activity of the opposite nature. 6 = Meet at least one obligation or responsibility before next participation. 7 = Select at least one undesirable situation and deal with it before next participation. 8 = Deal with a problem immediately after next participation. 9 = Repeat this exercise at least once per week.)

remember the nurse who said, "Your father is dead. Have a valium." She was at a loss when I said "No."

There are things that everyone can do that will help and things that will make it all worse. Suggesting the solution is valium is not beneficial. Honesty is the best policy. I always preferred the person who said "I want to help, but I don't know how" to the persons who tried to show expertise and empathy, and it was obvious they didn't know the slightest about what I was experiencing.

Grief is no time for others to satisfy personal curiosity. The ambulance technician who asked me if my mother wanted to die from cancer got a calm "no" response from me. I got traumatic delayed stress from his question. It took years of tortured reflection before I could satisfy myself that I had not, in some way, caused my mother to want to die. The question would have never even occurred to me had that "helping professional" kept his mouth shut. (My mother wanted very much to live. What she did not want was to die in a hospital and that was before the time of hospice programs.) So if you want to help and don't know how, then tell the person you love them. Tell the person that words cannot describe your feelings and then shut up. Don't ask if there was any pain. Don't ask if they wanted to die. Don't break down and cry on the victim's shoulder, dumping your grief on top of theirs.

The books say there are stages of grief—shock, denial, fault finding, anger, sorrow, depression, regret, resentment, acceptance. Perhaps I've added a few and can add a few more. For me, shock comes first. During this time I laugh and joke and take care of business. I know the shock stage is wearing off when I lose my ability to control body temperature. I'm feverish one minute and freezing cold the next. That is when I put a map in the car and give an extra set of keys to the neighbor, because when my temperature controls come back on, I enter disorganized thinking, absent-mindedness, which causes me to lose things. I get lost going places that I go everyday. Sleep deprivation and appetite curtailment begin on day one and continue for months. Emotional control is destroyed. I'm laughing one minute and crying the next. The first time or two I went through these symptoms, I made things harder on myself by fearing that I was going crazy and by getting angry with myself for doing the things I was doing. "I should be able to remember." "I shouldn't cry in front of people." "I should be stronger than this." "I should be sleeping." By the time my husband died, I knew how I reacted, which meant I only had to deal with the grief, not the fears of self-inadequacy. I had also learned little tricks. Like, if I get to sleep before 11:45 p.m., I will sleep. If I don't get to sleep by then, I must get up and focus my mind on something productive or I will be swallowed by a black hole. Grief at night is less productive and more painful than grief during the day.

I have also learned to protect myself on special occasions. Birthdays, holidays, anniversaries are days of doom unless I plan some very special, unusual event for them. Over the years the planning diminishes. Sometimes I have thought I was doing so well that I didn't need a special plan for a special day.

Sometimes it has been a miscalculation. But the pain after the first year is less intense and can be handled with short outbursts rather than being an all-day ordeal.

There is also fear stemming from recognition that other loved ones are capable of dying. My husband's death in a traffic accident made me want to run to the phone and check on the safety of my son every time he was given a ride by someone other than me. I had to fight hard not to place that call. I knew that if I called to check on him, I would be calling for the rest of my life. I didn't call. He came home okay, and continued to do so, until a time came when I didn't even think about calling.

Grief is not resolved in stages but in layers. The first layer of shock, anger, and frustration peels off and then the next layer, and then the next for years and years and years. Support from others can help the process. Again, don't dig or pry if you don't know what you are doing. Just be there.

Therapeutic Recreation can help. During the wood for brains stage, I am only capable of mechanical actions. Tell me what to do and I'll do it. Give me a jigsaw puzzle or a game without too many rules. It keeps my mind occupied and makes me think I'm functional. Both are helpful. Initially, don't ask me to paint or create. All that will come out is blackness, which will intensify my mood. After I have had a chance to rant and rave and scream and cry, then I can work through the rest of it by creating. Give me some good times and some laughs to balance out my pain. If I start talking about my grief, listen but don't feel a need to resolve anything. There is nothing anyone can say to change the situation. Don't feel a need to make me cry or stop me from crying. Just hand me a tissue. If you see I am totally blocked and denying that I hurt, send me to a Therapist with experience in dealing with grief. Let me know that my behavior is normal, and that my actions result from grief, not insanity. Allow me to heal at my own rate. Let me see others who have survived. If they can do it, then maybe I can do it too. Love me. Trust that better days are ahead for me. Other than this you can do very little for me. But in doing these, you have done a lot. The following is what I share with others after a death of a loved one:

CLIMB

When there seems to be no way,
Put the right foot in front of the left,
The left in front of the right,
Again and again all through the day,
Looking back you'll find progress
made, You'r making a way,
Creating a path to recovery.
The better view is at the higher grade.

I've got a lot of fight in me. I know it's in you too. So fight. Fight back by:

1. Getting up in the morning.
2. Eating when you are not hungry.
3. Sleep when sleep comes.

4. Buy a pair of sunglasses. Tears come during relaxed moments, like driving to work. Sunglasses hide the puffeys and once at work, getting busy forgets to hurt.

5. Tie your keys on your body and put a map in your car.

6. Take charge of your life. People say stupid things when trying to express concern. Allowing them to show their ignorance is awkward for both you and them. I always headed them off at the pass: "I know you are concerned. Thank you. Words cannot express it, can they?" This brings agreement and a big smile, and then it's back to business as usual. This greeting is not for close friends. It's for the bank clerk, the gas station attendant, the new employee fresh out of school, etc

7. Go places you usually go immediately. Go back to work, if only for a visit, as soon as possible. I have found that places I go before the shock wears off are easier to go to later. The longer the time lapse the harder to face.

8. Beware of self-blame. "If only I had...." nothing would have ended differently.

9. Feel the pain in measured doses. There's too much to deal with all at once. Imagine a closet. Put your pain in boxes and put the boxes in the closet and lock the door. Then go to the closet and take it out one box at a time. Feel it. Let it hurt. Let it go. Don't lock the closet door forever. The door to good is blocked until the closet is emptied.

10. It's unfair, so get angry. Chew your loved one out and God too anytime you feel like it. Don't apologize for doing it. The bond of love cannot be broken by a few ill words. God is big enough to understand.

11. It just takes time.

12. Get professional counseling. Join a support group.

13. I fought very hard to find a reason for going on. I found it only after my door of good opened and I stepped into my new life. Right now, your reason for going on may not be apparent. But there is a reason. It will be revealed when the time is right. Until then, go on because the smell of a flower is a very special thing. Go on just to prove to yourself that you can go on.

14. Bonds of love are never broken. They stretch into infinity.

450.0 TRUST OF SELF AND OTHERS

By the time one reaches treatment for addiction, all evidence and past learning point toward failure and inadequacy as a human being. The lack of trust in self is not as visible as the resulting lack of trust of others. But how can one trust others when one can't trust one's self?

450.01 New Games

New games have been designed to develop trust in self and others. Clients identified as needing to develop trust begin with participation in New Game formats. New Games alone are not strong enough to completely break the barriers of distrust.

450.02 Truth or Dare

Truth or Dare is an adaptation of Spin the Bottle. Participants sit in a circle. A bottle is placed in the center of the circle and the bottle is spun. When it stops spinning, the person it is pointing to must select either a "truth" or a "dare." If a "truth" is selected, the person must honestly answer an honest question asked by the person who spun the bottle. If a "dare" is selected, the person must do whatever stupid trick the spinner requests. Having completed either a "truth" or a "dare," the person spins the bottle and provides the next honest question or dare to the person at which the bottle points.

450.03 Oh No Not That Again I'd Love To

This session discusses the difference between assertive, passive, and aggressive responses. It then uses role plays to help clients practice assertive responses to meet leisure needs. Passive behavior often results from a lack of trust in self and others. Role plays help clients learn to manage situations and develop confidence in their abilities to handle situations. This session is formatted the same as Leisure Education for Family. [Ch8:105.3] Situations for role plays are developed to meet the specific need of the client. If the client has difficulty standing his or her ground with drinking buddies, then that is the focus of the role play. If the client has difficulty expressing personal needs and desires to others, then that is the focus of the role play.

460.0 RISK-TAKING

The success of the recovery process depends on the individual's ability to overcome fear. The greatest fear is the fear of the unknown. Within the vast expanses of the unknown, between the fear of the dark and the fear of non-acceptance, lies the fear of one's own inadequacy. When one's adequacy is doubted, it is difficult to trust others or feel accepted by others. There must always be distance—distance between the self and the self, between the self and others, between desire and action. If others get too close, they might discover the truth. They might discover that competence is only a facade.

Therapy involves development of a program with gradual increases in risk taking. Selected activities may be from activities routinely provided for other purposes or from specially designed activities. Use of a challenge courses is ideal.

470.0 ANTICIPATIONS AND EXPECTATIONS MANAGEMENT

Many clients experience anxiety as a result of unrealistic anticipations and/or expectations of an upcoming event. As trust of self and others increases, the anxiety decreases. [Ch11: 450.0] Clients can be taught to focus attention on pleasurable mental images each time they find themselves anticipating an event. Timing is also important in anticipations management. Too much unobligated time before an event leads to anxiety. An event planned too far in advance leads to anxiety. Individuals may learn how to manage anticipations and expectations through managing involvement in the Therapeutic Recreation Service. Learning a new leisure skill may cause anxiety. Hearing other clients talk about a Recreation Therapy session content for which the client is scheduled to attend may create anxiety. Learning to manage these situations develops abilities to manage anticipations after discharge.

470.01 Ain't It Awful?

Some people get into the habit of looking for the worst in every situation. The purpose of this session is to help participants become aware of this habit, to realize the internal feelings produced by negative thinking, and to give them practice at changing the habit. [Ch2: Learning The Lessons Too Well; Ch4: Children of Addiction]

Participants are divided into two teams. The activity leader serves as moderator. One team selects heads, the other tails. A coin is flipped to see which team begins. Each time the coin lands heads, the "heads" team begins. Each time the coin lands tails, the "tails" team begins. The moderator reads a newspaper headline or other statement about a current affairs controversy. The statement could be a reporting of an accident. It could be an arrest for a break-in. It could be a political scandal, or the greenhouse effect, or nuclear energy, or the slipping GNP, etc. The first team must give a statement about the situation that makes it seem worse than the original statement. Then, the second team must give a statement that is worse than the first team's statement. Play goes back and forth between the teams until a team comes up with the most awful statement, one that the other team can't make worse. The team giving the most awful statement wins a point. The moderator selects a new statement, flips a coin, and the process is repeated. Play continues until the moderator sees that all participants are depressed by the process. (They may be really into the play, but body language is showing the symptoms of negative thinking.) At this point the moderator asks partici-

pants to tune into their inner feelings and share how they are feeling. Play begins again, but there is a change. The moderator reads the first original statement, which began play. The coin is flipped. The first team must now come up with a reason why the event is good. They must find some positive aspect of the situation. Then the next team must find a better aspect of the situation. The team that gives the most positive statement that cannot be beat by the other team gets two points. Play continues until all statements given while looking for the most awful consequences have been also given most positive consequences. The game is processed. Participants are asked to tune into their feelings after finding positive results and compare those feelings to those encountered after the negative considerations. Participants are asked to apply the results of their findings to their lives.

470.02 Deriving Positives from Positive Expectations

Some persons allow their expectations to become so great that they set themselves up for disappointments. In this session clients are taught to think positive about an upcoming event but not too positive. The session begins with the leader building up the group. The leader tells them what a wonderful exciting event is in store for them. The leader acts so excited that everyone catches the excitement. Then the leader brings out the most boring game that can be found. Client reactions are discussed. Clients are encouraged to keep a open mind. It is important not to attempt to manipulate expectations by telling the self that the event will be terrible or fantastic. After the clients complete the discussion, they are challenged to play the boring game and find ways to make it fun and interesting. The point is that there are always choices. A person can choose to be bored or choose to discover interesting facets in a boring activity.

480.0 DECISION MAKING

Making decisions can be difficult for many. Trust of self is important. The more confidence a person has in his/her ability to make decisions the easier it is to make decisions. Practice in making decisions is helpful. Persons who take themselves and their situation too seriously may have great difficulty in making decisions. They assume that the results of their decision have significant consequences. In my opinion, the majority of decisions made in a lifetime have very little serious consequences. Most of our decisions are like deciding to purchase an apple or banana. Purchasing an apple only to find yourself hungry for a banana will not stop the world from turning. While most decisions have consequences, making the wrong decision is usually reversible. Activities that help the client to separate decisions that are irreversible (suicide) from decisions that can be changed are helpful. Helping the client to see consequences of decisions are helpful. Helping the client to reduce the perceived seriousness of most decisions is helpful.

480.01 No Decision Is A Decision

Some clients become so fearful of making the wrong decision that they refuse to make any decision at all. A game may be designed to show clients that decisions get made no matter what. When a decision is not made by the person, the person loses the power to influence the results of the decision. The passive approach to decision making leads to unmanageability.

480.02 Decision Making Practice

Clients who fear making decisions or always look to others to make decisions should be given practice at making decisions. A series of opposing choices are presented on cards. There is a set of cards for each player. The cards are things like: "Apples or Bananas." "Today or Tomorrow." "Beer or Vodka." "Two or Ten." "Marry or Stay Single." "Chinese Food or Italian Food." "Drink or No Drink." "Cut the Grass or Mow the Lawn." Obviously, some statements result in selection of a choice that is meaningless in the person's life. Selecting apples rather than bananas make no significant differences. Some choices have major impact, such as to drink or not to drink. Some choices are designed where both choices are bad ones such as the choice between beer or vodka. The game is a speed game. Participants make choices as quickly as possible. They stack selections they want to keep in one pile as decisions made. They discard the other. Though no instructions are given in advance, they are permitted to discard both choices. Another pile is made of choices that require further consideration. The first person to complete the restacking of the cards wins. Then the contents of the stacks are discussed. For the stack of choices requiring further consideration, the group discusses the type of additional information that may be needed to make the decision.

480.03 Failure to Deliberate

Some clients have fallen in a habit of making decisions too quickly. Snap decisions can be dangerous. Clients should always be encouraged to wait twenty-four hours before delivering a decision. Clients should be taught to use a decision tree or other method of reviewing positive and negative consequences of a decision. They should also try to think of alternative methods of achieving an objective. Too often, the client focuses on the presented choice and deliberates its consequences, forgetting that other options are available that might be much better.

490.0 ADVENTURE COURSE

The most significant way to attack a lack of self-confidence is through participation in an adventure program. TNT operates a program. The obstacle course used for the program is located on the grounds of the treatment facility. For this program to be operated safely and effectively, it is not enough to have a degree in Therapeutic Recreation. The activity leader should be a Therapeutic Recreation Specialist with special training and certification in adventure based program leadership.

References/Resources

Avedon, E., & Sutton-Smith, B. (1971). *The Study of Games.* NY: John Wiley and Sons.

Barcus, C. J., & Bergeson, R. J. (1972, First Quarter). Survival training and mental health: A review. *Therapeutic Recreation Journal.*

Blau, M. (1988, September 26). Learning the hard way: How to help children triumph over learning disabilities. *New York* 21, p. 74(15).

Erickson, S., & Harris, B. (1981). *The Adventure Book: A Curriculum Guide To School Based Adventuring With Troubled Adolescents.* Goshen, CT: The Wilderness School, Dept. of Children and Youth Services.

Faulke, W., & Keller, T. (1976, April). The art experience in addict rehabilitation. *American Journal of Art Therapy.*

Faulkner, R. W. (1989, August). *"Zanity Adventures For Learning Stimulation"* Unpublished copyrighted work.

Faulkner, R. W. (1989, August). *"Zanity Adventures For Decision Making."* Unpublished copyrighted work.

Funabiki, D., & Pringnitz, T. (1982, Fourth Quarter). Management of disruptive behaviors in therapeutic recreation settings. *Therapeutic Recreation Journal.*

Geiger, G., & Lettvin, J. Y. (1987, May 14). Peripheral vision in persons with dyslexia. *New England Journal of Medicine,* p. 1238(8).

Gibson, P. (1979, Second Quarter). Therapeutic aspects of wilderness programs. *Therapeutic Recreation Journal.*

Goldberg, H. K., Schiffman, G. B., & Bender, V. (1983). *Dyslexia: Interdisciplinary Approaches to Reading Disabilities.* New York, NY: Grune & Stratton.

Gunn, S. L., & Peterson, C. A. (1978). *Therapeutic Recreation Program Design: Principles & Procedures.* Englewood Cliffs, NJ: Prentice-Hall.

Hoper, C., Kutzleb, U., Stobbe, A., & Weber, B. (1975). *Awareness Games: Personal Growth Through Group Interaction.* NY: St. Martin's Press.

Hynd, G., & Hynd, C. Dyslexia: Neuroanatomic/neuro-linguistic perspectives. *Reading Research Quarterly.* 19, no. 4, pp. 482-98.

Levy, J. Director of Therapeutic Recreation and Staff Development, Lawerence Hall Youth Services, Chicago, IL. (Has done extensive work in the development of Therapeutic Games, most of which is unpublished at this time.)

Lytle, V. (1985, October). Edison, Rockefeller, Rodin, and the reading problem (detecting dyslexia in students) *NEA Today* 1, p. 10(2).

Manzo, A. V. (1987, January) Psychologically induced dyslexia and learning disabilities. *The Reading Teacher.*

McAvoy, L. H. (1982, Fourth Quarter). Management components in therapeutic outdoor adventure programs. *Therapeutic Recreation Journal.*

McKee, P. (1984, First Quarter). Effects of using enjoyable imagery with biofeedback induced relaxation for chronic pain patients. *Therapeutic Recreation Journal.*

Peterson, C. A. (1978). Therapeutic applications of new games. *Expanding Horizons V.* University of Missouri.

Segalowitz, S. J. (1983). *Two Sides of The Brain.* Englewood Cliffs, NJ: Prentice-Hall.

Stanovich, K. Z. (1988, December). Explaining the difference between the dyslexic and the garden variety poor reader. The phonological -core variable- difference model. *Journal Learning Disabilities* 21:590-604+.

Sugar, S. (1987, December). Trainings's the name of the game. *Training and Development Journal.*

Vandershaf, S. (1987, March). Dyslexia: recognizing shape, not sounds. *Psychology Today,* 21.

Vogar, E. W., Fenstermacher, G., & Bishop, P. (1982, First Quarter). Group oriented behavior management systems to control disruptive behavior in therapeutic recreation settings. *Therapeutic Recreation Journal.*

Weill, M. P. (1987, April). Gifted-learning disabled students: Their potential may be buried treasure." *Clearing House,* 50.

Wooten, H. E. (1977). The use of relaxation training and biofeedback as an adjunct to therapeutic recreation. *Expanding Horizons in Therapeutic Recreation IV.* University of Missouri.

Wright A. N. (1983, Second Quarter). Therapeutic potential of the outward bound process: An evaluation of a treatment program for juvenile delinquents. *Therapeutic Recreation Journal.*

CHAPTER 12

INDIVIDUAL CASES

THE CASE OF NARRON HIGH

(Leisure Independence Level: Independent)

The purpose of this unit is to integrate concepts previously discussed. Several fictitious characters have been developed to show how the fictitious Therapeutic Recreation service might impact on the treatment and recovery process. Activities, programs, services, have previously been discussed from a center-wide service delivery system viewpoint. This unit provides a view of the same system but from individual client viewpoints. Initial program plans are based on the type of data which is known about a client during the first few days after admission. Most information initially comes from the client, family, and staff observations. The information initially obtained from clients and family members is seldom detailed. The real story tends to surface throughout the treatment process. Data from staff observations combined with client responses to the assessment process usually provide an adequate starting point. The treatment plan should always be considered as tentative. Staff should be willing to change plans as more accurate information surfaces.

At TNT, clients complete the TRI Assessment immediately after admission, and again at discharge. If the treatment stay is longer than one month, sections of TRI are retaken. The sections that are repeated are the ones which are expected to change as a result of the treatment process. New treatment plans are developed as needed. In this unit, a composite TRI and treatment plan are provided.

At 33 years of age, Narron High was admitted for his first treatment attempt. While in Vietnam, Mr. High had been introduced to LSD and had become addicted to heroin. Since that time, he had used heroin whenever he could afford it. He had used other drugs and alcohol when he could not afford heroin. A year ago, fortunes of marriage brought him back into an affluent lifestyle and back into a bag of heroin for breakfast, a joint for lunch, and a six-pack of beer for dinner. Upon admission, he stated that he wanted to get straight for himself, knowing that if he continued to use he would lose his wife. (Naturally, a loss of the wife would result in a loss of emotional and financial security.)

The staff found Mr. High to be pleasant, outgoing, congenial and agreeable. He seemed to have good insight into his problems. Other patients found him to be friendly and helpful. Mr. High scored at the "Independent" level on the TRI Assessment system. (See Figure 12.1) He had high blood pressure at the time of admission, but that seemed to be a result of the addiction. After withdrawal, his blood pressure returned to within normal limits. There was some general weakness and deconditioning as a result of an inactive lifestyle. He also reported a history of difficulty sleeping. He had completed three years of college and was an avid reader and writer. He completed the entire TRI form within an hour and did not require assistance.

The TRI form indicated that Mr. High had a valid driver's license and a choice of cars to drive. He rated himself as "Semi-Independent" on Economic Situation, explaining that he had access to enough money to do most of the things he wanted to do, but it really was not his money. He rated himself as "Semi-Independent" on family support and added a comment, that

FIGURE 12.1

NARRON HIGH TRI TREATMENT PLAN						
Initial Assessment Results						
TRI Item:	Opinion of Client	Level TRS	Final Score (Level)	Wght. Score	Maximum Possible	Goal:
1 Physical	3	3	(3)	7.5	10	+ one level
2 Education	4	4	(4)	8	8	
3 Transportation	4	4	(4)	8	8	
4 Economic	3	3	(3)	6	8	+
5 Family Support	3	3	(3)	7.5	10	+ one level
6 Stress	2	2	(2)	5	10	+ one level
7 Play Status	4	4	(4)	12	12	
8 Problem Solving	4	4	(4)	10	10	Most important:
9 Leisure Skills	3	4	(4)	12	12	maintain leisure
10 Leisure Awareness	3	4	(4)	12	12	independence
		TRI Total Score:		88.0	out of 100	

things were temporarily strained at home. (His wife accompanied him on the day of admission. She stated that she was willing to do anything that might help. She stated that she knew he was drinking too much, and smoking some pot, but she never dreamed he might be using "anything else like. . .like . . . a hard drug." As much as she tried, she could not get the word "heroin" out of her mouth.)

Mr. High's lowest TRI score was stress- related. His play history status was scored Independent. He was able to think of nine different things to do with a newspaper which gave him an "Independent" score on problem solving. In terms of leisure, Mr. High had a wide variety of leisure skills but wanted more. He seemed to have an appreciation for the value of leisure but insisted he wanted to learn more. His overall TRI score of 88 was one-half point above the divider line between "Semi-Independent" and "Independent" leisure functioning.

Mr. High was the kind of guy that staff enjoyed being around. It would have been easy for the Therapeutic Recreation Specialist to pass the day exchanging pleasantries with him. But Mr. High did not need time spent with him as much as the clients rated in the "Dependent" and "At Risk" levels. His leisure lifestyle appeared adequate to meet his needs. In fact, this was a person accustomed to meeting his own leisure needs. Assisting him in meeting his needs while in treatment only risked forming unnecessary dependency on the facility, a habit which could lead to institutionalization. The Therapeutic Recreation Specialist decided to adopt the "if it isn't broken, don't fix it" approach.

Mr. High was placed in charge of his own Therapeutic Recreation program. The primary Therapeutic Recreation goal was to maintain Mr. High at his "Independent" level. His self- administered program included goals set by Mr. High. He wanted to increase his physical conditioning from "Semi-Independent" to "Independent." A second goal was to improve his ability to sleep. The third goal which Mr. High set was to improve his relationship with his wife.

The Therapeutic Recreation Specialist provided Mr. High with a schedule of available activities and explained the coding system.

To Increase Physical Conditioning:

211.3   How to Bowl
211.3   How to Golf
211.3   How to Participate in Team Swims
211.3   How to Play Competitive Water Games
211.3   How to Play Volleyball
221.3   How to Rumba Dance
221.3   Introduction to Martial Arts
221.3   Low- Impact Aerobics
231.3   Gardeneering
231.3   Working with Wood, Saws, and Hammers (234.3)
241.3   New Games for Fitness
241.3   Picnic Games for Moderate Exercise
241.3   Square Dance

251.3   Outdoor Gardening
271.3   Introduction to Ballet, Tap Dancing
311.3   Gym Schedule
321.3   Bowling
321.3   Water Fun
351.3   Nature Hike
351.3   Weight Room Schedule
391.3   High Risk (Diving, Horseback Riding, Adventure Courses)
391.3   Participation in Outdoor Activities

To Improve Relaxation for Sleep:

106.2   Alternative Methods of Relaxation
156.2   Overview of Relaxing with Music from Center Library
156.2   Relaxing with Nature
176.2   Relaxing with the Arts
216.2   Using Sports and Other Competitions to Reduce Stress
226.2   Relaxation through Physical Exercise
226.2   Relaxing with Water Exercises
236.2   Relaxing while Growing Things
256.2   How to Relax with Nature
256.2   How to Relax with Music (see Creative)
256.2   Relaxing with the Help of a Pet or Aquarium
326.2   Relaxing with Water Exercises
356.2   Relaxing with Music
356.2   Relaxing with Nature
356.2   Relaxing with the Help of a Pet or Aquarium
376.2   Relaxing with the Arts

To Improve Family Leisure:

105.3   Family Leisure
105.3   Meeting Son and/or Daughter Needs
145.3   Overview of Family Activities
215.3   Competitive Games for Family Fun
225.3   Non-Competitive Games For Family Fun
245.3   Family Activities
275.3   How to Develop Family Sing- A- Longs
315.3   Card Tournaments (Spades, Bridge) for Client and Family
315.3   Volleyball Tournaments for Client-Family Participation
345.3   Family Picnics
345.3   Live Entertainment and Dance Night
375.3   Talent and Non-Talent Competitions Open to Client and Family

Other Sessions of Possible Interest:

124.3   Overview of Health Club Memberships: How to Join and What They Offer

134.3   Overview of Hunting Clubs: How to Join and What They Offer

154.3   Overview of Travel Clubs and Guided Tours: How to Join and Advantages

174.3   Overview of Community Sources for Music Lessons

174.3   Overview of Community Sources for Dance Classes

194.3   Overview of Outdoor and Adventure Clubs: Finding, Joining, Advantages

234.3   Customizing Your Home

274.3   Ceramics

274.3   Crocheting/Knitting/Needlepoint

274.3   Painting Pictures/Pastels

274.3   Photography

274.3   Pottery

274.3   Stained Glass

274.3   Weaving

334.3   Interior Decorating

334.3   Woodworking Shop Hours

374.3   Art Room Schedule (Painting, Sculpture, etc.)

374.3   Photography Club

Mr. High selected activities that he felt met his goals. They included Skill Development sessions in physical exercise and Relaxation. Mr. High was given the responsibility to communicate the schedule of Skill Development sessions and Re-Creation events with his wife, after his Group Counselor gave him permission to contact her. Mr. High was invited to attend Leisure Education sessions, other Skill Development sessions and Re-Creation sessions, but these were not made part of his treatment program.

During treatment, Mr. High attended Skill Development sessions in swimming and in computers. Computer classes were not on the list, but availability and instructional manuals

were all that was needed to get him going during his free time. These were both new areas of interest for him. Whenever possible he was given an instruction book for a new game and asked to teach the game to other clients who had difficulty following written instructions. As he developed ideas for new leisure pursuits, he was given a phone book and asked to check out the details for himself.

Time usually taken up with Leisure Education sessions was diverted to time with the Vocational Rehabilitation Counselor. Since his primary source of income was his wife, it was felt that true independence could never be adequate without improving his own vocational skills.

Mr. High completed the treatment program and was discharged with a Leisure Independence score of 98, as measured by the TRI. This was a 10-point increase from his admission score. The primary goal was attained; he maintained his Leisure Independence during treatment. Mr. High found his sleeping patterns greatly improved and felt good being back in good physical condition. Mr. and Mrs. High attended Skill Development sessions and many Special Events together. Mrs. High's treatment program also included May Education and Anger Ventilation sessions. She could now say the word "heroin" and laugh about her previous inability to say it. She had also joined Nar-Anon. The combination of the above resulted in improved family support. (See Figure 12.2)

After discharge, Mr. High joined TNT's outpatient Addicted Vietnam Vets group and attended Narcotics Anonymous three nights per week. One night per week, Mr. and Mrs. High went on a date. The Vietnam group dealt with the specific characteristics of post-trauma delayed-stress syndrome. He discovered that the syndrome was characterized by frequent nightmares and sleep disturbance, by problems with emotional relationships and avoidance of activities, which leads to isolation. Post-Vietnam Stress is also characterized by hyperalertness, and feelings of guilt, anger, and depression. Employment problems, addiction, and poor self-image are also

FIGURE 12.2

NARRON HIGH TRI SUMMARY				
Discharge Assessment Results				
	Admission Score		Final Score	
TRI Item:	Level	Wght. Score	(Level)	Wght. Score
1 Physical	(3)	7.5	(4)	10
2 Education	(4)	8	(4)	8
3 Transportation	(4)	8	(4)	8
4 Economic	(3)	6	(3)	6
5 Family Support	(3)	7.5	(4)	10
6 Stress	(2)	5	(4)	10
7 Play Status	(4)	12	(4)	12
8 Problem Solving	(4)	10	(4)	10
9 Leisure Skills	(4)	12	(4)	12
10 Leisure Awareness	(4)	12	(4)	12
TRI Total Score: (Indep.)		88.0	(Indep.)	98.0 = 10 point gain

associated with the syndrome. Mr. High identified with these and discovered that many of the events of the past were a direct result of having the syndrome. The counselor who leads the Vietnam Group sent a referral to Therapeutic Recreation for outpatient recreation therapy. Mr. High's case was re-opened. It was found that his TRI scores remained independent. A program of recreation therapy was developed to meet the delayed stress needs. Mr. High joined inpatient groups to meet the identified needs.

Outpatient Recreation Therapy for Mr. High:

410.0   Situation Response Awareness
430.0   Ventilation of Anger
440.0   Managing Grief
450.0   Trust of Self and Others
480.0   Decision Making

After six months, Mr. High decided that he was cured. He was tired of going someplace every night. He began drinking. It was not long before life was as unmanageable as it was before entering treatment. Since it was all down the tubes anyway, he decided he might as well enjoy it and returned to heroin use. Upon re-admission, Mr. High described his situation as follows:

"A meeting a night puts a squeeze on the schedule. Recreation pursuits such as movies, bowling, and target practicing were moved from nights to Saturday afternoons. I thought I had my problem licked. I felt good. My family was happy. I could look back and see that all my problems had resulted from using drugs to control my feelings. I never wanted to use again. All my problems had resulted from drugs, not alcohol. So I started drinking a beer occasionally. Everything was fine for a while, but the next thing I knew I was back on heroin and drinking two six-packs a day. Everything good vanished from my life. I couldn't look at myself in the mirror. The first time I came for treatment, I did it to keep my wife, though I wouldn't admit it, not even to myself. This time I'm here because I hate seeing me like this, and I can't stop." Mr. High was detoxed and then discharged.

After that, he split his nights between NA and AA. He also joined the TNT After-Care program. After a few months he realized that his compulsion to use was triggered by affluence. With assistance from a TNT therapist, Mr. and Mrs. High developed a strict budget, all excess was placed in a special account. The account was used for leisure pursuits only.

Mr. High was contacted four years later. He had not used drugs nor alcohol. He now averages one AA and one NA meeting per week. "But it's harder to fit two meetings per week in now than it used to be to fit in seven. The number of things I like to do has increased dramatically, and my business continues to grow. My work would monopolize all my time if I didn't set some limits." Mr. High prefers high-risk outdoor activities. Since discharge he has learned to scuba dive, surf, and snow ski. He has a boat and enjoys speed boat racing and water skiing. During the last year he spent a week horseback

packing into a wilderness area in the Northwest, and several weekends shooting whitewater rapids. At the time of the interview, Mr. High and his family were planning a trip to Alaska, and he was getting a pilot's license. "Some people wonder how we can afford to do all this. I just spend as much on my leisure and home life as I used to spend on my drugs and booze. When I spent it on drugs, we were broke because I couldn't work and use too. Now I can spend it on fun and get twice as much done at work, so I'm coming out ahead of the game."

THE CASE OF COCA BUTTER

Leisure Level: Semi-Independent

The Therapeutic Recreation Specialist received a referral for Ms. Butter the first day she was in detox. The referral called for use of standard cocaine detox protocol. Ordinarily, the detox team handles the leisure needs listed on the standard protocols established for detox. Occasionally the team asked for consultation, but they seldom sent an actual referral. For this reason, the Therapeutic Recreation Specialist made a prompt response to the referral a top priority.

The detox team welcomed the Therapeutic Recreation Specialist with resounding applause. It seemed that Coca Butter was bounding with energy. She was also on suicidal precautions. The detox unit was short-staffed that day, making it impossible to free anyone up to escort Ms. Butter off the unit. On the unit, the other clients were feeling a need for a drink to tolerate Ms. Butter.

Ms. Butter was found huddled on the floor in a corner of the detox lounge. The lounge contained an artificial waterfall and soft lights. Ms. Butter had her arms wrapped around her knees and was sobbing and rocking. Another client walked into the lounge, saw Ms. Butter, glared, and walked out.

Ms. Butter's physical had been completed. She had no medical problems to restrict her activity. No suicidal attempts had been made since admission. The precautions were based on the fact that she had attempted suicide prior to admission. Ms. Butter had been found in her closet. She had apparently been hiding in her closet for quite some time. A neighbor came over to complain about Ms. Butter's dog barking. When no one answered the door, the neighbor had called the police. When the police found Ms. Butter, she ran from the closet to the bathroom and swallowed pills. The police took her to the emergency room and then she had been transferred from emergency to TNT detox.

The Therapeutic Recreation Specialist escorted Ms. Butter to the gym. At first Ms. Butter was guarded and extremely distrustful of the Therapeutic Recreation Specialist's motives. Since the interaction was unscheduled, nothing had been planned in advance. The Therapeutic Recreation Specialist picked up the first thing that came in view, a basketball, and tossed it at Ms. Butter. Ms. Butter caught it and bounced it a couple of times. The Therapeutic Recreation Specialist commented, "Looks like you have used one of those before." Ms.

Butter responded, "I have two brothers." A game of one-on-one ensued. The exercise seemed to relax Ms. Butter. After the game, the Therapeutic Recreation Specialist provided the routine introductions and gave Ms. Butter the assessment form to complete.

Ms. Butter was returned to the detox unit. The nurse responsible for Ms. Butter's case was informed of the nature of the interaction. The nurse was also asked to call the Therapeutic Recreation Specialist when Ms. Butter's energy seemed to build back to an undesirable level. The Therapeutic Recreation Specialist went back to the daily routine.

The Nurse called an hour later. Ms. Butter was starting to get rambunctious again. The Therapeutic Recreation Specialist made another trip to the detox unit. This time Ms. Butter was standing in a hall shouting at an aide. The Therapeutic Recreation Specialist asked if Ms. Butter needed another one-on-one. This time there was no hesitation. Ms. Butter was at the door.

During the second one-on-one, Ms. Butter was introduced to a Therapeutic Recreation assistant, who took the Therapeutic Recreation Specialist's place in the game. The results were the same. Ms. Butter relaxed. On the way back to the detox unit, the Therapeutic Recreation Specialist commented that the physical exercise seemed to help. Ms. Butter was also asked if any progress on the TRI assessment had been made. Ms. Butter said she had started it. She was encouraged to finish it as soon as she returned to the unit.

The next call from the nurse came three hours later. The longer period of time was attributed to progress in the cocaine withdrawal and Ms. Butter being occupied by completion of the TRI. Fortunately, the call came when Skill Development sessions were about to begin. The Therapeutic Recreation Specialist was concerned that another physical activity session might be too strenuous, too soon, for Ms. Butter. She was introduced to the computer video games. Ms. Butter remained there the remainder of the day. Afterward she was given a laptop computer, stocked with games and a set of headphones to use in her room. She was scheduled to join the morning exercise program and the afternoon Skill Development sessions for the remainder of her detox stay. She was also told to call Therapeutic Recreation at other times, when she felt the need for activity building.

Ms. Butter's TRI assessment indicated that she was at the low "Semi-Independent" level, gaining an overall score of 68.5. (A score of 62.5 is the dividing line between "Dependent" and "Semi-Independent.") Ms. Butter was rated "Semi-Independent" on most specific areas of the TRI. Her lowest score was on Family Relations. The Therapeutic Recreation Therapist felt it was too soon in the treatment process to deal with this one. Since Ms. Butter had been living alone prior to admission, and was planning on living alone after admission, there was no indicated need to rush into resolution of this area. Ms. Butter had her own car and valid driver's license and a good job, which she planned to return to. There were no problems to consider here either. Reviewing the other areas of need, the Therapeutic Recreation Specialist decided to establish a goal

to increase physical conditioning, since Ms. Butter was already responding to a physical activity program, and to improve leisure awareness. Ms. Butter had a number of leisure skills, but had confided she always felt guilty doing them. By giving Ms. Butter permission to call for physical activity any time she felt like it, the Therapeutic Recreation Specialist had written a prescription for the substitution physical activity for cocaine use. The potential for physical activity abuse was now great. Ms. Butter would have to be withdrawn gradually from physical activity and then the use of physical activity would have to be monitored. (See the following page for Figures 12.3 and 12.4)

Ms. Butter responded to the treatment regime. Suicidal precautions were lifted after two days. After three weeks, she was attending a physical exercise session once a day. The type of physical exercise varied from day to day. She was also developing passive interests. She continued to enjoy the computer games. They were removed from her room when she left detox. She was only permitted to use them once per week, to prevent abuse of these. Leisure awareness seemed to have reached the "Independent" level after attending the specified session.

The Therapeutic Recreation Specialist came to the treatment team meeting planning to pronounce Ms. Butter "cured" and establish a maintenance goal. The group therapist had a different plan in mind. It seemed Ms. Butter had a deep distrust of self and others which had not been resolved through the detoxification from cocaine. Other team members agreed. The Therapeutic Recreation Specialist developed a recreation therapy program to meet the needs identified by the team. Ms. Butter's needs seemed to involve a variety of problems. She was impulsive, yet failed to make decisions when needed. She was overly concerned about how she appeared to others. She had a tendency to speed through activities without paying attention to details. All of these seemed to feed her distrust. The recreation therapy intervention's primary goal was to develop trust in self and others. To accomplish this, Ms. Butter's program would involve sessions used for decision making, situation response awareness, and development of play behaviors. Many sessions would be videotaped for Ms. Butter to review with her group therapist. The recreation therapy program contained the following:

Week #1: To develop 450.0 Trust of Self and Others:

    450.01 New Games (2 sessions)
    407.15 Costume Party
    410.04 Finding What's Missing

Week #2: To Develop 450.0 Trust of Self and Others:

    480.01 No Decision is A Decision
    480.02 Decision Making Practice
    407.21 Songs of Youth
    407.16 Tele-Joke

FIGURE 12.3

COCA BUTTER TRI TREATMENT PLAN

Initial Assessment Results

TRI Item:	Opinion of Client	Level TRS	Final (Level)	Wght. Score	Maximum Possible	Goal:
1 Physical	3	3	(3)	7.5	10	+ one level
2 Education	3	3	(3)	6	8	
3 Transportation	4	4	(4)	8	8	
4 Economic	4	4	(4)	8	8	Most important:
5 Family Support	1	1	(1)	2.5	10	monitor potential
6 Stress	2	2	(2)	5	10	for process
7 Play Status	3	3	(3)	9	12	addiction
8 Problem Solving	3	3	(3)	7.5	10	
9 Leisure Skills	3	3	(3)	9	12	
10 Leisure Awareness	2	2	(2)	6	12	+ one level
		TRI Total Score:		68.5 out of	100	

FIGURE 12.4

COCA BUTTER TRI SUMMARY

Discharge Assessment Results

TRI Item:	Admission Score		Final Score	
	Level	Wght. Score	(Level)	Wght. Score
1 Physical	(3)	7.5	(4)	10
2 Education	(3)	6	(3)	6
3 Transportation	(4)	8	(4)	8
4 Economic	(4)	8	(4)	8
5 Family Support	(1)	2.5	(2)	5
6 Stress	(2)	5	(3)	9
7 Play Status	(3)	9	(3)	9
8 Problem Solving	(3)	7.5	(3)	7.5
9 Leisure Skills	(3)	9	(4)	12
10 Leisure Awareness	(2)	6	(4)	12
TRI Total Score:	(Semi-Indep.)	68.5	(Semi-Indep.)	86.5 = 18 point gain

Week #3: To develop 450.0 Trust of Self and Others:

    480.03 Failure to Deliberate
    407.12 Ridiculous Situations
    410.06 Creating Good Space
            Evaluation of Outcomes

Ms. Butter responded to the plan. With her group counselor's assistance, she was able to see how she had interacted with others and with herself. She found the courage to trust herself and to take social interaction risks without the use of cocaine. She was discharged and dealt with family relationships as an outpatient. She attended Cocaine Anonymous regularly.

THE CASE OF WILDIR I. SHROSE

(Leisure Level: Dependent)

Consider the case of Mr. Wildir I. Shrose. At the age of 29, he had been binge-drinking for 17 years. Upon admission, he was 6'2" and weighed 129 pounds. His coordination, balance, and agility were as good as that of any brittle wooden puppet. He could trip over an ant. At the sound of a pin dropping he would jump out of his skin. His left arm had been broken several times and finally pinned back onto his shoulder. The damage had resulted from a gunshot wound acquired while drinking, followed by an accident which occurred from trying to drive a motorcycle while drunk and while wearing a body cast. The arm and shoulder had also suffered from a number of slips and falls that occurred while drinking. His continued drinking had retarded mending. The cast had remained on for 18 months. When it was removed, his arm had "shriveled to nothing." The doctors has told him he would never use it again. Mr. Shrose refused to listen to the doctors before or after the cast was removed. His arm now had some minimal function. Mr. Shrose stated that he was unable to participate in any recreation activities due to the condition of his shoulder. As a result of the above, and severe withdrawal symptoms, his physical health was scored "At Risk."

The detox counselor observed that Mr. Shrose hid himself from others. His eyes hid in shadows created by long hair and a pulled-down hat. His body hid in oversized clothing. He quickly formed relationships with other clients and hid in the middle of a tight cluster of friends. He traveled through the treatment center's daily routine in the center of a tight knot of bodyguards. He also hid his feelings in an incredible web of humor. Staff desiring private conferences with Mr. Shrose would have to go find him, or reschedule appointments with him. He would not voluntarily keep an appointment for any private conference. After staff tracked him down, the inner man would be blocked or sidetracked, never emerging. Meaningful topics would be artistically avoided. When pressed for personal information he would take the offensive, attack, and run back to his bodyguards. Rather than risk offending him, some staff interacted with him at the friendly surface level. Some staff did not bother, justifying their position by saying, "He's hopeless, a dozen-plus admissions to other treatment facilities, I don't know why they even bothered to admit him." Interaction with all team members revealed basic patterns of denial.

It took four days for the Therapeutic Recreation Specialist to track him down, just to give him the TRI form and the customary welcome. Mr. Shrose's reading skills were assumed to be excellent, since the Therapeutic Recreation Specialist finally found him hiding in the library, reading a book. The Therapeutic Recreation Specialist dropped the routine welcome speech and engaged the client in a discussion of the book. The discussion of the book revealed that Mr. Shrose had a photographic memory, allowing him to read a 400-page book in an hour. Mr. Shrose quickly discounted his special talent by saying, "It's never done me any good, flunked out of every college in the state."

Since Mr. Shrose scored "Independent" in education, the Therapeutic Recreation Specialist asked him to complete the assessment without assistance. The next day the Therapeutic Recreation Specialist had to track Mr. Shrose down to get the form back. He had completed it. He had scored himself "Independent" in all areas. The Therapeutic Recreation Specialist confronted him by smiling and asking to see his driver's license. "I don't know where it is," he replied. The Therapeutic Recreation Specialist did not respond, only stood, blocking the exit path and looking into the shadow under his hat. Mr. Shrose laughed, "Last time I saw it was about 4 years ago when the judge said, 'Son, being drunk on four wheels is bad enough, but on two? You ain't never seeing this thing again.' That's where I lost it." Mr. Shrose was calmly given a blank TRI assessment

form and two choices: sit down with the Therapeutic Recreation Specialist and accurately complete it, or sit down and accurately complete it alone. He said he would do it alone. One hour later the Therapeutic Recreation Specialist found the accurately completed form slipped under her office door. The assessment appeared more realistic. This time, Mr. Shrose had rated himself "Independent" on education, play status, creative problem solving, leisure skills and leisure awareness, but the other scores had been reduced. The Therapeutic Recreation Specialist felt that some of the remaining scores were still too high. (See Figure 12.5)

The Therapeutic Recreation Specialist found Mr. Shrose hiding in a lounge. She and Mr. Shrose reviewed his assessment and completed the summary. Mr. Shrose had mixed reactions to the scoring process. He seemed interested, amused, and appreciative of the process. At the same time, he seemed to be anticipating an axe attack from some unknown source. The fact that he scored on the high side of "Dependent" surprised him. There seemed to be a flash of disbelief and hope which were quickly swallowed by witty negativity, "This means things could get a lot worse, but I don't know how."

Mr. Shrose said he could not remember doing any activities before he started drinking. While drinking he had played basketball before his arm "got in the way." Since then he had played poker. He said poker was a satisfying positive experience (except when he lost his Mad Dog money in the betting). He denied a need for more activities, and denied that drinking had any impact on the way he spent his time. His future plans were to do basically the same things as before, "just not drink while doing them." The Therapeutic Recreational Specialist calmly supported every person's right to disagree and then explained why she disagreed.

The Therapeutic Recreational Specialist summarized her conclusions as she entered the TRI scores into the computer, while Mr. Shrose observed. "The TRI shows some problems that I cannot help you solve, such as transportation. We seem to agree about your present physical status, but not about your potential. In my opinion, there are a number of activities that you can do in spite of the condition of your arm. You seem to think that participation in physical activities is hopeless. While you are here I would like you to attend physical restoration sessions. Start with the non-strenuous exercise program and build yourself back up. This week you will attend the session required of all clients plus the following:

401.0 Physical Restoration

- 101.0 Designing Your Fitness Maintenance Program For Use Now and After Discharge
- 101.1 It's Possible and It Feels Good to Be Physically Fit.
- 101.1 Physical Impairments Can Be Overcome.
- 401.01 Supervised Restoration
- 221.2 Aerobics Designed for Persons Over 60

FIGURE 12.5

	WILDIR I. SHROSE TRI TREATMENT PLAN					
	Initial Assessment Results					
TRI Item:	Opinion of Client	Level TRS	Final (Level)	Wght. Score	Maximum Possible	Goal:
1 Physical	1	1	(1)	2.5	10	+ at least one
2 Education	4	4	(4)	8	8	
3 Transportation	1	1	(1)	2	8	
4 Economic	3	3	(3)	6	8	Most important:
5 Family Support	3	1	(1)	2.5	10	leisure awareness
6 Stress	3	2	(3)	7.5	10	and physical
7 Play Status	4	4	(4)	12	12	conditioning
8 Problem Solving	4	4	(4)	10	10	
9 Leisure Skills	4	1	(1)	3	12	+ at least one
10 Leisure Awareness	4	1	(1)	3	12	+ at least one
		TRI Total Score:		56.5 out of	100	

When the doctor agrees that your physical condition has adequately progressed, you may select activities of interest. Try bowling with your right hand. Try ping pong with your right hand. We can discuss other activities when you get ready for them. The following is a list of activities I believe you will be capable of doing before you are discharged, if you choose to.

401.02   Disability Rehabilitation

211.2   Beach Ball Volleyball
211.2   How To Play Croquet
211.2   How to Play Miniature Golf
211.2   How To Play Shuffleboard
221.2   How to Swim for Fitness
221.2   Introduction to Tai Chi
221.2   New Games For Fitness
241.2   Low Cost Party and Family Games for Exercise
241.2   Picnic Games for Mild Exercise (Water Balloon Toss)
241.2   Social Dance Class (Slow Dancing)
251.2   Walking for Health and Fitness
311.2   Lazy Sports
321.2   Gym Schedule
321.2   Mild Morning Exercise
351.2   A.M. Walk
351.2   Open Swim Hours
351.2   Walking for Health and fitness
211.3   How to Bowl
211.3   How to Golf
211.3   How to Participate in Team Swims
211.3   How to Play Competitive Water Games
211.3   How to Play Volleyball
221.3   How to Rumba Dance
221.3   Introduction to Martial Arts

221.3   Low-Impact Aerobics
231.3   Gardeneering
231.3   Working with Wood, Saws, and Hammers (234.3)
241.3   New Games for Fitness
241.3   Picnic Games for Moderate Exercise
241.3   Square Dance
251.3   Outdoor Gardening
271.3   Introduction to Ballet, Tap Dancing
311.3   Gym Schedule
321.3   Bowling
321.3   Water Fun
351.3   Nature Hike
351.3   Weight Room Schedule
391.3   High Risk (Diving, Horseback Riding, Adventure Courses.)
391.3   Participation in Outdoor Activities

"It seems we disagree on other points," the Therapeutic Recreation Specialist continued. "I think you are here because of alcoholism. I think your health problems, transportation problems, family problems, and 12-plus admissions to alcohol treatment facilities have resulted from alcoholism. I don't think you can do the same things you did before without drinking. I think your free time is very empty except when you are drinking. When you are drinking, blackouts erase your free time. I think you need to look at the hows and whys of your free time. I would suggest evaluating your free time to make it rewarding and fun after discharge. Attending the Leisure Education sessions can help if you recognize the need for making changes. Many people are uncomfortable doing new things and meeting new people. Are you one of those people? Is that why it took five days to get to this point? Sometimes fear might get in the way by waiting to start new things after discharge. I suggest that you start new things while you are here. By discharge they sometimes will be familiar. There is a lot that can be done but nothing will help until the need to make changes is recognized and the impact that alcohol has on your life is understood."

Mr. Shrose sat for a moment and then summarized his points. "I don't need your damn recreation or your damned advice. Who do you think you are? Just get off my back."

A treatment plan was developed for Mr. Shrose at a treatment team conference. It was decided that the most important first step was to break down the denial. Even though Mr. Shrose had been in treatment 12 times, he still had not made it through step one. The force of his response to the Therapeutic Recreation Specialist was an indication of the pent-up anger lurking behind the friendly superficial facade. He would be required to attend the Recreation Therapy Ventilation sessions while working on step one. After that, the team would meet with him to establish further treatment goals. Hopefully he would then agree to participate in other aspects of the program. Though the treatment team had the power to require immediate participation from Mr. Shrose, they felt it more important to have him personally and voluntarily commit to the treatment program. (Required participation had not helped during his previous admissions.) It was agreed to require the activities that would begin the physical restoration process. His physical condition needed a lot of work. Waiting to start this might prevent completion of the program before discharge. The team also hoped that the program would prove to Mr. Shrose that he was capable of doing more, thus developing incentive to change. He seemed to be limited by his denial, his anger, his lack of self-confidence, his negative attitude, and that arm was a great excuse for the continuation of self-pity. It was also suggested that Mr. Shrose was a good candidate for the Recovery-Bound Program (TNT's version of a challenge or adventure course). At this time, his physical condition would not permit use of it. The initial treatment plan for Mr. Shrose included Recreation Therapy sessions for physical restoration [401.0], anger ventilation [440], and dealing with denial wherever it occurred.

The Therapeutic Recreational Specialist consulted the Medical Team Manager before implementing the Anger Ventilation sessions. The physician felt that Mr. Shrose might break something if he were involved in an activity requiring running or quick maneuvering. He felt that the risk of a heart attack was low. The activities selected were nerf ball throws and wet sponge smashes.

It took the treatment team less than one week to break down Mr. Shrose's denial. He finally "broke" in an Anger Ventilation session. Mr. Shrose's Group Therapist Treatment Team Nurse and Therapeutic Recreation Specialist participated in the ventilation sessions along with ten other clients. The group therapist maintained the role of moderator. The nurse assumed the role of heckler. The Therapeutic Recreation Specialist incited riot. The nurse would bring up some situation that had occurred on the unit, ridicule Mr. Shrose about it, then ask him if that was how he behaved with his wife or "was he so self-sufficient that he'd never been married?" Mr. Shrose twinged at this and the nurse zeroed in on the topic of

women and marriage. Each time the nurse made a comment, the group therapist would gently toss a Nerf™ ball to Mr. Shrose as the Therapeutic Recreation Specialist would shout something like, "Don't take that from her, show her how it makes you really feel!" Mr. Shrose began to break when he admitted he had been married, not once but several times. The nurse continued. The group therapist continued to smile and gently toss the ball to Mr. Shrose. The Therapeutic Recreation Specialist continued to shout, "Throw it hard!" Mr. Shrose began trusting and listening to the Therapeutic Recreation Specialist. He began throwing as he was told to throw. The nurse asked why he wouldn't talk about his marriages. Then the Therapeutic Recreation Specialist shouted, "Throw it and tell her how you feel!" Mr. Shrose shouted, "My wife won't let me near my kids. She hates me. I don't talk about it because I'm a miserable failure at marriage." The Therapeutic Recreation Specialist continued, "Tell her why you're a miserable failure." "Because I'm a damned drunk!" shouted Mr. Shrose. The group counselor calmly took control of the action, "You are not a drunk, Mr. Shrose," then continued as he walked closer, "You are an alcoholic." There was a pause as awareness seeped through the veil of denial. The Therapeutic Recreation Therapist and the nurse moved the other participants and the action away, as the group counselor sat down on the floor with Mr. Shrose. The group counselor continued, "Tell me something, when have you ever failed miserably without drinking?" "The last time I tried to quit drinking. That's why I'm here. I can't stay sober." "You're here because you don't know how to stay sober, not because you failed. You can't do it alone. We can't do it unless you will trust us and let us help you. I promise you this, if you will put as much energy into trying to stay sober as you have into drinking and fighting us, and holding onto your anger, you will stay sober. Your treatment team is meeting today at 3:00 p.m. If you want to help, come to the meeting and together we'll develop a treatment program. If you are not ready for help, don't bother to show. Don't answer me now, just think about it until 3:00 p.m." The group counselor held out his hand and Mr. Shrose hesitantly shook it. As Mr. Shrose walked to the door, the nurse came over to him. She said nothing but looked straight in his shadowed eyes and held out her hand. Mr. Shrose said nothing but paused, started to leave, returned and shook her hand before vanishing out the door.

The treatment team meeting began at 3:00 p.m. Mr. Shrose was waiting at the door when the team members arrived. Mr. Shrose agreed to the treatment plan, which included leisure education and a physical conditioning program, followed by the Recovery-Bound Program. Mr. Shrose also agreed to two Skill Development sessions of the Therapeutic Recreation Specialist's choice. The overall Therapeutic Recreation goal was to increase his leisure independence level from 59.5 to 76.5. This required an increase of two levels in physical conditioning, leisure skills, and leisure awareness.

Mr. Shrose not only attended, he participated in his treatment program. He attended the morning and evening exercise program. Within two weeks, his endurance, balance and agility increased to the level required for entering the Recovery Bound Program. He failed to appear at the scheduled time to begin the Recovery-Bound Program. His Therapeutic Recreation Specialist found him in the library. She met a verbal attack before she could open her mouth. "My problems is I'm a drunk! I'm not jumpin' through hoops for you or anybody else!" She responded, "You agreed to participate in two activities of my choice. There's a van leaving for the bowling alley. Be on the van or be on the Recovery-Bound Course."

He was on the van. At the bowling alley he tried to hide in his bodyguard friends. The first game played was called low ball. The object of the game is to get the lowest score possible. A gutter ball counts as a strike. Mr. Shrose agreed to participate when his bodyguards pressured him into trying. He got high score rolling straight gutter balls for the first eight frames. The Therapeutic Recreation Specialist began to think she had made a big mistake. Perhaps he really could not learn to bowl with his right hand. But Mr. Shrose began to laugh, "never knew the gutter could be worth so much!" The next two games were played by the regular rules. Mr. Shrose's approach looked like a stork that had escaped from a cartoon, but he scored a 70 on the second game and 190 on the third. The Therapeutic Recreation Specialist decided that anyone who can bowl a 190 could make it through the Recovery-Bound Program. The following day, the Therapeutic Recreation Specialist observed Mr. Shrose playing right-handed ping pong with one of his bodyguards.

The day before discharge, Mr. Shrose was scheduled for his discharge planning meeting with the Therapeutic Recreation Specialist. He arrived 10 minutes early. They repeated TRI assessment. All goals were attained. (See Figure 12.6) Mr. Shrose was now rated "Semi-Independent" with a score of 76.0. Mr. Shrose had increased in physical health five points. Leisure awareness and leisure skills had each increased six points. The major change was evidenced in the agreement of scoring between therapist and client. Mr. Shrose now recognized the impact of alcohol on his leisure, and recognized the need for making changes. Mr. Shrose admitted that his leisure while drinking and before drinking had been a negative experience. He also admitted that he was uncomfortable with the unfamiliar. "I promised to do two activities of your choice, what's the other one?" he asked. The Therapeutic Recreation Specialist responded, "Which ever one scares you the most." Mr. Shrose got up and walked out without a response. Two days later he attended a social dance class.

FOLLOW-UP SUMMARY

It took the follow-up coordinator several days to contact Mr. Shrose. Just as the coordinator began to wonder if he had fallen back into his old habit of hiding, he appeared at TNT. He had heard from a friend that TNT was trying to contact him. Since he had been able to catch an earlier flight than usual, he had some time and decided to stop by on his way home. The staff did not recognize him at first. He was now 185 pounds, and walked with quick, smooth, fluent movements. He had also cut his hair and lost his hat, revealing a handsome smiling face. The follow-up coordinator re-administered the TRI and found Mr. Shrose was now "Independent" on all items.

Mr. Shrose did not attend any of the center's programs after discharge. He did attend AA from discharge until present. Mr. Shrose remarried and lives with his wife and one son. He reports he is on good terms with his sisters and brothers, several ex-wives, and his two other sons. Working as a consultant for an international corporation, he was traveling all over the United States. Most of his free time now occurred on airplanes. He used it reading, talking with other passengers, and learning a foreign language by listening to cassettes. Weekend time was spent with family and friends in a variety of activities.

During his first year of sobriety, he and his AA sponsor started bowling on a league and had won several trophies. He had managed to adapt a gun for one-hand use and had joined a hunting club, though he spent more time playing cards than hunting.

FIGURE 12.6

WILDER I. SHROSE TRI SUMMARY					
Discharge Assessment Results					
	Admission Score		Final Score		
TRI Item:	Level	Wght. Score	(Level)	Wght. Score	
1 Physical	(1)	2.5	(3)	7.5	
2 Education	(4)	8	(4)	8	
3 Transportation	(1)	2	(1)	2	
4 Economic	(3)	6	(3)	6	
5 Family Support	(1)	2.5	(1)	2.5	
6 Stress	(3)	7.5	(4)	10	
7 Play Status	(4)	12	(4)	12	
8 Problem Solving	(4)	10	(4)	10	
9 Leisure Skills	(1)	3	(3)	9	
10 Leisure Awareness	(1)	3	(3)	9	
TRI Total Score: (Dependent)		56.5	(Semi-Indep.)	76.0 = 19.5 point gain	

"When I was first approached about my recreation habits, I thought the girl had lost her mind. I knew how bad it felt to have time on my hands, but I had no idea how good it could be to have some free time. I really see the value of it now. My problem is now I just don't have enough time to do everything I want to do. Sometimes I get running so fast I have to stop and say, 'what's most important? Do it and forget the rest.' A lot of times, what's most important is just being with my family."

THE CASE OF VAL EYUM YUM

(Leisure Level: Dependent)

Mrs. Yum was 47 and slightly underweight. A mother of two adult children, she coexisted with her husband. This career-oriented woman had a reputation for being a shrewd operator and an aggressive wheeler-dealer. In the business world she was applauded for seeing what she wanted and going after it until she got it. Mrs. Yum had built her career on the assumption that the correct response to a "no" is a new strategy, a new plan of attack. In her personal life she was seen by others as overpowering and difficult to be around unless she got her own way. She and her husband lived under the same roof. He lived in the lower floor of the house, while she lived in the upper floor. The only time they shared each other's company was during business-oriented social affairs. Both Mr. and Mrs. Yum were very conscious of their images in the public eye. Upon admission, she promptly threatened to sue the Center if word of her presence leaked out.

Mrs. Yum did not condone the abuse of alcohol. She requested a private room, and separate accommodations because she was not like "those people." She didn't have an alcohol problem. Her problem was her nerves. (Naturally, her request was denied.)

The detox counselor worked closely with Mrs. Yum's family to maneuver her into the admission. He was able to provide the treatment team with detailed information about Mrs. Yum. It seemed that 10 years before admission, a routine physical had revealed that Mrs. Yum was overweight. During the discussion of her weight problem, she had confided in her physician. She was having difficulty sleeping. Trying to balance the pressures of marriage, teenagers at home, and the pressures of her career were overwhelming her. She could handle it all during the day. But at night, her mind would not shut down. No matter what she tried, she would find herself cleaning out the refrigerator instead of sleeping. The next morning she would feel exhausted. All she saw in the mirror was a tired fat person staring back at her. She wondered how much longer she could cope without adequate rest. She hated herself when she was fat. The good doctor had listened as he wrote out a prescription. "Take one of these at bedtime, or when you're feeling tense. And these will help you control your diet. Overweight and stress is an unhealthy combination. It can lead to serious health problems. You should slow down. If you have any problems give me a call," he said. And so she did. One at night, and she slept all night. One before a battle

with a young entrepreneur pip-squeak, and she could sweep him under the carpet and still remain calm and in control. She was never hungry, thanks to the other pills the good doctor had prescribed. Each morning trip to the mirror was an exhilarating boost to the ego.

After a while the pills quit working. Sleep was difficult again. She reported this to the good doctor and he prescribed a slightly stronger dose. She was back in control and felt great. Over the years, stress took its toll (or so she thought). Her nervous condition continued to get worse. Why bother the good but busy doctor with her problems? She knew what he would say. It was just a matter of increasing the dose.

As time went by, it became necessary to consult the good doctor on a number of occasions for other problems. She was sleeping and looking good but was feeling sluggish. The good doctor prescribed amphetamines. After a while, Mrs. Yum began experiencing mood swings and the good doctor suggested a consult with a specialist. The specialist was a discreet psychiatrist who placed her on reserpine less than an hour after meeting her. Over the years, Mrs. Yum established rapport with several good doctors and always maintained an adequate supply of legally prescribed stimulants, depressants, antidepressants, and antipsychotic agents. She sometimes met herself at the door. She sometimes saw two Mrs. Yums in her mirror. But that's the price one has to pay for living a successful life with bad nerves.

One day she was called into her boss's office. To her surprise, her husband, her children, her boss, and the TNT detox counselor were sitting together in the office. They proceeded to explain to her that she was addicted to pills. They described crisis after crisis and insisted that they resulted from her abuse of prescription drugs. They told her that her nerves were fine except when she was experiencing withdrawal symptoms. She was shocked. But not half as shocked as when her boss gave her a choice. She could be admitted to TNT immediately using her sick leave and then come back to work when TNT said she was ready, or she would be placed on immediate leave of absence without pay. As soon as she agreed to the admission, her daughter handed Mrs. Yum's packed suitcase to the TNT Detox Counselor and she was on her way to the treatment facility.

Mrs. Yum had no leisure activities. Since early childhood, she had successfully avoided having any free time. She was a straight "A" student and a classic overachiever from the day she was born. Within 24 hours after admission she had found her way to the Therapeutic Recreation computer room and was developing programs for the promotion of spectrographic dialysis units. She had also unwittingly intimidated every client in the center, and half of the staff. It was obvious that Mrs. Yum required detox from work as well as from valium, quaaludes, librium, seconal, methedrine, reserpine, and so on. There was also the weight problem and sleeplessness, which had started the pill-popping dependency. It was also obvious that Mrs. Yum would be on detox for weeks. (See Figure 12.7, p. 208) Her lab report indicated a mixture of stimulants, barbiturates, and tranquilizers, with valium being the most preva-

FIGURE 12.7

VAL EYUM YUM TRI TREATMENT PLAN

Initial Assessment Results

TRI Item:	Opinion of Client	Level TRS	Final Score (Level)	Wght. Score	Maximum Possible	Goal:
1 Physical	1	1	(2)	5	10	+ at least one
2 Education	4	4	(4)	8	8	
3 Transportation	1	1	(4)	8	8	Most important:
4 Economic	3	3	(4)	8	8	leisure awareness
5 Family Support	1	2	(2)	5	10	
6 Stress	3	2	(2)	5	10	+ one level
7 Play Status	4	4	(1)	3	12	
8 Problem Solving	4	4	(2)	5	10	
9 Leisure Skills	1	1	(1)	3	12	+ at least one
10 Leisure Awareness	1	1	(1)	3	12	+ at least one
TRI Total Score:				53 out of	100	

lent. It would take days for the Medical Team Manager to be sure he had substituted the right mixture and quantities of drugs into her system before he could begin withdrawing the drugs. The reduction of drug amounts would have to be very gradual in order to prevent seizures (always a concern when barbiturates are involved). Mrs. Yum was in a total state of shock at the medical manager's news. She had never purchased a drug illegally. She knew nothing of how to buy them on a street corner. Now she was being told that the cocaine addict and the heroin addict, admitted on the same day, would be feeling fine in a few days and it was going to take her weeks!

Therapeutic Recreation planning and team treatment planning had begun weeks before Mrs. Yum was admitted. The detox counselor had contacted the Therapeutic Recreation Specialist before he had gone to pick up Mrs. Yum. The detox counselor had met with the employer and family on several occasions. He had a good idea of what she would be like. He had shared his opinions with the treatment team. Though nothing could be implemented until Mrs. Yum had been admitted and medically evaluated, several alternatives had been discussed and were ready and waiting. The detox counselor had warned that routine procedures would not be adequate to keep Mrs. Yum busy during detox. If she had one minute to think, she would run away. Mrs. Yum's dash to the computer room had validated the detox counselor's concerns. The detox counselor had gone to the crisis intervention meeting with a request from the Therapeutic Recreation Specialist. Mrs. Yum's dash to the computer room had come on the heels of her Therapeutic Recreation referral. The Therapeutic Recreation Specialist called Mrs. Yum's place of employment to activate the request. The next day a package arrived for Mrs. Yum. It was a feasibility study for a project which was dear to Mrs. Yum's heart. She had been given permission to develop the idea and present it when she returned to work, provided that she stayed at TNT and got "cured." The note in the package also reminded Mrs. Yum that if she didn't stay, there would be no

need to work on the project, since it was difficult to present proposals while standing in unemployment lines.

The Therapeutic Recreation Specialist found Mrs. Yum in her room happily working on the project. The reading materials, games, and TRI form, left the previous day, had not been touched. The Therapeutic Recreation Specialist was not able to get Mrs. Yum's attention until Mrs. Yum found out that the Therapeutic Recreation Specialist was responsible for her having the project. Rapport and rules were then quickly established. Treatment would have to come first. The TRI form would have to be completed (as well as assignments from other team members) before work on the project. Mrs. Yum was not informed that there was a goal to detox her from work as well as drugs. That would come later. [420.02]

In keeping with the goal, the Therapeutic Recreation Specialist visited Mrs. Yum each day. Each day the visit was kept light, social, and superficial. Each day the length of the visit was increased. Each day the Therapeutic Recreation Specialist assigned Mrs. Yum a leisure task that would take more time to complete than the previous day's task. Some of the tasks were to go for a walk, to eat lunch with someone and talk to them about anything except work, to listen to music, to watch TV for an hour, and to play a card or table game with one of the other clients. By the time drug detox had been completed, Mrs. Yum was splitting her time between work and leisure for the first time in her life.

During detox, the TRI form was assigned to Mrs. Yum, one item at a time. If it had been given to her all at once, she would have completed it all at once, with little thought involved. Mrs. Yum needed to slow down. Each part was reviewed and discussed with Mrs. Yum as it was completed.

Mrs. Yum began required leisure education sessions while still in detox. [100.0] The comparison of leisure habits before and during addiction revealed little that surprised the Therapeutic Recreation Specialist but much to surprise Mrs. Yum. Mrs. Yum had listed leisure activities such as studying for

FIGURE 12.8

VAL EYUM YUM TRI SUMMARY

Discharge Assessment Results

	Admission Score		Final Score	
TRI Item:	Level	Wght. Score	(Level)	Wght. Score
1 Physical	(2)	5	(3)	7.5
2 Education	(4)	8	(4)	8
3 Transportation	(4)	8	(4)	8
4 Economic	(4)	8	(4)	8
5 Family Support	(2)	5	(2)	5
6 Stress	(2)	5	(3)	7.5
7 Play Status	(1)	3	(6)	6
8 Problem Solving	(2)	5	(2)	5
9 Leisure Skills	(1)	3	(4)	12
10 Leisure Awareness	(1)	3	(4)	12
TRI Total Score: (Dependent)		53.0	(Semi-Indep.)	79.0 = 26 point gain

exams as her fun before becoming addicted, and preparing for business meetings as her fun during her addicted life. Initially Mrs. Yum did not see a need for more activities, stating that she never had enough time as it was. She viewed her workaholic habits as being positive both before and during her addiction. Both Mrs. Yum and the Therapeutic Recreation Specialist agreed that her addiction had not changed her patterns. Indeed, addiction had resulted from, and successfully sustained, an unhealthy lifestyle. (The Therapeutic Recreation Specialist did not make this point to Mrs. Yum. It was too early in the treatment process. Referring to work as unhealthy would have blown Mrs. Yum out of the water and set her recovery program back one hundred years.)

During completion of one leisure education form, Mrs. Yum placed a question mark next to the recognition of the impact of addiction on her lifestyle. The Therapeutic Recreation Specialist marked it as not appropriate. The question mark was a healthy sign. It indicated that the crisis intervention meeting and the admission had made some inroads into her denial system. She was not ready to accept her addiction, but she could no longer totally deny its existence. The Therapeutic Recreation Specialist saw no impact of addiction on Mrs. Yum's leisure because there was no leisure to impact upon. (This point was shared with Mrs. Yum, adding a little more confusion to Mrs. Yum's frame of mind.)

Mrs. Yum and the Therapeutic Recreation Specialist disagreed on desired treatment outcomes. Mrs. Yum's plan for the future was to go back doing the same workaholic things and just not use so many different types of prescription medications. The Therapeutic Recreation Specialist suppressed a desire to attack Mrs. Yum's statement. This again was a healthy step forward. Prior to admission Mrs. Yum had no intention of making any changes. Now she was conceding that some form of change was needed. The shift from discontinuing some drugs to all drugs would be best handled in group therapy after the detox phase. The Therapeutic Recreation Specialist focused discussion on the importance and need to

include leisure pursuits in Mrs. Yum's future plans. Mrs. Yum agreed, but it seemed to be only lip service. Since no leisure activities were listed, the Therapeutic Recreation Specialist did not comment on the drug enhancement aspect of the activities. The Therapeutic Recreation Specialist did strongly suggest that Mrs. Yum consider the impact of drugs on her plans and discuss this issue when she got into group therapy. The Therapeutic Recreation Specialist also said that she would make this issue known to Mrs. Yum's group therapist. That way if Mrs. Yum should forget to bring it up, the group therapist could remind her.

The same basic discussion prevailed after each part of the TRI was completed and after each required leisure education session was attended. Mrs. Yum denied the existence of leisure. The Therapeutic Recreation Specialist insisted that leisure existed and was necessary to life. There was a shred of light glimmering through a well of denial and a life of workaholism. Two new insights were gained. In reviewing the session on balance, Mrs. Yum indicated that she was comfortable doing unfamiliar things. When asked for examples, Mrs. Yum could not remember doing anything new or different. The Therapeutic Recreation Specialist suggested that spending her time in her room, working on her project was a way of avoiding new and unfamiliar situations. In the discussion of priorities, Mrs. Yum was masterful at setting priorities in her career life, but had never considered applying the same principles to the void she called her personal life.

When Mrs. Yum was released from detox, the Therapeutic Recreation Specialist used the TRI and information from the required leisure education sessions to open discussion of Therapeutic Recreation treatment planning. "We seem to have some basic differences in our approaches and philosophies about life. Yours is one of work and mine is one of play. I would like to learn more about your lifestyle and I would like you to learn more about mine." After this introduction, the Therapeutic Recreation Specialist got Mrs. Yum to agree to attend all additional Leisure Education sessions offered at

TNT. She also agreed to attend one of each type of Skill Development session offered. Sessions that dealt with relaxation and weight control were most appealing to her.

For Leisure Awareness and Skill Development:

100.1 Leisure as Related to Work and Substance Abuse

100.2 Drawing From Paradise

100.2 Haven't Got Time Or Won't Take Time? A Matter of Priorities

100.2 Leisure Values Clarification: Living verses Existing

100.2 Time, Priorities, and Leisure: Finding Time for Fun

100.3 Matching Needs, Skills, and Activities with Activity Analysis

100.3 Sources of Leisure Guilt

100.3 Will Yesterday's Fun Be Fun Tomorrow?

119.1 Overview of Other-Competitive Non-Physical and Physical Activities

129.1 Overview of Self-Competitive Non-Physical and Physical Activities

139.1 Overview of Productive Activities

179.1 Overview of Arts and Crafts.

179.1 Overview of Creative Writing Activities

179.1 Overview of Dance

179.1 Overview of Drama

179.1 Overview of Music and Song

189.1 Overview of Spiritual Activities

199.1 Overview of Outdoor Activities

199.1 Overview of Risk Taking Opportunities

For Stress Reduction:

106.1 What Causes Stress and What Causes Relaxation

236.1 Fishing

266.1 How to Design a Stress Free Environment at Home

266.1 How to Select Reading Materials Stress Reduction

276.1 How to Lip-synch to Vent Stress

276.1 How to Select Music for Stress Reduction

336.1 Indoor/Outdoor Gardening

For Maintaining Fitness:

211.2 Beach ball Volleyball

211.2 How To Play Croquet

211.2 How to Play Miniature Golf

211.2 How To Play Shuffleboard

221.2 Aerobics Designed for Persons over 60

221.2 How to Swim for Fitness

221.2 Introduction to Tai Chi

221.2 New Games For Fitness

241.2 Low Cost Party and Family Games for Exercise

241.2 Picnic Games for Mild Exercise (Water Balloon Toss)

241.2 Social Dance Class (Slow Dancing)

251.2 Walking for Health and Fitness

311.2 Lazy Sports

321.2 Gym Schedule

321.2 Mild Morning Exercise

351.2 A.M. Walk

351.2 Open Swim Hours

351.2 Walking for Health and Fitness

The overall goal for Mrs. Yum's Therapeutic Recreation treatment plan was to increase leisure independence by at least 11 points. Then her plan would be reviewed. The game-plan called for and increase of three points on leisure awareness through participation in leisure education, an increase of three points through Skill Development sessions, and at least a one-level increase in physical conditioning and stress management (2.5 points each). Since a concept of leisure was nonexistent, she would have to investigate a wide variety of activities before being able to select one or two which fit her needs and interests. Recreation Therapy goals were also established to support treatment team efforts. Mrs. Yum desperately needed to develop the ability to change gears, and to balance her life. This goal would not require additional programing but careful scheduling. She would not be permitted to work all day, or play all day, or attend therapy all day. Her schedule would be designed to develop a daily routine which included a wide variety of experiences every day. She needed to learn to balance working and playing, eating and sleeping, relaxing and exercising, as well as being useful and worthless. Session 100.0, leisure planning for today, would be attended daily.

Most of all, she needed to learn to play. She needed to leave her work behind and develop playful social relationships. The treatment team felt that if Mrs. Yum could learn to change her approach to her personal life, her family support would be greatly increased. The final measure of Mrs. Yum's growth along these lines would be voluntary participation in Re-Creation, not as a planner of some event, but as an equal participant with her peers.

The initial treatment plan was rewritten as Mrs. Yum progressed. She responded to most of the sessions that offered a potential for management of stress and weight without pills. Then she seemed to stall. A treatment team conference decided that there was one big fear which would have to be dealt with before further progress could be made. Mrs. Yum was still afraid of getting caught with nothing to do. She was assigned to session 420.01, Nothingness. Her group therapist co-led the session. During the session, Mrs. Yum became aware of her fear of having nothing to do for the first time. She also discovered that she could handle the situation.

Mrs. Yum became active in Re-Creation, but her style of interaction was abrasive to other clients and she did not seem to understand why, or what, or how. She was assigned to situation response awareness sessions 410.01 and 410.02. During I Yi Yi, she became aware of her directiveness. The session of Grab It was videotaped and she could not believe her eyes. She had never realized how she steamrolled over others before. After that, she was constantly catching herself participating in unwanted interactions and was continually stopping to rephrase statements. Other clients responded. Seeing that she was trying to change, they did what they could to help her. As the clientele tried to help her, she realized that being like them was not such a bad thing after all.

By discharge, Mrs. Yum had completed all required leisure education sessions and skill development sessions. (See Figure 12.8, p. 209) She had developed new leisure options for post-discharge. She stated that the turning point in her leisure comprehension came in a session that discussed dating. She had suddenly realized that she had always dated for the purpose of improving her social status and prestige. She had never dated for fun. She then realized that she had applied the same selection criteria to all her "leisure pursuits." At last, she understood that the end product of a true leisure pursuit was a pleasurable experience. Shortly after that she met true recreation during a scavenger hunt. She laughed for days. She could not believe something so stupid and childish could be so much fun and feel so good. After that, she was an active participant in every Re-Creation event offered. New clients had a hard time believing the stories; that this once was a cold-hearted, intimidating workhorse.

The most important leisure lesson came to Mrs. Yum on the day of discharge. She had a good time in treatment. At the same time, she had learned life-saving lessons about herself. She now knew that pills were not for her; she was an addict. But most amazing, with all this she had still found the time to complete her project for work. She walked out of the TNT door with her suitcase empty of pills but filled with quality work and leisure.

The follow-up coordinator found that the road was not smooth for Mrs. Yum after discharge. Her husband refused to share in her new-found leisure and her recovery. He refused to visit TNT while she was in treatment. He refused to seek counseling. He refused to attend Nar-Anon or Al-Anon. He refused to attend open NA or AA meetings. He disliked Mrs. Yum's attendance, living in constant fear that someone would discover his wife's secret. After two years of trying, Mrs. Yum finally accepted the thing she could not change. She could not change her husband's attitude. She divorced him and has re-created happily ever after.

THE CASE OF BUD M. WISER

(Leisure Level: Dependent)

Review of the computerized admission referral data led the Therapeutic Recreation Specialist to believe that Mr. Wiser could be handled with routine procedures. This belief was validated in the first meeting with Mr. Wiser. He implied that he was not impressed with life and was willing to do anything to change it. He was unable to complete the TRI Assessment

because his hands were shaking. The Therapeutic Specialist assured him that the shaking would go away. A meeting was scheduled for the next day. It was agreed that if Mr. Wiser's condition improved before the meeting, he would complete TRI. If not, then the Therapeutic Recreation Specialist would assist him in completing it. The next day, Mr. Wiser had responded to the withdrawal regimen and was feeling better. He had completed the TRI assessment by the next meeting. The Therapeutic Recreation Specialist used the allotted time to review the assessment results with Mr. Wiser and establish treatment goals. (See Figure 12.9)

Initially, the Therapeutic Recreation Specialist assumed that Mr. Wiser's physical condition and time constraints were the factors which had prevented the form's completion. The discussion of TRI changed the Therapeutic Recreation Specialist's mind. Mr. Wiser was found to avoid sensitive a issue: future plans. Recalling the admission data, the Therapeutic Recreation Specialist asked Mr. Wiser how long he had been retired. He had retired 3 1/2 years before admission. The Therapeutic Recreation Specialist asked, "How much did you drink before you retired?" Mr. Wiser responded, "I never touched the stuff." The change in satisfaction with leisure was reflected in Mr. Wiser's feelings about retirement as well as his addiction.

The Therapeutic Recreation Specialist asked Mr. Wiser to describe his job. He had been a production supervisor. He displayed a great deal of pride in his work, in the product he had produced, in the company he had worked for, and the awards he had won, as he talked about his job, relating story after story of humorous situations and of close friendships with other employees. Once he interrupted himself with, "I'm not boring you, am I? My wife has heard these so many times she leaves the room when I open my mouth."

When he finally stopped for a breath, the Therapeutic Recreation Specialist asked Mr. Wiser to describe his retirement. He paused, stared out the window, then shrugged his shoulders and said, "Well, you've heard the definition of being retired. To retire is to be tired twice. Too tired to work, and then tired again by not working. . ."

"Mr. Wiser, where were you when you started drinking?" "It was six months after I retired. My wife and I went to a neighborhood barbecue. I sat around watching everybody else. They were drinking and having a good time. Someone offered me a beer and I took it. Somehow everything seemed better after that. I got to drinkin' a beer now and then around the house, then a six-pack, then, well then it all got out of hand. It would be nice to go back to feeling the way I did at that neighborhood barbecue."

In a caring tone, the Therapeutic Recreation Specialist confronted the client, "Mr. Wiser, you are addicted to alcohol now. There's no going back to drinking just one. But, I think you can go back to feeling the way you did at that neighborhood barbecue, and the way you felt when you were working, without drinking." Mr. Wiser looked at the Therapeutic Recreation Specialist with hope and disbelief. The Therapeutic Recreation Specialist continued to explain the aspects of

FIGURE 12.9

			BUD M. WISER TRI TREATMENT PLAN			
			Initial Assessment Results			
TRI Item:	Opinion of Client	Level TRS	Final (Level)	Wght. Score	Maximum Possible	Goal:
1 Physical	2	2	(2)	5	10	+ at least one
2 Education	3	3	(3)	6	8	
3 Transportation	2	2	(2)	4	8	Most important:
4 Economic	3	3	(3)	6	8	leisure awareness
5 Family Support	2	2	(2)	5	10	+ one level
6 Stress	2	2	(2)	5	10	
7 Play Status	2	2	(2)	6	12	
8 Problem Solving	2	2	(2)	5	10	+ one level
9 Leisure Skills	1	1	(1)	3	12	+ at least two
10 Leisure Awareness	1	1	(1)	3	12	+ at least two
		TRI Total Score:		48 out of	100	

Therapeutic Recreation that would help Mr. Wiser adjust and find meaning in his retirement. Mr. Wiser said he was willing to try anything.

The primary goal was to move Mr. Wiser from the "Dependent" level to the "Semi-Independent" level. This would require an increase of over 19 points or more on the TRI scale. The majority of the gain could be made by increasing Mr. Walker's leisure awareness. As that improved, his leisure skills and physical status would be easier to improve. Improvement in those areas should also lead to improvements in family status. There were other areas that could easily be improved but rather than getting too spread out, it was decided to concentrate on leisure awareness and skills first. Once Mr. Wiser was at least "Semi-Independent" in these areas, then another goal would be established in a different area if needed. (It was possible that his physical health, family support, and problem solving scores would increase as a result of the overall treatment process.) Activities were selected to help Mr. Wiser realize how dependent he had become on his work, as well as to provide a system of withdrawal from work-like activities.

420.0   Process Addiction Treatment
    410.04   Finding What's Missing
    100.3   Will Yesterday's Fun Be Fun Tomorrow?
    100.1   Leisure As Related to Work and Substance Abuse

420.002 Process Addiction Withdrawal
    230.0   Client Selection of Productive Activities

101.0   Designing Your Fitness Maintenance Program For Use Now and After Discharge
    420.03   Process Addiction Monitoring

Mr. Wiser's treatment goals were met through routinely provided leisure education, skill development, and Re-Creation sessions. Mr. Wiser was given a TRI form for his wife to complete. She scored "Independent" in leisure skills and in leisure awareness. Mrs. Wiser had no problems developing leisure plans. She had developed a highly individualistic leisure lifestyle after 27 years of marriage to a workaholic. She loved her husband, but she resented his drinking and his dependency on her. Most of all, she resented her husband moping around the house with nothing to do, when she had so much she wanted to do. Mrs. Wiser's frustration was a result of the addiction and of the upset to her independent leisure caused by Mr. Wiser's retirement.

Mr. Wiser's group therapist held a conference with Mr. and Mrs. Wiser. Mrs. Wiser's leisure frustrations surfaced during the meeting. The issues were resolved within the same conference. Before retirement, Mrs. Wiser drove her husband to work and kept the car. She disliked using the car when Mr. Wiser might need it. Now that he was home all the time she felt like her wings had been clipped. When she took the car, she always felt like she had to rush back home. When she rushed back, what did she find? Mr. Wiser passed out drunk. Mr. Wiser had no idea that transportation was a problem. He quickly suggested the purchase of a second car. The other leisure issues were resolved as the Group Therapist helped Mr. and Mrs. Wiser identify frustrating time slots in their daily routine. For example, it drove Mrs. Wiser nuts trying to cook with Mr. Wiser always under foot. Mr. Wiser needed something he could do alone when Mrs. Wiser was cooking. It drove Mr. Wiser nuts to have to stop it when his wife yelled, "Dinner's ready." So Mr. Wiser agreed to come up with a list of things he would enjoy doing and yet could set aside at a moment's notice. The group therapist suggested that bouncing the leisure needs around in a leisure education session would be good way to develop a long list of things to do. Mr. Wiser followed up on the suggestion the next day.

FIGURE 12.10

	BUD M. WISER TRI SUMMARY				
	Discharge Assessment Results:				
	Admission Score		Final Score		
TRI Item:	Level	Wght. Score	(Level)	Wght. Score	
1 Physical	(2)	5	(3)	7.5	
2 Education	(3)	6	(3)	6	
3 Transportation	(2)	4	(3)	6	
4 Economic	(3)	6	(3)	6	
5 Family Support	(2)	5	(3)	7.5	
6 Stress	(2)	5	(3)	7.5	
7 Play Status	(2)	6	(3)	9	
8 Problem Solving	(2)	5	(2)	5	
9 Leisure Skills	(1)	3	(3)	9	
10 Leisure Awareness	(1)	3	(4)	12	
TRI Total Score: (Dependent)		48	(Semi-Indep.)	75.5 = 27.5 point gain	

The leisure education session turned into a brainstorming session. Mr. Wiser came away with a list of activities for each of his problem time slots. Many other participants came away with interesting activities for problem time slots they didn't even know they had.

(At TNT, treatment and Therapeutic Recreation are team efforts. Each member of the team has been cross-trained in the other's discipline. The group counselor had not planned to discuss leisure with the Wisers but the timing was right. He felt free to seize the golden moment because of the trust and communication that existed between the group counselor and the Therapeutic Recreation Specialist. A turf protection battle was not sparked by pursuing the trail of frustration which led into leisure land. The Therapeutic Recreation Specialist was neither threatened nor concerned by the situation, knowing the group counselor would refer the Wisers back to Therapeutic Recreation should the group counselor get beyond his scope of expertise.)

Originally Mr. Wiser's treatment team estimated a six-week treatment stay. He spent five days in detox and had the first step completed two days later. Two weeks later, he was in the final stages of achieving all established treatment goals. It was decided that his other needs could be met through outpatient programs. The team agreed to send Mr. Wiser on a trial weekend pass. If things went OK, he could be discharged early.

The trial visit went smoothly. The Wisers spent the first afternoon shopping for jigsaw puzzles, golf balls and clubs, and a second car. While Mrs. Wiser fixed dinner, Mr. Wiser worked on a puzzle. After dinner they went to an AA meeting together. The next morning Mr. Wiser practiced putting while Mrs. Wiser fixed breakfast. They spent some time together "chatting" after breakfast. If only they had bought a car. Mrs. Wiser wanted to go to church and Mr. Wiser wanted to go to another AA meeting. But instead of one giving into the other's desire, they found a solution. Mrs. Wiser took the car,

dropping Mr. Wiser at a friend's house. The friend was an AA who had talked Mr. Wiser into the treatment admission. Mrs. Wiser picked him up after the meeting. Mr. Wiser seemed confident upon his return to TNT. Mr. Wiser was discharged three days later.

By discharge, Mr. Wiser had made larger gains than originally anticipated. (See Figure 12.10) Mr. Wiser was admitted at the "Dependent" level with a TRI score of 48 and was discharged at the "Semi-Independent" level with a TRI score of 75.5. During his brief treatment stay, he had increased nine points on leisure awareness and six points on leisure skills. His physical condition had increased one level and problem solving, although the same level, showed improvement as a result of the withdrawal process. He also increased one level in family support as a result of the group therapist's work, and being married to a naturally tough, honest lady who loved him very much.

His leisure discharge plans included all the things listed during the leisure education, plus AA, golf, and volunteer work. Mr. Wiser's volunteer work consisted of visiting various businesses and having coffee with employees who were preparing for retirement. This is part of a retirement counseling service offered to businesses by TNT. As such, Mr. Wiser was under the direction and supervision of TNT's Therapeutic Recreation, but spent most of his time away from TNT. His new job was to help others avoid the pitfalls of retirement.

Mr. and Mrs. Wiser never got around to buying a second car. At After-Care, they reported that the issue had resolved itself. In fact there was never a real need for a second car. Mrs. Wiser's wings had been clipped by her failure to express her needs to her husband, and her fear of what might happen to a drunk Mr. Wiser if left alone.

THE CASE OF TINA BOPPER

(Leisure Level: Dependent)

At 15, Tina played a game of judge's choice and won a trip to TNT. At her trial, she had said she preferred jail but the judge said it had not done her any good the last time, that the jail space was needed for those who might be rehabilitated by the imprisoning experience. She had run away from home at age 12. "My folks told me to be in by 10. I wasn't and couldn't see any reason to go home to get harassed for it. My folks just didn't understand. Always on my case about something. So I split, just hitched a ride and did fine until that stupid trick flashed his badge."

Tina's drug of choice was anything she could get off on. Uppers, downers, booze, hallucinogens, or a combination. It didn't matter. Whatever someone had to offer, she'd take it for whatever price asked.

A sheriff's car delivered her to TNT. Her primary link to the outside world was her parole officer, who was treated as a member of her treatment team. The Therapeutic Recreation Specialist's first impression of Tina was formed during the admission process. Tina was leaning against a wall with arms folded and fists clenched. Tina blended with the plastered surface. She did not resemble a child, but an ancient inner city wall with its original purpose long forgotten. Tina's expressions sprayed across her hardened surface, like graffiti on a subway's skin. When Tina saw the swimming pool, a flash of silent excitement danced across her facade. It vanished as her nurse pointed the way to her new room.

When Tina's nurse informed Tina that she would have to keep her own room neat and clean, Tina flew into a rage. Her nurse dodged out of the door, being hit by foul verbal abuse, but narrowly missed by a flying chair. The nurse called for backup and waited for the room to land before re-entering. Seeing that she was out-numbered, Tina quietly slumped into a chair and stared at the floor. The nurse continued to inform Tina of the rules, picking up where she had left off, without a change of tone or inflection. There was no response from Tina until the nurse finished and the entourage started out the door. "Hey! Wait a minute!" The nurse stopped and looked back at Tina. "What are you going to do about this mess?" demanded Tina. The nurse smiled at Tina and said calmly, "Here at TNT we follow old Chinese proverb, he who screws it up, cleans it up."

Tina's lab work came back clean. She had been permitted to go cold turkey while in jail. The Medical Team Manager approved immediate transfer to the adolescent unit, pending resolution of her shattered room. At the recommendation of her parole officer, she was placed on full runaway precautions. (The TNT adolescent unit is a locked ward. Clients on full runaway precautions are not permitted off the unit. Partial runaway precautions permit the client to go to the cafeteria for meals or to recreation areas, when accompanied by a staff member. The majority of adolescents are initially on some form of runaway precautions.)

It took Tina three days to put her room back together. She was then transferred to the adolescent unit. While Tina was cleaning her room, the detox counselor was busy locating Tina's parents. He found her parents living in a small community 50 miles from the center. The detox counselor told Tina's mother that Tina was at TNT. She sounded relieved. Her parents agreed to come to TNT for a meeting with Tina's treatment team.

Tina's nurse recommended that it would be best not to give Tina any opportunities to act out for a while. In accordance, the Therapeutic Recreation Specialist used the interview process to complete the TRI assessment. The TRI revealed that Tina was in good health. She rated "Independent" on education even though she had discontinued her formal education. She was in the 7th grade when she ran away from home, but had been in many accelerated classes. At the time of the interview, she had no driver's license and no one to depend on for transportation. She had no means of financial support other than prostitution. "There isn't much time or money left over after my pimp takes his cut." Family support was scored "At Risk." "I think I've seen them once since I ran away. My pimp had this system. When the cops would get me, he'd have a couple of his friends come in, say they were my parents. The cops would always fall for it. Once as I was leaving, I thought I saw Mom and Dad coming in to get me." The Therapeutic Recreation Specialist had asked Tina how she felt when she thought she saw her parents. For a moment, Tina's wall slipped down, "I wanted to run and hide. It would kill them to see me like this." Then she made a quick recovery as her wall slammed back into place: "I'll see them in Hell right along with you and that tight ass Nurse and the rest of the do gooders in this world!"

She had been living in a city with a wide variety of leisure resources. The Therapeutic Recreation Specialist had some concern that there were no leisure resources available to this child if she were living in the same city as her pimp. Her Therapeutic Recreation Specialist also wondered what a 15-year-old might do to legally support herself. There was also a question of why Tina left her parents. Being told to be in by 10 did not sound like an unreasonable request.

Tina's discharge destination was unknown. Her parole officer was in favor of a geographic cure. He saw no hope for Tina if she returned to the same environment. According to TRI, Tina had good problem-solving skills, though it was easy to question how anyone with good problem-solving skills could find such self-destructive solutions for her own life. Tina was knowledgeable of a wide variety of leisure skills. She knew how to horseback ride, to play golf, tennis, football, basketball, volleyball, swim, and play card and table games. She also knew how to play the piano and dance. She used to spend her summers at a lake. After hearing the long list of leisure skills, the Therapeutic Recreation Specialist was about to mark her "Independent" in leisure awareness, too. Instead the Therapeutic Recreation Specialist asked Tina how she felt when doing these things. Tina answered, "Alone." (See Figure 12.11)

FIGURE 12.11

TINA BOPPER TRI TREATMENT PLAN

Initial Assessment Results

TRI Item:	Opinion of Client	Level TRS	Final (Level)	Wght. Score	Maximum Possible	Goal:
1. Physical	4	(4)	10	10	maintain
2 Education	4	(4)	8	8	
3 Transportation	1	(1)	2	8	Most important:
4 Economic	1	(1)	2	8	family support
5 Family Support	1	(1)	2.5	10	at least two
6 Stress	0	(0)	0	10	evaluate
7 Play Status	0	(0)	0	12	evaluate
8 Problem Solving	3	(3)	7.5	10	
9 Leisure Skills	4	(4)	12	12	
10 Leisure Awareness	1	(1)	3	12	+ at least one
	TRI Total Score:			47.0 out of 100		

Tina's treatment team met to pull the pieces together. A psychologist had been called into the case for testing. The tests revealed a girl above-average in intelligence, trapped in an angry rage. The rage was directed toward males. The source of the anger toward males was cause for speculation. The pimp was a male, the police officer who arrested her was a male, and the judge who sentenced her was a male. It was also pointed out that the anger may have existed before the arrests, before Tina ran away from home.

After these individuals shared their information, Mr. and Mrs. Bopper joined the meeting. In arranging the appointment, the detox counselor had only told the parents that Tina was at TNT, that she was safe. The team brought Mr. and Mrs. Bopper up-to-date as gently as possible. Initially both parents were shocked and angry. Tina's father was overheard grumbling to his wife, "How could you let this happen?" But when asked to repeat his statement to the group, he said "I was just wondering why this happens to kids these days. I gave her a good home, everything she needed." The team took time to give support and assurance to the parents before proceeding to specific questions. The parents were asked to describe specific situations that occurred before Tina left home. Mrs. Bopper described a situation as her husband listened. He nodded his head to confirm the accuracy of his wife's report. He then stood up and excused himself from the room. The Detox Counselor followed him out of the room and offered Mr. Bopper a cup of coffee, support, and time to regroup. With tears in her eyes, Mrs. Bopper continued to describe situation after situation. She was then asked to leave the room, while the team discussed treatment options.

The nurse was the first to speak. "Anger at the pimp, or, at Daddy?" "Both," agreed the treatment team. Dad was a classic well-intentioned, loving, avoider. He was quick to blame others. He couldn't seem to face his own feelings of guilt and self-condemnation. It was sad. He had nothing to feel guilty about. It was obvious that he loved his daughter. Tina had not

been able to interpret his actions into feelings of being loved and accepted. It would take a great deal of therapy before he would be able to face himself and let go of his fears. And avoiders tend to avoid therapy. It would take a great deal of therapy before Tina could accept him as he was. Any attempt to bring the two together until one or both had gotten well into the recovery process would only add fuel to the fire. Visitation would not be permitted for a while.

Tina's mother was a different story. Mrs. Bopper was well on the way to recovery. She had joined Al-Anon six months before Tina left home. Mrs. Bopper had faithfully continued with her Al-Anon attendance even though she thought she might never see her daughter again. Mrs. Bopper had also attended a Tough Love group for a while. At the moment she was shaken to the quick by finding her daughter, and by learning of the prostitution. Tina's addiction was no surprise. The team felt that Mrs. Bopper could provide positive support for Tina in the near future.

The treatment team brought Mr. and Mrs. Bopper back into the meeting. While the team had been discussing options, the detox counselor had been introducing Mr. and Mrs. Bopper to other parents who were coming in for a group session. The team managed to talk them into joining the sessions. Mr. and Mrs. Bopper agreed to take Tina home after discharge provided that the team felt it was the best alternative.

The parents stayed in the meeting as the team mapped out plans to get Tina from where she was to discharge and home. Naturally the first steps were basic, get rid of the denial and anger, become willing to accept help. Next she needed to accept herself. She also needed to feel accepted. While at TNT, attempts would be made to get Tina back into the education system and back to her own grade level. She would have to develop avenues other than sexual ones for gaining acceptance. She also needed to grow from being a woman back to being a child. Learning how to play would help. It was decided that the Recovery-Bound Program would play a key role in meeting her needs.

The treatment planning process brought hope and excitement to Mr. Bopper. He made the mistake of saying, "What can I do to help my little girl?" The team gave him a rigorous schedule of therapy, education, and recreation. He accepted the schedule without hesitation but turned white when he saw that his schedule included participating in the Recovery-Bound Program with his daughter. He began to falter, but the Therapeutic Recreation Specialist stopped him cold, "She needs your acceptance. She needs you there to cheer her on. Most of all, you need what this program can teach. I don't think you have ever turned your back on your daughter. Are you going to start now when she needs you the most?" Mr. Bopper agreed. (He was in excellent health and could financially afford to take the time.)

430.0   Ventilation of Anger
490.0   Adventure Course
402.02   Attitude Adjusters

Tina made rapid progress. Anger ventilation sessions began the day after the treatment meeting and continued throughout her treatment stay. As part of her required selection of skill development classes, she chose painting. Painting classes also became an outlet for Tina's anger. During initial classes, she painted ugly scenes in angry colors using aggressive brush stokes. When a picture was finished she would throw water or paint on it and destroy the scene completely. Tina quit destroying the pictures when she started painting scenes of sunlight breaking through angry clouds. By discharge, her pictures were filled with people sharing in a sunlit experience.

Originally, the Therapeutic Recreation Specialist was unable to determine the levels for TRI Items dealing with stress management and play history status. As Tina calmed down, the Therapeutic Recreation Specialist was able to observe Tina and discuss the two areas with Tina. She was found to be "Semi-Independent" on both.

In group therapy, she was prepared to meet her mother first. Even though Tina had been informed by her group counselor that her parents knew her basic situation, she was still apprehensive. Preparation included group therapy time devoted to the situation, and dramatic role-play of the upcoming event. The meeting went smoothly. Tina shared her deep, dark secrets with her mother. But her mother, instead of having a heart attack, simply asked what Tina was going to do about it, and pledged her support to the recovery process. When the group therapist felt Tina's mother's support was in place, he had Tina's status changed from full to partial runaway precautions.

Tina's meeting with her father was more difficult but equally effective. They said nothing to each other. Finally Mr. Bopper walked over, put his arm around her and said, "I just want you to get well. You'll always be my girl." At that, Tina cried her eyes out. The next day, Tina found her Dad on the Recovery-Bound Course. By the end of the course, they had learned to trust each other as well as themselves. She was taken

off partial runaway precautions at the end of the Recovery-Bound Program. Tina's view of herself changed; she became disenchanted with her appearance. She made several visits to the TNT style salon. A change in hairstyle was easy. Too much make-up was a habit that took some time to break. Tina negotiated a loan from her parents. One of the beauticians at the style salon went with Tina to purchase new clothes. With the beautician's assistance, Tina purchased clothing which was appropriate for her age group yet reflected her maturity.

As part of the family therapy, Tina's parents were given a full line of leisure education sessions. The sessions were the same as offered to inpatients. But the sessions did not explain what Tina needed from leisure. They helped Mr. and Mrs. Bopper understand their own personal leisure needs. Through this process, they discovered that they had done very little as a family. Mr. Bopper had always met his needs though his work. Mrs. Bopper never had a chance to take desired lessons as a child. She had always tried to meet her interests through her daughter's leisure. Mr. Bopper vowed to participate in more family leisure. Mrs. Bopper decided to learn to play the guitar. Both decided to consult Tina about which leisure interests she desired to pursue in the future.

Tina and her parents attended family recreation sessions. During a picnic, the Therapeutic Recreation Specialist managed to get Tina and her parents talking about past leisure experiences. Though the years Tina's parents had sent her to prestigious camps, to "the right" social events in the community. Tina always thought they were doing it to get rid of her. Her parents were speechless after Tina expressed this feeling. The Therapeutic Recreation Specialist helped her parents find their words. For the first time, Tina realized that her parents had sent her to all those "leisure experiences" because they loved her and were trying to do what they thought was best for her. She also realized that they missed her when she was away. Before regret and remorse could set in, the Therapeutic Recreation Specialist moved the focus of the discussion from the past to the future. How did Tina feel about returning home to the same leisure pursuits? "I didn't feel like I fit in before. Now, after all this has happened, I'll feel even...even...I can't pretend the past three years never happened. That would be a lie, and my recovery depends on my honesty..." At this point Tina became too emotional for words. Tina's parents did not know how to handle their emotions nor Tina's. A good deal of hidden agenda had been brought out into the open and time was needed to process the new information. The Therapeutic Recreation Specialist summarized the points that had been made, and got a commitment from everyone to explore the uncovered feelings in group therapy sessions. The family also agreed to continue discussing the issues together. By discharge, Tina would have a leisure option plan developed which would include time spent in leisure pursuits with her parents, time spent in leisure pursuits with a peer group, and time alone. The plan would be agreeable to her parents. By this time the picnic had turned into a free-for-all square dance. Tina and her parents joined a modified square dance called a Triples dance. In Triples, basic traditional square dance calls are used but three people are partnered together instead of two. Mr. and Mrs. Bopper and Tina danced together, bonding their commitment to joint leisure pursuits.

The original goal for Tina's school program was to get her back to her grade level. Initially, the Education Specialist felt that Tina had missed too much formal education to ever rejoin a regular school program. But Tina was bright. Learning was easy for her. She caught on to new concepts quickly. Participation in the recreation therapy learning stimulation sessions rekindled Tina's interest. Tina also realized that she had rejected education to get even with her father, and because she feared becoming a workhorse like him. By discharge, Tina had options. With private tutoring, she could return to school only one grade behind her age group. Or she could attend night school and finish preparation for a G.E.D. Tina decided to return to school, keeping night school as an option should things not work out.

Tina also participated in leisure education and a wide variety of skill development and Re-Creation sessions. She joined the TNT drama club. Painting and creative writing were also fond interests. During her free time she could usually be found poolside.

The treatment team reviewed her case one final time. Tina seemed ready to go home. Her parents seemed ready to have her home. Yet, there was one need still unmet. Over the course of treatment it had become clear that Tina had spent her life crying out to her father, "Look at me. Look at me!" Had Mr. Bopper really stopped to look at Tina? The Team decided to use Tina's drama club activities as a way to meet this need and see how Mr. Bopper now responded to his daughter. The Therapeutic Recreation Service arranged a special event in which the drama club produced a skit. Tina was given the leading role. It was held at night, and many families attended, including Mr. and Mrs. Bopper. Tina played the part of a very wild and rebellious gangster. Yet she built into the role a sense of humor and hope. At the end of the show the cast took their bows. There was a standing ovation. Tina beckoned to her father to come up on the stage. He was hesitant, but a therapist gave him a push. Tina gave him a hug on stage. Mr. Bopper hugged her back though he was flushed with embarrassment. After the audience began to leave, Tina's therapist joined them. "What are you feeling right now Mr. Bopper?" Mr. Bopper looked at the therapist. "I'm very proud of this girl." The therapist replied, "Tell her that, not me." Mr. Bopper looked at Tina, "I'm very proud of you!"

At discharge, Tina was given two photos, one of herself at admission and one taken on the day of discharge. It was hard to believe the pictures were of the same person. Tina was also given an award by community government. She was awarded the title of Miss Super-girl, in recognition of her ability to "change her world in a single treatment attempt." At discharge, her TRI Score reflected the changes. (See Figure 12.12)

Tina's TRI score increased 31 points from admission to discharge. She entered at the "Dependent" level and was discharged at the Leisure "Semi-Independent" level. She had made gains in transportation status, family status, leisure skills, and leisure awareness. The other increases were a result of accurately placing her level in the area of stress management and play history status.

After discharge Tina followed through on her options. She reentered high school and was able to adjust. While at school, she became active in the school's drama club. Drama club members accepted her for her talents. She was never a social debutante, but her parents were happy with her just the way she was. She participated in leisure activities with her parents and her peer group. Her peer group was an active Young People's AA group in her town. The Young People's group provided many recreation opportunities as well as the needed support system for recovery. Once a week her parents would drive her to the big city. They would eat dinner together or shop together, or visit TNT. Mr. and Mrs. Bopper would drop Tina off at an NA meeting. Tina would catch a ride back home with an NA member who lived in their community but worked in the big city.

FIGURE 12.12

TINA BOPPER TRI SUMMARY				
Discharge Assessment Results				
	Admission Score		Final Score	
TRI Item:	Level	Wght. Score	(Level)	Wght. Score
1 Physical	(4)	10	(4)	10
2 Education	(4)	8	(4)	8
3 Transportation	(1)	2	(1)	2
4 Economic	(1)	2	(2)	6
5 Family Support	(1)	2.5	(4)	10
6 Stress	(0)	0	(3)	7.5
7 Play Status	(0)	0	(3)	9
8 Problem Solving	(3)	7.5	(3)	7.5
9 Leisure Skills	(4)	12	(4)	12
10 Leisure Awareness	(1)	3	(2)	6
TRI Total Score:	(Dependent)	47	(Semi-Indep.)	78 = 31 point gain

Tina also found time to be alone. She once commented, "It's funny. I used to go to the lake with people, but feel so alone. Now I can go there by myself and I never feel alone. I've always loved the water, but I could never sit still long enough to enjoy it. Now I can stay there all day long and feel perfectly content."

THE CASE OF TWEETY BOPPER

Tweety Bopper entered TNT in the exact same way and under the same conditions as Tina Bopper. Same age, same problems. Her parents appeared to be the same as Tina's too. The same treatment program was established. The treatment team was planning to return Tweety to live with her parents. Tweety's program for recovery progressed the same as Tina's, but then it stalled. It seemed the anger would wane, but never disappear. The father's attempts to reach out to Tweety were condoned for a while and then the anger would return, and Tweety would reject all those who were reaching out to her.

The treatment team met and compared notes. A pattern was clear. Tweety would get better. Her father would enter the scene. Tweety would react and become violent. The violence seemed self-destructive. Tweety was placed on suicidal precautions and was scheduled for re-evaluation by the psychologist. The Therapeutic Recreation Specialist was asked to observe Tweety's interactions and behaviors during leisure and to make a detailed report to the psychologist. The report included the time of observations, the clients and staff Tweety interacted with, and the type of interactions.

Based on the psychological test results and the Therapeutic Recreation Specialist's report, Tweety's group counselor assembled a group of clients that Tweety appeared to trust. The group gathered in a private area of the Therapeutic Recreation facility for a little game of "Truth or Dare." Tweety's Therapeutic Recreation Specialist co-led the session with Tweety's group counselor. [Ch11:450.02]

The game began on a superficial level. It quickly got deeper and deeper. Tweety usually took the dares rather than risking the truth. Finally, a client dared Tweety to tell the truth. She said she would on the next turn. On the next turn, Tweety was asked, "What is your problem with your Dad?" She at first gave a superficial answer, but the group saw through it and rejected it. Eventually the truth came out. Tweety's Dad had been sexually involved with Tweety since she was three years old. Tweety's mother apparently was deep in denial. The only protection Tweety's mother had provided was sending Tweety away to take lessons, or away to summer camps.

The treatment team was reconvened. The old plan to return Tweety to live with her parents was scuttled. All parent visiting privileges were revoked. The psychologist would confront the parents and see what type of treatment and/or legal action would be required for Mr. and Mrs. Bopper. The facility's attorney would also be consulted to review options. Meanwhile the group counselor would continue to deal with Tweety. On the heels of the recent breakthrough, the team

agreed that Tweety would soon begin entering the grief process. She would be dealing with the death of her youth. The Therapeutic Recreation Specialist would prepare sessions to assist her through this phase. [Ch11: 440.0]

Tweety responded to the change of plans. Tweety's parents did not. It was decided to declare emancipation for Tweety and then send her to a group home after discharge. When Tweety learned of the change of discharge destination, she became motivated to recover. Suicide precautions were lifted. Her treatment program was back on course.

Tweety made good progress. It was observed that she often allowed her feelings about her parents to influence the way she interacted with others. Recreation Therapy sessions for Situation Response Awareness and for Trust of Self and Others were added to her program. [Ch11:410.0, 450.0] Reviews of videotapes from these sessions helped Tweety to see her behaviors. With practice she was able to change her interaction patterns.

Tweety was discharged to TNT's transitions center, then finally to a group home. During the post-discharge time, Tweety continued therapy at TNT, which included attendance in Leisure Skill Development sessions and Re-Creation sessions. She got a job and finished school at nights. She then continued her job and attended college part-time.

THE CASE OF GEORGE DIKKEL

(Leisure Level: At Risk)

George Dikkel was 57-years-old. He had been drinking for the last 30 years. A previous treatment attempt had resulted in six months of non-drinking. "The worst six months I ever spent in my life," he confided. "To be honest I don't know which is worse, being drunk or being sober." Mr. Dikkel had been drinking on a daily basis prior to admission. "They tell me I had the DTs. All I know is, one day I was home and the next thing I knew I opened my eyes and saw a nurse staring at me. I had all kind of tubes stuck in me. They told me I'd been there four days and my heart had stopped once. I was in the hospital for awhile before they sent me over here."

Mr. Dikkel lived with his wife on their farm. The farm was located in a rural area, miles and miles from the bright city lights. Mr. Dikkel had been married since age 17. "My wife and me quit school to raise a family. Times were hard but we got 'em raised. They're all gone now. Some years I get a Christmas card from them." All four of his children lived out of state. Mrs. Dikkel had not visited him since he was admitted to the hospital. "I want to go back home after I get out of here but my wife says we're finished. She's said it before, but she always comes back."

A discussion of leisure revealed that Mr. Dikkel saw free time as a problem with no solution. "I don't like having time on my hands. That was the worst thing about being in the hospital…and not drinking too. There was nothing to do. Just sitting and waiting for nothing. Listening to the old lady

FIGURE 12.13

GEORGE DIKKEL TRI TREATMENT PLAN
Initial Assessment Results

TRI Item:	Opinion of Client	Level TRS	Final Score (Level)	Wght. Score	Maximum Possible	Goal:
1 Physical	1		(1)	2.5	10	+ one level
2 Education	1		(1)	2	8	
3 Transportation	1		(1)	2	8	Most important:
4 Economic	1		(1)	2	8	leisure skills
5 Family Support	1		(1)	2.5	10	
6 Stress	2		(2)	5	10	
7 Play Status	1		(1)	3	12	
8 Problem Solving	1		(1)	2.5	10	
9 Leisure Skills	1		(1)	3	12	+ at least one
10 Leisure Awareness	3		(3)	9	12	+ at least one
		TRI Total Score:		33.5	out of 100	

complain and watching her watching me." He could not associate a single positive experience with free time. He understood the impact of empty time, but had no alternatives. Mr. Dikkel said he was willing to try anything the Therapeutic Recreation Specialist thought might help.

A treatment team conference clarified his situation. (See Figure 12.13) The detox counselor had contacted his wife. Mrs. Dikkel was filing separation papers. "He can go any place he wants, do anything he wants, so long as he doesn't come back here. I don't care if he's drunk or sober. We're finished!" Mrs. Dikkel had not yet shared this information with Mr. Dikkel. The treatment team agreed that a half-way house would be appropriate placement after discharge. The nurse agreed to be in charge of coordination between husband, wife, lawyer, and half-way house. The rest of the team should avoid the topic until the nurse managed to get the wife to break the news to Mr. Dikkel.

Mr. Dikkel was active in Therapeutic Recreation, attending almost every activity provided. Then, did not attend for two days-- the two days after his wife mailed his separation papers to him. But by the time his discharge date arrived, Mr. Dikkel seemed to have accepted his plight. "I'm not happy about it all. I came real close to leaving and going home and telling her to get out. Then I thought about it. The nurse was right. It wouldn't do any good to leave early. One of the guys in my dorm is going to the same half-way house I am. We get along OK so there'll be somebody there I know. I think the best thing I can do is give it a shot and see what happens."

Mr. Dikkel, assisted by leisure education sessions and individual leisure counseling, was able to develop realistic plans for post-discharge leisure. (See Figure 12.14, p. 220) He would be staying at a half-way house within driving distance from the treatment center. A leisure counseling session was used to visit the half-way house and the city's senior citizen recreation building, which was two blocks from the half-way house. Mr. Dikkel planned to spend some of his daytime hours at the senior citizen building. His evenings were reserved for

AA meetings. Weekends concerned him most. He had developed a woodworking hobby while in treatment. Building on some almost forgotten carpentry skills, he was now making small wooden toys. He decided to continue his hobby on weekends.

TRI DISCHARGE SUMMARY

Five years later, Mr. Dikkel was still living at the same half-way house but there had been many positive changes in his life. At age 62, he was in excellent physical condition. For the last year he had been employed as assistant manager of the half-way house. He was still active at the senior citizen center but the time spent there had been reduced. His woodworking hobby had become a source of income for him and the half-way house. It had also become an excuse to travel. "Some of the other boys who live here got interested in woodworking so we set up a shop in the basement. We got to making so many things that we didn't have any place to put them. John over at the senior citizen building told us to bring them to their craft fair. We did and sold almost all of them. We put the money in a fund. We use the fund to buy supplies, and pay travel expenses. We take off and go to a couple craft fairs a year and sell our stuff. Last winter we went to a fair in Florida. Everything we made we spent on the trip plus some, but we sure had a good time."

At the time of the follow-up, Mr. Dikkel had not had a drink for four years. "Things went along OK for a while after I left the center. My wife changed her mind and I went back to live with her. Next thing I knew I was right back to drinking. My AA sponsor helped me dry out. I thought I could drink just one and I found out I couldn't. In just a few weeks I was worse than I ever was. Then one day, after I got straightened out, I just looked around and I knew if I stayed there I'd get drunk again. I realized I didn't like farming, and I didn't like living with my wife. Don't know if I ever did. So I packed up and moved back

FIGURE 12.14

	GEORGE DIKKEL TRI SUMMARY			
	Discharge Assessment Results			
	Admission Score		Final Score	
TRI Item:	Level	Wght. Score	(Level)	Wght. Score
1 Physical	(1)	2.5	(2)	5
2 Education	(1)	2	(1)	2
3 Transportation	(1)	2	(1)	2
4 Economic	(1)	2	(1)	2
5 Family Support	(1)	2.5	(1)	2.5
6 Stress	(2)	5	(2)	5
7 Play Status	(1)	3	(1)	3
8 Problem Solving	(1)	2.5	(1)	2.5
9 Leisure Skills	(1)	3	(3)	9
10 Leisure Awareness	(3)	9	(4)	12
TRI Total Score: (At Risk)		33.5	(Dependent)	45.0 = 11.5 point gain

here. Things have been getting better ever since. My children are remembering they have a Daddy now. We write all the time. One came to see me and one has called me a few times. Things are still rocky with 'em but it's getting better. I didn't realize they had to leave the state to get away from my drinking. They still have some resentments, but I can tell they're proud of me too."

THE CASE OF JOHNNY WALKER

(Leisure Level: At Risk)

Since Mr. Walker was unable to read, the Therapeutic Recreation Specialist completed the TRI assessment during the first meeting after completion of detox. Before that time, Mr. Walker's severe withdrawal symptoms that would have limited participation in organized recreation after discharge. Having no driver's license, Mr. Walker depended on his feet for transportation. He lived in a rural area where recreation opportunities were few and far between. Community recreation programs in his area were geared toward children's summer needs. Mr. Walker had worked and lived in the back room of a gas station, but had been fired due to his inability to sober up. "When the boss man found me trying to pour a quart of oil in the gas tank, he said I had to go." Termination of employment also terminated his living accommodations.

The client's stress management, play history status, and problem-solving skills, as measured by TRI, were minimal. His understanding of leisure was limited as demonstrated by his response to the question, "What do you do when you are not working." "Nothing." "Nothing? You must do something. What do you do?" inquired the Therapeutic Recreation Specialist. "Well, I drink." "What would you do if you didn't drink?" Mr. Walker responded, "Oh, I don't know...I don't know what I'd do just sitting and staring at those four walls. Not working's bad enough when I'm drinking. What would I do? Go crazy."

Leisure skills consisted of fishing, watching television, and playing checkers. The last time he played checkers was about 20 years ago. As far as he could remember, he had been fishing only once in the last five years. (See Figure 12.15)

Mr. Walker's treatment team had a productive debate before establishing treatment goals. It was unrealistic to assume that Mr. Walker could reach the "Independent" or even the "Semi-Independent" level within the usual six-week treatment stay. Extending Mr. Walker's stay long enough to make him "Independent" might backfire into institutionalization. It was realistic to bring him up to the "Dependent" level in six weeks or perhaps "Semi-Independent" in 10 weeks. With the deck stacked against him, should they take the time to prepare him for living alone in the community, or should they just send him to a half-way house? The detox counselor had shared with the team that Mr. Walker had lived in a half-way house years ago, and hated it. The team finally decided to prepare Mr. Walker to live in the community, saving the half-way house as a fall-back position. Additional time could be provided through the use of the transition center. He would need assistance in meeting his leisure needs, as well as basic needs for food, shelter, and clothing. The goal of Therapeutic Recreation programing was to increase his leisure level to "Semi-Independent" through concentrating on improving his physical condition, his leisure awareness, and his leisure skills. Leisure skills would have to be carefully selected. The "right" activities for Mr. Walker, would not require money, transportation, or educational preparation. The "right" activities for Mr. Walker could be performed alone, in a small confined area. He would also need a heavy concentration of social activities to compensate for the time he would be spending alone. (Even though Mr. Walker was not returning to the gas station, his new abode would probably look a lot like his old one.)

The Therapeutic Recreation Specialist decided to start by involving Mr. Walker in activities which appeal to people with strong work ethics. He would probably reject participation in any activity which seemed too playful until he completed the

FIGURE 12.15

JOHNNY WALKER TRI TREATMENT PLAN

Initial Assessment Results

TRI Item:	Opinion of Client	Level TRS	Final Score (Level)	Wght. Score	Maximum Possible	Goal:
1 Physical	1		(1)	2.5	10	+ at least two
2 Education	1		(1)	2	8	
3 Transportation	1		(1)	2	8	
4 Economic	1		(1)	2	8	
5 Family Support	1		(1)	2.5	10	
6 Stress	1		(1)	2.5	10	
7 Play Status	1		(1)	3	12	
8 Problem Solving	1		(1)	2.5	10	
9 Leisure Skills	1		(1)	3	12	+ at least two
10 Leisure Awareness	1		(1)	3	12	+ at least two
	TRI Total Score:			25.0 out of	100	

leisure education series. Developing skills in leisure activities couldn't wait until Mr. Walker had completed the Leisure Education series. Since he couldn't read, it would take him at least three weeks to complete the leisure education series. There would not be enough time between the end of leisure education and discharge to equip Mr. Walker with the needed leisure skills.

108.1 Leisure Planning Assistance
231.2 Gardeneering (Specialized)
221.2 Aerobics Designed for Persons over 60
234.1 Cooking Class
362.1 Jigsaw Puzzles and Non-Word Mazes
105.1 Value of Leisure Aloneness
155.1 Overview of Collecting Things
155.1 Overview of Individualized Leisure Pursuits (Hobbies, Puzzles, Games)

It was found that Mr. Walker grew up on a farm and enjoyed growing things. Gardeneering was scheduled for one of his first skill development sessions. Gardeneering is usually designed for clients who are in better physical condition. The gardeneering session was reviewed by the doctor, and the portions that Mr. Walker could do were selected for a starting point. This information was carefully communicated to the leader of the gardeneering program. In gardeneering he learned to adapt his knowledge of farming to small areas which might be found in an apartment complex. He learned to grow vegetables and other plants indoors. Mr. Walker also participated in bachelor cooking classes. He had never taken an interest in cooking. He was suffering from malnutrition. He had always waited for someone else to cook for him, when he was not drinking. (He was too drunk to eat when he was drinking.) In cooking class, he learned to enjoy preparing food.

He was given an exercise program that gradually increased his strength and endurance. By discharge he was in excellent physical condition. To maintain his physical condition,

he was given a program of walking and jogging. These activities would not require expensive equipment, other people, or facilities. Mr. Walker could easily continue the program after discharge.

As Mr. Walker responded, his program was upgraded. By the first month treatment plan review, Mr. Walker had completed all required leisure education sessions. It was decided that he might have time to benefit from the creative problem-solving series. He also needed to get in the habit of maintaining his physical condition.

For Maintaining Fitness:

251.2 Walking for Health and Fitness
324.1 Home Exercise Programs Club

408.0 Creative Problem-Solving

408.21 Color Me Not
408.22 Read Me Not
408.23 Create-a-Game
408.24 Half Deck
408.25 Sentence Malpractice and Old Story New Ending
408.26 Ana-Ma-Grammy
218.2 How To Play Backgammon
228.2 How to Play Computer Games
268.2 Math Games (How Many Ways to Add # to Get Given #)
278.2 Drama: How Many Different People Can You Be
278.2 Mime and Mimicry
278.2 Trash Art
278.2 Using Modeling Clay (How Many Shapes Can You Make?)
368.2 Backgammon and Other Game Check-Out
378.2 Mime and Mimicry Club
102.0 Guest Speaker: Adults Expanding Knowledge

Though Mr. Walker's score had increased 19 points, he was still at the "Dependent" level of the TRI scale. The team decided to transfer Mr. Walker to the transition center. This would permit continuation of the treatment plan, yet allow Mr. Walker more freedom and responsibility for self-care. While at the transition center, Mr. Walker continued to receive assistance in daily leisure planning. He found an AA sponsor and the relationship seemed to be meeting Mr. Walker's needs.

Mr. Walker used a weekend pass to visit a number of places to live. An AA member provided transportation and guidance. While on pass, Mr. Walker responded to an ad in a newspaper for a roommate. Another ad described an independent living community. It was designed for senior citizens who required some supervision but still wanted to live alone. He also checked a motel that rented rooms by the week, and an apartment or two. He found a job at a gas station and decided to rent the motel room since it was nearest to the gas station and on the bus route. Mr. Walker was discharged from the transition center. (See Figure 12.16) Unmet goals could be completed through outpatient services.

After discharge, Mr. Walker used the TNT wake-up service. Many times he would leave messages for the TNT staff to contact him. Many times the stated need was for a new recipe. The cooking class instructor always responded to his call. Nine times out of 10, Mr. Walker didn't need a new recipe as much as he needed to hear a friendly voice and a pep talk. The ingredients were always supplied.

After a year, Mr. Walker got on his feet financially. He then contacted Therapeutic Recreation and asked for additional outpatient services. He said he was happy with his motel room garden, and eating his own cooking, but there was something missing in his life. He was lonely. The Therapeutic Recreation Specialist interviewed him. He was ready for social interaction but didn't know how to go about it. The Therapeutic Recreation Specialist developed an outpatient program for him that met his needs.

After two years, Mr. Walker contacted the Therapeutic Recreation Specialist again. He was now happy with his motel room that now looked like a jungle. His cooking was known throughout the AA community, but there was still something missing. The Therapeutic Recreation Specialist found that he needed a purpose, a goal in his life. After a referral to a vocational counselor and a goals clarification session, Mr. Walker decided he was happy with his job and his life. What he wanted was to learn to read. With the support and encouragement of the Therapeutic Recreation staff, and his AA friends, Mr. Walker, at 49 years of age, enrolled in a basic education program at a nearby community college. After that Mr. Walker quit contacting the TNT staff. But the staff never lost track of Mr. Walker. There was always a story floating through the AA community about a great dinner concocted by a great guy named Johnny W.

FIGURE 12.16

JOHNNY WALKER TRI SUMMARY

Discharge Assessment Results

TRI Item:	Admission Score		Final Score	
	Level	Wght. Score	(Level)	Wght. Score
1 Physical	(1)	2.5	(3)	7.5
2 Education	(1)	2	(1)	2
3 Transportation	(1)	2	(1)	2
4 Economic	(1)	2	(2)	4
5 Family Support	(1)	2.5	(1)	2.5
6 Stress	(1)	2.5	(1)	2.5
7 Play Status	(1)	3	(1)	3
8 Problem Solving	(1)	2.5	(1)	2.5
9 Leisure Skills	(1)	3	(3)	9
10 Leisure Awareness	(1)	3	(3)	9
TRI Total Score: (At Risk)		25	(Dependent)	44.0 = 19 point gain

References/Resources

Bourne, P. G. (1970). *Men, Stress, and Vietnam.* Boston: Little Brown.

Disabled American Veterans, Vietnam Veterans Outreach Program, Washington, DC.

Figley, C. R., & Sprenkle, D. H. (1978). Delayed stress response syndrome: Family therapy implications. *Journal of Marriage & Family Counseling.*

Figley, C. R. (Ed.). (1978). *Stress Disorders Among Vietnam Veterans.* NY: Brunner/Mazel.

Lifton, R. J. (1973). *Home From The War; Vietnam Veterans: Neither Victims Nor Executioners.* NY: Simon & Schuster.

Missing In America: The Hidden Minority of Vietnam Veterans: Project Return-Vets, Portland, OR.

Shatan, C. (1973). The grief of soldiers. *American Journal of Orthopsychiatry,* 43.

Shatan, C. (1973). How do we turn off the guilt? *Human Behavior,* 2.

Wilson, J. P. (1977). *Identity, Ideology, & Crisis: The Vietnam Veteran in Transition, Part I.* OH: Cleveland State University.

Wilson, J. P. (1978). *Identity, Ideology, & Crisis: The Vietnam Veteran in Transition, Part II.* OH: Cleveland State University.

Women In The Wake Of War. Service Center, Church Women United, Cincinnati, OH.

CHAPTER 13

BACK TO THE REAL WORLD

Programs and activities suggested in this text have been based on provision in a model center that does not exist. Fantasy provided unlimited resources. If I were reading this text, I would get excited about all the options. Then I would eventually look at my real world setting and feel overwhelmed, perhaps even depressed. No one can do it all. The goal is to do the best that can be done *within the given limitations*. Implementation of quality services happens one day at a time, one step at a time, one activity at a time. Progress often happens in the midst of chanting the Serenity Prayer.

The real world demands quality service at quantity prices. I hear Therapeutic Recreation Specialists cry, "There is no money." That is not true. There is no longer money for meaningless expenses. There is no place for penny-wise/pound-foolish ventures. But there will always be money for a program that is effective and efficient.

Many effective and efficient programs have been discontinued. This has happened because the providers of the programs have failed to communicate the value of their programs to the persons who provide the money. "If they could just see the good." They can't see, nor should they be forced to interrupt their work schedule to traipse down to the activity. It is the Therapeutic Recreation Manager's job to communicate the good which the program does. To do this, it must first be asked, who is "they"? Then it must be asked what do "they" expect, desire, and how do "they" see? How do "they" communicate? What language do "they" use? When "they" look at a service do "they" see numbers, dollar signs, or outcomes? A quality administration will see all three, and demand all three. The days of random application are gone, thank God. The days of predictable and repeatable programming are here to stay.

A program seldom starts where it wants to be. But no one ever starts someplace else. Each of us must begin where we are. That's true for a service as well as an individual. By reading this book, you have told me that you don't want to be where you are. You want to provide a bigger and better service. Great. But start by making the most of what you have. Turn what you have into a clean, lean fighting machine. Create a demonstrated track record. Help staff in other services "see" what you are doing. Help them meet their goals. Set desired outcomes for each program that meet the expectations of your supervisor(s). Then ask permission to take a small cost-effective step toward making it better.

Patience is truly a virtue. Take time to learn the right times and methods for making changes. The results will amaze you. Doors will open that have been locked since time began. Submit cost-saving proposals when the census is low. Submit cost-increasing proposals when the census is high. Don't complain about anything if your organization is facing bankruptcy.

Progress never results from procrastination. Taking it slow means taking a step. It does not mean staying where you are. Simply reading this text has done no one any good (except those of us who profit from the sale of the book). Improved thinking must be turned to action. The remainder of this chapter are suggestions of activities which can be implemented now within specified limitations. The lists are still too long. Try to pick just one new activity and implement it. When it is functioning, pick another.

NO SPACE

Select activities which match the available space. Attempting to play football in a day room is not only frustrating to clients, it is unsafe. Packing a group in like sardines ends all chances of leisurely exchanges. The group will only remember discomfort. If a room only holds three, then a room only holds three.

Think about space requirements before ordering equipment. Something large and bulky may look like fun, but if it consumes floor space which is at a premium, then look for another way to provide fun. Storage space is as important as activity space. One closet only holds so much.

Art, Drama, Writing, and Discussion require less space than sports. If space is limited, then look to the creative areas of programming. Physical exercise during treatment is important. Look to hallways for hiking for exercise. Look to jumping jacks and exercises that stay in one place.

Room-to-room parties and special events do not require large areas to mass. A cart with refreshments and balloons can take the fun to the client rather than making the client come to the fun. Roving musicians can serenade from door to door. A small room can be maximized. Instead of bringing everyone in at once, rotate a series of small groups through the activity, one after the other. (Be sure to document the process. Let administration know that the cost of staff time is greatly increased by this process.) The bottom line is, no space is no excuse.

NO MONEY

Well, there has to be some money. Be sure you know exactly how much money you have to spend. If every dollar counts, watch your dollars as well as your pennies. Don't take on an activity that costs $10 if there is another activity that will do the same thing for $5. Remember you often get what you pay for. Buying cheap equipment often results in a more expensive replacement. Consider maintenance and repair costs too. Games that easily lose playing pieces are no good to anyone. Buy extra playing pieces whenever possible.

Take care of the supplies you have. Routine maintenance pays. Remember there was leisure even during the years of the great depression. The day when leisure equals cents is the day when leisure lacks sense.

INADEQUATE STAFF SKILLS

It is my opinion that at least one Certified Therapeutic Recreation Specialist is needed. I don't think it is unrealistic to require additional training in alcoholism counseling. Certification in both Therapeutic Recreation and alcoholism counseling is rare, but ideal. Management requires more than certification. Management requires management skills. Our profession's past difficulty in communicating our needs and value is most likely a reflection of the lack of business skills possessed by individuals practicing in our field. Management skills may be acquired by getting a master's degree in Therapeutic Recreation Administration. Skills may also be acquired through participation in Therapeutic Recreation management schools that provide a crash course one week per year. Until adequate skills are developed, consultation from qualified Therapeutic Recreation Professionals will prevent costly errors. Networking is no replacement for consultation or training, but it can help overcome obstacles.

The most important skills for effective provision of programs are process skills. A Therapeutic Specialist must be able to communicate, to observe, and to interact therapeutically. Group dynamics are a must. Skills in establishing and making use of therapeutic relationships are mandatory. The ability to see the client's self-worth and to interact with dignity and integrity are imperative.

Many Therapeutic Recreation Specialists lack activity skills. None of us ever possess all the activities skills there are. Leisure is simply too broad an area to be covered by any one individual. Go with the activity skills you have. Whenever possible, pick up skills in leading a basic activity outside your activity interest area. Clients therapy needs can be met through any interest category if the leader is skilled. A service of all physical activity is limited in appeal but not limited in capacity to help. A service of all art is also limited in appeal but not in ability to meet client recovery needs.

Where there is a need to provide variety that staff cannot meet, look to volunteers, students, audiovisuals, and high tech. There may be a need for specialized activity skills one hour per week. This hardly justifies a full-time position. When all other resources are exhausted, if the need still cannot be met, then decide whether meeting the need is really mandatory. If it is, see if it can be met by establishing a liaison with a community college or other community agency. If not, then a part-time staff member can be hired. Having documented the exhaustion of all other possibilities increases the likelihood of consideration.

NO STAFF

Having more staff is not always a solution. More staff means more supervision. More staff means more training, more expenses, more office space and supplies, and more overhead in the personnel and business departments. Too often, acquiring more staff means acquiring more work, so the results never really change.

Living within the limitations is important. Develop a program that can be effective. Make it happen for a few if not for all. Try to address the most important needs of each client, not all the needs of each client for all the clients. Do not become a workaholic. The more demanding the job, the greater the need for personal play off the job.

After an administration realizes the need for additional staff, yet has turned down several requests for additional staff, "they" may be in the mood to spend money on supplies and equipment. Non-staff expenditures are far less expensive. Equipment never asks for a raise. Try to get approval for a video library. Such a library can greatly expand diversity without significant cost, especially if the videos are purchased one at a time.

A video library can meet individual needs which cannot be met with hands-on programming. Sometimes a client has an interest in something which requires several others to perform. Small caseloads result in wide diversity. It is seldom that enough clients with common needs and interest are available to conduct a group meeting on a specific interest. The video library permits pursuit of a specific leisure interest even though no other clients display interest in that area. How-to videos also provide assistance where expertise is not possessed by staff.

Few quality videos exist in Therapeutic Recreation at this time. But where there's a will, there's a way. The following is a list to stimulate thought.

For Leisure Education Videos, see if local college cinema students may be enticed to create some. Local libraries and clubs may be willing to contribute:

114.4	Overview of Affluent Leisure Competitions (e.g., Polo)
119.1	Overview of Other-Competitive Non-Physical and Physical Activities
124.3	Overview of Health Club Memberships: How to Join and What They Offer
129.1	Overview of Self-Competitive Non-Physical and Physical Activities
134.1	Patio Vegetable Gardening
134.3	Overview of Hunting Clubs: How to Join and What They Offer
134.4	Custom Home and Living Space Designs
134.4	Overview of Affluent Leisure (Travel, Fishing in Alaska)
139.1	Overview of Productive Activities
144.4	Overview of Volunteerism, and Philanthropy

145.2   Overview of Social Activities
145.3   Overview of Family Activities
154.3   Overview of Travel Clubs and Guided Tours: How to Join and Advantages
155.1   Overview of Collecting Things
155.1   Overview of Individualized Leisure Pursuits (Hobbies, Puzzles, Games for One)
156.2   Overview of Relaxing with Music from Center Library
156.2   Relaxing with Nature
157.1   Overview of Joining Creative Writing Clubs, Little Theatre, Guilds
162.2   Reading and Math-Mazes, and Puzzles
164.1   Overview of Taking Advantage of Public Education Channel of the TV
164.4   Overview of Travel Planning: Meeting AA Worldwide
171.3   Introduction to Ballet, Tap Dancing
172.2   Overview of Creative Writing and Poetry
174.3   Overview of Community Sources for Dance Classes
174.3   Overview of Community Sources for Music Lessons
174.4   Overview of Affluent Leisure (Opera, Concerts, Theatre)
174.4   Overview of Creative Hobbies Which are Expensive.
176.2   Relaxing with the Arts
179.1   Overview of Arts and Crafts
179.1   Overview of Creative Writing Activities
179.1   Overview of Dance
179.1   Overview of Drama
179.1   Overview of Music and Song
189.1   Overview of Spiritual Activities
194.3   Overview of Outdoor and Adventure Clubs: Finding, Joining, Advantages
199.1   Overview of Outdoor Activities
199.1   Overview of Risk Taking Opportunities

For Skill Development Sessions, video sources for the following are noted in Chapter 9:

221.2   Aerobics Designed for Persons Over 60
221.3   Low-Impact Aerobics
221.4   High-Impact Aerobics
224.1   Home Exercise Programs
271.3   Introduction to Ballet, Tap Dancing, Jazz and Modern

Consult Your Local Public Education Television Channel for Sources for the following:

211.3   How to Bowl
211.3   How to Golf
211.3   How to Play Competitive Water Games
211.3   How to Participate in Team Swims
211.4   How to Play Tennis
212.2   How to Speed Read
221.2   How to Swim for Fitness
231.3   Working with Wood, Saws and Hammers
234.1   Cooking Class
234.2   Cake Decorating
234.2   Calligraphy
234.2   How to Sew Clothes
234.2   Tie Your Own Flies for Fishing
234.3   Customizing Your Home
235.1   Crocheting/Knitting/Needlepoint
236.1   Fishing
245.2   Cooking for Large Groups
245.3   Family Activities
274.1   Drawing
274.1   Paper-Mâché Projects
274.1   Rubbings
274.1   Flower Arranging
274.2   Clay Modeling/Sculpture/Carving
274.3   Ceramics
274.3   Painting Pictures/Pastels
274.3   Photography
274.3   Pottery
274.3   Stained Glass
274.3   Weaving
278.2   Trash Art
278.2   Using Modeling Clay: How Many Shapes Can You Make?
279.2   How to Design Living Spaces
279.2   How to Make Costumes and Your Own Patterns
279.2   How to Tie Dye
251.2   Walking for Health and Fitness.
251.3   Outdoor Gardening
256.2   How to Relax with Music (see Creative)
256.2   How to Relax with Nature
256.2   Relaxing with the Help of a Pet or Aquarium
257.1   Joining Creative Writing Clubs, Little Theatre, Guilds.
259.1   Collector's Corner
259.2   Outdoor Photography
264.4   How to Make a Travel Plan
265.1   How to Operate a Computer for Fun
271.4   Introduction to Folk Dancing (275.0)
272.2   Creative Writing and Poetry
276.1   How to Select Music for Stress Reduction
277.1   Home Made Rhythm and Kazoo Band
278.2   Mime and Mimicry
279.0   How to Make Music a Therapeutic Force
279.2   How to Act and Participate in Drama
279.2   Script Writing
279.2   How to Play Keyboard, Guitar and Drums
279.2   How to Write a Song
299.2   How to Rock Climb and Rappel
299.2   Diving
299.2   How to go Whitewater Rafting Safely
299.2   How to Camp Out and Cook Over an Open Fire

NO TIME

Do a time-analysis study. Determine the amount of time spent in paperwork, getting to and from activities, setting up for activities, and answering the phone. Determine the time lost from interruptions, and the time cost of meetings. Streamline all of the above. Where things can't be improved, document the issue or area and send it to your supervisor. This documentation should include the average length of time waste identified, the source of time loss, an estimate of dollar cost over a year, and an alternative which is less than the annual cost. For example, the loss of a minute isn't much. An hourly wage of $5 isn't much. (Note that $5 in wages is usually $10 when indirect expenses are added in.) A minute of a $5 per hour job costs $.83. That's not much. Loss of one minute, five days a week for 52 weeks is $21.67. That's a new basketball. If the staff's wage is $10 an hour then that's $43.33 a year, and if that $10 wage is wasted 10 minutes a day, that's $433.34 a year. Little losses add up fast.

The greatest expense is time. If there is a lack of time, find a quicker, shorter assessment system. Gathering information that you don't have time to implement is meaningless. Standardize. Doing something new takes longer than doing something familiar. Manage distractions. A phone message recorder will pay for itself in the first few months of operation. Computerize. Organize. Time spent looking for supplies helps no one. Keep supplies on carts. There is no time to pull it out and put it back. Wherever possible, code with numbers. In this text, a "4" means independent. Writing a "4" is faster than writing "independent." As long as "4" is defined so that everyone knows what it means, nothing but waste has been lost by using it. Buy in quantities. Not only is there usually a discount for purchase of several at once, but the time consumed by placing the request and checking in the new supplies is reduced. Buy games which are manufactured, rather than creating self-made games. The time required to construct a good game is far greater than the cost of the most expensive game.

Be time-wise. Cut the waste. Put your energies where they will do the most good. Accept the things that cannot be changed. Do what you can and let the rest go. Give your energy to the client who is ready for help. Let the client who can help him/herself, help him/herself.

SHORT STAY

If a client is only in treatment for a week, then little can be done. But a little is better than nothing. For Recreation Therapy to be effective, time is required. Sessions may need repetition. Don't start things you have no time to finish. Leisure Education, Skill Development, and Re-Creation can have impact in a limited period of time.

Suppose there is only one hour a day for five days. If I only had five sessions, I would use the first day as a Leisure Education session combined with group assessment and self-evaluation of needs and interests, using the TRI. I would boil down and provide a brief introduction to Therapeutic Recreation and the Service. [Ch8:100.0] Individual treatment needs would be identified and written up after the session. The second day would be used to provide a second Leisure Education session, based on needs identified on the first day. I would be sure to present a boiled down concept of the need for balance and have participants select options for a daily leisure plan. [Ch8: 100.0] The third day could be used to develop skill in planning sessions and problem solving by preparing for a Re-Creation session to be held on the fourth day. The fourth day would be used for participation in the group-selected Re-Creation session. The fifth day would be used to process the week's work and learning. On the last day I would stress the addiction tree and the need to structure leisure time after discharge. If possible I would also use the last day to provide referral to community resources for continued leisure growth. The fifth day would summarize progress made during the week. Discharge summaries can be written after the fifth day. A week is not much time, but progress can be made.

Needs which cannot be met through such a short-stay program should be documented at the time discharge summaries are written. Keep a list of activities from which the client could benefit, that there has not been time to offer. Try to find a community agency willing to meet those needs. Propose an outpatient program to meet the identified needs.

ONE-MAN DEPARTMENT, SHORT STAY, NO SPACE, NO MONEY

Even in the face of combined limitations, there is still room for quality programming. Put yourself through the creative problem solving sessions noted in this book. Close your mind to closed doors and seek alternatives. There are thousands of activities which can be successful within the given limitations. The following list contains only activities which do not require more space than a day room might provide. There are no activities listed which require expensive supplies or equipment. The list is still long and the Therapeutic Recreation Specialist will have to pick and choose.

For Leisure Education:

100.0   Introduction to Recreation and the
         Therapeutic Recreation Service
100.0   Your Leisure and Internal Chemical Needs
100.0   The Balancing Act
100.0   Beware! The Tree of Addictions Grows:
         Substance Abuse and Leisure Abuse are
         Interrelated

100.0   Leisure Planning for Today
100.1   Leisure as Related to Work and Substance
        Abuse
100.2   Haven't Got Time Or Won't Take Time?
        A Matter of Priorities
100.2   Drawing From Paradise
100.2   Leisure Values Clarification: Living
        versus Existing
100.2   Time, Priorities, and Leisure/Finding
        Time for Fun
100.3   Sources of Leisure Guilt
100.3   Will Yesterday's Fun be Fun Tomorrow?
100.3   Matching Needs, Skills and Activities
        with Activity Analysis
100.4   Maintaining Leisure Independence During
        Treatment
101.0   Designing Your Fitness Maintenance
        Program for Use Now and After Discharge
101.1   It's Possible and It Feels Good to Be Physically Fit
101.1   Physical Impairments Can be Overcome
102.0   Guest Speaker: Adults Expanding Knowledge
102.2   It's Never Too Late to Learn
103.1   Discovering Leisure Close By and Mail Order
103.2   Assertive Car Pooling for Leisure Pleasure
103.3   Transportation a Factor of Leisure Discharge
        Planning
104.0   Fun and Money
104.1   Leisure at a Reasonable Price
104.2   Developing a Leisure Budget
104.2   Economic Changes Mean Leisure Adjustments
104.2   Leisure Opportunities at Your Library and
        Other Public Facilities
104.3   The Average Cost of Leisure
104.4   Are You Getting Rich to Enjoy or Relapse?
105.1   Value of Leisure Aloneness
105.2   Fun and the Opposite Sex
105.2   Family Leisure What is it, How Does it Work?
105.3   Family Leisure
105.3   Meeting Son and/or Daughter Needs.
106.0   Coping with Burnout
106.1   What Causes Stress and What Causes Relaxation
106.2   Alternative Methods of Relaxation
106.3   Matching Leisure Relaxers to Stress Producers
107.1   Childhood Play: Lessons Learned About
        Leisure
107.2   Recall Memories Associated with
        Balloons and Cotton Candy
107.3   Appropriate Times and Places for Kids Play
108.1   Leisure Planning Assistance
109.0   What's the Risk?
109.2   Learning New Things and Learning
        Creative Activities
109.4   Leisure Rap

For Skill Development Sessions:

200.0   Finding and Taking Target Heart Rate
214.1   Let's Play Cards and Table Games
217.1   How to Laugh and Make it Funny
218.2   How To Play Backgammon
221.2   Aerobics Designed for Persons Over 60
224.1   Home Exercise Programs
232.2   Writing Letters for Freebies
234.2   Cake Decorating
234.2   Calligraphy
234.3   Customizing Your Home
245.1   How to Start Pen Pal Letter Writing
247.1   Playing Pictionary™ and Charades
247.1   Shouting Contests
247.1   Yarn Spinning and Telling Fisherman's
        Tales
249.2   Planning Alcohol/Drug Free Social
        Gatherings
251.2   Walking for Health and Fitness
254.1   How to Go Fly A Kite
255.1   How to Play One-Player Games
256.2   How to Relax with Music (see Creative)
256.2   How to Relax with Nature
259.1   Collector's Corner
264.4   How to Make a Travel Plan
377.1   Rhythm and Kazoo Band
378.2   Mime and Mimicry Club
389.4   Spiritual Club
349.4   Leisure Rap: What's New in Family
        Activities
349.4   Leisure Rap: What's New in Water Fun
        Games
359.4   Leisure Rap: What's New in Collecting
        Things
359.4   Leisure Rap: What's New in Individual
        Activities
369.4   Leisure Rap: What's New in Computer
        Fun
369.4   Leisure Rap: What's New in High Tech
379.4   Leisure Rap: What's New in Creative
        Activities
389.4   Leisure Rap: What's New in Spiritual
        Activities
399.4   Leisure Rap: What's New in High Risk
        Activities.
399.4   Leisure Rap: What's New in Outdoor
        Activities
(Special Events)
345.0   Theme Parties
345.2   Picnic and Special Event Planning
345.3   Family Picnics
399.3   Marshmallow Cook Out

(Library)

362.2   Games That Practice the 3 R's
362.2   Reading and Math Volunteers Schedule
362.3   Library/Audio Visuals Unsupervised
362.3   Library Unsupervised
362.1   Jigsaw Puzzles and Non-Word Mazes
362.1   Picture Library and Comic Books
362.2   Crossword Puzzles
362.2   Magazine Library and Comic Books
362.3   Book Library With Topics for Each
          Interest Category
362.4   Instructional Library of Leisure Pursuits
382.1   Assisted Reading of AA and Spiritual Materials

(Non-supervised Activities)

389.1   Spiritual activities Schedule
389.4   Chapel/Church Hours
364.1   Public Education Channel Schedule
368.2   Backgammon and Other Game Check-out
368.3   Chess and Other Game Check-out
368.4   Divergent Thinking Challenges and
          Games Check-out
374.1   Crafts Room Schedule (Paper-Mâché, Trash Art
          Projects)

For Recreation Therapy:

402.0   Learning Stimulation
402.01   Learning Disability Identification
402.02   Attitude Adjusters
402.03   Games for Success
402.04   Behavior Modification
402.05   Creative Applications
402.06   Learning of Value
403.20   Assertive Transport Improvement
405.0   Family Relationships
405.01   Songs of Relationships
405.02   Haveta-Supposedta-Can't:
405.23   Drama for Family Roles and Fun
407.0   Restoration of Developmental Play Behaviors
407.11   Creative Writing About Events in a Child's Life
407.12   Ridiculous Situations
407.13   Drama: Role Playing Kids Play
407.14   Pot and Pan and Noise Making Things
407.16   Tele-Joke
407.21   Songs of Youth
408.0   Creative Problem Solving
408.21   Color-Me-Not
408.22   Read-Me-Not
408.23   Create-a-Game
408.24   Half Deck
408.25   Sentence Malpractice and Old Story New Ending
408.26   Ana-ma-grammy
408.28   Traditional Games
408.31   New Pathways
408.33   Impromptu Adventures
408.34   Trash Art

410.0   Situation Response Awareness
410.01   I Yi Yi
410.02   Grab It
410.09   Music's Self Fulfilling Prophecy
420.0   Process Addiction Treatment
420.01   Nothingness
420.02   Process Addiction Withdrawal: Detox
420.03   Process Addiction Monitoring
440.0   Managing Grief
450.0   Trust of Self and Others
450.02   Truth or Dare
450.03   Oh No Not That Again I'd Love To
460.0   Risk Taking (Through Art and Social Interaction)
470.0   Anticipations and Expectations Management
470.01   Ain't It Awful?
470.02   Deriving Positives from Positive Expectations
480.0   Decision Making
480.01   No Decision is A Decision
480.02   Decision Making Practice
480.03   Failure to Deliberate

The list still seems overwhelming. To narrow the list, select criteria. The most important thing to do is help the client understand the connection between leisure and addiction. If limitations are severe, create Leisure Awareness through Leisure Education sessions, and then refer to other sources of assistance. If a client knows he/she has a need, and where to go for help, well, that's the best that can be done in constricted conditions.

OVERWHELMING CLIENT STAFF RATIO

When each Therapeutic Recreation Specialist is responsible for 100 or more clients, the Therapeutic Recreation Specialist becomes a consultant rather than a therapist. Training of staff belonging to other services is imperative. They will have more hands-on experiences with the clients. Identifying clients who are "Independent" in Leisure Functioning and who have leisure skills is also imperative. They will be in charge of leading most Skill Development and Re-Creation which occurs. If the population is not "Independent" in leisure when they enter treatment, then make sure some of them get there before discharge. Nothing provides more health and hope to a new client than seeing a client preparing for discharge who has his/her act together. [Ch10:Community Government, Style Shop, Break Times, Club and Rap Sessions] If Skill Development sessions are required, don't try to teach 100 clients how to play a game at the same time. Teach the staff who escorts the clients to the activity, and teach the "Independent" clients. Let them teach the rest of the clients. [Ch9]

Negotiate with administration a percentage of clients for whom you will provide in-depth services. Use the assessment process to select that percentage which needs your service the most. If more clients need you than there is you to give, then that's administration's problem, not yours. Remember, doing too much looks exactly the same as doing nothing at all. [Ch8; Ch11]

Ever tried to do an effective discussion session with 100 clients at once? Is it possible? Yes. Provide pre-training to the staff and "Independent" client leaders. Break the 100 into 10 groups of 10. Place one pre-trained leader in each group. Use a microphone and stand where all can be observed. (If you have an assistant, allow the assistant to float from group to group to make sure none of the groups get off track.) Present the topic for discussion from the microphone. Allow the group leaders to handle the discussion. Keep the groups on track by breaking the discussion into small, short, simple segments. Have a person from each group summarize to the other groups the points discussed after each segment is concluded.

Create a quality audiovisual library. Make sure clients have an opportunity to use it. Make sure clients know what resources are available. A homemade video of the Therapeutic Recreation Service and library resources is most effective. It saves staff time and does a better job too.

FINAL COMMENTS

1. The purpose of this text is to describe the role of Therapeutic Recreation in the treatment of substance addiction. As such, it has focused on the miracle elixir known as recreation. This should not be construed to imply that recreation alone can "cure" alcoholism or drug addiction.

2. Addiction is a disease. The development of a healthy independent leisure lifestyle will not restore an alcoholic to a life of social drinking. Once the disease has caused changes within the individual's body, the person is always just one drink away from a drunk. Recreation alone will not keep an alcoholic from drinking nor an addict from using. A healthy leisure lifestyle makes the pill of abstinence easier to swallow.

3. Therapeutic Recreation cannot and should not take the place of group therapy. Recreation and group therapy cannot take the place of Alcoholics Anonymous or Narcotic Anonymous, or any of the other established group support mechanisms. This text attempts to recommend a hand-in-hand approach: Therapy, Therapeutic Recreation, and a 12-step program, together in the treatment phase.

4. This text suggests that the end product of treatment is recovery. And recovery means an AA or NA member with a healthy leisure lifestyle. Recovery is waking up in the morning thankful for life.

5. This text has offered a variety of specific activity recommendations. Remember, no two individuals are exactly alike. A client may resemble one discussed in this text, but don't jump to conclusions. Your client's needs may be extremely different from the needs of one described in this text. Many drug types have not been fully discussed. For example, "ice" may require protocols that were not discussed. To select an appropriate program, consider the drug's family tree and the internal systems that are being manipulated. An appropriate selection will result from these considerations.

6. Reality is but a perception, unique to each individual. Let your perception be filled with seasoned hope. Let it be filled with acceptance. Let honesty and balance rule each hour.

7. Strive to accept the limits and boundaries. I cannot change the world. I can change me. I cannot cure another's pain. I can release my own. I cannot make another change his path to mine no matter how prudent it seems to try. I can respect another's choice though different from my own. I can always practice what I preach.

8. At all costs, keep your own leisure healthy.

9. Having personally experienced the value of leisure, help other staff to do the same.

10. Help your clients realize the difference between living and existing.

11. Start today. One day at a time.

12. Until we meet, may the wind be soft and gentle and always at your back.

APPENDIX

POLICY: VIDEO RECORDING

Each client shall sign a release form permitting use of photographic equipment and video recording at the time of admission. A list of clients refusing to sign such a form will be maintained within the Therapeutic Recreation Service. Clients who do not give permission to be photographed or recorded will not attend sessions in which pictures are taken or recordings are made.

The photographs and video recordings are made for the sole purpose of therapeutic benefit to clients. The standard release form does not give the facility the right to use video recordings or photographs for any form of public demonstration. A separate and specific form of release must be used for these purposes.

All photographs and videotapes made of clients will be destroyed after client has received maximum therapeutic benefit from them.

Sample Video Recording Release Form:

I _____ hereby give TNT staff permission to videotape record me during my treatment, and to take pictures as desired. I understand that the sole purpose of such recordings is to help me see myself. I understand that therapists working with me may also view the tapes. I understand that other clients may see these tapes with my knowledge and permission. (For example, if a tape is made in a group setting, then all clients in that group may see that tape.) I understand that the only purpose of this tape is therapeutic benefit and it will not be used for any other purpose without my knowledge and permission. I understand that the tape will be destroyed after therapeutic benefits have been gained. I also understand that I have the right to sue for breach of confidentiality if the tape is used in any way other than that specified above.

_____
Client's Printed Name

_____
Client Signature   Date

_____
Witness   Date

JOB DESCRIPTION

JOB TITLE: Therapeutic Recreation Team Manager

RESPONSIBLE TO: Center Coordinator

RESPONSIBLE FOR: Therapeutic Recreation Team which includes Therapeutic Recreation Personnel, Swimming Personnel, Non-Paid Students and Volunteers assigned to Therapeutic Recreation Services.

DESCRIPTION OF WORK:

The Therapeutic Recreation Team Manager is responsible for overall planning, development, budgeting, staffing, and administration of the Therapeutic Recreation Service and Swimming Program. Responsibilities include recruiting, influencing, motivating, educating, scheduling, evaluating, and controlling assigned staff. The manager is responsible for all actions and functions of the Therapeutic Recreation Service and Team. Responsible for operating Services within the guidelines, policies, procedures and philosophies of the organization. The TR Team Manager functions as a member of the Management Team in developing, maintaining, communicating, and evaluating overall policies, procedures, and guidelines for the Center. Also responsible for the development and maintenance of productive communication channels within the Therapeutic Recreation Team and between Therapeutic Recreation and other teams.

MORE SPECIFIC DUTIES INCLUDE:

1. Establishing standard operating procedures for Therapeutic Recreation consistent with organizational policies and procedures.
2. Recruiting, hiring, supervising, developing, educating, evaluating, and terminating staff as situation warrants. Monitoring employee performance and developing employees to their full potential are essential aspects of the position. Hiring and firing is done with the knowledge and consent of the Management Team.
3. Establishing sound expense and reimbursement practices to financially support Therapeutic Recreation functions. Establishing and following a budget for services and programs provided. The TR Team Manager has authority to purchase any equipment or supplies deemed necessary when funds are available; however, expenditures which exceed budgeted amounts are considered grounds for dismissal.
4. Maintaining safe operating procedures to assure safety for all participants. This includes routine safety reviews of equipment, supplies, facilities, programs, activities, and staff.
5. Participating in and conducting meetings as appropriate to assure effective communications. Taking all steps necessary to develop and maintain a team approach to treatment.
6. Participating in studies and ongoing review of data to improve effectiveness, efficiency, and quality of services provided.
7. Actively providing Therapeutic Recreation Services as time permits, providing backup coverage for vacationing Therapeutic Recreation Staff.
8. Participate in the organization and conduct of education experiences for the Service, the Organization, and the Community. Educational experiences include improving public understanding to the disease of addiction as well as the use of Therapeutic Recreation Practices related to the disease of addiction.
9. Providing quality experience for Therapeutic Recreation students.
10. Taking rotating administrative call as needed.
11. Utilizing computerized programs and data to operate the service and perform position functions.
12. Attending Community Meetings and being responsible to the needs of the clientele.
13. Serving as a Leisure Consultant to Employee Recreation Club and providing services as required.
14. Coordinating swimming program and supervising swimming pool staff.

HOURS OF WORK:

Vary from week to week to permit full contact and review of a seven day a week, twenty-four hour a day service.

EDUCATION AND EXPERIENCE REQUIREMENTS:

Masters degree in Therapeutic Recreation Administration from an NRPA accredited college or university curriculum. In addition to Masters, a Bachelor degree in Therapeutic Recreation is required, or at least one year of work as a Therapeutic Recreation Specialist. At least nine hours of course work in substance abuse, psychology, counseling or the equivalent. At least twelve hours course work in management, business, computer operations, accounting, and/or marketing, or the equivalent. At least three years experience in a management role. It is desirable that the experience in Therapeutic Recreation was concurrent with the experience in management. At least three years experience working with persons with alcohol and/or drug addiction. Personal experience with alcohol/drugs as a user or a family member is acceptable, however person must demonstrate a minimum of three years sobriety or clean time.

OTHER SKILLS AND ABILITIES REQUIRED:

Progressive and dynamic knowledge of Therapeutic Recreation and Participatory Management required. Optimism and innovativeness essential. Ability to communicate honestly, openly, and effectively, in verbal and written form essential. Skills in evaluation, budgeting, and computer programming/operation desirable but not mandatory. Must have strong working knowledge of group dynamics and application to Therapeutic Recreation Practices. Must have organiza tional skills. The ability to translate philosophical principles and ideals into practical action is also essential. Must be able to demonstrate safe driving practices. Must be able to maintain client confidentiality. Ability to exercise good judgment mandatory.

CERTIFICATION REQUIREMENTS:

Certification as a Therapeutic Recreation Specialist (C.T.R.S.) with National Council for Therapeutic Recreation Certification or the equivalent. Certification as an Alcoholism Counselor or the equivalent desirable.

JOB DESCRIPTION

JOB TITLE: Therapeutic Recreation Specialist 1, 2, 4, and 5

RESPONSIBLE TO: Therapeutic Recreation Team Manager

RESPONSIBLE FOR: TRS 1: Therapeutic Recreation Technician B.
TRS 2: Therapeutic Recreation Technician D.
TRS 4: Therapeutic Recreation Technician B. when TRS 1 is absent.
TRS 5: Therapeutic Recreation Technician D. when TRS 2 is absent.
Also Volunteers, Interns, Other Technicians and Assistants when assigned.

DESCRIPTION OF WORK:

This is highly skilled rehabilitative work with clients whose abilities to cope with tasks of living are threatened or impaired by the disease of alcohol and/or drug addiction. Work involves initial evaluation of level of functioning, leisure independence, periodic re-evaluation for assigned clients, and designing and implementing treatment plans that resolve identified problems for assigned clients. Treatment goals and programs are designed to restructure time, provide options for alcohol/drug free activity, and to regenerate physical condition. Primary goal of work is to improve leisure independence levels through provision of Leisure Education/Counseling sessions, and Recreation Therapy with assigned clients and families as needed. Develops leisure discharge plans. Treatment plans are carried out through the provision of group Leisure Education sessions, and/or small group or individual Recreation Therapy and Leisure Counseling sessions as needed. Functions as a member of a therapy team to accomplish designated team goals which are specific to the recovery program of each client and may include: improve emotional control, communication skills, frustration tolerance, self-understanding, motivation, coping with stress, relation, understand disease concept of addiction, etc. Functions as a member of the Therapeutic Recreation Team to develop and maintain Therapeutic Recreation Services and facilities which are responsive to the needs of the TNT Center and clientele. Though primary focus of work is on the clients's post discharge needs, work includes planning, organizing, and conducting Re-Creation events in consultation with clients and the Therapeutic Recreation Team. Provides Skill Development sessions which develop clients skills, allowing them to participate in special events at the highest level of leisure independence possible. Works closely with other Therapeutic Recreation Staff to produce an atmosphere which is conducive to leisure and rehabilitation. Maintains safety in all aspects of work. Assists and supervises Therapeutic Recreation Technician and others when assigned, in the conduct of their duties. Responsible for routine functions of supervision for such persons including: monitoring, advising, evaluating, developing, etc. Contact with outpatients, clients after discharge & during after-care, family members, and the public is provided when assigned and as needed.

MORE SPECIFIC DUTIES INCLUDE:

(Each Therapeutic Recreation Specialist is responsible for the following. Therapeutic Recreation Specialist 1 and 2 perform duties primarily in connection with inpatient clients. Therapeutic Recreation Specialists 4 and 5 perform duties primarily in connection with out-patient clients, transition center clients and after-care clients.)

1. Introducing clients to Therapeutic Recreation concepts while they are in detox.
2. Using TRI to evaluate clients and family needs, within 48 hours of admission.
3. Using computerized formats to interpret assessment data, develop treatment plans, and schedule activity for a maximum of 44 assigned clients.
4. Sharing insights and progress of assigned clients with treatment staff through computerized systems and through staff conferences.
5. Planning and conducting four Leisure Education sessions each week.
6. Planning and assisting in the conduct of two skill development sessions each week.
7. Planning and assisting Therapeutic Recreation staff and clients in the conduct of one special event each week.
8. Providing one Leisure Education session for clients each week.
9. Scheduling and conducting Leisure Counseling, Recreation Therapy, and Skill Development sessions as required to accomplish treatment objectives.
10. Using computer to summarize activity, keep attendance, review progress, develop discharge summaries, etc.
11. Assuming responsibility for the safety of all staff and clients within an activity under his/her supervision.
12. Promoting and maintaining good working relations within Therapeutic Recreation and between Therapeutic Recreation and other Staff.

13. Assisting in routine operations and procedures as assigned by TR Team Manager to permit effective and efficient operations of the service as a whole.
14. Participating in meetings to update staff on client progress and approach changes, gain input from client representatives, give input and receive feedback on Center and Service decisions.
15. Participating in education and professional development activities on a regular basis.
16. Other duties as assigned.

HOURS OF WORK:

TRS 1: 40 hours per week Sundays - Thursdays (usually mornings and afternoons)
TRS 2: 40 hours per week Tuesdays - Saturdays (usually mornings and afternoons)
TRS 4: 40 hours per week Sundays - Thursdays (usually afternoons and evenings)
TRS 5: 40 hours per week Tuesdays - Saturdays (usually afternoons and evenings)

EDUCATION AND EXPERIENCE REQUIREMENTS:

Bachelors degree from an NRPA accredited college or university with a major in Therapeutic Recreation. At least nine credit hours should be in substance abuse, psychology, or counseling. Degree must include at least 400 hours of fieldwork or internship experience. Minimum of two years experience in a Therapeutic Recreation Treatment setting. At least two years experience working with alcohol/drug abuse clientele. Persons may substitute personal experience with alcohol/drug abuse for the two years of work experience in an alcohol/drug treatment setting, but must demonstrate three consecutive years of sobriety/clean time prior to the hiring date.

OTHER SKILLS AND ABILITIES REQUIRED:

Must possess a wide variety of leisure skills and a firm knowledge of the value and role of leisure. Strong working knowledge of group dynamics and application to Therapeutic Recreation Services. Ability to exercise good discretionary judgment in the conduct of duties. Ability to perform work within organizational boundaries. Ability to translate philosophical principles and ideals into practical and efficient action. Ability to relate and communicate effectively with clients, families, Therapeutic Recreation personnel, and other staff. Ability to document observations and activities accurately and consistently. Ability to influence others positively. Ability to supervise and to motivate others is essential. Skills in computer use desirable, but not required. Must have the capacity and willingness to learn computer operations. Must be able to demonstrate safe driving practices. Must be able to maintain client confidentiality. Knowledge of the disease concept of addiction desirable, must have the willingness to view addiction as a disease.

CERTIFICATION REQUIREMENTS:

Certified Therapeutic Recreation Specialist (C.T.R.S.) or the equivalent. Certification as Alcoholism Counselor preferred but not required.

JOB DESCRIPTION

JOB TITLE: Therapeutic Recreation Specialist 3

RESPONSIBLE TO: Therapeutic Recreation Team Manager

RESPONSIBLE FOR: TRS 3: Therapeutic Recreation Assistant A.
Also Volunteers, Interns, other Technicians and Assistants when assigned.

DESCRIPTION OF WORK:

This is highly skilled rehabilitative work with clients whose abilities to cope with tasks of living are threatened or impaired by the disease of alcohol and/or drug addiction. Treatment goals and programs are designed to restructure time and provide options for alcohol/drug free activity, and to regenerate physical conditioning. Primary goal of work is to improve leisure independence levels through provision of Recreation Therapy with assigned clients and families as needed. Assigned clients may be from inpatient, outpatient, after-care, or transition center. Treatment plans are carried out through the provision of specific interventions such as the Recovery-Bound Program. Functions as a member of the Therapeutic Recreation team to accomplish designated goals, and consults with other teams as needed. Outcomes for client involvement include improving emotional control, communication skills, frustration tolerance, self-understanding, motivation, coping with stress, relation, understand disease concept of addiction, revision of developmental play behaviors, etc. Functions as a member of the Therapeutic Recreation Team to develop and maintain Therapeutic Recreation Services and facilities which are responsive to the needs of the TNT Center and clientele. Work also includes planning, organizing, conducting Re-Creation events, in consultation with clients and the Therapeutic Recreation Team. Provides Skill Development sessions which develop clients skills, allowing them to participate in special events at the highest level of leisure independence possible. Works closely with other Therapeutic Recreation Staff to produce an atmosphere which is conducive to leisure and rehabilitation. Maintains safety in all aspects of work. Assists and supervises Therapeutic Recreation Technician A and others when assigned, in the conduct of their duties. Responsible for routine functions of supervision for such persons, including monitoring, advising, evaluating, developing, etc. Contact with outpatients, clients after discharge, and during after-care, family members, and the public is provided when assigned and as needed. Functions as Therapeutic Recreation Team Manager when TR Team Manager is absent.

MORE SPECIFIC DUTIES INCLUDE:

1. Coordinating and conducting the Recovery-Bound Program.
2. Using TRI to evaluate progress and outcomes, and communicating results to appropriate Therapeutic Recreation Specialists.
3. Using computerized formats to interpret assessment data, develop treatment plans, and schedule activities.
4. Conducting anger ventilation, trust development, relaxation, process addiction treatment, play restoration, and other Recreation Therapy sessions as needed.
5. Planning and conducting Leisure Education sessions when needed.
6. Planning and assisting in the conduct of skill development sessions when needed.
7. Planning and assisting Therapeutic Recreation staff and clients in the conduct of one special even each week.
8. Assuming caseload responsibilities for Therapeutic Recreation Specialists 1, 2, 4, and 5, when needed.
9. Assuming responsibilities and duties of Therapeutic Recreation Team Manager when needed.
10. Provide training to other staff as needed.
11. Assuming responsibility for the safety of all staff and clients within an activity under his/her supervision.
12. Promoting and maintaining good working relations within Therapeutic Recreation and between Therapeutic Recreation and other Staff.
13. Assisting in routine operations and procedures as assigned by TR Team Manager to permit effective and efficient operations of the service as a whole.
14. Participating in meetings to update staff on client progress and approach changes, gain input from client representatives, give input and receive feedback on Center and Service decisions.
15. Participating in education and professional development activities on a regular basis.
16. Other duties as assigned.

HOURS OF WORK: TRS 3: 40 hours per week are routinely scheduled as needed.

EDUCATION AND EXPERIENCE REQUIREMENTS:

Bachelors degree from an NRPA accredited college or university with a major in Therapeutic Recreation. At least nine credit hours should be in substance abuse, psychology, or counseling. Degree must include at least 400 hours of fieldwork or internship experience. Minimum of two years experience in a Therapeutic Recreation Treatment setting. At least two years experience working with alcohol/drug abuse clientele. Persons may substitute personal experience with alcohol/drug abuse for the two years of work experience in an alcohol/drug treatment setting but must demonstrate three consecutive years of sobriety/clean time prior to the hiring date. Training in a recognized adventure course program mandatory.

OTHER SKILLS AND ABILITIES REQUIRED:

Must possess a wide variety of leisure skills and a firm knowledge of the value and role of leisure. Strong working knowledge of group dynamics and application to Therapeutic Recreation Services. Ability to exercise good discretionary judgment in the conduct of duties. Ability to perform work within organizational boundaries. Ability to translate philosophical principles and ideals into practical and efficient action. Ability to relate and communicate effectively with clients, families, Therapeutic Recreation personnel, and other staff. Ability to document observations and activities accurately, and consistently. Ability to influence others positively. Ability to supervise and to motivate others is essential. Skills in computer use desirable but not required. Must have the capacity and willingness to learn computer operations. Must be able to demonstrate safe driving practices. Must be able to maintain client confidentiality. Knowledge of the disease concept of addiction desirable, must have the willingness to view addiction as a disease.

CERTIFICATION REQUIREMENTS:

Certified Therapeutic Recreation Specialist (C.T.R.S.) or the equivalent. Certified Adventure Course Instructor. Certification as Alcoholism Counselor preferred but not required.

JOB DESCRIPTION

JOB TITLE: Recreation Assistant A and C

RESPONSIBLE TO: Therapeutic Recreation Team Manager

RESPONSIBLE FOR: Volunteers when assigned.

DESCRIPTION OF WORK:

This work involves secretarial and receptionist duties as well as the provision of activities for clients as directed. Responsible for the provision of skill development sessions which acquaint clients with the basics of computer operations, library, and audio-visual functions of the service. Also conducts morning exercise sessions as directed. Provides area supervision which includes monitoring and controlling equipment and facility use. Maintains library and assists clients in reading selections. Programs and operates Therapeutic Recreation computers to meet service needs. Provides input into Center's management and operations.

MORE SPECIFIC DUTIES INCLUDE:

1. Conduct morning exercise program. (Assistant A: twice per week, Assistant C: five times per week.)
2. Provide Skill Development for Employee Recreation Club upon request.
3. Supervise area when not performing other functions.
4. Provide skill development sessions. (Assistant A: three times per week in activities such as games, art and/or music. Assistant C: two times per week in activities such as computer games, basics, and programming.)
5. Prepare audio visual equipment, and written materials for sessions and meetings as needed.
6. Introduce new clients, staff, and visitors to routines as needed.
7. Maintain and update files and bulletin boards as needed.
8. Perform safety checks on equipment as directed.
9. Coordinate skill development sessions for guest instructors.
10. Coordinate style salon.
11. Use computers to file records, reports, and review daily routines as needed.
12. Schedule and coordinate workshops offered by Therapeutic Recreation staff as needed.
13. Other duties as assigned.

HOURS OF WORK:

Assistant A: 26 hours per week. (2:30 p.m. - 6:30 p.m. Wednesdays; 6:30 a.m. - 5:30 p.m., Fridays: 8:00 a.m. - 5:30 p.m. Saturdays and Sundays.

Assistant C: 40 hours per week, beginning Mondays and ending Fridays. (6:30 a.m. - 4:40 p.m. Mondays - Wednesdays; 6:30 a.m. - 3:00 p.m. Thursdays; 6:30 a.m. - 11:00 a.m. Fridays.)

EDUCATION AND EXPERIENCE REQUIREMENTS:

Assistant A: Minimum of one year college course in Recreation, or Therapeutic Recreation. Course work in Therapeutic Recreation desirable. Experience working in an Alcohol/Drug Addiction Treatment Center, and in a Therapeutic Recreation Service preferred.

Assistant C: Associate of Arts degree in Computer Science or in a related field. Course work in Therapeutic Recreation desireable. Minimum of one year of paid experience working as a secretary, receptionist, computer programmer or the equivalent. Experience working in an Alcohol/Drug Addiction Treatment Center, and in a Therapeutic Recreation Service preferred.

OTHER SKILLS AND ABILITIES REQUIRED:

Must have strong working knowledge of computers. Must be able to organize and systematize service communications and documents. Must be skilled in communicating accurate observed behaviors to others, and in carrying out assigned tasks. Must have working knowledge of group dynamics and demonstrated concern for people. Knowledge of, and able to instruct skill development sessions as indicated above. Must be able to conduct exercise sessions as directed. Must be able to demonstrate safe driving practices. Must be able to maintain client confidentiality. Must have a philosophy of Therapeutic Recreation which is compatible with the Center's philosophy.

CERTIFICATION REQUIREMENTS: None.

JOB DESCRIPTION

JOB TITLE: Therapeutic Recreation Technician B and D

RESPONSIBLE TO: TRT B.: Therapeutic Recreation Specialist 1
TRT D.: Therapeutic Recreation Specialist 3

RESPONSIBLE FOR: Volunteers and when assigned.

DESCRIPTION OF WORK:

This skilled rehabilitative work, involves the provision of activities for clients, as directed by the Therapeutic Recreation Specialist. Responsible for the provision of skill development sessions which acquaint clients with the basics of a variety of leisure pursuits. Area supervision includes monitoring and controlling equipment and facilities use. Participates in and encourages spontaneous activity between clients during voluntary recreation times. Responsible for developing Re-Creation activities requested by clients which support the Center's and Service's objectives. Involves clients without visitors in skill development and recreation during critical visiting hours. Assists clients in the conduct of Community Government as needed. Maintains equipment in safe working condition, performing repairs as needed. Operates computers to maintain records, file reports, and to review daily routines. Drives Center's van to transport clients to and from AA/NA meetings. Provides input into Center's management and operations.

MORE SPECIFIC DUTIES INCLUDE:

1. Conduct evening exercise programs for relaxation purposes when assigned.
2. Transport clients to AA/NA meetings when assigned.
3. Provide Skill Development and/or Recreation for Employee Recreation Club when assigned.
4. Supervise area and provide Re-Creation opportunities five times per week.
5. Assist in the development and conduct of Special Events when assigned (not more than twice per week.)
6. Assist with Kids Group once per week when and as directed.
7. TRT B: Provide Skill Development four times per week in activities such as sports, games, and collecting as directed.
8. TRT D: Provide Skill Development Sessions in activities such as art, music, and dance as directed.
9. Maintain equipment in safe working condition as directed.
10. Communicate with Therapeutic Recreation Team as needed.
11. Provide interactions with clientele as directed by supervisor.
12. Perform other duties as assigned by supervisor.
13. Participate in education and Center management upon request.

HOURS OF WORK:

TRT B.: 40 hours per week, beginning Sundays and ending Thursdays. (2:30 p.m. - 11:00 p.m. Sundays, Mondays, Tuesdays; 3:00 p.m. - 9:00 p.m. Wednesdays; 12:30 p.m. - 11:00 p.m. Thursdays.)

TRT D.: 34 hours per week, beginning Wednesdays and ending Saturdays. (2:30 p.m. - 11:00 p.m. Wednesdays; 12:30 p.m. - 8:30 p.m. Thursdays; 1:00 p.m. - 11:00 p.m. Fridays and Saturdays.)

EDUCATION AND EXPERIENCE REQUIREMENTS:

Minimum of an Associate of Arts degree with major in Therapeutic Recreation, or completion of major course work for Bachelor Degree in Therapeutic Recreation. One year experience working in the field of Therapeutic Recreation and experience working in an Alcohol/Drug Addition Treatment Center preferred.

OTHER SKILLS AND ABILITIES REQUIRED:

Must be capable of independent action within established guidelines. Must be able to implement objectives set by supervisor. Must be skilled in communicating accurate observed behaviors to others, and carry out treatment plan objectives as directed. Must have good working knowledge of group dynamics. Must be able to shift from competitive to non-competitive leadership styles as dictated by client's needs. Knowledgeable of and able to instruct a wide variety of activities (TRT B: Sports, Games etc. TRT D.: Arts, Music, Drama, Dance.) Must be able to assist clients in achieving relaxation through exercise techniques. Must be able to learn routine computer operations and equipment maintenance procedures. Must be able to demonstrate safe driving practices. Must be able to maintain client confidentiality. Must have a philosophy of Therapeutic Recreation which is compatible with the Center's philosophy.

CERTIFICATION REQUIREMENTS:

Certified TRT by the National Council for Therapeutic Recreation Certification, or the equivalent. Unrestricted valid driver's license, with no moving traffic violations during past two years. SCHEDULE: Basic for Clients During Treatment.

BASIC SCHEDULE FOR TNT CLIENTS DURING TREATMENT PHASE

TIME	MONDAY		TUESDAY		WEDNESDAY		THURSDAY		FRIDAY		SATURDAY		SUNDAY	
Wake-up 6:30	6:00 a.m. exercise		6:00 a.m. exercise		6:00 a.m. exercise		6:00 a.m. exercise		6:00 a.m. exercise		6:30 a.m.		6:30 a.m.	
7:00 7:30 8:00 8:30	/////	/////	/////	/////	medications breakfast		medical sign-up community meet		/////	/////	/////	/////	/////	/////
	Groups 1-4	Groups 5-8	Groups 1-4	Groups 5-8	Groups 1-4	Groups 5-8	Groups 1-4	Groups 5-8	Groups 1-4	Groups 5-8	Groups 1-4	Groups 5-8	Groups 1-4	Groups 5-8
9:00 9:30 10:00	leisure educ. session	group therapy session	leisure educ. session	group therapy session	leisure educ. session	group therapy session	leisure educ. session	group therapy session	leisure educ. session	group therapy session	exercise	exercise	spiritual exercise	spiritual exercise
10:30 11:00 11:30	group therapy session	leisure educ. session	group therapy session	leisure educ. session	group therapy session	leisure educ. session	group therapy session	leisure educ. session	group therapy session	Leisure educ. session	family educ. or free	family educ. or free	12 steps 12 trad.	12 steps 12 trad.
12:00 12:30 1:00	/////	/////	/////	/////	/////	/////	LUNCH		/////	/////	/////	/////	/////	/////
1:30 2:00 2:30	addiction educ. session		addiction educ. session		addiction educ. session		12 steps and 12 trad.		addiction educ. session		family leisure session	free free free	free free free	family leisure session
3:00 3:30 4:00	skill develop. and rec. therapy		skill develop. and rec. therapy		skill develop. and rec. therapy		skill develop. and rec. therapy		skill develop. and rec. therapy		skill develop. session	free free free	free free free	skill develop. session
4:30 5:00 5:30	/////	/////	/////	/////	/////	/////	DINNER		/////	/////	/////	/////	/////	/////
6:00 6:30 7:00	family therapy or free		family educ. or free		recreation special event		couples group or free		free free free		lecture lecture lecture	free free free	free free free	lecture lecture lecture
7:30 8:00 8:30 9:00 9:30	transport to AA/NA in town return		AA/NA at center		AA/NA at center		AA/NA at center		transport to AA/NA in town return		AA/NA at center _____ recreation special event		AA/NA in town return _____	
10:00 10:30	exercise		exercise		exercise		exercise		exercise				exercise	
Lights out	11:30 p.m.		11:30 p.m.		11:30 p.m.		11:30 p.m.		12:30 a.m.		12:30 a.m.		11:30 p.m.	

TYPICAL SCHEDULE FOR THERAPEUTIC RECREATION TEAM MANAGER

TIME	MONDAY	TUESDAY	WEDNESDAY	THURSDAY	FRIDAY	SATURDAY	SUNDAY
6:30	exercise		exercise				
7:00	discussion with		managers meet				
7:30	ex. leader		" "				
8:00	comm. meet		comm. meet				
8:30	update		managers meet	update			
9:00	leisure		managers meet	leisure		1st. Sat. of mo.:	
9:30	education		management	education		exercise	
10:00	session		functions	session		family educ.	3rd. Sun. of mo.:
10:30	leisure			leisure		session	exercise
11:00	education			education		re-creation	re-creation
11:30	session			session		program	program
12:00	lunch		lunch	lunch		supervision	supervision
12:30	lunch		lunch	lunch		"	family leisure
1:00	twice per mo.	update, then	TR meet	TR meet	addiction	family leisure	skill develop. and
1:30	special	recovery bound	TR meet	TR meet	education	education	recovery bound
2:00	out-patient	adventure	TR meet	TR meet	session	skill dev.	supervision
2:30	programming	course	TR meet				
3:00	skill dev. and/or	program	management		skill dev.		
3:30	rec. therapy	"	functions		or R. T.		
4:00	" "	"	"				
4:30	documentation	"	report				
5:00	report	report					
5:30		dinner					
6:00		dinner					
6:30		leisure educ. for		4th. Thurs. of mo.:			
7:00		out-patient		evening program			
7:30		family					
8:00		leisure				2nd. Sat. of mo.:	
8:30		education				recreation	
9:00		documentation				special	
9:30		meet ex. leader				event	
10:00		exercise					
TOTAL:	10 hrs.	8.5 hrs.	9.5 hrs.	5 hrs.	3 hrs.	average 4 hrs.	

BASIC SCHEDULE FOR THERAPEUTIC RECREATION SPECIALISTS 1 AND 2

Time	MONDAY		TUESDAY		WEDNESDAY		THRUSDAY		FRIDAY		SATURDAY		SUNDAY	
	TRS #1	TRS #2	TRS #1	TRS #2	TRS #1	TRS #2	TRS #1	TRS #2	TRS #1	TRS #2	TRS #1	TRS #2	TRS #1	TRS #2
8:30	update		update	update	update	update	update	update		update				
9:00	leisure		leisure	leisure	leisure	leisure	leisure	leisure		leisure				
9:30	educ.		educ.	educ.	educ.	educ.	educ.	educ.		educ.				
10:00	session		session	session	session	session	session	session		session				
10:30	leisure		leisure	leisure	leisure	leisure	leisure	leisure		leisure				update
11:00	educ.		educ.	educ.	educ.	educ.	educ.	educ.		educ.				TR tec.
11:30	session		session	Session	session	session	session	session		session				and area
12:00	lunch		lunch	lunch	lunch	lunch	lunch	lunch		lunch				supv.
12:30	lunch		lunch	lunch	lunch	lunch	lunch	lunch		lunch				1 to 1
1:00	evals.		conference	evals.	TR meet	TR meet	TR meet	TR meet		report		TR tec.	1 to 1	
1:30	evals.		conference	evals.	TR meet	TR meet	TR meet	TR meet		conference		family	family	
2:00	evals.		conference	evals.	TR meet	TR meet	TR meet	TR meet		conference		leisure	leisure	
2:30	report		report	report						conference		session	session	
3:00	skill		1 to 1	skill	skill	1 to 1	evals.	evals.		skill		skill	skill	
3:30	dev.		1 to 1	dev.	dev.	1 to 1	evals.	evals.		dev.		dev. and	dev. and	
4:00	or R. T.		1 to 1	or R. T.	or R. T.	1 to 1	evals.	evals.		or R. T.		1 to 1	1 to 1	
4:30	area			area	dinner					area		dinner	dinner	
5:00	supv.			supv.	dinner					supv.		dinner	dinner	
5:30					prep. for							wknd.	wknd.	
6:00					recreation							leisure	leisure	
6:30					special							reviews	reviews	
7:00					event							.	.	
7:30														
8:00												prep. and	.	
8:30												rec. sp.		
9:00												event		
TRS #1	8 hrs.		7 hrs.		9 hrs.		8 hrs.		off		off		8 hrs.	
TRS #2		off		8 hrs.		7 hrs.		7 hrs.		8 hrs.		10 hrs.		off

BASIC SCHEDULE FOR THERAPEUTIC RECREATION SPECIALISTS 3 AND 4

TIME	MONDAY		TUESDAY		WEDNESDAY		THRUSDAY		FRIDAY		SATURDAY		SUNDAY	
	TRS #3	TRS #4	TRS #3	TRS #4	TRS #3	TRS #4	TRS #3	TRS #4	TRS #3	TRS #4	TRS #3	TRS #4	TRS #3	TRS #4
8:30	update		update			update			update	update				
9:00	leisure		leisure			leisure			leisure	leisure			twice per	
9:30	educ.		educ.			educ.			educ.	educ.			month:	
10:00	session		session			session			session	session			recovery	
10:30	leisure		leisure			leisure			leisure	leisure			bound	
11:00	educ.		educ.			educ.			educ.	educ.			adv.	
11:30	session		session			session			session	session			Program	
12:00	lunch		lunch			lunch			lunch	lunch			for	
12:30	lunch		lunch			lunch			lunch	lunch			out-pt.	
1:00	recovery	twice	recovery	update	TR meet	TR meet	TR meet	TR meet	special	conf.			family	
1:30	bound	per. mo.	bound	evals.	TR meet	TR meet	TR meet	TR meet	projects	conf.			commu-	
2:00	adv.	spec.	adv.	evals.	TR meet	TR meet	TR meet	TR meet	"	conf.			nity	
2:30	course	out-pt.	course	evals.	TR meet	TR meet			"				organiza-	
3:00	program	program	program	1:1	skill	out-pt.	skill	skill	skill	skill			tions	
3:30	"	as	"	1:1	dev. or	orienta-	dev.	dev.	dev.	dev.				
4:00	"	needed	"	1:1	R. T.	tion	or R. T.	or R. T.	or R. T.	or R. T.				
4:30	"		"		dinner	report	dinner	dinner		area				
5:00	report	out-pt.	report	dinner	dinner	report	dinner	dinner		supv.				
5:30		evals.		dinner	prep. for		out-pt.	out-pt.						
6:00		out-pt.		leisure	rec.		rec.	leisure						
6:30		rec.		ed. for	spec.		therapy	educ.						
7:00		therapy		out-pt.	event		session	kids						
7:30				Family			family	group			twice per			
8:00				leisure			leisure				month:			
8:30				educ.			report	report			rec. spec.			
9:00											event			
TRS #3	8 hrs.		8 hrs.		6 hrs.		7 hrs.		7 hrs.		off		4 hrs. avg.	
TRS #4		4/8 hrs.		8 hrs.		8 hrs.		8 hrs.		8 hrs.		4/0 hrs.		

BASIC SCHEDULE FOR TECHNICIANS "A," "B," "C," AND "D"

TIME	MON C	MON B	TUE C	TUE B	WED C	WED D	WED B	THU C	THU D	THU B	FRI C	FRI D	FRI A	SAT A	SAT D	SUN A	SUN B
6:00	updt.		updt.		updt.			updt.			updt.						
6:30	exer.		exer.		exer.			exer.			exer.						
7:00	pro. 1		pro. 1		pro. 1			pro. 1			pro. 1						
7:30	pro. 2		pro. 2		pro. 2			pro. 2			pro. 2						
8:00	prep.		prep.		prep.			prep.			prep.						
8:30	updt.		updt.		updt.			updt.			updt.	pro. 3		updt.		updt.	
9:00	pro. 3		pro. 3		pro. 3			pro. 3			pro. 3	pro. 3		exer.		pro. 2	
9:30	"		"		"			"			"	"		pro. 1		exer.	
10:00	"		"		"			"			"	"		pro. 2		exer.	
10:30	"		"		"			"			pro. 4	"		pro. 3		updt.	
11:00	"		"		"			"				"		"		pro. 3	
11:30	eat		eat		eat			eat			eat			eat		eat	
12:00	eat		eat		eat			eat			eat			eat		eat	
12:30	pro. 2		pro. 3		prep.			prep.			pro. 3			pro. 3		pro. 3	
1:00	pro. 3		"		TR.Mt.	TR.Mt.	TR.Mt.	TR.Mt.	TR.Mt.	TR.Mt.	updt.	updt.		"		"	
1:30	"		"		"	"	"	"	"	"	pro. 3	pro. 3		"		"	
2:00	prep.		prep.		"	"	"	"	"	"	"	"		prep.		prep.	
2:30	updt.	updt.	updt.	updt.		pro. 3	prep.	sfty.	pro. 3	pro. 3	prep.	prep.		lead.		lead.	
3:00	lead.	lead.	lead.	lead.		lead.	lead.	pro. 4	lead.	lead.	lead.	lead.		skill	updt.	skill	
3:30	skill	skill	skill	skill		skill	skill		skill	skill	skill	skill		dev.	pro. 3	dev.	
4:00	dev.	dev.	dev.	dev.		dev.	dev.		dev.	dev.	dev.	dev.		pro. 1	"	pro. 1	
4:30	pro. 4	pro. 1	pro. 4	pro. 1		pro. 1	pro. 1		pro. 1	pro. 1	pro. 4	pro. 1		pro. 3	prep.	pro. 3	
5:00		eat		eat		eat	eat		eat	eat		eat		pro. 4	lead.	pro. 4	prep.
5:30		eat		eat		eat	eat		eat	eat		eat			skill		updt.
6:00		pro. 3		pro. 3		prep.	prep.		pro. 3	prep.		pro. 3			dev.		skill
6:30		"		"		rec.	rec.		"	lead.		"			pro. 1		dev.
7:00		"		"		sp.	sp.		"	kids		"			prep.		pro. 1
7:30		tran-		prep.		evnt.	evnt.		"	gp.			tran-		rec.		tran-
8:00		sport		emp.		pro. 1	pro. 1		"	"			sport		sp.		sport
8:30		to and		rec.		pro. 3	sfty.		"	"			to and		evnt.		to and
9:00		from		pro. 3		"	"		"	"			from		"		from
9:30		AA		"		"	pro. 4		"	"			AA		"		AA
10:00		pro. 1		pro. 1		pro. 1			pro. 4	pro. 1			pro. 1		pro. 1		pro. 1
10:30		exer.		exer.		exer.				exer.			exer.		exer.		exer.
11:00		pro. 4		pro. 4		pro. 4				pro. 4			pro. 4		pro. 4		pro. 4
A							1.5 hrs.						9.5 hrs.	6.5 hrs.		8.5 hrs.	
B		8 hrs.		8 hrs.	8 hrs.		8 hrs.			9.5 hrs.							6.5 hrs.
C	10 hrs.		9.5hrs.					8 hrs.			4.5 hrs.						
D						9.5 hrs.			8.5 hrs.			7.5 hrs.			8.5 hrs.		

pro. 1 = protocol #1 (procedures for recording client participation in activity)

pro. 2 = protocol #2 (procedures for collection and dissemination of information, equipment, supplies, etc.)

pro. 3 = protocol #3 (procedures for creating Re-Creation opportunities while supervising recreation facilities, assisting clients, typing, filing, manning phone, operating audio visual equipment, assisting activity leaders as needed, etc.)

pro. 4 = protocol #4 (procedures for recording the days activity, noting supply needs, client interactions, etc.)

updt. = update (brief computer review and contract with other therapeutic recreation staff about client needs and plans for the day.

prep. = prepare area, equipment, supplies for next activity.

sfty. = performing safety checks, repair, and maintaining equipment.

TYPICAL SCHEDULE OF SKILL DEVELOPMENT FOR A WEEK

STAFF	MONDAY	TUESDAY	WEDNESDAY	THURSDAY	FRIDAY
TEC A					250.0 Individual
TEC B	270.0 Art	270.0 Art	270.0 Art	270.0 Art	
TEC C	265.0 Computer Oper.	260.0 Intellectual Pursuits			
TEC D			230.0 Cooking	230.0 Fishing	230.0 Gardening
TRS 1	240.0 Social		240.0 Social		
TRS 2		270.0 Drama			270.0 Creative Writing
TRS 3			290.0 Risk Activities		211.0 Other Competitive
TRS 4				200.0 Music	270.0 Music
TR MGR	250.0 Individual Pursuits				
OTHER	221.0 Swimming	211.0 Swim Races	221.0 Swim Fun	211.0 Swim Races	221.0 Swim Fun
OTHER		250.0 Guest Speaker			

TYPICAL SCHEDULE FOR RE-CREATION

EXERCISE	FACILITIES	WED. SPECIAL EVENT	SAT. SPECIAL EVENT

Mon.-Fri. : 6:30-7:00 a.m.
Mon.-Fri. : 10:00-10:30 p.m.
Sat. : 9:00-10:00 a.m. and
    11:00 p.m.
Sun. : 9:30-10:00 a.m. and
    10:00 p.m.
	Mon.-Sun. : Noon-1:30 p.m.
	    4:30-8:00 p.m.
	Sat. and Sun. : 10:30 a.m.-Noon
	Beauty Shop: Fri.-Sun.
	    by appointment
		Week 1: Addict of the Century Roast
		Week 2: Non-Talent Show
		Week 3: Picnic
		Week 4: Sobriety Dance and Sing
			Week 1: Dance with Buzzz Boys
			Week 2: TNT Actors Club
			Week 3: Bowling Night
			Week 4: Pool Party

TYPICAL ROTATION OF LEISURE EDUCATION SESSIONS FOR 9 A.M. TIME SLOT

TIME	MONDAY	TUESDAY	WEDNESDAY	THURSDAY	FRIDAY
WEEK 1	100.0 Leisure and Chem. 100.2 Values Clar. 102.0 Guest Speaker Clients admitted by Wed. Week 1 Scheduled: 100.0 Wed., Thurs., and Fri.	100.0 Adct. Tree 100.3 Match Needs Sk. 103.1 L. Close By	100.0 Intro. 101.0 Design Fitness 104.0 Fun Money	100.0 Balance Act 100.1 What is It? 105.1 L. Aloneness	100.0 L. Pin. Today 109.0 What's Risk? (Caseload Dependent)
WEEK 2	100.0 Leisure and Chem. 100.2 Time Priorities (Caseload Dependent) Week 1 Admissions: 100.0 on Mon., and Tues.; 101.0 on Wed. Sessions most needed Thurs., and Fri.	100.0 Adct. Tree 100.3 Yesterday Fun 105.2 Family L. Clients admitted by Wed. Week 2 Scheduled: 101.0 Wed. 100.0 Thurs., and Fri.	101.0 Heart Rate 101.1 Fitness 106.1 Stress	100.0 Balance Act 100.1 L. Work and CD 107.1 Child Play	100.0 L. Pin. today 109.2 New and Creat. (Caseload Dependent)
WEEK 3	100.0 Leisure and Chem. 100.2 Draw Paradise (Caseload Dependent) Week 1 Admissions: Scheduled for remaining sessions which are appropriate.	100.0 Adct. Tree 100.3 Sources Guilt 103.3 Transport Factor Week 2 Admissions: 100.0 on Mon., Tues., and Wed. Most needed sessions on Thurs., and Fri.	100.0 Intro. 101.1 Design Fitness 104.0 Fun Money Clients admitted by Wed. Week 3 Scheduled 100.0 Wed., Thurs., and Fri.	100.0 Balance Act 100.1 What is It? 105.1 L. Aloneness	100.0 L. Pin. Today 109.0 What's Risk? (Caseload Dependent)
WEEK 4	100.0 Leisure and Chem. 100.2 Values Clar. 102.0 Guest Speaker Week 1 Admissions: Completing required sessions and are involved in self selected activity.	100.0 Adct. Tree 100.3 Match Needs, Sk. 103.1 L. Close By Week 2 Admissions: Scheduled for remaining sessions which are appropriate.	101.0 Heart Rate 100.1 Fitness 106.1 Stress Week 3 Admissions: 100.0 Mon., and Tues. 101.0 Wed. Most needed Thurs., and Fri.	100.0 Balance Act 100.1 L. Work and CD 107.1 Childs Play Clients admitted by Wed. Week 4 Scheduled: 101.0 Wed. 100.0 Thurs., and Fri.	100.0 L. Pin. Today 109.0 New and Creat. (Caseload Dependent)
WEEK 5	100.0 Leisure and Chem. 100.2 Haven't Got or (Caseload Dependent) Week 1 Admissions: Discharged.	100.0 Adct. Tree 100.3 Yesterday Fun 105.2 Family L. Week 2 Admissions: Completing required sessions and are involved in self selected activity.	100.0 Intro. 100.0 L. Pin. Today 104.0 Fun Money Week 3 Admissions: Scheduled for remaining sessions which are approp.	100.0 Balance Act 100.1 What is It? 105.1 L. Aloneness Week 4 Admissions: 100.0 Mon., Tues., Wed. Most needed Thurs., and Fri.	100.0 L. Pin. today 109.0 What's Risk? (Caseload Dependent) Clients admitted Wed. Week 5 Scheduled 100.0 Wed., Thurs., and Fri.
WEEK 6	100.0 Leisure and Chem. 100.2 Draw Paradise (Caseload Dependent)	100.0 Adct. Tree 100.3 Sources Guilt 103.3 Transport Factor Week 2 Admissions: Discharged.	101.0 Heart Rate 100.0 L. Pin. today 106.1 Stress Week 3 Admissions: Completing required sessions and are involved in self selected activity.	100.0 Balance Act 100.1 L. Work and CD 107.1 Childs Play Week 4 Admissions: Scheduled for remaining sessions which are appropriate.	100.0 L. Pin. today 109.2 New and Creat. (Caseload Dependent) Week 5 Admissions: 100.0 Mon., and Tues. 101.0 Wed. Most needed Thurs., and Fri.

OTHER SOURCES

Addiction Research Foundation, Central Office, 33 Russel Street, Toronto, Ontario, Canada, M5S 2S1

Alcoholics Anonymous, Box 459, Grand Central Station, New York, NY 10163.

Al-Anon Family Group Headquarters, Inc. P.O. Box 182, Madison Square Station, New York, NY 10159-0182.

ATRA, American Therapeutic Recreation Association, 2021 L. Street NW, Suite 250, Washington, DC 20038.

Center of Alcohol Studies, Rutgers University, New Brunswick, NJ

Disabled American Veterans, Vietnam Veterans Outreach Program, 807 Maine Ave. SW, Washington, DC 20024.

Hazeldon, Box 176, Center City, MN 55012

Leisure Enrichment Service, P.O. Box 1190, Seaside, OR 97138.

Nar-Anon Family Group Headquarters Inc., P.O. Box 2562, Palos Verdes Peninsula, CA, 90274.

Narcotics Anonymous World Service Office, Inc.: CA.

National Clearinghouse for Alcohol & Drug Information, P.O. Box 2345, Rockville, MD 20852, Phone: (301) 468-2600. (References followed by numbers such as (32251/91546) are available in abstract form from National Clearinghouse. The first number indicates record number, with second being the accession number.)

National Council on Alcoholism, 2 Park Ave., New York, NY 10016.

NCTRC, National Council for Therapeutic Recreation Certification, 49 S. Main St., Suite 005 Spring Valley, NY 10977.

NTRS, National Therapeutic Recreation Society, a branch of National Recreation & Park Association, 3101 Park Center Drive, Alexandria, VA 22302-1593.